DEVELOPING CAREER COUNSELING AND ASSESSMENT

Second Edition

DEVELOPMENTAL CAREER COUNSELING AND ASSESSMENT

Second Edition

Linda Seligman

SAGE Publications
International Educational and Professional Publisher
Thousand Oaks   London   New Delhi

For information address:

SAGE Publications, Inc.
2455 Teller Road
Thousand Oaks, California 91320
E-mail: order@sagepub.com

Sage Publications, Ltd.
6 Bonhill Street
London EC2A 4PU
United Kingdom

Sage Publications India Pvt. Ltd.
M-32 Market
Greater Kailish I
New Delhi 110 048 India

Printed in the United States of America

Library of Congress Cataloging-in-Publication Data

Seligman, Linda
    Developmental career conseling and assessment / Linda Seligman.—
2nd ed.
        p. cm.
    Includes bibliographical references and index.
    ISBN 0-8039-5803-X — ISBN 0-8039-5804-8 (pbk.)
    1. Vocational guidance. I. Title.
HF5381.S475 1994
650.14—dc20   94-13646

        98 99 00 01 10 9 8 7 6 5 4

Sage Production Editor: Diana E. Axelsen

Contents

Preface   ix

1. Overview of Career Counseling and Development   1
   History of Career Counseling and Development   1
   Theories of Career Development   5
   A Lexicon of Career Counseling   25
   Factors Affecting Career Development   38

2. The Use of Assessment in Career Counseling   63
   History of Assessment in Career Counseling   63
   Benefits and Limitations of Testing and Assessment   66
   Selecting Appropriate Tests and Inventories   68
   Understanding Tests and Test Manuals   74
   Pitfalls of the Assessment Process   91
   Interpretation of Test Results   97
   Client Rights in Assessment   108

3. Tools of Assessment   109
   Overview   109
   Ability Tests   110
   Interest Inventories   135
   Personality Inventories   151
   Computer-Assisted Assessment   165
   Nonstandardized Methods of Assessment   166

4. Childhood: Years of Identification and Differentiation   168
   Early Childhood Development   168
   Development During the Middle Childhood Years   170
   Children's Career Development   178
   Developmental Accomplishments of Childhood   185
   Counseling for Self-Esteem and Differentiation   186
   Career Education   186
   The Role of the Counselor in the Elementary School   196

Case Study of Laura Ashton: A Young Girl Seeking
Identification and Differentiation   198

5. Early Adolescence: Years of Growth and Searching   207
Overview of Early Adolescent Development   207
Career Development   214
Career Counseling With the Early Adolescent   221
Developmental Milestones of Early Adolescence   232
Career Development Objectives for Early Adolescence   233
The Role of Assessment in the Counseling of Early Adolescents   234
Case Study of Hector Gomez: An Early Adolescent Engaged in
Growing and Searching   236

6. Adolescence: Years of Realism and Separation   249
Emotional Development During Adolescence   249
Developments in Thinking Ability During Adolescence   253
Attaining Maturity in Adolescence   254
Adolescent Career Development   254
Formulating Educational Plans and Decisions   267
Developmental Goals   272
Counseling the Adolescent Toward Realism and Separation   272
Career Counseling With Adolsecents   274
Case Study of Bob Questor:
Searching for Realism and Separation   286

7. Young Adulthood: Years of Compromise
and Commitment to a Lifestyle   302
Overview of Young Adult Development   302
Development of a Generation   310
Gender and Career Development   312
The Young Adult as Worker   320
The Young Adult as College Student   325
Counseling to Facilitate Compromise and Commitment   336
Case Study of Kerry Kelly:
A Young Woman in Search of Herself   346

8. Middle Adulthood: Years of Consolidating
and Redirecting   358
Middle Adult Years: A Time of Transition   358
Development During the Middle Adult Years   359
Career Development During the Middle Adult Years   376
The Adult as Student   388
Overview of the Middle Adult Years   390

Counseling the Adult During Midlife 391
Two Case Studies of Anita Hirsch and Fred Newman:
   Adults in Midlife 401

9. Later Adulthood: Years of Adapting and Extending 416
Older Adults—A Growing Segment of the Population 416
Emotional Development in the Later Years 418
Social and Interpersonal Changes During the Later Adult Years 423
Theories of Coping With Aging 426
Career Development During the Later Years 429
Capabilities of Older People 434
Retirement 435
Counseling the Older Person 443
Case Study of Elizabeth Hepburn:
   A Woman Engaged in Adapting and Extending 450

10. The Future of Career Counseling and Assessment:
Trends and Application 461
State of the Art 461
Overview of Changes in the Field 462
Expectations of Career Counseling 463
Changes in the Workplace 464
The Multicultural Workforce 467
Changes in the Process of Career Counseling and Assessment 468
Career Counseling in Groups 470
The Importance of the Family in Career Development 471
Barriers to Career Development 473
A Field of Continuing Change 474
The Content and Process of Career Counseling 475
Skills of the Career Counselor 482
Case Study of Senesie Robinson: For the Reader's Analysis 484

Appendix A: National Career Development Association
Ethical Standards 497

Appendix B: Sources and Resources for Career Counselors 508

Appendix C: Acronyms for Tools of Assessment 513

References 516

Index 546

About the Author 571

Preface

The first edition of this book was published in 1980. In the years between the writing of that book and this revision, the field of career counseling and assessment has grown and evolved in many ways. However, the life span developmental approach to career counseling that was just beginning to gain widespread acceptance in 1980 has continued to provide the bedrock for most theories and techniques for understanding and facilitating career development.

That career development is a lifelong process, extending throughout the life span, is well established. In addition, perspectives on career development have continued to expand and become increasingly holistic, with most career counselors now considering leisure activities, family and interpersonal goals, and the mental health of their clients as important aspects of career counseling.

In addition, emphasis on counseling diverse populations has continued to be an important aspect of career counseling as the workforce has become increasingly multicultural. Greater attention also has been paid, in recent years, to people with special physical or intellectual needs.

Assessment has continued to be an important aspect of career counseling, and as some of the criticisms of testing expressed during the 1970s have been addressed, the role of assessment in career counseling has achieved a new level of appreciation and sophistication. The rapid growth of computer-assisted career counseling as well as the many new tests and inventories that have been developed also have enhanced the importance of assessment in the counseling process.

Although the field of career counseling has undergone many changes since the first edition of this book, the purpose of this book remains the same. This book was written to help counselors, psychologists, and teachers to understand the lifelong process of career development and become better able to use counseling and assessment to facilitate that process. This book also can help readers gain greater awareness of their own career development.

I would like to express my appreciation to some of the people who contributed, directly or indirectly, to the writing of this book:

I would like to thank the administrators, faculty, and staff at George Mason University, especially Barry Beyer, Larry Bowen, and Arthur Chickering, for giving me the time and resources I needed to write this book.

I would like to thank Roberta Cordingly and Merle Wexler for contributing case studies for use in this book.

I would like to thank the people who volunteered to share their time and their lives to serve as the case studies in this book.

I would like to thank my family and friends, especially my husband Robert Zeskind and my friend Bettie MacLennan, for their caring and support while this book was being written.

Finally, I would like to dedicate this book to my mother, Florence Scolnick Goldberg, a truly remarkable woman.

Linda Seligman
George Mason University
Fairfax, Virginia

ONE

Overview of Career Counseling and Development

History of Career Counseling and Development

No other technique for the conduct of life attaches the individual so firmly to reality as laying emphasis on work; for work at least gives . . . a secure place in a portion of reality, in the human community. (Freud, 1962, p. 27)

Along with his many other contributions to our understanding of human development, Freud recognized the importance that work has in reflecting our sense of ourselves, shaping who we are, organizing our days, providing us friends and colleagues, helping us feel productive and creative, and establishing our place in the world. Freud saw that work, along with love, is one of the two central forces directing our lives.

Modern theorists in career counseling agree. As Yost and Corbishly (1987) stated, "In Western society, work is a major source of status, identity, and gratification" (p. 2). The average person spends more time at work than at any other single activity except sleep. Since the 1970s, counselors and career development theorists have recognized that our careers are inextricably intertwined with the rest of our lives and that career counseling must take a holistic view of people.

Parsons's Trait-and-Factor Theory

In its early years, however, theories of career choice and development took a more circumscribed view. Most credit Frank Parsons and his 1909 book *Choosing a Vocation* with the inception of the study of career development. Parsons has been called a "trait-and-factor" theorist because he based his ideas on the assumption that "people possess stable and relatively unchanging characteristics (traits), including interests, special talents, and intelligence" (Yost & Corbishly, 1987, p. 4). He developed a systematic process for selecting a career that does not diverge greatly from many modern approaches to career choice:

1. First, have a clear understanding of yourself, aptitudes, abilities, interests, resources, limitations, and other qualities.
2. Second, a knowledge of the requirements and conditions of success, advantages and disadvantages, compensations, opportunities, and prospects in different lines of work.
3. Third, true reasoning on the relations of these two groups of facts. (Parsons, 1909, p. 5)

Parsons assumed that if this three-step process was followed correctly, high job performance as well as occupational satisfaction would be the expected outcomes.

Despite the extensive study of human behavior around the early 20th century by such theorists as Francis Galton, Alfred Binet, G. Stanley Hall, and James Cattell, the relatively narrow focus of the trait-and-factor approach dominated the field of career development until the 1950s. Trait-and-factor theorists, influenced by the study of individual differences, sought to measure empirically those variations in personality, interests, and abilities and to relate those traits to career plans that would make a good fit. The trait-and-factor approach is based on the assumption "that optimal career outcomes for both the individual and the organization can best be facilitated through a congruence between the individual's characteristics and the demands, requirements, and rewards of the organizational environment" (Betz, Fitzgerald, & Hill, 1989, p. 26). Although most career choice researchers no longer believe in the concepts of the ideal job or the unchanging nature of human attributes and consider such influences as family background, development, and environment as factors in career choice, the influence of the trait-and-factor approach is still felt in modern theories, such as those developed by Holland (1966) and others.

The trait-and-factor approach now has been shaped by developmental and social learning models and has evolved into a Person × Environment approach (Chartrand, 1991). Assumptions of this approach include concepts such as the following:

1. People are capable of rational decision making.
2. Meaningful individual and environmental differences can be identified and assessed.
3. Matching of person and environment increases the likelihood of a positive outcome.
4. People seek out environments that are congruent with their personalities.

Career Development Organizations

Although Parsons died before the publication of his influential book, the impact of his ideas was immediate and far-reaching. In 1910, the First National Conference on Vocational Guidance was held in Boston to provide a forum for sharing ideas on career counseling. At the third meeting of this conference in 1913, the National Vocational Guidance Association was formed. The first organization for counselors, it has continued to provide leadership and focus to the field of career counseling up to the present, now under its new name, the National Career Development Association (NCDA), a division of the American Counseling Association (ACA). The journal of NCDA, originally named the *Vocational Guidance Quarterly*, now the *Career Development Quarterly*, has been a primary source of information on this field.

In 1966, the National Employment Counseling Association became another division of ACA of importance to career counselors. Originally aimed at counselors employed at local, state, and national levels of the U.S. Employment Service, this organization has since broadened its scope and now has over 1,500 members, interested in the field of career counseling (Smith, Engels, & Bonk, 1985).

The nature of the field of career counseling was further developed in 1984 with the initiation of the National Career Counseling Credentialing Examination, given under the auspices of ACA (Smith & Karpati, 1985). Counselors who pass this examination and who meet other relevant criteria are eligible for certification as career counselors.

Career Counseling in the 1930s: Depression Era

The 1930s were the years of the Great Depression. Unemployment was high in the United States, and immigrants to this country had a particularly difficult time finding jobs during those years. Several developments during the 1930s improved economic prospects while concurrently contributing to the development of the field of career counseling. In 1933, the Wagner-Peyser Act established the U.S. Employment Service to facilitate placing people in available jobs. In that same year, the Civilian Conservation Corps (CCC) was founded to provide employment to large numbers of people out of work due to the depression. Workers involved in CCC projects made important contributions to the United States through their development of the national parks and other resources.

Employment needs of some of the immigrants to the United States were addressed by the B'nai B'rith Vocational Service Bureau, formed in 1938 to provide counseling, placement, and rehabilitation to Jewish immigrants. Fifty years later, related organizations provide similar services to Jewish immigrants coming from the Soviet Union to the United States.

Several publications of importance to career counseling were issued during these years. In 1939, the first edition of the *Dictionary of Occupational Titles* was published by the United Stated Employment Service. That volume, based on a trait-and-factor approach of linking person and job, will be discussed in greater detail later in this book. At about that same time, the first edition of the *Mental Measurements Yearbook*, a compendium of tests and inventories designed to assess abilities and personality, was published. That book, which also will be discussed later, facilitated the work of trait-and-factor counselors by giving them a ready source of information on measurement tools that they might use to gain greater understanding of people.

Probably the most important contribution of the 1930s to the theory of career counseling was the publication of E. G. Williamson's 1939 book, *How to Counsel Students*. Based on Parsons's trait-and-factor approach, Williamson developed an approach to career counseling that he called *directive counseling*. His approach consisted of the following six steps: analysis, synthesis, diagnosis, prognosis, counseling, and follow-up. Williamson's approach, although narrower and more programmed than many of the modern approaches to career counseling, contains similar ingredients to those approaches.

Career Counseling in the 1940s: World War II

World War II and its aftermath had a profound impact on career development and counseling. During the war, tests proliferated and increased in influence because of their use to classify recruits into positions that would ideally maximize their potential. After the war ended, the influx of veterans into jobs and colleges led to an increase in counseling services. In 1944, the Veterans Administration (VA) established centers to provide career and related counseling to men and women having difficulty making and implementing occupational plans after their departure from the armed services. VA benefits enabled many to attend college and added an older and more experienced group of students to the college population. This seasoned group of students tended to be goal oriented and required an expansion of previously available career counseling and placement services.

The role of women before, during, and after World War II has historical importance in women's career development. Before the war, most women worked briefly in traditionally female-dominated careers (e.g., teaching, secretarial services) and then became full-time homemakers. With the drafting of large numbers of men into the armed forces, women not only assumed increased responsibility at home but were needed to fill the jobs vacated by the men. The image of Rosie the Riveter embodied the new role occupied by many of these women. However, when the men returned from the war, most of the women were relieved of their jobs to make room for the men and were expected to resume their roles as full-time homemakers. They did this with varying degrees of comfort, and this stint as full-time wage earner in a nontraditional position seemed to plant a seed in the minds of many of these women that came to fruition years later with the Women's Movement of the 1970s and its emphasis on broadened opportunities for women. Women's changing role in the workplace will be discussed later in this chapter.

Carl Rogers is the person who probably made the greatest impact on the field of counseling in the 1940s with the 1942 publication of *Counseling and Psychotherapy*. Rogers, in contrast to Williamson, espoused what he called a nondirective approach to counseling in which the client took the lead in the counseling process. The primary goal of the counselor was to promote the client's self-confidence and self-esteem. Although Rogers did not directly address the process of career counseling, he broadened and humanized our view of the counseling process and paved the way for the work of Donald Super in the next decade.

Theories of Career Development

Since Frank Parson's (1909) writing, many theories have been advanced to explain how people make career plans and choices and, ideally, move toward a rewarding career and lifestyle. Research is currently ongoing on more than 10 theories of career development, and no one point of view has emerged as the ideal theory of career development. To be of greatest value, a theory of career development should both describe and explain that process. The theory should help counselors as well as the people they seek to help to understand and assess career development and to facilitate positive and rewarding career choices.

At present, even the most useful theories are incomplete, not well substantiated by research, or still in the process of being developed and studied. Most provide useful frameworks for understanding but contribute only minimally to the process of facilitating career development. However, shortcomings of theories of the 1950s, 1960s, and 1970s, such as their limited attention to the relationship between work and leisure activities and work and family life and their assumption that success and happiness can readily be attained through work, have largely been overcome by the theories of the 1980s and 1990s. Most modern theories of career development consider not only occupational preferences but also leisure, personal, and social choices (Gysbers, 1984). In addition, most refer to *life* career development, reflecting their comprehensive emphasis. Despite a continuing need for research on the current broader theories of career and lifestyle development, these theories can be extremely useful in increasing self-awareness, guiding and improving the process of career counseling, promoting more rewarding career choices, contributing to the prediction of future development, and promoting further research.

Developmental Theorists

Although their perspectives and emphases may vary, most theorists accept the developmental nature of the process of making career plans and view that developmental process as an ongoing and continuous one, extending throughout the life span. The developmental viewpoint seems to have European origins, emphasizing the importance of focusing on the whole person. It holds that people are capable of being happy and successful in a number of jobs and that satisfaction is a function of overall lifestyle (Zaccaria, 1970). The developmental approach to understanding people became well accepted in the United States in the 1950s and 1960s through the work of Erik Erikson as well as of career development theorists such as Donald Super. Developmental theories generally view career maturation in terms of stages and life tasks. Researchers espousing a developmental point of view recognize that people may need counseling at any point during the life span but that the nature of both their difficulties and the help that they need typically is related to their stage of development.

The best known proponents of theories of career development are Ginzberg, Ginsburg, Axelrad, and Herma (1951) and Super. Both Super and Ginzberg and his colleagues were influenced by Buehler's (1933) view of development as consisting of five life stages: growth, exploration, establishment, maintenance, and decline (Super, 1957b). Super also was influenced by his own study of the British working-class movements of the 19th century and his involvement with unemployed men and women during the Great Depression (Super, personal communication, January 26, 1989). Super and Ginzberg and his colleagues based their initial translations of Buehler's theory into the realm of careers primarily on research into the career development of a relatively small group, composed largely of White males of the 1950s. Although both theories have been revised over the years, it should be borne in mind that the career development of a given person may vary considerably from these models, particularly if that person is a woman or the member of a culturally disadvantaged or minority group.

Ginzberg, Ginsburg, Axelrad, and Herma

Ginzberg et al. (1951) based their ideas on a study of males from upper middle-class urban Protestant and Catholic families. Their findings led them to view career development as a process that could be divided into three broad stages. They suggested that the first of these, the fantasy stage, extended from ages 6 to 11. Pleasure and fantasy were viewed as the primary determinants of career preferences during these years, because children in this age group had little awareness of obstacles to their career development. During these years, play became increasingly work oriented and career preferences emerged.

The second stage, the tentative period, spanned the years from 11 to 17 and was made up of three substages. According to Ginzberg and his colleagues, 11- and 12-year-olds tended to reject earlier fantasy choices and focused on future goals linked to present *interests and joys*. By 12 or 13, most children had begun to take account of their *abilities and capacities* when stating their career goals. About the age of 14, *values* became a more prominent determinant of career aspirations, and by age 15 or 16, career plans represented an integration of values, capacities, and interests. Young people in this age group were seen as having an awareness of the need to make occupational choices, to take on adult responsibilities, and to make the transition from school to employment.

The third stage, the realistic period, began at age 18 and consisted of *exploration*, followed by *crystallization* or commitment to a career goal, followed by *specification* or specialization within the chosen field.

Ginzberg has made two significant revisions to his theory. In 1972, he emphasized the open-ended nature of the career development process and advanced a view of people going through a process of optimization in which they weighed the apparent satisfactions of career options against their costs to determine their final choices. In 1984, Ginzberg retracted his earlier view of career development as an irreversible process and stated that he now saw it as a process that extended throughout life.

Despite the important contribution made by Ginzberg's developmental approach, his theory has several shortcomings. It is a descriptive theory and does not really provide much direction to the process of facilitating career development. It says little about the process of moving from one stage to another, about impediments to that process, or about how that process might differ for people who are not White males.

Super and the Career Pattern Study

Super's (1957b) developmental theory, based largely on his Career Pattern Study, which has followed the development of a group of males since 1951 when they were in the ninth grade, differs from Ginzberg's theory in several respects. Super emphasized the importance of the self-concept in career development and viewed the expression of an occupational preference as a reflection of how people viewed themselves as well as an expression of their efforts to implement and actualize their self-concepts (Super, Starishevsky, Matlin, & Jordaan, 1963). For Super, career satisfaction was related to the extent to which people could find outlets for their interests, abilities, values, and personality traits and also to the extent to which they could implement and actualize their self-concepts. As Super and his colleagues stated, "In expressing a vocational preference, a person puts into occupational terminology his idea of the kind of person he is; that in entering an occupation, he seeks to implement a concept of himself; that in getting established in an occupation he achieves self-actualization" (p. 1).

Super's original model of the 1950s seems to have more relevance than that of Ginzberg and his colleagues, developed during the same time period. Super's research was based on a group of 100 ninth-grade boys from Middletown, New York, chosen because the town seemed representative in terms of occupations and socioeconomic status not only of New York State as a whole but also of other small American cities. Also, Super's model extended throughout the life span, acknowledging the lifelong nature of career development (Super et al., 1957). The 100 boys in the Career Pattern Study were studied further when they were 21, 25, and 36 to yield information on the process of career development (Super, 1985).

Super and his colleagues (1957) postulated a five-stage model of career development. Stage 1 is the growth stage that extends from birth to age 14 and includes the fantasy, interest, and capacity stages mentioned by Ginzberg. Super's second stage, exploration, extends from age 15 to age 24 with reality playing an increasing role in career development. The exploration stage includes three substages, tentative (ages 15-17), transition (ages 18-21), and trial (ages 22-24). Stage 3 in Super's model is the establishment stage, involving early trial and shifting (25-30), followed by stabilization (31-44). The middle years compose Stage 4 in Super's model, the maintenance stage, and in the original model was followed by the years of decline (65 on), which included deceleration (65-70) and retirement (71 on).

Super's research (1957a) led to the definition of four common career patterns for men and seven for women. The four types of career patterns that characterized male career development are the following:

1. *The stable career pattern.* These people seemed to skip the trial work period to go directly from school into a type of work in which they have continued. The pattern was characteristic of professionals, managers, and some skilled, semiskilled, and clerical workers.
2. *The conventional career pattern.* In this pattern, people progressed from initial employment through trial positions to stable employment, most characteristic of managerial, skilled, and clerical workers.
3. *The unstable career pattern.* Characterized by a trial-stable-trial sequence in which establishment was delayed or inhibited by occupational change, this pattern was most typical of semiskilled, clerical, and domestic workers.
4. *The multiple-trial career pattern.* Characterized by frequent job changes with little indication of establishment, this pattern was also most typical of semiskilled, clerical, and domestic workers.

Super (1957a) found the following patterns to characterize women's career development:

1. *The stable homemaking career pattern.* An early marriage was anticipated and achieved with little meaningful employment experience.
2. *The conventional career pattern.* Brief employment was replaced by full-time homemaking as the primary endeavor.
3. *The stable working career pattern.* An occupation was entered after leaving school that became the focus of the woman's career.
4. *The double-track career pattern.* These women sought to combine employment and homemaking. This pattern was most characteristic of women at the extremes of the occupational scale.
5. *The interrupted career pattern.* Employment preceded and followed a significant period of time out of the labor force for homemaking and child rearing.
6. *The unstable career pattern.* This pattern is the same for women as for men, but shifting was more likely to occur between homemaking and employment than from one job to another.
7. *The multiple-trial career pattern.* This pattern is the same as for men.

Since Super's study in the 1950s, the proportion of people following each of these patterns has changed, especially reflecting growth in the number of women following the stable working or double-track patterns and the declining number following the stable homemaking pattern. Patterns of men and women also are less disparate than they were in the 1950s, with growth in the number of men who are homemakers and in the number of dual-career couples. However, these patterns still provide a useful framework for conceptualizing variations in career development and reviewing options.

Perhaps in part because Super himself has remained an active and creative researcher well beyond what he had originally viewed as the start of the years of decline, he has reconceptualized his developmental approach so that it is broader and more flexible. Super (1982) now writes of a "life-career rainbow" that involves an interaction of nine major life roles (child, student, leisurite, citizen, worker, pensioner, spouse, homemaker, parent) and an integration of activities over the life span. He views the combination of roles, their sequence, and their changing importance for each person as instrumental in defining that person's career development (Super, 1984). Super also writes of minicycles encompassed in maxicycles, individual periods of change sparked by personal milestones in career development, such as a midlife career change. He has come to view the life span as a process of change with multiple decision points. For adults, Super stresses career adaptability rather than career maturity (Whiston, 1990). Super's ideas, especially with ongoing revision by himself and his colleagues, still have considerable relevance, and Super has continued to be a leader in the field of career development. Super's (1982) current research, the Work Importance Project, begun in 1978 and conducted in 14 countries, has led to the development of a broad range of inventories to clarify work values and role salience. These will be discussed later in this book.

However, Super's work, too, presents some unanswered questions. For example, research of the 1980s has indicated that many people who come from families where physical abuse or substance abuse was prominent have negative and inaccurate self-concepts. Does implementation of the self-concept via career choices for these people lead to satisfaction, or does that sequence hold true only for people with positive and realistic self-concepts? Research is needed to answer that question and others.

Tiedeman and O'Hara and Miller-Tiedeman

Tiedeman and O'Hara (1963) advanced another developmental view of career development. Based on Erikson's eight psychosocial crises and drawing on the work of Ginzberg and Super, their theory focused on ego development as well as on the self-in-situation and self-in-world. Tiedeman and O'Hara postulated a two-stage model of career development with each stage having substages as follows:

I. Anticipation or preoccupation period
   A. Exploration—awareness of options develops
   B. Crystallization—options are explored, narrowed
   C. Choice—decisions are made
   D. Clarification—plans are implemented
II. Implementation or adjustment period
   A. Induction—entry into the world of work
   B. Reformation—modification of goals and environment
   C. Integration—becoming an established member of the workforce

Probably the greatest contribution of Tiedeman and O'Hara's ideas was exploration of the struggle many workers experience in balancing individual needs and the demands of the workforce. This issue is further examined in the more recent ideas of Miller-Tiedeman (1988). Influenced by phenomenological and existential ideas and termed "constructive-developmentalism" (Savickas, 1989), Miller-Tiedeman has advanced a life career theory, viewing life as a learning process, and advocating the belief that people construct their own reality and meaning. Miller-Tiedeman's work promotes the development of a systematic problem-solving process, drawing on cognitive abilities, ego differentiation, developmental tasks, and resolution of psychosocial crises. By promoting the development of self-awareness, meaning making, and choices, this approach seeks to help people lead more self-directed, decision-guided lives and to promote a sense of purpose, direction, and completion in life. The approach views career development as only one aspect of the process of development, and emphasizes the importance of individuality and taking control of one's life.

Gottfredson: Circumscription and Compromise

Another modern developmental theory has been advanced by Gottfredson (1981). Expanding on Super's earlier emphasis on the role of the self-concept in career development, Gottfredson postulated a theory of circumscription and compromise to explain occupational goals. According to Gottfredson, people have self-images, including who they believe they are, who they believe they are not, and who they would like to be. They also have cognitive maps of the world of work and its occupations. Drawing on these two visions, "People assess the compatibility of occupations with their images of who they would like to be and how much effort they are willing to exert to enter those occupations" (Gottfredson, 1981, p. 547). Occupational alternatives, then, equal perceptions of job-self compatibility plus perceptions of job accessibility, according to Gottfredson. She has advanced a four-stage model to describe the evolution of people's images of themselves and the world of work:

1. *Orientation to size and power.* Between ages 3 and 5, children grasp the concept of being an adult and associate power with size and adulthood, which is associated with occupational roles.
2. *Orientation to sex roles.* About the ages of 6, 7, or 8, most children develop a fairly rigid gender self-concept.
3. *Orientation to social valuation.* Between the ages of 9 and 13, children become able to deal with abstractions, become aware of social class and economic factors, and develop a fairly good awareness of their own abilities and emotions.
4. *Orientation to internal, unique self.* Beginning about age 14, adolescents begin to sort through occupational possibilities, eliminating those that are perceived as inappropriate for their gender, too low in prestige, or

incompatible with their social class self-images and the amount of effort they want to put forth to attain their occupations. Occupations that survive this initial screening then are considered in terms of their compatibility with people's perceptions of their interests, personality, values, and capacities. Finally, in late adolescence, the availability of preferred career opportunities is considered and a zone of acceptable alternatives is identified.

After people enter the world of work, compromises almost inevitably continue. These involve "giving up certain aspects of one's career goals that are of lesser importance to retain those aspects that are of higher priority to the individual" (Leung & Plake, 1990, p. 399). According to Gottfredson (1981) interests typically are sacrificed first, then prestige level, and finally gender appropriateness. In other words, those criteria that achieved importance last are sacrificed first. "Compromises continue until eventually most people report being in the type of work they want" (p. 549).

Research on Developmental Theories

The concept of career development as a lifelong process with identifiable stages seems to have achieved almost universal support and acceptance. Researchers also seem accepting of the importance of self-concept in the process of career choice. The more recent ideas of Tiedeman and Miller-Tiedeman and of Gottfredson, however, still are in the early stages of research. For example, although several studies have supported Gottfredson's emphasis on interests, prestige, and sex type as salient influences on career decision making, Leung and Plake (1990) found prestige to be the preferred factor whereas Hesketh, Elmslie, and Kaldor (1990) found interests to be a more important factor.

Personality and Need Theories

A second important group of theories of career choice and development are the personality and need theories. The evolution of these theories has paralleled that of the developmental theories and the two have sometimes overlapped, sometimes conflicted, and often complemented each other. A consideration of both categories of theories will probably lead to the fullest understanding of how career development happens and how it can best be facilitated.

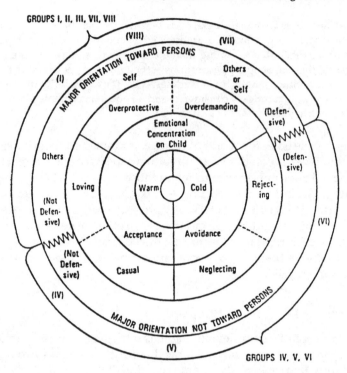

Figure 1.1. Ann Roe's Circular Model: Early Determinants of Occupational Choice

Reprinted from "Early Determinants of Vocational Choice," by Ann Roe (*Journal of Consulting Psychology*, 1957, 4, 216). Copyright © 1957 by the American Psychological Association.

Roe's Theory of Career Choice

Ann Roe's groundbreaking model drew general attention to the relationship between early needs and subsequent career development. The essence of Roe's theory, derived from Maslow's theory of needs, is that the nature of people's orientation toward others is related to the nature of the parent-child relationships they experienced. Roe believed that the nature of people's person orientation will be reflected in their career objectives, as they seek to satisfy needs raised in childhood that have not yet been satisfied (Roe, 1956, 1964). She hypothesized, for example, that people who came from accepting, demanding, or protective families would gravitate toward person-oriented occupations, whereas those who came from neglecting, rejecting, or casual homes would prefer to work with data or things.

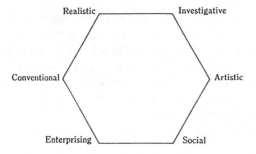

Figure 1.2. Holland's Hexagonal Model

Research has given only limited support to Roe's theory, developed primarily through nonempirical methods. However, Roe was instrumental in promoting the classification of occupations by both level and field. Her work also drew attention to the importance of family influence and early development at a time when most career counselors tended to focus on people outside of their environmental context. In addition, several instruments and programs have been developed, based on or stimulated by Roe's theory, including the Family Relations Inventory developed by Brunken and Crites, the Roe-Siegelman Parent-Child Relations Questionnaire, the Hall Occupational Orientation Inventory, the COPSystem Interest Inventory, and the Vocational Interest Inventory developed by Lunneborg (Zytowski, 1986).

Holland's Model of Congruence

One outgrowth of Roe's (1957) theory was an eight-group circumplex model that she used to illustrate the relationship between family environment and career choice (see Figure 1.1). Her circumplex model may have provided the blueprint for the hexagonal model John Holland (1991) used to illustrate his theory (see Figure 1.2). According to Zytowski (1986), Roe's model has been replaced by Holland's empirically based model of the relationship between personality and career choice. Holland (1966) accepted the developmental nature of career plans and decisions and, in fact, viewed the childhood years as important in determining the nature of people's career choices. Holland also embraced many of the tenets of the trait-and-factor model, including his perception of interests and aptitudes as relatively stable and his effort to facilitate an optimal match of person and occupation.

However, Holland placed greatest emphasis on the role of personality and views himself as taking a person-environment perspective (Holland, 1987a). He defined six modal types, organized in a hexagonal configuration, that could be used to describe both personal orientations and occupational environments.

His six types consist of the following:

1. *Realistic*. People in which the realistic type predominates prefer to work with their hands and enjoy objective and concrete tasks. They are often mathematically oriented.
2. *Investigative*. Investigative people are thinkers who tend to excel in academic and scientific areas. They typically are confident, intellectual, and independent.
3. *Artistic*. Artistic people, according to Holland's definition, tend to be creative and original and excel in verbal and artistic areas. They tend to be sensitive, impulsive, and introspective and prefer being alone or in small groups to being in large social gatherings.
4. *Social*. People in this group generally enjoy working with and helping others. Their strengths include their verbal and interpersonal skills. They tend to be sociable, cheerful, achieving, and conservative.
5. *Enterprising*. Enterprising individuals also are people oriented but are more concerned with dominating and persuading than with helping. They tend to be adventurous, extroverted, and sociable.
6. *Conventional*. People in this group tend to be concerned with social approval and to be conservative, conforming, and sociable. They tend to enjoy business, computational, and clerical occupations.

Although most people are not pure types, most can be characterized more by one of these personality types than they can by the other five. The Self-Directed Search (SDS), an inventory developed by Holland (1987b) based on his theory of the relationship between personality and career development, can be used to help people identify their dominant, secondary, and tertiary types. Holland hypothesized that people in similar occupations have similar developmental histories and personalities, resulting from people's tendency to seek occupational environments that are consistent with their personalities. Holland further believed that people who established careers that were congruent with their personal orientations were more likely to be satisfied and successful in their work and to have more stable careers. Research has provided support to Holland's assumption; Gottfredson and Holland (1990) found that "person-job congruence *did* have substantial correlations with job satisfaction in a well-defined homogeneous sample" (p. 396).

Along with *congruence,* calculus, consistency, differentiation, and identity are key concepts in Holland's (1985) theory. *Calculus* "suggests that the personality types and vocational environments can be ordered according to a hexagonal model. In this model, the distances between the personality types are inversely proportional to the supposed relationships among the types" (Erwin, 1988, p. 158). The construct of calculus has been well supported by research.

Holland (1985) believes that people whose dominant and secondary environments are adjacent on the hexagon (e.g., realistic and investigative) manifest greater consistency of personality pattern than do people whose first two environments are distant from each other (e.g., realistic and social). Holland also believes that *consistency,* as measured by proximity of environments, correlates with career satisfaction and persistence.

Differentiation refers to the numerical difference between a person's highest and lowest score on Holland's scales. The greater the difference, the more the differentiation (Brown, 1987). Highly differentiated people are expected to have greater occupational and educational achievement, stability, and satisfaction (Erwin, 1987). High differentiation, combined with consistency, seems likely to facilitate selection of career goals that are congruent with a person's personality patterns.

Vocational *identity,* the fifth and least well-defined of Holland's major constructs, is a measure of clarity of career goals and self-image derived from Erikson's concept of identity. Leong and Morris (1989) defined vocational identity as "an awareness of, and ability to specify one's own interests, personality characteristics, strengths, and goals as these relate to career choices" (p. 117). Having a strong vocational identity is believed to facilitate career decision making as well as confidence in those decisions and is associated with being well organized, self-confident, rational, socially comfortable, and wanting to use one's creativity and abilities effectively. Vocational identity, then, is a sort of overall measure of adjustment. *My Vocational Situation,* an inventory developed by Holland (Holland, Daiger, & Power, 1980), can be used to measure identity.

Holland's theory has been extensively studied and evaluated over the past 25 years and has considerable heuristic value for counseling both males and females (Holland, 1987a). The SDS facilitates identification of type. Extensive materials developed to accompany the SDS encourage development of knowledge of self and occupations and the compatible matching of the two. Other inventories, including the Harrington/O'Shea System for Career Decision-Making and the Strong Interest Inventory, have used Holland's hexagonal framework to organize information. (All of these inventories will be discussed later in this book.)

At the same time, some shortcomings to Holland's theory remain. Continued research is needed to give full support to his constructs. Also, Holland and his colleagues touch only lightly on such issues as how personality types develop, how decisions can best be made, how career roles and life roles interface, and the usefulness of Holland's model for people from non-Western cultures.

Theories Derived From Personal Counseling

As the field of career counseling has broadened to encompass life planning, the distinction between career counseling and personal counseling has diminished. Counselors focusing on career concerns seem to be drawing increasingly on approaches to general counseling in their work.

Person-Centered Career Counseling

A prominent example of this trend is the use of person-centered counseling to help people with career concerns. The person-centered approach is derived from the ideas of Carl Rogers. Rogers emphasized the importance of the self-concept and the uniqueness of each person. He believed that many personal problems stem from low self-esteem and advanced a counseling approach designed to improve self-esteem through the counselor's acceptance and understanding of the client. Person-centered career counseling also has been heavily influenced by existential and humanistic theories and, in keeping with those theories, helps people to discover goals and meaning that are relevant to them. Mark J. Miller (1988b) views the ultimate goal of person-centered career counseling as clarification and implementation of the self-concept through an occupational role that will provide a means of self-expression and fulfillment. As Bloland and Walker (1981) stated, "Of all available choices, life work may be the most critical to self-definition" (p. 199). Homan (1986), writing from an existential point of view, supported this position: "Vocation is the organizing, existential principle of the concept of work . . . Vocation . . . reflects the matrix of meaning that one attributes both to one's career and to oneself" (pp. 14-15).

In person- or client-centered career counseling, tests, inventories, and career information are de-emphasized. When inventories or information are used, process and dialogue are usually more important than content. Clients participate actively in the process of deciding whether tests will be used, what tests will be used, and what meaning they have. Clients' use of their own resources is emphasized, and self-directed rather than counselor-directed or test-directed behavior and decisions are encouraged. In this way, clients' ability to exercise free choice and accept responsibility for their actions is encouraged. Key assumptions in this approach are that (a) people know what is best for themselves, (b) labeling or diagnosis is unnecessary, (c) the counselor should focus on the person first and the data second, (d) the best occupational information comes from people employed in the occupations of interest, and (e) career counseling should help people implement their self-concepts through career choice (M. J. Miller, 1988b). Counselor interventions to promote the process of career choice include genuineness, acceptance, open questions, reflection of feelings, and other techniques designed to develop self-awareness and decision making. If a client's personal concerns seem to be intruding on his or her career development, those problems would receive the counselor's attention. The counselor is in a responsive mode, with the client as the initiator (Freeman, 1990).

Cognitive-Behavioral Approaches to Career Counseling

Another group of approaches to career counseling, derived from general theories of counseling, are the cognitive-behavioral approaches. These models look at people's thinking processes and hypothesize that learning is accomplished by what people tell themselves (Peterson, Sampson, & Reardon, 1991). Self-defeating beliefs can interfere with career development. Changes in both behavior and emotions, then, are believed to occur by effecting changes in self-talk and thinking processes (Richman, 1988).

Cognitive-behavioral approaches place particular emphasis on understanding and improving how people make decisions. Gelatt's (1967) decision theory offers a sequential approach to understanding how decisions are made:

1. The person sees that a decision is needed.
2. Data collection and consideration of options are undertaken.

3. Data are used to determine possible courses of action and their probable consequences.
4. Values are considered in assessing desirability of outcomes.
5. Options are evaluated further and a decision is made.

Counselors can help people through this systematic process of decision making by exploring their readiness to make decisions, their self-images, their understanding of their world of work, their usual style of decision making, and their ability to follow the steps in this model.

Gati (Gati & Tikotzki, 1989), too, looked at the process of decision making and suggested that decisions are made in one of three ways (see also Carson & Mowsesian, 1990).

Expected Utility Model. Gati viewed this as a compensatory, rational model. At the outset, a person determines criteria and prioritizes them. Options are then reviewed in a linear fashion, with those options offering the best combination of expected value and probability of achievement being seen as the best choices.

A variation on this model is the sequential elimination model. In this noncompensatory model, the person would list all relevant aspects of careers and rank them according to importance. For each aspect, a range of acceptable qualities would be identified. Finally, alternatives would be evaluated according to these guidelines, until a small number of options are identified as most desirable.

Gati viewed the expected utility model as the best way to make decisions from the point of view of decision theory but recognized that it might be unrealistic to expect most people to go through such a systematic process.

Conjunctive Model. This is a noncompensatory model in which minimal criteria are initially determined. An alternative then is explored, until it fails to meet the minimal criteria. Then another alternative is generated and explored.

Within-Attributes Model. This is another noncompensatory model in which options are screened with respect to one criterion (e.g., interests). All options that pass this initial screen are then reviewed according to the next criterion (e.g., abilities).

According to Gati, most people using computerized career guidance systems use noncompensatory strategies that seem to be the best strategy for large-scale decisions. The compensatory process, however, seems more appropriate when deciding between two options (Gati & Tikotzki, 1989).

Learning and Social Influence Theories

In light of the importance of decision making in career development, career counselors should probably familiarize themselves with research on learning styles. Research conducted primarily during the 1970s and 1980s has indicated that people learn and absorb new information in a variety of ways. Inventories have been developed to assist teachers and counselors in identifying the learning styles of their students and clients and developing more effective ways of communicating with them. One of these inventories, the Learning Styles Inventory (Kolb, 1976, 1984), delineates the following four learning styles:

1. *Accommodators* are people who are flexible and responsive to new situations but who have difficulty taking a broad view and seeing the importance of a piece of information.
2. *Divergers* are imaginative and insightful but have difficulty making decisions and moving forward.
3. *Convergers* use deductive reasoning effectively and efficiently and are more comfortable dealing with data and things than with people.
4. *Assimilators* use theory and inductive reasoning well but may have difficulty with practical application.

Understanding a person's learning style can be helpful, especially to the cognitive career counselor. That knowledge can help the counselor determine how best to present information and how to promote exploration of self and alternatives.

Dorn (1988) advanced a social influence approach to career counseling. According to his point of view, when people seek counseling, they typically feel powerless and attribute their difficulties to factors beyond their control. Dorn suggests that the counselor can modify this helpless feeling by encouraging people to reattribute their difficulties to factors over which they do have control. Drawing further on the theory of social influence, Dorn suggests that the counselors' reattributions are more likely to be accepted if counselors increase their social power base by presenting themselves as expert, trustworthy, and socially attractive.

Krumboltz, Mitchell, and Gelatt (1976) view career development as a lifelong learning process that takes place in a social context. They view that process as involving four factors: genetic endowments and special abilities, environmental conditions and events, learning experiences, and task approach skills. They, too, pay particular attention to learning and thinking. Sometimes, learning experiences can lead to the development of distorted cognitions related to career development: For example, "Career development involves only one decision that should be made at a specific time," or "Work should satisfy all my needs," or "If only I get a college degree, then I will be happy" (Lewis & Gilhousen, 1981). Mitchell and Krumboltz (1987) found that cognitive restructuring was effective in reducing anxiety about career decision making, encouraging occupational exploration, and promoting satisfying decisions.

Cognitive-behavioral career counselors and learning theorists use a broad repertoire of techniques in their work, techniques that also might be integrated effectively into other approaches to career counseling. Examples of these techniques are the following:

1. giving information
2. guided career fantasies and images
3. promoting awareness of learning styles
4. modeling
5. exploration and modification of dysfunctional belief systems
6. training in problem solving
7. self-observation of behavior
8. rewards and consequences (Keller, Biggs, & Gysbers, 1982)
9. reinforcement
10. setting goals
11. time management
12. assertiveness training

Sociological/Environmental Theories

As the boundaries between theories of career counseling and theories of general counseling have loosened, so have the boundaries between the person and the environment. Most career development counselors and theorists now recognize the importance of considering the person in context and exploring the influences of the family, socioeconomic environment, ethnic origins, community, and workplace. Some theories seem to give even greater attention to the context than they do to the person. Although most of these theories of career development are rather general and rudimentary at this time, they emphasize the importance of considering the person in context.

Impact of Family Counseling on Career Counseling

Although no systematic approach to family-based career counseling has yet obtained a prominent place in the literature, many techniques drawn from family counseling have found their way into career counseling. Adlerian approaches to family counseling have contributed the exploration of birth order and earliest memories to the repertoire of interventions used by career counselors. The ideas of Murray Bowen (1978) and his systems approach to family counseling have led to an interest in exploring family career history, expectations, and differentiation as part of career counseling. Those dimensions seem particularly important in adolescents and young adults who are undecided or indecisive about their career goals. Over time, other concepts and techniques from family counseling seem likely to be incorporated into career counseling with the establishment of the life span approach to understanding career development.

Happenstance in Career Choice

Another perspective on the impact of context on career development is suggested by M. J. Miller (1983). He pointed out that career planning rarely is a purely logical process but is usually influenced by social events, accidents, illness, economic change, and biological events. Counselors and their clients should be aware of the role of chance in career development and should be prepared both to take advantage of unanticipated opportunities and to cope with disappointments that occur despite the best planning.

Commonalities in Career Development Theories

Theories of career choice discussed in this chapter have been organized into the following categories: trait-and-factor theories, developmental or self-concept theories, personality and need theories, theories derived from general counseling, learning and social influence theories, and sociological/environmental theories. These categories reflect the major emphases of theories of career development. Career theorists differ as to the factors they see as most important in career choice, how active a role people are seen as playing in their own career development, and the importance of the developmental aspect of career choice (Hesketh, 1985). Many commonalities exist among these theories, however, including the following:

1. Career development is a process that follows relatively predictable stages throughout the life span. However, the nature of those stages varies between people. Counselors, then, should consider both general and unique individual processes of development.
2. Career information and counseling can be useful at multiple transitions and choice points throughout the life span.
3. Career development is influenced by many personal factors, including gender, family background, biology, personality, thinking and learning styles, values, interests, and abilities. All of these, both obstacles and resources, should be explored during career counseling to maximize self-awareness and facilitate career maturity.
4. The self-image is a particularly important influence on career choices. Accuracy of self-concept can facilitate the making of rewarding career choices.
5. External factors such as time, society, environment, geography, economics, and chance also influence career development and should be considered during career counseling.
6. People whose career choices are congruent with their personalities and who have well-defined and prominent personality patterns seem particularly likely to have stable and satisfying careers.
7. Career counseling should focus not only on occupational preferences but also on social and family goals, leisure interests, geographic choices, and other aspects of the lifestyle to reflect not just career planning but life planning.
8. Major goals of career counseling include developing people's sense of responsibility and empowerment so that they can make independent, purposeful, and deliberate career choices that are likely to be attainable and rewarding.

Theories of career choice are far more comprehensive, complex, and well-grounded in research than they were in the days of Frank Parsons (1909). However, we still have not developed one universal approach to facilitating career development, nor have we developed a formula to clearly guide our application of interventions. As Savickas (1989) put it, "We know that career interventions generally have positive effects. Now we need to determine which interventions work with whom under what circumstances" (p. 107). Most career counselors, then, will probably find themselves taking an eclectic approach in which they integrate several theories to provide a framework for their research and interventions. Beyond that, they probably will draw on their own abilities, training, and personalities as well as on the attributes of their setting and the individual needs and learning styles of their clients to develop an approach to counseling a particular person that seems most likely to be effective. The balance of this book is designed to provide counselors with the understanding and tools they need to develop effective approaches to career counseling and assessment.

A Lexicon of Career Counseling

The field of career counseling has developed its own terminology. Understanding the vocabulary of the profession is important in understanding its concepts.

Career. This is a sequence of roles or positions, including work, leisure, volunteer, and educational pursuits. *Career* may encompass several occupations or vocations and many jobs or positions. However, people have only one career, extending from early childhood through retirement. *Career* has been defined as "the evolving sequence of a person's work experiences over time" (Arthur, Hall, & Lawrence, 1989, p. 8) and as "the total constellation of psychological, sociological, educational, physical, economic and chance factors that combine to shape the career of any given individual over the life span" (Hoyt, 1991, p. 23). Careers have multiple functions for both people and society. Super (1957a) perceived careers as satisfying three major personal needs:

1. human relations needs (e.g., socialization, recognition, independence, status)
2. activity needs (e.g., structure, stimulation, creativity, use of skills)
3. livelihood needs (e.g., security, compensation)

Identity needs, such as self-awareness, self-confidence, self-definition, and self-actualization, also could be added to that list. For society, careers sustain the economy and provide needed products and services. For people, careers give form and substance to their lives.

Occupation/Vocation. This is a definable work activity found in numerous and varied settings. For example, counseling is an occupation; there are many types of counselors, employed in a variety of settings, including schools, colleges, and mental health centers.

Job. This is defined as a group of related or similar positions in a particular place of employment. Career counselor at State University is a job.

Position. A position is a group of tasks, duties, or activities performed by one person. Coordinator of career counseling at State University is a position.

Work. Hoyt (1991) provided a useful definition for work: "conscious effort, other than having as its primary purpose either coping or relaxation, aimed at producing benefits for oneself and/or oneself and others" (p. 23).

Career Development

Career development is a term that came into general use in the 1960s and was broadened in definition through the 1970s. During the 1980s, theorists in the field broadened the term even further and spoke of *life career development* (Gysbers, 1984). In this book, life career development is viewed as a process that encompasses the total life span and includes all of a person's roles and positions. Career development includes not only paid employment but also leisure activities, volunteer work, time spent on education, and time spent at home caring for a family.

Career development is not just a decision to enter a particular line of work; it reflects a person's accumulated life experience and inevitably has a profound effect on all aspects of that person's life. The family life and leisure activities of the physician, machinist, teacher, concert pianist, and freelance writer are likely to differ because of the differences in their working lives. Their occupational choices, then, are really lifestyle choices.

Although career development varies from one person to another, there is general agreement about several characteristics of career development.

1. It is a continuous process of choices and adjustments.
2. It is multidimensional.
3. The rate of career development differs from one person to the next.
4. Career development can be described in terms of typical stages with certain milestones or developments associated with each stage.
5. Career development is commonly characterized by relatively predictable growth and continuity, with early development being predictive of later development.
6. Career development involves an interaction of environment, experience, and individual potential leading to the evolution of a self-concept and a corresponding lifestyle.

Gribbons and Lohnes (1968) identified five styles of career development:

1. *Floundering*—changing occupational choice from one cluster of occupations to another with no advancement in achieved level.
2. *Trial*—changing occupational choice within a group of related occupations, leading to a refinement of career goals.
3. *Stagnation*—remaining developmentally stationary for too long with resulting deterioration of status or opportunity.
4. *Instrumentation*—goal-directed change.
5. *Establishment*—stabilizing in a rewarding career.

Although life career development will be described in this book according to age-related stages, the probability of individual variation in career development must be borne in mind. Taylor (1972) pointed out that there are actually three kinds of stages: stage as a metaphor (e.g., leaving home), stage as a paraphrase for age (e.g., the 30s), and stage as a symbol for an event that is significant within a period of life (e.g., menopause). People who experience significant life events, such as marriage or the birth of children, at a time much before or much after these events are experienced by their age peers may be developmentally more like those experiencing these same events than they are like their age group. The sequence and duration of stages, then, can vary. Although patterns of life career development commonly do correlate with age, their relationship to individual life patterns and experiences certainly also should be considered.

Career Maturity

Career maturity has been defined as the ability to successfully negotiate the tasks and transitions inherent in the process of career development and the readiness to make age- and stage-appropriate career choices (Yost & Corbishly, 1987). Therefore, career maturity is both a process and a descriptive term. Measures of career maturity, to be discussed later in this book, have been developed. Scores on those measures seem to be related to general intellectual ability (Westbrook, Sanford, Merwin, Fleenor, & Renzi, 1987), raising questions about exactly what career maturity really is.

Super (1983), one of the first researchers to write of career maturity, has suggested *career adaptability* as a more appropriate term than career maturity. According to Super, the process of career adaptability has five elements:

1. *Planfulness*—independence, ability to learn from experience and anticipate the future, and self-esteem.
2. *Exploration*—asking questions and gathering information, using resources, and participating in school, the community, the workplace, and the family.
3. *Information gathering*—on the world of work, occupational preferences, and occupational and other life roles.
4. *Decision making*—making choices according to sound principles of decision making.
5. *Reality orientation*—developing self-knowledge; realistic options; consistency of preferences; clear values, interests, and objectives; and work experience.

Gribbons and Lohnes (1968) studied the career development or readiness for career planning of young people and found four patterns of career maturation:

1. constant maturity—consistent pursuit of a stated and realistic goal
2. emerging maturity—passage through the appropriate developmental stages and tasks
3. degeneration—progressive deterioration of hopes and accomplishments, accompanied by frustration and loss of status

4. constant immaturity—persistent fixation on unrealistic goals, with no evident progress

Positive career maturation will generally be characterized by an array of lifelong processes, including (a) increasing self-awareness, (b) increasing knowledge of relevant options, (c) increasing congruence between self-image (abilities, interests, values, personality) and career goals, (d) increasing realism of career goals, (e) increasing competence for career planning and success, (f) improving career-related attitudes (achievement orientation, independence, planfulness, commitment, motivation, self-efficacy), and (g) increasing success and satisfaction with one's life career development.

Career Satisfaction

In the 1940s and 1950s, people cited security as what they most wanted from their jobs (Strauss, 1976). Both the Great Depression and World War II were fresh in the minds of those workers, and the prospect of regular employment, in itself, offered great gratification. However, by the 1970s, most people listed interesting work as what they most wanted from their jobs. Since then, the emphasis on career satisfaction has grown.

Most people hope to have careers that will be rewarding to them. They believe in work, are committed to the process of working, and would work even if it were not financially necessary (Yankelovich, 1978). Most people, indeed, report success in achieving occupational satisfaction. In a Gallup poll, 28% of respondents said they were completely satisfied with their jobs, 60% were mostly satisfied, 9% were mostly dissatisfied, and only 3% reported feeling completely dissatisfied. At the same time, there has been growing evidence of employee dissatisfaction. Hackman and Oldham (1981) attribute this to the declining challenge offered by many jobs as well as to dated management policies and practices.

Career development has a great effect on the overall happiness of people and may determine whether they will regard themselves as successes or failures. Many studies have been conducted to determine the concomitants of career satisfaction. Dawis and Lofquist (1984) advanced a theory of work adjustment that suggests that satisfaction results from a correspondence between individual needs and the nature of the work environment. They viewed work adjustment as being the sum of the worker's satisfactoriness and the level of occupational satisfaction. Dawis and Lofquist found that occupational satisfaction was strongly related to involvement on the job, morale, and overall life satisfaction and only minimally related to on-the-job performance and productivity.

Other studies have confirmed this finding of only a slight relationship between career satisfaction and success. Cytrynbaum and Crites (1989) suggest that this is due to the presence of a moderator variable, perhaps social or environmental circumstances.

Holland (1966) suggested that occupational satisfaction depends on a congruence of personality (including both interests and abilities) and work environment. The literature has provided considerable support to the relationship between congruence and satisfaction, stability, and achievement (Betz et al., 1989).

Gottfredson and Holland (1990) found that the single most efficient predictor of job satisfaction for a group of bank tellers was a measure of expected satisfaction. Gottfredson and Holland concluded: "The simple expedient of asking people if they will be satisfied with a job generates efficient predictions of subsequent job satisfaction" (p. 396).

Looking at the question from the other side, Borgen, Amundson, and Harder (1988) found that underemployment (in other words, lack of congruence between abilities and work activities) had a negative impact on personal relationships, self-esteem, mood, and optimism about the future. Underemployment, apparently a problem for 25% to 50% of recent college graduates, has been correlated with an increased rate of suicide. Even in cases in which people's incomes were substantial, dissatisfaction was associated with tenure in jobs that failed to make good use of people's skills. This finding is consistent with earlier studies that suggest that nearly all people seem to value intrinsic work-related rewards, such as achievement and independence, more than extrinsic ones, such as salary and flexible hours (Weaver, 1975).

T. Adler (1989) found that gender was another important determinant of occupational satisfaction. In a study of recent college graduates, Adler found that men in male-dominated occupations congruent with their college majors were particularly satisfied with their work. Women, too, generally were more satisfied in male-dominated occupations, except for those women in female-dominated occupations that were highly congruent with their college majors. Least happy were those women in female-dominated occupations that were not congruent with their majors and, therefore, presumably not making good use of their abilities.

Quinn and Baldi de Mandilovitch (1980) reviewed 16 studies on the relationship between education and career satisfaction. For people with a college degree, overall career satisfaction, particularly in the areas of challenge and financial rewards, was significantly related to education. This is consistent with Super and Bohn's (1970) earlier finding that people in higher-level jobs tend to be more satisfied than are people in lower-level jobs.

Expectations of success seem important in determining both expectation and experience of satisfaction. Barak, Librowsky, and Shiloh (1989) found strong correlations between perceived ability to succeed in one's career and anticipated satisfaction.

In recent years, there has been increasing labor-management cooperation to develop programs to improve the quality of the working life. Programs include features such as arbitration, increased options in health and pension plans, educational benefits, increased vacation and sick days, improved retirement and unemployment benefits, more flexible schedules, job restructuring, job sharing, more stimulating work roles, and increased employee voice in determining one's work-related tasks. In addition, employee assistance programs have increased dramatically in number. These programs are designed to help people with problems such as substance abuse, family conflict, finances, and supervisor-employee conflict and to indirectly reduce absenteeism and turnover rates.

What people find satisfying in their work differs. Some seek achievement and recognition, whereas others seek socialization or stimulation. Similarly, people's sources of satisfaction differ. Some derive their greatest satisfaction from their families or leisure activities, whereas others are most gratified by their careers. These multiple sources of satisfaction help to address the problems presented by tedious and unstimulating jobs and underemployment. However, counselors should not minimize the importance of career satisfaction in people's lives and should consider the factors cited in this section when helping people find greater satisfaction through their careers.

Career Success

Career or occupational success typically has been assessed by measuring some combination of satisfaction and performance. Reeves (1970) suggested discussion of the following questions to measure career success:

To what extent has your career been

1. using and developing, but not exceeding, your physical capacities?
2. meeting your economic, social, and geographic needs?

3. making full use of your abilities, without exceeding their limits or curtailing their development?

4. contributing to your experience and credentials?

5. satisfying and expanding your interests on the job as well as allowing sufficient opportunity for satisfaction outside of the job?

6. making good use of your personal strengths, minimizing your weaknesses, and generally encouraging positive personality development? (p. 214)

Garfield (1986), writing about so-called peak performers, suggested that a cluster of personal attributes were highly correlated with success. According to Garfield, peak performers do the following:

1. have a purpose in life

2. formulate plans to accomplish their goals

3. don't get trapped in a comfortable plateau for long

4. take reasonable risks after determining what the consequences are likely to be

5. base their self-confidence on their history of using their skills successfully

6. solve problems rather than placing blame

7. prepare for future events by rehearsing them mentally with a positive outcome

8. enjoy taking control

9. are concerned with both quality and quantity of performance

10. train and make good use of those around them

Reeves's (1970) questions provide a useful guide for assessing success, whereas Garfield's characteristics determine how well people are contributing to their own successes and, if appropriate, can identify ways to increase their chances for success. Although these general guidelines are useful, counselors should ascertain the individual goals of a particular person. Some people may measure success by salary and promotions; others, by the creativity and impact of their work. Success, then, for a particular person, can best be measured by the degree of fulfillment of that person's salient goals and needs.

The Role of Leisure in Career Development

Most career counselors recognize that effective career planning looks beyond educational and occupational choices and considers the interface between career and personal goals. According to Weiner and Hunt

(1983), there is a general consensus among career counselors that the definition and scope of the term *career* has changed considerably. Newer definitions of career equate it with the concepts of life/work or lifestyle planning, concepts that recognize other areas such as health, leisure, interpersonal relations, and personal goals as being linked to career.

McDaniels (1984) goes so far as to define career as "the totality of work and leisure one does in a lifetime" (p. 35). He defined leisure as "relatively self-determined activities and experiences that are available due to discretionary income, time, and social behavior; the activity may be physical, intellectual, volunteer, creative or some combination of all four" (p. 35).

Leisure counseling is now an emerging specialty, designed to help people make rewarding use of their free time. Life span career counselors, too, should attend to their clients' use of leisure time. McDaniels (1984) found that average weekly leisure time ranged from 23 hours for dual-career parents to 43 hours for retired people. Even those with extensive job and family responsibilities seem to have considerable time for leisure pursuits. Younger workers and students place particularly strong emphasis on leisure. However, without thought and planning, many or all of those hours may be spent watching television, the primary leisure activity in the United States. Only 58% of the population reports deriving a great deal of satisfaction from leisure time (McDowell, 1981). Nevertheless, manifested activities certainly go beyond television viewing for most. The top-ranked leisure activity is spending time with family and friends. Nearly one half of adults are involved in some type of volunteer work. Over 96% of the population engage in an athletic activity at least once a month.

McDowell (1981) viewed leisure as "a powerfully integrative aspect of life" (p. 11) and stated that leisure could promote well-being by contributing to a sense of fulfillment. Leisure can promote development of a positive identity; increase sense of optimism; provide enjoyment; offer opportunities for achievement, learning, and development of self-esteem; serve as an arena for socialization and intimacy; provide challenge, distraction, and relaxation; improve health; and complement or compensate for other life endeavors. Counselors can facilitate the process of life/work planning by encouraging people to (a) assess their use of leisure time, (b) identify leisure activities likely to be rewarding, (c) select and schedule activities that complement occupational roles (e.g., can be done in available time and fulfill needs or goals that are not being met well through work), and (d) evaluate their overall involvement in work and leisure to develop a rewarding career path. Conflicts between work demands and leisure interests should be examined, with compromises or changes made as needed.

Career Indecision

Many people seen by career counselors are experiencing career indecision, an uncertainly about what career options they want to pursue. Savickas (1989) surveyed recent literature on this construct and suggested that people with career indecision could be categorized into the following three subgroups.

Group one. People who feel no pressure to make decisions: Although they usually have good problem-solving skills and are confident that they will eventually make rewarding career choices, they lack information about their options. Van Matre and Cooper (1984) termed these people "undecided-decisive"; Kaplan and Brown (1987) called these people "undecided rather than "indecisive" and viewed them as making a developmentally appropriate choice to defer commitment to a career path until they had gathered more information.

Group two. People who manifest some immaturity and anxiety about their careers, experiencing moderate to severe indecision.

Group three. People who manifest considerable immaturity in career development and who are highly anxious about their indecision, people Van Matre and Cooper call undecided-indecisive: These people seem unable to make decisions, even though they have the necessary data; they typically have a low sense of self-efficacy about their ability to make good career decisions (Kaplan & Brown, 1987).

Differentiating between these three groups seems important for the career counselor because different interventions are indicated for each group. Typically, people in group one require only brief intervention focusing on information giving and self-awareness, perhaps using computer-assisted career guidance, workshops, or self-help programs to promote greater awareness of self and the world of work and to develop effective decision-making skills.

Counseling for people in groups two and three should pay some attention to anxiety and self-efficacy. Those in group two require more intensive career counseling than do those in group one; inventories as well as individual help with planning can increase readiness to make decisions, promote self-awareness, reduce anxiety, and facilitate sound decision making. Interest inventories are very useful for people who are undecided and seem to predict eventual occupational choice as well for those who are undecided as they do for those who are decided (Bartling & Hood, 1981).

People in group three may not be ready for career-focused interventions. Rather, they usually will need personal counseling first to help them overcome barriers in their career development. Replacing avoidance with more constructive coping abilities to reduce anxiety is one likely avenue to improving their career maturity.

Although career indecision is likely to be prevalent among people seeking career counseling, Newman, Fuqua, and Minger (1990) observed that many people who describe themselves as decided about their career choices have some discomfort about those choices and may have made choices under pressure or out of a desire to please without adequate information about themselves or the world of work. Van Matre and Cooper (1984) have called these people "decided-indecisive," as distinguished from the "decided-decisive" people who feel a sense of closure and comfort with the career decisions they have made. Decided-indecisive people, too, are likely to benefit from career information and counseling.

Career indecision is receiving increasing attention in the career counseling literature. Counselors helping people with career decisions should identify the nature of their client's indecision; view that indecision in the context of the client's stage of career development, sense of self, and level of work importance; and use that information to plan interventions that are most likely to be helpful.

Career-Related Stress

Stress is another dimension of career development that has received increasing attention in recent years. Some occupations are inherently more stressful than others. One study indicated that the most stressful occupations, in order, are (a) firefighter, (b) race car driver, (c) astronaut, (d) surgeon, (e) NFL football player, (f) police officer, (g) osteopath, (h) air traffic controller, (i) mayor, and (j) jockey, whereas the least stressful occupations are (a) musical instrument repairer, (b) industrial machine repairer, (c) medical records technician, (d) pharmacist, (e) medical assistant, (f) typist/word processor, (g) librarian, (h) janitor, (i) book-keeper, and (j) forklift operator (Krantz, 1988). Job situations particularly likely to engender stress are those that place severe and prolonged physical and psychological demands on workers while at the same time offering them little support or opportunity to control the demands being placed on them. Role conflict and ambiguity, boredom on the job, shift work, and lack of rewarding work also can contribute to stress at work (Zunker, 1990).

Stress is a function of the person as well as the job. People who are low in self-esteem, have high anxiety, tend to be passive, withdraw from social supports, and have little commitment to their work, are more likely to experience stress and its frequent by-product, a feeling of being burned out or stagnated (Bruhn, 1989). People experiencing personal or professional transitions are particularly vulnerable to stress.

Adult clients, many of whom will have a substantial work history, often seek career counseling because of work-related stress. If these people can effect changes in their jobs, such as increasing their involvement in decision making and their sense of control, making greater use of support systems, and maintaining a realistic level of demands, their stress is likely to diminish. Personal changes, such as understanding the nature and cause of stress, clarifying what can and what cannot be changed, improving coping mechanisms, developing a greater sense of self-efficacy, and maintaining a sense of humor, can also contribute to stress reduction. Stress can be used productively as a motivation to change and, with help in seeing their options and improving both their own coping skills and the nature of their jobs, people can improve their career development through career counseling focusing on stress reduction.

Career Self-Efficacy

Self-efficacy has been defined by Kaplan and Brown (1987) as the belief that one can successfully perform behaviors needed to produce certain outcomes and accomplish certain plans. Self-efficacy seems to be related to self-esteem, and both constructs seem positively correlated with engaging in goal-directed behavior, gathering information productively on the self and on career options, perceiving a broad range of occupational options, and conducting an effective job search (Blustein, 1989; Steffy, Shaw, & Noe, 1989). Self-efficacy, then, another relatively new term in the career lexicon, seems to be an important construct for the career counselor to consider because of its close tie to positive career development.

Motivation and Level of Aspiration

Work-related motivation is the drive to fulfill one's needs through career experiences. Many have written about salient needs. Maslow (1943) established a needs hierarchy that begins with physiological needs and ends with self-actualization. Maslow suggested that basic needs must be filled first before people could attend to fulfillment of higher needs. People have two categories of basic needs in their careers: extrinsic compensation (e.g., salary, benefits, security) and intrinsic needs (e.g., achievement, recognition) (Zunker, 1990). These and other frameworks offer a structure for examination and discussion of work-related motivation.

Motivation is a complex dimension, composed of factors in both the self and the job. Farmer (1985) reported that three major factors contributed to motivation: (a) background, including gender, geography, socioeconomic status, race, age, and ability; (b) environment, particularly support and encouragement for pursuing a particular career path; and, most important of the three, (c) personality and self-concept. Work-related motivators include economic rewards, personal enjoyment, and opportunity to make a contribution to society.

Motivation is a key determinant of how much effort people put into their work, the level of aspiration they establish for themselves, and their degree of success. Motivation seems likely to be enhanced when personal drives are congruent with work attributes. When motivation is low, according to Hoyt (1991), work becomes drudgery. When it is high, career commitment is strong, level of aspiration is high, and a sense of mastery is valued and experienced (Farmer, 1985).

Katzell and Thompson (1990) suggest seven strategies for improving motivation that might be used as part of career counseling and that are particularly likely to be useful strategies for managers who want to increase employee motivation:

1. Ensure that personal goals and values are relevant to the organization and job.
2. Improve performance incentives and rewards.
3. Reinforce positive performance.
4. Set goals that are specific, clear, and attainable while also being challenging and attractive.

5. Ensure that workers have adequate personal, social, and material resources.

6. Use interpersonal and group process, team development, and focus groups to increase morale and motivation.

7. Improve the quality of work life via better hours, more attractive work conditions, or other means.

Factors Affecting Career Development

Career development has been defined earlier in this chapter. Considerable research has focused not only on defining career development but on looking at factors that have an impact on that process. Six general factors have been identified as influencing career development (O'Neil et al., 1980). These include familial factors, societal factors, socioeconomic factors, individual factors, and psychosocial and emotional factors.

Familial Factors

Probably the most important determinant of people's career development is their family background. Early childhood experiences, role models established by both mother and father, birth order and, career paths both present and absent in the family, as well as career paths both encouraged and discouraged by the family are some of the dimensions of the family that influence career development.

Penick and Jepsen (1992) found that family functioning seemed more important in determining vocational identity than did achievement, gender, or socioeconomic status. Families that were extremely enmeshed, disengaged, conflicted, or laissez-faire seemed to limit development of vocational identity and involvement in career planning.

Generally, children, especially sons, are encouraged to (and do) select careers that equal or surpass those of their parents in status or prestige. Especially for males, patterns of mobility seem to be strongly affected by their fathers' occupations, with farmers' sons tending to stay in farming, sons of blue-collar workers either remaining in blue-collar positions or moving into white-collar fields, and sons of white-collar workers remaining in white-collar fields. Sons tend either to duplicate the type and level of their fathers' work in their own occupational choices or to move upward in terms of the status of their chosen careers (Bailey &

Stadt, 1973). Some occupations, notably the physical and social sciences and the medical professions, seem to run in families.

Paternal earnings have been found to correlate with sons' expected earnings, suggesting that sons with high-salaried fathers will aspire to well-paying occupations, whereas those with less economically successful fathers may not aim so high. Abilities and interests sometimes have little bearing on these aspirations. Similarly, parental pressure toward college attendance often is a stronger determinant of educational aspiration than is ability or interest.

Women actually seem to have more career mobility than do men because their socioeconomic status typically is moderated not only by their own careers and those of their parents but also by the careers of their spouses. Because women do not yet have earnings commensurate with those of men, even for equal work, the male's occupation rather than the female's usually will determine the family's socioeconomic status.

Mothers, as well as fathers, have a strong influence on the career development of their children, particularly on the career attainment of their daughters. This influence is especially evident in early studies, conducted when women were less likely to pursue careers. Baruch (1970) found that college women whose mothers had desired to establish themselves occupationally had higher self-esteem and a stronger sense of competence than did college women whose mothers had not aspired to occupational accomplishment. Baruch (1974) also found that daughters of employed mothers were more likely to use their mothers as role models. Daughters of career-oriented women, then, tend to feel better about themselves and about the role of women than do daughters of non-career-oriented women.

One task facing counselors is helping people formulate career plans that are not primarily a reflection of parental modeling or pressure and that are realistic and likely to be rewarding. Accomplishing this involves both increasing people's awareness of their own strengths and preferences and helping them to understand and deal with family models and messages.

Although children commonly strive to equal or surpass parental levels of educational and occupational success, the career plans of some may be influenced by a fear of competing with the parents or a strong personal need to defy or differ from parental choices and preferences. In these cases, too, choices may not take adequate account of interests or abilities and may be self-destructive.

Roe's theory (1956) of career choice and development emphasized the importance of child-rearing patterns on children's subsequent career development. Although studies of Roe's ideas have not provided consistent support, several studies have demonstrated the impact of child rearing and early childhood experiences on career development. Medvene and Shueman (1978) found that people who were reared in families in which the dominant parent was perceived as avoiding seemed to gravitate toward non-person-oriented careers. Orleans (1970) concluded that maternal stimulation promoted an interest in creative fields, whereas an authoritarian mode of parental discipline led people to seek out work environments that provided structure and security.

A related variable that seems to affect career development is parents' personality. DeWinne, Overton, and Schneider (1978) classified parents and their college-age children according to Holland's (1991) hexagonal model of personality. They found that parents' personality types were related to the personality types of both their sons and their daughters, with the paternal personality type exerting a greater influence than the mother's. Lopez (1989) found a negative correlation between the amount of intrafamily conflict in the family of origin and college students' adjustment to college. Women were especially affected by this dynamic. Career indecisiveness in college students also seemed related to family background and was more prevalent among students from families that were either enmeshed or disengaged; those from families with moderate levels of cohesiveness had the least indecisiveness.

Birth Order

Just as career development is influenced by parents, so it also is influenced by siblings and birth order. Alfred Adler (1931) first brought the importance of birth order to popular attention. He viewed oldest or firstborn children as responsible and achieving; they were expected to feel dethroned with the birth of the second child and to work hard to overcome feelings of insecurity and maintain a superior position. Second or middle children also were expected to be ambitious, but their strivings were colored by the realization that they could never really surpass their older siblings. As a result, second borns typically choose an area of accomplishment that is very different from that of their firstborn siblings so that they are not in direct competition. Adler saw youngest children as typically pampered and spoiled; they were not expected to develop the ambitiousness of older children.

Over the years, many studies have supported Adler's ideas about birth order. Breland (1974) studied high school students taking the National Merit Examination and found that those who were firstborn or from small families generally scored higher than did both later borns and those from large families. Levine (1976) suggested that children from small families typically perform better academically than do children from large families because the former receive more attention, advice, and information. That theory may help to explain the higher achievement of people who are firstborn. For a time, they are only children and are not required to share their parents' teaching, intellectual stimulation, and encouragement with siblings.

A study of firstborn and later-born elementary students suggested that the firstborn also had a higher level of academic motivation that led to better performance in school (Adams & Phillips, 1972). The authors of that study concluded that parents had higher expectations for their firstborn children and that the children were striving to meet their parents' expectations.

Bradley (1982) obtained similar results in a study of adults. According to Bradley, people who are firstborn tend to be high achievers in structured occupations. Male firstborns are overrepresented among astronauts, chemists, anthropologists, and army officers and underrepresented in the skilled trades, music, agriculture, and social service. Female firstborns are overrepresented among translators, chemists, and registered nurses and underrepresented in artistic and creative occupations. On the other hand, second borns, especially those 1 to 4 years younger than their older siblings, are overrepresented in creative and artistic occupations. Second borns who are more than 4 years younger than their older siblings tend to act more like firstborns, perhaps because the competition is not so acute.

Birth order also may have an impact on career development because of its connection to family resources. Although parents may have adequate funds to send one or two children to college, their resources may be depleted by the time the later-born children are ready for higher education. The parents may already be planning for their retirement at that time, and later-born children may be reluctant to ask parents to finance their college educations. On the other hand, the oldest child may be ready for college before the parents have had time to accumulate adequate savings.

Clearly, family background and birth order can have an impact on career development in many ways. Career counselors should help their clients to examine these factors to better understand their career development. A systematic way to approach this is through the use of a family career tree, similar to the genograms used by Murray Bowen (1978) and others in family counseling. The family career tree provides a vehicle for recording family career paths and facilitates identification of patterns and influences. The use of this tool will be illustrated later in this book.

Socioeconomic Factors

Socioeconomic factors represent a second group of influences on career development and include environment, socioeconomic status, racial and ethnic background, gender, and supply and demand of the job market.

Environment

Environment can influence career development in at least three ways. It influences people's exposure to occupations, the settings in which they feel comfortable, and the messages they receive about acceptable career paths. During the 1960s, several researchers (Anderson & Apostal, 1971; Sewell & Orenstein, 1965) noted that people from small towns tended to have limited occupational information, to establish a narrow range of options for themselves, and to select career paths that did not involve extensive stimulation or contact with people. On the other hand, aspirations tended to rise with the population density, and people from urban backgrounds usually selected career paths that involved considerable competition and pressure to achieve. This pattern seems to have persisted. People tend to gravitate toward occupational environments that are reminiscent of those in which they grew up and probably feel most comfortable. However, these choices may be made with a limited view of options and may not adequately reflect interests and abilities.

Environment also exerts a considerable influence on available opportunities and employment rate. In general, overcrowded urban areas and extremely rural areas offer the fewest opportunities, but that varies, depending on the particular occupation that has been selected.

When exploring people's career development, counselors should inquire about environmental origins and preferences. Many people overlook the influence of geography, but research has shown that it can play an important role in career development. Counselors also should help people ensure that their career goals can realistically be achieved in their chosen place of residence. If not, changes may be in order.

Socioeconomic Status

Socioeconomic status seems to exert an influence on career development that is similar to that of family background. In general, the higher people's socioeconomic origins, the higher their aspirations (Dillard & Perrin, 1980). Several explanations have been advanced for the limited aspirations and career development of many people from lower socio-economic backgrounds, including low self-esteem, lack of strong male role models, limited career information, inadequate finances, lack of encouragement to succeed, and negative stereotypes. All of these expla-nations are certainly true in some cases, but no one explanation has emerged as the reason for the limited career achievement of many from lower socioeconomic environments.

The term *at-risk* has been used increasingly for people from disad-vantaged backgrounds (Spokane & Hawks, 1990). This term describes people who have been exposed to a range of risk factors, such as poverty, abuse, divorce, disability, and unstable living situations. As a result, they are prone to leave school prematurely and to encounter difficul-ties in their careers. Although programs designed specifically to pro-mote the career development of the at-risk population are still in the early stages, there is general recognition that these people need to feel more empowered and optimistic about their options. Programs that incorporate their cultural and linguistic backgrounds, provide consis-tency and structure, and offer academic help as needed seem particu-larly likely to be effective.

Race and Cultural Background

By the year 2000, ethnic minorities will constitute approximately one third of the population in the United States. African Americans repre-sent 12% of the labor force; Hispanics, 10%; and Asians and other minor-ity groups, 4%. These percentages are expected to increase, particularly for Hispanics (Fullerton, 1989). Minority group members are over-represented among the poor, among high school dropouts, and in occupations declining in employment. They are underrepresented in higher education and in high-growth occupations (Hawks & Muha, 1991).

People from minority ethnic backgrounds generally are not as success-ful as others in developing careers that lead to high-level positions and economic rewards. This is particularly true of African Americans and Hispanics. Of course, there are many exceptions to this pattern. How-ever, the 1983 census indicated that only 4.7% of executives, adminis-trators, and managers in the United States were African American, and only 2.8% were Hispanic (Fullerton, 1989).

Unemployment rates of racial minorities are typically much higher than those of Whites (Thomas & Alderfer, 1989). In 1986, unemployment rates for African American high school graduates aged 18 to 19 was 40.6%; for young White high school graduates, the unemployment rate was 13.8% (Hoyt, 1989).

Hispanics. Hispanics, a diverse group of people, are the fastest growing minority group in the United States as well as one of the country's youngest groups (Arbona, 1990). Of the Hispanics in the United States, 47% are below the age of 23, whereas only 35% of the general population is below that age. Hispanics seem to have limited occupational mobility due to a combination of factors, including socioeconomic status and limited opportunities. Low educational attainment is a major determinant of their disadvantaged position. Approximately 50% of Hispanic young people leave high school before graduation. Many attribute this to discrimination and a lack of bilingual programs in the schools.

Information about the career development of Hispanics is limited (Arbona, 1990). The expectations of young people seem very much influenced by those of their parents, and young people seem aware of barriers and stereotypes they are likely to encounter. In general, Hispanics are more satisfied with their work than are African Americans but less satisfied than are people from ethnic majority groups. The career satisfaction of people from a Hispanic background seems more related to status than income. Those who are satisfied with other areas of their lives also tend to be satisfied with their careers. The lowest levels of career satisfaction are found among those with high school diplomas; they generally believe they have not been well rewarded for their educations. Hispanics who complete high school are as likely to attend college as are high school graduates from other groups, but Hispanics are more likely to attend 2-year institutions. Their level of aspiration is likely to decline in college, particularly for men in 2-year institutions. Men who attend 4-year institutions, and particularly those who succeed in graduating from college, seem to manifest achievement and career-related attitudes and behaviors similar to what is observed in the career development of Whites.

Women from a Hispanic background often experience considerable conflict between their career and marriage aspirations. These women consistently enter traditional careers, despite feminist work values, and tend to give priority to the homemaker role over the worker role. Those exceptional Hispanic women who break from tradition and make a commitment to a profession report having had family support, strong maternal role models, and attendance at integrated schools.

Hispanic students, especially females, are less likely to seek career information from parents and counselors than are African American or White students (Orum, 1982). Instead, they look to teachers, friends, and other sources of information. Career counselors might consider what they could do differently to reach more of these students.

Chicano students have been found to be less realistic about career planning than are White students (Pinkney & Ramirez, 1985). Their decisions about college and career choices are colored by their concern about loss of cultural identity, and decision making seems more complex for Chicano young people than for White young people.

Similar findings emerged from a study by Dillard and Perrin (1980). They found that Puerto Rican and African American high school boys actually had higher career aspirations than did White high school boys who made more realistic occupational choices but that there were no significant differences in career expectations among the three groups. What this meant, then, was that the Puerto Rican and African American boys had a greater gap between their aspirations and their expectations than did the White boys, a situation likely to lead to greater discouragement.

African Americans. In addition to the aspiration-expectation gap, African Americans experience many of the same career problems as do Hispanics, including high unemployment and low economic rewards. Although the level of education among African Americans has been rising over the past 20 years, their economic gains have not kept pace with their educational gains. Education has been a less significant determinant of income for African Americans than it has been for Whites.

Cheatham (1990) explored cultural messages that African Americans generally receive and concluded: "African tradition has no central emphasis on the individual; rather, the individual's being is authenticated only in terms of others" (p. 337). African American families stress affiliation, interdependence, and relationships; work is perceived as a group effort. These messages may make it difficult for an African American young person to develop individual goals and to operate effectively in competitive academic and occupational environments.

African American men and women are very underrepresented in mathematical and scientific occupations, whereas African American women are overrepresented in education, social science, and social welfare fields (Kammer, Fouad, & Williams, 1988). Here, too, cultural messages seem to limit options. African American women, unlike Hispanic women, seem to have little difficulty developing career-oriented identities, and they enter the workforce in high numbers. However, the low economic rewards they often receive, combined with their family responsibilities, often make them pessimistic about their likelihood of achieving rewarding careers.

Asian Americans. Asian Americans typically manifest different patterns of career development than do members of other minority groups. They tend to be more successful, academically and economically, and express even greater interest in career counseling than do Whites, who are more likely to seek career counseling than are either African Americans or Mexican Americans (Leong, 1985). However, Asian Americans, too, experience what Leong has called "occupational segregation" in that they prefer structured, logical, concrete, and impersonal fields and tend to choose occupations in physical science or technical trades. Three quarters of Asian Americans pursuing graduate study do so in science or engineering. They are underrepresented in fields that draw heavily on verbal-persuasive and social skills. In addition, Asian Americans seem to have lower levels of career maturity and are more likely to externalize responsibility for career decision making than are those from a non-Asian background. Asian Americans also have a tendency to emphasize the extrinsic rewards of their careers, money and security, and may overlook the importance of intrinsic sources of satisfaction (Leong, 1991). Although Asian American cultural values have led to considerable occupational success, those values also may limit career options and lead to choices that may not best reflect the interests and abilities of a particular person.

Native Americans. Although little is known, thus far, about the career development of Native Americans, several studies provide important information. Lauver and Jones (1991) found that Native American high school students had a lower sense of self-efficacy than did White or Hispanic students in similar settings. Self-efficacy is generally associated with perceived career options. The Native American students, therefore, may see themselves as having fewer career options than do students from other cultural backgrounds.

Native Americans, like African Americans and Hispanics, come from a culture where cooperation typically is emphasized over competition. Consequently, they may have difficulty coping with academic and occupational competition and dealing with taking tests and other individual endeavors (Hood & Johnson, 1991).

Understanding and Improving Minority Career Development

Several explanations have been advanced for the difference between careers of people from majority groups and those from minority groups in the United States. Racial prejudice is the most obvious one; people in White-dominated occupations and businesses may be reluctant to admit members of minority groups just as the minority group members may be reluctant to seek entry into fields where they feel little assurance of acceptance, let alone mentoring or encouragement. People from minority groups may feel a sort of bicultural conflict; to fit into White-dominated fields, they may feel pressure to reject the styles and values of their origins that probably have considerable importance to them. In addition, people from minority backgrounds are aware of the likelihood of encountering barriers in their careers and so may focus more on factors outside themselves than on their inner strengths and needs. This process may lead them to develop aspirations that are too high or too low for their abilities and that do not become more realistic over time (Cosby, 1974). People from minority groups often perceive a gap between their aspirations and their expectations and are pessimistic about achieving their goals. The self-perpetuating cycle of economic depression is another factor in the career difficulties of people from minority groups; their family incomes tend to be lower than those of majority groups, making it more difficult for them to pay for college educations and more likely for the children to leave school early to contribute to the support of the family.

Counselors should be aware of the effect of race and cultural background on both opportunity and attitude. They also should be aware that "few studies have examined whether vocational development theories and interest inventories researched primarily with white samples are meaningful for Spanish-speaking individuals" (Harrington & O'Shea, 1980, p. 246) as well as for people from other minority groups.

In general, it is safe to conclude that people from minority backgrounds benefit from finding ways to set goals that are commensurate with their abilities and interests while at the same time maintaining their ethnic identity and community ties. Helping people from minority backgrounds find mentors who have accomplished this often difficult balance is one way to help. High school programs, providing special services and support to minority students, have demonstrated success. One such program targeted minority students with special aptitude in math and science; 64% of those students receiving extra help and encouragement at the high school level went on to study math or science-related fields at the college level (Kammer et al., 1988). Counselors also should ensure that minority group members have equal opportunities and access to services. They are less likely than Whites to seek out and receive counseling so may need an outreach approach to providing services.

Hawks and Muha (1991) made four recommendations for facilitating the career development of minorities that encompass many of these considerations:

1. Foster intrinsic motivation in students by emphasizing student-generated versus counselor- or teacher-transmitted knowledge.
2. Incorporate the student's language and culture in educational programs.
3. Involve the minority community, especially parents, in the program.
4. Advocate for students by viewing problems primarily as a result of the system versus a flaw within the student. (pp. 255-258)

Gender

Gender differences in career aspirations and expectations seem to be even stronger than ethnic ones (Arbona & Novy, 1991). The career aspirations and options of both men and women are influenced by assumptions of what are appropriate career choices for each gender and by the percentage of people of each gender in occupations.

Women

Nearly half of the labor force in the United States is female, and the average education levels of men and women are approximately equal (12.8 years of education) (Backover, 1991). Between 1970 and 1980, the percentage of women in professional and managerial positions nearly doubled (Hoyt, 1989). Clearly, women are advancing in their careers. However, full-time female employees earn 34% less than do their male counterparts. Even in the field of counseling, the disparity is evident.

Women hold 59% of the positions yet earn 19% less than do men in the field.

It is not surprising that women, like people from minority groups, often perceive a discrepancy between their aspirations and their expectations and see themselves as unlikely to realize their career goals. As Fitzgerald and Crites (1980) stated, "Females consistently select occupations that are unrealistically low in terms of their aptitudes and interests" (p. 47).

According to Spokane and Hawks (1990), social constraints seem to affect both women and minority groups in the following ways:

1. They limit consideration of career options. Most women focus on occupations in which women are well represented, primarily clerical, teaching, and service occupations, and give little consideration to scientific, mechanical, or managerial occupations.
2. They reduce both expectations and likelihood of achieving aspirations.
3. They increase the importance of external factors in career planning.
4. They increase the number of factors that must be considered as well as the complexity of career planning.
5. They increase the need for structured career counseling.

Although the Women's Movement and social and economic changes have led to an increase of women in the labor force as well as to greater acceptance of women seeking employment in both traditional and nontraditional fields, those changes have created other problems. Many women now feel pressure not only to establish successful and exemplary families and homes but also to achieve occupational success. In 1988, 65% of women with school-age children and 56% of women with children under the age of 6 were employed outside the home; these percentages are increasing (Tinsley & Tinsley, 1989). This challenging double role may necessitate some difficult compromises for many women.

Fitzgerald and Crites (1980) observed that many women delay achievement of establishment and maintenance stages to focus on a homemaking stage in their career development. Although this process has been moderated by the increasing age at first marriage, the tendency to delay childbearing, and the declining birth rate, most women continue to view marriage and child rearing as important aspects of their lives.

Schwartz (1989), observing that women in management have a much greater turnover rate than do their male counterparts and are more likely to modify their career paths in limiting ways, advanced the controversial proposal that two career paths should be made available to women. One path, designed for career-salient women, should afford equality of opportunity and compensation equal to that of their male counterparts, whereas the other path, for women Schwartz has called "baby-trackers," would allow flexible schedules and modified compensation for those seeking to combine career and family. This proposal has been criticized, primarily because it penalizes career-oriented women who head households. However, Schwartz's proposal does emphasize the importance of career counselors taking a life span perspective with their female clients and helping them to clarify and plan for both occupational and family goals.

Recent research, spearheaded by the writing of Carol Gilligan (1982), has drawn attention to some fundamental personality differences between men and women. Gilligan defined three stages in the development of women's identity. In Stage 1, egocentrism dominates. In Stage 2, women become oriented toward self-sacrifice and pleasing others. Finally, in Stage 3, women recognize the legitimacy and importance of their own concerns and succeed in integrating their wish to please and help others with their drive to satisfy their own needs. Some women are discouraged by social and family pressures from moving beyond Stage 2 and fail to explore their own interests and abilities (Enns, 1991). Counselors can promote women's career development by encouraging them to expand and explore their identities and build their self-esteem while at the same time maintaining their emphasis on responsiveness, social approval, and caring. As McBride (1990) put it, "Learning to make independent choices and to grow toward self-mastery does not mean that women should ignore their affiliative needs. Being autonomous means choosing to take care of oneself as well as give to others" (p. 25).

Changes in women's career development are both developmental and historical. These trends were highlighted by a study in which women were interviewed as college freshmen in 1968, were followed up in 1981, and were compared with women who were college freshmen in 1983 (Harmon, 1989). The first group of women in their 30s were more like the 1983 college students than they had been in 1968. Both groups were more committed to work; 73% of the 1983 freshmen and 67% of the women in midlife expected to work for most of their lives, whereas in 1968, only 29% of the young women expected to work for most of their lives. The aspirations of the older women changed over time and shifted away from social service occupations and toward involvement in business. The younger women had less traditional aspirations and expressed greater interest in mathematics, science, and medical service. Women's values also seem to have shifted since the 1960s; Pine and Innis (1987) found that women of the 1980s were far less interested in altruism and social welfare and were more concerned with power, authority, money, and status.

Although women are considering more career options, women continue to express the greatest confidence in their self-efficacy or ability to successfully perform traditional occupations, such as teaching, nursing, and secretarial work, in which females predominant (Rotberg, Brown, & Ware, 1987). Self-efficacy, along with interest, are among the strongest predictors of perceived career options. As long as women believe they are less capable of achieving success in male-dominated occupations, they will continue to eliminate from consideration a broad range of potentially rewarding fields.

Role models seem to play a particularly important role in women's career development. Hackett, Esposito, and O'Halloran (1989) found that women's role models, especially parents and teachers, were significantly related to the women's career salience, their level of educational aspiration, and the extent to which their career choices were nontraditional. Messages received from important males, especially fathers and teachers, could have either a positive or a negative impact on women's interest in nontraditional careers.

According to Fitzgerald and Crites (1980), "The potential career development of women, although not fundamentally *different* than that of men, is a great deal more complex due to that combination of attitudes, role expectations, behaviors, and sanctions known as the socialization process" (p. 45). Counselors seeking to facilitate women's career development should take account not only of the factors considered in this section but of such dynamics as fear of success, decline in women's academic self-confidence, lower tendency to take risks, and vicarious sources of achievement. False beliefs about women in the workplace (e.g., women take more sick leave than do men, men do not like to work for female supervisors, and maternal employment is harmful to children), held by employers, counselors, and even the women themselves, present further barriers to women's career development and should be considered in counseling.

Men

Because men provided the focus for most studies of career development during the 1950s and 1960s, more probably is known about the career development of men than is known about women. However, in the 1970s and 1980s, the focus shifted and women's career development received special attention. In the 1990s, there seems to be a growing recognition that men, too, have special needs and concerns in their career development. Current studies of career development, then, are considering the differences as well as the similarities in the career patterns of men and women.

Skovholt and Morgan (1981) identified eight issues that seem to have a significant impact on the career development of men:

1. sex role stereotypes
2. the relationship of self-esteem to occupational success
3. achieving a balance between work, relationships, and recreation
4. avoidance of nontraditional or female-dominated occupations
5. maintaining dual careers in marriage and managing competitive feelings toward one's spouse
6. finding a suitable mentor despite feelings of competitiveness toward the male mentor and avoidance of female mentors
7. midlife changes in career values
8. negotiating retirement successfully without loss of self-esteem

Many of these issues are similar to those experienced by women, although the specifics may be different. Both genders must contend with sex role stereotypes, face the challenge of balancing personal and professional aspects of their lives, manage discomfort in nontraditional occupations, cope with the pressures of dual-career marriages, seek appropriate mentors, and accommodate to value changes in midlife.

Unlike women, men report self-efficacy for both traditional and nontraditional occupations (Betz & Hackett, 1981). Nevertheless, men typically shun such occupations as nurse, librarian, primary school teacher, and secretary in which the female gender is predominant. Reasons for avoidance of these occupations include a reluctance to accept lower pay and status for their work, a fear that they may be viewed as inadequate or even homosexual if they enter these professions, concerns about discrimination and comfort with colleagues, as well as issues of self-esteem (Hayes, 1987). This foreclosure of opportunities is unfortunate because these nontraditional occupations may be more compatible with some men's personal needs. Men also may gain a positive advantage by being part of the male minority in a profession, just as women may gain similar attention by being part of a female minority in a male-dominated profession.

Chusmir (1990) found that men who choose female-dominated occupations possess many of the same traits as do women in those fields while at the same time feeling comfortable with themselves and their masculine sexuality. Nontraditional men are more likely to be firstborn, members of racial minority groups, well educated, liberal in outlook, and raised by traditional mothers. They tend to emphasize intrinsic motivation, have social and esthetic values, and have a broad view of appropriate gender roles for men. They generally are committed to their careers and satisfied with them.

Men's goals seem to have a different focus than do women's. Whereas women seek affiliation, men are drawn by autonomy, mastery, and competition as ways to establish a sense of power and achievement (Gallos, 1989). Interestingly enough, the single most critical factor in men's job failure is their inability to get along well with others (Fitzgerald & Crites, 1980). Through their lack of attention to interpersonal skills and relationships, then, men may undermine their career efforts.

Men, as well as women, seem likely to benefit from career counseling that encourages their examination of their abilities and interests, helps them consider and minimize the influence of sex role stereotypes, and helps them to balance and integrate occupational and personal areas of their lives. In addition, men, too, encounter expectations in themselves as well as in employers, counselors, friends, and family that may be difficult for them to meet. Examination of those expectations can lead men to plan more rewarding and realistic careers.

Individual Factors

The third group of factors that influence career development, individual factors, includes such dimensions as self-expectancies, self-esteem, abilities, interests, attitudes, and achievement needs.

Self-Esteem

Self-esteem, emphasized by Super's theory of career development (Super et al., 1963), has received considerable support as a major determinant of career patterns and choices. Greenhaus (1973) found that people who were high in self-esteem tended to have positive attitudes toward work; they enjoyed thinking about and planning for their careers and viewed work as a vehicle for self-expression. Consequently, such people were more highly motivated to plan appropriate careers and were more likely to view their chosen career paths as satisfying and rewarding.

High self-esteem seems to lead to both better career planning and more satisfaction with the implementation of the plans. Although many factors enter into the development of self-esteem, counselors can foster self-esteem and a realistic self-concept by encouraging, expecting, and reinforcing realistic levels of achievement. Counselors also might meet with the parents of their young clients to help the parents promote a positive self-concept in their children by appreciating the children's abilities and encouraging positive and realistic attitudes toward achievement.

Abilities and Interests

Although intelligence, aptitudes, and interests will be considered in greater detail in Chapter 3, they are cited here as factors that affect career development. Generally, the greater the correspondence between people's abilities, interests, and aptitudes and the requirements of their occupations, the greater will be their satisfaction, their performance, and their stability. However, these correlations are not high, and gratification of personal needs seems to be at least as important in determining career satisfaction as the correspondence between the nature of people's work and their interests and capacities.

When assessing abilities, one should pay particular attention to people with special needs, those who have physical or learning disabilities, or those who are gifted. Although much has been written in the education literature about these people, information on their career development is thus far limited. However, some information is available that should be considered by career counselors working with these special groups.

Some of the literature paints a pessimistic picture of the career development of people with disabilities. According to Brolin and Gysbers (1989), "The vast majority of students with disabilities never attain a satisfactory level of career development consistent with their capabilities" (p. 155). On the other hand, Dahl (1982) stated, "Very few occupations fail to offer opportunities for seriously handicapped people. Of course, this does not imply that each handicapped person is a legitimate candidate for every job. (Such an assumption is never made for the nonhandicapped, either)" (p. 45). The challenge for the counselor, then, is to help people with disabilities identify and maximize their potential through appropriate career planning.

The following common barriers to the career development of people with disabilities have been identified, followed by suggested strategies for overcoming those barriers (Dahl, 1982; Hagner & Salomone, 1989):

1. *Barrier*—low expectations of accomplishment held by both the people with disabilities and potential employers

   Strategy—giving information on academic and occupational accomplishments of people with disabilities, use of role models and advocacy groups, reinforcement of successful experiences to build self-esteem
2. *Barrier*—inadequate skill development

   Strategy—accurate assessment of strengths and weaknesses, opportunities for exploration and gathering of information, careful planning of appropriate and occupationally relevant training, use of transitional employment settings and job coaches if needed
3. *Barrier*—challenging physical settings

   Strategy—modify physical settings as needed, discuss limitations and abilities openly with disabled people to determine exactly what changes would be beneficial
4. *Barrier*—communication problems

   Strategy—provide information about aids to communication, simplify communication, use alternate modes of communication (e.g., interpreter, writing)
5. *Barrier*—limited experience and skill in decision making

   Strategy—involve people with disabilities as fully as possible in making decisions that affect them and encourage families to follow a similar model, develop and present choices, teach decision-making skills
6. *Barrier*—academic discouragement and low rate of high school completion

   Strategy—provide relevant and appropriate academic programs that maximize opportunities for success and teach useful skills

Since 1978, a life-centered career education curriculum has been used in school districts throughout the country (Brolin & Gysbers, 1989). Designed to develop competencies in daily living, personal-social skills, and occupational abilities that will be needed after high school graduation, it is only one of many programs that have been developed to promote the academic involvement and career development of people with disabilities. Legislation such as the Carl D. Perkins Vocational Education Act of 1984 has provided funding for career development programs and services for students with disabilities.

Although general theories of career development seem to have some relevance to people with disabilities, counselors also should consider the unique needs of these people and develop approaches to working with them that meet those needs. Nonrestrictive counseling that is readily available, builds on clients' strengths and potentials, broadens their criteria for decision making, encourages self-esteem and independence, and makes good use of community resources as well as vocational rehabilitation and other governmental programs designed to help people with disabilities is likely to be helpful.

Career counseling with gifted people seems to have received even less attention than career counseling for people with disabilities, at least in part because general theories of career counseling probably have considerable relevance for the gifted. One dynamic that should be considered when counseling people who are gifted is their multipotentiality. Often, these people have a broad range of interests and excel in many areas. The greatest challenge they may face in their career development is narrowing their focus and identifying the specific career path that is likely to be most rewarding.

Personality

Many theorists in the field, including Holland (1987) and Roe (1956, 1964), have found that people in the same or closely related occupations tend to have similar personalities. Personality includes many dimensions relevant to career development: interpersonal orientation, values, motivation, stability, and willingness to take risks are only a few of these. Personality traits certainly influence the nature of people's career plans. According to Dawis and Lofquist's (1984) theory of work adjustment, occupational satisfaction is primarily a function of correspondence between psychological needs and the pattern of reinforcement provided by the work environment. Assessment procedures, discussed in subsequent chapters, can be useful in helping people develop understanding of their own personalities. Career counseling should consider the interface between people's personalities and their career plans, although the relationship between personality and career development is complex and ill defined.

Prestige

By the end of elementary school, most students have developed a fairly clear idea of the amount of prestige associated with a large number of occupations and by the end of high school, most students have an image of the kind of people found in their preferred occupations. The possession of such occupational images or stereotypes does not seem to bear much relation to knowledge or experience, although, certainly, the accuracy of these images is related to career information. Regardless of their accuracy, these images have been found to influence career decisions. In light of this, counselors should explore these images with their clients so that expectations are in line with reality.

Counselors also should be familiar with the literature on prestige rankings to facilitate their exploration of that dimension with their clients. Prestige rankings have changed little over the past 60 years and are very similar when made by either men or women (Thomas & O'Brien, 1984). In general, the prestige rank of an occupation is correlated with the level of ability and amount of effort required to perform that occupation (Villemez, 1974). Highly ranked occupations include, in order, physician, lawyer, nuclear engineer, architect, electrical engineer, chemist, biological scientist, psychologist, city manager, and legislator (Parker, Chan, & Saper, 1989). Occupations that rank low in terms of prestige include street vendor, newspaper carrier, hand packer, lost-and-found clerk, washing machine operator, automobile service station attendant, garbage collector, bookbinder, bus driver, and short-order cook. Occupations that have gained in prestige over the years include farmer and grocer whereas carpenter, barber, and soldier have lost prestige (Thomas & O'Brien, 1984).

Prestige rankings often are associated with personal qualities that people attribute to those engaged in certain occupations. For example, physicians are often viewed as intelligent, truthful, and affluent. Prestige rankings also reflect underlying attitudes toward desirable work conditions. White-collar work is often perceived as superior to manual labor and receives higher prestige ratings. Counselors can help their clients to elucidate their career preferences by discussing their individual prestige hierarchy, their images of people in occupations of interest, and their underlying assumptions about the nature of desirable work.

The World of Work

One of the biggest factors in career planning is the world of work, the job market. Constantly changing and somewhat unpredictable, it can have a strong effect on people's satisfaction with their careers simply by exerting an influence over what career paths the laws of supply and demand allow them to pursue. Although individuals can exert little control over the economy, they can maximize their chances of achieving their desired career goals by understanding current employment trends. Counselors, too, should become aware of economic and employment trends so that they can keep their clients well informed and help them factor economic trends into their career planning.

Many people in the present workforce entered the labor market during the 1960s, years when the economy was expanding and the job market was improving. Optimism about employment opportunities was great during those years, and college graduates were all but assured of positions commensurate with their training. Schools and colleges increased in number, college enrollment increased, and, in the minds of many, a college education become the way to achieve success.

Although many continue to maintain this optimistic view, the changed economic situation of the 1970s and 1980s has affected the career goals and plans of many people. Unemployment rates between 7% and 9% have been common in recent years. These figures do not take into account the hidden unemployed: those who would like to reenter the labor force after a long absence, those entering the labor force for the first time, and those who have been unemployed for so long that they have exhausted their benefits or given up their efforts to locate employment.

The last-hired, first-fired formula, the difficulty in locating suitable entry-level jobs, and discrimination have resulted in particularly elevated unemployment rates for women, members of minority groups, and young people. In 1986, for example, the unemployment rate for young African American men who had graduated from high school was 40.6% (Hoyt, 1989). At about the same time, unemployment for college graduates was 2.5%. Some unemployment is inevitable, notably the so-called frictional unemployment, reflecting temporary difficulties of matching new workers, such as recent high school and college graduates, to available jobs. However, widespread and prolonged unemployment, especially due to job loss, the major cause of unemployment, can be both emotionally and financially devastating. The growing homeless population, including many families with children, reflects the impact of a tight employment market.

Trends in the Labor Force

Although the 1980s were economically better than the 1970s and labor force projections are positive through the 1990s, the economy is affected by many factors that are difficult to anticipate, such as the availability of sources of energy and natural resources, business cycles, fads, technological changes, natural disasters, and wars.

Overall growth of the labor force is expected to continue but to slow over the next decade, with a 1.2% annual growth rate anticipated

(Fullerton, 1989). Due to a combination of slower growth and delayed retirement, the average age of the workforce is expected to increase from 35.9 in 1988 to 39.9 in 2000. The workforce also is becoming better educated, due primarily to a great increase in people receiving degrees from community colleges. The rate of high school completion has also continued to increase, with 75% completing high school and an additional 8% receiving a general equivalency diploma (GED). Over 20% of the workforce has completed at least 4 years of college. Similarly, the average skill level required of occupations will increase. On-the-job training may become more available as problems in recruiting new workers with the needed qualifications develop (Offerman & Gowing, 1990).

The percentage of women receiving college degrees, participating in the workforce, and holding professional and managerial positions has increased greatly since the 1970s. In 1986, 70% of women aged 24 to 54 were in the labor force; that percentage is expected to increase to 80% (Hoyt, 1989). By 2000, women are expected to constitute 47.5% of the labor force (Fullerton, 1989) and 60% of new workers (Offermann & Gowing, 1990). Among African Americans, women are expected to outnumber men in the labor force.

A great increase of minority persons in the labor force is predicted, due to a combination of immigration and birth rate; between 1986 and 2000, the percentage of African Americans in the labor force is expected to increase by 29%, Hispanics by 74%, and Asians and Pacific Islanders by 70% (Hoyt, 1989). In contrast, the percentage of White workers is expected to increase by only 14.6% during that same time period (W. B. Johnson, 1987).

Changes in the Job Market

To understand the world of work, one must become familiar with both long- and short-range trends. Several economic trends have persisted since the 19th century. The changing distribution of the workforce is one such long-term trend. In 1879, 48% of American workers were farmers. By 1974, only 3% of American workers were farmers. Technological advances have led to a decrease in the percentage of jobs demanding primarily physical skills and manual labor, whereas the percentage of professional and technical jobs has increased. According to Hoyt (1987), America has moved from an agricultural society to an industrial society to being "primarily a service, information-oriented, and high technology society" (p. 270). The percentage of people who are self-employed has decreased to approximately 10%, largely because competition from franchises and chain stores has made the small business, a risky venture (Olney, 1988). At the same time, small businesses continue to furnish most new jobs (Hoyt, 1987).

Between 1986 and 2000, 21 million new jobs are anticipated, reflecting a 19% increase in the job market (Hoyt, 1989). Of these, 90% will be in service industries rather than in goods-producing industries, and most will be jobs offering low wages. Over one third of these new jobs, however, will require some form of postsecondary education, reflecting a pattern of job growth at both ends of the skill spectrum.

The U.S. Department of Labor has predicted that the greatest number of job openings will be in the following areas: retail sales, food service, nursing, cleaning and custodial work, managerial and executive positions, cashiering, truck driving, and office work. The fastest growing occupations are paralegal personnel, medical and physical therapy assistants, computer programming and repair, podiatrists, medical record technicians, and employment interviewers. Occupations that have declined in employment include those in agriculture, forestry, fishing, secretarial services, leather and textile work, and production fields.

Of course, growth in employment opportunities varies from one region to another. Greatest growth in opportunities as well as population is expected to be in southern and western regions of the United States; on the other hand, with the exception of New Hampshire, most northeastern and north central states are losing population.

Brand (1990) identified six factors that underlie most of the changes in employment patterns anticipated for the 1990s:

1. Growth in the use of computers and other technology will lead to a great increase of jobs in these areas.
2. Changes in business practices due to increased competition (especially from international markets) as well as efforts to cut costs have led to decreases in secretarial services and greater use of legal and accounting services.
3. Increased emphasis on research and development to remain competitive and efficient will lead to increased employment opportunities in engineering, natural sciences, and electronics.
4. Population growth, primarily of young people and the elderly, will lead to an increased need for teachers and people in medical professions.
5. A greater emphasis on outpatient medical care as well as an increase in surgical procedures will lead to a need for more technicians and rehabilitation specialists.

6. Increased emphasis on personal safety will necessitate increased employment in law, law enforcement, and corrections.

Changes in Work Life

The nature of the typical work life has been changing in many ways. Earlier retirement, coupled with increased holidays and a longer life span, has meant that most men spend less time in the labor force and have more time for leisure. Women, on the other hand, are spending more years in the labor force.

Although the average work week declined from 53 hours in 1900 to 40 hours in 1970 (Kreps, 1973), it has not declined significantly since then. Of the workforce, 25% spends more than 40 hours on the job. Rapid inflation and higher standards of living seem to have led many workers to extend their hours both for advancement and more pay. Of workers, 5% have more than one job (Olney, 1988). Generally, people's second jobs differ from their first jobs, and although economic need is the most important reason for having a second job, enjoyment is the next most frequently given reason. Career planning, then, needs to consider the possibility of multiple concurrent jobs.

One of the most positive trends in the world of work has been employers' growing awareness of the special needs of their employees, reflected by increasing development of programs to improve the quality of work life. Employers, as well as counselors and employees, are increasingly taking a holistic view of work and considering the interaction of personal and professional goals and activities. The following are examples of special programs that have been established to improve the quality of work life:

1. career counseling and planning
2. choice of benefits (e.g., increased salary, vacation, health care benefits, stock options)
3. compact work week (e.g., four days, 40 hours)
4. cooperative bargaining
5. employee assistance programs
6. employee rotation and job exchange programs
7. flexible career ladders
8. flexible or variable work schedules (e.g., working 7 a.m.–3 p.m. or 10 a.m.–6 p.m. in lieu of regular work hours)

9. home-based employment, particularly useful in allowing women to maintain occupational continuity while rearing children
10. job restructuring
11. job sharing
12. lateral and temporary transfers
13. leave for family medical problems, including caring for elderly parents
14. on-site child care
15. paid educational leave, tuition reimbursement, and on-the-job training
16. participatory management
17. personal growth workshops (e.g., stress management, assertiveness training)
18. physical fitness programs and equipment at the place of employment, sometimes including incentives for developing healthier lifestyles
19. quality circles, small groups of co-workers who meet to develop ways to improve the work setting, productivity, and the quality of work life
20. reduction in forced relocation and assistance provided to facilitate family adjustment and employment of spouse when relocation does occur
21. sabbaticals, often providing pay for volunteer work with charitable organizations
22. smoke-free work environments

Relatively few people are now troubled by unpleasant working conditions, long hours, or arduous work. The quality of working life has been improving for many years, and indications are that trend will continue. Nevertheless, the complexity of the world of work, the many options open to people, and the great variety of people make career counseling and development a challenging endeavor.

TWO

The Use of Assessment in Career Counseling

History of Assessment
in Career Counseling

Assessment in career counseling is used primarily for two purposes, guidance and selection. Just as the origin of career counseling can be attributed to Frank Parsons and his 1909 book *Choosing a Vocation*, so can the origin of assessment for guidance purposes be attributed to Parsons. He was the first to emphasize the importance of accurate measurement in career counseling (Wakelee-Lynch, 1990). Measurement has continued to be an important component of career counseling throughout its history. Claiborn (1991) wrote of the current role of assessment in counseling: "We consider psychological measurement to be an essential component of all kinds of counseling. We value it both as a source of diagnostic information *about* clients and as a stimulus to self-exploration and self-understanding *for* clients" (p. 456).

Intelligence testing began with the 1916 publication of Lewis Terman's individual intelligence test and was further developed when Arthur Otis published the first group intelligence test based on the Army Alpha and Army Beta tests developed during World War I. Modern versions of Terman's and Otis's tests, the Stanford-Binet Intelligence Scale and the Otis-Lennon School Ability Test, are still widely used.

The use of assessment for selection was firmly established by the military during the First and Second World Wars when testing was used as an efficient way to match military personnel to jobs. For example, during World War II, the Air Force used the Army General Classification Test to identify potential pilots and navigators.

In the 1920s and 1930s, the field of assessment broadened in scope and extended beyond the measurement of abilities. E. K. Strong, Jr. published his Vocational Interest Blank in 1927, the precursor of today's Strong Interest Inventory (SII). Inventories designed to assess personality first appeared in the 1930s.

By the 1950s, assessment was generally accepted as an integral part of career counseling. Reflecting the prevailing attitude, Super (1952) concluded that people were more likely to be satisfied if they were in occupations that required patterns of interests, personality, values, and abilities that were consistent with their own characteristics. The use of tests and inventories was an important way to maximize that correspondence, and Super and Crites (1962) found that counseling with testing was superior to counseling without testing.

During the 1970s, however, attitudes toward testing changed. Goldman (1972), assessing the role of testing in the counseling process, wrote: "Some would say that not only has the marriage between tests and counseling failed but that it was never even consummated. Whatever the marital metaphor, it seems clear that this marriage has not yet been a successful or happy one" (p. 213).

Concerns about assessment expressed during the 1970s focused on the possible negative impact of testing on women and people from minority groups. Testing was perceived as reinforcing role bias and limiting opportunities. Some alleged that interest inventories kept men and women in traditional occupations (Holland, 1980). Intelligence tests, too, were blamed for curtailing the educational opportunities of African Americans and other people from minority backgrounds by measuring culturally linked factors. Some alleged that tests measured nothing but the ability to take tests and had little predictive power (Snyderman & Rothman, 1987). In 1980, the landmark case of *Larry P. v. Riles* led to the banning of intelligence tests for determination of placement in special education programs in California (Linn, 1986). However, at the same time that the use of tests was being questioned, the number of states requiring minimum competency testing of high school students jumped from 8 to 38.

Clearly, the field of testing and assessment was in a state of confusion during the 1970s. The American Personnel and Guidance Association, now the American Counseling Association (ACA), attempted to resolve the controversy by issuing the following statement: "Testing is not a policy nor a set of beliefs or principles. Testing is a technique for obtaining information . . . as a technique, testing itself is a neutral. It is a tool that serves the ends of the users" (1972, p. 385). It is up to the counselor, then, to make effective use of tests.

During the 1980s, criticisms of testing diminished, whereas the role of testing continued to expand. Several developments contributed to this shift in attitude. Tests and inventories have been modified so that gender and racial bias has been reduced. Emphasis of ability testing has increasingly been on higher-order skills such as thinking and writing rather than on minimum competencies, on the individual rather than on the group, on holistic assessment and self-assessment, and on qualitative rather than quantitative assessment (Linn, 1986; Watkins & Campbell, 1990). The resurgence of interest in and commitment to testing, then, has been accompanied by a more humanistic philosophy that stressed the importance of the individual and viewed assessment as a process that should serve the best interests of that person.

Surveys conducted during the 1980s indicated that helping professionals were extensively involved in assessment and saw it as an important part of their role. Watkins, Campbell, and McGregor (1988) surveyed 630 counseling psychologists and found that 66% were involved in objective testing, administering an average of seven objective tests and two projective tests each week. The counseling psychologists tested an average of 12.4% of their clients and used testing for three primary purposes: 49.2% used tests to assess psychopathology, 43.9% used tests for career counseling, and 36.5% used tests to assess intelligence and ability.

School counselors, as well as counseling psychologists, make extensive use of tests. A survey of test usage in Grades 7 through 12 indicated that 93% of the schools used career guidance inventories, primarily at the high school level; 76% used achievement test batteries, primarily in Grades 7 and 8; 66% used aptitude tests; and 16% administered personality inventories (Engen, Lamb, & Prediger, 1982). Of guidance directors, 70% reported that if more time and funds were available, they would include even more testing in their school's counseling program.

Predictions suggest that use of assessment, especially in career counseling, will increase (Piotrowski & Keller, 1984). Several changes in the assessment process are anticipated. According to Watkins and Campbell (1990), "Future efforts in this area will focus on (a) using and interpreting available tests within the context of cultural boundaries and (b) developing and validating culturally specific tests and assessment methods" (p. 193). Use of computerized career guidance and assessment should increase the accessibility of tests and inventories and facilitate counselors' use of those tools. In addition, continuation of a humanistic perspective of assessment is anticipated.

Benefits and Limitations of Testing and Assessment

An overview of the historical development of assessment makes clear that tests are powerful tools that have potential to both enhance the counseling process and to harm people's self-images and opportunities. Counselors need to be familiar with both the benefits and the limitations of testing so that they can determine when to test, how to present the assessment process, and how to use the test results constructively.

What tests and inventories probably do best is to summarize a person's responses to a standard set of questions or statements and present those responses in a more useful form, generally by categorizing the responses and comparing them with the responses of others who have taken the same instrument. Tests, then, present an objective and standardized measurement of a person's behavior at a specific point in time.

Tests can best answer *what* questions such as, "What are this person's salient interests?" or "What are her academic strengths and weaknesses?" Tests also can be used to answer *how* questions such as, "How well is this person likely to perform at a very competitive university?" and "How do this person's interests compare with others who have been successful in his chosen occupation?" Test data do not usually provide answers to *why* questions such as, "Why is this person having difficulty making career choices?" and "Why is this person's academic performance far below what would have been predicted from test scores?" Only by integrating test data with other information and insights obtained during the counseling process can answers be provided to the why questions that will really lead to effective career planning.

Results of tests and inventories, then, should always be considered in a holistic context, in combination with other data about the person. When combined appropriately with other data, tests and inventories can be used to accomplish the following:

1. promote more relevant and focused discussion
2. stimulate and guide exploration and information seeking

3. clarify self-concept by providing information on strengths and weaknesses, likes and dislikes, and personality traits

4. facilitate counselor's understanding of the client

5. indicate the likelihood that certain events will happen

6. promote translation of interests, abilities, and personality dimensions into career terms

7. generate options and alternatives

8. facilitate the ordering or ranking of options, thereby improving decision making, goal setting, and planning

Eyde, Moreland, and Robertson (1988) suggest that the following seven factors are integral to the sound use of testing:

1. conducting a comprehensive assessment, leading to an interpretation that integrates test scores with history and other data

2. conducting a test administration that follows sound principles of assessment as well as the directions in the test manual

3. ensuring accuracy of scoring

4. having psychometric knowledge and using that in interpreting test results

5. maintaining the integrity of the test results, not overstating their significance, and making their limitations clear

6. making appropriate use of test norms when interpreting test results

7. presenting test data in the context of an effective counseling process

Tests and inventories can contribute a great deal to the effectiveness of career counseling. At the same time, counselors should bear in mind the risks and limitations of testing. Tyler (1984), in an article titled "What Tests Don't Measure," cited the following limitations of testing:

1. Tests cannot measure unique characteristics; they measure only traits common to many people.

2. Tests provide little information on development or dynamics.

3. Tests do not provide information on background or context.

4. Intelligence, personality, abilities, and interests are not static; tests do not provide information on whether and how they might change over time.

Although these and other limitations are inherent in tests, they need not have an adverse impact if tests and inventories are used properly by counselors. According to Snyderman and Rothman (1987) who surveyed over 1,000 psychologists and educational specialists, the greatest problems in testing are the counselors' misinterpretation of and over-reliance on test scores in elementary and secondary schools. The counselor, not the test, is the key ingredient in career counseling and assessment. As Anastasi (1992) stated,

> A conspicuous development in psychological testing during the 1980s and 1990s is the increasing recognition of the key role of the test user. Most popular criticisms of tests are clearly identifiable as criticisms of test use (or misuse), rather than criticisms of the tests themselves. Tests are essentially tools. Whether any tool is an instrument of good or harm depends on how the tool is used. (p. 610)

Selecting Appropriate Tests and Inventories

Testing should be an integral part of the counseling relationship. Before making the decision to use tests or inventories, counselors should ask themselves the following questions:

1. What are the goals of the counseling process?
2. What information is needed to accomplish those goals?
3. Have available sources of information such as the client's own experiences and self-knowledge, school records, and previous tests been used effectively and fully?
4. Does it seem likely that assessment can provide important information that is not available from other sources?
5. How will this client respond to and be affected by testing?
6. What questions can be answered by the testing?

Counselors and their clients should collaborate on establishing the goals of the counseling process and monitoring progress to determine whether, when, and what sort of testing and assessment would be most appropriate. Although clients generally do not have the necessary knowledge to participate in the selection of specific inventories, they should be involved in making the broader decisions about testing. This collaboration will help them to develop realistic expectations about what they can hope to learn from assessment and will help to reduce test-related anxiety and increase motivation.

Attitudes Toward Assessment

People often bring with them into counseling strong feelings and preconceptions about testing. Some view assessment as less threatening than counseling and may state that they have come to see a counselor because they would like to take an interest inventory, rather than acknowledge their need for counseling. Using a request for testing as a pretext for gaining access to personal counseling seems particularly common among young people who may attach some stigma to the process of counseling and do not want to appear different from their peers.

A common misconception is the belief that testing can provide people definitive answers to their questions. They may request testing to determine whether they will succeed at college, how intelligent they really are, or the one right occupation for them. Such requests often come from people who are experiencing low self-esteem and a sense of identity confusion. They may have derived little self-awareness and self-confidence from their inner resources and now are looking outside of themselves for answers.

Some people enter counseling with a very negative view of the testing process. Perhaps they associate testing with their academic experiences and are reminded of previous failures or anxiety-provoking situations. These people may be resistant to testing and may even terminate the counseling relationship if they anticipate that testing may be part of the counseling process.

Before deciding to use testing as part of career counseling, the counselor should explore, with the client, that person's assumptions and previous experiences with testing. Counselors should not immediately agree to a client's request for a particular type of test, nor should they immediately agree to eliminate any testing from the counseling process. Both extremely favorable and extremely negative client attitudes toward testing most likely reflect misunderstanding of that process and the information it can yield. The counselor's first goal when discussing testing should be to ensure that clients are favorably disposed toward testing yet realistic about what it can offer them.

Counselors, as well as clients, sometimes have unwarranted views of testing. Some counselors view testing as a routine or preliminary part of the counseling process. Although some routine testing can be useful in a school setting to assess the overall level of academic achievement or to identify those students who seem to be having academic or personal difficulties, the process of regular group testing sometimes is abused. In such situations, test takers may be given little prior information about the purposes or nature of the testing process and may have little or no opportunity to discuss their reactions to the testing process. As a result, for some of the students, motivation may be low and discomfort, high. Feedback on results of group testing can be another source of problems. Scores may be provided on a computer-generated form that is mailed home to the students' parents. Opportunity for individual interpretation and discussion of questions may be limited, if available at all, and both parents and students may be harmed by misinterpreted test scores or inappropriate emphasis given to scores. On the other hand, some counselors avoid testing, viewing it as an intrusion into the counseling relationship. They fail to appreciate how assessment can enhance the counseling process.

Planning the Assessment Process

Formulating specific questions to be answered through assessment can facilitate the overall planning of the testing process. Before counselors can formulate those questions and use testing appropriately, they must establish a positive relationship with their clients, agree on tentative goals for the counseling relationship, explore the clients' attitudes toward testing, and gather relevant data about the clients via interviews and available records. Only then can counselors determine what questions still need to be answered, how testing will affect the counseling relationship, and which tests would be most useful.

Hood and Johnson (1991) suggest six basic questions that should be answered when planning the assessment process:

1. Who will be making the assessment?
2. What is being assessed?
3. Where will the assessment process take place?
4. When will that process occur?
5. Why is assessment being undertaken?
6. How will it be conducted?

Biggs and Keller (1982) suggest the following three-stage process to establish the groundwork for meaningful assessment:

1. *Orientation to testing.* Initiate the counseling relationship and begin to develop rapport, examine the client's motives and preconceptions, dispel unrealistic expectations, explore presenting concerns and their context, promote self-evaluation, discuss the client's feelings about assessment.

2. *Induce a high level of client control and involvement.* Clarify with the client the rationale for assessment and identify questions that test data might help answer, involve the client in test selection, help the client perceive assess- ment as a way to increase self-knowledge and self-control.
3. *Improve clients' thinking about their concerns.* Develop client self-awareness, clarify the nature of concerns, facilitate integration of test data with current knowledge about the self, improve realism of thinking, increase the congruence of self-image.

Results of tests and inventories, used in conjunction with other relevant information, can be used to help answer the following specific questions:

1. What are my chances of success in those educational activities that I am considering?
2. How congruent are my present career plans with my interests, abilities, values, and personality?
3. What academic and occupational alternatives merit further exploration or consideration?
4. How do my interests compare with those of people who are employed in and satisfied with certain occupational choices?
5. What can I do to maximize my chances for success in a particular endeavor?
6. What is making it difficult for me to formulate satisfying and realistic career plans and what can I do to facilitate my career development?
7. What short- and long-term career/life plans seem to offer me the greatest promise for success and satisfaction?

Counselors and clients should work together to determine those questions that they hope testing will help answer. They then are ready to identify the types of tests and inventories they will use.

Sometimes multiple measures provide richer and more reliable information than does one measure alone, particularly if those measures take different approaches to gathering information. For example, data on interests can be gathered by asking people about their interests, having them keep a record of how they spend their leisure time, administering a quantitative computer-scored interest inventory, and using a qualitative measure of interests such as a card sort. Similarities and differences emerging from these multiple sources of information can confirm the strength of interests that appear repeatedly and focus discussion on interests that appear in only one or two measures. Identifying discrepancies between expressed interests and inventoried interests, for example, can promote productive exploration. Although counselors should not overwhelm their clients with tests and inventories, the use of multiple measures can be far more informative than reliance on only one source of data.

Selecting Tests and Inventories

Counselors have the responsibility of selecting instruments they are qualified to administer and that seem most likely to help the clients, to prepare the clients adequately for the counseling process, to ensure that the testing experience is a positive one, to make sure the tests have been properly scored, to provide an accurate and useful interpretation of the test results to clients, and to take any other steps necessary to be sure that the testing enhances the counseling process and helps people achieve their counseling goals.

Selecting the type of test or inventory may be fairly easy, but selecting the one or two best tests or inventories to use with a particular person may be difficult. Chapter 3 of this book reviews the types of tests and inventories that are available and provides brief descriptions of some of the most useful and popular inventories to facilitate their selection.

Many factors must be considered when evaluating the usefulness of a test or inventory, including (a) counselor's qualifications for administering the inventory and comfort in using the inventory; (b) ease of administration, scoring, and interpretation; (c) attractiveness of the instrument; (d) relevance to the purpose of the assessment; (e) available norms; (f) cost; and (g) validity and reliability.

Sources of Information on Tests

Several sources of information are available to help counselors gather the information they need to locate appropriate tests and inventories. Counselors might begin their search for useful tests and inventories with one of the comprehensive sources on available instruments.

The *Mental Measurements Yearbook* (*MMY*) was originally developed by O. K. Buros. The *MMY* has gone through at least 10 editions since its inception in 1938. The 10th edition (Conoley & Kramer, 1989) includes 569 reviews of 396 tests that were published or revised since the publication of the 9th edition. Both the *MMY* and *Tests in Print*, a companion volume, are published by the University of Nebraska Press and are the oldest and best established sources of information on tests.

Test Critiques, published by Test Corporation of America, comprised five volumes in 1986 and reviewed over 500 tests. New volumes of *Test Critiques* are issued every few years. Cumulative and subject indexes facilitate counselors' use of this multivolume set.

Tests: A Comprehensive Reference for Assessments in Psychology, Education, and Business is a companion to *Test Critiques*. *Tests* offers a listing of over 3,000 tests used in counseling, special education, psychology, and business. Tests of personality, development, and abilities are briefly described, and information is provided on their time of administration, scoring, norms, cost, and publisher. This volume provides factual information, whereas *Test Critiques* provides evaluations.

ETS Test Collection, compiled by the Educational Testing Service, is an array of over 200 annotated bibliographies on tests. Counselors can order bibliographies in specific areas such as achievement batteries or values.

Review of one or more of these general sources of information on tests and inventories can enable counselors to pinpoint specific instruments that might be of interest to them. More information on individual tests and suggestions of appropriate instruments can be obtained from the test reviews in counseling journals. The *Journal of Counseling and Development*, *Measurement and Evaluation in Counseling and Development*, and *Career Development Quarterly*, all published by the ACA, are particularly rich sources of information on instruments of interest to career counselors. Informal sources of information, such as conversations with colleagues, can also provide suggestions about potentially useful instruments.

Once tests of interest to the counselor have been identified, counselors will probably want to obtain catalogs from the publishers. The catalogs will provide current information on qualifications of the test users, the various forms of the tests that are available, and the cost.

Publishers offer for sale specimen sets of many of their tests, and this is a useful third step for counselors selecting appropriate instruments. Specimen sets typically include one copy of the test, a key or scoring voucher so that the test can be scored, and a copy of the test manual. Counselors may complete the sample test themselves so that they have the opportunity to assess how long administration is likely to take, what the test items are like, and what reactions people are likely to have to the experience of taking that test. Having the test scored or scoring it themselves can provide counselors not only with some useful information about themselves but also a clear idea of the sort of information that is provided by the test. Completing the scoring process can help counselors assess how time-consuming and difficult that process is and, if the test is sent away for scoring, how long it will take to receive results. The test manual, however, will probably be the richest source of information on a test and will enable counselors to decide if and how they will use the test.

Understanding Tests and Test Manuals

Nearly all standardized tests and inventories have an accompanying manual that provides information on the nature, administration, and development of the test. Counselors should read the test manual with care, both to determine whether a particular inventory will meet their needs and to obtain information on the proper administration of the inventory. Review of the test manual, along with self-administration of the test itself and review of the catalog description of the test, should provide counselors with answers to their questions about a test.

The following information usually can be obtained from the test manual:

1. What training and/or qualifications are needed to administer this test?
2. What is the purpose of this test? What is its theoretical basis?
3. Are alternate forms of this inventory available? What are the differences between the forms?
4. How much time is required for the administration of each form of this instrument?
   a. Can the test administration be divided over several sessions or is it recommended that it be completed in one session?
   b. If this is an ability test, how much does it assess speed and how much does it assess power?
5. Is this test designed for administration to groups or to individuals? Is there a limit to how many people can be tested with this instrument at the same time?
6. How is the test scored?
7. What is the reading level of each form of the test?
8. For what ages, grades, or groups is the test suitable? For what groups are norms available?
9. What have studies shown about the validity of this instrument?
10. What have studies shown about the reliability of this instrument?
11. In what forms are scores on this test presented?

12. What safeguards have been built in to minimize the effects of response sets and untruthful answers?
13. What efforts have been made to minimize culture and gender bias in the test?

Finding Answers in the Test Manual

Qualifications of the Test User

Test user qualifications have been developed to identify who is and who is not competent to use a specific test. Publishers and professional associations disseminate these standards to make tests available to qualified users and prevent their use by others.

The amount of training required to administer and interpret tests varies greatly from one test to another. Objective or standardized tests usually are easier to administer than projective tests. Standardized tests specify uniform testing procedures, have an objective system of scoring, and usually present information on normative data, validity, and reliability. Standardized tests typically present a circumscribed number of responses from which people select their answers. Multiple-choice and true-false formats are common in standardized tests. Administration of these tests typically involves providing instructions on taking the test, perhaps overseeing examinees' completion of several sample items, answering questions, timing the testing process, and making sure good testing conditions are maintained, such as a quiet and temperature-controlled room. Examinees generally mark their own answers on answer sheets that have been provided, and the test administrator is not directly involved during the testing process.

Projective tests, on the other hand, usually are far more difficult to administer. These tests present ambiguous stimuli, such as ink blots or pictures, and ask test takers to produce individual and subjective responses. Projective tests such as the Rorschach Test and the Thematic Apperception Test, discussed further in Chapter 3, require considerable expertise to administer. Examiner and examinee are engaged in an interactive process during administration of most projective tests, with each step or question being predicated on the examinee's previous responses.

Expertise required to score inventories also varies. Scoring of most objective inventories is not difficult. Computer or machine scoring is available for most objective tests, either locally or by mailing them to the test publisher. Those that are to be hand scored typically require little more than careful clerical skills and, in fact, objective tests often are scored by the test takers themselves or by support staff with the counselor's direction and supervision. Scoring of projective tests is more difficult, requiring decisions and judgments that can be made only by professionals who have extensive knowledge of the particular instrument.

Interpretation is the third factor that must be considered when skill level of the test administrator is determined. Objective tests can rival projective tests in the complexity of their interpretation. Tests such as the SII and the Minnesota Multiphasic Personality Inventory, although simple to administer and scored by computer, are challenging to interpret and require the expertise of a trained counselor or psychologist.

Most of the tests that counselors employ are objective in nature. Unless the counselors have participated in special programs or workshops or have taken courses beyond the master's degree, most counselors will not be qualified to administer projective tests. Some objective tests, too, will not be available for their use because the interpretation of those tests requires specialized training. The test catalog usually is the easiest place to locate information on credentials required of the test administrator, although that information will probably also be contained in the test manual and in test reviews.

Typically, test publishers establish levels of expertise and indicate the level required for purchase of each test. The National Computer System (NCS), for example, has three levels of products. Purchase of Level A products requires a graduate degree in applied psychology or a closely related field, a graduate course in abnormal psychology or psychopathology, and the equivalent of 1 year of experience in administering Level A products under qualified professional supervision. Level B1 products can be purchased and used by anyone with a graduate degree in applied psychology or a closely related field and a graduate course in abnormal psychology, psychopathology, or tests and measurement. Level B2 products have the lowest experience requirements. Their use and purchase requires a bachelor's degree in psychology or a closely related field and course work in psychological assessment. NCS sponsors workshops on using the tests they publish that can substitute for some of the required credentials.

Before A, B1, or B2 level tests can be purchased from NCS, prospective test users must complete a form describing their training and experience. Personnel at NCS review the form and assign a purchase level and a number to applicants that reflects what tests they are eligible to purchase and use. This system of establishing levels of expertise and certifying the qualification level of prospective test purchasers is typical of large test publishers.

Clearly, counselors must adhere to publisher guidelines as to which tests they can use and should not use tests that are beyond their level of expertise. However, counselors' assessment of their own expertise is at least as important as that of the publishers. Even if counselors are qualified on paper to administer an inventory, they must be sure, for themselves and their clients, that they have adequate familiarity with the administration, scoring, and interpretation of the inventory. If counselors are using instruments for which they have not received specific training, they should be sure to familiarize themselves with the test manual as well as with recent reviews of the test. Taking the test themselves can help counselors to anticipate questions or difficulties that may arise when they administer the instrument to their clients. Seeking supervision from a colleague with more experience in using a particular test is another way for counselors to gain needed expertise and be sure they are interpreting test information accurately.

The Purposes of Tests

Probably the most important piece of information about a test is its intended purpose. Tests can be categorized into those that measure *cognitive* or *affective* variables. Cognitive tests typically pose questions that have correct or incorrect answers. Such tests are designed to assess intelligence, mastery or achievement of a particular subject or body of knowledge (e.g., mathematics, spelling, French), or aptitude for success in a particular area. Tests that measure affective variables, on the other hand, ask for ideas, preferences, self-descriptors, and opinions. Because there are no correct responses to those items or questions, these tests might more properly be called *inventories*, a term many people find less threatening than *tests*. Affective inventories measure such variables as personality, interests, and values.

In addition to determining exactly what is being measured by the test or inventory, counselors should determine whether a test is *diagnostic* (designed to describe or categorize behavior or attitudes) or *prognostic* (designed to predict). Only by ascertaining exactly what information the test was designed to provide can counselors determine whether the test is suitable for their purposes.

Counselors also should determine the theoretical basis underlying the development of the test. The Myers-Briggs Type Indicator (MBTI), for example, is based on a conception of personality originally advanced by Carl Jung. According to Jung, personality can be described by four bipolar dimensions. The MBTI, discussed in greater detail later in this book, is an inventory that yields scores on those four bipolar dimensions. One of the theoretical underpinnings of the SII is that people are more likely to be satisfied and successful if they enter occupations in which they have highly similar interests to people who are already satisfied and successful. Understanding the theory behind the test is integral to making appropriate use and interpretation of the inventory.

How inventory items are constructed usually grows logically out of the theory underlying the test. Counselors should familiarize themselves with how items were developed. *Empirical* and *rational* approaches are the most common in test development. Empirical tests are those developed on the basis of experience. A pool of test items will be submitted to people specially selected to represent the groups that the test developer wants to measure. Those items that significantly differentiate one group from another will be incorporated into the test. The SII was developed in this way; it comprises test items that differentiated people in various occupations from each other and from people in general. The rational approach to test construction, on the other hand, begins with a description and analysis of behavior and leads to the formulation of items based on that analysis. The California Occupational Preference System Interest Inventory was developed in this way. The spectrum of interests was first divided into broad occupational clusters, and items were then written to correspond with the clusters.

Most counselors adopt a theory of career development in their work, probably borrowing heavily from one or more of the theories discussed in Chapter 1. They should be sure that the theoretical underpinnings of the tests and inventories they use are compatible with their theory of career development.

Test Forms

Most tests and inventories are available in several forms. Forms may differ according to the type of scoring used, the age or grade level of the test takers, the reading level of the test, or the length of administration. The MBTI, for example, includes a whole family of inventories. The basic inventory is designed to be administered to an adolescent or an adult and to be hand scored by a counselor. A brief version is available that can be self-scored, ideal for use in workshops. A computer-scored version is available for counselors who use the inventory in quantity and want to save time. A narrative interpretation of a person's scores is available as well as an analysis of a couple's MBTI scores, highlighting likely areas of compatibility and difference. In addition, a children's version of the MBTI also is available. Test catalogs are the best source of information about the variety of forms of a test that are available. Counselors must decide, then, not only which test or inventory to use but which form is likely to be best for a client.

Timing the Test Administration

Test manuals will indicate approximately how much time is required for the administration of a test and will indicate if the test is time limited. Generally, tests of aptitude, achievement, and intelligence are designed to be given during a specified length of time, whereas inventories of interests or personality are untimed. Timed tests may be constructed so that they allow ample time for most people to complete all test items (power test) or they may be designed so that only the most capable can complete all test items within the specified time limit (speed test). Counselors should determine whether they are more interested in measuring the skills or the rate of performance of their clients and should select tests accordingly. Counselors who are interested primarily in an individual client, particularly if that person is uneasy with the testing process, has some disabilities, or is not a native speaker of the language in which the test is written, might do best to select a power test. On the other hand, counselors who are under time pressure to obtain a rough measure of relative standing of a large group of people, seeking a general measure of the academic performance of a class, or doing a preliminary screening for either gifted students or those with potential academic problems might find a speed test to be the most efficient source of information.

In interpreting tests, counselors should differentiate between people who completed a test but made many errors and people who did not finish the test but made few errors. Although the two groups may have achieved similar scores, their abilities and areas of strength and weakness probably differ.

Under some circumstances, counselors may be tempted to deviate from standardized procedure for test administration. They may consider allowing a person with limited time to complete a test at home, or they may be inclined to give a few extra minutes to a person with low self-esteem or learning problems who is having considerable difficulty with a timed inventory. It is almost never a good idea to deviate from standardized methods of test administration. Altering the administration of a timed inventory invalidates the score because the scoring system has been based on a standardized administration. Allowing people to complete tests at home, particularly measures of ability, can also invalidate the results as well as jeopardize the counseling relationship. Testing often is an emotionally charged experience for the client. Therefore, this experience should take place in the presence of a counselor or someone else who is qualified to answer questions and alleviate anxiety. People who have an uncomfortable experience completing a test or inventory at home may not be motivated to do their best on the instrument or may even decide to terminate the counseling relationship because they became very anxious while completing the inventory.

If standardized procedures are unavoidably violated, such as by an emergency that occurs during the testing, counselors should probably contact the test publisher to determine how to proceed. Starting a timed ability test over again can invalidate the score because students would have had previous exposure to some of the questions. Having the students pick up where they left off might also invalidate the procedure because they have had an opportunity to talk to each other and might have become distracted by the interruption. Clearly, problems emerge when standardized procedures are violated; counselors should take steps to ensure that those procedures are followed whenever possible and should recognize that tests that do not follow standardized procedures may not provide accurate information.

Group Versus Individual Administration

Most tests used by counselors are designed so that they can be administered either to one person at a time or to a group of people. Generally, the test manual will indicate whether there are any limits on the size of the group that can comfortably be administered a particular test at one time. Although group administration usually is more efficient than individual administration, it is not always as useful. Counselors should consider whether a person has sufficient motivation, self-control, and self-confidence to perform optimally in a group-testing situation or whether individual testing might be indicated to reduce the threat posed by the testing and encourage the person to respond to the inventories with honesty and effort.

Scoring the Test

Tests are generally scored either by hand, using keys or templates, or by machine. Hand scoring can be done at the counselor's convenience but may be complicated and time-consuming and may require clerical help if large numbers of tests are being administered. The likelihood of errors or loss of tests increases, too, with the number of people who are processing the inventories. Hand scoring also may not yield as much information as machine scoring, particularly when compared to the information available in a narrative report. However, hand scoring does have several advantages. It is less expensive in terms of costs paid to the test publisher; however, that economic advantage may not be present when the cost of the counselor's time is considered. Results can be obtained more rapidly than from tests that need to be sent away for scoring; anywhere from a few days to a few weeks must be allowed in turnaround time for tests that are mailed away for machine scoring, whereas hand scoring can yield immediate results. Some hand-scored instruments such as the Self-Directed Search (SDS) can be scored by the client, with some direction provided by the counselor; this involvement in the scoring process can increase the person's interest in the test and can help to demystify the testing process.

Two approaches are available for the machine scoring of tests. Tests can be mailed away for scoring. Typically, scoring costs will be prepaid, with the cost of scoring built into the cost of the test form, although with some tests, scoring can be paid for each time a test is sent in for processing. Costs can be reduced by prepaying for the scoring of a group of tests, even if they are to be scored one at a time.

Increasingly, test publishers have made software available to purchasers, so that they can use their own computers to score tests on site. This process has many advantages; it is rapid, efficient, and convenient, and it poses little risk of error or loss. Cost, however, will probably be the primary determinant of whether this method of scoring is used. The initial expenditure for scoring software usually is quite high. However, that initial expenditure also allows the purchaser to use the software on a large number of tests. The examiner also will need to have terminals and other computer hardware available for administration and scoring of the inventories. If large numbers of an inventory are to be administered in a relatively short period of time (months rather than years), on-site computerized scoring may prove to have the lowest per-test cost. However, the high initial outlay of this option may be prohibitive.

When deciding what approach to scoring a test they should use, counselors should first ascertain what approaches are available. Some inventories cannot be hand scored (e.g., the SII), whereas others cannot be machine scored. Once the counselor has determined what forms of scoring are available, consideration of cost of scoring in terms of both processing and counselor time, number of tests being used in a given time period, speed with which scores are needed, facilities, support staff, and amount of data needed will indicate the best method of scoring.

Reading Levels of Tests

Test manuals generally will indicate both the age group and the reading level for which a test has been designed. Some tests may be unsuitable for people whose reading levels are considerably below average even though those people are in the age group targeted by the test. Giving people tests that are far too difficult for them can increase their negative feelings toward the testing process, the counseling relationship, and even themselves. Instead, counselors should seek out tests at the client's reading level or in the client's native language. If these are not available, alternate approaches to information gathering should be used.

Counselors have been known to read untimed tests to people that would otherwise have been too difficult for them. However, this approach is questionable at best because it deviates from the method of administration on which the test was standardized.

Norms

Norms are sets of scores that allow the comparison of the test scores of one person or a group such as a class or a school with the distribution of scores obtained by various sample groups. Sample groups for which norms have been developed may be described in terms of age, gender, education, occupation, location, or background. Norms may be national and based on a sample selected to be representative of a particular group of people throughout the country (e.g., college freshmen) or they may be local and based on a sample representing a school, community, or region. Members of a sample group may be selected at random or may have been selected to conform to predetermined demographic requirements. Large sample groups usually are more desirable than small sample groups because their test performance is more likely to be representative of the population from which they were selected. Kline

(1975) recommended that sample groups of adults consist of at least 3,000 people.

Counselors usually want to compare the scores of people they have assessed with sample groups that are very similar to their clients or who represent a group that the clients are thinking about joining, such as college students or people engaged in a particular occupation. Test scores will be most meaningful to counselors and clients if they can be compared with the scores of a relevant sample. The nature of the normative samples provided in test manuals, then, should be carefully examined by the counselor who is assessing the suitability of a test.

Validity

Validity is the one most important attribute of a test. Validity indicates how well a test measures what it purports to measure.

Four types of test validity exist. *Face validity* indicates only whether a test looks as though it measures what it claims to be assessing. Some believe it is a misnomer to call this validity. *Content validity* usually involves an examination of test items by experts in the field to determine whether, according to those experts, the items are measuring what is claimed. *Construct validity* compares test scores with other measures of the behavior or knowledge that the scores are supposed to reflect, to determine if the test really is a good measure of a particular characteristic. Hood and Johnson (1991) have identified the following four types of construct validity: (a) *convergent validity*—the similarity of scores on a given test to scores on other measures of the same construct; (b) *divergent validity*—the difference of scores on a given test from scores on measures with which they would be expected to differ; (c) *internal consistency*—to what extent items on the test are related to each other and to the total score; (d) *treatment validity*—to what extent the test results make a difference in the client's treatment.

Criterion-related validity, the fourth type of validity, indicates how closely the test corresponds to some criterion or standard. Two types of criterion-related validity have been identified: (a) *predictive validity*—how effective the test is at anticipating a future outcome, for example, how well aptitude test scores of high school students predict college grades; and (b) *concurrent validity*—relationship of test scores to an empirical measure, for example, the performance of a group of English teachers on a measure of verbal skills.

Statistically, validity is expressed in terms of a correlation coefficient that may range from 0.00 (no relationship) to +1.00 or –1.00 (a perfect relationship). In general, the higher the validity, the better the test. Test authors are generally satisfied with validities above .40. Even a validity correlation coefficient of .30 can improve prediction by approximately 30%. Counselors should consider the types of validity that have been studied for a particular instrument and their relationship to the reasons for the testing as well as the levels of the validity coefficients.

Reliability

The reliability of a test indicates how consistent that test is. Two types of reliability have been identified: internal consistency and stability over time.

Internal consistency generally is assessed via the split-half method. Performance on one half of a test is compared with performance on the other half. This can readily be determined by scoring a test twice, once based only on the odd-numbered items and once based only on the even-numbered items. The relationship between performance on the odd-numbered half and performance on the even-numbered half provides an indication of the internal consistency of the test content. Another measure of internal consistency can be obtained by analyzing the intercorrelations between all tests items (interitem consistency).

Stability over time typically is measured by administering a test twice to a group of people, with the administrations separated by a specified length of time. The relationship of scores from the two administrations yields a reliability coefficient reflecting stability over time. However, the effects of practice and memory enter into the process and can affect the results. To reduce that effect, alternate or parallel forms of an instrument can be given, with some people receiving Form A before Form B and others receiving Form B before Form A. Reliability scores derived from the alternate-form approach are less likely to be affected by practice and memory, but equivalence of forms must be established to provide reasonably accurate reliability coefficients. The split-half method also can be used to determine stability over time, with the administration of each half separated by time. This method, too, has shortcomings; the shorter test is likely to yield lower reliability scores. However, a formula is available to correct for this. In general, reliability declines as the length of the interval between test administrations increases, whereas reliability increases with the length of the test (Lyman, 1971). Speed tests usually have higher reliability than do power or performance tests.

Reliability, like validity, is expressed in terms of a correlation coefficient that can range from 0.00 to +1.00 or –1.00. The following provides a guide to the interpretation of correlation coefficients, although their significance varies with the number of people involved in the validation or reliability studies (Herr & Cramer, 1972):

Correlation Coefficient (r)	Interpretation
.00-.20	Negligible relationship
.20-.40	Low to moderate relationship
.40-.70	Substantial or marked relationship
.70-1.00	High to very high relationship

Although validity always is an important component of measurement, reliability may or may not be important. If the counselor is concerned with measuring day-to-day changes, such as in level of depression or anxiety, stability over time may not be important. However, if interests are being measured for use in long-range career decisions, reliability is very important. By reviewing the test manual, counselors can determine whether the level of reliability emerging from studies of a given test is adequate for their purposes.

The lower the reliability of a test, the higher the *standard error of measurement (SEM)*. This is another term that should be familiar to counselors who use tests in their work. Reliability focuses on groups, whereas the *SEM* focuses on the individual. According to Hood and Johnson (1991), the *SEM* "represents the theoretical distribution that would be obtained if an individual were repeatedly tested with a large number of exactly equivalent forms of the same test" (p. 33) and allows counselors to develop "bands of confidence" around people's obtained test scores. Chances are two out of three that a person's true score on a test will fall within one *SEM* of his or her achieved score and 95% that the true score will fall within two *SEMs* above or below the achieved score. That test scores will vary from one administration to the next is almost inevitable. However, the *SEM* gives counselors an idea of how much change they should expect if a person were to take a test a second time and also how much confidence to place in the achieved score.

Types of Test Scores

Although there are a few tests, such as the SDS, for which interpretation is based on raw scores, most tests use tables or statistical procedures to convert raw scores into measures that are more conducive to comparison. Age or grade equivalents, percentiles, standard scores, and stanines are common ways of presenting test data.

Age- or *grade-equivalent scores* are commonly used in tests of intelligence or ability that are designed to be administered to children. Such scores indicate the age or grade level that would be expected to perform on the test in a way comparable to that of a particular test taker. By comparing people's age or grade scores with their actual age or grade, the counselor can determine whether test takers have performed as well, better, or less well than others of their age and grade have performed on the test. The Wide Range Achievement Test is an example of a test that allows the translation of raw scores into both age and grade scores.

Grade equivalents are commonly used in tests of educational achievement. A number representing the grade, followed by a decimal representing the 10 months of the school year, is used to indicate a child's performance; for example, 4.5 would represent the fifth month of the fourth grade. Although these scores are relatively easy to interpret, they do not mean that the child could actually perform class work at the specified grade level; rather, the score is an indication of how the average student in the achieved grade would score on the given test.

Percentile scores or *ranks* probably are the most frequently used method for reporting scores on standardized tests. Percentile ranks generally range from 1 to 99 with a median of 50 and indicate a person's relative standing within a particular group—in other words, the percentage of people in a reference group who scored lower than the test taker when their scores are rank ordered.

Percentile scores may be expressed in terms of *percentile bands* that encompass a range of scores extending from +1 to –1 *SEM* away from a person's achieved score. Chances are two out of three that a person's true scores lie within +1 or –1 *SEM* of that person's achieved score. Hanna (1988), as well as other writers, recommends percentile ranks as a method of transmitting scores; they are easy to understand, free of jargon, and involve a linear or rectangular scale, more familiar to most people than the so-called normal or bell-shaped curve that can be confusing. Counselors should be sure, however, that people do not misinterpret percentile score as percentage of correct answers. Also, counselors should realize that small differences in percentile scores are more important in the middle range than they are at the extremes. The Differential Aptitude Tests are an example of an inventory that uses percentile ranks and bands.

Standard scores are a way of organizing test scores into a normal distribution so that they can readily be interpreted. They reflect the difference between a person's raw score and the mean score of the group on which the test was normed. Standard scores are based on the *standard deviation*, the most dependable measure of variability (Hood & Johnson, 1991). One standard deviation from the mean encompasses 34.13% of the population; the second standard includes 13.59% of the population; the third standard deviation includes 2.14%; and the fourth standard deviation includes 0.13%. A score that is one standard deviation above the mean, therefore, is better than approximately 84% (50% + one standard deviation or 34.13%) of the test takers in the reference group. The SII, the Graduate Record Examination, and the Scholastic Aptitude Test (SAT) are examples of tests that use standard scores.

Various forms of standard scores are used, perhaps the most common of which is the *t* score, which allows the conversion of raw scores into a scale with a mean of 50 and a standard deviation of 10. Scores usually range from 20 to 80. A relative measure of a person's score then can be obtained by assessing its distance from the mean.

Stanine scores, derived from a combination of the words *standard* and *nine*, are another form of standard score. Stanine scores divide all possible scores on a given test into nine levels. Except for Stanines 1 and 9, which are open-ended, each of the nine levels is one half a standard deviation in width. Normally distributed stanines, then, have a mean of 5 and a standard deviation of 2.

Yet another form of standard score is the *z* score. Somewhat confusing because of their use of decimals and negative scores, *z* scores are not commonly found in reporting of test scores. A *z* score of zero indicates the mean, whereas a *z* score of +1.5 reflects a score that is 1.5 standard deviations above the mean of the reference group.

In interpreting scores, counselors should ascertain whether a test is *ipsative* because that will color the meaning of the test scores. Ipsative instruments are forced-choice tests that use test items to yield scores on more than one variable. Interpretation of scores on such an instrument should take account not only of a score on a given variable but of the strength of that score relative to scores on other variables. Scores on such tests generally will be balanced; if one score increases, others must decline. Ipsative inventories not only compare a given person with other people but also compare the relative strength of a group of variables, such as interests, for that person. The Kuder tests are examples of ipsative instruments.

Response Sets and Untruthful Answers

Inaccurate responses may result when test takers are inattentive or uninterested in the testing process or when they have difficulty understanding test items or test directions. An effort to present a particular impression also may color test results. Although most people try to present an honest and accurate picture of themselves through the tests they take, pressures and habits sometimes lead to distortion in responses. People commonly have response sets or habitual ways of responding to questions. They may tend to agree more than they disagree or vice versa. They may feel more comfortable selecting a moderate or neutral response or may enjoy endorsing extreme positions and attitudes. They may choose the more socially desirable of two responses. People also may "fake good" or "fake bad" or slant responses in a given direction so that test results are more likely to reflect a desired image.

For example, one young man, descended from a large family of physicians and strongly encouraged to pursue a career in medicine, deliberately provided positive responses to all inventory questions related to medicine so that he could tell his parents that the inventory had confirmed the family hopes for him. However, as trust developed in the counseling relationship, he acknowledged that he had not responded accurately to the inventory and, in fact, had little interest in pursuing the study of medicine. Family pressure and a wish to please his parents previously had prevented him from expressing and pursuing his strong interests in art and music.

Although test writers usually try to minimize inaccurate and distorted responses by equating the social desirability of paired test items and creating test items so that a positive or extreme response does not always mean the same thing, inaccurate responses, whether deliberate or inadvertent, cannot completely be eliminated. However, many instruments such as the Kuder Occupational Interest Survey and the Edwards Personal Preference Schedule have built-in scales that can give counselors some idea of the consistency and acceptability of the test takers' responses. Elevated scores on these scales suggest that a great deal of weight should not be placed on those test results and indicate that counselors should explore further the client's attitude toward the counseling and assessment process before proceeding.

Culture, Race, and Gender Bias

During the 1970s, tests received a great deal of criticism for bias. Sedlacek (1977) described three kinds of bias that could affect the assessment process. *Content bias* occurs when the language, illustrations, or content of a test are oriented more toward one cultural, ethnic, or gender group than toward another. *Atmosphere bias* can be present in the administration of an inventory; the interface of the backgrounds, race, and gender of examiner and test taker and their perceptions of and attitudes toward each other have been shown to affect the performance of the test taker. *Use bias* occurs when test results are interpreted in such a way as to discriminate against any ethnic, cultural, or gender group or to influence people to limit their consideration of career options solely or primarily on the basis of their gender or culture.

Test bias can appear in many forms, both blatant and subtle. Early forms of the SII included different questions for men and women, with the men's form being printed in blue and the women's in pink. Many illustrated inventories for young children contained few pictures of African Americans or Asians and portrayed boys and girls engaged only in traditional activities and occupations. Females were depicted as homemakers or teachers and males were shown as physicians or engineers. Although such gender stereotyping may, indeed, have reflected common roles for each gender, most authorities now seem to agree that such portrayals limited options. Such blatant stereotyping is rarely found today.

Considerable efforts have been made since the 1970s to develop tests that are either free of bias or are fair in their treatment of people, regardless of their gender or cultural group. Several principles have guided these efforts. Of course, test items and illustrations have been recast to avoid stereotyping. Tests and interpretive material now generally use plural pronouns (they, them) rather than singular, gender-linked pronouns (he or she). Separate tests for males and females rarely are found, and both males and females almost always are afforded the opportunity to respond to the same test items.

Most studies seem to agree, however, that same-sex norms are more useful than other-sex or combined-sex norms in helping people identify a broad range of viable career options (Diamond, Harmon, & Zytowski, 1976). Although the use of combined-sex or other-sex norms may, at least on the surface, seem to be inherently less gender biased than the use of same-sex norms, research has not found that to be the case. In fact, scores based on opposite-sex norms seem to exaggerate traditional differences, leading to stereotyped results. For example, a young woman with a relatively high interest in mechanical engineering may not achieve a high score when her responses are compared with males, many of whom have an interest in that area. However, when she is compared with other women, her interest will emerge clearly. Counselors should not assume that a test contains gender bias, then, because same-sex norms are emphasized. However, a justification should be offered in the test manual for the use of same-sex norms. In addition, the test protocol also might compare a person's scores with those obtained by a normative group of the other gender and should present scores in a way that does not foster gender bias.

Not all researchers agree with the use of same-sex norms. Holland (1987b), for example, has not followed that procedure in the development of the SDS. Holland believed that men and women are primarily seeking reassurance about an aspiration they already hold rather than seeking new options when they seek career counseling and assessment (Holland, 1980). Consequently, he concluded that combined gender norms, presenting a holistic view of the world of work, provide the most useful and realistic information.

Although separate gender norming is well established, race norming is quite controversial (Gottfredson & Sharf, 1988). Some believe it will expand opportunities for people from minority groups, whereas others suggest that separate race norming will lead to the development of unrealistic aspirations and, in employment settings, the hiring of unqualified people. Continued research is needed in this area.

Although considerable progress has been made in identifying and describing cultural and gender bias and reducing its impact on test takers, researchers have had little success developing tests that are entirely free of bias. As Thorndike (1978) stated at a court case involving the cultural bias of intelligence tests,

> Everybody would acknowledge that we have no conceivable way of directly measuring native ability. What we measure is the developed ability that the individual possesses at a given level and point in time. . . . I'm not quite sure what would be meant by a culture fair test. Any test is based upon and uses the medium of a culture. It cannot do otherwise. We cannot test people in a vacuum. . . . If you are going to have a social setting in which the minority and the major bulk of the population are going to function jointly in a common setting, then it seems to me that it is probably inappropriate to provide separate treatment for the minority groupings in the one context when you are not going to deal with them as a separate group in another. ("Exhibit C: I.Q. trial," 1978, p. 9)

The solution to dealing with gender and culture bias does not seem to be to eliminate all tests as some suggested in the 1970s or to concentrate on developing inventories that are culture free. Rather, the solution seems to involve refining established tests and developing new ones that have demonstrated their validity regardless of the background or gender of the test taker and that do not perpetuate discriminatory attitudes and limitations. In addition, as Watkins and Campbell (1990) stated, "Future efforts in this area will focus on (a) using and interpreting available tests within the context of cultural boundaries and (b) developing and validating culturally specific tests and assessment methods" (p. 193).

Counselors can contribute to the reduction of bias in testing in two important ways. When selecting a test, they should pay special attention to the discussion of gender and culture bias in the test manual. They should review the nature of the available norms to ensure that the test authors have appropriately addressed issues of bias in the development of the test and that the test is suitable for their clients. In addition, in their interpretation of test results, counselors should make use of self-report and qualitative data and should focus on the person as well as on his or her environment. A holistic approach, drawing on multiple sources of data, seems most likely to reduce the negative influence of test bias.

Pitfalls of the Assessment Process

Tests have been much criticized for many years. In the 1950s, the scientific validity of tests was questioned. In the 1960s, person-centered counselors viewed testing as incompatible with the process of psychotherapy. In the 1970s and 1980s, tests were condemned for their ethnic and gender bias.

At the same time, tests have been widely used for many years. In the 1960s, between 150 and 250 million standardized tests were administered annually in United States schools, for an average of three to five standardized tests per student per year (Kirkland, 1971). Criticisms levied against tests during the next decades did little to diminish the assessment process, largely because the 1970s and 1980s were a period of considerable concern about the effectiveness of American education. Increasing numbers of schools introduced testing programs to assess the competency levels of their students and, in some cases, to determine whether students should be promoted or graduated. During the last half of the 1970s, the number of states requiring minimum competency testing of students increased from 8 to 38 (Linn, 1986). During the 1980s, nearly half of all 2- and 4-year colleges required an admissions test of their applicants (Franco, 1983). Tests such as the SAT and the SII that are good predictors of future events have contributed to continued widespread testing. Testing also has been increased as a result of the growing attention that schools have been paying since the 1970s to career education and counseling and the accompanying development of many new and improved instruments designed to reduce bias and facilitate the process of career development. In addition, knowledge about learning styles and thinking skills increased during the 1980s and led to increased emphasis on assessing higher-order skills.

Testing will probably continue to be an important aspect of the counselor's role, despite its limitations. Counselors can reduce the negative aspects of testing in their own work by becoming aware of the possible drawbacks to testing. The following are some of the criticisms that frequently have been levied against tests:

1. Tests have been used to place harmful and sometimes inaccurate labels on people, especially on children who may be diagnosed as mentally retarded or learning disabled when, in reality, their cultural background has limited their performance on standardized tests. Such labeling can damage self-esteem, interfere with the provision of appropriate help, and influence the lifelong social and occupational status of the person.

2. Tests can place limitations on the educational and occupational aspirations and opportunities of people, especially females and those from lower socioeconomic or multicultural backgrounds.

3. Tests can foster a narrow concept of ability and can limit diversity and reduce opportunities for creative and unusual thinkers and for those whose abilities are not focused in the academic arena.

4. Testing can be dehumanizing and can foster a process of evaluation that is inflexible and impersonal and that does not take sufficient account of individual needs.

5. Adequate safeguards may not be provided to ensure privacy: Test data sometimes may be released to parents, teachers, or employers without the test takers' knowledge or permission and without ascertaining that these people are able to understand and make appropriate use of the test data.

6. Misunderstood or misinterpreted test data can have powerful adverse effects on people's self-images and future plans. Although people seem to be more receptive to positive test data and to remember them longer than they do negative test data, most adults who have taken tests reported that the tests had influenced their lives (Goodyear, 1990; Kirkland, 1971).

7. Test results may be overemphasized and overgeneralized and may be erroneously viewed as evaluating the worth of people and their likelihood of future success.

8. Testing can cast people in dependent roles in which they feel subordinate to the computer as well as to the counselor and so are reluctant to express points of view that are discrepant with the test results.
9. Test interpretation can erroneously view the person out of context and, consequently, can be misleading.

Proper administration and interpretation of assessment information can greatly reduce or eliminate the prevalence of these pitfalls.

Administration of Tests

The administration of tests and inventories is an integral part of the assessment process, as are selecting and interpreting tests. Such non-intellectual factors as anxiety, attentiveness, persistence, emotional lability, achievement motivation, and physical health all have been found to affect test performance as does the behavior of the examiner (Snyderman & Rathman, 1987). Johnson and Hummel (1971) found, for example, that test anxiety was negatively correlated with performance on ability tests of fifth-grade students and that expressions of approval and disapproval by test administrators affected examinee performance. A correlation also has been found between very low anxiety and poor performance on achievement tests (Karmos & Karmos, 1984). On the other hand, Kinnie and Sternlof (1971) found that the level of children's inventoried intelligence could be increased by familiarizing them with adults similar to those who would be administering the tests, the language and materials that they would encounter during the test administration, and the nature of the testing situation. Practice and coaching have been found to improve test performance of people who have little recent experience in taking tests, although their effect on the sophisticated test taker generally is limited (Benson, Urman, & Hocevar, 1986).

Although most approach testing with interest and motivation, Karmos and Karmos (1984) found that over one third of students in Grades 6 through 9 whom they studied viewed achievement tests as a waste of time, whereas 22% said they did not care much about getting the right answers. Males and low achievers were overrepresented in those groups.

Research on test administration, then, suggests that performance can be maximized if people are helped to see the relationship between their goals and the testing process, when they do not attribute excessive power to the test results, when they are comfortable with the examiner, when they know what to expect during the testing session, and when efforts have been made to clarify and reduce sources of anxiety inherent in the testing process. Clients should be involved in planning their assessment and should know what tests they will be taking, why those particular tests have been selected, what information is expected to be provided by the testing, how the results will be used, and to whom they will be available.

Although situational variables generally do not have a great effect on test performance, they still should be taken into account when planning the assessment process. Testing sessions should be scheduled at a time and place that are likely to evoke positive attitudes toward the assessment process. Length of each testing session should be planned so that chances of fatigue or loss of interest are minimized. Testing probably should be postponed if test takers are feeling very tired or ill. The testing room should be quiet and well lighted, and seating should be comfortable and provide an adequate surface for the test materials. Necessary supplies, including pencils and a clock, should be available. Security of tests should be maintained, particularly for ability tests, and, in most cases, test takers should not be given an opportunity to review an inventory until the actual testing session has begun. At that time, standardized procedures such as time limits and use of certain writing implements (e.g., the No. 2 pencil) should be followed scrupulously. Directions should be given clearly and administrators should not discourage people from changing answers they believe to be incorrect. The belief that one's first response usually is correct is a myth; in reality, studies have found that changing answers thoughtfully results in increased scores (McMorris & Weideman, 1986).

If possible, the test administration should be conducted by the counselor with whom the test taker has already established a relationship. This will not only facilitate the test administration but also can provide the counselor with some valuable information. The manner in which people approach and deal with taking tests often reflects their attitudes and personalities. Counselors should take note of whether their clients arrive on time for a testing session, the number and nature of their questions, their apparent level of comfort and attention, and their speed in completing the inventories. If counselors observe signs of anxiety or lack of motivation such as a late arrival for the test administration or a hasty completion of an inventory, these behaviors should be kept in mind when the results of the testing are interpreted and might be discussed with the clients.

Counselors also should examine test takers' completed answer sheets before they leave the room. Some inventories are invalidated by the omission of a few responses; by checking answer sheets, counselors can spot omissions and can encourage people to respond to those questions, if permitted by the timing of the inventory and the guidelines of the test manual. Counselors should make sure that responses on the answer sheets are sufficiently clear and dark and reflect understanding of the test directions. Counselors also should look for unusual patterns of response that may signify a loss of interest or motivation. People sometimes begin a test administration with a positive attitude but experience a decline in motivation because of the level of difficulty or apparent irrelevance of the test material. Such a shift in attitude may be reflected in an answer sheet that begins with a seemingly random pattern of responses and then shifts to a pattern of responses that suggests a design or predetermined sequence of responses. A test protocol that reflects more correct answers in the beginning than it does toward the end of the test may be another indication of the emergence of a negative attitude toward the testing process, unless the test is one that becomes more difficult as it progresses.

Computer-Based Assessment

Many tests and inventories are available in computer-based or computer-assisted versions. Hansen (1986) identified five levels of computer-assisted assessment:

1. computerized scoring of inventories
2. computer-generated interpretive reports
3. computer-administered inventories and computerized career guidance programs
4. graphics, used to assess psychomotor skills and skills specific to certain jobs
5. comprehensive computerized assessment, in which the computer administers the tests, computes the scores, transforms raw scores into scaled scores, and provides the results and their interpretation

Determination of needs and resources, including funds and space, as well as the services available for the tests they use most, will help counselors decide which level of computer assistance is appropriate for them.

Computer-based testing offers many advantages over paper-and-pencil assessment (Madsen, 1986; Vansickle, Kimmel, & Kapes, 1989; Wise & Plake, 1990). Computer-based assessment can

1. be cost-effective, although the initial expenses may be high
2. afford people an active role in the testing process
3. require less testing time for many inventories
4. provide immediate feedback
5. gather more information, such as a record of answers that were changed and latency of time response for each item
6. provide greater standardization of administration
7. offer additional format options, such as graphics, simulations, and motion
8. offer more strategies for testing (e.g., can allow respondent to change an answer after receiving immediate feedback, can promote learning with an answer-until-correct instruction)
9. offer scoring that saves time and paper
10. allow testing that is individualized or adapted to particular needs (e.g., ending the testing when a specified number of consecutive errors have been made to reduce test-taker frustration and discouragement)
11. improve test-retest reliability, possibly because the computerized presentation of one item at a time improves focusing and accuracy
12. store information for later retrieval, review, or comparison with other pieces of information

In general, computer-based assessment is an efficient, statistically sound approach to testing that is well received by both counselors and clients (McKee & Levinson, 1990). However, some concerns have been raised about computer-based assessment. Computer anxiety is common and may afflict counselors as well as clients (Madsen, 1986). Staff training as well as orientation of clients to the computer should be done with care, to be sure that anxiety does not scare off potential users. Privacy both of administration and results may be compromised by computer-based assessment, and steps should be taken to protect confidentiality of users. Computerized assessment may seem even more powerful than paper-and-pencil tests, and people may put too much faith in the feedback of the computer (Eberly & Cech, 1986). People with considerable confusion about their career direction or personal difficulties that are inhibiting their career development may feel alienated or discouraged by computerized assessment. The computer may raise more questions for them than it answers. In addition, printed and computerized versions of the same inventory are not always comparable. As Dimock and Cormier (1991) stated, "A computerized version of a standard paper-and-pencil test should not be assumed equivalent to the original test without definite evidence that it is equivalent. Without such evidence, the results of a computerized test should be interpreted with caution" (p. 125). However, if these concerns are appropriately addressed, respondents are likely to prefer computerized assessment to paper-and-pencil formats and to be more honest in providing answers when interacting with a computer (Koch, Dodd, & Fitzpatrick, 1990).

Computer-based assessment is an important aspect of a comprehensive and well-integrated counseling program. People should be screened before being introduced to the computer to be sure they are not in crisis and are sufficiently clear about their needs and questions to benefit from the computerized testing. They should be oriented to the process to allay anxiety. Finally, they should have ample opportunity to meet with a counselor following the computer-based assessment to review the information they obtained, to have their questions answered, to help them relate the information obtained from the computer to information they already have about themselves, and to develop career plans that are likely to be realistic and rewarding.

Interpretation of Test Results

Tests are neutral. They may be an effective method of communicating knowledge, increasing self-awareness, and facilitating sound planning, or they may be a way of stereotyping, limiting options, and reinforcing negative self-images. Tests, like almost any powerful tool, have a potential for both benefit and harm. The burden of ensuring that the testing process helps rather than hinders development generally falls on counselors. It is up to counselors to ensure that both the testing that they perform and the testing programs that are conducted by their schools or agencies are beneficial. Although selection of inappropriate tests and poorly conducted test administrations can invalidate test results and make the testing process a waste of time, the interpretation phase of the testing process has the greatest potential for harm as well as for benefit. In a review of 44 studies conducted since 1950, Goodyear (1990) concluded that people who received test interpretations experienced greater gains than did those who did not.

Written Interpretation of Test Results

Although, ideally, test results should be disseminated in face-to-face situations, circumstances sometimes dictate another approach to giving information. A school or college counselor may have to give test results to an entering class of hundreds of students. A counselor may act as a consultant, providing assessment of a person at the request of another mental health professional who may not be familiar with career-related testing. In cases such as these, results will probably be transmitted in writing. Even in such cases, steps can be taken by the counselor to maximize chances of people's making appropriate use of the test data. An assembly or group meeting might help students interpret the written results and integrate those results into their self-images in useful ways. Opportunity for people with questions to meet individually with the counselor also should be extended.

In the case of a report written to a referral source, counselors can take a holistic approach to transmitting data. For example, a comprehensive and integrated assessment report may have the following format:

1. description of client, including physical appearance, affect, presenting concerns, interaction with counselor, attitude toward assessment
2. reason for counseling or referral
3. relevant background information
4. goals of assessment process
5. description of inventories and other assessment procedures used
6. behavioral observations of client during the testing process
7. summary of test results and their significance for the client
8. integration of test data with other information on the client
9. recommendations
10. summary

Some impersonal approaches to assessment are unethical. For example, some services offer both testing and interpretation of personality and abilities by mail to the general population. Counselors should not participate in such unethical practices and are encouraged to work for their elimination.

Face-to-Face Interpretation of Test Results

Ideally, test interpretation should take place in person, particularly if the testing was done as a part of career counseling. The following principles of effective face-to-face test interpretation are well established:

1. Be well acquainted with the clients, their backgrounds, their present needs, and the goals of the testing process.

2. Know the tests that have been used.

3. Prepare for the interpretation, focusing on information that will meet the goals of the testing process and that is personally meaningful to the client.

4. Present information clearly and accurately, without jargon or technical terms.

5. Interpretation should be a collaborative process, with the clients participating actively throughout.

6. Emphasize a holistic approach that presents test data in the context of what is already known about the clients.

7. Avoid making decisions or judgments for clients.

8. Be aware of and explore the clients' needs and their reactions to the information that is being presented.

9. View testing as part of a process of promoting people's self-esteem, self-awareness, career development, decisions, and action.

10. Keep in mind that the primary goal of the assessment process is "empowerment of the individual" (Duckworth, 1990, p. 203).

Counselors, then, should begin the interpretation process with preparation. They should review both the test manual and the client's test protocol to be sure that any questions that may arise can be answered and that clients will not receive incorrect information. Counselors should consider the relationship between the test results and other information that has been obtained about the client, taking particular note of any discrepancies. They should consider the original goals of the counseling and assessment process and identify information that will further the accomplishment of those goals.

Although a test interpretation should be an open and honest sharing of test results, the counselor should not feel compelled to discuss every score in depth. The counselor should gear the test interpretation to the needs and concerns of a particular person and the goals of the counseling relationship. The counselor should focus on those facets of the test results that seem most likely to clarify self-concept and facilitate decision making.

Guidelines for Interpretation

During the process of interpretation, counselors should emphasize descriptive or comparative terminology rather than numbers. Positive aspects of the test results should be highlighted, to encourage development of self-esteem and optimism. Counselors should not distort the results or omit important information to avoid damaging a person's self-image, although, of course, tact and sensitivity in presentation of information is important. If sufficient thought went into the selection of an instrument, then the counselor should have decided that the outcome of the administration of that instrument would be worthwhile to the client, regardless of the nature of the scores that are achieved. Counselors should not use tests simply to enhance a person's self-esteem. Counselors rarely can predict with confidence how a person will score on an inventory or how a person will react to a test score. Generally, discussion rather than testing is indicated to help people with low self-esteem unless at least part of those negative feelings are due to a lack of information and feedback about the self.

When discussing tests with clients, counselors should try to maintain their objectivity. Although, inevitably, counselors as well as clients will have some reactions to a test protocol, counselors should guard against imposing their values and intuitions on their clients. Although a counselor may think that it would be a mistake for a bright high school student to formulate career plans that do not involve attending college, that is a decision for the student to make. Neither counselors nor tests can predict the future with certainty. At the same time, for counselors to foster the belief that people can become anything they want to be as long as they are willing to work hard is to perpetuate the Horatio Alger myth and to do people a disservice.

Counselors can help people to make sound decisions by encouraging them to consider all options and their probable outcomes in both the long and short range and to explore carefully how they arrived at their decisions. Counselors' interventions should be carefully phrased so that they encourage realistic thinking without making decisions for clients or making either positive or negative value judgments about people's choices. For example, counselors might tell people with poor academic records and low scores on ability tests that they are likely to be less capable of handling college course work than are typical college students and that they will probably have to work hard to keep up with their classmates. Counselors should not tell such students that they are not college material and that they should choose occupations that do not require a college education. Should those people elect to apply to college despite the obstacles, counselors should not try to change their plans but, rather, should help their clients prepare themselves as well as possible for entry into college as well as develop contingency plans if they are not admitted to college or find they are unable to handle the academic demands of college.

Approaches to Interpretation

When interpreting tests, both counselors and clients should view tests as only one source of information, the accuracy of which cannot always be ensured. Test data should not be overemphasized but should be considered in light of data already obtained and should be incorporated into the total picture of the client. What Goodyear (1990) has called *integrative counseling* seems preferable to test-centered interpretations. According to Goodyear, the interpretation process should emphasize discussion and exploration. Counselors should not abandon their fundamental skills, their empathy, reflection of feeling, open questions, encouragement of specificity, and acceptance just because they are engaged in the process of test interpretation. Although, generally, teaching and giving information will be part of the counselors' role when they are engaged in test interpretation, the role of counselor always should predominate.

Several approaches to test interpretation have been found effective. Whichever approach is selected, that approach should be used in such a way as to elicit people's feelings about test results that are both discrepant from and consistent with their views of themselves. The test results should be used to promote people's self-awareness, to identify and clarify options, and to promote realistic and rewarding planning. Although a trait-and-factor model underlies the development of many tests, the trait-and-factor process will probably not predominate during the interpretation. Tests should not be used to persuade people either to enter a particular occupation or to rule out occupational options that have not been supported by the testing. Test data, alone, cannot be relied on to guide people into appropriate occupations. Generally, test data take little or no account of factors such as motivation or background and can do little to integrate interests, abilities, values, and personality. This work must be accomplished through the dialogue of the counseling sessions.

Goldman (1971) defined four types of test interpretation: (a) *descriptive* (what is this person like?), (b) *genetic* (how did the person become like this?), (c) *predictive* (what paths seem most likely to be realistic and rewarding for this person?), and (d) *evaluative* (what should this person do?). In determining which approach to use in presenting test data, counselors should consider what types of interpretation are likely to be most useful. A profile analysis presenting a range of scores or the results of several tests often is helpful in providing a description that can then readily be compared with the person's self-image and other information that has been gathered. Genetic interpretations require an integration of test data and background information such as a developmental history and school grades; in focusing on such an approach to interpretation, counselors would de-emphasize the test results and concentrate on exploration. Predictive interpretations often rely heavily on a comparison of people's test results with those of relevant norm groups and might use regression analysis to make a prediction from several pieces of information. An evaluative interpretation would integrate several techniques of interpretation. Profile analysis and normative data both would be important but so would an analysis of people's backgrounds and resources, their reactions to the test results, and their decision-making skills.

The following steps probably should be incorporated into most approaches to test interpretation:

1. review of tests taken and discussion of client's reactions to the testing process
2. review of objectives of assessment process
3. counselor's presentation of first inventory, perhaps the one that is easiest to understand, most positive, or most consistent with the client's self-image, including nature of data presented, scoring process, limitations of the inventory
4. presentation and processing of client's scores, focusing on what is personally meaningful to the client
5. integration of test data with background and other available information
6. discussion of client's reactions to the information and exploration of questions
7. integration of data from all inventories into a holistic view of the person
8. summarization by client of information obtained and how that meshes with other information
9. concluding opportunity for client to ask questions, express concerns and reactions, with counselor being sure that the client has an accurate and comfortable understanding of the test data
10. planning for the next step in the counseling

Steps 3 through 6 would be followed for each inventory.

A focused test interpretation may extend over one or more sessions, depending on the number of inventories that have been administered. Although counselors probably can plan approximately how many sessions will be needed to focus on interpretation, discussion of test data is not limited to those sessions but should be woven into subsequent counseling sessions as clients develop and refine their plans.

Using Prediction in Interpretation

One effective method of test interpretation gives people the opportunity to predict their inventoried results after they have completed the testing but before they are actually informed of the outcome. This method is particularly useful in highlighting discrepancies between people's views of themselves and the way they are portrayed by the test results. The prediction approach seems to increase people's interest in the test results because they are motivated to learn not only what information is provided by their test scores but also how their views of themselves coincide with the test results. This method can increase relevant discussion of test results and can help counselors to focus on those aspects of the test data that are likely to have the greatest impact on clients. For example, counselors cannot safely assume that people will always be pleased by high scores on ability tests and disappointed by low scores on such tests. Some people are invested in maintaining an image of themselves as weak students, whereas others may fear that high test scores will lead their families and teachers to expect too much from them. Clients' predictions of their test results enable counselors to better anticipate reactions to actual results and can help clients be more open about their feelings.

Prediction as well as interpretation of test results generally will be facilitated if the counselor can supply a blank copy of the form on which the results have been recorded; clients can then indicate, on the form, their guesses as to where their scores will fall. People need not be asked to predict exact numbers or percentiles if that process would be too confusing or too complicated. Rather, they can be asked to predict the ranges (high, medium, or low) into which each of their scores will fall or, if the relative strength of their scores is important, they might be asked to guess the rankings or order of their scores. Specific numerical scores generally are not important in the process of test interpretation and should be de-emphasized. What is important is the relationship and level of scores, the implications for the client's present functioning and future objectives, and the congruence of the scores with the person's self-image. In light of the imperfect validity and reliability of all standardized counseling tests, numerical scores are unlikely to remain constant from one test administration to the next. The significance of the scores, rather than the scores themselves, should receive primary emphasis during the test interpretation.

Gestalt Approaches to Interpretation

In addition to the prediction approach, a variety of approaches to test interpretation have been advanced. Sodetz and Vinitsky (1977) suggested three ways of interpreting test results. These approaches were derived from the Gestalt approach to counseling and were designed to promote people's active involvement in understanding their test results. The first approach involves the Gestalt technique of the empty chair. People are encouraged to enact a dialogue between the types of people they imagine would be represented by their highest and lowest scores. In the second approach, a guided fantasy, people describe what their lives might be like as the type of people represented by their high and low scores. Behaving like an exaggerated version of these hypothetical people is a third approach to helping clients understand their test results, their reactions to those results, and the implications of those results for their career planning. These Gestalt approaches seem particularly useful with people who have difficulty viewing their test results as meaningful to them or who have difficulty verbalizing their reactions to the test results.

Interpretation in Group Settings

A group setting can be as effective as one-to-one counseling for the communication of test interpretations, although most people prefer an individual interpretation (Goldman, 1971). Group test interpretation can make efficient use of the counselor's time and also can increase discussion and involvement as well as client insight, self-awareness, and reality testing. People who may have had little initial interest in discussing their test results with a counselor may become very interested in the process of comparing their results with those of their peers and in helping others in the group to understand their scores and relate their results to their self-images and plans. The group process may provide a vehicle for increasing peer contact and improving understanding and communication skills as well as for transmitting test results.

The technique of predicting scores can be just as effective in a group setting as it is in an individual counseling setting. Productive discussion typically decreases for awhile after test results are distributed in a group as people curiously examine their own protocols and those of the other group members. The preparation involved in the process of prediction seems to help people scan their results with more understanding, keep their focus primarily on their own scores rather than on those of other group members, and facilitate the rapid resumption of the process of exploring the meaning of the test results and their implications.

Goldman (1990) emphasized the importance of learning about the self in a developmental context, especially in group counseling. Group career counseling will probably take place in fairly homogeneous groups (e.g., high school students, adult career changers), and educating participants about typical developmental processes they are experiencing as well as encouraging them to talk about commonalities and differences in their development can facilitate the integration of test data with other information.

Counselors who are using a group setting for test interpretation should be cautious about discussions of measures of ability. Group members who did not perform as well as some of their peers may feel uncomfortable and self-conscious about discussing their ability scores, and that process may be detrimental to their self-esteem. Group counseling seems to be a more appropriate vehicle for the discussion of interest, values, and some nonpejorative personality inventories than it is for the consideration of ability tests. Even when tests that do not have right or wrong answers are being discussed, counselors should be sure that no one's interests, goals, or personal style are devalued by other members of the group and that all group participants have adequate opportunity to ask questions and discuss their interpretations of and reactions to their scores.

Reactions to Interpretation

People's reactions to the process of test interpretation seem to have a great deal to do with the counselors' approaches to that process. People often have negative reactions to the interpretation process and have difficulty integrating the results into their views of themselves and their futures if they have not been given enough time to discuss and explore their reactions to those results. People seem to benefit most from the testing process and its subsequent interpretation if their participation in that process has been maximized. Consequently, interactive and hands-on approaches like the prediction model and those derived from Gestalt counseling seem particularly useful.

Social learning theory suggests that the level of competence that people attribute to their counselors also will affect their attitude toward the testing process and their willingness to make constructive use of the test results. People will probably consider more seriously information provided by counselors whom they perceive as competent, genuine, and trustworthy. Counselors should be alert to the possibility that people are accepting or rejecting test interpretations because of their source rather than because of the value and meaningfulness the information has for them.

Client intelligence and personality are also related to the use that people are able to make of test data. Goodyear (1990) found that more intelligent people seem to remember test data with greater accuracy. He also found that certain personality types (e.g., investigative and realistic types, as measured on the SDS) benefited more from test interpretation than did other personality types (e.g., social, enterprising, or artistic). Presentation of test information should be geared to the particular person, and terminology, format, and method of involving the client in the interpretation should all reflect understanding of the client's attitudes toward testing and that person's learning style.

Just as some people can be resistant to understanding test data and integrating it into their self-images, some people can place too much confidence in the results of a test. Goodyear (1990) cited a Barnum Effect that had been identified in the literature: People who were "given bogus test interpretations that contained universally true information gave credence to those interpretations" (p. 247), especially when the interpretations were positively worded. For some people, the printed word, especially when produced by a computer, seems to have greater power than the spoken word. The overreliance on test results seems particularly likely among people with low self-esteem who are floundering or undecided in their career choices. They may be hopeful that some outside source of wisdom, an inventory or a counselor, can show them the path to happiness. Counselors can guard against the development of such an overreliance on test data by emphasizing the limitations of testing, particularly for people who are not White males from middle-class American backgrounds. Talking in terms of probabilities rather than making definite statements is another way for counselors to communicate the uncertainty of test results.

Counselors should explain to their clients how test results were derived. That process can help to demystify the testing process and elicit questions or reservations that people may have. If a competent interpretation and discussion of test results, relating them to other information obtained about the person, still leaves a person feeling confused and unhappy with test results, counselors may want to review selected test items with the person to promote understanding of how scores were derived. (This process may not be possible if the inventory has been computer scored because the counselor may have little idea of the relationship between responses and scores.) Discussion of individual test items also may be useful if an unresolved disparity exists between the test results and either the clients' views of themselves or the counselor's views of the clients. By ascertaining what questions were particularly difficult for a person or the thought process that was behind some of a person's responses, client and counselor can gain greater understanding of both the person and the test results and can determine how much credibility should be placed the test results.

On occasion, test results seem to be valid but do not seem to make sense to people in terms of the images they have of themselves. It may be that the test results are in error, or it may be that the people are not yet ready to relinquish inaccurate views of themselves. When this occurs, counselors should not persist in stressing the value of the test results, nor should they indicate that either the clients or the tests are wrong. Emphasis should be shifted from the tests to other approaches to assessment and conversation (e.g., school grades, activities), and care should be taken lest this situation have an adverse effect on the counseling relationship or on the person's attitudes toward counseling and testing.

Concluding the Interpretation

At the conclusion of the process of assessment and interpretation, counselors should evaluate the experience and its cost-effectiveness. Most counselors develop a repertoire of tests and inventories that match both the typical needs of the people whom they counsel and their own approaches to test interpretation. By evaluating each assessment they conduct, counselors can determine which tests seem most useful to them, which should be discarded or replaced with alternatives, and probably most important, which approaches to interpretation seem effective.

Tyler (1984) provided an excellent summary of the process of interpretation.

Out of this discussion emerges one guiding principle for users of tests. What test scores give us are clues to be followed as we deal with children and adults for whose welfare we have some responsibility. The scores mean something, but in order to know what, we must consider each individual case in an empathic way, combining test evidence with everything else we know about the person. The practice of basing important decisions on test scores alone is unsound; so is the policy of dispensing with tests altogether. (p. 50)

Client Rights in Assessment

In conducting a test administration and interpretation, counselors should bear in mind both ethical standards and client rights. Appendix A includes ethical standards relevant to the assessment process. Loesch (1975) developed a list of children's rights in assessment. His work has been expanded on here to develop the following list of rights for people of all ages who are being tested or assessed:

1. The right to know in advance of testing why they are being tested, how the testing will benefit them, how the test data will be used, and how much time and money the testing will cost them.
2. The right to participate in planning and scheduling the testing.
3. The right to be free of unnecessary and outdated tests.
4. The right to be tested in an atmosphere that is free from distractions and conducive to positive test performance.
5. The right to be assessed via the most appropriate instruments and techniques available.
6. The right to a complete, comprehensive, clear, and honest explanation and analysis of test results and their application to them as individuals.
7. The right to discuss their test results with people competent to interpret their test protocols, relate test data to other available data, and answer any questions.
8. The right to have their confidentiality protected.
9. The right to further counseling or assessment if indicated.

THREE

Tools of Assessment

Overview

Thousands of tests and inventories, as well as nonstandardized methods of assessment, are available to counselors. Such an array of options can be overwhelming, despite available sources of information. This chapter will present an overview of the major types of assessment tools, discussion of their appropriate selection and use, and descriptions of important and frequently used inventories. (Additional information on specific inventories is provided in the case studies presented in Chapters 4-10.) Six broad categories of assessment tools are available:

1. ability tests, including tests of achievement, aptitude, and intelligence
2. interest inventories
3. personality inventories, including measures of self-esteem and values
4. measures of career development, including inventories of decisiveness, career information, and work-related attitudes
5. computer-based assessment and information programs
6. nonstandardized approaches to assessment

In addition to these categories, composite inventories or assessment systems are available, integrating two or more approaches to assessment. Evaluation of abilities and interests probably is the most common combination.

Patterns of test usage vary, depending primarily on setting, but also on budget, local and agency guidelines, and personal preference and experience. For example, school counselors make the greatest use of the Armed Services Vocational Aptitude Battery (ASVAB), not only because it provides useful information but also because it is available without charge and because free assistance with its administration and interpretation is provided by military recruiters (Engen et al., 1982). School counselors also have made extensive use of the Differential Aptitude Tests (DAT), the General Aptitude Test Battery (GATB), the Strong Interest Inventory (SII), and the Kuder family of interest inventories. Assessment of abilities and interests seems to predominate in school assessment programs.

In private practice and mental health settings, however, assessment of personality and intelligence are usually most important, although assessment of interests also receives attention. The most frequently used inventories in those settings include the Minnesota Multiphasic Personality Inventory (MMPI), the SII, and the Wechsler Adult Intelligence Scale (WAIS), all used by more than 50% of counseling psychologists (Watkins et al., 1988). Psychologists and counselors in college settings also use the MMPI, the SII, and the WAIS extensively. Their most frequently used inventory was the SII, whereas those in mental health settings made the greatest use of the MMPI. Types of assessments conducted do not seem to have changed much over the past 30 years, especially in mental health settings, although the tools themselves have changed considerably (Lubin, Larsen, & Matarazzo, 1984).

Ability Tests

Achievement, intelligence, and aptitude tests all can be categorized as measures of ability. All three draw on some combination of innate ability and learning acquired through both formal and informal education and experience. Typically, the questions that appear on the three types of tests look very similar; counselors will not always be able to determine from the content of a test whether it was designed to measure achievement, intelligence, or aptitude. One way to conceptualize the differences between the three types of inventories is to think of *achievement tests* as looking backward to assess how much people have learned about a given subject or how much they have gained from a course or from some part of their education. *Intelligence tests* can be thought of as focusing on the present and measuring current levels of abilities. *Aptitude tests*, on the other hand, look forward to predict how well a person will succeed in a particular endeavor, perhaps a college curriculum, a job, or an occupation. The major differences between the three types of instruments, then, are in their development, their systems of scoring, the normative samples that they use, and the interpretations of the scores achieved on the tests.

Primary purposes of ability testing include the following:

1. assessing degree of mastery of a body of knowledge and certifying credentials (e.g., for high school graduation, licensure as a counselor)
2. identifying people who need remedial intervention
3. determining a person's likelihood of succeeding in an academic or occupational endeavor

Bias in Assessment of Abilities

Although tests of abilities increase accuracy and efficiency in determining skills and predicting likelihood of success for a group of people, they do not necessarily present a true picture of a given person. Consequently, they have been criticized for serving the needs of the organization more than those of the individual and for perpetuating gender and culture bias. Gender-linked, as well as racially linked, patterns of performance on ability tests have been identified. For example, women generally score higher than men on tests of verbal ability, whereas men excel on measures of numerical ability and tend to have more extreme test scores than do women (Hood & Johnson, 1991). African Americans score approximately one standard deviation below White Americans on most standardized tests of cognitive ability. Of course, the distribution of scores contains considerable overlap with 20% of African Americans scoring above the White mean and 20% of Whites scoring below the African American mean.

The problem of test bias does not seem to stem primarily from a lack of test validity. Although most experts in the field of assessment recognize that many tests are somewhat racially and socioeconomically biased, they also hold generally positive views of the validity and usefulness of most intelligence and aptitude tests (Snyderman & Rothman, 1987). As Hood and Johnson (1991) concluded, "In general, results have shown that ability tests are equally valid for both minority and majority groups" (p. 211). However, the patterns of difference can damage self-esteem and limit options. How should counselors deal with this issue?

According to Gottfredson and Sharf (1988), the major overarching debate in assessment, particularly in the area of employment testing, is, "How deeply troubled should we be over the policy question of what to do when valid tests have an adverse impact?" (p. 226). Although a definitive answer to this question has not yet been given, counselors can take steps to reduce the negative impact of valid ability tests. Several principles should be borne in mind when assessing abilities. First, whenever possible, the welfare and best interests of the individual should be paramount. Second, although gender- and racially linked patterns of performance on ability tests have been identified, those patterns do not mean that some groups are basically less intelligent than others. As Tyler (1984) stated, "We cannot conclude on the basis of test results that any racial, cultural, or socioeconomic group is superior or inferior to any other. All we can do is to estimate how well an individual will function in the culture for which the test is appropriate" (p. 48). As long as counselors recognize, and communicate to their clients, that tests of ability have only this circumscribed significance, we can go a long way toward eliminating the primary problem in ability assessment and misinterpretation of and overreliance on test data.

In addition, counselors and their clients should view ability test results as only one piece of information. These tests provide little insight into motivation, persistence, and attentiveness, factors that can contribute considerably to academic and occupational performance. Viewing the test results from a holistic perspective can increase appropriate use of the test data. Considering both individual personality and culture are particularly important. Cultural background, for some groups, is likely to influence attitude toward testing and test results. Asian Americans, for example, typically put considerable effort into preparing for and performing on tests and inventories and may overemphasize the importance of tests of ability. Native Americans, on the other hand, may have only limited experience in taking tests and may find the competitive nature of that process incongruent with their views of the world. Their more casual attitude toward assessment may result in scores that do not adequately reflect their abilities.

Many standardized tests of ability, as well as of interest and personality, are available in languages other than English, with Spanish language versions being particularly common. These inventories may be more appropriate for use with people who are not native-English speaking. Counselors dealing with a bilingual population should check whether the tests they use most are available in languages other than English.

Counselors also can minimize the possible negative impact of ability inventories by helping people focus on other sources of information about their abilities and by exploring with them their self-concepts.

Self-efficacy, defined as "a person's beliefs concerning his or her ability to successfully perform a given task or behavior" (Betz & Hackett, 1981, p. 400), has been found to be a primary determinant of perceived occupational options. Women are more likely to have high self-efficacy for traditional occupations, such as teaching or nursing, and low self-efficacy for nontraditional occupations, such as mathematics. These limiting patterns can be reinforced by tests of ability that demonstrate that a given woman does, indeed, have strong verbal skills and weak numerical skills compared with the general population. A more accurate picture of a woman's relative strengths and weaknesses may be obtained by comparing her with other women rather than with people in general and by taking a broad look at sources of information on her competencies.

Achievement Tests

Achievement tests are designed to evaluate the degree of mastery or ability already attained, generally from relatively standardized experiences. Achievement tests are usually designed to assess the outcome of school learning. They can be used for the following:

1. to provide an objective measure of how much a person has learned from a given experience
2. to indicate the relative standing in a group (classroom, school, nationwide sample) of a person's level of learning
3. to indicate whether and in what educational areas a person is in need of remediation
4. to indicate in what areas a person seems to have marked ability

Two types of achievement tests are available: criterion-referenced tests and norm-referenced tests. *Criterion-referenced* tests do not compare a person's level of performance with that of others but, rather, seek to ascertain whether an individual test taker has achieved certain educational goals. *Norm-referenced* achievement tests, on the other hand, determine the relative standing of a person's ability by comparing the scores achieved by that person with those achieved by a normative reference group. Because achievement tests are generally designed to assess school learning, those reference groups are likely to be defined by such criteria as grade level, age, or amount of education.

Teacher-made tests are achievement tests in that they are designed to measure how much students have learned from a unit of study or from a period of learning, such as a semester or a school year. Generally, such instruments have not been standardized, however, and so their validity and reliability are open to question.

Most achievement tests focus on one skill or ability, such as verbal reasoning, spacial relations, or French. Groups of achievement tests often are combined into a battery of tests, designed to provide a comprehensive picture of a person's abilities. The Wide Range Achievement Test (WRAT) is a widely used example of such an instrument. That test consists of three parts, measuring achievement in spelling, arithmetic, and reading. Most test batteries can be administered either as a whole or in part, depending on the goals of the assessment process.

Despite controversy over their potential bias, achievement tests are well established and accepted. According to Karmos and Karmos (1984), "Standardized achievement test scores are becoming increasingly more important, with current emphasis on accountability, minimum competency, and basic skills in schools" (p. 56). Proposals have been advanced for a national examination that high school students will need to pass to graduate. The goals of such an examination are maintenance of acceptable standards of teaching and learning in the schools and improvement of student motivation. As presently envisioned, such an examination might include portfolios of creative and other accomplishments as well as performance-based assessments and examinations completed throughout a person's educational career (Moses, 1991). The examination could be used to indicate minimum competency, proficiency, or excellence in skills and could be retaken if not passed the first time.

Concern has been expressed that the establishment of national achievement standards could limit freedom in teaching and curriculum development. Counselors can play an instrumental role in state and national programs of competency testing. Counselors may be called on to establish school- or countywide programs to assess achievement in which they are responsible for selecting the appropriate instruments, helping teachers to administer and interpret the tests, and ensuring that the results are used for the benefit of both the students and the school. Counselors should strive to ensure that such assessment programs are not instituted in a hasty and haphazard manner to meet public demand but are developed and used in a way that is consistent with the principles of sound counseling and assessment.

In addition to conducting large-scale programs to test achievement, counselors may decide to use achievement tests as part of individual or group career counseling when they have reason to believe that school grades or tests do not accurately reflect a person's level of academic ability or when people have been away from an academic environment for many years and have little information about the levels of their abilities.

Although the primary purpose of achievement testing is assessment rather than prediction, some achievement tests can be used to predict college performance or to provide differential predictions of success in specific subject areas. Achievement tests seem to predict future levels of academic achievement as well as or better than intelligence tests but, generally, have not been good predictors of occupational success (S. G. Cox, 1971). This is at least in part because achievement tests do not take account of factors such as stability, maturity, and motivation that, of course, contribute to occupational success. As Betz et al. (1989) put it, "Abilities are necessary but not sufficient for acceptable job performance" (p. 28). In fact, it seems as damaging to job performance to be overqualified for a job as to be underqualified for the job; being overqualified can lead to boredom and discouragement and consequent poor performance.

Despite their limitations, achievement tests continue to be used in employment settings. However, they are usually used to measure specific job-related skills (such as typing) for nonprofessional jobs. Testing of applicants for managerial and professional positions is more likely to focus on the assessment of interests, personality, and integrity. These uses of assessment also are controversial and will be discussed later.

When interpreting scores on achievement tests, as well as on other tests of ability, only the standard error of measurement (*SEM*) above the scores received is important (Kline, 1975), whereas with inventories of personality and interests, both the *SEM* above and below the achieved score should be considered. Generally, personality and interest inventories are less reliable than measures of ability and have more potential for error because there are no right or wrong responses. Nevertheless, counselors should not assume that achievement tests provide a valid indication of either a person's future performance or of that person's present performance. A person may be capable of demonstrating certain skills on a standardized achievement test but may not be consistently willing or able to use those skills successfully in the classroom or work setting. Although, generally, a positive correlation has been found between inventoried achievement and classroom performance in comparable areas, many factors, including emotional difficulties, poor motivation, family disapproval of academic endeavors, and a classroom situation that is not conducive to learning, can lead to disparities between inventoried and teacher-evaluated levels of performance. From the fifth grade on, personal factors gain considerable importance in determining achievement, and shifts in level of performance may result. Self-concept seems to be one of the most important determinants of achievement, particularly during adolescence when girls' self-esteem declines, whereas boys' self-esteem increases.

Achievement test scores may be significantly lower than school grades as well as significantly higher. When test scores are lower, a lack of test motivation or interest may be the cause. Karmos and Karmos (1984) found that although most students viewed achievement tests positively, 36% of students studied in Grades 6 through 9 viewed the tests as a waste of time and may not have been motivated to expend much energy in performing as well as they could on the tests. This negative view of achievement tests was particularly prevalent among males and people with low levels of achievement who, perhaps, had been discouraged by a history of poor performance on similar instruments. Counselors should take note of students or clients who seem to have negative or inaccurate views of their own abilities or who manifest significant differences between their school grades and their inventoried achievement. Such people may not be performing up to their capacities because of low self-esteem, family concerns, learning disabilities, or other factors and may benefit from counseling and additional assessment.

Examples of Achievement Tests

Assessment of Basic Skills

1. *Basic Achievement Skills Individual Screener (BASIS)*. This inventory is an individually administered achievement test, published by Psychological Corporation, that measures skill development in reading, mathematics, spelling, and writing. It can be used for students in Grades 1 through 12, requires less than 1 hour for administration, is relatively easy to administer, and seems to have considerable technical support (Ysseldyke, 1985).

2. *Peabody Individual Achievement Test—Revised (PIAT—R)*. Another achievement test for Grades 1 through 12, the PIAT—R measures written expression, general information, reading recognition, reading comprehension, mathematics, and spelling. It is published by the American Guidance Service (AGS).

3. *Vineland Adaptive Behavior Scales.* This instrument, published by AGS, measures personal and social skills in people from birth to age 18 years, 11 months as well as low functioning adults. Test profile includes a composite score in addition to scores in communication, daily living skills, socialization, and motor skills and is particularly useful with young children who are having academic and interpersonal difficulties.

4. *Wide Range Achievement Test (WRAT).* The WRAT is a widely used measure of abilities that is fairly easy to administer and score, requiring only 15 to 30 minutes. Published by Jastak Associates, it yields scores on reading, spelling, and mathematics that can readily be transformed into grade equivalents, age-normed percentile ranks, and standard scores. Despite its widespread use, concerns have been expressed about the validity and reliability of this instrument as well as what it actually measures (Reid, 1986). Some evidence is available that the WRAT underestimates abilities (Owen & Erchul, 1987).

Assessment of Academic Achievement

Many test batteries have gained acceptance and extensive use as broad-based measures of academic achievement. Nearly all schools have testing programs in which students are given an extensive nationally stand-ardized achievement test every few years (e.g., 3rd, 6th, and 10th grades) to determine not only individual levels of mastery but also the effectiveness of the school district. Such test batteries typically require at least 2 or 3 hours for administration and include six or more subscales, designed to present a comprehensive picture of academic achievement. For example, the Comprehensive Assessment Program: Achievement Series includes subtests in vocabulary, reading comprehension, computation, mathematics concepts, mathematics problem solving, spelling/capitalization/punctuation/grammar, word attack, and reference and study skills. A variety of forms of these test batteries are available so that school districts can use variations of the same test with children at all grade levels, thereby facilitating comparison and assessment of progress. In addition to the Comprehensive Assessment Program (published by Scott, Foresman), examples of this type of test include the Comprehensive Test of Basic Skills (CTB/Macmillan/McGraw-Hill), the Kaufman Test of Educational Achievement (AGS), Metropolitan Achievement Test (Psychological Corporation), Iowa Test of Basic Skills

(Riverside), and the Curriculum Referenced Tests of Mastery (Charles E. Merrill).

1. *Scholastic Aptitude Tests (SAT).* The SAT tests, published by Educational Testing Service (ETS), include both aptitude and achievement tests. The aptitude tests are discussed later in this chapter. Typically, achievement tests are taken in three academic areas of a person's choice, such as French, history, and chemistry. These tests are designed to reflect the mastery an applicant to college has achieved in these areas, as one piece of information the college can use in evaluating admission qualifications. These tests currently are undergoing revision and the SAT II is expected in 1994. The revised SAT achievement tests will probably offer an essay as an optional test and will offer examinations in new subject areas such as Japanese, Chinese, and English proficiency (Avasthi, 1990).

2. *Graduate Record Examination (GRE).* Like the SAT, the GRE (published by ETS) has both aptitude and achievement components. Twenty advanced achievement tests are offered in conjunction with the GRE. Although these are taken by fewer people than the aptitude component of the GRE, they are used to demonstrate competence in the particular area of study, such as psychology, that a person plans to pursue in graduate school.

3. *College-Level Examination Program (CLEP), Advanced Placement Program (APP), and Proficiency Examination Program (PEP).* All three of these programs are designed for people to demonstrate their proficiency, by examination, in college-level course work. Satisfactory performance on these inventories can afford people college credit and enable them to take advanced courses without completing the prerequisites. The PEP program, administered by the American College Testing (ACT) program, includes tests in areas such as the arts and sciences, nursing, business, and education. The APP program is primarily for very bright high school seniors, whereas the CLEP program seems directed primarily toward people who are reentering school after an absence and want to obtain credit for learning they achieved while out of school. The CLEP and APP programs are administered by the College Entrance Examination Board.

Aptitude Tests

Aptitude tests are designed to predict a person's ability to learn or profit from an educational experience or the likelihood of a person's success in a given occupation or course of study. Although, generally, achievement is developed quite rapidly, aptitude grows slowly and results from daily living and learning (Angoff, 1988). Hood and Johnson (1991) defined aptitude as the "ability to acquire a specific type of skill or knowledge" (p. 67). Aptitude tests are most commonly used to select people for educational programs or jobs or to help people gain a greater understanding of their potentials in order to facilitate career planning and decision making. Scholastic aptitude is especially important in gaining entrance to college and graduate school and, consequently, to many professions.

Many counselors make extensive use of aptitude tests to help people decide whether they have the potential needed for specified educational or occupational goals, to identify occupations that their clients could probably learn if they had the interest and the opportunity, and to increase self-awareness.

Although achievement and aptitude tests may appear indistinguishable, they are differentiated by their normative samples. Achievement tests are usually normed on people who have undergone relatively standardized and similar experiences; they have completed the same number of grades in school or have completed the same courses. Aptitude tests, however, are normed in situations where learning experiences may be uncontrolled or even unknown. Aptitude tests are concerned with how much the presence of certain abilities relates to future success, regardless of how those abilities were developed.

Aptitudes seem to take shape during childhood and then remain fairly stable throughout the adolescent and adult years. It has long been established that although skills may change, usually aptitudes are not significantly affected by adult work experiences and are affected in only a limited way by educational experiences (Super & Bohn, 1970).

Aptitude test scores can be excellent predictors of school grades. However, generally, correlations between aptitude tests and career success and satisfaction have not been high. In part, this is because preparation for entry into an occupation and subsequent performance in that occupation often require rather different abilities. For example, in the field of medicine, success in preparation depends largely on mastery of academic courses, whereas success in performance also depends on interpersonal skills and business acumen. The limited relationship between inventoried aptitudes and occupational performance also can be explained by the moderate correlation between aptitudes and interests; people's interests and their strengths often lie in different areas. People sometimes assume that if only they can identify their strongest aptitudes and which occupations are most related to those aptitudes, they will know which occupations are best for them. Although there is some tendency for people to be drawn to occupations that are consistent with their aptitudes, especially if they value those aptitudes, interests and aptitudes do not necessarily coincide and people who formulate career plans based on aptitudes alone are likely to be disappointed.

The relationship between interests and abilities is complex and can vary considerably. The two can have a reciprocal relationship, with good performance leading to increased interest and interest leading to improved performance, or the two may be relatively unrelated. Generally, research has found that interests are the strongest determinant of the direction and intensity of people's efforts, whereas their abilities determine their level of attainment (Zytowski, 1970b). In other words, interests will have the greatest effect on career choice and aptitudes will be the major determinant of success. Counselors, then, should discourage people from making career plans based exclusively on either interests or abilities. Rather, they should help their clients look for areas of inter- face between the two, thereby maximizing chances of having successful and satisfying careers.

Types of Aptitudes

Two types of aptitudes have been identified, *simple or specific aptitudes* and *complex aptitudes*. Tests have been developed to measure each type. An example of a specific aptitude is clerical speed; it is readily measured and defined and has an obvious and direct relationship to many types of work. Most professions or occupations that require higher education, however, require a cluster of complex aptitudes, the nature and interaction of which are often difficult to define. Although tests are available to select people for preparation for professions such as law, medicine, or teaching, such tests are typically highly sophisticated instruments related to success in the course work required to prepare for these professions but that bear an uncertain relationship to success in the professions themselves. For many other professions, no aptitude tests are available. Counselors and clients, then, must try to estimate a person's suitability for such professions on the basis of previously demonstrated success and on measures of complex aptitudes designed to predict success in college or in graduate school. In light of the weak relationship between aptitude and satisfaction, more accurate predictions of success and satisfaction are likely to result from information drawn from a range of personal and intellectual factors, including the person's history, than from a measure of abilities alone.

Generally, measures of specific aptitude are most useful when a person has had no previous relevant experience that can provide a basis for estimating future success. Although aptitudes are relatively unaffected by training or experience, relevant past experience affords a valuable source of information about a person's capacity to succeed in a particular endeavor and often eliminates the need for aptitude testing in that area.

The following list represents some of the specific or special aptitudes for which tests have been developed:

1. sensory abilities (e.g., vision, hearing)
2. motor abilities (e.g., manual dexterity)
3. mechanical aptitude
4. spatial relations
5. clerical ability (speed, accuracy)
6. artistic ability (appreciation, production)
7. musical ability
8. creativity
9. language aptitude

Most *multi-aptitude* batteries offer the advantages of tests of both specific and complex aptitudes. Multi-aptitude batteries consist of a group of tests of specific aptitudes that may be given either singly or in combination. An overall measure of aptitude can be derived by combining scores from a group of tests in the battery. However, if only one test is indicated for a given person, that test can be meaningfully administered and interpreted apart from the rest of the test battery. Discrepancies between people's numerical and verbal aptitudes as well as between their inventoried aptitudes and either their inventoried achievements or their classroom performance should be noted; they can indicate learning, emotional, or motivational difficulties.

Use and Selection of Aptitude Tests

Counselors can most readily locate suitable aptitude tests by referring to *Tests in Print, Tests,* and the *Mental Measurements Yearbooks (MMY)*, all discussed in Chapter 2. The nature of the norm groups used in developing an aptitude test is particularly important in determining the relevance of the test for a given person or group. Counselors should be sure that the aptitude tests they are using have been standardized on groups that reflect the educational or occupational goals of their clients. Counselors should not overgeneralize from aptitude test results and should keep in mind that such results generally predict success in training better than they do success in a job or occupation. Being very familiar with the manuals for aptitude tests will help counselors avoid drawing unwarranted conclusions.

Counselors also should be aware that the validity of aptitude tests varies greatly, depending on the nature of both the tests and the aptitudes. The validity of tests of creativity, for example, has been called into question, whereas most tests of clerical aptitude have fairly high levels of validity. Many of the most valid aptitude tests are not available for administration by the counselor. Tests such as the GRE, the SAT, the Miller Analogies Test (MAT), and the Law School Aptitude Test (LSAT) can be administered and scored only by the organizations that develop and publish them. However, counselors should be familiar with the nature and interpretation of these instruments so that they know when to recommend these tests to their clients and can understand and interpret their clients' scores on these inventories.

Ralph Nader and others have been critical of colleges that rely heavily on aptitude tests to determine admission and pay little attention to such personal traits as perseverance, wisdom, idealism, and creativity (Robinson, 1983). Although high school grades, reflecting motivation and other personal characteristics as well as ability, are the best predictors of college performance, use of aptitude test scores in conjunction with grades can improve accuracy of prediction and is particularly useful for people who have not attended a public high school in recent years. This would include older clients as well as people who attended competitive private schools where average grades may not actually reflect average ability. Indications are that many college officials do view aptitude tests as only one indication of probable college performance. Although 61% of 4-year public colleges require an admissions test, 65% of admissions officials viewed high school performance as either the single most important factor or a very important factor in the admission decision (Franco, 1983).

Aptitude tests may be encountered in employment settings as well as in academic or counseling settings. Testing is sometimes used in business or industry to identify good candidates for hire or promotion.

Testing in those settings differs from aptitude assessment in other settings; in business and industry, the emphasis is on selection; external constraints, such as Equal Employment Opportunity Commission guidelines, must be followed; and brevity and economy are usually very important considerations (Vale, 1990).

Measures of Academic Aptitude

1. *Armed Services Vocational Aptitude Battery (ASVAB).* By the late 1980s, the ASVAB was being administered to over 1.3 million students in 14,000 high schools (Prediger, 1987). This 2.5-hour comprehensive test battery, provided free of charge to interested high schools by the U.S. Department of Defense, yields three academic composite scores (verbal, mathematical, and academic ability) as well as four occupational composite scores (mechanical and crafts; business and clerical; electronics and electrical; and health, social, and technology). Although one purpose of this instrument is military recruiting, the ASVAB seems very useful to 11th- and 12th-grade high school students who want help in clarifying their abilities and relating them to job families that have similar ability profiles. A workbook and other accompanying materials, providing interpretive information as well as linking scores to Holland's hexagon, discussed in Chapter 1 and the DISCOVER program to be discussed later in this chapter, facilitate interpretation of test profiles.

2. *Career Occupational Preference System (COPS).* Available from EdITS, the COPS is a comprehensive career counseling program that includes a measure of aptitude as well as measures of interests and values. This system is discussed further in Chapter 5.

3. *Differential Aptitude Tests (DAT).* Published by Psychological Corporation, the DAT is a well-established aptitude test battery. First published in 1947, the DAT has gone through at least five editions. Separate tests measure verbal reasoning (VR), numerical ability (NA), abstract reasoning, perceptual speed and accuracy, mechanical reasoning, space relations, spelling, and language usage. VR and NA scores can be combined to yield a measure of scholastic ability. The DAT is available in two forms: Level 1 includes Grades 7 through 9 and adults who are expected to have below-average abilities, and Level 2 is for Grades 10

through 12 and adults with average or better aptitudes. Both versions of the DAT can be purchased with a grade-appropriate career planning package, including an interest inventory, designed to facilitate course selection and career planning. Completion of the entire DAT requires approximately 3 hours for the paper-and-pencil version. A computerized adaptive edition also is available that requires about half the time, because the computer tailors the test to the individual student's ability level. Both computer and paper-and-pencil versions yield a profile with percentiles comparing the test takers with both males and females in the same grade.

4. *Peabody Picture Vocabulary Test—Revised (PPVT).* This 10- to 20-minute inventory, published by AGS, is particularly useful in assessing the verbal or scholastic aptitude of people with limited English proficiency—the very young, the disabled, and the foreign-born. This test requires no reading or writing and can be used as an indicator of placement.

5. *Tests of Adult Basic Education (TABE).* This widely used test was designed to assess adults' basic skills (reading, mathematics, language skills). Published by CTB/Macmillan/McGraw-Hill, the TABE is available in four levels, (easy, medium, difficult, and advanced) and can be used to predict scores on the GED (high school equivalency examination) as well as academic performance. It is especially useful for adults with limited education who are considering completing their high school education and possibly entering college.

Aptitude Tests for College Admissions

1. *Scholastic Aptitude Test (SAT).* This well-established instrument, published by ETS, has been used since 1926 to provide information about people seeking admission to college. The SAT is the most widely used standardized test in the United States and is taken by 1.7 million high school juniors and seniors annually (Avasthi, 1990). Generally taken during the junior or senior years of high school, the SAT is a 3-hour multiple-choice examination that measures verbal and mathematical aptitude. With a reliability of about .90, this instrument, especially considered in conjunction with high school grades, is a good predictor of

college performance. Potential scores range from 200 to 800. Presently, the verbal score averages about 425 nationwide, and the mathematical score, at least somewhat linked to learning in that subject, is about 465 with a *SEM* of about 30 to 35. Originally, the mean was estimated to be 500 on each test, and many colleges look for a combined applicant score of at least 1,000. Average scores on the SAT have long been viewed as a broad measure of the educational level of American high school students.

Scores on the SAT declined through the 1960s and 1970s but reversed themselves and have increased during the 1980s (Zajonc, 1986). Continued increases in SAT scores throughout the 20th century have been predicted. A disparity has long been observed between the scores of White and non-White test takers and between males and females on the SAT, and the instrument has been criticized for being biased against women and people from minority groups. However, scores for non-Whites have been increasing faster than scores for Whites, gradually closing the gap (Wainer, 1988).

Psychological Corporation has published materials designed to help people prepare for the SAT: the *College Admissions Practice Test for the SAT* and the *Diagnostic College Admissions Program for the SAT*. Several publishers also have issued workbooks to facilitate preparation for the SAT, and preparation programs are widespread. Although coaching for examinations such as the SAT and the GRE are controversial and are unlikely to produce substantial gains, most people benefit from familiarity with the examination and tend to perform better when taking it for a second time (Hood & Johnson, 1991).

A revised version of the SAT is scheduled for publication in 1994. The SAT II, as it will be called, is expected to be a 2.5-hour test of verbal and mathematical reasoning that emphasizes critical reading and reasoning, data interpretation, and problem-solving skills (Avasthi, 1990). Calculators may be used during the examination, and a writing test will no longer be mandatory. Some view these changes as likely to reduce the bias in the test, whereas others see them as merely cosmetic.

2. *Preliminary Scholastic Aptitude Test (PSAT).* The PSAT (also published by ETS), generally taken early in the 11th grade, is a sort of practice version of the SAT. It familiarizes test takers with the type of items and formats they will encounter on the SAT and allows prediction of SAT scores by adding a zero to achieved PSAT scores, ranging from 20 to 80 for verbal and mathematics scores. The PSAT is also used as the qualify-

ing test for the National Merit Scholarship program; high performance on the PSAT (the top 1% of each state) can, therefore, lead to some financial aid for college.

3. *American College Testing Program (ACT)*. A broad-based aptitude inventory like the SAT, first published in 1959, the ACT is used by approximately 2,400 U.S. colleges, primarily in the Midwest. Approximately 1 million ACT tests are administered each year (Carvajal, McKnab, Gerber, Hewes, & Smith, 1989). In 1989, the enhanced ACT assessment program was developed, which includes four academic tests (English usage, mathematics usage, social studies reading, and natural science reading) as well as an interest inventory. Possible scores on the ability tests range from 1 to 36 with a mean of 18 and a standard deviation of 6. The ACT program, too, has a preliminary version, the P-ACT, generally taken during the 10th grade, that includes a study skills assessment, an interest inventory, and a student information section in addition to versions of the ACT aptitude tests.

4. *Graduate Record Examination (GRE)*. Also published by ETS, the GRE is to college students as the SAT and ACT are to high school students. The GRE includes measures of verbal ability (GRE-V), quantitative ability (GRE-Q), and analytical ability (GRE-A). This highly reliable instrument is required for admission to many graduate schools.

5. *Miller Analogies Test (MAT)*. Published by Psychological Corporation, this 50-minute test consists of 100 analogies and is another much used and reliable predictor of success in graduate school.

Several tests have been developed to predict success in specific professional fields: These include the *Law School Aptitude Test*, the *Medical College Admission Test*, the *Graduate Management Aptitude Test*, and the *Dental Aptitude Test*, among others.

Measures of Occupational Aptitude

1. *General Aptitude Test Battery (GATB)*. This extensively studied aptitude test battery was developed by the U.S. Employment Service

and was distributed by state employment services. The GATB provides assessment in nine areas: general learning ability, verbal aptitude, numerical aptitude, spatial aptitude, form perception, clerical perception, motor coordination, finger and manual dexterity, and occupational aptitude. This 2.5-hour test battery is designed for adolescents and adults in Grades 9 and above who are aiming primarily toward occupations that require specific vocational preparation. The GATB is based on an analysis of 460 occupations and yields scores on 66 occupational aptitude patterns. Droege and Boese (1982) said of the GATB, "No other aptitude measure has an occupational validity data base of this size" (p. 228). Information on aptitudes provided by the GATB covers 97% of the nonsupervisory/nonprofessional occupations in the *Dictionary of Occupational Titles* (U.S. Government Printing Office), most of which are in unskilled, semiskilled, trades, or crafts areas. Primary uses of the GATB include counseling and placement for people in state employment services, vocational-technical schools, vocational rehabilitation programs, and secondary and postsecondary schools.

Despite the history of over 40 years of use of this instrument, controversy erupted in the 1980s over its use. African American and Hispanic people tended to score lower on the GATB and so were not being referred for desirable jobs as frequently as were Whites. Once this was recognized, adjustments were made in the scores of people from minority backgrounds so that they benefited from referral and rehabilitation programs as much as did people from majority backgrounds. However, this, too, was seen as discriminatory (Helwig, 1989). As a result of this controversy, the Department of Labor suspended use of the GATB for 2 years, beginning in 1991. The future of this valuable instrument, then, is uncertain. If its use is reinstated, counselors should remember that the predictive power of the GATB is not very great and should use that inventory as only one source of information about a person's ability. Particular care should be taken in interpreting results of the GATB for women and for people who are older, have disabilities, or are from minority or multicultural backgrounds.

2. *The Minnesota Clerical Assessment Battery (MCAB).* One of the first computerized tests for personnel selection to be commercially available, the MCAB (from Psychological Corporation) is a relatively comprehensive clerical battery that assesses six aptitudes (typing, proofreading, filing, business vocabulary, business mathematics, and clerical knowledge) in approximately 1 hour.

Intelligence Tests

Since their inception, there has been a mystique surrounding intelligence tests. Many have erroneously believed that these tests measure innate ability and that people have an intelligence quotient (IQ) that is with them at birth and that remains constant throughout their lives. People often are eager to know their IQ scores and tend to place so much emphasis on these scores that many school counselors, psychologists, and others using intelligence tests have been reluctant to divulge those scores, although they have little or no reluctance to disclose aptitude or achievement test scores.

Nature of Intelligence

Intelligence testing is grounded in Francis Galton's (1883) study of individual differences. Many authors have developed definitions of what is measured by intelligence tests in an effort to demystify those instruments. Wechsler (1958), well known for his development of intelligence tests, defined the IQ as a measure of a person's capacity to act purposefully, to think rationally, and to deal effectively with the environment (Samuda, 1975). Tyler (1984) viewed intelligence as the ability to learn and adapt to life's changing demands. Weinberg (1989) suggested that there are three facets to intelligence: reasoning and practical problem-solving ability, verbal ability, and social intelligence. A survey of psychologists found that most viewed intelligence as a combination of abstract thinking or reasoning, problem-solving ability, and the capacity to acquire knowledge (Snyderman & Rothman, 1987). Others have viewed intelligence tests as measuring general educational ability and the ability to cope with one's culture.

Intelligence tests, therefore, measure a heterogeneous group of abilities that are determined by a combination of heredity, background, and education. Level of inventoried intelligence can and does change throughout the life span of most people, depending on their overall development and experiences. Deliberate efforts to increase inventoried intelligence have been fairly successful when implemented in early childhood (Angoff, 1988). An IQ, then, is at best a measure of a person's current intellectual functioning. Although a series of scores derived from intelligence tests administered over a period of years can provide valuable information about a person's intellectual development, the score from a single administration of an intelligence test says little about what the test taker has been like or will be like or why the present score was achieved. Nevertheless, according to Barrett and Depinet (1991), "A review of the literature shows that intelligence tests are valid predictors of job success and other important life outcomes. Cognitive ability is the best predictor of performance in most employment situations and this relationship remains stable over extended periods of time" (p. 1016).

Types of Intelligence Tests

Individual and group intelligence tests are available. Individual intelligence tests are designed to be given to one person at a time. Generally, they yield both a general measure of intellectual functioning and scores in several aspects of intelligence, consistent with Spearman's (1904) finding that intelligence could be described as "g" or general intellectual ability or could be divided into many factors. Some aspects of intelligence commonly assessed by these instruments include verbal and numerical reasoning, judgment, memory, abstract thinking, and learning ability. Typically, g, or the IQ, is reflected by a composite of a person's scores on the various subtests encompassed by the whole test. A score of 100 is usually the mean on intelligence tests, with the average range extending from approximately 90 to 110. Scores below that would indicate lower than average intelligence, whereas higher scores would reflect high intelligence. Scores below 70 are usually regarded as reflecting mental retardation, whereas scores of at least 130 or 140 may qualify people for placement in special programs for the gifted. Although most who use intelligence tests view the tests as adequately measuring the most important aspects of intelligence, they are less supportive of the value of dividing intelligence into multiple factors (Snyderman & Rothman, 1987).

Individual intelligence tests were developed before the group tests and are the best known, including such instruments as the Stanford-Binet Intelligence Scale (Riverside) and the Wechsler Preschool and Primary Scale of Intelligence (WPPSI), the Wechsler Intelligence Scale for Children (WISC), and WAIS, all available from Psychological Corporation. The Stanford-Binet Intelligence Scale, the oldest of the accepted individual measures of intelligence, has been described as a "mainstay of school and clinical psychology practice since early this century" (Reynolds, Kamphaus, & Rosenthal, 1988, p. 52). The latest revision, published in 1986, assesses three levels of abilities: general intelligence; crystallized abilities, fluid-analytic abilities, and short-term memory;

and verbal reasoning, quantitative reasoning, and abstract/visual reasoning. Designed for ages 2 through adulthood, administration of the Stanford-Binet may have 3 to 13 subtests, depending on individual performance. Subtest as well as composite scores have a mean of 100 and a standard deviation of 16. The three Wechsler tests (WPPSI, WISC, and WAIS) also yield subtest scores as well as verbal, performance, and full-scale IQ scores. Watkins et al. (1988) found that over 63% of counseling psychologists use the Wechsler intelligence scales and that they are among the five most frequently used tests in student counseling centers, private practice, and mental health clinics. Either the Stanford-Binet or a Wechsler intelligence scale is almost always included in any comprehensive psychological assessment that involves testing.

Group intelligence tests. Although individual intelligence tests generally provide a more detailed and more valid picture of a person's intelligence than do group intelligence tests, they are far more time-consuming to administer and score than are group intelligence tests and require considerably more training and experience. Although some counselors have been trained in the use of individual intelligence tests, most counselors make greater use of group intelligence tests. Consequently, it is that variety of intelligence tests that will be emphasized in this book.

The Otis-Lennon School Ability Test (OLSAT), originally published in 1918, probably is the best known group intelligence test. Published by Psychological Corporation, the OLSAT was designed to measure cognitive abilities that relate to success in school. Seven levels of the OLSAT are available, encompassing Grades K through 12, with a spiral arrangement of test items in which a difficult item is followed by an easy item, thereby minimizing discouragement. The OLSAT has a mean of 100 and a standard deviation of 16 and yields verbal, nonverbal, and total scores that can be presented in percentile ranks or stanines based on age and grade. The OLSAT is highly correlated with measures of achievement and probably yields a score that is more tied to educational experiences than do the individual intelligence tests (Ahmann, 1985).

Several nonverbal tests of intelligence have been published in recent years in reaction to criticisms of intelligence tests being culturally biased. The nonverbal tests are useful in testing people with language handicaps as well as people from non-English-speaking backgrounds. Examples of popular nonverbal tests of intelligence are the Test of Nonverbal Intelligence (TONI), a 20-minute inventory for ages 5 to 85+; Cattell's Culture-Fair Intelligence Test; and Raven's Progressive Matrices. Nonverbal intelligence tests typically do not rely heavily on school learning. However, nonverbal intelligence tests are usually less reliable than verbal ones and may provide misleading information for people who are aspiring to educational or occupational goals that demand a high level of verbal ability. Many verbal tests can be adapted for use with special populations. Materials, including audiocassettes and Braille and large-type versions, as well as authorization of extended time limits for testing are available for many verbal tests of all types to allow their appropriate use with people who have special needs.

Development of Intellectual Abilities

Level of inventoried intellectual functioning seems to be greatly affected by family attitudes and composition. Families that emphasize achievement and independence and foster a desire to learn are more likely to produce children with high levels of intellectual ability. Girls with brothers, boys with much older sisters, firstborn children, children from intact families, and those from small or affluent families seem to be in situations that facilitate positive intellectual development (Rees & Palmer, 1970; Zajonc, 1986). Although African Americans tend to score lower on standardized measures of intelligence than do Whites, this seems to be due to differences in family background, environment, and educational experiences rather than to race as has been alleged by some researchers. Studies have shown that when African American children were placed for adoption in homes that were better than average in terms of parental intelligence, income, education, occupational standing, and the parents' desire for children, the children's inventoried intelligence rose markedly; this suggests that intelligence is strongly connected to environment (Fields, 1977). As Weinberg (1989) put it, genes do not fix behavior and performance but "establish a range of possible reactions" (p. 101). Weinberg suggested that the range of potential intelligence test scores in a given environment is approximately 20 to 25 points, as much as the entire normal range of intelligence.

Intellectual development shows some stability by the age of 7 and becomes fairly stable by about the age of 12 (Hopkins & Bracht, 1975). Until that time, scores on intelligence tests can vary widely, and little faith should be placed in the predictive value of infant or early childhood intelligence tests. IQs based on verbal tests and on individual intelligence tests generally have greater stability than do those derived from nonverbal or group intelligence tests. However, even after early adolescence, great changes in environment, family situation, opportunity for learning, and emotional adjustment can have a considerable impact on intellectual development and functioning.

The circumstances of a test administration can also affect intellectual performance. Moore and Retish (1974), for example, found that African American children achieved higher levels of inventoried intelligence when they were tested by African American examiners than they did when the examiners were White.

Appropriate Use of Intelligence Tests

Intelligence tests, like other ability tests, have been much criticized for their shortcomings and abuses. The criticisms came to a head during the 1970s and were reflected in the 1976 resolution of the American School Counselors Association governing board, calling for a discontinuation of standardized group intelligence tests. The resolution made the following criticisms of the use of intelligence tests:

1. Intelligence tests have been used to categorize people; they ignore individual diversity.
2. Intelligence tests do not measure what they claim to measure; they are not adequate to measure the complexities of human intelligence.
3. Intelligence tests are based on White middle-class culture and values and are therefore biased. In some cases, they classify people according to socioeconomic status or race rather than according to intellectual ability.
4. Intelligence tests are used across the nation in such a way as to permanently affect the self-images of those tested. Intelligence testing may alter the aspirations of those tested and the expectations of their teachers.

The landmark case of *Larry P. v. Riles*, resolved in 1980, alleged that intelligence tests had discriminated against people from minority groups. That case led to a ban on the use of intelligence tests for placement in special education programs in California (Linn, 1986).

These criticisms of the rampant misuse of intelligence tests seem to have been justified. However, intelligence tests can provide useful information:

1. They can facilitate selection of students for gifted and talented programs or other programs offering the opportunity for advanced or accelerated course work.

2. They can provide a measure of functioning that is less linked to educational experiences than most achievement tests and many aptitude tests and, therefore, provide a different source of information on abilities.
3. A disparity between school performance and inventoried intelligence can be helpful in identifying children who are performing below capacity as well as those who are stretching their abilities and may feel great pressure to achieve academic success.
4. Intelligence test scores correlate significantly and positively with many variables relevant to career development such as occupational success, career maturity, levels of occupational and education aspiration, academic performance, and likelihood of attending and graduating from college (Levine, 1976). Most people are aware of their intellectual abilities and gravitate toward career paths that are consistent with those abilities.

Since the 1970s, patterns of use of intelligence tests have changed greatly in an effort to control and improve the use of those tests. During the 1980s, criticism of intelligence testing declined as intelligence tests were used less frequently and more judiciously (Snyderman & Rothman, 1987). Schoolwide testing of intelligence now has all but disappeared, and most testing is done with individuals or small groups, with the specific purpose of the testing predetermined.

Counselors make less use of intelligence tests than they do of the other types of tests, especially when they are dealing with adults who have already demonstrated their abilities through years of educational and occupational endeavor. Counselors should be comfortable with intelligence tests, however, for their own use, for understanding psychological reports they may receive about their clients, and for knowing when a referral for intelligence testing is warranted.

Intelligence tests are closely related to both aptitude and achievement tests, and people's scores on all three types of instruments tend to be highly correlated (Angoff, 1988). Counselors should be sure that they are not administering an intelligence test when what they really want is an aptitude test. Usually, measures of aptitude are more appropriate for prediction, and people often find them more acceptable and less threatening. Both intelligence and aptitude measures correlate more highly with success in training than with success on the job, and intelligence tests, like aptitude tests, are not good indicators of overall career success or satisfaction.

When considering the use of an intelligence test, counselors should take particular note of the groups on which it was normed. If those groups are not comparable to groups to which their clients presently belong or to which they aspire, the test may be discriminatory or irrelevant to the client. However, if the test was normed on groups that do not represent the clients' background or present group membership but do reflect their future goals, the test may well have value. For example, if a person from a lower socioeconomic background is considering applying to a highly competitive university, an intelligence test may be useful, in combination with other information, in assessing whether that person's intellectual ability is comparable to that of the average student at that university. When intelligence tests are administered, examiners should be alert to circumstances that might call into question the validity of a score. The attitudes of the test takers and the interaction between test takers and examiners should be noted. Some believe that nonintellectual factors, such as anxiety, attentiveness, persistence, emotional lability, achievement motivation, and physical health, can have a marked impact on inventoried intelligence (Snyderman & Rothman, 1987).

The interpretation of an intelligence test score should involve the thoughtful integration of test data with information on a person's level of motivation, background, academic performance, and other test data. Intelligence tests, like other tests of ability, are usually timed tests, so speed as well as knowledge and thinking may be reflected by a score. Discussing inventoried intelligence in terms of ranges rather than specific scores can promote a more accurate and less threatening understanding of the meaning of the test results. Such an understanding of the significance of an intelligence score also can be facilitated if the score is discussed in terms of the information it provides about a person's standing in a group and the relationship of the score to school grades, inventoried achievement and aptitude, accomplishments, and future academic goals.

In interpreting intelligence tests taken by people who do not come from White middle-class backgrounds, counselors might think of *knowing differently* rather than knowing less. Such people often possess a different body of knowledge than do middle-class White people, knowledge that is not adequately tapped or reflected by most standardized tests of intelligence. Although intelligence tests may be useful in estimating the chances of success of such people in a particular educational or occupational endeavor, intelligence tests do not reflect innate ability or true intellectual capacity.

Interest Inventories

Interests are constellations of likes and dislikes. They are manifested through the activities people pursue, the objects they value, their topics of reading and conversation, and their patterns of behavior. Three major types of interests have been identified: expressed, manifest, and inventoried. *Expressed interests* are the preferences people report when they are asked what they enjoy. Expressed interests may be hypothetical and reflect how people believe they would react to certain objects or activities as well as how people recall feeling when they had certain experiences. *Manifest interests* are those that are embodied in people's lifestyles. They can be elicited by asking how people spend their leisure time, what courses or special projects they have selected, what books or television programs they prefer, and what sort of work they do. *Inventoried interests* are identified by a person's pattern of scores on a standardized interest inventory.

The correlation between expressed and inventoried interests is moderate, and sizable discrepancies between the two are not uncommon. Walsh and Hanle (1975) found that, often, a lack of congruence between expressed career goals and inventoried preferences reflected career immaturity. Similarity, a discrepancy between expressed and manifest interests may characterize people who have limited self-awareness, dissatisfaction with their lifestyles, or personal difficulties. For example, a young man who reports that his interests are sports and popular music but who spends most of his time reading and listening to opera may think that he will not be accepted by his family or peers if he expresses interests that are not consistent with theirs. Generally, incongruence between any of the three types of interests should be explored during the counseling process.

Expressed occupational aspirations and interests have greater predictive validity than do inventoried interests. However, people sometimes may answer direct questions about their career-related interests from a position that is affected by limited self-awareness, a lack of career information, a stereotyped and biased view of the world of work and their future role there, and aspirations that others have imposed on them. Expressed interests can indicate a wish to be in a particular occupation and to acquire its prestige or its financial rewards without indicating genuine interest in the activities involved in the performance of the occupation. Predictive validity of expressed interests can be increased by asking people to report two or more occupational aspirations or by looking at the interface of expressed aspirations and inventoried interests

(Holland, Gottfredson, & Baker, 1990). Validity of prediction is related to certainty level of expressed occupational choice, so counselors should be sure to explore that dimension (Noeth & Jepsen, 1981). Although using interest inventories as part of career counseling can help to clarify occupational goals, counselors should not underestimate the importance of simply asking people about their career goals. Despite the sophisticated technology of testing, self-report is the best source of information on interests.

Development of Interests

Interests, like personality traits, tend to crystallize later than do abilities. Interests that are expressed or demonstrated during childhood or early adolescence are usually quite unstable and should not be used as the basis for definite and long-range career planning. Interests during those years may be greatly influenced by family and social background, peer group interests, and educational and recreational activities and opportunities. Interests seem to grow most in areas of greatest experience. It is not just coincidence or genetics, for example, that outstanding young tennis players often have parents and siblings who also are skilled tennis players. Because of the typical instability of early interests, most interest inventories designed for children or early adolescents provide information on broad occupational and educational areas and do not translate interests into specific occupations. Young people's interest in social service may be measured, for example, but would not be assessed in terms of specific occupational categories, such as counselor, nurse, or teacher.

Once young people pass the middle teens, their interests stabilize enough to play a major role in career planning. Their expressed interests reflect greater self-awareness and independence of thought. Their manifest interests, too, become a more reliable indicator because the teenagers have a broader range of opportunities and experiences. Swanson and Hansen (1988) gave an interest inventory (the Strong-Campbell Interest Inventory) to a group of 18-year-old college freshmen and then tested them again every 4 years for 12 years. They concluded that "there was a remarkable degree of interest stability over all three time intervals" (p. 185), with individual differences in stability related to self-ratings of stability. Many sophisticated and valuable interest inventories, discussed later in this book, have been developed to assess the interests of people from age 16 or 17 through adulthood.

Longitudinal studies conducted by Super and his colleagues in the past suggested that women generally have more stable interests than do men, although interests are never completely fixed for either gender and marked change between the ages of 18 and 25 is not uncommon (Super & Crites, 1962). Super and his colleagues also found that some of the development of interests seemed to be undone during the transitional stages that occurred about ages 25 and 55. Interests of people in the middle adult years often reflected new self-awareness and discovery and were more like those of adolescents than they were like young adults.

Super (1985) found that expressed occupational preference was a better predictor of occupational choice for people from upper classes than it was for people from the middle class. Perhaps social and class pressures on members of the upper classes limit their opportunity to select occupations that are congruent with their inventoried interests; cultural values may be more important to them than actualization of interests. Although we do not know whether those findings of over 30 years ago are still true in today's society, where men and women have greater equality, class barriers are less rigid, and change at midlife is more acceptable, those patterns provide a useful perspective for viewing and evaluating interests.

Research has found that interests are a major determinant of both college major and occupational choice and, along with people's beliefs about their abilities, are usually the most important considerations in these decisions (Betz & Hackett, 1981). Generally, interests have been found to exert a more important influence on occupational choice than do aptitudes. Because the relationship between interests and abilities is only moderate, many people select occupations for which they may not have great ability. Although interest in one's work increases effort and motivation, it does not fully compensate for a lack of ability. As a result, interest is not a consistent predictor of occupational success (Thomas, Morrill, & Miller, 1970). On the other hand, congruence of interests and career choice *is* related to both satisfaction and stability (Betz et al., 1989).

Development of Interest Inventories

Two methods of developing interest inventories have been widely used. One method compares the interests of the test taker with the interests of people engaged in a variety of occupations. This method is based on the finding that people in an occupational group have similar interests, are drawn to each other and the occupation because of these interests, and are more likely to find satisfaction in occupations in which their interests are similar to those of the typical satisfied worker. The second method is based on activity similarity rather than on people similarity and assesses the relationship between a person's preferred and disliked activities and the activities involved in the performance of occupations. Interest inventories developed in this way are usually easier to interpret and more appropriate for people of high school age or younger, whereas the more complex inventories, based on people similarity, are more appropriate for people of college age or older. The Kuder General Interest Survey (KGIS) is an example of an interest inventory that is based on activity similarity, while the Kuder Occupational Interest Survey (KOIS) is based on people similarity. The SII incorporates both of these approaches. Both of these methods of test development draw heavily on the trait-and-factor theory of career choice.

Interest inventories have been in use for more than 60 years, and the validity and reliability of the best of them have been well established, based primarily on their ability to predict eventual occupational choice. Typically, short-term hit rates, accurate prediction of college majors or occupational choices a few years after a person takes an interest inventory, are over 50%, whereas the long-term prediction rate is over 30% for well-established interest inventories. This rate of accurate prediction is nearly as high for people who report being decided about their careers as for people who are undecided (Bartling & Hood, 1981; Knapp, Knapp, & Knapp-Lee, 1985). However, the accuracy of prediction is considerably higher for people whose expressed and inventoried interests are congruent than for those for whom they are not congruent.

Use of Interest Inventories

Although expressed interests are the most valid predictor of occupational choice, most people report wanting to learn more about their career options (Feller, 1991), and interest inventories can help them do that. They are particularly useful for people who report being undecided about their career goals but who do not seem to have significant emotional difficulties that are impeding their career development. The following are some of the goals that can be accomplished or furthered by interest inventories:

1. promote awareness and clarification of interests
2. introduce unfamiliar occupations

3. increase knowledge of the world of work
4. highlight discrepancies between interests and abilities and between interests and expressed occupational goals
5. translate interests into occupational terms
6. organize interests in meaningful and useful ways
7. stimulate career thought and exploration
8. provide insight into the nature of a person's academic and occupational dissatisfaction
9. increase the realism of one's career goals
10. reassure people who have already made appropriate tentative career plans
11. facilitate conflict resolution and decision making

Even in the case of the minimally threatening and very useful interest inventories, counselors should be cautious in their interpretations. As Tyler (1984) observed, "Interest inventories do not measure how much interest the person has in anything, but only what direction his or her interests have taken. . . . scores can best serve as starting points for discussion, . . . as facilitators or aids to thinking" (p. 49).

When discussing interests, then, considerable exploration is usually indicated, especially of interests or occupational areas with which people have had little experience. Counselors should be sure they are making full use of the career-related ideas and experiences their clients already have had before they turn to interest inventories for further information. Counselors should examine whether the clients have an accurate view of the work performed in the occupations that interest them, the lifestyle that generally accompanies that occupation, and both the positive and negative aspects of the occupation. Both expressed and inventoried interests always consist of likes as well as dislikes; both can provide useful information about occupational options that are likely to be rewarding.

Counselors should not assume that an occupation means the same thing to everyone. People often attribute different qualities and activities to the same occupation. Consequently, people with similar interests may translate them into different career goals, and people with different interests may aim toward very similar careers. For example, some people may express an interest in medicine because they enjoy helping people, whereas others may select a career in medicine because of an interest in science and research.

Often, people's inventoried interests reflect high interest in occupations that, at least initially, hold little interest for them and are surprising.

Counselors can encourage people to take a broad view of occupations in an effort to ascertain how their patterns of high and low scores correspond to what they believe to be true about themselves rather than accepting an immediate rejection of an occupation. For example, a person's interest inventory may reflect high similarity to people employed as funeral directors. If this occupation had not previously been considered, it might cause some discomfort and might be rejected without consideration. However, a discussion of what funeral directors do might clarify the person's interest in occupations that combine art and business. Another person who had high inventoried interest in military occupations may have an interest in structured roles, although military service may not be appealing. Much can be learned about a person's occupational interests and preferences by taking a close look at inventoried interests.

The prediction approach to interpretation, discussed earlier in this chapter, seems especially fruitful as a first step in interpreting interest inventories. Generally, subsequent discussion of interest profiles would move from broad scales to narrow ones, looking at percentages and patterns of likes and dislikes. Small differences should not be overemphasized, and other information about the person should be woven into the discussion of the interest inventory. Often, interpretation will culminate in the identification of a small group (3 to 6) of occupations of interest that the client will explore further.

Approximately 10% to 20% of test takers achieve flat profiles on interest inventories, reflecting little differentiation of interests (Pinkney, 1985). This may indicate people who have broad and loosely related interests, who have little academic or occupational motivation, who have negative or restricted thinking about their future options, who have limited experience or exposure to the world of work, who are unwilling or unable to make a commitment, or who have significant emotional difficulties. These people typically present a challenge to the career counselor. Depending on the counselor's assessment of the reasons for the flat profile, such clients might benefit from personal counseling or the use of a nonstandardized approach to interest clarification before they can make good use of the results of an interest inventory.

One of the most challenging aspects of interpreting interest inventories constructively is differentiating interest from ability. Sometimes, people will confuse interests and abilities and will misinterpret high inventoried interest as a reflection of strong potential ability for an occupation. Although some people have interests and abilities that are congruent, that is frequently not the case, and studies generally show a negligible relationship between inventoried interests and assessed abilities (Hood & Johnson, 1991). Information from interest inventories must be considered in conjunction with other data about a person, especially information on the person's abilities. If there is overlap between people's interests and their abilities, career planning may be fairly straightforward. However, if the two are not congruent, counselors can help people to translate their interests into a broad range of career options in an effort to identify occupations that are realistic in light of their abilities. For example, a person who achieves high inventoried interest in such occupations as physician, pediatrician, and school psychologist but who seems to have neither the motivation nor the interest for graduate study might be able to express the interests in medicine and helping children through such fields as nursing, child care worker, or medical technician.

On occasion, translation of people's interests into occupations that are congruent with their abilities seems very difficult. An example of this might be a person whose interests point in the direction of musical performance but who has shown little talent in this area. In such a case, work and leisure activities can be structured in such a way as to complement each other. Although vocational and avocational interests often coincide, it is possible for people to find expression for one cluster of interests in their work and for another through their leisure activities.

Interest inventories, for the most part, assess intrinsic sources of satisfaction and indicate the likelihood that people will enjoy a particular type of work. However, extrinsic satisfactions, such as working conditions, salary, and lifestyle, inherent in a given job or occupation are also important. The relative importance of intrinsic versus extrinsic satisfactions and of the various types of extrinsic satisfactions are more clearly reflected by values inventories that will be discussed later in this chapter. Counselors should be sure that they discuss both intrinsic and extrinsic sources of satisfaction with their clients to determine reactions to all aspects of an occupation.

Bias and Distortion in Interest Inventories

When interpreting interest inventories, counselors should be aware that faking is possible on these inventories and that scores can be influenced by either conscious or unconscious desires to make a particular impression. The ease of faking varies from one interest inventory to the next, depending on how transparent the scoring system is.

Although interest profiles can be deliberately modified, people usually report their interests truthfully.

Potential for gender and ethnic bias and stereotyping must be considered in selecting and interpreting interest inventories as it must with inventories of abilities. However, Hansen (1987) concluded, "The data available suggest that at least some interest inventories, developed on White U.S. normative samples, are sufficiently valid for international and cross-ethnic use and that the world of work is organized around a structure that is similar to Holland's hexagon and reasonably invariant across cultures" (p. 163). Hood and Johnson (1991) agreed: "Interest inventories can be used with minority clients with the same amount of confidence as with Whites, with the possible exception of those coming from particularly disadvantaged backgrounds" (p. 215). Research on the use of interest inventories with people with disabilities also presents a positive picture: "The occupational interests of adult handicapped persons can be differentiated and structured in a way that corresponds closely with the interest dimensions found in studies of other populations (e.g., college students, high school students, non-handicapped adults)" (Brookings & Bolton, 1986, p. 173).

Despite this optimistic picture, researchers still struggle with how to cope with ethnic- and gender-related patterns of interest. For example, most Asian Americans focus their career goals on business, science, mathematics, and engineering, with few considering law, social science, and the humanities. African Americans tend to have high inventoried interest in occupations that involve helping others but usually manifest little interest in science or research (Miller, Springer, & Wells, 1988). Hispanic women tend to have high inventoried interest in areas such as business and research, areas in which they are underrepresented in the labor force (Harrington & O'Shea, 1980). Women's interests, in general, tend to gravitate toward social and artistic endeavors, whereas men in general have interests that focus on business and science.

Researchers seem agreed that interest inventories should be interpreted in such a way as to expand options rather than reinforce stereotyped roles and limited role models. Exactly how this should happen, however, is unclear, and considerable debate has focused on whether use of same-sex, combined-sex, or opposite-sex norms is most helpful. Holland (1980) minimized the impact of gender bias in interest inventories, stating that most high school students taking interest inventories are seeking reassurance on an aspiration they already had rather than seeking new options. Holland found no evidence that interest inventories had a negative impact on self-image or goals; at the same time, he felt they had little potential to make a real dent in people's long-held stereotyped beliefs. Other researchers disagree. Although same-sex norms may have a higher predictive validity and be more reflective of the real world of work, use of raw scores, combined-sex norms, or opposite-sex norms, in addition to same-sex norms, can suggest a less traditional range of occupational options (Hanson, Noeth, & Prediger, 1977). Perhaps the soundest approach for counselors to take is to recognize that traditional gender and cultural roles will exert a powerful influence over people's careers but, at the same time, to encourage exploration of nontraditional areas of interest and opportunity.

Important and Representative Interest Inventories

A great many interest inventories are available. Included here are brief descriptions of some of the best established and most useful interest inventories.

1. *Career Assessment Inventory (CAI)*. This inventory, developed by Charles B. Johansson and published by National Computer Systems (NCS), is available in both enhanced and vocational editions. The enhanced version, for people in junior high school or older, asks respondents to rate 370 items (activities, school subjects, and occupations) on a 5-point like/dislike scale. Results provide information on interest in the six Holland (1987) themes, 25 basic interest area scales, 111 diverse career groups, and four nonoccupational scales. The vocational version is briefer and easier to read but follows a similar format to the enhanced version. Aimed at people interested in occupations such as skilled trades requiring less than a 4-year college degree, this inventory is particularly useful for people in vocational/technical schools and occupations. Combined gender scores help to reduce gender bias in results. This inventory has many similarities to the SII discussed later but provides separate versions for professional and vocational interests. Generally, test-retest reliabilities in the .80s and .90s have been achieved.

2. *Career Directions Inventory (CDI)*. Published in 1986 by Research Psychologists Press and developed by Douglas N. Jackson, this inventory is designed to facilitate the educational and career planning of high school and college students and adults. Respondents select their most and least preferred choices from 100 triads, reflecting interests in skilled and trade as well as professional occupations. Scores are provided in

seven general occupational themes (realistic/practical, enterprising, artistic/communicative, social/helping, investigative/logical, conventional, and serving) as well as 15 basic interest scales. This relatively new inventory seems particularly useful for high school or college students with little career direction.

3. *College Major Interest Inventory.* This specialized interest inventory, published by Consulting Psychologists Press and designed for high school and college students, includes 399 items that identify educational interests, achievement aspirations, and academic self-concept.

4. *Geist Picture Interest Inventory.* Although not widely used, this inventory, available from Western Psychological Services, might be particularly helpful to people who are nonnative English speakers or who have language limitations. Respondents indicate preferences from pictures, presented in clusters of three, that reflect work or leisure interests. Information on 11 general interest areas is provided.

5. *The Harrington O'Shea Career Decision-Making System (CDM).* Published by AGS, this interest inventory for people of high school age or older seems to be growing in use. Its theoretical basis, that people are more satisfied with their careers when personality style and work setting are congruent, is similar to Holland's (1966) theory of career development (Loughead, 1988). Items assess occupational preferences, academic preferences, future educational plans, work-related values, and reported abilities. Information is provided on 283 occupations, organized into 18 career clusters, that employ the vast majority of the workforce.

6. *Individual Career Exploration (ICE).* This inventory for Grades 8 through 12, published by STS, is based on Roe's (1957) map of the world of work. Information is provided on interest in eight occupational groups (service, business contact, organization, technology, outdoor, science, general culture, and arts and entertainment) and distinguishes interest by level (professional and managerial, semiprofessional and small business, semiskilled labor). A picture version of this inventory is available for Grades 3 through 7 to promote children's thinking about activities they might like to do, places they might like to work,

tools they might like to work with, and jobs they might enjoy and find interesting. Although not much used at this point, this inventory is one of the few based on Roe's ideas and has the advantage of being self-scoring.

7. *Interest Determination, Exploration and Assessment System (IDEAS).* This short, self-scored interest inventory, published by NCS and developed by Charles B. Johansson, presents 128 items that respondents rate on a 5-point like/dislike scale. Norms are provided for Grades 7 through 9, 10 through 12, and adults. Linked to both the *Occupational Outlook Handbook*, published regularly by the U.S. Department of Labor, and Holland's hexagonal conception of occupational environments, IDEAS organizes interests into 16 broad categories. Derived from the CAI, IDEAS seems particularly useful for students in the early stages of career exploration (Bauernfeind, 1991a).

8. *Jackson Vocational Interest Survey (JVIS).* Developed by Douglas N. Jackson and published by Research Psychologists Press, the JVIS is geared particularly to college-bound students in Grades 9 and up. It presents 289 job-related activities in pairs; respondents select the more interesting item in each pair. Scores are provided on 10 general occupational themes (expressive, logical, inquiring, practical, assertive, socialized, helping, conventional, enterprising, and communicative), 17 clusters of college majors, and 32 occupational clusters. Studies report good test-retest reliability for this inventory (Bauernfeind, 1991b).

9. *Kuder General Interest Survey (KGIS).* An earlier version of the KGIS, the Kuder Preference Record, was first published in 1948, making it one of the oldest and best-established interest inventories. The KGIS, developed by Frederick Kuder and published by Science Research Associates, uses a forced-choice triad format to yield a verification or validity score as well as scores on 10 relatively independent scales (outdoor, mechanical, computational, scientific, persuasive, artistic, literary, musical, social service, and clerical). Its broad categories of information, sixth-grade reading level, and availability in a self-scoring version make it particularly useful in junior high school classes. However, it is fairly lengthy, requiring 45 to 60 minutes of testing time, and scoring should be carefully supervised to ensure accuracy (Lampe, 1985).

10. *Kuder Occupational Interest Survey (KOIS)*. This more sophisticated Kuder interest inventory (also published by Science Research Associates) was first published in 1966 and is based on similarity of respondents' interests to those of people in occupational criterion groups, whereas the KGIS is based on an activity similarity approach. The KOIS, designed for high school and college students as well as for adults, provides scores on the same 10 scales as the KGIS and also provides interest scores for over 100 occupations and 48 college majors. Occupations and majors of highest interest are rank ordered in the profile of results, thereby facilitating interpretation. The forced-choice or ipsative triad format, with respondents indicating their most and least preferred options on 100 items, intended to reduce response bias, is used in the KOIS as well as in the KGIS. Some test takers find that format difficult. Self-scoring is not available for the KOIS; machine scoring must be used. David P. Jepsen (1985) wrote about the form DD version of this inventory:

> The KOIS-DD does well and perhaps better than any other interest inventory what it was designed to do—namely to assist students in differentiating among a limited group of occupations on the basis of similarity of interest patterns. Claims that go beyond the constraints of this simple but important purpose are not substantiated by data or theory. (p. 219)

See Chapter 6 for further discussion of this inventory.

11. *Ohio Vocational Interest Survey—II (OVIS—II)*. The OVIS—II, published by Psychological Corporation and described by Harmon (1985) as "carefully constructed and well-presented" (p. 224), consists of 253 activity items that respondents evaluate on a 5-point like/dislike scale. Scoring yields information on interest in 23 occupational clusters, based on a data/people/things conception of the world of work, linked to the 20,000 occupations in the *Dictionary of Occupational Titles*. Perhaps the greatest strength of the OVIS is its accompanying materials; the OVIS—II includes an introductory filmstrip, the questionnaire, the report form, a second filmstrip on interpretation, and a workbook, *Handbook for Exploring Careers*, to facilitate application of the inventory results. Norms for this inventory are available for Grades 7 through 9, 10 through 12, and first- and second-year college students.

12. *Self-Directed Search (SDS)*. Developed by John Holland and first published by Psychological Assessment Resources (PAR) in 1971, the

SDS "has received wide acceptance among professionals in the areas of psychology, counseling and other related fields" (McKee & Levinson, 1990, p. 331). This inventory is used by over 250,000 people each year (Prediger, 1981). The basic version of the SDS can be used with ages 15 to 70 (Bauernfeind & Kandor, 1988). Form E (easy) is available for people with limited reading ability, and foreign language versions (e.g., Spanish, Vietnamese) also are available. The SDS is based on Holland's (1987b) theory of the importance of congruence of person and environment in career development, which is discussed in greater detail in Chapter 1.

The SDS consists of 228 items, divided into three sets of six scales, corresponding to Holland's (1987b) six occupational environments. Although the SDS is generally viewed as an interest inventory, items ask not only about interest in activities and occupations but also about self-assessed competencies. The inventory can be self-scored and yields a three-letter occupational code, reflecting a person's three highest occupational environments in Holland's hexagon. For example, ISA would be the occupational code for someone whose highest interest was in the investigative area, followed by the social and then the artistic areas.

Extensive supplementary materials are available to facilitate use of the SDS. The *Jobs Finder* lists 500 jobs with their two-letter Holland codes. The *College Majors Finder* lists over 900 college majors alphabetically and by Holland code. The *Occupations Finder* provides a similar listing of approximately 1,500 occupations with accompanying educational requirements and *Dictionary of Occupational Titles* codes so that people can readily obtain more information on occupations of interest. The *Dictionary of Holland Occupational Codes* is a listing of over 12,000 occupations and their codes. *You and Your Career* is a supplementary booklet that facilitates use of the SDS scores in career planning.

The SDS is one of the few interest inventories that uses raw scores to report and compare interests. Holland saw this format as having more predictive validity (Prediger, 1981).

Although Holland suggested that the SDS could facilitate the career decision making of approximately 50% of the population without the help of a career counselor, most seem to view the SDS as contributing to the efficiency of that process but continue to emphasize the importance of using the SDS with the help of a counselor (Krieshok, 1987; McKee & Levinson, 1990). This inventory is discussed further in Chapter 6.

13. *Strong Interest Inventory (SII)*. Formerly known as the Strong Vocational Interest Blank and the Strong-Campbell Interest Inventory, the SII, published by Consulting Psychologists Press, is the best established and most widely used interest inventory in the United States (Vansickle et al., 1989). The men's form was first developed by E. K. Strong in 1927-28; the women's form, in 1933-35. The present version asks about respondents' likes and dislikes for 325 items. A narrative report, as well as a profile of results, can be obtained from the publisher to facilitate interpretation of this rich inventory. Appropriate for high school and college students and adults, the SII has been used in career counseling, outplacement counseling, college major selection, leadership development, retirement counseling, team building, and leisure counseling. The 1985 SII profile presents scores in four ways:

1. General Occupational Themes organize overall occupational orientation according to Holland's (1991) hexagon.
2. 23 Basic Interest Scales reflect occupational and leisure interests and dislikes.
3. 207 Occupations Scales compare test takers' interests with men and women who are happily and successfully employed in the given occupations, one third of which do not require college degrees for entry.
4. Administrative and additional indexes help identify unusual or invalid profiles and provide information on reactions to continued education and to people-oriented occupations.

The SII has good predictive validity as well as good exploration validity, the ability to increase the diversity of a person's career options (Campbell, 1987). Scores for each gender are compared with both same-sex and opposite-sex norms to reduce bias, although same-sex norms are emphasized. Although the SII probably is the richest of the interest inventories, its complexity can be overwhelming. It is best used for people who have already given considerable thought to their career development, who are ready to think in specific occupational terms, and who can work closely with a counselor in understanding and making use of this inventory. The SII will be discussed further in Chapter 8.

14. *U.S. Employment Service Interest Inventory (USES-II)*. This inventory, developed by the Department of Labor, is used primarily in assessing the interests of vocational rehabilitation clients. Interest scores are provided on 12 scales: artistic, scientific, plants and animals, protective, mechanical, industrial, business detail, selling, accommodating, humani-

tarian, leading-influencing, and physical performing. According to Bolton (1988), "Profile reliabilities and indices of interest score stability for the highest three scores were supportive of the use of the USES-II in occupational exploration activities and in vocational counseling applications" (p. 116).

15. *Vocational Interest Experience and Skill Assessment (VIESA)*. Part of the ACT Career Planning Services program, VIESA was designed to link information on experiences, interests, and values. It is available in two forms, Level 1 for Grades 8 through 10 and Level 2 for Grade 11 through adult. Based on the data/ideas and people/things dimensions and Holland's (1985) and Roe's (1957) typologies of careers, scores on the VIESA are linked to 450 occupations in the *Occupational Outlook Handbook* that employ over 95% of the labor force in the United States. The VIESA can be administered and self-scored in 45 minutes. This has been viewed more as a teaching tool than an interest inventory (Hood & Johnson, 1991).

16. *Wide Range Interest-Opinion Test (WRIOT)*. This pictorial interest inventory requires no reading or language understanding and claims to be free of culture and gender bias. Its use with educationally disadvantaged and mentally retarded people has been recommended (Zunker, 1990). Responses to 150 sets of three pictures provide scores on 18 interest clusters and 8 general attitude clusters.

Career Planning Programs

Interest inventories are available by themselves or as part of comprehensive career planning programs that also may include inventories of abilities, values, personality, or career maturity. The following are some of the most widely used career planning programs.

1. *ACT Career Planning Program (CPP)*. The CPP consists of four parts: an inventory of interests, an inventory of experiences, an assessment of self-rated abilities, and six timed ability tests. Totaling 173 minutes of testing, this program can be divided into three sessions. The program is available in two forms, Level 1 for Grades 8 through 10 and Level 2 for those above Grade 10. Results are organized according to Holland's (1985) occupational themes. This program is used by over

200,000 people per year, most of whom are high school juniors, and for the most part has received positive reviews, although some have been overwhelmed by the massive amount of information that is produced.

2. *COPSystem Career Guidance Program.* The COPSystem, published by EdITS, includes tools to assess interests, abilities, and values. Abilities are assessed in the COPSystem by the Career Ability Placement Survey (CAPS), consisting of eight 5-minute ability tests and an accompanying career planning guide. The Career Orientation Placement and Evaluation Survey (COPES) is a 20 to 30-minute work values inventory for people in Grade 7 through adult that translates values into the COPS career clusters. The COPS Interest Inventory is available in four editions: the COPS Interest Inventory, a 168-item survey of occupationally relevant activities based on Roe's (1956) classification of occupations that can be used with adolescents and adults; the COPS form R, a simplified single-sex inventory; the COPS II Intermediate Inventory for junior and senior high school students; and the COPS—P for those considering primarily professional occupations.

The COPS was developed "to meet the need for a brief inventory of interests providing systematic measurement of job activity preferences in terms of clusters of meaningfully related occupations (Knapp & Knapp, 1984, p. 1). Scores are provided in 14 interest clusters. A *Career Briefs Kit* is available to facilitate linking of inventoried interests to college majors and occupations. According to Kane (1989), the interest inventory is especially good for organizing the career preferences of young adults into coherent clusters and is best used to encourage career exploration rather than for decision making. The COPS has been recommended for vocational rehabilitation counseling (Brookings & Bolton, 1986). The interest inventory has generally received positive reviews. The COPSystem is discussed further in Chapter 5.

The COPSystem can be used in total or as individual components. Extensive supplementary materials, linking test results to the *Occupational Outlook Handbook*, are available to facilitate use.

3. *Differential Aptitude Test Career Planning Program (DAT CPP).* The DAT, discussed earlier in this chapter, can be purchased with an accompanying Career Planning Questionnaire (CPQ). The DAT and the CPQ can be used either separately or together. When used together, the integrated results can help people, especially those in the early stages of career exploration, to link interests and abilities.

Selecting an Interest Inventory

Selecting the best interest inventory from the wide range of useful and well-regarded instruments can be challenging. Factors to consider include age, reading ability, and level of career maturity of the client; reliability of the inventory; cost; ease of administration and interpretation; availability of special editions; reading level of the inventory; underlying theory of career development; supplementary materials; method of reducing culture and gender bias; nature and presentation of information; goals of the assessment (e.g., promoting exploration, confirming career choices, refining plans, expanding options); and counselor preference.

The most widely used interest inventory, by far, is the SII, but the Kuder interest inventories, the CAI, the SDS, and the COPS Interest Inventory also are widely used (Engen et al., 1982). The SII and the CAI have been commended for their ability to suggest nontraditional as well as traditional occupations for women (Galassi, Jones, & Britt, 1985). Each of the popular interest inventories has special features. Counselors are encouraged to review manuals and evaluations for at least four or five interest inventories to familiarize themselves with the available features and to help them select the best inventory for their purposes.

Personality Inventories

Personality has an important impact on career development and success as do interests and abilities. A person with good social skills who enjoys creative challenges will probably not find rewarding employment on an assembly line, whereas a person who tends to be shy and withdrawn, avoiding ambiguity and conflict, will not gravitate toward working in customer relations in a large business. Although the literature supports the consideration of personality as part of career counseling, the research on the relationship between personality and career development gives little clear direction as to how to explore personality and its impact on career development.

Influence of Personality on Career Development

According to Spokane and Hawks (1990), career decisions seem to have a "transactional fluid quality" that is moderated by personality style, self-esteem, and anxiety (p. 112). Personality influences how people approach making career decisions, their estimates of their likelihood of succeeding at particular endeavors, the nature of their performance on their jobs, their relationships with supervisors and co-workers, and their enjoyment of their work. However, research has not yet found the direct correspondence between personality and occupation that it has between interests and occupations.

The many studies conducted on the occupational distribution of personality types, as measured by the Myers-Briggs Type Indicator (MBTI) (see *Journal of Psychological Type* for examples), make clear that nearly all occupations have several characteristic personality types that are overrepresented, whereas others are underrepresented. For example, counselors are most heavily concentrated in the MBTI NF (intuitive, feeling) type of personality, whereas business leaders are far more likely to be TJ (thinking, judging) types (McCaulley, 1990). However, counselors who urge people with NF preferences to become counselors and those with TJ preferences to go into business are misunderstanding the relationship between personality and occupations.

Although members of the same occupational groups tend to be more like each other in terms of their personality traits than are people engaged in different occupations, a wide range of personality types can be found in any occupation. Personality seems to have a greater bearing on the sequence of career decisions that are made and on how career development is refined rather than on the specific occupational choices themselves. For example, a person with a TJ preference on the MBTI but an interest in counseling might well enter and succeed in the profession of counseling but might focus on the administrative and research aspects of the profession rather than on the interpersonal ones. In a sense, interests are the array or menu of choices that are considered by people, whereas personality determines how they view that menu and which courses they select at a given time.

Another reason for the lack of a strong relationship between personality and occupational choice is the nature of personality inventories. Generally, measures of personality are less reliable, less valid, more subject to faking, less well integrated with theories of career development, more subject to contamination by situational effects, and more threatening than measures of abilities and interests. In addition, personality inventories may provide information on preferences rather than on actual behavior. In light of all this, it is not surprising that correlations between personality inventories and inventories of abilities and interests are not high.

Nevertheless, Holland and others have demonstrated that people whose occupational environments are congruent with their personality styles tend to be more satisfied with their careers. Personality inventories can be useful, then, in helping people identify work settings in which they are likely to be successful and also in helping people understand the nature of dissatisfaction or disappointment they might be experiencing with their careers. An example is the case, presented in Chapter 8, of a man who was unhappy, although successful with his career in business because it failed to meet his needs for helping and communicating with others.

Selection and Use of Personality Inventories

Personality inventories can be a useful addition to career counseling, as long as those inventories are both chosen and used with care. When selecting a personality inventory, counselors should pay particular attention to levels of reliability and validity, methods of test construction designed to minimize or detect faking, the nature of the questions, and the personality variables that are measured. Personality inventories sometimes evoke feelings of anxiety or anger in people who believe that they might be exposed or given negative information about themselves. In light of this, ample time should be allowed for people to explore and discuss their reactions to the personality scores and both similarities and differences between how they were depicted by the personality inventory and the images they have of themselves.

Although racial bias is seldom an issue in personality measurement, many personality inventories, especially the projective inventories, probably have little relevance to people from non-Western backgrounds (Hood & Johnson, 1991). In addition, particularly with women as well as with people from multicultural backgrounds, counselors should carefully discuss the clients' own stereotyped or negative views of themselves that might be inhibiting factors in their career development.

Personality inventories, like measures of ability and interest, should not be overemphasized and always should be considered in conjunction with other available data. Because most personality inventories are not directly linked to career options, counselors will have to make good use of their insight and exploratory skills in helping people apply personality data to themselves and their careers.

A battery of various types of tests and inventories often can be very helpful to people who are having difficulty formulating and implementing sound career plans. Used in an integrated fashion, interest inventories can be can be viewed as providing information on the *what*; personality inventories, on the *why*; and ability tests, on the *how* of career development. However, the importance of using all these powerful tools with knowledge, wisdom, sensitivity, and caution cannot be overemphasized.

Types of Personality Inventories

For purposes of this book, the term *personality inventory* will be used broadly to include any inventory that measures personal, social, emotional, behavioral, or maturational dimensions of a person. These inventories can be divided into the following categories:

    I. General personality inventories
    II. Clinical personality inventories
       A. Objective tests
       B. Projective tests
    III. Specialized personality inventories
       A. Values inventories
       B. Inventories of self-esteem
       C. Wellness and leisure inventories
       D. Other inventories of personality
    IV. Measures of career maturity and development

General Personality Inventories

General personality inventories are designed to provide a broad-based picture of the personalities of people who are not assumed to have significant emotional difficulties. A survey of 48 master's degree programs in counseling psychology indicated that objective personality measurement was seen as a crucial skill, and 38% of the programs surveyed anticipated a growing interest in the use of objective personality assessment, both general and clinical (Piotrowski & Keller, 1984). The most used general personality inventories include the California Psychological Inventory (CPI), the 16 Personality Factor (16PF), the Edwards Personal Preference Schedule (EPPS), and the MBTI (Watkins et al., 1988). General personality inventories are useful in providing counselors and their clients with a broad look at personality, mapping out a person's preferred style of coping. Many of these inventories deliberately use nonpejorative language to maximize comfort with scores, whatever they might be.

1. *Adjective Checklist (ACL)*. Published by Consulting Psychologists Press, this 20-minute inventory consists of 300 adjectives. Recently developed interpretive reports for this inventory allow people to provide comparative descriptions of how they see themselves, their ideal selves, and how they are perceived by a spouse or significant person in their lives. Scores provide information on overall personality as well as on behavioral tendencies and psychological needs. This will be discussed further in Chapter 9.

2. *California Psychological Inventory (CPI)*. Developed by Harrison C. Gough and published by Consulting Psychologists Press, this well-established inventory was first published in 1956 and revised in 1987. The CPI was one of the first inventories to assess personality traits within the general population. The CPI provides information on 20 basic aspects of personality and four lifestyles (alpha—dependable, enterprising, outgoing; beta—reserved, responsible, moderate; gamma—adventurous, pleasure seeking, restless; and delta—private, withdrawn, disaffected) (Van Hutton, 1990). Special-purpose scales, including managerial potential, work orientation, leadership, and creativity, are particularly useful in career counseling. This inventory seems helpful for assessing personal style, goals, motivation, and drive of high school and college students. According to Van Hutton (1990), this inventory is "one of the best of its kind . . . has been researched extensively and is potentially useful for counselors" (p. 76).

3. *Edwards Personal Preference Schedule (EPPS)*. The EPPS, published by Psychological Corporation, was derived from a needs theory developed by Murray and his associates (Murray & Kluckhohn, 1953) and was developed to measure 15 relatively independent normal personality variables. The EPPS consists of 225 pairs of statements; respondents choose the statement in each pair that they believe to be more characteristic of themselves. The format and interpretation of this inventory is difficult, and despite extensive research, it has received mixed reviews. Although well known, its use in career counseling seems to be declining.

4. *Myers-Briggs Type Indicator (MBTI)*. Published by Consulting Psychologists Press and based on Carl Jung's theory of personality, the MBTI was developed by Katharine C. Briggs and Isabel Briggs Myers, a mother and daughter. The MBTI is now one of the most widely used invento-

ries for normal populations (McCaulley, 1990). It is used not only in career counseling but also for leadership training and team building, personal counseling, relationship enhancement, and personal growth workshops. Its appeal lies, at least in part, in its assumption that all personality preferences are equally valuable. The MBTI yields scores on four bipolar dimensions: introversion-extroversion, sensing-intuition, thinking-feeling, and judging-perceiving. Combinations of these scores are translated into 16 personality types. The goal of the MBTI is to help people discover, understand, and appreciate their natural styles. Further information on the MBTI will be provided in Chapter 8.

Although use of the MBTI in career counseling remains experimental (Healy, 1989), numerous studies have been conducted relating the MBTI to other measures of personality and interest, and most people seem to respond positively to the MBTI, viewing it as providing information they can use in their career decision making. Levin (1990) suggested that the MBTI could complement the SII by providing "within occupation information" (p. 1), guiding choice of setting and specialization. Supplementary materials facilitate the use of the MBTI in career counseling. A *Narrative Report for Organizations* gives information on the effect of a person's preference scores in the work setting, including preferred styles of communication, leadership, and problem solving. An atlas of the MBTI is available, indicating type distribution of many occupations. A children's version, the *Murphy-Meisgeier Type Indicator for Children*, is available for use in Grades 2 though 8.

5. *Sixteen Personality Factor (16PF).* The 16PF is part of a family of general personality inventories published by the Institute for Personality and Ability Testing (IPAT). The 16PF, first published in 1949, was developed by R. B. Cattell as a measure of normal adult personality. It yields scores on 16 basic dimensions of personality, viewed as independent and meaningful measures (Fleenor, 1986). A computer-interpreted version of the 16PF, the Personal Career Development Profile (PCDP), compares the test takers' 16PF profile with those of people in a broad range of occupations and provides other information relevant to career development, such as ways of coping with stress and problem solving. Although the validity of the PCDP has not yet been established, it may prove to be a useful enhancement to the 16PF.

Versions of the 16PF are available for people under the age of 16, among the few general personality inventories designed for children that have been extensively researched. The *High School Personality Ques-*

tionnaire, discussed in Chapter 6, was designed for ages 12 to 18; the *Children's Personality Questionnaire,* for ages 8 to 12; and the *Early School Personality Questionnaire,* for ages 6 to 8. Although the validity of these inventories has not yet been well established, they are widely used, relatively easy to administer and score, and useful in promoting self-awareness and providing information on behavioral styles, interpersonal relationships, self-perceptions, and coping mechanisms of young people (Drummond, 1986).

6. *Vocational Preference Inventory (VPI).* Developed by John Holland, the VPI (available from Consulting Psychologists Press) is a personality inventory linked to his hexagonal model of occupational and personal environments. Used less than the SDS, the VPI is best used in individual career and clinical counseling settings and yields more information on personality than does the SDS.

Clinical Personality Inventories

Clinical personality inventories are those designed especially to provide information on the emotional difficulties of troubled people. Although career counselors will make little use of these inventories, they should be familiar with them for use when appropriate. They are widely used and important tools for assessment. These inventories can be either objective or projective. Objective inventories have a predetermined system of scoring that is clear and straightforward, whereas the projective tests usually yield more ambiguous results and their scoring and interpretation may require extensive training. Typically, projective tests are used by psychologists rather than by counselors.

1. *Minnesota Multiphasic Personality Inventory—II (MMPI—II).* The MMPI, published by NCS, is the inventory most used by counseling psychologists (Watkins et al., 1988). The classic objective test of personality, the MMPI is the most researched psychological test (Hood & Johnson, 1991). The MMPI, revised in 1989, consists of 567 true-false items designed to identify symptoms and diagnose pathology. Scales focus on areas such as depression, potential for addiction, level of adjustment, and psychosis. Of particular interest to career counselors is the Minnesota Report Personnel Selection System, an interpretive scoring system of the MMPI that can be used to screen applicants for high-risk, high-stress occupations, such as law enforcement officer, physician, or

firefighter. Duckworth (1991) called the MMPI "the best that psychometric expertise has to offer" (p. 566).

2. *Millon Clinical Multiaxial Inventory—II (MCMI—II)*. Another comprehensive and objectively scored clinical personality inventory, the MCMI—II, published by NCS, was developed by Theodore Millon, who specializes in the study and treatment of personality disorders. The MCMI—II, described as useful and generally valid (Millon, 1992), is particularly appropriate for the diagnosis and treatment of people with personality disorders.

3. *Specialized Clinical Inventories*. A broad range of specialized inventories has been developed in recent years to assess specific emotional or behavioral difficulties. Important, representative, and useful examples include the Beck Depression Inventory (Psychological Corporation), the State-Trait Anxiety Inventory (Consulting Psycholgists Press), and the Eating Inventory (Psychological Corporation).

4. *Projective Tests*. These tests typically present test takers with ambiguous stimuli, such as ink blots, drawings, or sentence stems, and ask for their perceptions or reactions to the stimuli. Considerable clinical skill is needed to administer and interpret these inventories. They are usually given by psychologists as part of a diagnostic assessment of a person with significant emotional or academic difficulties. Frequently used projective tests include the Rorschach Technique, the Thematic Apperception Test, and the Rotter Incomplete Sentences Blank, all published by Psychological Corporation; the House-Tree-Person exercise; and the Bender Visual Motor Gestalt Test, from the American Orthopsychiatric Association. Only about one third of counseling psychologists use projective tests (Watkins et al., 1988).

Specialized Personality Inventories

Values Inventories. "Work values have long been recognized as a critical concept in career planning and development" (Pine & Innis, 1987, p. 280). Clarification of work values can be instrumental in helping people make rewarding career choices. In their theory of work adjustment, for example, Dawis and Lofquist (1984) and their colleagues suggested that the better the match between workers' values and the reinforcers of a job, the better would be the workers' adjustment. Satisfaction with one's career development also has been viewed as being positively correlated with satisfaction of needs and values (Betz et al., 1989). Values can be influenced by personal, sociological, cultural, economic, and historical factors. Overall, the 1980s saw a growth in the United States in the value of self-fulfillment and helping others. At the same time, however, the competitive employment market led to increased emphasis on economic rewards and power among college students. Since the 1960s, opposite shifts have been noted in the values of men and women. Whereas women are focusing increasingly on power, achievement, and financial rewards, the value men place on self-actualization, beauty, and altruism is increasing.

Values tend to stabilize during middle adolescence and by the middle school or high school years, identification and exploration of values can promote career development (Sampson & Loesch, 1981). However, value shifts in midlife are common as people focus more on their individual needs and are less influenced by societal values and expectations (L. V. Yates, 1990).

To incorporate values effectively into career counseling, counselors need to help people clarify their values and also help them gather the occupational information they need to determine the likelihood of given career paths being congruent with their values. Zytowski (1970a) divided work values into three categories that continue to provide a useful framework for discussion:

1. extrinsic values (e.g., security, prestige, economic return)
2. intrinsic values (e.g., independence, creativity, personal growth, learning, responsibility)
3. concomitants (e.g., surroundings, associates, management, supervision)

A growing number of values inventories have been developed to help counselors and their clients identify and clarify values.

1. *Career Orientation Placement and Evaluation Survey (COPES).* Part of the COPSystem, the COPES, discussed further in Chapter 5, was designed to measure work and personal values relevant to career motivation. Designed primarily for students in junior high, high school, and the early years of college, this instrument assesses values on eight scales (e.g., leadership vs. supportive, recognition vs. privacy) and has been viewed

as a moderately good values measurement inventory, although its use in conjunction with other sources of information was emphasized (Mueller, 1985).

2. *Hall Occupational Orientation Inventory.* Published by Scholastic Testing Service (STS), the HALL, discussed further in Chapter 6, is based on the theories of Abraham Maslow and Ann Roe as well as on the U.S. Department of Labor information on worker traits and job characteristics. The HALL views work as a way of achieving psychological fulfillment. Available in three versions (Intermediate for Grades 3-7, Young Adult/College, and Adult Basic with simplified reading), supplementary materials facilitate the relationship of values to occupations.

3. *Minnesota Importance Questionnaire (MIQ).* Based on Dawis and Lofquist's (1984) studies of job satisfaction and published by Vocational Psychology Research, this tool measures 20 work needs and six broad factors (achievement, comfort, status, altruism, safety, and autonomy).

4. *The Salience Inventory (SI).* Developed by Donald Super and D. D. Nevill and published by Consulting Psychologists Press, this inventory grew out of Super's (1982) International Work Importance Study. It assesses participation, commitment, and values expectations in five roles: studying, working, community service, home and family, and leisure activities. The SI can help people to look at the relative importance of their roles and determine whether the way they spend their time is consistent with their values and preferences.

5. *The Values Scale (VS).* Another product of the international research of Nevill and Super and published by Consulting Psychologists Press, the VS provides information on 21 scales measuring values or satisfaction that people seek in life (use of abilities, achievement, advancement, aesthetics, altruism, authority, autonomy, creativity, economic rewards, lifestyle, personal development, physical activity, prestige, risk, social interaction, social relations, variety, working conditions, cultural identity, physical prowess, and economic security). Drummond (1988) concluded, the VS is a "potentially useful instrument in career and developmental counseling even though the instrument now has some technical problems" (p. 138).

In addition to inventories focusing primarily on work values, many inventories are available that focus on personal values. Well-known examples of these inventories include the Study of Values by Allport, Vernon, and Lindzey (1960); the Survey of Personal Values and the Survey of Interpersonal Values by Gordon (1960a, 1960b); and the Personal Orientation Inventory by Shostrom (1963). All seem to be useful as springboards for discussion but have psychometric limitations (Kavanagh, 1980). In addition, Moos (1987) has developed several surveys of environmental values and preference that can provide another view of people's work-related needs, particularly in cases of people who are dissatisfied with their careers.

Inventories of Self-Esteem. Since the 1950s research of Donald Super, career counselors seem to agree that self-esteem and self-efficacy are important determinants of career choice. Chiu (1988) defined self-esteem as "the evaluative component of the self-concept" (p. 298). People may have interests and abilities that point in a particular career direction, but unless they can envision themselves successfully and happily engaged in that occupation, they are unlikely to pursue it. Discussion probably is the primary vehicle for exploration of self-image. Inventories of self-esteem seem more suited to research or classroom screening purposes and may not have sufficient reliability or validity for use with a single person. Caution should be used, then, when interpreting inventories of self-esteem. The following are widely used self-esteem inventories.

1. *Coopersmith Self-Esteem Inventories (SEI).* Available in forms for ages 8 to 15 and for adults, this inventory (published by Consulting Psychologists Press) measures the evaluation that people generally hold of themselves. Chiu (1988) report positively on the reliability and validity of this instrument.

2. *Piers-Harris Children's Self-Concept Scale.* This well-known inventory, available from Western Psychological Services, can be used for children in Grades 3 through 12 and was written at a third-grade reading level.

3. *Tennessee Self-Concept Scale.* This inventory, published by Western Psychological Services, is for people age 12 and up. Its goal is to measure a multidimensional construct of self-concept (physical self, moral-ethical

self, personal self, family self, and social self) and has been found very useful in counseling (Gellen & Hoffman, 1984).

Wellness and Leisure Inventories. Career counseling has increasingly become a holistic endeavor, helping people establish health, leisure, personal, and family goals that are compatible with their career goals. Especially for counselors working with adults, inventories of wellness and leisure can provide a useful source of information. The following represents a selection of these inventories: the Wellness Inventory, published by Wellness Associates; the Lifestyle Assessment Questionnaire (LAQ), developed by Elsenrath, Hettler, and Leafgreen (1988) and published by the National Wellness Institute; and the Lifestyle Coping Inventory, also published by the National Wellness Institute. The LAQ is typical of these and yields information on the following 10 dimensions: physical fitness, nutrition, self-care, drugs and driving, social-environmental, emotional awareness, emotional control, intellectual, occupational, and spiritual.

Other Inventories of Personality. Counselors attempting to facilitate the career development of students might benefit from assessing the *academic habits and attitudes* of their clients, especially if a disparity is evident between abilities and goals. According to Hughes, Redfield, and Martray (1989), "approximately 44%-75% of the variability in academic achievement is unexplained by intelligence test scores or standardized test data" (p. 137). Several useful inventories are available. The Study Attitudes and Methods Survey, for example, assesses six factors associated with academic success: academic interest-love of learning, academic drive-conformity, study methods, study anxiety, manipulation, and alienation toward authority. Available through Ed-ITS, this inventory can help students in junior high school, high school, or college to eliminate nonacademic barriers to their scholastic success. A similar inventory is the Survey of Study Habits and Attitudes, also from EdITS.

Thinking, learning, and decision-making style are other factors that can interfere with academic performance. These factors have been receiving increasing attention in recent years as their impact on performance is appreciated. Tools such as the Decision Making Inventory, published by Marathon Consulting Press, and Kolb's (1976) Learning Style Inventory, published by McBer, can facilitate teaching and placement of students that will maximize their chances for success.

Counselors working primarily with adult clients frequently will encounter presenting problems of discouragement, frustration, and confusion about goals and direction. Useful inventories for *adults in midlife transitions* include the Occupational Stress Inventory, published by PAR, and the Maslach Burnout Inventory and Staff Burnout Scale, published by Consulting Psychologists Press. The Maslach Burnout Inventory, much studied over the last 10 years, is a brief inventory that assesses emotional exhaustion, depersonalization, and lack of personal accomplishment, key ingredients in burnout.

Counselors working with businesses or employment agencies may encounter *integrity tests*, given by employers to assess prospective workers' attitudes toward honesty, reliability, and rules in the workplace. Although approximately 40 such tests exist, they are quite controversial and many believe they have been used unfairly (Wakelee-Lynch, 1990).

Career counselors also might want to be aware of the growing number of inventories designed to assess *marital satisfaction and adjustment*. Often, people seek career counseling as a result of marital difficulties that raise their awareness of their need for other sources of satisfaction and income. Although career counselors are not likely to make much use of these inventories, unless they have special training in family counseling, they might be working collaboratively with a family counselor who is helping a client with relationship problems.

Measures of Career Maturity and Development

Savickas (1984) defined career maturity as "readiness to cope with vocational development tasks" (p. 222). Career maturity seems related to vocational identity, a construct that has been defined as "an awareness of, and ability to specify one's own interests, personality characteristics, strengths, and goals as these relate to career choices" (Leong & Morris, 1989, p. 117). Sometimes people will seem to be stuck in terms of their career development. They may have little awareness of themselves or of the world of work and may experience unusual difficulty in making decisions. One of the growing number of inventories of career maturity may be useful to clarify the barriers encountered by these people and help counselors determine how best to help them.

1. *Adult Career Concerns Inventory (ACCI).* Developed by Super, Thompson, and Lindeman (1988) and published by Consulting Psychologists Press, the ACCI measures concerns related to the adult career development stages of exploration, establishment, maintenance, and disengagement as described by Super. The ACCI is based on Super's concept of career adaptability in adults and can be useful with adults who need help in understanding, managing, rethinking, and changing their careers (Super et al., 1988). According to Whiston (1990), "The ACCI has the potential to be a very useful instrument, depending on future research" (p. 79).

2. *Assessment of Career Decision Making (ACDM).* Originally developed by Vincent Harren and published by Western Psychological Services, this instrument was designed to help high school and college students identify their decision-making styles and measure their progress in adjusting to school, choosing a career, and choosing a major. R. W. Johnson (1987) wrote of the ACDM, "[this instrument] accomplishes the purpose for which it was intended as well as does any other measure of career development" (p. 568).

3. *Career Decision Scale (CDS).* Developed by Samual H. Osipow and published by Psychology Assessment Resources, the CDI was designed to identify barriers in the educational and occupational decisions of high school and college students. According to Allis (1984), "The CDS is a useful counseling tool for focusing an individual's attention on which circumstances are causing the indecision and for directing efforts aimed at ameliorating those particular issues" (p. 100).

4. *Career Development Inventory (CDI).* A tool that grew out of Super's Career Patterns Study, the CDI, published by Consulting Psychologists Press, was designed to facilitate the career decision making of adolescents and young adults, people in the exploratory stage of career development. The CDI measures four basic dimensions of career maturity: planfulness, exploration, decision making, and information.

5. *Career Maturity Inventory (CMI).* Developed by John Crites and published by CTB/McGraw-Hill, the CMI measures both career maturity and career decision-making ability. Although this inventory has been much used and studied, concern has been expressed about the

close relationship between career maturity, as measured on the CMI, and cognitive development. More research seems indicated on this potentially useful instrument.

6. *My Vocational Situation (MVS).* The MVS, developed by John Holland, has been described as a short, easily scored instrument "that attempts to assess problems with career development in the following three areas: vocational identity, occupational information, and barriers to an occupational goal" (Lucas, Gysbers, Buescher, & Heppner, 1988, p. 163). This inventory is being used with increasing frequency in career counseling. See Chapter 6 for more information.

Computer-Assisted Assessment

Computers are playing an increasing role in assessment. Many of the inventories described in this chapter are available in computer-assisted versions with administration, scoring, and even interpretation available through an on-site computer. In addition, several computer-based career information systems (CBCISs), including assessment tools and information giving, are becoming widely available, especially in high schools and colleges.

The two CBCISs that seem to have received the most attention in the literature are DISCOVER and SIGI (System of Interactive Guidance and Information) Plus. DISCOVER, published by the ACT program and described as a complete career planning system is available for junior high and middle school students, for high school students and for college students and adults. Able to be used by groups or individuals, DISCOVER, like most of the other CBCISs, requires no prior experience with computers. DISCOVER for High Schools is similar to the other two versions and includes seven modules: beginning the career journey, learning about the world of work, learning about yourself, finding occupations, learning about occupations, making educational choices, and planning next steps.

SIGI Plus, available through ETS, is a comprehensive program consisting of nine modules: introduction, self-assessment, search/what occupations might I like, information on nature and requirements of occupations, skills needed for occupations and self-ratings, preparing to enter an occupation, coping/can I do what is required, deciding, and next steps/putting the plan into action.

Other CBCISs include Career Exploration and Planning Program, available from Meridian Education Corporation; Career Information System from the University of Oregon; C-LECT from Chronicle Guidance Publications; CHOICES from the Canada Systems Group; and the Guidance Information System, available through Houghton Mifflin.

Although a CBCIS can be costly, at least $2,000 for the first year of use, in settings where career counseling with large numbers of people is done, the system can be an invaluable aid to both counselors and clients, increasing the efficiency of counseling and giving people more control and independence over their efforts to increase their self-awareness and their knowledge of the world of work and to formulate viable career plans.

Nonstandardized Methods of Assessment

Although assessment in career counseling generally means the use of published and standardized inventories, many nonstandardized approaches are available that can enhance the counseling process. Not only can they promote exploration and self-awareness, but, especially with people who are uncomfortable with standardized inventories or who might be harmed by stereotyping inherent in those inventories, nonstandardized approaches to assessment can build rapport and advance counseling goals. The following are some of these methods.

1. *Vocational Card Sort (VCS).* The VCS consists of a group of cards listing occupations, purchased or developed by the counselor, that can be used with individuals or groups to clarify career-related interests, values, and needs. Participants initially sort cards into three piles—occupations I would consider for myself, those I would not consider, and those that are questionable. Then each pile is taken one at a time and subsorted, with each pile reflecting a common reason why the person would or would not consider those occupations (Dewey, 1974). Goldman (1990) described the VCS as the most well-developed qualitative method of assessment available to career counselors. Commercially available versions of the card sort include the Missouri Occupational Card Sort (Career Planning and Placement Service, University of Missouri—Columbia), the Occ-U-Sort (Publishers Test Service), and the Non-Sexist Vocational Card Set (see Non-Sexist Vocational Card Set in Appendix B). The use of a VCS will be discussed in Chapter 9.

2. *Daydreams and Mental Imagery.* These can be useful in clarifying career goals and seem to be increasing in use (Skovholt, Morgan, & Negron-Cunningham, 1989). Nearly everyone daydreams about the future, and those dreams can be a useful source of information. Images can be elicited in many different ways. People can simply be asked about their occupational daydreams. They can be led through systematic relaxation followed by guided imagery that is designed to help them imagine their future career paths. Drawing pictures of future roles or assuming those roles in a group career counseling setting are other approaches. Some people are reluctant to participate in these activities; they may find them uncomfortable, difficult, or inappropriate in the counseling process. Counselors can increase cooperation by explaining the rationale for these activities, giving people an opportunity to discuss their reactions to these exercises, and providing patience and prompts that are likely to elicit occupational fantasies.

3. *Lifeline.* This is another useful tool (Goldman, 1990). In this exercise, participants draw a horizontal line to reflect an average level of satisfaction. Then they draw a line looking something like a fever chart with peaks reflecting happy and rewarding experiences and valleys mirroring disappointments. The height of a peak or valley would reflect the impact of the experience it represents. A lifeline can be developed that encompasses both a person's life to date and the future that person anticipates. Considerable material for discussion should be generated by this exercise.

4. *Genograms.* Genograms are useful devices not only for describing family relationships but also for delineating family roles, educational experiences, career patterns, and sources of success and satisfaction (Okiishi, 1987). An understanding of family careers can help people clarify the impact that family messages and role models are having on their career and can facilitate understanding of and commitment to personally rewarding career choices.

Many other exercises are available to facilitate career development. In addition, counselors can feel free to be creative in developing their own exercises. Although many of these exercises are enjoyable, counselors should ensure that the goals of counseling guide the use of these qualitative tools and that ample time is allowed to process the strong reactions they might evoke in people.

FOUR

Childhood

*Years of Identification
and Differentiation*

Freud called the years from ages 6 to 12 the latency period and viewed this stage of development as a relatively quiescent one. Research since that time, however, suggests that the early school years are ones of significant growth and change. These are the years when the foundation is built for future academic and social accomplishments and when attitudes and competencies are established that will have a lasting effect on career development.

Early Childhood Development

Before entering prekindergarten or kindergarten, most children have little contact with teachers and no contact with counselors. Counselors rarely have an opportunity to contribute to the development of children during the first 3 to 5 years of life, except through the parents. However, counselors still need some understanding of developmental trends during the early years so that they are better able to assess children's progress when they do begin school and come into contact with teachers and counselors. Even at 3, 4, or 5 years of age, children bring with them years of emotional, physical, and intellectual growth that takes place under the influence of families and communities.

According to Erikson's (1963) well-established model of human development, children already have passed through two of the eight developmental stages and are in the third stage when they enter school. The first stage revolves around the development of what Erikson called basic trust. Generally, children who spend their first few years acquiring some independence and mobility in an environment that is safe and secure, meeting their important needs, will develop the ability to trust. This first stage, extending from birth to about 18 months of age, probably affects the nature of children's future interpersonal relationships and their feelings about themselves and their environments. Children who pass through this stage in a positive way are likely to become optimistic, open, and positive as they mature (Hamachek, 1988).

Erikson termed the second stage or crisis in his model autonomy versus shame and doubt. Proper toilet training seems crucial to successful negotiation of this stage that extends from 18 months to about 3 years of age. Children who learn that they can successfully control their bodily functions and who feel gratified by these early achievements tend to develop self-confidence and self-reliance. They have learned that they need not be entirely dependent on their parents but can exert self-control, and as they mature, they are likely to become assertive, independent, and task oriented. At the same time, they are likely to develop the capacity for loving, cooperative relationships. All of these traits can make important contributions to children's social, academic, and occupational futures. However, those children who come to view bodily functions and their own lack of self-control as shameful are likely to develop doubt, anxiety, and low self-esteem.

Initiative versus guilt is the third and last of the preschool stages in Erikson's model, extending from about the age of 3 to age 6. Crucial to this stage are the nature of children's identification with their same-gender parents and the children's freedom to explore and imagine. This stage, too, is important in the development of children's self-images and self-esteem. Those children who develop confidence in their own initiative are more likely to enter school ready to enjoy the challenge of that new experience. They will probably be self-starters and good leaders and will have a sense of direction and energy (Hamachek, 1988). They will have developed a conscience or a sense of right and wrong that will enable them to monitor their own behavior with little assistance. The importance of this stage to people's eventual roles as worker, colleague, and supervisor is obvious.

In addition to their emotional development, children entering school bring with them certain skills that they have acquired during their early years at home. Most have learned to play cooperatively and know how to participate as members of a group. They have coped with jealousy, anger, and anxiety and have begun to learn to deal effectively with negative feelings. They have experienced several roles (child, grandchild, friend, sibling) and have had to adjust to role changes, perhaps with the arrival of a new sibling or through changes in the expectations their parents hold for them. They have experienced both achievement and failure and already have begun to assess their potential and need for achievement. Considerable growth has taken place in both thought and language, although at the time of school entry, thinking is still based largely on what can be seen and language is still primarily focused on the self.

Development During the Middle Childhood Years

Children entering school are individuals in many ways. They have characteristic personalities and have patterns of coping and responding. However, children aged 4, 5, or 6 are egocentric, and most know little of the world outside of their families and neighborhoods. When they enter school, children become part of new social systems. They must adjust to school and peer groups without the security of parental protection. For most children, this adjustment involves the development of both their self-awareness and their ability to empathize and communicate with others.

Self-Concept and Self-Esteem

During the middle childhood years, most children are very concerned with reward and approval, especially from parents and teachers. Because children have not yet developed clear standards of their own, they tend to accept the standards of those around them. For most, parental standards are most important. Children who come from homes that are warm, accepting, and encouraging of individuality as well as consistent in enforcement of realistic standards and appropriate limits seem most likely to develop positive self-concepts. Children who have high self-esteem "respect themselves and consider themselves worthy . . . feel competent . . . and have a sense of belonging" (Chiu, 1987, p. 36). Children who come from backgrounds where the expectations are meager, inconsistent, or unattainable tend to lose confidence in themselves and may fail to develop high self-esteem.

Peer group standards and approval become important during the elementary school years and also contribute to the development of self-image. Chiu found that children's self-esteem correlated with teacher and sociometric ratings of their popularity and concluded: "The more socially successful individual may be expected to be higher in self-esteem and the less socially successful individual to be lower in self-esteem" (p. 40).

The peer group establishes its own system of rules and values, with companionship and a sense of belonging being the rewards for acceptance of peer group standards. Peer group approval can not only enhance the self-esteem of children who are liked and admired but can also be destructive to the self-images of children who are unwilling or unable to meet peer group standards.

Identification with role models is an important vehicle for self-concept development during childhood. Up to the time of school entry, most children have few models and tend to form their strongest identifications with their same-gender parents. Once they begin school, however, a variety of models, both adults and peers, are readily available for identification and emulation. Although parental identification remains strong, with a positive relationship with the mother particularly connected to self-esteem at this age, children develop their self-awareness and clarity of self-image by comparing themselves with others and trying to be more like those they admire and see as powerful.

By the age of 9 or 10, most children have a relatively clear and differentiated self-concept (Seligman, Weinstock, & Heflin, 1991). Freiberg (1991b) found that at the age of 8 or 9, 60% of girls and 67% of boys are confident, assertive, and have positive feelings about themselves. Most children in middle childhood are not beset by the self-doubts and anxiety that are so prevalent during adolescence. At the same time, a marked increase in the rate of suicide for children as young as 10 years of age has been noted (Jackson & Hornbeck, 1989). Some children, then, are having significant emotional and interpersonal difficulties during the relatively benign years of middle childhood.

Research has shown that both individual and group interventions can successfully improve self-esteem. Morse, Bockoven, and Bettesworth (1988) studied children both immediately and 6 months after they had experienced an 8-week program of affective education using Developing Understanding of Self and Others (DUSO-2-R). They found that the children made significant and enduring changes in self-esteem, social skills, and independence. Self-esteem, then, can be nurtured through planned activities conducted by teachers and counselors, and these activities seem particularly useful during the middle school years when self-esteem is being established.

Social Development

Erikson (1963) labeled the crisis of the middle school years (ages 6 to 12) industry versus inferiority. Successful resolution of this crisis seems to involve not only self-concept development but also social development. Children learn new skills and tools during these years and become more confident of their own abilities. They learn to take pride in their work; to use persistence, creativity, and feedback to solve problems; and to establish a balance of work and play in their lives. This is a crucial stage in terms of career development because it is the time when most children learn to appreciate the importance of education and competence and develop images of themselves as workers. They learn cooperation and division of labor and become aware of the consequences of failing to do their share on a team or on a project.

The role of the peer group in the development of children's social skills is as important as it is in the development of their self-concepts. During the childhood years, the most influential peer groups are composed primarily of children of the same gender and seem to derive some of their power from establishing guidelines for gender-appropriate behavior. However, the significance of the peer group varies, depending on the age and gender of the child.

Harry Stack Sullivan's (1954) classic research still provides one of the best descriptions of childhood socialization. Sullivan divided the social development of the elementary school years into two stages: the juvenile era and preadolescence. The juvenile era encompasses the first few years of school. During those years, socialization and acculturation are primarily accomplished through the peer group. Group games are particularly important and enjoyable to the child, especially games that are dramatic, exciting, or ritualized.

Sullivan described the preadolescent period as extending roughly from the ages of 9 to 12. During these years, one special friend assumes greater importance than the peer group as a whole. Although most children have a series of best friends during these years, they are intensely loyal and devoted to each friend in turn. This "chumship" stage, as Sullivan called it, signals the decline of early childhood egocentrism and the growth of children's capacity for empathy. They are now concerned with the welfare of someone other than themselves. This stage is important in developing children's capacity for intimacy, altruism, and collaboration.

Although girls tend to have only one or two best friends at a time whereas boys may have several, both are experiencing similar developmental changes. These changes are reflected in their recreation. Group games decline in popularity during these years, and team sports and games involving individual ability and planning are preferred.

Development in Thought
and Judgment During Childhood

Before they enter school, children's thinking passes through two stages that Piaget (1963) termed the "sensori-motor" and "preoperational" stages. During these stages, children base their thinking on what they can see or on what they would like to believe. They make little use of logic or hypothesis, and thoughts may seem inconsistent.

About the age of 6 or 7, the thinking of most children enters the concrete operational stage. Children can now use logic, base their thinking on experience, and imagine points of view other than their own. They can classify, order, and think systematically, although they have yet to develop the ability to hypothesize and still tend to focus on one element at a time. However, their thinking no longer is limited by their perceptions.

Most children enter the third stage of thought, the formal-operations stage, during the years between the ages of 10 and 12. Although some children in this age range are still influenced by preoperational thinking, most show evidence of developing the ability to hypothesize, consider alternate solutions, and perceive when more information is needed. Typically, thinking during these years is less rigid and stereotyped than it is in both younger and older children, and children in the middle years of childhood tend to be very receptive to new ideas (Minuchin, 1977; Seligman et al., 1991).

Between the ages of 7 and 10, most children are intensely moral. They view the world as being governed by rules and are anxious to learn those rules so that they can feel more comfortable in their environments. Rules must be followed in behavior as well as in games, and, often, children will become frustrated and angry if they see that someone is not following the rules. They may appeal to adults to intervene and restore the order they need if other children do not seem to be following the rules properly.

Although most children have developed a strong sense of justice and fairness by the age of 8 or 9, children's administration of justice is based on rules rather than on thought and often is very rigid. Children between the ages of 8 and 10, for example, tend to view all lies as equally wrong and do not distinguish between a lie that is told to avoid hurting another and a lie that is told to deliberately hurt or cheat. By the age of 11 or 12, most children have developed sufficient empathy and understanding of cause-and-effect relationships to enable them to incorporate consideration of motivation and circumstance into their moral judgments. However, until that point, adults should realize that, often, children's apparent harshness and cruelty is a reflection of their incomplete moral development and their need for security, consistency, and control.

Development of Achievement Motivation

The elementary school years seem to be the time when the foundation for future achievement is established. According to Dweck (1986), "Motivational processes have been shown to affect (a) how well children can deploy their existing skills and knowledge, (b) how well they acquire new skills and knowledge, and (c) how well they transfer these new skills and knowledge to novel situations" (p. 1046). The development of an achievement-oriented personality may occur as early as ages 5 to 9 and by the fifth grade, future high and low achievers can be differentiated (Solomon, Scheinfeld, Hirsch, & Jackson, 1971). For most people, their motivation to achieve will have a strong effect on their educational and occupational success. The attitudes toward achievement of elementary school children, then, warrant considerable attention.

Some children, identified as at-risk, are particularly in need of help. These children have experienced a range of risk factors, such as poverty, abuse, family separations, disability, or cultural conflict. As a result, they are more likely to leave school before graduation and are more susceptible to later career difficulties (Spokane & Hawks, 1990). Providing help during the elementary school years may well have a significant positive impact on the futures of these at-risk children. Several approaches have been shown to contribute to the development of positive achievement motivation.

Ameliorate Emotional Difficulties. Society is becoming increasingly aware of the prevalence of physical abuse, sexual abuse, and substance abuse. Children who are depressed or anxious or who have poor attendance because they are living in abusive home environments are not likely to perform well in school. Although school counselors may not have the resources or expertise to help these children, elementary school counselors and teachers are in a good position to observe symptoms of abuse and depression and can then take appropriate steps to obtain help for the child by meeting with the parents, making a referral for mental health services, or, if necessary, contacting child protective services or other groups that are available to handle abusive situations.

Establish Realistic Goals, But Also Expect Children to Perform Up to Capacity. Counselors, parents, and teachers all need to have a clear and accurate understanding of a child's ability and then develop expectations that seem likely to reflect both achievement and success. Establishing clear steps to the achievement of goals and involving children in setting goals and in the evaluation processes can increase motivation. Low or negative expectations and disturbing failures can impair the desire to achieve. The classroom, then, should provide a helpful and supportive environment for learning and experimentation, and mistakes should de-emphasized and viewed as potential learning experiences for the child. Efforts should be made to maintain children's confidence in their learning abilities and their interest in school and avoid raising excessive school-related anxiety.

Parents can contribute to the development of children's achievement motivation by demonstrating interest in their children's schoolwork, encouraging and rewarding their children's achievements, providing surroundings that stimulate and support the children's efforts to achieve (e.g., a quiet place to study, available reading books and reference materials), and having appropriate expectations of success. Some overestimating of children's abilities seems to have a positive effect on children's self-confidence and ambitions. However, parental expectations and aspirations can have a negative effect on their children's achievement motivations if the parents' aspirations for their children are con- siderably higher than their expectations or if their high hopes are not presented in a supportive and accepting context.

Provide Special Programs and Services Early. Research has shown that Head Start and similar programs, providing early educational experiences, can have a significant positive impact on children's later adjustment to school and their achievement motivation and persistence (Scarr & Weinberg, 1986). Programs for low-achieving and underachieving students during the elementary school grades can be similarly helpful. In a review of the literature, N. S. Wilson (1986) concluded that programs associated with successful outcomes were more likely to be structured, behaviorally oriented, at least 12 sessions in length, group focused, and voluntary and to include study skills instruction and parental involvement.

Gifted children have special needs just as do at-risk children. Teachers and parents may not realize that the intellectual and emotional development of these children may take place at different rates and they may not be emotionally ready to handle the high expectations that others have of them. Gifted boys, in particular, commonly have difficulty screening and managing stimuli and may easily become overstimulated (Blackburn & Erickson, 1986). During the fourth and fifth grades, gifted children often have trouble conforming to the structure of the school and may respond with boredom, inattention, and eventual underachievement, affecting about 50% of gifted children in this age group.

The special needs of each gender should be taken into account when encouraging the development of achievement motivation. Generally, mastery, skill development, and independence are reinforced more in boys, whereas affiliation and interpersonal and communication skills seem more likely to be reinforced in girls. Consequently, although girls actually earn better grades than do boys during their early school years, girls tend to achieve for approval, whereas boys are more invested in attaining competence. Girls also tend to be less confident of their abilities than boys and have lower expectations of academic success.

A combination of positive feedback and success experiences can compensate for some of the discrepancies between the development of achievement motivation in girls and boys. For example, girls' need for social approval can be used in such a way as to reinforce feelings of competence and drives for mastery. Counselors can help girls to separate achievement from affiliation by encouraging independent as well as group endeavors. The goal of these efforts is not to make girls just like boys; that stands little prospect of success and can have just the opposite effect by communicating to girls that they need to be different. Rather, the goal is to help girls feel good about both their interpersonal and academic accomplishments and maintain positive images of their competence.

Development of Gender and Sex Role Identity

The development of gender identity seems to begin very early. Within the first few years of life, children develop an awareness of their own gender and by the age of 4 or 5, have formulated ideas on gender-appropriate roles and behavior. Up until about the age of 9, children tend to be very concerned with learning how their gender is supposed to behave and conforming to perceived social expectations for their gender. Models will be sought to guide behavior, and children may emulate a friend's parent, a teacher, a sports figure, or a television star who is admired. Children's sex roles are likely to be rigid and stereotyped during these years, regardless of their family background or experience, and this may be discouraging to parents who have worked hard not to limit the roles of their sons or daughters. However, this rigidity seems to be another reflection of the children's need for guidelines and structure during these years. In an effort to achieve consistency, children may try to bring interests, attitudes, and behaviors into conformity with their stereotyped sex roles. Boys tend to emphasize their aggressive and athletic sides, whereas girls emphasize nurturing, aesthetic, and verbal interests.

Between the ages of 9 and 11, however, children seem to have less need for structure and their conceptions of appropriate sex role behavior relax and broaden; they become more individualized, less dependent on the peer group, and more interested in the other gender (Marantz & Mansfield, 1977). During these years, the impact of schools and families that emphasize a broad range of roles and opportunities for both genders will become evident.

One study of the sex role attitudes of boys and girls in Grades 3 through 6 reflected differences in the relationship between self-esteem and sex role attitudes for each gender (Hughes, Martinek, & Fitzgerald, 1985). Girls who were assertive and believed in multiple roles for women had higher self-esteem than did girls who maintained traditional views of women's roles and believed that women's place was in the home. On the other hand, boys with traditional sex role attitudes tended to have higher self-esteem than did boys with nontraditional views. The authors concluded that the study "suggested a relationship between self-esteem and traditional career choices that is positive for boys and negative for girls" (p. 61) and that "for girls the relationship between self-esteem and nontraditional attitudes is reliably established as early as the primary years in school" (p. 63).

Although most teachers and counselors today are aware of the importance of avoiding sex role bias and many schools bring in speakers and offer programs specifically designed to communicate broad and flexible definitions of gender role, subtle messages may continue to give boys and girls different expectations about their opportunities. For example, Freiberg (1991a) noted that teachers seem to give boys more attention, ask them more questions, and give them more feedback in the classroom. Assignment of chores and expectations of children's play activities are other ways in which stereotyping can unintentionally be transmitted.

Although sex role bias has been condemned largely because of its inhibiting effect on females, the findings of Hughes and colleagues (1985) suggest that boys, too, may suffer the impact of stereotyping if it leads boys with more flexible attitudes to view themselves negatively. In some ways, achieving a positive gender identity may actually be more difficult for boys than for girls. Because most children are still reared primarily by their mothers, the mother becomes the first object for identification. Girls may maintain this identification, but boys must shift the focus to their fathers. Disapproval is greater of boys who act girlish than of girls who act boyish. Boys also may receive more mixed messages than do girls regarding desirable behavior; boys are supposed to be compliant and obedient in the classroom but assertive and energetic outside. Boys may, therefore, need at least as much help as girls in establishing clear, satisfying, and flexible gender identities. Both boys and girls seem to develop the broadest view of sex roles when distinctions between male and female activities are minimized and learning and experience via a wide range of activities is promoted so that individual interests and abilities can emerge and grow.

Children's Career Development

Career development has its roots in the early childhood years. During these years, children develop a view of themselves as workers, evaluate their potential for achievement and the importance that achievement has for them, and begin to acquire those skills that will determine their later success in school and work. The foundations are established for the development of interests and values, and attitudes are formed that affect later occupational and social adjustment. Knowledge is gained of the world of work and of how one might best fit into that world.

Super (1957b) and Ginzberg and his associates (1951), discussed in Chapter 1, were among the first to recognize that career development is a lifelong process that begins in childhood. In the 1970s, the development of career education in the schools helped teachers and counselors to operationalize their awareness that the seeds of adult career development are sown in childhood. Today, most school districts seem to at least acknowledge the need for career education in the elementary schools, although the nature and extent of such programs vary widely. Similarly, most counselors seem aware that they can make a contribution to a child's later occupational success by facilitating career development during childhood.

Fantasy Stage

Children begin to form conceptions of the world of work long before they enter school. They observe the activities of their mothers and fathers at home and listen to their discussion of successes and disappointments at work or at school. Children may notice different patterns of behavior in each parent; one may be away from home each day, whereas the other may be away for only part of the time or may be a full-time homemaker. Children observe the work of people in the neighborhood and watch the workers in the stores when they are taken on shopping trips. By the time children enter school, most are aware that many different kinds of jobs exist and that people have some choice as to what kind of work they will do.

Career development during most of the elementary school years is dominated by what has been termed the fantasy stage. Super (1957b) viewed this stage as extending from the age of 4 to age 10, whereas Ginzberg et al. (1951) placed the fantasy stage between ages 6 and 11. Children express many occupational choices during these years. Often, their earliest choices are derived from parental roles and occupations, whereas later choices tend to be based on the occupations of their heroes. Common occupational choices include football player, television performer, teacher, and doctor. Most boys select active, physically oriented occupations, and most girls express a preference for people-oriented, helping occupations (M. J. Miller, 1989). Workers who seem powerful, skillful, brave, and action oriented are particularly appealing to this age group. Typically, these choices bear little or no relation to children's capacities or activities but, rather, reflect what sounds exciting and pleasurable. Gottfredson (1981) termed this first stage of career development the stage of orientation to size and power and saw it as the stage in which children grasped the concept of being an adult.

Children's occupational preferences expressed during the early and middle childhood years reflect their experiences and knowledge. They have little awareness of barriers or requirements to occupational entry. Needs and wants dominate choices. At the same time, children do tend to rule out occupations that, even at this young age, do not seem gender appropriate. As early as the age of 4 or 5, children see differences in men's and women's roles and begin to make judgments as to appropriate behavior and roles for each gender. Gottfredson termed this second stage of career development, taking place between the ages of 6 and 8, orientation to sex roles, characterized by the development of a gender self-concept.

By the age of 4 or 5, children are also able to articulate personal goals. Most report wanting to marry and have children, and some research has indicated that even at this early age, children report anticipating marriage at a realistic age, having a reasonable number of children, and having viable ideas on combining work and family (Seligman, Weinstock, & Owings, 1988).

During the early years of childhood, home environment and parent-child relations are important factors in career development. Children who came from positive environments, as reflected in drawings of their families, were more likely to be able to articulate plans for both their personal and professional futures than were children who came from troubled families or families with little communication and closeness, especially if those children seemed to have a weak relationship with their fathers (Seligman et al., 1988).

The fantasy stage is a valuable one in that it offers children the opportunity to try out a variety of adult roles without risk. Children seem to derive satisfaction from assuming the powerful roles of their heroes and perhaps borrowing some self-confidence from their idols during this time. Adults should encourage the fantasizing of these years and should avoid introducing reality prematurely. They also should not be dismayed by what may seem to be inappropriate occupational choices, because preferences expressed during these years generally are short-lived.

Interest Stage

When children are between the ages of 10 and 12, their fantasy-based occupational choices diminish and, generally, are replaced by occupational preferences more closely linked to interests. Children become more aware of their likes and dislikes and begin to translate them into career goals. Although both the 12-year-old and the 7-year-old may report that they want to be baseball players, the reasons for their choices probably differ. The 7-year-old may view baseball players as heroes and may crave their competence and apparent importance; this choice often is unrelated to the child's interest in or ability to play baseball. The 12-year-old, however, is in the interest stage of career development and probably is aspiring to a career as a baseball player because baseball is a favorite activity.

Occupational Self-Concepts

By the age of 9, children are well on their way to formulating concepts of their own competencies. Over 80% of 9-year-olds can state things they do well, 75% can indicate how well they perform a specific task in relation to others, and 42% can describe ways they can improve their abilities (M. J. Miller, 1989). Although they also have some awareness of their limitations, 9-year-olds have a better grasp of their strengths (J. Miller, 1977). By the age of 9, most have been involved in a broad range of work-related activities and are familiar with a range of visible occupations. However, children of this age also do not realize that they will have primary responsibility for their career development, and they tend to attribute those decisions to parents and other authority figures.

During the interest stage, children's occupational self-concepts become clearer and better articulated. Influence of parental role models declines and reality testing and other influences on career development increase. By the age of 10, most children have given considerable thought to their futures and have narrowed their occupational preferences, at least temporarily, to only a few options. By the age of 12, most have made tentative occupational choices and can explain the reasons for their choices. Although children in this stage have an awareness of their parents' aspirations for them, many also feel free to express goals that differ from those aspirations (Seligman et al., 1991). Children in this stage have a fairly good understanding of the nature of occupations that interest them and can report, with reasonable accuracy, how much education they would need to enter their chosen occupations. When asked about changes in their occupational aspirations, about half report changes, usually from mastery-related to interest-related occupations.

Career Maturation

Although stages of career development do seem to be related to age, patterns of career maturation vary. Typically, girls, children with well-educated parents, and children with average or better intelligence move from the fantasy to the interest stage earlier than do boys and children with below-average intelligence, although young boys seem to have a clearer idea of their strengths than do young girls (J. Miller, 1977). Even mature preadolescents, however, are generally not able to engage in long-range career planning.

Exposure, as well as developmental readiness, is important to the early acquisition of career information. Children's knowledge of occupations increases as they grow and gain awareness of a greater variety of occupations. This contact can occur through reading, films, and television as well as through direct observation of workers. During the 1970s, books and television programs aimed at a young audience were much criticized for presenting a distorted picture of the world of work in which professional, managerial, and service occupations were overemphasized; skilled trades and clerical and sales occupations were underemphasized; and men and women were presented in traditional roles (Leifer & Lesser, 1976; Tennyson & Monnens, 1973). Since the 1970s, conscious efforts have resulted in portrayal of a broader spectrum of occupations and less traditional roles for men and women in television and in print. Today, women are portrayed as lawyers, physicians, and journalists, and men are depicted in the roles of teacher and home-maker as well as in more traditional roles.

Influence of Values
on Career Development

Values, as well as interests, are a significant determinant of occupational preference during the later elementary school years. Gottfredson (1981) called the third stage of career development, orientation to social valuation, the time between the ages of 9 and 13 when children develop the ability to grasp abstract concepts and to understand social class, abilities, and emotions. The development of occupational values seems to be well underway by the time children are in the fourth or fifth grade. Children in Grades 4 through 6 were found to have developed attitudes toward earnings, occupational status and prestige, working conditions, and opportunities for independence and self-expression through work (Gottfredson, 1981; Kuldau & Hollis, 1971).

Children develop ideas of the prestigiousness of occupations early, and some children can rank occupations by prestige as early as the first grade (Gottfredson, 1981). By the age of 9 or about the fourth grade, most children have developed conceptions of job prestige hierarchies that are similar to those of high school students and adults (R. R. Miller, 1986). Children who already have eliminated some occupations that they view as unsuitable for their gender now circumscribe their choices further, ruling out occupations they believe to have unacceptably low prestige or income or seem incompatible with their social class self-concept.

Children's gender, race, and socioeconomic status have little effect on their occupational prestige rankings. Most children attribute the highest status to occupations such as physician and Supreme Court judge that are viewed as lucrative and able to make an important contribution to society. They perceive occupations involving manual labor, an arduous lifestyle, and potentially unclean conditions (e.g., construction worker, groundskeeper) as low in prestige. By the sixth grade, children have clear ideas of the salaries associated with many occupations, and economic considerations become an important factor in determining their occupational daydreams (Gottfredson, 1981).

Personal Goals
and Family Interactions

Most 10-year-olds have fairly clear personal goals. Most expect to marry and have children, with the majority anticipating marriage between the ages of 20 and 30 and wanting to have two children (Seligman et al., 1991). Both the boys and the girls interviewed by Seligman and her colleagues envisioned combining occupational and family life.

Paternal influence seemed less important than it had been to the 5 year olds, perhaps because power is now less important, whereas a positive relationship with the mother is correlated with having a positive self-image and being able to articulate family-related goals. Children who were closer to their fathers seemed most interested in action-oriented play and pastimes, whereas those children who were closer to their mothers were more interested in people and interactions (Seligman et al., 1991).

Roe (1964) hypothesized that the nature of child-rearing practices experienced by children had an effect on their later occupational choices. Her theory is discussed in greater detail in Chapter 1. Although only limited support has been given to Roe's findings, parental attitudes and behaviors often do seem to exert a very early and powerful influence over children's subsequent career development. For example, a positive correlation was found between aspirations and expectations that parents held for their children and the aspirations and expectations the children held for themselves (Brook, Whiteman, Persach, & Deutsch, 1974). Because most parents want their children to equal or surpass their occupational accomplishments, it is not surprising that most children aspire to occupations that require at least as much education as their parents' occupations.

Gender and Career Development

Gender seems to exert a powerful influence on children's occupational choices and perceptions, perhaps because during the childhood years children are developing a sex role identity and are very concerned with adhering to the social guidelines for their gender. By the age of 4 or 5, children have well-developed universal sex role stereotypes that stabilize by the time the children are 6 or 8 years of age (Farmer, 1985). Children tend to dichotomize the world of work into men's occupations and women's occupations and quickly eliminate occupations they do not see as gender appropriate. Although such thinking is limiting to boys as well as girls, girls are especially prone to engage in occupational foreclosure based on gender, and both boys and girls perceive girls as having fewer career options (R. R. Miller, 1986). Children's awareness of occupations is also influenced by gender, and both boys and girls are more familiar with occupations that are viewed as traditional for their own gender (M. J. Miller, 1989). Although children's occupational gender bias does seem to decrease as they gain greater exposure to adult workers and lose some of their need for order and structure, early occupational choices that were in conformity with traditional gender roles seem to be more persistent than nontraditional choices.

Gender also seems to influence the development of self-esteem during the childhood years. In assessing their competence, for example, 9-year-old boys were more likely to see themselves as more capable than their peers, whereas girls of the same age generally saw themselves as less skilled (M. J. Miller, 1989). Although both boys and girls in the middle childhood years tend to have clear, positive, and differentiated self-concepts, male self-esteem begins to surpass that of females very early (Seligman et al., 1991).

Overview of Career Development

Occupational choices made during the elementary school years have been shown to be determined by many factors, including interests, values, perceptions of occupational status, social class, self-image, achievement motivation, gender, and parental aspirations and occupational levels. Although most children will change their occupational goals before adulthood, some will have chosen their future occupations during these years. Careers in science and medicine are often planned as early as the elementary school years. Whether or not children's career plans persist into adulthood, the childhood years are important ones in the process of career development, and considerable attention to the early stages of this process is warranted.

Developmental Accomplishments of Childhood

The elementary school years are years in which most children accomplish a great deal in terms of their physical, emotional, and intellectual growth as well as their career development. Typically, growth is complex and uneven during these years. Individual differences are considerable and should not be underemphasized by counselors or teachers. However, a common core of growth experiences has been identified that is shared by most of the children in this age group.

Havighurst's (1972) classic book, *Developmental Tasks and Education*, provides a basis for identifying the developmental tasks of children, aged 6 to 12. However, these tasks have been modified here to meet the demands of modern society and to take account of children's career development. The following are developmental tasks of this age group.

1. learning physical skills necessary for common games, chores, and activities
2. developing fundamental skills in reading, writing, mathematics, and the acquisition of new learning
3. developing social skills that enable one to get along with both peers and authority figures
4. developing conscience, morality, and values
5. developing thinking and planning skills
6. developing positive attitudes toward the family, social groups, and institutions
7. developing broad, flexible, and satisfying gender role identity

8. developing attitudes that are conducive to competence, cooperation, and achievement

9. acquiring an awareness and appreciation of one's own developing interests, values, abilities, and personal qualities

10. acquiring basic understanding of workers, their roles, the importance of work in society, and the relationship of interests and values to occupational choice

11. achieving a sense of personal independence and uniqueness as well as an appreciation of individual differences

Counseling for Self-Esteem and Differentiation

The elementary school counselor is a growing phenomenon. In 1964, the equivalent of 1,500 full-time counselors were in elementary schools in the United States. In 1970, 16,800 counselors were in the elementary schools. In the 1980s, many states enacted legislation requiring at least a part-time counselor in all elementary schools. Nevertheless, many elementary schools still have no counselors, and where there are counselors, they are likely to be confronted with a very high counselor-student ratio. For counselors in the elementary school to engage in worthwhile counseling relationships with all of their counselees is impossible in most settings. However, career education does offer counselors a vehicle for providing help to large numbers of students.

Career Education

Career education involves the integration into the curriculum of information, concepts, and experiences designed to promote career development and help students formulate realistic and satisfying career plans and self-concepts. Career education sometimes has been confused with vocational education and has been criticized for detracting from the broad goals of education by emphasizing only work-related skills. Career education also has been criticized for detracting from academic study and promoting premature decision making. These criticisms represent a misunderstanding of the aims of career education. Career education seeks to expand and strengthen the educational process so that it has a greater impact on personal growth and development. Career education does not try to nudge students into early occupational plans;

rather, it seeks to help them develop greater knowledge of themselves, the world of work, and the relationship of the two so that students have a greater opportunity to develop rewarding career plans. It seeks to develop skills and readiness, including autonomy, self-esteem, an internal locus of control, and a future perspective, so that when appropriate, people can make sound decisions (Super, 1983).

Career education was introduced in 1971 by Sidney Marland, then the U.S. commissioner of education. He conceived of career education as an ongoing process that was infused into the entire educational system. Career education is based on the assumption that career development is a lifelong process that can be facilitated by the acquisition of greater knowledge about the self and the world of work.

Marland's (1974) ideas were implemented by the Ohio State Center for Vocational and Technical Education, which developed a framework for career education consisting of eight key elements:

1. career awareness—knowledge of the broad range of occupations and career paths
2. self-awareness—knowledge of the facets of the self
3. appreciations, attitudes—awareness of the self in relation to others and to society
4. decision-making skills
5. economic awareness—knowledge of economic trends and principles, including supply and demand, production, distribution, and consumption
6. skill awareness and beginning competence
7. employability skills—social and communication skills relevant to career planning
8. educational awareness—appreciation of the relationship of education to implementation of career plans and goals

In 1984, the American School Counselors Association urged school counselors to "assume leadership in implementing developmental career guidance programs for all students, beginning no later than kindergarten" (Hoffman & McDaniels, 1991, p. 163). Super (1983) agreed with this position and expressed the belief that developments made during childhood were integral to career maturity. Widespread acceptance of the importance of career education in the elementary school seems present today.

The following are the major goals of career education:

1. promoting relevant exploration of the self and the world of work

2. developing decision making and thinking skills

3. enhancing, elaborating, and clarifying the self-concept

4. promoting identification of one's own interests, capacities, personality, and values and an awareness of their relationships to the world of work

5. developing skills for communication, coping, conflict resolution, and cooperation

6. developing a commitment to learning, achievement, and personal growth

7. increasing actual and perceived competencies and control over one's own life

8. developing appreciation of work and its importance in society

9. reducing stereotyped and distorted thinking about occupations and people's options and opportunities

10. facilitating the development and implementation of viable career plans and a rewarding lifestyle

Career Education in the Elementary School

Although these goals apply to career education at the elementary school level as well as at the middle and high school levels, the focus and emphasis of career education, of course, will differ, depending on the ages and needs of the participants. The primary goal of career education with young children is increased awareness of themselves, of their society, and of the world of work. Although early occupational choices should be viewed as an important expression of children's interests, attitudes, and feelings, career education during the elementary school years should not be designed to encourage occupational choices and decisions. On the contrary, career education with children should involve an expansion of possible options, not a narrowing of possibilities. Limitations, abilities, and aptitudes should be de-emphasized. As M. J. Miller (1989) put it, "the words, 'you can't' or 'that's not possible,' do not belong in elementary school career development and guidance activities" (p. 169).

Important goals of career education with elementary school children include the following:

1. increasing understanding of and interest in the relationships between school subjects, leisure activities, and occupations

2. helping children identify and differentiate their values, interests, and abilities

3. promoting understanding and appreciation of individual differences

4. providing the knowledge, understanding, attitudes, and competencies that children need to function in their current life roles (e.g., son or daughter, family member, sibling, student, classmate, friend, peer group member, team member, classmate, leisurite [Hoffman & McDaniels, 1991])
5. increasing feelings of security, autonomy, and curiosity
6. promoting development of positive work habits, attitudes, and listening and cognitive skills
7. facilitating positive self-esteem, self-confidence, and identity development
8. increasing understanding of the meaning and importance of work
9. developing an awareness of occupational groups
10. creating an awareness of community resources
11. preparing children to make choices and cope with changes they will encounter in middle or junior high school

Career education during the elementary school years is most likely to be effective if it is geared to the developmental stages of the children. During the fantasy stage, identification with appropriate role models can be encouraged. Efforts should be made to broaden children's knowledge of workers and their roles. Social skills and work habits are developing rapidly during this stage, and their development can be facilitated. Activities that reinforce a sense of mastery, internal control, and moderate risk taking can be particularly beneficial (M. J. Miller, 1989). However, young children have little tolerance for ambiguity and little facility for abstraction and integration. In addition, children may be too young to respond positively to interventions to reduce gender stereotyping. Career education programs geared to children in the fantasy stage, then, should be clear and concrete and should emphasize activity and creativity.

By the time children enter the interest stage of career development, they are more flexible in their thinking and more able to integrate and hypothesize. Career education, during that stage, should focus on increasing self-awareness, identifying interests and values, reducing gender stereotyping, increasing independence and a sense of control over one's life, and expanding understanding of the institution of work.

An example of a sound model of career education has been implemented by the state of Virginia. Career education in each grade has a focal theme:

1. Kindergarten/Grade 1—understanding the self
2. Grade 2—understanding the self and others

3. Grade 3—understanding self, goals, and behavior
4. Grade 4—making personal choices and decisions
5. Grade 5—understanding the changing self and developing effective communication skills (Hoffman & McDaniels, 1991)

Career Education to Reduce Stereotyping

Career education that exposes both boys and girls to a broad range of leisure and occupational opportunities can be particularly useful in reducing gender stereotyping. Modeling can be effective in reducing children's foreclosure of occupational options because of gender. R. R. Miller (1986) suggested exposing children to atypical models of familiar occupations (e.g., a woman firefighter) during the early elementary school years and broadening the variety of atypical models during the later elementary school years. Speakers, photographs, films, stories, field trips, and games are all vehicles for providing models.

Cooper and Robinson (1989) found that the career aspirations of college-age women were related to their childhood interest in masculine-oriented play and activities. Women planning to study mathematics, science, and engineering had had more masculine-oriented childhood interests than did more traditional women, although the feminine-oriented interests of the two groups did not differ significantly. Cooper and Robinson concluded that "masculine childhood activities play a role in the development of skills necessary for achievement in various careers" (p. 338) and encouraged counselors to support girls' involvement in masculine and androgynous interests, emphasizing a holistic approach to personal development.

Cultural and ethnic occupational stereotypes also should be addressed through career education. According to R. R. Miller (1986), "A major goal for the upper elementary grades should be to counteract the effects of occupational elimination based on social class inappropriateness" (p. 251). Here, too, exposure to a broad range of atypical models can be useful in reducing stereotyping.

Children's Responses to Career Education

Children seem very receptive to career education and, generally, are interested in understanding their own career development. Young children are eager to become adults, and thinking about themselves in adult roles is exciting to most. Extensive studies conducted during the development of career education programs demonstrated that career education helps children appreciate their roles in society, gain understanding of adults, clarify their self-concepts, increase their knowledge of the world of work, and feel more positive about both themselves and their education (Hosie, 1975; O'Bryant & Corder-Bolz, 1978; Roth, 1973; Shelver, 1976; Vincenzi, 1977). A meta-analysis of 18 studies of Grades K through 12 career education programs concluded, "Career education works" (Baker & Popowicz, 1983, p. 185).

Content of Career Education Programs

Comprehensive career education programs typically include the following common core experiences:

1. individual and group counseling, to promote personal growth, self-awareness, and coping skills as well as to address problems of adjustment and behavior
2. assessment of abilities, personality traits, and interests
3. provision of occupational and educational information
4. indirect services to teachers, parents, and community members, including training, consultation, coordination of services, and referral

Walz and Benjamin (1984) identified eight characteristics of systematic and effective career guidance programs. Typically, these programs are

1. organized, sequential, and comprehensive, involving cooperation between grades, schools, community resources, and businesses
2. based on the developmental needs of the participants
3. designed to achieve measurable, realistic, and specific objectives
4. structured with a built-in evaluation component, providing ongoing and summative feedback
5. set up to use a variety of resources and methods
6. delivered by appropriately trained personnel
7. focused on process as well as results, providers as well as recipients of the program
8. planned by a guidance committee with representatives from all concerned groups (e.g., counselors, teachers, administrators, parents)

In addition, to maximize effectiveness, career education should be infused into the academic curriculum and should enhance academic learning by making it more relevant and stimulating. Career education programs that adhere to these guidelines are likely to be successful, not only because they are developmentally appropriate and make good use of resources and personnel but also because their ease of evaluation makes them flexible and easy to change as needed.

Many resources and methods have been developed to facilitate the process of career education with children of elementary school age. A sampling of resources suitable for this age group is presented here:

I. Classroom and group activities
   A. Field visits can be made to observe workers in their places of employment.
   B. Speakers can brought in to talk about their career development and work activities. (Parents are a good source of speakers.)
   C. Age-appropriate exercises or discussions can be designed to promote self-awareness, decision-making and thinking skill development, and values clarification. Topics might include Deciding What to Do on Weekends, What I Like Best About My Friends, The Kind of Person I Am, My Favorite Day, and What Makes My Family Special. Thought-provoking incomplete sentences can be assigned, such as I Wish . . . , Someday I Will . . . , and When I Am Grown Up I Will Be. . . .
   D. The classroom can be transformed into a simulated work site where children apply for jobs, are interviewed, and are given jobs to perform.
   E. Children can role-play adults in particular occupations, enacting both the work and leisure roles of those adults.
   F. The relationships that school subjects and leisure activities have to careers can be discussed.
   G. Stories, plays, and films depicting nontraditional as well as traditional role models can be presented.
   H. Students can conduct interviews of parents and other workers, with results presented to the class.
   I. Students can keep diaries or journals of their own experiences and observations.
   J. Drama, mental imagery, music, puppets, poetry, and creative play experiences (e.g., dollhouses, sand, costumes) can encourage children to try on new roles and experiences.
   K. Computer word processing and graphics can facilitate children's expression of their ideas and images.
   L. Shadowing, in which individual students spend time with a worker, observing the worker's activities and participating, as much as possible, in planning and executing those activities, can broaden students' perspectives of particular occupations.

    M. Students can discuss and explore their perceptions of adult occupational roles and lifestyles, comparing and clarifying ideas.

    N. Games such as What's My Line? can encourage students to think about a range of occupations.

II. Commercial products

    A. Developing Understanding of Self and Others (DUSO) uses DUSO the dolphin and extensive supplementary materials to promote positive self-concept development, self-awareness, and understanding of relationships, for Grades K through 4 (available from the American Guidance Services [AGS]). DUSO materials also are available to prevent sexual abuse of children (Body Rights Kit) and to prevent drug abuse (Drug Free Program).

    B. PEEK: Peabody Early Experiences Kit includes 1,000 activities designed to promote cognitive, social, and language development in preschool children and older learning disabled children (AGS).

    C. I Am Amazing is a program designed to promote self-esteem as well as health and safety in preschoolers (AGS).

    D. My Friends and Me promotes social skills and self-esteem development in 4- to 5-year-old children (AGS).

    E. *The Bookfinder* is a listing of children's books that can be used to promote self-awareness and personal development (AGS).

    F. Positive Action is a curriculum for children in Grades K through 8, consisting of many brief lessons designed to build self-esteem, particularly good for use in a schoolwide homeroom program (from Positive Action).

    G. Toward Affective Development is a program designed to promote positive emotional growth, for Grades 4 through 6 (AGS).

    H. *Play, Learn, Grow!* is an activities book published by CTB/Macmillan/ McGraw-Hill.

Many assessment tools are available to the counselor working with young children. The following lists include some of those tools that seem likely to be useful to counselors of this age group:

III. Inventories of career maturation, interests, and personality

    A. Individual Career Exploration (ICE), published by Scholastic Testing Service, is based on Roe's (1956, 1964) theory of career development and divides occupations into eight groups and three levels. A picture form is available for Grades 3 through 7, designed to promote thinking about activities that children might like to do, places they might like to work, tools they might like to work with, and jobs that sound enjoyable and interesting.

    B. Vineland Adaptive Behavior Scales: Classroom Edition, available from AGS, is designed "to assess the personal and social sufficiency of individuals from birth to adulthood" (Stevens, 1986, p. 112), providing scores in four domains (communication, daily living skills, socialization, and motor skills).

C. CFKR Career Materials has produced a variety of tools for assessing and promoting the career maturity of children. Useful products include the JOB JUNGLE (for career awareness), Looking at MYSELF (to promote self-esteem), E-WOW (to identify career-related interests), the JOB-O E, Careerville (to provide information on career clusters and choices), and Work Windows, designed to teach positive work habits and promote knowledge of the world of work.

D. The Career Awareness Inventory (CAI) includes items on occupational role models, personal assessment of career knowledge, and societal functions of workers. The inventory is designed to measure and stimulate children's career awareness and is available in two levels: elementary for Grades 3 through 6 and advanced for Grades 7 through 12.

E. Measures of self-esteem include the Coopersmith Self-Esteem Inventories, Culture-Free Self-Esteem Inventories, Piers-Harris Children's Self-Concept Scale, Rosenberg Self-Esteem Scale, Tennessee Self-Concept Scale, Behavioral Academic Self-Esteem Scale, Inferred Self-Concept Scale, and the Self-Esteem Rating Scale for Children (Chiu, 1988).

F. The Children's Personality Questionnaire provides a profile of 14 personality dimensions for children aged 8 to 12 (from the Institute for Personality and Ability Testing).

IV. Measures of abilities

A. The Kaufman Test of Educational Achievement, published by AGS, comes in two forms, brief and comprehensive, and two levels, Grades 1 through 3 and 4 through 12. The brief form measures achievement in mathematics, reading, and spelling; the comprehensive form, in mathematics application, reading decoding, spelling, reading comprehension, and mathematical computation. Worthington (1987) called this "a very worthwhile new instrument" (p. 327).

B. The Wide Range Achievement Test (WRAT), published by Jastak, is another measure of achievement, assessing spelling, mathematics, and reading for ages 5.0 through adulthood, probably the briefest of those available.

C. Comprehensive Tests of Basic Skills, published by CTB/Macmillan/McGraw-Hill, are available in 11 levels for Grades K through 12.9. Subtests vary, depending on level, but typically include vocabulary, comprehension, language mechanics and expression, spelling, study skills, mathematics computation, concepts and application, science, and social studies.

D. The Peabody Individual Achievement Test, published by AGS, provides six subtests measuring written expression, general information, reading recognition, reading comprehension, mathematics, and spelling, to measure achievement for young people from ages 5 to 18.

E. The Basic Achievement Skills Individual Screener (BASIS), published by Psychological Corporation, is an individually administered achievement test for Grades 1 through 12, measuring skill development in reading, mathematics, spelling, and writing. Ysseldyke (1985) called this "an attractive alternative to the Wide Range Achievement Test and the Peabody Individual Achievement Test" (p. 91).

F. The Test of Nonverbal Intelligence (TONI), published by AGS, is a 20-minute inventory for people aged 5 to 85+, disabilities designed to be a nonverbal measure of intelligence and reading ability for people with language handicaps or limited mastery of English.

G. The Peabody Picture Vocabulary Test, published by AGS, is a brief measure of verbal ability and scholastic aptitude. It, too, requires no reading or writing and is particularly good for the very young, people with disabilities, or non-English speakers.

H. The Kaufman Brief Intelligence Test (K-BIT), published by AGS, is a 15- to 30-minute test for people aged 4 to 90 that measures vocabulary and ability to solve new problems. It yields a composite intelligence score.

I. Several tools for early childhood assessment are published by CTB/Macmillan/McGraw-Hill; these include the Developing Skills Checklist, Early School Assessment, and the Primary Test of Cognitive Skills.

Career Education for Children With Disabilities

Research on the career development of young people with disabilities is discouraging. Brolin and Gysbers (1989) concluded, "The vast majority of students with disabilities never attain a satisfactory level of career development consistent with their capabilities" (p. 155). Over 30% leave school prior to graduating from high school, and only 15% locate jobs with salaries above the minimum wage. Legislation, such as the Carl D. Perkins Vocational Education Act of 1984 and the Job Training Partnership Act of 1982, has enhanced options and funding over the years for career development programs for people with disabilities. However, the responsibility of initiating and planning such programs falls to counselors and teachers.

A model program, initiated in 1978 and presently adopted by many school districts, is the Life-Centered Career Education Curriculum (LCCE). The LCCE is a comprehensive career development program, extending from kindergarten through the 12th grade and is designed to promote development of 22 competencies in daily living and personal, social, and occupational functioning that the students will need after leaving school. The LCCE program aims to develop what is called "the total worker," encompassing four roles: employee, worker in the home, volunteer worker, and participant in avocational activities. Broad-based programs such as the LCCE, infused into the academic curriculum, seem likely to have a very beneficial impact on students with disabilities.

The Role of the Counselor in the Elementary School

The role of the elementary school counselor is a multifaceted one. G. M. Miller (1988) found that it included the following eight roles, in order of importance: counseling and consultation, coordination, professional development, career assistance, organization, educational planning, assessment, and discipline. Wilgus and Shelley (1988) asked a group of elementary school counselors to keep diaries of their activities. On the whole, their time was divided in the following ways: individual counseling (19% of counselors' time), miscellaneous duties (administration, lunch duty, and other, 15%), staff consultation (14%), guidance and counseling meetings (9%), parent contact (8%), group counseling (7%), recognition programs (5%), classroom programs (5%), nonguidance meetings (4%), individual testing (4%), classroom observation (3%), parent education (3%), group testing (3%), referrals (2%), and staff development (1%). Although contact with individual students is clearly the counselors' first priority, it is surprising how much of their time is devoted to activities that do not involve direct student contact.

The model of counseling that seems most effective with children during the elementary school years is one that emphasizes development, prevention, consultation, and group work. The primary goal of counselors in the elementary schools should be to help children develop those strengths that will facilitate positive growth and development.

Typically, counseling with children has three foci:

1. *Self-concept development*—helping children to develop self-awareness, to differentiate themselves from their families and friends and to develop a positive view of themselves.
2. *Reality testing*—helping children gather information about their environments and societies, clarify and reduce stereotypes and misconceptions,

sharpen perceptions, and facilitate development of an accurate picture of the world and their options and places in it.

3. *Skill development*—effecting improvement in decision-making skills, communication skills, academic abilities, coping skills, planning abilities, and other life skills.

The elementary school counselor's role should not be primarily that of working with a small number of troubled children; rather, the focus of the counseling should be on helping all children to maintain positive development. Consequently, group and consultation approaches must be employed to enable counselors to have an impact on large numbers of children.

Although some career education will be done by counselors, they often serve as consultants to teachers who are introducing career education into the curriculum. Counselors should be familiar with both the school subjects and the methods of career education to help teachers facilitate the career development of their student. Teachers sometimes view career education as an infringement on their classroom work. Therefore, counselors should be able to help teachers appreciate the importance of career education and integrate it into their curricula without detracting from the academic material.

Counselors can also serve an important function by consulting with teachers on the common problems of this age group or on how to deal with a particular child. Teachers may be having difficulty with classroom management or may be uncertain about how to deal with a withdrawn child or a disruptive and uncooperative child. Although the counselor may want to observe these children in the classroom or see them individually for assessment and counseling, often, such problems can be resolved via consultation with the teacher.

Group counseling is particularly effective with elementary school children because of the importance the peer group has for them. Often, children are quite receptive to group counseling because it offers another opportunity for peer contact, whereas they may resist individual counseling because they do not want to be perceived as different from their peers. Modeling is important during these years, and group counseling offers a child the opportunity to learn from multiple models. Caution must be exercised when conducting group counseling experiences with children to limit group size and duration of sessions and to safeguard confidentiality. However, when properly conducted, group counseling can have a strong and powerful impact on children's development.

Case Study of Laura Ashton

A Young Girl Seeking Identification and Differentiation

The following case study exemplifies some of the developmental patterns seen in children as well as and counseling and assessment procedures used with children in elementary school. Laura Ashton had been referred to the school counselor because of her inconsistent peer relationships. At times, Laura seemed to interact well with the other children. However, at other times she vacillated from attempting to dominate them to withdrawing tearfully from group play.

No evidence of social maladjustment was present when Laura came to see the counselor. A small, slender girl with large glasses and a short, unruly haircut, Laura had an inquisitive expression and a great deal of energy. She began her session with, "Thanks for calling me in. It got me out of a math class."

Background

At the time of the counseling, Laura was 10 years old and in the fourth grade. She had been having difficulties in school since kindergarten and, after a frustrating year in first grade, was evaluated for learning disabilities. According to that evaluation, Laura had a specific learning disability with deficits in visual-motor integration. Her achievement was significantly below grade level in reading, arithmetic, and written expression, and she was recommended for special education services. According to the report, she would need continuous and intensive remediation and compensation in deficit areas. Laura spent second and third grades in a highly structured self-contained classroom with a low pupil-teacher ratio. This year, she was being mainstreamed and had been moved into a general classroom. She had a mentor to help her keep up with the class, and other forms of special help were provided to ease Laura's transition.

Laura lived in a suburban community near a large city. Both parents were employed full-time, her mother as a medical technician, her father as an automobile salesperson. Both worked long hours, and Laura's maternal grandmother often cared for Laura and her brother Kevin after school. Kevin, aged 8, was in the second grade. An outstanding student, he excelled in both academics and athletics.

Laura's father had a history of learning problems as a child as had one of his brothers; however, no special education programs were offered to them. Laura's father had left high school in his junior year to contribute to the support of his large family. Her mother had completed 2 years at a community college.

Laura's Perceptions

Laura's description of herself initially focused on aspects that displeased her. "I'm short, the shortest girl in the class, and I have to wear glasses. The worst thing about me is that I have trouble in school; I just can't get an A in math!" However, with some coaxing, she spoke about more positive aspects of her life. Laura had been taking ballet lessons since she was 2 years old and was about to present a recital. She had a large collection of porcelain dolls as well as a German shepherd. This summer she had gone to space camp and told her counselor proudly that she wanted to be an astronaut like one of her uncles. She also reported that she loved making up stories and offered to tell the counselor her latest story about the "skweshy mooshy creatures" who lived under lily pads.

Laura presented a positive picture of her family. "Mom and Dad work a lot, but they always say good-night and read me a story before I go to bed, even if they work late. On Saturdays, we go to the park and play ball." Her brother was not portrayed quite so positively. "Kevin can really be a pain. Once he broke one of my dolls. And he's almost as tall as I am."

Obviously, friends were an area of concern for Laura. "They make fun of the way I make letters and always choose me last for games. Sometimes they laugh at me when I ask questions in class." She was confused about why children did not seem to like her when "they don't even know me." At a time when many of the girls her age are moving into dyadic rather than group relationships, Laura was unable to cite a special friend.

Clearly, Laura had gotten some negative messages from her peers, almost certainly an important source of some of her own negative views of herself. For most children Laura's age, the peer group has a powerful influence on self-image and self-esteem. The group enables children to see themselves as others see them and to develop a more realistic view of themselves. In Laura's case, she had received some negative feedback from her peers who may have been impatient with her learning difficulties, and this had a considerable impact on her.

Laura needed little coaxing to talk about school. "I know I have a learning problem," she said. "My parents explained it to me. It doesn't mean I'm dumb or anything, but it takes me longer to learn some things." She reported enjoying physical education, art, and writing. Mathematics and reading were perceived as being the most difficult subjects for her. Outside interests included ballet, playing with her dog, and watching programs about outer space.

Laura was expected to come home right after school and check in with her grandmother before going out to play. She had regular household chores, including setting the table and making her bed, and was expected to complete her homework before dinner. Little opportunity was afforded her to develop her relationships with other children. When she did have an opportunity to play with other children, she enjoyed playing school with Laura as the teacher, playing with dolls, playing soccer, and playing board games. Learning and following the rules were important to Laura, and she stated that she got angry with herself when she made a mistake. Her tendency to be self-critical and perfectionistic may make her a difficult companion. As Laura put it, "They say I'm bossy, but I just want to follow the rules."

This academic year, Laura was not only mainstreamed but was placed in a creative writing group for gifted and talented children. Here, ideas were more important than spelling, and Laura spoke fondly of her teacher and the stories the class members told each other. However, she also reported that her teachers seemed to expect more from her than they did from the other children.

Career Development

Laura expressed several tentative career goals: becoming an astronaut or a teacher or working in a hospital. Clearly, Laura had been influenced by role models, her uncle the astronaut, her teachers, and her mother who worked in a hospital. Laura did not seem to feel limited by her gender and was able to use a male role model and aspire to a traditionally male-dominated career, space research. All three choices seemed to Laura to reflect prestige and power, elements that she craved in her present life. Although these choices bear a relationship to Laura's interests, the primary appeal of her choices seems to be in the special roles they embodied. She had little sense of training requirements for these occupations, except that, "You have to study hard and go to college."

Because career development is viewed as the establishment of personal, family, and occupational goals, leading to a rewarding lifestyle, Laura was asked to project herself into the future, to talk about the kind of life she would like to have when she was an adult and what she thought would be important to her at that time. Like most children her age, Laura had given some thought to herself as an adult and had begun to develop a system of personal and occupational values. "I want to get married and have two children and lots of dogs, maybe live on a farm. I want to go to college like my mom. Someday I'd like to write a book for children." Clearly, values of family closeness, creativity, education, and nature were already emerging.

Obstacles to Development

Although Laura seemed to have a fairly clear idea of what she wanted in the future, several factors emerged during counseling that were interfering with her optimal functioning in the present and that might affect her future. Laura seemed to hear negative messages more clearly than positive ones, and she focused on her areas of difficulty rather than on her strengths. Generally, her peer relationships were not rewarding, and she could benefit from improving her interpersonal skills. During the years when Laura and others of her age are engaged in the development of what Erikson (1963) termed industry versus inferiority, Laura lacked adequate opportunity for socialization, the close friendships, and the confidence in her own abilities that, generally, are important ingredients in the development of a sense of industry. Nevertheless, Laura seemed to be motivated and hardworking. When asked how she dealt with difficult math problems, she replied, "I just practice more." With some continued assistance from family and school to help Laura from becoming discouraged and to develop her social skills and self-esteem, Laura should be able to successfully negotiate these years of transition.

Assessment of Laura Ashton

Although several thousand tests are available that are appropriate for use with children of elementary school age, most of these are tests of ability and are designed more for the purposes of teachers than for those of counselors. With interests, values, and personality in flux during these years, only limited attention has been paid to the testing of children's career and personal development. Although caution must be exercised when assessing children's abilities or personalities to avoid labeling and stigmatizing them, testing can be helpful in clarifying the strengths and difficulties of children and in helping counselors to better meet their needs.

In testing children, the nature of the test administration and the relationship between the children and the examiner can have a powerful effect on the test results. Especially in light of Laura's low academic self-esteem, efforts were made to present the assessment process in a supportive and positive way, to ensure that Laura felt relaxed and comfortable in the testing situation and that she knew exactly what was expected.

Observing test-taking behavior is important with children. More than most adults, children provide clues to their motivation, work habits, and test-taking attitudes by the way they participate in the assessment process. Laura, for example, tended to ask many questions during the administration, often beginning her questions even before the examiner had a chance to finish explaining the directions. Laura was very concerned about whether or not her answers were correct or appropriate and was frequently self-critical.

Assessment of Abilities

Generally, aptitude testing is less useful with children than is intelligence and achievement testing. Aptitude testing is for purposes of prediction. Because the time when major choices and decisions must be made is quite a few years away, prediction is usually not an important aspect of counseling with young children. In addition, aptitudes are not well developed or differentiated during these years. School grades are perhaps the most useful measure of abilities. Comparison of school grades, intelligence test scores, and achievement test scores can provide enlightening information on how children are using their abilities.

Laura's report cards through the third quarter of fourth grade reflect nearly perfect attendance as well as above-average grades. Grades for achievement were largely Bs with Laura receiving As in art, written communication, and physical education and Cs in spelling and oral communication. Effort, citizenship, and study skills were generally rated as good. Clearly, Laura is holding her own in her new classroom.

The most widely used and discriminating tests of intelligence for children are the Stanford-Binet Intelligence Scale (4th edition, Riverside Publishing Company) and the Wechsler Intelligence Scale for Children, now in its third edition (WISC-III, Psychological Corporation), one of the Wechsler family of tests. Both of these are individually administered and require approximately an hour of working time. The Otis-Lennon School Ability Test (6th edition, OLSAT, Psychological Corporation) is a widely used alternative and is more efficient because it can be administered to groups but yields less detailed information. All three inventories can be used from elementary school to high school. The OLSAT is available in seven versions, from kindergarten through grade 12. The Stanford-Binet and WISC-III each comes in only one version; the administrator selects the tasks or subtests to use depending on the age and anticipated ability level of the person to be tested.

Generally, counselors are not trained to administer the Wechsler and Stanford-Binet tests. However, they may receive results of those tests for their clients. Laura had recently been given the WISC-III by a school psychologist and received a verbal IQ score of 113, a performance IQ of 108, and a full-scale IQ of 112. Her verbal and full-scale scores fell in the above-average range, and her performance score was in the average range. Laura's intelligence test score and her school grades, then, seemed congruent, an indication that Laura is making good use of her intellectual potential at school.

However, another inventory, administered to Laura at school, presented a somewhat different picture. The Woodcock-Johnson Psycho-Educational Battery II (WJII) (Teaching Resources Corporation) is an individually administered test that evaluates cognitive ability and scholastic achievement (Sweetland & Keyser, 1986). It is particularly useful in assessment of learning disabilities and for instructional planning. Five subtest scores were reported for Laura in terms of age and grade equivalents, standard scores, and percentiles:

Subtest	Age	Grade	Standard Score	Percentile
Reading	7.9	2.6	82	12
Mathematics	10.3	5.0	102	55
Written language	8.2	3.1	84	14
Knowledge	11.2	5.8	108	70
Skills	8.8	3.5	88	22

Clearly, Laura's abilities have not developed evenly, as is characteristic of people with learning disabilities. Her scores in mathematics and knowledge are well above average, whereas the other three scores are below average, with her reading score reflecting particular difficulty in that area. Although Laura's school grades suggest that she is doing a fine job of overcoming and compensating for the difficulty she has in reading, at present, reading is a challenging area for her. Fortunately, her learning disability was diagnosed early, and appropriate help has been provided. This should curtail the impact that her learning disability has had on her development. However, Laura's presentation in the interview as well as her responses on the personality inventory to be discussed later in this chapter indicate how much this bright, motivated young girl has been affected by her learning disability.

Personality and Interest Assessment

For the elementary-school-age child, personality and interests are almost inseparable. Changes in interests seem to be associated with personality development.

The primary purpose of using personality/interest assessment with children as a part of the counseling process is to help children develop greater self-awareness and to facilitate the planning of relevant exploratory experiences. Unless the child is being seen in a mental health setting, counselors will generally not be seeking an in-depth analysis or diagnosis of the psychological functioning of the child but, rather, will be using inventories that can be discussed with the child to promote self-esteem, self-knowledge, and personal growth. Although many personality inventories are available that have long been used to describe the personality dynamics of children, most of these inventories (e.g., the Rorschach Test, the Children's Apperception Test, and the Early School Personality Questionnaire) yield information that requires considerable training and experience to interpret and cannot readily be shared with the child. Few inventories are available to describe the personality dimensions of the average school-age child in a meaningful and valid way. Those instruments that are available are largely still in the experimental stages and do not provide adequate norms or data on validity and reliability.

Although counselors may want to use such inventories to add some direction or focus to a counseling relationship, the uncertain reliability of such instruments should be borne in mind, and their results should be interpreted tentatively and with caution. The results of such inventories should be compared and integrated with other available information on the child, and care should be taken to avoid placing undue emphasis on the data. Counselors should also be aware that the personalities and interests of children are typically in a state of flux, and labeling or basing decisions with far-reaching implications on personality testing of children should be done with great caution. Although useful inventories to assess interests are more available than those to assess personality, with those inventories, too, the counselors' goal should not be to facilitate current planning or decision making; rather, the inventories can be most useful in determining what knowledge or experiences are needed to improve career development and to identify inventoried interests that are not congruent with expressed or manifest interests and that might, therefore, warrant further exploration.

Two inventories were used to obtain additional information about Laura's career awareness and personality. The JOB-O E (elementary) career awareness inventory (CFKR Career Materials, 1990) is the version of the JOB-O for children in Grades 4 through 6, also available as the JOB-O for Grade 7 through adult and the JOB-O A, the advanced edition for career decision making. The JOB-O E is considered an instructional activity that can be administered to groups or individuals. Focusing on six job groups (Group 1—mechanical, construction, and agricultural workers; Group 2—scientific and technical workers; Group 3—creative and artistic workers; Group 4—social, legal, and educational workers; Group 5—managers and sales workers; and Group 6—administrative support workers), paralleling Holland's (1987) six occupational environments discussed in Chapter 1, the inventory assesses interests, promotes self-exploration, and provides information. When they complete the inventory, students have an assessment of their level of interest in the six job groups as well as a list of 18 jobs of interest to them, three from each of the six different groups. They also select two occupations to explore and research. The inventory promotes parental involvement by suggesting that the children ask their parents, "What are the four most important things I should think about in career planning?"

Although Laura was able to find occupations in each of the six groups that interested her, a disparity was evident between the job groups she preferred and the specific occupations that most interested her. Her preferred job groups included Groups 3 and 4. Occupations she thought she would like best under the creative and artistic group included photographer, fine artist, and writer, and she was interested in teacher, nursing aide, and waitress in the social, legal, and educational group. However, the occupations she was most interested in exploring included astronaut and oceanographer. Completion of the JOB-O seemed to increase Laura's awareness of the importance of science and mathematics to several of her preferred occupations, and she volunteered that she wanted to get a book about being an astronaut to follow up on the discussion of that occupation.

Laura's interests were very broad, encompassing social, artistic, and scientific areas. Perhaps this reflects several origins of her interests. Creative and artistic areas reflect her present interests and skills, social and educational areas reflect family occupations that have been sanctioned for her, and her interest in becoming an astronaut may reflect the influence of a powerful role model as well as Laura's own wish for more power and prestige. This breadth of interests can be used as a springboard to encourage experiences and learning that will eventually help her narrow her career focus. At present, however, her varied interests can be used positively to promote both personal and intellectual growth.

Although data from teachers suggested that Laura was doing well in school, her own verbalized view of herself seemed quite negative, raising concern about a problem with self-image. Consequently, the Piers-Harris Children's Self-Concept Scale (Piers & Harris, 1983) was used as a measure of Laura's personality because of its emphasis on self-image. Designed for use in Grades 4 through 12, the Piers-Harris consists of 80 first-person statements. Respondents indicate whether each statement describes them. The inventory provides scores in six areas as well as a total score. Computer scoring yields a chromagraph or color-coded profile of scores, as well as a printed narrative, facilitating interpretation. According to Chiu (1988), the Piers-Harris is "the most psychometrically sound instrument for assessing children's self-esteem" (p. 299).

According to the narrative, Laura's overall level of self-concept was much below average compared with a U.S. sample of public school children. Based on her self-report, she would be expected to feel very ineffective and self-doubt across a wide range of cognitive and interpersonal situations. Laura's scores in all six areas were well below average. Her score in behavior was the highest, for her, suggesting some positive feelings about her behavior in school and her ability to get along with others. However, responses in intellectual and school status, physical appearance and attributes, anxiety, popularity, and happiness and satisfaction reflected few positive feelings, with her attitude toward her physical appearance being particularly negative. Although single responses, in themselves, have little interpretative value, a sampling of items selected by Laura clearly convey the flavor of her self image: It is usually my fault when something goes wrong. I am dumb about most things. My looks bother me. I am often sad. I wish I were different. My classmates make fun of me. I am unpopular.

Recommendations

Clearly, Laura has been both open and consistent in her inventories and verbalized views of herself. Despite her good performance at school, the special programs she has been involved in, and the encouragement she has received from parents and teachers, Laura's learning disability and her transitions into and out of special education classes have had a strong negative impact on her. She feels different from and inferior to the other children and blames herself for her academic difficulties. The special academic help she has been receiving now needs to be combined with some social and psychological help, ideally a combination of individual, family, and group counseling.

Individual counseling, along with some family sessions, could promote Laura's self-expression as well as develop her self-confidence and interpersonal skills. Family members could be coached in ways to develop Laura's sense of self-efficacy without giving her too much responsibility or setting unattainable goals. Once some progress has been made, group counseling or participation in psychoeducational groups at school with children who are likely to offer her understanding and acceptance should help Laura apply what she is learning about how to relate better to others. Participation in a peer counseling program and in special programs for creative children are other possible avenues for building self-esteem and providing Laura an opportunity to build skills and clarify interests. Conferences with teachers can help them to better understand the needs of this young girl, so bright and engaging and yet so low in self-esteem.

Although the case study presented here is that of one person, counselors can use a similar combination of discussion and assessment, either individually or in a group situation, to determine the developmental needs of a group or class of students and can then work with students, parents, and teachers to provide appropriate growth experiences. Although this will probably be more complex and challenging with groups than with one child, the career education model, discussed earlier in this chapter, can provide counselors and teachers a viable structure for accomplishing these goals.

FIVE

Early Adolescence

Years of Growth and Searching

The next phase of development can appropriately be termed *the years of growth and searching*. These are the years of preadolescence and puberty, the years when both physical and emotional growth accelerate, often leaving early adolescents feeling confused and alone, searching for a new and clearer definition of who they are and who they want to be. Beane (1986) has coined the term *transescence* to describe this age group, emphasizing the importance of change and transition.

Overview of Early
Adolescent Development

Although, typically, the changes described in this chapter span the years from the ages of 11 to 14, they represent a stage in which rates of maturation tend to vary greatly. It is not uncommon for young people to be slow to enter or reluctant to leave this stage of development. This is a more turbulent stage than the previous one, and some young people may strive to hold onto the stability they have achieved in childhood and resist involving themselves in the characteristic floundering of early adolescence. They may experience so much difficulty consolidating the physical and emotional changes of this period that they may linger and delay entry into the next phase, almost as though they were saying, "I've barely made it through this stage. How can I possibly negotiate the next one?" Others experiencing difficulty with this stage may manifest a pseudomaturity, demonstrating behaviors and appearances more characteristic and appropriate for an older age. Use of alcohol and illegal drugs, sexual activity and pregnancy, and affiliation with cults and other extreme groups, accompanied by an angry rejection of previously held family and social values may be expressions of this pseudomaturity. These young people seem to want to negotiate early adolescence by skipping over its important developmental tasks and moving directly to late adolescence or early adulthood. However, the importance of developmental continuity seems reflected in some of the poor choices of these hurried young people. Whether passage through early adolescence is rapid, delayed, or timely, this is a difficult age for most, characterized by increasing self-consciousness, unstable self-concepts, and discouragement (Gottfredson, 1981).

Physical Development

Physical change is probably the most dramatic aspect of development during these years. Rapid physical growth and sexual maturation occur. The average girl will begin to menstruate at about the age of 12 or 13, and the average boy will reach a parallel point in his development about a year and a half later. (These milestones are occurring earlier; 150 years ago, the average age for menarche was 16.)

The impending adulthood of these children now is difficult to deny. Parenthood and physical intimacy are within reach, and both the young adolescents and their parents must cope with these dramatic changes. Crushes, especially on adults and media stars, are common and seem to offer a safe route to fantasies of intimate relationships and of the adult roles of spouse and parent. Thoughts of oneself as spouse and parent naturally lead to thoughts of oneself as provider and homemaker, and concern about planning for future careers is heightened during this stage.

Whether people in this age group achieve physical and sexual maturity early or late does not affect the time of their entry into the early adolescent stage of development as much as it colors their attitudes toward themselves and their development. Because there is so much variation in rates of maturation, early adolescents almost inevitably feel different from their peers. Comparison and self-evaluation are rampant, and even the most typical young adolescent probably feels some dissatisfaction with the self.

Early maturers tend to feel self-conscious and awkward, and girls seem to have particular difficulty fitting in with their peers (Livson & Peskin, 1980). They may date earlier, and involvement with older boys may lead to decisions and experiences for which they are ill prepared. Girls who date early may miss the peer group involvement and self-exploration of these years and may make a premature commitment to a traditional female role, focusing on marriage and parenting because of the prestige their early dating has brought them. Although pregnancy rates have been declining during the 1970s and 1980s for older teenagers, rates for younger adolescents have risen from 13.5 to 16.6 per 10,000 from 1973 to 1983 (Jackson & Hornbeck, 1989).

Early maturing boys seem to fare better; their size may be associated with athletic success and admiration by both male and female peers, leading to growth in confidence and social skills. However, boys who begin to date early may regard their girlfriends as mother figures and may develop a pattern of dependent and imbalanced relationships (White & Speisman, 1977).

On the other hand, the late maturer may feel inadequate and left behind. Delayed maturation is particularly difficult for boys, who may engage in acting-out and attention-seeking behavior to compensate for their small size. Late maturing girls fare better; their more gradual maturation seems to promote adaptation to their changing selves, and they are often perceived as more feminine and popular among their peers.

Self-Image and Self-Concept

According to Gottfredson (1981), "Self-concept refers to one's view of oneself, one's view of who one is and who one is not" (p. 547). Most young adolescents engage in considerable self-examination and develop an increasingly accurate picture of themselves. They become more aware of how they differ from others and how they are perceived by others, leading to greater congruence between young adolescents' self-concepts and the way they are seen by others.

At the start of the early adolescent years, most are in the stage that Erikson (1963) labeled industry versus inferiority. In this stage, early adolescents develop their capacity for cooperation and productive work. Most develop confidence in their ability to achieve mastery and competence, learn new skills, and function as group members.

As they progress through the early adolescent years, most young people move into the stage Erikson termed identity versus role confusion. Although the struggle to achieve a sense of their own identity is not resolved for most until late adolescence or early adulthood, gener-ally, young adolescents will be engaged in finding out who they are and what they want to do with their lives. The process of individuation is a difficult one for most. It requires giving up the image of oneself as a child and finding an identity that may, at least initially, be less comfortable and more demanding.

Although, generally, the early adolescent years are marked by an overt movement away from the family and toward the peer group, the family remains an important force in shaping and supporting the child's search for identity. Ideally, the family will provide a continued source of encouragement and security, promoting reasonable independence without threat. Parental approval is crucial during this phase, and young adolescents need to believe that their parents love and approve of their children's maturing selves as much as they did their childish selves.

Academic demands, nature of performance, and feedback are also important in shaping the self-image of young adolescents. Beane (1986) found that in middle schools, self-esteem was especially related to the character of the teachers, the nature of the learning activities, and the social experiences of the students. Among this age group, gifted stu-dents who, presumably, had received positive messages about their academic abilities had the highest academic *and* social self-concepts, whereas those with special learning problems had the lowest self-concepts. Self-confidence and academic achievement seem to have a circular relationship; Beane (1986) concluded, "Self-confidence in learn-ing is a key to being successful in school" (p. 190). This relationship between academic accomplishment and social self-concept was par-ticularly marked for boys, who draw more heavily on social experi-ences in building their self-image (Colangelo, Kelly, & Schrepfer, 1987). In general, boys in this age group have better self-esteem than do girls, particularly in terms of their academic self-cconfidence and job com-petence (Aubrey, 1977; Kelly & Jordan, 1990).

Bayer (1986) observed that self-concept could be modified by posi-tive (enhancing) or negative (deleterious) experiences and was able to improve the self-concepts of a group of seventh graders through a series of twelve 50-minute group sessions that emphasized affective learning experiences that the students had chosen, developed, and explored. Teacher-directed experiences were not nearly so successful. According to Bayer, then, classroom experiences are most likely to succeed in improving the self-concepts of early adolescents if those experiences foster trust in self and others, self-direction and autonomy, spontaneity, and cooperation. Calsyn, Pennell, and Harter (1984), too, found that affective education in the classroom could increase self-esteem as well as improve interpersonal relations, particularly for girls. They recommend programs of at least 10 sessions, implemented by the students' regular classroom teachers. Attention to the affective development of young adolescents seems of considerable importance, especially in light of the increasing suicide rate for 10- to 14-year-olds (Jackson & Hornbeck, 1989).

The process of individuation and increasing independence often leads to significant growth in career maturation. Young adolescents become more aware of their special interests and aptitudes and develop a sharper awareness of likes and dislikes. Some economic independence may be available for the first time, and, often, part-time employment can be secured delivering papers, babysitting, or mowing lawns. No matter how unrelated these tasks may be to a person's eventual career, such early work experiences are likely to have a positive effect on career maturation. They provide a firsthand view of the world of work and enable young adolescents to see themselves as productive, autonomous, and responsible. They learn to appreciate the balance of rewards and obligations inherent in all work.

Importance of the Peer Group

Typically, the process of individuation is tempered during early adolescence by increased involvement in peer group activities. Heterosexual relationships grow in importance as do friends perceived as having high status (Thornburg, 1986). Fearing isolation and rejection and confused by rapid physical and emotional changes, many young adolescents immerse themselves in the peer group and assume the identity, values, and norms of prestigious members of that group until the adolescents are comfortable enough with their changing selves to establish and assert their own values. In working with this age group, counselors should be aware of group pressures that may affect the attitudes and behaviors of its members. Peer pressure and approval are important factors in determining level of achievement, socialization patterns, and family interaction. One of the counselor's tasks, then, in working with this age group is to facilitate the emergence of individual values without threatening the sense of security and identity offered to the early adolescent by the peer group. Counselors may find themselves becoming annoyed and frustrated by the pressure toward peer conformity and the revolt against authority that commonly occur during early adolescence. This pressure may lead some young people to minimize or conceal intellectual or personal strengths that might be viewed as different or unacceptable by the peer group. Modeling oneself after stereotyped role models and peer group standards seems to be a common way for early adolescents to reduce anxiety engendered by the increased array of options and choices available to them (Thornburg, 1986). However, the peer group identification is a useful sort of defense mechanism that will diminish, in most young people, after it has served the purpose of providing support and structure during a tumultuous period.

Development of Thinking and Values

During early adolescence, considerable intellectual as well as physical growth takes place. At about the ages of 11 to 13, the formal operations stage of thought gains importance over concrete thinking processes, improving the ability to use problem-solving and decision-making strategies, deductive reasoning, reflective thinking, abstraction, logic, introspection, generalization, and hypothesis (Thornburg, 1986). Early adolescents can use assumptions and have developed an understanding of cause-and-effect relationships and general properties. They are now more able to project themselves into the future and anticipate the consequences of complex choices and decisions. Judgment is considerably improved, and morality reflects awareness of the importance of inner controls and an emerging and individual system of ideals. No longer are right and wrong perceived as being determined by power. Egocentricity declines and empathy for others increases as does the ability to accept divergent points of view. Although the development of skills associated with the formal operations stage of thought continues through the high school years and beyond, most young adolescents begin to manifest adultlike thinking. To facilitate the development of their thinking skills, promote satisfying decision making, and encourage self-confidence, adolescents should be involved as much as possible in any planning that affects them.

Values clarification, too, is progressing at a rapid rate during these years (Tinsley, Benton, & Rollins, 1984). Work-related values become relatively stable, and the values of eighth or ninth graders will, for the most part, persist into adulthood (Sampson & Loesch, 1981). Therefore, considerable attention should be paid to the nature and formation of these values. Although all early adolescents are in the process of defining and developing a mature system of values, they are not all equally conscious of this process. One of the tasks of people working with this age group is to help them become aware of their values and be able to articulate and refine them as well as relate them to their present and anticipated lifestyles.

Middle School/Junior High School Environment

Changes in the school environment both complement and complicate the process of emotional development during the early adolescent years. During the 1970s and 1980s, educators became increasingly aware that the personal and academic needs of young adolescents are special and different from those of elementary and high school students. This realization has been reflected in the growth of middle schools, typically, encompassing Grades 5 through 8, designed to bridge the gap from elementary to secondary school. Farinholt (1977), writing on the increasing prevalence of middle schools, stated that the goals of these schools should include increasing self-knowledge and self-differentiation by individualizing learning, emphasizing cooperation and a sense of pride and ownership rather than competition, and maximizing success and involvement in academics. In a similar vein, Beane (1986) suggested that middle or junior high schools should promote positive interpersonal relations, communication, and respect for the individual. Beane emphasized the importance of student support networks for young adolescents. Peer tutoring, student assistants, support groups, and student involvement in school leadership and curriculum development are ways of facilitating student interaction and involvement in the schools. Both Beane and Farinholt view middle schools as places where personal development is facilitated by the academic environment. Schools can contribute to the need of the typical early adolescent for gradual and positive development of self-concept, self-confidence, and independence.

Whether early adolescents enter junior high or middle schools, they will probably experience a shift from the one-room/one-teacher model of education to the multiple-room/multiple-teacher model. School life now is more like working life and more is demanded. Students are responsible for being in class on time and satisfying the diverse demands of a number of people. Typically, homework assignments increase, and, now, early adolescents must manage out-of-school time to accommodate homework, chores, recreation, family activities, and perhaps part-time jobs. In addition, early adolescents are now afforded broader exposure to role models. Male teachers are more available in the schools, and exposure to other adult role models in the community increases as the children's range of activities expands.

During the middle school years, most adolescents experience a renewed interest in school, perhaps because of the challenging transition from elementary school to middle or junior high school. These years, then, present an optimal time for young people to develop a sense of themselves as competent and productive students and to develop qualities of responsibility and diligence that are conducive to success in both school and work. Students should be helped to derive gratification from their accomplishments and to feel proud of their abilities.

For many, the first decisions with implications for the future will be made during these years. The early adolescent may have to make decisions about the study of foreign languages, the selection of elective courses, and whether to pursue an academic curriculum. Less formal decisions such as whether to become involved in after-school sports or clubs, what topics to investigate in book reports and research papers, and which subjects to emphasize in one's homework preparation also have significance for the future and merit attention from parents, teachers, and counselors. Ideally, these adults can help early adolescents make choices that will promote competence, maturity, independence, self-awareness, and understanding of the world, as well as a sense of collaboration and cooperation. Teachers and counselors can best accomplish these goals with early adolescents by being patient, interested, understanding, and aware of developmental and individual needs, avoiding messages that might embarrass, limit, or stereotype these young people.

Career Development

The career development of young adolescents is closely related to their emotional and physical development, and the two really cannot be separated. Just as early adolescents are searching for guidelines and models in the personal realm, they are also searching in the world of work. Their efforts to acquire good work habits (industry vs. inferiority) and to develop an accurate and positive sense of themselves (identity vs. role confusion) are central to both their emotional development and their career development.

Stages of Career Development

Ginzberg et al. (1951) divided the early adolescent years into two sub-stages of career development: the interest stage, which extends from age 11 to age 12, and the capacity stage, which extends from age 12 or 13 to age 14. Most early adolescents will be in the interest substage as they enter this phase of development, although some will still be in the fantasy stage and others will be moving into the capacity stage.

During the interest stage, young people are concerned with answering the question, "What do I like to do?" As they move into the capacity stage, that question is replaced by, "What can I do well?" In the capacity stage, people become more aware of their strengths and weaknesses and realize that ability and aptitude must be considered along with interest when making career plans. This realization can have a disconcerting effect on some; they become aware that they really cannot become anything they want and feel anxious about the importance of making sound career plans. The young adolescent whose self-image is still developing may feel confused and even discouraged by this emphasis on abilities. Increased floundering and premature and hasty commitment to career goals are different ways that young adolescents cope with this anxiety.

The introduction of the notion of ability as an important factor in career planning often leads to decreased identification with parents. Typically, young adolescents feel a need to broaden their horizons, and other role models (teachers, neighbors, friends' parents) gain in importance. External standards, too, assume greater significance, and early adolescents tend to become more interested in evaluating and determining their aptitudes and abilities, to see how they compare to occupational and academic criteria and requirements.

By the end of the early adolescent years, many young people will have successfully negotiated the capacity stage or what Super (1957b) called the growth stage and will have progressed onto what Super termed the tentative substage of the exploration phase of career development (Cole, 1982). That stage will be discussed in greater detail in the next chapter. It represents an integration of many of the concerns of the earlier stages—interests, ideals, abilities, and values—and is an effort to answer the question, "What will I do with my life?"

Gottfredson (1981), like Super (1957b) and Ginzberg et al. (1951), viewed the early adolescent as moving between two important stages of career development. The third stage in Gottfredson's model of career development, orientation to social valuation, encompasses the ages of

9 to 13, the years when children develop their understanding of abstract concepts, including social class, prestige, abilities, and their own feelings. They become aware of the interrelationship of education, occupation, wealth, and social status. Their insight into these important concepts enables them to eliminate occupations with unacceptably low prestige that are incompatible with their social class self-concept (R. R. Miller, 1986). Most will be ready to move into Stage 4, orientation to internal, unique self, about the age of 14 and continue the process of elimination that will eventually define their career goals.

Career Maturation During Early Adolescence

Super (1985) found that developmental patterns observed in ninth-grade boys had a significant correlation with their career development as adults. Parental socioeconomic status, children's academic performance, sense of harmony in their lives, and nature of self-concept all correlated with career establishment at age 25 and were good predictors of later occupational status. Clearly, then, attention should be paid to describing and promoting the career development of early adolescents. Studies suggest the following characteristics of the career development of young people in this age group (Aubrey, 1977; Farmer, 1985).

1. They can identify some of their strengths and limitations as well as their interests.
2. They can name things they would like to do better.
3. About 70% have a current hobby, sport, or activity that they think would help them obtain employment, and they understand that there is a link between academic and leisure pursuits and eventual employment.
4. They can list at least a few factors to consider in choosing a job, although most cannot list as many as five factors.
5. Most can express tentative occupational preferences, although only a small percentage feel certain of their occupational choices. Fluctuation between one definite choice and uncertainty is typical.
6. Most have an awareness of the occupational prestige hierarchy and can rank occupations along a prestige continuum similar to that of adults, using a broad range of criteria (e.g., service to the community, financial and psychological rewards, educational requirements, the nature of the work, and the power of the position).
7. Level of occupational aspiration is fairly well established between Grades 4 and 8.

8. Interest in lower-level occupations declines; most of early adolescents' primary occupational choices require postsecondary education.
9. Most have general information about many occupations.
10. They have some understanding of the process and challenges of job seeking.
11. Three quarters believe that, eventually, they should make the final decisions about their careers.

In general, then, early adolescents with satisfactory career maturity can distinguish between interests, values, and abilities and have good awareness of their own interests, values, and abilities. The images they have of themselves are congruent with their expressed occupational preferences. They are concerned about and interested in the process of making career plans and accept the need for planning and the responsibility of making career-related choices and decisions. They have some knowledge of the world of work, including the nature of many occupations, their academic requirements, and their prestige levels. Early adolescents with career maturity recognize the importance of information in career decision making and are open to exploring the world of work via increased self-awareness, information gathering, and relevant experiences, including involvement in extracurricular activities and part-time jobs. They are aware that career planning and decision making are developmental processes that are already underway.

Although the 1950s research of Super and Ginzberg and his colleagues still seems quite relevant to our understanding of the career development of the early adolescent 50 years later, longitudinal studies shed light on modern trends in career development. Prediger and Sawyer (1986) compared a large national sample of 8th, 10th, and 12th graders in 1973 with a similar group in 1983. Among the 8th and 11th graders, shifts in interest were noted, with interest in social, health, and personal service careers declining from 1973 to 1983, whereas interest in technologies and trades became the top interest group, using Holland's (1987a) career clusters (see Chapter 1). In 1983, both age groups were less certain about their occupational choices and seemed to have a greater awareness of options as well as an increasing recognition that most people change jobs throughout their lives. In addition, schools seemed to be having a substantially greater impact on students' career development than they had in 1973. Exploration and information gathering are the primary career development goals for the middle school years, rather than commitment and choice, and this pattern seems reflected by career development patterns noted in this group in the 1980s, perhaps an indication that overall career maturity is increasing.

Influences on Career Development

Many influences, including gender, ethnic and socioeconomic background, family, and environment, can have a powerful influence on the career development of young people (Osipow, 1968).

Gender

At the start of the early adolescent years, girls seem less affected by gender bias and stereotyping than they are at earlier and later ages. They have outgrown the inordinate need for structure that led to rigid gender stereotyping during the early elementary school years, and they have not yet entered the years when pressures toward dating and marriage seem to contribute to an increase in stereotyped thinking. Generally, they are still performing well in school and have not yet given much evidence of the decline in performance in traditionally masculine areas such as mathematics and science that is prevalent during the high school years. By the end of the early adolescent phase, however, a trend toward inhibited academic and occupational motivation is evident in many girls.

Kelly and Jordan (1990) found that, generally, eighth-grade girls had lower self-ratings than did eighth-grade boys in academic self-concept and job competence. This was as true of gifted young people as it was of those of less ability; although the gifted girls seemed to plan more for their careers than did the gifted boys, the girls had lower career aspirations. Gottfredson (1981) found a similar relationship between gender and career choice. She observed that during early adolescence, boys' occupational preferences increased in prestige, whereas girls' declined, seeming to pass each other in the process.

Fitzgerald and Crites (1980) found that from the eighth grade on, females seem to have more career maturity than do males. In fact, girls seem to reach a peak of interest in planning for college and their future careers between the ages of 11 and 14. These years are, therefore, a time when most girls will be particularly receptive to discussing their career plans, and it is an appropriate time to focus on expanding options. This is important because, despite their more advanced career maturity, "Females consistently select occupations that are unrealistically low in terms of their aptitudes and interests" (p. 47). Research by Gilligan

(1982) and others on the personal and moral development of females sheds lights on this disparity. Although both males and females seem motivated by a desire for achievement, they define achievement differently. Typically, females seek excellence in the social arena as reflected by love, approval, and social approbation, whereas males are more focused on mastery and power. In the girls, expressiveness and concern for others emerge as strong skills and values, and for the boys, independence and power are emphasized. Occupational interests reflect these patterns, with girls developing increasing interest in nurturing and people-oriented occupations, such as teaching and nursing, whereas boys manifest interest in occupations that reflect their values, such as law enforcement, athletics, and heavy equipment operation (Gottfredson, 1981). Girls are more outer directed and judge themselves more by the feedback they receive from others, whereas boys seem more inner directed (Fitzgerald & Crites, 1980). Girls' performance in school, often more stable and acceptable than boys', is driven more by their wish for approval than for excellence, whereas boys' academic strivings often reflect their wish for mastery. Other dynamics, such as a fear of success, a lower propensity for risk taking, and family and societal messages about appropriate gender roles also may contribute to the inhibition of some girls' occupational aspirations.

By the time they are in junior high school, both genders understand sex type and levels of occupations and use those dimensions to define a zone of acceptable careers. Barriers to interest in nontraditional careers during these years include need for peer acceptance, lack of nontraditional role models, and low self-esteem and self-efficacy, especially with respect to skills in mathematics and science (Lapan & Jingeleski, 1992; McKenna & Ferrero, 1991). However, girls with mothers who work outside the home, young people living in urban and suburban areas, and those who are assertive and high in self-efficacy show more interest in nontraditional occupations than do those with mothers who are homemakers, who live in rural areas, or who tend to be passive and low in self-esteem.

Ethnic and Socioeconomic Background

Just as gender affects career maturity, so does ethnic and socioeconomic background. Most early adolescents from all socioeconomic levels aspire to high occupational levels. However, those from minority or disadvantaged backgrounds seem more aware of the obstacles they might encounter, have fewer role models that reflect their aspirations, and are less optimistic about their chances for success.

A study of the career maturity of ninth graders (Westbrook, Sanford, Merwin, Fleenor, & Gilliland, 1988) found a relationship between scholastic aptitude and career maturity and between race and career maturity, with White boys and girls achieving higher maturity scores than did African American boys and girls. Although the White students, as well as the females, seemed more able to appraise others' aptitude more accurately, no ethnic or gender differences were found in the ability to appraise oneself.

Parental support has been found to have a stronger influence on aspirations than friends' plans, teachers' encouragement, or social status (Farmer, 1985). A high correlation has been found between the education of parents and the education of their children. Most parents want their children to be more successful than they themselves have been, and by early adolescence, most young people express career goals that are consistent with the aspirations their parents hold for them. However, exploration of the antecedents of the aspirations of the young adolescents is important to ascertain whether the aspirations are a reflection of parental pressure or truly reflect the young person's own abilities, interests, and values.

Most studies of the relationship between early adolescent career goals and background variables have focused on the relationship between the career of the father and the occupational aspirations of the child. However, the educational and occupational development of the mother also seems to be an important influence, particularly on her daughters. Maternal achievement, as well as parental attitudes toward women in the workforce, are important factors in determining those careers that are viewed as acceptable to the young adolescent female.

Farmer (1985) found that, generally, young people from urban areas had higher levels of career aspiration than did those from rural areas, whereas those from higher socioeconomic levels tended to have higher levels of aspiration than did those from lower levels, particularly for people from ethnic minority groups, although academic achievement was at least as important a variable as background. Career maturity, too, seems related to background, with urban and rural youth typically having less career maturity than do those from suburban areas.

Career counseling can be helpful to inner-city, rural, and suburban young people, but counselors should remember that their needs may be quite different. The inner-city youth who may be overwhelmed by possibilities is likely to need help in narrowing and defining viable career objectives, the rural youth with limited role models will often need help in broadening options, and the suburban youth may well need help in reassessing a premature career decision, made in response to family and environmental norms and pressures

Career Counseling
With the Early Adolescent

Cole (1982) described early adolescence as a critical time for career development, a time when young people are questioning their futures, are open to new ideas, and are eager to explore their own interests and capabilities. In addition, the middle or junior high school years present most early adolescents with the first point at which they must make choices that have implications for their future careers. They may have to select courses, decide which high school to attend, or decide whether or not to pursue a college preparatory curriculum. Often, leisure interests, hobbies, and athletic pursuits become well established during these years. In a classic longitudinal study, Super and Bohn (1970) found that young people who were confused and floundering over their career plans in the eighth grade were more likely than not to be in the same position 6 years later when they were 20 years old and had been out of high school for 2 years. Clearly, then, both the need for and the interest in counseling with a career development focus is present in this age group.

Although most early adolescents do verbalize occupational goals, counselors should not assume that these goals will persist into high school and beyond, nor should they encourage students in this age group to make firm career plans. Super and Bohn found that only one sixth of the boys in their Career Patterns Study expressed the same occupational aspirations in the 12th grade as they had in the 9th grade. Although some early adolescents are ready to make career decisions, others have only limited career awareness and will not be ready to formulate mature career plans for many years. The middle school years should be years of exploration rather than commitment, and counselors should encourage that exploration rather than the making of early decisions. Change should be viewed as the norm for this age group, and all reasonable options should be kept open to facilitate that process.

At the same time, early occupational choices should not be ignored. Choices of broad career field and occupational level made in early adolescence often do persist beyond high school, and for some young people, specific occupational choices will be enduring. In addition, whether or not the early adolescents' career aspirations are maintained, those aspirations provide useful information on self-image and interests and a good starting point for discussion.

The primary goal of counseling with early adolescents should be to help them reach the point at which they have clear and accurate self-images, can make decisions without undue difficulty, and are involved in exploration of themselves and the world of work. Usually, to accomplish this, counselors must first attend to the emotional development of these young people. Many early adolescents feel isolated and inferior during these years, and until the counselor helps them deal with these negative feelings, little growth can be expected in career development. The process of ameliorating low self-esteem and fostering a sense of belonging will lead naturally into the development of requisite skills and attitudes for career maturation because the essence of career maturity corresponds with the hallmarks of mental health at this age. These include an open, accurate, and positive view of oneself and one's world, positive interpersonal relationships, and an acceptance of increased independence and responsibility.

In assessing the emotional development of early adolescents, counselors should recall that during these years, rate of development varies widely from one person to the next and should not assume, for example, that all 13-year-olds have shifted their attention from their interests to their abilities. Emotional factors may lead some 13-year-olds to aim toward fantasy occupations that they cannot hope to attain, whereas others may already have made mature, realistic, and enduring career plans.

Approaches to Counseling

Individual counseling, developmental group counseling, consultation with parents and teachers, career education, and career resource centers all have an important place in promoting the emotional and career development of early adolescents. *Individual counseling*, perhaps leading to a referral by the school counselor, often will be the method of choice when an early adolescent seems to be experiencing prominent emotional difficulties or is in crisis. Troubled young people who have difficulty accepting themselves can benefit greatly from realizing that they are accepted by an adult authority figure. However, early adolescents tend to be self-conscious and are fearful of appearing strange or different. A negative reaction to individual counseling may result from their feeling stigmatized by that process (M. J. Miller, 1988a). The ambiguity often posed by the process of individual counseling also can be disconcerting to young adolescents who very much want to know what is expected of them and what is going to happen. Use of a relatively structured approach, coupled with the use of hands-on materials and clear information on the counseling process, will often make individual counseling an acceptable and useful process to this age group.

However, the importance of the peer group and the strong interest of most early adolescents in learning more about themselves and their world, coupled with a wish to avoid the potential stigma of individual counseling and the pressures of the large caseloads of most school counselors, will lead many to emphasize *developmental group counseling*. Group counseling can be particularly effective in promoting positive interpersonal skills, so important during this phase. Counselors should remember, though, that early adolescents may have considerable resistance to exposing themselves to their peers, especially to peers of the other gender, and conversation may tend toward the superficial without skillful counselor intervention. In addition, counselors must be sure that scapegoating or ostracizing of a different member, a common occurrence in early adolescent groups, does not take place.

Developmental counseling groups are ideal vehicles for teaching skills that will enhance career maturity. Skills such as decision making, problem solving, communication, developing leisure activities, increasing self-knowledge, and values clarification are appropriate foci for developmental counseling groups for early adolescents. Because most early adolescents must make some educational decisions that will influence their futures, counseling with this age group must have a practical aspect to help the immature and troubled young person as well as the mature adolescent make sound decisions. The assurance with which early adolescents express their preferences may bear little relation to the realism and appropriateness of their choices. One task of the counselor, then, is to promote examination of the decision-making process and those factors that contributed to a decision to help young people assess the soundness of their choices. Decisions should be geared toward expanding options and opening doors rather than narrowing or limiting alternatives. For example, moving from a college preparatory curriculum to specific vocational preparation is usually easier than moving from a concentration in business or vocational education into a liberal arts curriculum. Those adolescents who consider college a possibility should probably select a college preparatory curriculum in junior high and high school, even though many will eventually decide not to attend college. This is part of the process of broadening options and helping young people make decisions based on thought and exploration rather than on impulse or limited alternatives.

Because, generally, values stabilize during the middle school years, this stage of development is the time when values should receive particular attention. The late 1960s and early 1970s brought *values clarification* to the fore with the work of Raths, Harmin, and Simon (1966); Kirschenbaum; and others (Abramowitz & Macari, 1972). Values have been defined as beliefs that a person is proud of and willing to affirm, chosen from alternatives with regard to possible consequences, free from outside pressure, and reflected in consistent action. Values can help answer questions such as these: Who am I? Where am I going? What is important to me? What do I want to do? What are my options? What decisions will be best for me? Although values clarification now seems to have faded in importance, the process of helping young people clarify their values is often included in *affective education* programs, based on the ideas of Carl Rogers (1942) and Abraham Maslow (1943). Studies of these programs at the sixth- and seventh-grade levels concluded, "Affective education can improve the self-esteem and interpersonal skills of children" (Calsyn et al., 1984, p. 138).

Teachers and counselors engaged in affective education should guard against persuading, limiting choices, evaluating, moralizing, or imposing their own values on their students. Teachers and counselors need to be aware of their own biases and should avoid communicating them to their students. Their role should be an accepting and encouraging one that promotes exploration, self-examination, and self-awareness. Facilitators of affective education groups also should be careful that peer norms do not limit honesty and individual development. Affective education can be made particularly relevant to career development if counselors encourage group members to examine relationships between values and interests and values and abilities.

Parent conferences and special programs for parents are another approach to promoting career development. Many parents have difficulty recognizing that young adolescents are capable of anticipating the future and are quite concerned about their adult roles. Counselors can serve an important function by meeting with parents and children together to foster dialogue and cooperative planning. Counseling with early adolescents and their parents should focus on how decisions affecting the children are being made as well as what decisions are being made. This process can improve parent-child communication and facilitate the development of decision making that meets the needs of early adolescents for independence, competence, and responsibility yet maintains the close parent-child tie that remains important during these years.

Typically, *career education* is a large-scale program, designed to promote career maturation. Group and individual counseling as well as consultation with parents may be components of career education. However, it is usually conducted at a broader level, the classroom, the grade level, or the entire school. Multifaceted in nature, career education programs combine teaching and counseling interventions and usually involve close collaboration of all school personnel.

Rubinton (1985), describing a career education program implemented in middle schools in New York, stated, "The middle and junior high school years . . . are crucial years for students to be involved in career education" (p. 249). The New York program, called Career Exploration for Youth, consisted of four components:

1. *Children's program.* This included an examination of myths about careers and biases for and against familiar careers, exploration of unfamiliar and nontraditional careers, development of career-related options in cluster areas of interest, direct participation in career experiences, exposure to role models, and exploration of the relationship of careers to values.
2. *Parents' program.* The goal of this component of the program was to familiarize parents with the processes of career decision making and development and enable them to facilitate those processes in their children.
3. *School personnel program.* The focus here was teaching principles of career education and ways of infusing career education into the classroom.
4. *Recreation.* This program was for the children and was conducted on four Saturdays for 2 hours.

Despite its brevity the program was shown to increase career awareness, self-knowledge, and facility with decision making.

Career resource centers are another popular approach to facilitating career development at the middle and junior high school levels. Common ingredients of these centers include descriptions of occupations, projections of occupational outlooks, information on postsecondary education and training, information on careers in the military, descriptions of apprenticeship and internship programs, lists of resource people in various careers, information on the education and career development of special populations, resources on financial aid for college, guides for interviewing and résumé writing, tests and inventories useful in promoting self-awareness, lists of local job openings, and computer terminals with career development programs that can be used with little supervision (Zunker, 1990). These centers can be used for structured programs with groups of students or can be used on a drop-in, as-needed basis.

Role of the Career Counselor
With Young Adolescents

Although the literature on career development programs in middle and junior high schools describes many resources and procedures for counselors to use, some counselors may find a disparity between what they would like to do and what they are required to do. Tennyson, Miller, Skovholt, and Williams (1989) surveyed junior high school counselors and found they saw their most frequent roles as conferring with a teacher about a student, participating in a case conference, and informing parents about a school program. M. J. Miller's (1988a) survey of middle school counselors in schools identified by the U.S. Department of Education as exemplary ranked the following, in order, as important factors in counseling: (a) counseling and consultation, (b) coordination, (c) career assistance, (d) professional development, (e) organization, (f) educational planning, (g) assessment, and (h) discipline. The disparity in the findings of the two surveys suggests that middle/junior high school counselors may not spend as much time in direct contact with the students as they think is optimal. This seems to be reflected in early adolescents' attitudes; Aubrey (1977) found that most do not view teachers and school counselors as resources on occupational information.

Recently, some states have attempted to address this disparity by revamping school counseling programs so that paperwork is reduced and at least a predetermined minimum number of hours of direct counselor-student contact is maintained. New Hampshire's Comprehensive Counseling and Guidance Program is an example of a statewide initiative to establish school counseling programs that are more responsive to people's needs (Carr & Hayslip, 1989). Initial strategies of program development included establishment of a local advisory committee; time and task analyses; needs assessments via surveys of students, parents, teachers, and community members; development of desired student outcomes; and a competency-based guidance program action plan. Four components were central to the program: (a) a guidance curriculum of competencies to be attained by students at various stages of their development; (b) personal, social, educational, and career planning with students and their parents; (c) responsive counseling, consultation, and referral; and (d) management support and monitoring to ensure accountability.

One of the challenges facing counselors at this level, then, is planning programs that are realistic and likely to be implemented that also seem likely to be effective in addressing the needs of early adolescents. Understanding the nature of both positive career development and common problems in development that are likely to arise among young people in this age group can facilitate counselors' efforts at program planning.

Research has identified many dimensions that are likely to have an impact on early adolescents' career maturation. A consideration of some of these provides guidelines for counselors seeking to promote career development of this age group.

Exploring and developing abilities. Aubrey (1977) found that 13-year-olds were particularly interested in improving themselves in and learning about areas of achievement not modeled in their families. For example, those whose parents had not completed high school were particularly interested in improving their academic abilities, whereas those with parents who had gone to college were more interested in improving their athletic ability. Whether this reflects rebellion or curiosity, counselors should help early adolescents explore and develop abilities in endeavors that both mirror and diverge from those of other family members.

Information about careers. Although most early adolescents have general information on occupations, their knowledge of occupational roles, benefits, and requirements is limited, as is their awareness of factors to consider in formulating career plans. Providing specific information on occupations, then, should be an important component in career development activities with this age group.

Enhancing self-esteem. Typically, impairment in girls' self-esteem appears during the middle school years, limiting career options and perhaps leading to early choices that do not make good use of abilities. Counselors should provide experiences, recognition, and feedback that are likely to enhance self-esteem, particularly for girls, and should counteract the effect of sex-based occupational foreclosure for both males and females (R. R. Miller, 1986).

Realistic career aspirations. The establishment of strong social class stereotypes and a rigid occupational prestige hierarchy often take place during early adolescence, leading to the formulation of aspirations that may exceed abilities and later opportunities. Harris and Wallin (1978) found that a much higher percentage of seventh graders expressed occupational choices that required a college education than were likely to graduate from college. According to R. R. Miller (1986), a major goal for this age group "should be to counteract the effects of occupational elimination based on social class inappropriateness" (p. 251).

Flexibility in career development plans. Career maturity varies considerably among early adolescents and is affected by many factors, including academic achievement, geography, socioeconomic status, family background, and ethnicity. Career development programs, then, should be flexible and modified to meet individual needs. Extra help should be provided, particularly to special education students, those from minority ethnic backgrounds, those who are at-risk of leaving high school before completion, and any others who may manifest impaired self-esteem or career development.

Encouraging self-responsibility. A study of ninth graders (Bernardelli, 1983) suggested that an internal locus of control was positively correlated with career maturity, which, in turn, was correlated with occupational information-seeking behavior. However, most early adolescents do not have a strong sense of responsibility for themselves. In light of these findings, encouragement of inner directedness, competence, and responsibility should contribute positively to career development.

Resources to Promote
Early Adolescent Career Development

Since the early 1970s, many publishers have been developing materials designed to facilitate the career development of early adolescents. A review of recent test catalogs or a visit to the annual convention of the American Counseling Association can help counselors to select materials that are in keeping with their needs and budgets.

Many young adolescents have the ability and motivation to make good use of printed as well as audio and visual career information, if they are given some help in selecting the material and relating the information to themselves. Because of their interest in new role models, early adolescents tend to be particularly receptive to reading biographies of successful people in various occupations. Many young teenagers are intrigued by computers and enjoy and benefit from computerized programs designed to promote self-awareness and knowledge of the world of work. In addition, exercises and programs presented by counselors can be particularly powerful in involving young people and helping them to personalize the information that is presented. A comprehensive career education program that presents information and promotes learning in a variety of ways seems most likely to reach the greatest number of students and to have the strongest impact. The following is a list of suggested programs and resources that seem likely to be useful at the middle and junior high school levels.

Career Education Exercises and Programs

1. Creating a life line, participants draw a graph of past and anticipated highs and lows in their lives, noting when important events occur.
2. In group role-play, participants assume the identities of famous people, people they admire, or hypothetical people in occupations of interest to them. Discussion and socialization occurs while they remain in role.
3. In a group role play, participants act as if an anticipated goal has already happened (e.g., marriage, graduation from law school, parenthood, teaching a class).
4. Students take part in a group discussion of a typical day, a special day they have experienced, or an ideal day.
5. Participants write a news release about themselves, describing their accomplishment of a major goal they have for themselves.
6. Participants write their autobiographies, including both past and future events.
7. Participants identify their major roles (e.g., daughter, student, friend, sister, tennis player, waitress) and then hypothetically give up one role at a time, beginning with the least important role. When all roles have been given up, they are then reassumed, one at a time. This process of role stripping helps people understand the importance of roles as well as realize the many roles they have already developed.
8. A career day/week/fair is planned in which parents and others from the community visit the school and talk about their careers, college and

vocational school representatives visit and provide information, and other activities are scheduled to focus attention on career development. Atypical role models in terms of gender, ethnic and socioeconomic background, and disabilities are particularly valuable.

9. Shadowing or mentoring is arranged, in which students are paired with someone employed in an occupation of interest to them. The students spend time at the person's place of business, becoming acquainted with the sort of work that is done. Students are taught how to observe and analyze the experience beforehand and are given the opportunity to process it afterward.

10. Play "What's My Line?" with participants assuming interesting occupational roles.

11. Show movies and other films that depict a range of career roles and then have students discuss the characteristics, benefits, and limitations of each role. Photographs or magazine pictures can be used if films are not available.

12. Students maintain file folders or prepare presentations and reports on occupations of interest to them.

13. Students create a family tree, listing family members by occupation as well as by name, and then discuss patterns and family messages about career choices.

14. Present students with lists of occupations and help them rank order them or sort them into groups according to a variety of criteria (e.g., most prestigious, most enjoyable, most exciting, most lucrative).

15. Job bank and/or work-study programs can be established, to help students locate part-time and vacation employment.

16. Topics for classroom or small group discussion might include the following:
    a. setting goals
    b. using leisure time
    c. identifying values/interests/abilities/personality traits
    d. understanding self-concept
    e. career clusters
    f. defining occupational prestige
    g. family career patterns
    h. occupational myths (e.g., the one perfect occupation)
    i. selecting courses and majors
    j. looking ahead to college
    k. career choice and planning
    l. making the most of potential

17. Skill development classes might include the following:
    a. finding a job
    b. career exploration

    c. peer counseling/tutoring
    d. problem solving
    e. assertiveness
    f. building interpersonal relationships
    g. developing leadership skills
    h. decision making

Commercially Available Resources

  I. Books
    A. *Dictionary of Occupational Titles* (Superintendent of Documents, U.S. Government Printing Office, Washington, DC 20402)
    B. *Occupational Outlook Handbook* (Superintendent of Documents)
    C. *Encyclopedia of Careers* (Hopke, 1990)
    D. *101 Careers: A Guide to the Fastest Growing Opportunities* (New Careers Center)
    E. *Jobs 1990* (New Careers Center)
    F. *Children's Dictionary of Occupations* (Meridian Education Corporation)—describes over 300 occupations, designed for children in Grades 3 through 8
    G. Vocational biographies, especially of women, ethnic minorities, and people with disabilities who have achieved career success
    H. Catalogs from colleges and other postsecondary schools
 II. Career information
    A. Occupational briefs (Chronicle Guidance Publishers)
    B. *Who Am I? Looking at Self-Concept.* This film and cassette kit for Grades 5 through 9 uses multi-ethnic scenes and characters to promote awareness of self-concept, its development, and its impact on one's life. Ways of improving self-concept and dealing with relationships with family and friends are considered. (Sunburst Communications)
    C. *Feelings Grow Too.* These are filmstrips and cassettes designed to help children in Grades 5 through 9 to understand the emotional changes that accompany puberty (Sunburst Communications).
      1. *Friends: How They Help . . . How They Hurt.* This is for use in Grades 5 through 9 (Sunburst Communications).
      2. *Anger: The Turbulent Emotion.* This is for use in Grades 5 through 9 (Sunburst Communications).
    D. Vocational biographies. Available are nearly 700 biographies that show how real people developed their careers. This company also has information on college finding, job seeking, and career planning.
    E. *The Whole Work Catalog* (New Career Center). This is a very useful compendium of career information and reference books in the following categories:

1. job hunting (e.g., preparing résumés, obtaining references, writing cover letters)
2. career choice—information on occupational outlook, new employment opportunities, geographic distribution of jobs, career paths, salaries, internships, sources of information on a broad range of occupations, books on specific career areas (e.g., *Career Choices for Students of Psychology*)
3. comprehensive books of career information
4. books on self-employment
5. career development videos on specific occupations and general topics of relevance (e.g., self-awareness, the world of work)
6. improving work-related skills

F. *Career Choices*. This is a workbook with accompanying instructor's and counselor's guide to help adolescents and young adults with career decision making (Advocacy Press).

G. *Positive Action*. This is a comprehensive, school-based curriculum designed to build self-concept; it includes many 15- to 20-minute classroom lessons and a teacher's manual, available for Grades K through 6 and Grades 7 and 8 (Positive Action).

H. The American Guidance Service has many books and programs available to promote affective development, socialization, self-esteem, and family life for early adolescents. These include *Homework Coach*, designed to improve the study skills of 12- to 20-year-olds.

III. Computer-based career guidance systems

A. *DISCOVER for junior high and middle schools*. This is a computer-based career planning system for group or individual use, designed to facilitate planning for high school, improve self-esteem, promote career development and planning, and increase knowledge of self and the world of work (American College Testing Program, Educational Services Division).

B. *Career Exploration and Planning Program (CEPP)*. This is another comprehensive computerized career information delivery system, describing 4,000 high employment occupations as well as career roles in the military, linked with several major inventories of interests and abilities (Meridian).

Developmental Milestones
of Early Adolescence

Characteristics or milestones can be identified that typify healthy early adolescent development. Counselors might look for these when assessing the career and emotional development of the young people with whom they are working and formulate plans to facilitate growth in those areas where maturation seems to be slow. Particular attention should be given to career maturation because, during the high school years, career decisions with potentially long-range implications must be made.

Early adolescents who are emotionally healthy and mature can be expected to do the following:

1. accept themselves as worthwhile and have a positive self-image that is relatively clear and accurate
2. have acquired basic habits of industry—be able to work diligently, productively, and cooperatively and gain gratification from making good use of their potentials
3. accept and adjust to their changing physical and emotional selves and use their minds and bodies effectively
4. be able to view life as a continuous and developmental process, appreciate the influence of the past, live in the present, and formulate realistic plans for the future
5. establish relationships with family, teachers, peers, and others that are rewarding but that allow early adolescents independence and a sense of their own uniqueness
6. develop a system of values and a sense of personal and social morality and responsibility
7. develop self-control and a capacity for deferred gratification
8. engage in rewarding leisure activities
9. become able to deal with abstractions and generalizations, organizing knowledge in meaningful ways
10. remain open to learning new roles without undue limitations imposed by gender, background, or disabilities

As Jackson and Hornbeck (1989) put it, the goal of middle school education is the development of "thinking, productive, caring, healthy youth" (p. 835).

Career Development Objectives
for Early Adolescence

Although career and emotional development are intertwined, a more detailed and specific list of career development milestones for this age group is provided to facilitate career counseling and education at the middle/junior high school levels. Early adolescents with positive career maturation will do the following:

1. gain awareness and understanding of interests, aptitudes, values, and personality traits in themselves and others and become eager to learn more about these aspects
2. use these qualities as a basis for initiating an exploration of relevant careers
3. examine and gain insight into the effects of family background, socio-economic status and ethnic background, environment, gender, early learning, and heredity on present interests, abilities, values, personality, and aspirations
4. become aware of their own level of aspiration
5. view career development as a comprehensive process that extends throughout the life span and affects all aspects of one's life
6. develop decision-making, planning, communicating, and problem-solving skills
7. assume responsibility for their own career-related decisions
8. develop some understanding of the American system of economy, business, and technology and an appreciation of the impact these factors can have on career development
9. appreciate work as a rewarding and enduring institution
10. appreciate and consider a broad variety of jobs, occupations, and careers
11. realize that different occupations have different requirements and provide different rewards
12. become aware of imminent academic choices and their relationship to postsecondary school options
13. become familiar with resources providing career information
14. obtain prevocational experiences via part-time jobs, volunteer work, leisure activities
15. develop tentative career goals

The Role of Assessment in the Counseling of Early Adolescents

The assessment process is an important aspect of counseling the early adolescent. These are action-oriented years when physical rather than verbal means of communication may be more comfortable for the child. In addition, the process of seeking independence and individuality leads many early adolescents to turn from their parents to their peers when seeking confidantes. These factors may make young people in this stage of development somewhat uncomfortable and unskilled at discussing their thoughts and feelings with an adult. Assessment can, therefore, serve as a useful vehicle to promote discussion and can bring to light concerns and ideas that can more easily be put on paper than confided to the counselor.

The major goals of the assessment process with early adolescents are closely related to the goals of the counseling process with this age group. Broadening options and developing self-awareness and self-esteem are primary. Assessment can contribute to these goals by identifying abilities and interests that have not yet come to the attention of early adolescents or their teachers, enabling their translation into expanded and rewarding activities.

Assessment during early adolescence is designed not so much to facilitate commitment to plans but to help people deal with any obstacles that might get in the way of their making sound choices and plans in the future. For that reason, particular attention should be paid to the emotional well-being of the early adolescent. Personal difficulties experienced during these years may lead young people to aim toward career choices that grow out of strong emotional needs or self-doubts and are not congruent with interests and aptitudes.

In addition, this is an important time for clarification and development of abilities. Adolescents' achievements in high school almost certainly will have an effect on their readiness for postsecondary school education and admission to college, which will, in turn, have some bearing on future career success. To increase the early adolescent's chances of having a rewarding experience in high school, problems in academic performance, negative attitudes toward school, low self-esteem, and impaired interpersonal relationships should be identified and ameliorated as soon as possible. Concerns such as these often come to light via the assessment process.

Although most early adolescents are interested in discussing their future plans, few have much understanding of the role of assessment in helping people formulate realistic and rewarding career plans. Some in this age group will have developed a negative view of tests and associate them with failure and anxiety. The assessment process, for early adolescents, will almost invariably be initiated by the counselor rather than by the student and must be presented with care. Assessment should not begin until a comfortable counseling relationship with a satisfactory degree of rapport has been established. Many early adolescents are routinely tested shortly before or after entry into junior high or middle school. Routine schoolwide administration of achievement test batteries during the seventh or eighth grades, for example, is widespread

(Engen et al., 1982). School files should be reviewed before planning an assessment to avoid superfluous testing.

Early adolescents should be involved in planning the assessment process as much as possible. Although they may not question the reason for the assessment and generally will comply with a counselor's request that tests and inventories be completed, efforts should be made to help young people understand the relationship between the counseling and assessment processes. Motivation and openness will probably be increased and suspiciousness decreased if early adolescents can regard the assessment process as a way of helping themselves to increase self-understanding rather than as a means of judging or evaluating them. They should be informed in advance that the results of the assessment will be discussed with them and also should know who else (for example, parents, teachers, school psychologist, therapist) will have access to the results.

Early adolescents, as a group, are responsive to and interested in counseling with a focus on career development. They are eager to learn more about themselves and their environments and feel a need for skills that will enable them to cope more effectively. The successful counselor will attend first to early adolescents' emotional needs and development and then will promote the integration of personal and career development, using a variety of tools and resources. The early adolescent years are years of change and flux, and both counselors and young people should acknowledge this and expend efforts to make those changes positive and rewarding. If this occurs, it can have the effect of developing an optimistic outlook in early adolescents and helping them approach future milestones with anticipation and good judgment.

Case Study of Hector Gomez

An Early Adolescent Engaged in Growing and Searching

The case of Hector Gomez is presented to illustrate the process of counseling and assessment with an early adolescent. Reflected in this case are not only age- and stage-related dynamics but also developmental patterns related to Hector's socioeconomic background and family of origin as well as to his life experiences.

Background

Hector is a 13-year-old Hispanic male who is in the eighth grade. Hector's parents had married when his mother was 19 years old and his father was 25. Hector's father was a successful businessman from a South American country who had traveled widely, with and without his family, developing international markets for a South American corporation. Hector's mother had never been employed outside of the home, but Hector reported that now that the children were older, she spoke of establishing a business to market South American crafts. Hector was the oldest of three children. His sisters were 11 and 9 years of age.

Hector had lived in the United States for a year when he was in elementary school and now had been back in the United States for 5 months, completing the first two quarters of eighth grade here. He spoke English fluently, as well as Spanish and French. A tall, stocky boy, dressed in the designer jeans and athletic shoes most coveted by his age group, he presented a very positive appearance.

Hector had been referred for counseling because his teachers thought he might benefit from some help in facilitating his adjustment to his new school. Although he had been performing well academically, his teachers reported that Hector was sometimes aggressive and belligerent, particularly toward the boys who were smaller than he. This behavior seemed to occur under two circumstances: when Hector was performing better at a task than most of the other children and when Hector was having more difficulty at a task than most of the other children.

Hector presented himself right on schedule for his meeting with the counselor. When he was told that the purpose of the interview was to talk about his adjustment to his new school, he quickly responded with a lengthy description of his life in South America and how much he missed his friends and extended family there. According to Hector, the family had a large home in South America with extensive grounds where he was able to have his own horse. A tennis court nearby gave him opportunity to improve his tennis skills, and he had been a member of a local tennis team before the family came to the United States. Another source of pride and interest for Hector was his new computer, purchased for him recently by his father.

Hector verbalized many interests, most of them involving challenge, activity, and use of motor skills. He was presently on the school basketball team and described himself as a good player who tried to spend as much time as possible practicing so that he would be even better. In South America, he had played soccer as well as tennis but stated that he preferred basketball to soccer because the smaller number of players on the team made his own role even more important. As a child, Hector had imagined himself becoming a professional soccer player, reflecting both interests and power motives. However, he stated that he realized he probably was not skilled enough for that profession and, perhaps reflecting parental input, said, "I want a more stable job, where you're not always traveling around."

Hector seemed to enjoy competition. However, he set high standards for his own performance and became unhappy when he made a mistake.

Hector reported little interest in the academic aspects of school. As he put it, "School can really get boring, but I know I have to get good grades to be successful in life." Education was a strong family value, and Hector's parents expected him to allow ample time for homework in his schedule. To return to the school he had been attending in South America, he must pass a reentrance examination after his return, and both Hector and his parents viewed his return to this academically oriented and highly competitive school as essential to his development. Hector stated that physical education and shop were his favorite times of day at school. He enjoyed staying busy and active and preferred activities that involve using his hands and his body.

Hector reported a close relationship with all his family members but seemed to be closest to his mother. His father often played tennis with him and took him along on business trips, privileges that were not extended to his sisters, making Hector feel that he and his father had a special bond. Hector reported missing his father when he was away on extended business trips but enjoyed the sort of celebration, with stories and presents, that would ensue when his father returned from a long trip. He viewed his parents as strict but loving and stated that if he misbehaved or did not complete his school work, his parents would punish him by withdrawing privileges such as watching television and playing computer games.

Hector believed that he got along well with the other children in his class and cited two special friends: one boy who excelled at tennis and basketball and another boy who excelled academically but who had little athletic ability. Hector reported, with pride, that he taught that boy to play tennis and seemed proud of the admiration and appreciation he received from helping his friend.

Career Aspirations

Hector had some very definite ideas about what he planned to do in the future. A cousin of his had had a brain tumor successfully removed when she was 3 years old, and since then, Hector has hoped to become a brain surgeon. He spoke admiringly of how a famous brain surgeon had been brought in to perform the delicate surgery and how the surgeon had saved his cousin's life. When asked what appealed to him about becoming a brain surgeon, Hector cited the recognition, the skills, and the high salary of a brain surgeon as attractions, as well as the ability to save lives and help people. Hector seemed aware that becoming a brain surgeon was a long, challenging process and stated that if he could not become a brain surgeon, he wanted to be a physician of some sort, perhaps a pediatrician or a gastroenterologist. He thought that both of those fields would allow him to help people, use his hands, and receive recognition for his work.

Clearly, Hector has established high levels of aspiration for himself in aiming toward a career as a brain surgeon. The prestige associated with this occupation as well as its positive impact on his family seems to have had considerable influence on Hector's choice. Values play an important part in Hector's goals, with a career as a physician enabling him to achieve several of his goals: helping others, having power, obtaining recognition, and being well paid for his work. Interests and abilities seem less important determinants of Hector's choices. Although he recognized that surgeons must work skillfully with their hands and thought that he might be successful as a surgeon because of his skill and enjoyment in using his hands, he seemed to have little genuine understanding of the training and experience of a surgeon. Hector did not report a strong interest in science and expressed little fondness for academics in general. Although Hector's career goals certainly should not be discouraged, he might benefit from some help in reality testing to determine whether he really is interested in pursuing the extensive academic training required to become a physician.

The omission of athletics, Hector's strongest interest, from his career aspirations is noteworthy. When asked about this, Hector replied that although his parents encouraged his participation in team and individual sports right now, they had told him that athletics was not a good career choice because of the instability and uncertainty of such an endeavor. They encouraged him to aspire to a more academically demanding career that drew on his intellectual abilities rather than his physical ones.

These messages reflect several aspects of Hector's life. Typically, the firstborn male in a family, especially in a family with a relatively high socioeconomic status and a Hispanic background, will be expected to be a high achiever. As the only boy in his family, Hector will be carrying on the family name and is probably expected to bring honor and recognition to the family. Although Hector has internalized many of these family values and has high expectations of himself, as does his family, the pressure he is feeling to succeed, especially in areas such as science and mathematics that reportedly hold little interest for him, may be contributing to his outbursts of anger in the classroom as well as leading him to premature foreclosure of some opportunities. Broadening out Hector's range of options and engaging him in some information gathering and occupational exploration might prove useful. Whether those experiences confirm his choice of a career in medicine or point him in another direction, they will help him to make a choice that reflects his own interests, abilities, values, and personality.

Broadening his options might also help Hector with his interpersonal relationships and his acceptance of himself. Although he does seem to have considerable self-confidence, particularly about his athletic abilities, his low tolerance for frustration and unrealistically high expectations of himself were sometimes evident. When asked what happened when he makes a mistake, Hector responded quite openly: "I'm pretty hard on myself. It really makes me feel dumb to make a mistake, and sometimes I act like somebody else really made the mistake. It's not so bad making a mistake on the basketball court because usually I do pretty good, but when the teacher calls on me in math and I don't know the answer, it really gets me mad. I try to just forget about it, play some ball, or take a nap, and sometimes that helps, but other times I just get mad at somebody."

Assessment of Hector

Hector's teachers described him as hardworking, responsible, and competitive, although they also felt that his extensive involvement in formal and informal athletic activities might be keeping him from maximizing his academic potential. His grades for the first two quarters of eighth grade reflected good, although somewhat inconsistent, ability. Hector received As in industrial arts, health and physical education, and percussion; Bs in English, history, and science; and a C+ in mathematics. Hector's grades reflect his own self-estimates; his highest grades are in those subjects that are less academically oriented and that involve use of his hands. He has the most difficulty with mathematics. However, in light of the fact that Hector has spent little time in the United States and has been in his present school for only 5 months, he seems to be performing quite well.

No standardized tests of Hector's abilities, interests, or personality were available. Consequently, a comprehensive assessment program was planned to provide better understanding of Hector.

The COPSystem (Career Occupational Placement System), published by EdITS (San Diego, California) was selected to provide a broad-based and coordinated picture of Hector's abilities, interests, and values. The COPSystem is described by its publishers as "a career awareness unit providing interest, ability, and work value scores keyed to occupational clusters, job information and curriculum." Scores provided by all the inventories that are part of the COPSystem, the CAPS ability battery, the COPS interest inventory, and the COPES work values survey, are linked to 14 occupational clusters:

1. science, professional
2. science, skilled
3. technology, professional
4. technology, skilled
5. consumer economics
6. outdoor

7. business, professional
8. business, skilled
9. clerical
10. communication
11. arts, professional
12. arts, skilled
13. service, professional
14. service, skilled

These clusters are based on Roe's classification of occupations into major groups and levels within each group. The COPSystem Comprehensive Career Guide facilitates interpretation and comparison of scores as well as giving direction to information gathering and planning. Extensive support materials for the COPSystem, including a career briefs kit, a career cluster booklet kit, and occupational cluster charts, have been developed based on the *Occupational Outlook Handbook* and other information from the U.S. Department of Labor. These materials enable school and career counselors to use the system as part of a career education program, promoting self-awareness as well as career development. Machine-scoring as well as self-scoring forms are available, allowing assessment of large groups and of individuals. The COPSystem was originally developed for use with people in junior high school, high school, and college. Since its inception, the COPS II has been developed for the elementary school grades or for people with reading or motivational difficulties, and the COPS-P (professional level) is available for adults and college students.

Abilities

The Career Ability Placement Survey (CAPS) includes eight 5-minute tests, providing a rapid measurement of aptitude in the following areas: mechanical reasoning, spatial relations, verbal reasoning, numerical ability, language usage, word knowledge, perceptual speed and accuracy, and manual speed and dexterity. Scores in the eight areas are presented in terms of stanines, scores ranging from one to nine. National norms for the CAPS are available for intermediate, high school, and community college students. The CAPS has been correlated with the Differential Aptitude Tests (DAT) and the General Aptitude Test Battery (GATB), two well-established aptitude tests.

Hector's highest stanine scores on the CAPS, sevens, were in verbal reasoning and numerical ability. His score in spatial relations fell in the 6th stanine and his score in mechanical reasoning fell slightly below average, in the 4th stanine. His other four scores all fell in the 5th or middle stanine.

Interestingly, Hector's scores are quite different from what he predicted prior to being given his results. He had predicted that his highest score would be in mechanical reasoning (actually his lowest score), and he was very surprised that his highest scores were in verbal and numerical areas. When these ability scores were plotted on the CAPS Career Profile, relating CAPS scores to the 14 occupational clusters, all of Hector's scores fell in the middle range or slightly higher. Although no marked strengths emerged, neither does Hector seem to have any significant intellectual deficits. His ability levels were high enough to suggest that he had an opportunity for success in all 14 areas. Although caution should be exercised in interpreting this instrument in light of Hector's bilingual background, his inventoried abilities and his school grades are congruent in portraying him as an average to above-average student. No irregularities appeared in his responses or discussion of the inventory, supporting its accuracy.

Several aspects of the results of this inventory suggest that career exploration and education might be important to Hector at the present time. Hector's scores are not very congruent with his expressed interests. Perhaps Hector's frequent changes in academic environment have negatively affected his attitude toward the academic subjects and, were he in a stable and comfortable environment, greater interest and ability in the basic academic subjects might emerge. Hector might benefit from exposure to more rewarding academic experiences and from an increased opportunity to develop his self-awareness. Another concern raised by the CAPS was the disparity between Hector's scores (somewhat above average) and the high academic demands of his present career aspiration, brain surgeon. Although no definite determination can be made at present, Hector may not have the high grades and academic abilities he will need for a career in medicine. Although he should not be dissuaded from his present career goals, exposing Hector to occupational information relevant to his inventoried scores on the COPSystem might help him to make more realistic choices. Hector's scores on the CAPS also suggest an explanation for his frustration in school. He may be setting unrealistically high academic goals for himself and may be having difficulty accepting that, at least at present, he is not an outstanding student.

The CAPS is only one of many inventories available to assess the abilities of children in the intermediate grades. Others include the DAT (Psychological Corporation), now available with an accompanying interest inventory, the Career Planning Questionnaire (CPQ); the Iowa Tests of Basic Skills (Riverside); the Kuhlmann Anderson Tests (Scholastic Testing Service); the Comprehensive Tests of Basic Skills (CTB/Macmillan/McGraw-Hill); the Stanford Achievement Test (Psychological Corporation); the Otis-Lennon School Ability Test (Psychological Corporation); and the Metropolitan Achievement Tests (Psychological Corporation).

Interests

Interests, like almost everything else during the early adolescent years, tend to be in a state of flux and do not stabilize in most people until the ninth grade or later. Counselors should be cautious in interpreting the inventoried interests of this age group and should anticipate considerable change.

Both interests and abilities are important to early adolescents when they formulate their tentative career plans, and interest inventories offer a way to help young people in this phase of development to examine and explore their interests and perhaps to discover new areas of interest. Interest inventories can provide an important service in expanding early adolescents' views of themselves and the world of work and in suggesting appropriate exploratory experiences. However, an examination of interests always should begin with a discussion of expressed and manifest interests. Interest inventories should be regarded as a tertiary source of information at this stage.

The tendency for early adolescents to have difficulty reacting objectively to inventories is particularly evident in their reactions to measures of interests. For some, the information provided by the inventory is immediately rejected if it differs from their expressed interests because of the threat posed by an inventory that may seem to know more about them than they do about themselves. For others, the association of tests with authority leads to an exaggeration of the importance and validity of the results. In discussing the results of interest inventories with early adolescents, exploring their attitudes toward the instruments can promote an appropriate degree of acceptance of the results.

The Career Occupational Preference Survey (COPS) Interest Inventory, part of the COPSystem, was used to assess Hector's interests. The Interest Inventory consists of 168 items describing occupationally relevant activities (Brookings & Bolton, 1986). Twelve items are included for each of the 14 scales. Interest is indicated on a 4-point Likert-type scale ranging from *like very much* (4) to *dislike very much* (1). Kane (1989) viewed the COPS as especially good for organizing career preferences and for encouraging career exploration but less useful as a decision-making tool. Because Hector's needs focused more on exploration than decision making, the COPS seemed an appropriate measure of his interests. The COPS uses a free-response format rather than an ipsative one. Although people seem to prefer the format of the COPS, it can result in extreme and misleading scores. Extensive normative data are available for the COPS as for the other instruments in this system. In addition, many validity studies link the COPS to information on choice of major, occupational group scores, and scores on other interest inventories. Typically, completion of the COPS requires 20 to 30 minutes. A profile sheet facilitates the translation of raw scores into percentile scores.

Before Hector's scores on the COPS were discussed with him, the 14 occupational clusters were reviewed, and he was asked to predict his highest and lowest interest areas. He guessed that science, professional would be his highest score, consistent with his expressed interest in becoming a brain surgeon, whereas he viewed the clerical, service, and arts areas as likely to be his lowest scores. When his reasoning was explored, Hector seemed to reject clerical, service, and arts areas not only because of lack of interest but also because he viewed those fields as being low in prestige and more appropriate for women than for men. As he interpreted the categories, "Clerical is like secretaries, arts is dancers and painters and stuff like that, and service is teachers and nurses. Mostly women are in jobs like that. Teachers and secretaries don't make very much money, I know that. I just wouldn't like those kinds of jobs." Having people predict their scores before they are presented can provide useful insights into self-image and rationale for preferences.

Hector's inventoried interests were quite consistent with his predictions. His highest interest was in science, professional (95th percentile) with technology, professional second (75th percentile). Nearly all his other scores were quite low with outdoor; business, skilled; arts, skilled; and service, skilled being at about the first percentile. Hector's profile is a very well-differentiated one, with strong highs and lows. Clearly, he is rejecting several occupational areas while also indicating a preference for professional over skilled occupations.

According to the COPS Profile and Guide, the science, professional cluster includes occupations in medical-life science, mathematical science, and physical science. Several occupations in the cluster such as surgeon, programmer, and engineer are consistent with other sources of information on Hector's interests, whereas other occupations such as statistician, chemist, and botanist probably hold little interest for Hector. Technology, professional includes occupations in four areas; aeronautical-marine, civil-construction, electrical, and mechanical-chemical. Related courses of study include industrial arts, science, and mathematics, a mix of Hector's expressed likes and dislikes.

Hector was pleased with the results of this inventory because they seemed, to him, to confirm his career aspirations. Counselors should bear in mind that most interest inventories can be deliberately slanted toward or away from specific occupations, although most people present honest responses. However, the possibility remains that Hector responded in such a way as to reflect his interest in becoming a brain surgeon. Whether or not some faking had occurred, the results of the inventory are sufficiently broad to facilitate exploration. Educational experiences such as informational interviews, biographies, and field visits to help Hector become familiar with some of the other occupations in his high interest areas would help to expand his range of options and stimulate his thinking.

Values and Personality

The Career Orientation Placement and Evaluation Survey (COPES), the third part of the COPSystem, was used to assess Hector's values. This work values survey requires 20 to 30 minutes to complete and provides scores on eight bipolar value scales:

1. investigative/accepting
2. practical/carefree
3. independence/conformity
4. leadership/supportive
5. orderliness/noncompulsive
6. recognition/privacy
7. aesthetic/realistic
8. social/self-concern

The inventory consists of 128 pairs of statements. For each one, respondents indicate which item in each pair best completes the statement, "I value activities or jobs in which . . . ." Although the COPES has been called a moderately good inventory for the measurement of values, Mueller (1985) cautioned that reliability for the inventory was fairly low, with substantial intercorrelation among some scales. The COPES seems best used as part of an assessment package, as it is here, rather than alone. A self-interpretation profile and guide facilitates translation of scores into percentiles.

Hector's strongest work values, as reflected on the COPES, were leadership (94th percentile) and recognition (92nd percentile). All other scores fell in the second or third quartile. Leadership and recognition are values that are consistent with Hector's verbalized goals of power and prestige. However, typically, they correlate more strongly with interest in business and enterprising areas than with scientific or investigative areas (EdITS, 1990).

Another view of Hector's personality was obtained through the Tennessee Self-Concept Scale (Western Psychological Services). This inventory consists of 100 self-descriptive statements, designed to allow people aged 12 or over to present the picture they have of themselves. Scores are presented for overall level of self-esteem, self-criticism, identity, self-satisfaction, behavior, physical self, moral-ethical self, personal self, family self, social self, and variability. Although considerable study has been done on the validity and reliability of this instrument, it, too, is best used as part of an assessment package, providing information to complement other sources of data.

Hector's overall levels of self-esteem and self-criticism were in the average range. However, his self-concept scores reflected considerable variability, suggesting significant inconsistency in his self-image. Highest scores included self-satisfaction, physical self, and identity. Generally, Hector has positive self-esteem and is particularly proud of his physical abilities. On the other hand, his scores were rather low in behavior and moral-ethical self, suggesting that he has some concern about the way he acts and may sometimes view himself as a bad person. Despite Hector's external bravado, he seems to be concerned about his behavior, as are his teachers, and some self-doubts may be troubling him. Although, generally, his self-image is sound, the few low scores on this measure of self-concept may be useful in opening discussion of these shared concerns and in involving Hector in some short-term counseling.

Synthesis of Inventories and Counseling Recommendations

The COPSystem includes a summary profile sheet that allows the results of all three inventories—the CAPS, the COPS, and the COPES—to be plotted on a single form and related to the 14 occupational clusters (see Figure 5.1). Hector's abilities, interests, and values were strong in the area of technology, professional. Although his interest was strongest in science, professional, Hector's values and abilities were not consistent with that area. On the other hand, his values were consistent with such areas as business, service and arts, professional, areas that were not consistent with his abilities or interests. Although career exploration, for Hector, probably should focus most on promoting self-awareness as well as deepening his understanding of professional occupations in technology, the breadth of his abilities, interests, and values warrants consideration of a wide range of options, of course, including Hector's expressed interest in the field of medicine.

In addition to career education and exploration, Hector seems likely to benefit from some short-term counseling, perhaps involving a combination of individual, family, and group interventions. Individual counseling, perhaps with his school counselor, would afford Hector the opportunity to develop better ways of coping with anger and frustration, a clearer and more realistic self-image, and an opportunity to explore and address areas of low self-concept. The school counselor also might want to schedule a meeting with Hector's parents, to involve them in helping him avoid putting excessive pressure on himself and promoting the process of self-discovery and career exploration. In addition, involvement in a peer counseling program or in a personal growth group at school might enable Hector to form more comfortable relationships with his peers, to facilitate his own acceptance of himself, and to help him feel more established in his new school.

This is a copy of your COPSystem profile for your records. You may tear out this sheet and copy your profile from page 2. Be sure to fill out all the blanks and print your name at the bottom of this sheet.

SUMMARY PROFILE SHEET FOR THE CAREER OCCUPATIONAL PREFERENCE SYSTEM—FILE COPY

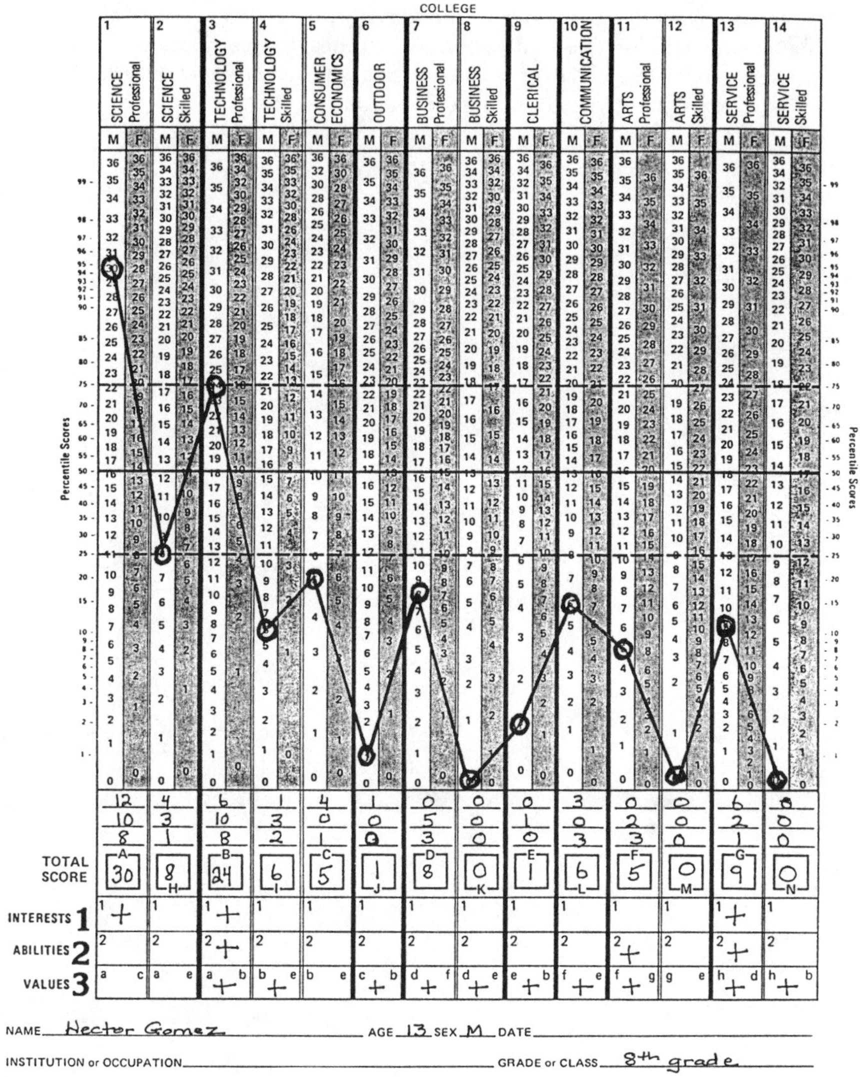

Figure 5.1. COPS Profile Summary for Hector Gomez

Reproduced with permission. COPS Interest Inventory Profile, from the COPSystem Comprehensive Career Guide, copyright © 1992, EdITS, San Diego, CA.

Clearly, Hector is a young man with many strengths and resources. However, assessment has helped to clarify some potential barriers to his career and personal development. With some help, however, it seems likely that Hector will be able to draw on his abilities, interests, and personal strengths and values and to achieve a positive educational experience, leading to establishment in a rewarding occupation.

SIX

Adolescence

Years of Realism and Separation

Emotional Development During Adolescence

Adolescence is a difficult period for many young people, a time of rapid change, confusion, and uncertainty. Many adolescents experience anxiety and discomfort as they struggle to develop separateness from their support systems of childhood and make viable plans for productive and independent lifestyles. However, the challenges of these years can also lead to exhilaration and satisfaction, as adolescents develop rewarding and mature plans and relationships.

Erikson (1963) termed the focal conflict of the high school or adolescent years identity versus role confusion, extending from about the age of 12 to age 20. He described adolescents as searching for continuity and meaning in their lives and in themselves. At a time when independence and separation from their parents, schools, communities, and friends is probably imminent, young people often feel a great need for support and continuity. They are seeking to know and integrate all aspects of themselves—their interests, values, abilities, emotions, bodies, and experiences—so that they can answer the question, "Who am I?" Hallmarks of successful resolution of the so-called identity crisis include development of a positive and stable self-concept, realistic goals, a sense of responsibility for one's own life, flexibility and the ability to handle change, acceptance of oneself and others, and the ability to achieve closeness (Hamachek, 1988).

Developmental Personality Changes

Adolescents tend to be very demanding of themselves and others and hold rather romantic ideals. Their idealism offers them a framework from which to evaluate their experiences and give greater shape to their identities. Idealism also helps adolescents to overcome some of the isolation and alienation they experience by providing a point of view that they share with others in their age group.

Adolescence is a period of transition. Young people of high school age are unsure whether they are children or adults, and that confusion is shared by most of those around them. Adolescent behavior is likely to be impulsive, inconsistent, and unpredictable. Young people in this age group are in the process of finding out what is right for them and are going through trial and error experiences to do so. The process of adolescent identity formation often seems to be characterized by "one step forward, two steps back," as the adolescent shifts between mature and childish behavior. This discontinuity may also result from biological, social, intellectual, and emotional development proceeding at different rates in the same person. However, contrary to popular thought, most adolescents do not undergo severe emotional stress. Only 10% to 20% of adolescents exhibit severe emotional disturbance, the same percentage as is found in the adult population (Powers, Hauser, & Kilner, 1989).

Adolescence is a period of developing and changing self-image. Although a positive self-image may have been formed in childhood, typically, adolescents perceive themselves as different from their childhood selves, and earlier self-concepts may be questioned. Physical changes must be incorporated into the self-image along with changes in attitudes and feelings. Adolescents tend to look to others, usually their peers, for validation and understanding and are very concerned with how they are perceived.

This concern with the attitudes and perceptions of others helps adolescents to form mutually rewarding friendships. Their capacity for empathy and devotion has developed so that they are now capable of providing the support, caring, and encouragement valued by their friends. Intimacy, along with autonomy, is a major issue for adolescents.

Although adolescents value friendships with young people both of their own gender and of the other gender, they are acutely aware of real and imagined differences between the two genders. Gender stereotyping is common during this stage as both boys and girls search for modes of behavior that will promote peer acceptance.

Values development, which intensified during the middle and junior high school years, continues, with the ages between 14 and 18 being particularly important in formation of values (Tinsley et al., 1984).

Relationships With Parents

Often, the parent-child relationship is the arena where adolescents wage their battles for identity and independence. Both adolescents and their parents may have ambivalent feelings about the process of maturation and separation. Most adolescents seem eager to be free of parental restraint yet are uncertain of their ability to handle independence without parental support and structure. The parents, on the other hand, know that their children need to establish their own lifestyles at this time. However, sometimes parents are reluctant to give up their close involvement with their children's lives and remain concerned with protecting their children from possible hurt and disappointment. Unfortunately, few families can talk openly about these mixed feelings, perhaps because one way for adolescents to assert their independence is to withhold their thoughts and feelings from their parents.

Although those adolescents who have experienced gratifying and trusting relationships with their parents are generally more likely to effect a mature separation, the early and middle phases of adolescence are almost inevitably characterized by increased negativity toward parents, along with increased family strain (Powers et al., 1989). Mother-daughter conflict is particularly pronounced and seems to be a way for adolescent girls to accelerate their maturation. Parents should be willing to negotiate and need to recognize the increased maturity and responsibility of their children. At the same time, appropriate guidance and setting of limits is still in order. As Powers et al. put it, authoritative parenting that allows increasing personal jurisdiction seems superior to authoritarian parenting in developing adolescent autonomy and positive parent-child relations. Parental acceptance, empathy, and support are also important in promoting autonomy. Individuated family relationships that allow adolescents freedom to formulate their own identities are likely to lead to greater self-esteem and improved interpersonal relationships.

By the 12th grade, most adolescents will have passed through the most difficult period of conflict with their parents. Success in obtaining more independence and establishing other sources of help and support enables adolescents to perceive their parents more positively and accurately and to resume closer relationships with them.

Peer Relations

The development of peer relations in adolescence seems to parallel that observed in children during the elementary school years. When young people enter high school, the peer group has great importance, just as it did for children in the first few years of school. At both points in development, the peer group seems to serve similar functions; it offers support, sets standards, and lends a sense of identity until group members have established a clearer sense of themselves.

Peer group norms, models, and values provide an alternative to those of the family, thereby facilitating independence from the family. Although parental standards remain important to adolescents, often, those standards are reviewed in light of peer group norms. This may lead to excessive conformity to peer standards.

Toward the end of high school, many adolescents have developed enough confidence in themselves to leave the security of the peer group and begin to develop intimate and committed relationships with selected individuals. This parallels the chumship stage that emerges toward the end of elementary school, although now the special friends usually are of the other gender rather than of the same gender. A substantial percentage of adolescents, however, do not make much progress in establishing their sense of identity and self-confidence during the high school years and move into young adulthood in a continued state of identity confusion and group dependence.

Gender-Related Patterns of Development

Although both boys and girls experience the struggle for identity, intimacy, and independence during adolescence, some patterns of development are gender-related. Even the brightest and most capable girls seem to have more difficulty maintaining positive self-esteem than do boys (S. Wilson, 1982) and tend to be more cautious and limited in their perceived opportunities. As the girls' affiliative needs develop, their avoidance of competitive and risky opportunities increases as does their struggle to integrate interpersonal and achievement-oriented goals and interests. Although adolescent girls seem to mature more rapidly than boys and have less overt difficulty with social adjustment and establishment of autonomy, they also seem to be more anxious and dependent than their male counterparts.

Boys, on the other hand, seem to experience more conflict surrounding school and family. Their academic performance is less consistent than that of girls, they engage in more acting out and antisocial behavior, and they seem less comfortable accepting the changes of adolescence than do girls.

Other Areas of Difficulty

Academic difficulties often surface for both boys and girls during adolescence. School is now demanding, requiring more initiative and responsibility, and may be viewed as part of the adult world that is limiting the freedom of the adolescent. Awareness of differences is sharpened, for most, during adolescence, and young people with learning difficulties or other special attributes may have more trouble than most with self-acceptance, peer relations, and adjustment. Adolescents who mature physically at a different rate than most of their friends may have similar concerns. Issues of sexual identity and behavior also are prevalent during adolescence, and concerns about physical and emotional intimacy are common.

Developments in Thinking Ability During Adolescence

At about the age of 11 or 12, most children enter what Piaget (1963) termed the formal operations stage of thinking. This stage evolves slowly over the next 5 or 6 years. By high school, most young people are capable of generating and evaluating hypotheses and using deductive logic (Powers et al., 1989; White & Speisman, 1977). Their capacity for abstraction and introspection has increased, and they can reflect with insight on their own abilities and personalities. They can separate reality from possibility and are better able to maintain objectivity. Generally, they have become more philosophical and can generate theories and ideas. Their time perspective has improved; they can engage in cognitive rehearsal, can envision themselves in the future, and can think in terms of a life plan. Their capacity for empathy has also improved, and they have more insight into the thoughts and feelings of others. Overall, adolescents manifest considerable growth in thinking ability, and by the high school years, most have developed those intellectual abilities that are crucial to the formulation of sound future plans.

Adolescents also show growth in their capacity for moral and ethical thinking. Prior to adolescence, most operate on a conventional level of morality. They verbalize conformity to societal expectations and maintain cultural norms without evaluating their validity or reason for being. During a transitional phase, adolescents may challenge and even violate cultural norms while, at the same time, criticizing themselves and others for doing so. By the later high school years, however, most young people begin to define and implement their own ethical codes.

Attaining Maturity in Adolescence

Adolescent maturation is both a linear and a circular process. Relatively invariant stages of development and maturation have been identified by Erikson, Piaget, and others and have been described in this book. In addition, patterns of development are affected by society and the age in which the young person is maturing. Vondracek and Schulenberg (1986) term this a "developmental-contextual approach." This approach takes a holistic view of the person, the context, and their relationships, looking at dynamic interactions in development. Mature adolescents of the early 21st century will probably have much in common with mature adolescents of earlier years, including such qualities as self-esteem; individuation; a sense of direction; good relationships with parents, peers, and others; and empathy. However, adolescent development also affects and is affected by its cultural and temporal context. Modern adolescents, for example, seem to mature earlier and are more pragmatic and more androgynous in their thinking and planning than their parents were as adolescents. Both internal and external forces impinging on development should be considered to fully understand the adolescent.

Adolescent Career Development

Erikson (1963) viewed the ability to formulate viable and rewarding career plans as central to the satisfactory resolution of the adolescent identity crisis. He stated, "The sense of ego identity, then, is the accrued confidence that the inner sameness and continuity prepared in the past are matched by the sameness and continuity of one's meaning for others, as evidenced in the tangible promise of a 'career' " (p. 261). For adolescents, then, a career seems to serve as a vehicle for actualizing the self-concept and for integrating both past and present aspects of themselves. However, Erikson also stated, "In most instances . . . it is the inability to settle on an occupational identity which disturbs young people" (p. 262). Counselors should, therefore, pay considerable attention to the career development of adolescents because it seems to be so relevant to their overall maturation during these important and often difficult years.

Overview of Career Development

Career development seems to accelerate with age during adolescence and is an important dynamic by high school (M. J. Miller, 1987; Mitchell, 1977). Most 17-year-olds have discussed their career plans with others and express a need for help with career planning, although they view themselves as responsible for formulating their career plans. Most express occupational preferences and have become more knowledgeable about job duties, psychosocial aspects of work, worker attributes, preparation required for entry into occupations, and approaches to career planning. However, they continue to be unclear about the skills or abilities needed for their chosen professions, and, often, information is not sufficient for occupational commitment during the adolescent years.

Status and prestige, important elements in early adolescent career development, continue to be important in later adolescence. More than two thirds in this age group are primarily interested in professional occupations. Values, too, are an important ingredient in career preference, becoming more intrinsic during the high school years (Post-Kammer, 1987). However, many young people are hazy about how their values are reflected in occupations and are attracted to high prestige fields without knowing much about the nature of those occupations.

Generally, the career plans of high school students reflect greater congruence with their self-concept, fuller information about their options, and more sources of information than do those of middle and junior high school students. Despite this growth, many need continued reality testing and exploration of themselves, their abilities, their interest, and the world of work before they can make sound career plans.

Many adolescents feel parental, peer, societal, and self-pressure to make the one "right" career choice. They may be tempted to commit themselves to an occupation to facilitate their definition of themselves and their futures and to relieve their career anxiety. This pressure toward adulthood may lead to hasty and unwise choices. Although adolescents are expected to make tentative career plans, continued expansion of options is often more appropriate for this age group than is commitment (D. A. Jepsen, 1975).

Stages of Adolescent
Career Development

Ginzberg et al. (1951) viewed career development during the high school years as consisting of two stages. The first of these is the values stage, which usually takes place during the ages of 15 and 16. During these years, adolescents broaden their occupational perspectives, become more aware of the range of factors involved in career planning, and develop a clearer and more accurate self-concept. They become particularly concerned with their own values and the importance of contributing to society. As the need to make future choices becomes more pressing, adolescents have an increased tendency to look toward the future and anticipate later lifestyles.

The second stage described by Ginzberg and his colleagues is the tentative stage, which begins about the age of 17, as the high school years are coming to a close. Adolescents turn their attention from subjective to objective factors, becoming less concerned with their own interests, abilities, and values and more concerned with reality factors, such as the job market and occupational opportunities. Options are assessed and tested in a more systematic fashion, and tentative choices are made as young people move toward the realistic period, which begins about the age of 18, a time when most will begin in earnest to implement their career plans.

Super (1957b) viewed the high school years as constituting the first substage of the exploration stage, which extends from about the age of 15 to about the age of 24. The exploration stage is a time for developing greater awareness of the self and the world of work and for trying out new roles. According to Super's classic research, 15- to 17-year-olds are usually in the tentative substage of this period.

Super (1963, p. 84) viewed *crystallization* as the primary career development task of the adolescent years (14-18) and described that process as involving the following attitudes, behaviors, and characteristics:

1. awareness of the need to crystallize
2. use of resources

3. awareness of factors to consider in career planning
4. awareness of contingencies that may affect goals
5. differentiation and clarification of interests and values
6. awareness of present-future relationships
7. formulation of general career preferences
8. consistency of preference
9. possession of information about the career preferences
10. planning for the preferred career
11. wisdom of the preference

In more recent research, Super (1985) recommended that the high school years be used as a time for wide-ranging but increasingly realistic exploration, unlike the aimless drifting that he perceived to characterize the development of many adolescents. Super's Career Patterns Study demonstrated the close connection of high school experiences and later career development, emphasizing the importance of positive career development during adolescence.

According to Gottfredson (1981), at about the age of 14 adolescents enter Stage 4 in her model of career development, orientation to internal, unique self. During this stage, adolescents continue to eliminate occupations perceived as unsuitable. Such occupations may be viewed as inappropriate for their gender, too low in prestige, incompatible with their social class self-concept, or requiring excessive effort. Usually, capable students raise their aspirations during this stage, whereas the less capable tend to lower them. This narrowing process leads to the development of a zone of acceptable occupational alternatives that adolescents then consider in light of their personality, interests, values, and capacities. Congruence of perceived personality between self and incumbents in an occupation becomes particularly important as adolescents integrate multiple complex factors in identifying their career choices. Similarly, goals for marriage and children are clarified and factored into career planning. Finally, by the end of high school, reality factors, including availability of jobs, receive strong consideration.

Although different theorists have attached different labels to the career development that occurs during the high school years, most seem agreed that career development during this period is characterized by increased exploration and planning, by greater self-awareness, by a narrowing of options, and eventually by a shift in focus from the self to the world of work as career planning becomes increasingly realistic.

Career Maturity in Adolescence

Career maturity during adolescence has been found to correlate with other important variables, both during adolescence and later in life. Super's Career Patterns Study (1968, 1985) found that adolescent career maturity was positively correlated with later career satisfaction, career status and success, career stability, use of assets, educational and occupational level, and realism of occupational choice. Measures of career maturity used by Super included agreement between expressed occupational goals and inventoried abilities and knowledge of preferred occupation.

More recent studies confirm these findings. Niles and Herr (1989) found that a combination of 12th-grade career attitude maturity, grade point average, involvement in school activities, self-awareness, occupational awareness, and part-time work experience were related to career certainty, maturity, satisfaction, and progress during the exploration stage at the age of 25.

During adolescence, career maturity increases systematically with age and seems to consist of two relatively independent ingredients: career-related knowledge and career-planning behaviors (McNair & Brown, 1983; Noeth & Prediger, 1978). Career maturity seems related to overall level of maturity and coping ability and is reflected by academic achievement and positive self-esteem. Background and parental influence are also important determinants of career maturity. In recent years, the growth in career education in the schools has made schools a more important influence on career development, reflected in a significant increase in the percentage of high school students involved in school-based career exploration (Prediger & Sawyer, 1986).

Career maturity also seems related to work values, with values becoming increasingly intrinsic with maturation. This relationship is particularly characteristic of adolescent girls, who place considerable importance on intrinsic values, such as achievement and altruism, but who also value way of life and security. Adolescent boys, too, have both intrinsic and extrinsic work values, emphasizing achievement, intellectual stimulation, way of life, and economic returns. However, generally, girls value achievement and variety more than do boys, whereas boys value way of life, management, economic rewards, and independence more than do girls (Post-Kammer, 1987). Although some studies have found no gender difference in career maturity, some have concluded that adolescent girls' career maturity was more advanced than was that of boys their age (McNair & Brown, 1983; Pedro, 1982).

Determinants of career maturation also reflect gender differences. For boys, age was the most important determinant of career maturity (King, 1989). For girls, age also is related to career maturity, but variables such as family cohesion and having an internal locus of control seem even more important. These patterns seem to support Gilligan's (1982) concept of the relational component of identity in females. Girls formulate their identities by connecting with people; boys, by establishing their independence.

Ethnic as well as gender differences in career maturity have been observed. McNair and Brown (1983), for example, found that White adolescents scored higher than African American adolescents on measures of career maturity.

Career maturity among adolescents seems to be characterized by the following attitudes and behaviors:

1. acquisition of career and educational information, leading to systematic exploration of the world of work
2. sound ability to use decision-making skills
3. awareness of a preferred lifestyle
4. development of a clear, positive, and realistic self-image
5. formulation of tentative career plans and goals that are congruent with the self-image and the preferred lifestyle

Making Occupational Choices During Adolescence

By the time they leave high school, most adolescents have formulated tentative career plans. Nearly all will decide whether to continue their education or seek employment and will make application for either work or school. Although adolescents are aware of the need to make these decisions long before the decisions must actually be implemented, the formulation of occupational choices during adolescence is a difficult process for many, one that is influenced by a wide variety of factors. Understandably, adolescents who are experiencing some confusion about their own identities may find it difficult to translate their self-images into occupational choices. Consequently, they may delay making decisions and leave themselves inadequate time for wise planning when decisions finally must be made.

Career Motivation

Farmer (1985) identified three clusters of factors determining motivation: (a) background factors (e.g., socioeconomic status, ethnicity, gender, age, skills, geography), (b) personal factors (self-esteem and personality traits), and (c) environment, especially support and encouragement from parents and other important people. Motivation, in turn, affects nature and level of aspiration, sense of mastery, and career commitment.

According to Farmer, career motivation is influenced three times as much by personal as by background and environmental factors, with self-concept being particularly important. Adolescents who have a fear of failure, little academic success in high school, low self-esteem, or a poorly integrated sense of identity may have particular difficulty developing sound career plans. On the other hand, young people who have been achievement oriented in high school, see themselves as having a range of appealing options, are self-confident and assertive, and have strong intrinsic values, a sense of independence and mastery, and good academic and intellectual abilities seem more likely to formulate timely and appropriate occupational and postsecondary educational plans.

Both counselors and young people should bear in mind, however, that career goals expressed in high school are likely to change. Noeth and Jepsen (1981) found that even among high school students who described themselves as very sure of their occupational choices, only 43% had maintained those choices 2 years later.

Influences on Career Development

People

Although personal factors seem to be the most important influence on career choice and development during adolescence, familial factors, including mother's and father's roles and early childhood experiences probably have the second greatest influence, being a particularly important determinant of occupational expectations (McNair & Brown, 1983; O'Neil et al., 1980). Jackson and Meara (1977) found that boys whose fathers were adequate role models when the boys were seniors in high school had higher levels of aspiration and achievement than did boys who did not have adequate paternal role models. Parental support of adolescents' aspirations exerts a more powerful influence on those plans than do friends' plans, teachers' encouragement, and social status. The quality of parent-child relationships, family interaction patterns, and the interest and expectations that parents have for their children's futures are important components in children's career development (Whiston, 1989). Parents may influence young people directly through advice and instructions or indirectly via role modeling. Despite the tendency for many adolescents to express disagreement with parental values, adolescents, particularly boys, often make their career choices in accord with aspirations held for them by their parents (Dillard & Campbell, 1981; Farmer, 1985; King, 1989).

Teachers' support is also an important influence on motivation, whereas friends' plans have a strong influence on level of aspiration (Farmer, 1985). Perceived support from parents and significant others for women to enter the workforce is particularly important in the development of adolescent girls' occupational aspirations.

Experiences

Experiences as well as people influence career development. This includes work experience, leisure activities, and exposure to occupations and lifestyles. Increasing numbers of teenagers are working on a part-time or temporary basis while attending high school. This is due to many factors: the increased availability of jobs in shopping malls and fast-food restaurants, the implementation of work-study programs in the high schools, economic pressures on families, and adolescents' growing interest in independence and the means for acquiring clothes, cars, and other symbols of their identity.

Adolescent work and leisure experiences seem to be positive influences for some and negative influences for others. Generally, adolescents who acquire employment experience have higher grades and better self-esteem than do those who do not have such experiences (Gade & Peterson, 1980). Although high school work experience does not usually, provide direct preparation for entry into future occupations, it can offer an opportunity to acquire firsthand knowledge of the world of work and to experience the role of worker. According to M. J. Miller (1987), direct observation is the primary source of occupational information, supporting the importance of work experience. On the other hand, positive employment experiences may hamper career maturation by influencing adolescents to discontinue their education and accept the most readily available employment. Leisure experiences, too, can broaden interests and clarify and enhance self-esteem but can also distract adolescents from their academic accomplishments and lead them to de-emphasize the importance of academic achievement.

Clearly, leisure activities, part-time and vacation employment, and work-study programs can all make a significant contribution to the career development of adolescents. However, ideally, such activities should be planned so that they do not discourage or limit options but, rather, help adolescents view themselves and the world of work more positively and more knowledgeably. Experiences that have a purpose and objective; are challenging and relevant to the person's values, interests, abilities, and personality; expand availability of role models, experiences, and skills; and offer opportunities for success and accomplishment seem particularly likely to enhance career maturity, self-esteem, and identity development.

Socioeconomic and Ethnic Background

Socioeconomic and ethnic variables have also been shown to influence adolescent career development. Their influence seems to be transmitted largely through accessible role models. Young people from lower socioeconomic backgrounds, for example, see few models of high occupational status in their families or neighborhoods. Consequently, they tend to have lower occupational aspirations and less awareness of the world of work than do their more affluent peers (McNair & Brown, 1983). A study by Dillard and Perrin (1980) that controlled for socioeconomic status and focused only on adolescents from middle- and lower-income group, found that males from minority ethnic groups (African American and Puerto Rican) had higher career aspirations than did Anglo males. This suggests that socioeconomic status rather than minority group status inhibits career aspirations. However, ethnic group membership and socioeconomic status can combine in their impact on career development. For example, Lauver and Jones (1991) compared the career self-efficacy of Native American, Anglo, and Hispanic high school students from rural communities and found that the Native Americans perceived themselves as having the fewest career options and had the lowest sense of self-efficacy. Similar findings emerged from Lee's (1984a) study of rural African American, White, and Native American high school students. In that study, self-concept had a negative impact on the career choices of the Native Americans, whereas it had a positive impact on the career choices of the White and African American adolescents. Lee (1984b) also found that for all these young people from rural backgrounds, extrinsic values such as salary and stability of employment, reportedly, were a greater influence on occupational choice than were intrinsic values.

The influence of socioeconomic status can vary, depending on gender. McNair and Brown (1983) found that higher socioeconomic status had a negative influence on the career aspirations of adolescent males, perhaps reflecting their doubts about their abilities and their efforts to model themselves after their fathers. However, socioeconomic status had a positive impact on the career aspirations of adolescent girls, perhaps because their background exposed them to more models of women who had achieved successful professional careers.

Ethnic-related differences in family patterns have also been found to moderate influences on career development. For example, the African American mother's aspirations for her children seem to be very important for adolescent boys and girls, even more important than their father's aspirations (Dillard & Campbell, 1981). This pattern was not found among Puerto Rican or Anglo adolescents and probably reflects the matriarchal nature of many African American families, where the mother's income is essential to the family.

Ethnic-related patterns of occupational preference have also been identified. Miller et al. (1988), using Holland's (1985) occupational typology (described in Chapter 1) found that African American high school students had stronger interest in social, conventional, and enterprising areas than did White students. Social occupations such as teaching and counseling were of particular interest to African Americans, probably because they saw those fields as acceptable in terms of both prestige and accessibility.

An indirect influence of ethnic background emerges in adolescent scores on standardized tests. For example, in 1985 average scores of White young people on the Scholastic Aptitude Test (SAT) were 449 (verbal) and 475 (mathematics), whereas those of African American young people were 372 and 429. A multitude of factors, including quality of education, role models, and experiences, have led to a relatively consistent pattern of Whites outperforming non-Whites on most tests and consequently having more postsecondary educational options.

Gender

Gender is another important influence on career development during the adolescent years. Typically, females achieve higher grades during the high school years than do males. However, females are underrepresented in the most prestigious professions. The career development of adolescent females seems to differ from that of adolescent males in such a way as to limit the occupational options of women.

One of the major determinants of gender difference in career development is self-esteem. At the age of 8 or 9, 60% of girls and 67% of boys are confident, assertive, and have positive self-esteem. By the age of 16 or 17, only 29% of the girls and 46% of the boys can be described in that way (Freiberg, 1991b). Girls also experience a corresponding decline in their interest in science and mathematics and are less likely than boys to aspire to professional fields (M. J. Miller, 1987). Girls are more likely than boys to select occupations that underuse their aptitudes and interests (Pedro, 1982). They gravitate toward occupations of medium prestige and, typically, exclude from consideration numerous occupations at both ends of the prestige spectrum because they are perceived as either unsuitable for women or too demanding for them.

On the other hand, adolescent girls manifest more career maturity than do adolescent boys and seem more certain of their occupational choices (Vondracek, Hostetler, Schulenberg, & Shimizu, 1990). Clearly, a different career planning process takes place for adolescent girls than for adolescent boys. According to Fitzgerald and Crites (1980), "The potential career development of women, although not fundamentally *different* than that of men, is a great deal more complex due to that combination of attitudes, role expectations, behaviors, and sanctions known as the socialization process" (p. 45). They view the adolescent female as her own greatest barrier to career development. Young women often limit themselves by choosing helper or assistant roles, emphasizing choices in social/artistic/clerical areas, and avoiding nontraditional roles out of fear that such choices may cause them to be perceived as unfeminine or undesirable by males.

Often, choices offering security and familiarity in adolescence are rejected years later. The identity confusion of the adolescent years leads many girls to adopt a traditional role for themselves. However, as they mature and develop a clearer sense of themselves, perhaps finding that their personal lives have progressed differently than anticipated, they are more able to pursue nontraditional career goals without being much affected by any social disapproval and gender bias they may encounter.

Gender and ethnic background seem to interact in their influence on career development. African American girls maintain their self-esteem better than do White girls, who maintain self-esteem better than do Hispanic girls (Freiberg, 1991b). African American girls seem to receive more family and community reinforcement and encouragement than do girls from other backgrounds.

Socioeconomic status, too, seems to interact with gender in influencing career development. For example, Lauver and Jones (1991) found that rural high school girls seemed less bound by traditional gender roles than did their male counterparts.

Having high abilities seems to expand options for young women. Kerr and Colangelo (1988) concluded that, in general, the higher the ability, the less the gender differences in choices of major and occupation, with many academically talented young women choosing traditionally male-dominated areas. S. Wilson (1982) studied gifted high school students and found that both males and females expressed greatest interest in male-dominated occupations, such as medical doctor, biologist, and accountant. However, females were more likely to select practical and familiar occupations, such as accountant, whereas males were more likely to select unfamiliar fields, such as astronomy. About 50% reported no discrepancy between their actual career goals and their ideal careers. However, the young women who did report a discrepancy attributed it to lack of finances for required education and their own lack of talent or intelligence; the young men who reported a discrepancy attributed it more to external forces such as parental pressure or lack of financial rewards of their ideal occupation. Kerr and Colangelo (1988) also found that gifted girls had unusually high uncertainty about their career choices. A follow-up study of adults who had been identified as gifted and talented in high school indicated that over 25% of the women (and fewer of the men) felt they had not lived up to their educational potentials (Post-Kammer & Perrone, 1983). Even among the gifted, then, the females are more likely to limit their choices because of perceived shortcomings in themselves.

Overall, the actual occupational choices of adolescent women are less prestigious and more heavily populated by female workers than their fantasy choices. For adolescent males, however, both fantasy and actual choices are primarily in traditionally male high-prestige areas, areas that the young women fantasized about but did not expect to attain (Koski & Subich, 1985). This aspiration-expectation gap may lead young women to make career plans that will be disappointing in future years.

According to Kerr (1983), both gifted and other young women limit their occupational choices out of a belief that they must choose between career and family goals. However, as Kerr stated, "Gifted young women's perception that a career and family cannot be combined successfully is indeed an unfortunate and inaccurate one. Homemaking does not seem to lead to as much life satisfaction for gifted women as having a career or combining career and family" (p. 37).

There are positive signs that the tendency for young women to inhibit their career options may be diminishing. Leung and Plake (1990) concluded, "Cultural changes in the past decades have produced a group of young women who are aware of the need for women to be employed and are considering less traditional careers" (p. 405). Amatea, Clark, and Cross (1984) found no difference between high school males and females on occupational and marital role salience. In addition, adolescent males are increasingly indicating an expectation to share parenting and career responsibilities equally with their future spouses (Farmer, 1983).

Gender stereotyping leads young men to limit their career options just as it does young women. Farmer (1983) found that 35% of high school girls expressed occupational choices that were nontraditional for their gender, whereas only 3% of high school boys expressed nontraditional choices. Although more concern has been expressed about this pattern in girls because it often limits them to occupations that are lower in prestige, influence, and remuneration, this pattern can also be harmful to males in preventing them from choosing occupations that are more compatible with their interests and abilities than are occupations that are traditional for their gender.

Other Influences on Career Development

A multitude of other influences, including intellectual and physical strengths and limitations, the time period in which young people are maturing, and chance can have an impact on career development. For example, adolescents of the 1990s are more likely to have employed mothers and parents who are supportive of women in the workforce than were adolescents of previous generations. Trends toward smaller families, delayed childbearing, more single-parent families, and increasing involvement of men in child rearing have resulted in most modern young women seeking to integrate career and family goals. Amatea et al. (1984) found that 82% of young women in high school planned to work and have a family concurrently. The growth in career education programs in the school should lead to greater awareness of options for both males and females (Prediger & Sawyer, 1986). Although this wealth of options certainly has a positive side, having too much to choose from can be overwhelming. Frequently, this dynamic has been observed in gifted adolescents (Blackburn & Erickson, 1986). Increasing opportunities, then, may increase the need for counseling to help young people narrow options appropriately. To facilitate this, counselors need to consider a broad range of factors that may have an impact on a person's career development and explore important influences with that person.

Formulating Educational Plans and Decisions

High School

High school is a time when important career-related decisions must be made. Students must decide whether to complete high school, whether to continue their education beyond high school, where they would like to continue their educations, and whether to seek full-time or part-time employment. Although pressure to make these decisions is particularly intense during the junior and senior years of high school, typically, these decisions reflect years of career development and can be anticipated many years earlier. Critical factors in these decisions include family background and the match between students' personalities and the academic environment. In some communities, the emphasis on a college education is so strong and pervasive that few young people will even consider other options, whereas in other communities, the young person who completes high school is unusual, and little financial or emotional support is available to those who consider college.

The percentage of people who complete high school has been increasing over the years. In 1900, only 4% of young people in America completed high school. According to the U.S. Department of Education, approximately 75% graduated from high school in 1990. This number is even higher when those who complete the high school equivalency examination are considered. For example, by 1986, 91% of the class of 1980 had their high school diplomas. Clearly, then, completing high school is the norm today. Although the percentage of high school leavers is low, the numbers are high. Approximately 1 million young people leave high school before graduation each year (Larsen & Shertzer, 1987). High school completion rates are particularly low for young people from ethnic minority groups or from lower socioeconomic and urban backgrounds. Dropout rates for Native Americans are as high as 85% and range between 70% and 80% for Puerto Rican youth (Bloch, 1989).

Larsen and Shertzer (1987) described the process that leads up to leaving school before graduation: (a) loss of interest in school, (b) falling grades, (c) skipping classes, (d) conflict with school authorities, (e) acting out, (f) suspension, (g) parental involvement, (h) conflict escalates, and (i) adolescent leaves school. Approximately 50% of those who drop out of high school have been held back at least one grade, and 80% of those who repeat first or second grade will leave school before graduation. Most of these people are of average intelligence, and at least 11% have the ability to complete college. Lack of ability, then, is not a major determinants of their leaving school. Similarly, research has not found school leavers to be significantly more emotionally disturbed or lower in self-esteem than those who complete high school. Rather, the high negative correlation between the socioeconomic status and educational levels of the parents and the likelihood of their children leaving high school prematurely suggests that social and family messages and expectations are the primary determinant of school leaving.

Typically, those young people who leave high school before graduation have the greatest difficulty in finding satisfying employment because of the limited options that are available to them. Despite the decline in the numbers of school leavers, the large number of those who do leave high school before graduation and the difficulties they encounter in the labor force justify paying special attention to potential high school leavers. Increased awareness of the difficulty and discouragement commonly encountered by high school leavers when they enter the workforce has led many schools and communities to develop special programs to make school more meaningful and rewarding for potential dropouts. Larsen and Shertzer (1987) and Bloch (1989) suggested the following procedures:

1. Identify potential dropouts early, monitor academic progress and attendance, and respond quickly when problems become evident.
2. Provide the students with support groups and extra encouragement and attention from teachers and counselors.
3. Encourage involvement in extracurricular activities.
4. Involve potential dropout in work-study programs that enable them to earn money while spending less time at school and more at work and in on-the-job training.
5. Provide career counseling and information that is designed to promote motivation, realistic goal setting, awareness of the world of work, and career development.
6. Individualize educational programs to address special needs and interests.
7. Schedule exit interviews for those who do drop out and offer them referrals and continuing help.

Recent attention has been paid to some affluent people who have, in a sense, adopted a school or class, promising college tuition to those who complete high school and providing tutoring, mentoring, and other forms of help to the young people while they are in school. Although sufficient benevolent millionaires are not likely to be found to address the needs of every school, this model of personal interest, creating a sense of specialness and realistic goals, may be adapted for use in schools without such endowments.

Collaborative programs between high schools and community or 4-year colleges can be beneficial to both potential dropouts and persisters who may be bored with the high school environment. Classes may be established at either the high school or the college, with arrangements made for students to receive college credit for some of their work. This process may well increase motivation and facilitate students' entry into college.

High school equivalency examinations have long been available to help people who left high school before graduation, worked for awhile, and now want their high school diploma. Brief evening courses are widely availably to help such people pass their high school equivalency examinations.

Clearly, many options are available to students who are dissatisfied with high school. Counselors should try to anticipate the special needs of such students and help them become aware of both the adverse effect that leaving high school is likely to have on their occupational choices and the alternatives to leaving school before graduation.

Education After High School

Many plans and decisions must be made by high school students before they continue their education beyond high school. First, they must decide whether they want to continue their education. If they decide to seek further schooling, they must decide on the nature of the programs they will pursue and where they will take courses. They also must deal with the requirements of their future educational institutions, which may include admissions tests, interviews, and the payment of tuition and fees. More than one half of all high school graduates will proceed on to college, and many others will enroll in specialized schools to prepare them for entry into their chosen occupations. Rapid growth in enrollment in 2-year colleges has been evident in recent years. From 1971 to 1988, the number of associates degrees awarded increased by 51% (U.S. Department of Labor, 1990).

Many factors contribute to the decision about whether or not to continue school after high school. Here, too, socioeconomic background and family models and messages are critical. The peer group also exerts a strong influence on educational goals. High school students whose friends are planning to continue their education beyond high school tend to view a college education as desirable and are more likely to continue their own education than are those students whose peer groups are not college oriented. Academic aptitude and achievement also tend to be positively correlated with likelihood of continuing one's education.

Unfortunately, the educational and occupational goals of many high school students are unrealistic. Even those with realistic goals may have difficulty implementing their goals. Many counseling programs have been developed, beginning during the middle school years, to facilitate students' planning and transition from high school to postsecondary education (Hanselman, 1989; Matthay, 1989; Phifer, 1987). Common steps or ingredients in these programs include information about the following:

1. promoting decision-making skills
2. clarifying self-image and future goals
3. increasing awareness of institutions and their majors and characteristics as well as ways to gather more information (e.g., interviews, visits, reviewing catalogs)
4. identifying factors that may influence choice of college or major
5. the college application process, focusing on criteria of the colleges, standardized testing programs, completing appli- cations for admission, gathering letters of recommendation, and negotiating the college interview
6. the costs of postsecondary education and facilitating application for financial aid if appropriate
7. making the final choices and decisions
8. implementing educational decisions

Whenever possible, parents as well as young people should be involved in the process of making decisions and planning for future education to be sure that parents and children are communicating with each other clearly and to help young people understand the influence of their parents on their future plans.

Despite the availability of career counseling in the schools, most high school students do not consult their school counselors about college choice. Matthay (1989) found that only 16% of high school students consulted their school counselors about college choice, reporting that they perceived the counselors as too overworked and not sufficiently informed to afford them much assistance. This is unfortunate because a strong correlation has been found between satisfaction with the assistance received with college planning and satisfaction with the college choice.

A survey of college freshmen (Matthay, 1989) yielded the following ranking of helpful resources on college planning:

1. visits to colleges
2. college catalogs
3. parents, other family members
4. school counselors
5. friends who attend college
6. college admissions representatives
7. admissions interviews
8. college guides and directories
9. college fairs
10. high school teachers

Counselors should be aware of the many sources of information that are useful and available to would-be college students and should help young people gain access to these resources.

Although students tend to view the process of choosing a college as a very important decision, Bowen (1977) found that choice of college did not seem to be as significant as some believe. His research indicated that, generally, differences between colleges and differences in their effects on students were modest, although students who lived in dormitories showed significantly more personal development than did those who remained at home with their parents. Most young people apply to only one or two colleges, most continue their education at their chosen institution, and most attend college within 50 miles of their home. Although counselors should be prepared to help students gather information about colleges and review the relevant factors before making their choices, counselors might also allay some of the anxiety that students are feeling about the process of college choice by advising them that the effect of college on a person depends more on the person than on the college.

Developmental Goals

Adolescence is a time when both emotional and career development progress at rapid rates. In the next stage, young adulthood, most will have to be independent and responsible for themselves. Adolescence is the period when those attributes that will facilitate the establishment of an independent and rewarding lifestyle should emerge. Healthy adolescent development typically includes the following accomplishments (Hamachek, 1988; Havighurst, 1972; Tennyson, 1981):

1. developing a clear idea of one's own values, personality, interests, and abilities as well as the capacity for continued self-examination
2. achieving emotional independence from parents and peers while maintaining mature, accepting, close, and positive interpersonal relations with both
3. developing a coherent, stable, and positive sense of identity
4. developing a sense of social belonging, commitment, and responsibility
5. developing skill, flexibility, and confidence in handling everyday tasks
6. acquiring clear and accurate knowledge of occupational and educational options
7. developing a capacity for sound planning and decision making
8. formulating tentative career goals that seem likely to be realistic and rewarding
9. taking responsibility for the establishment of a rewarding and enjoyable adult lifestyle

Counseling the Adolescent
Toward Realism and Separation

Adolescents' Attitudes
Toward Counseling

Although high school probably is the place where people have the greatest access to counseling, many young people do not receive adequate counseling during their high school years (Matthay, 1989). Research indicates that counseling services at the high school level are reaching more students. From 1973 to 1983, a 32% increase, from 50% to 66%, was found in 11th graders who reported receiving at least some help in career planning. At the same time, there was a decrease from 78%

to 71% of 11th graders who wanted help with career development. That decline apparently was due to the increase in students receiving career counseling (Prediger & Sawyer, 1986). Nevertheless, students continue to report receiving inadequate help with their career development.

Perhaps neither students nor counselors are reaching out to each other enough. Students report seeing counselors as overworked and limited in their information, whereas counselors seem to perceive themselves as responding appropriately to student needs. How can these conflicting impressions be reconciled? Many young people make premature and unrealistic career decisions during the high school years. That process is one way for them to give some structure to their lives, thereby relieving some of the stress and anxiety typically associated with the identity confusion of adolescence. This perceived pressure for rapid decisions, in combination with the adolescents' shift of focus away from parental and authority figures and toward the peer group, may lead adolescents to devalue counselors who seek to promote thought and self-exploration rather than quick solutions. Counselors need to realize that most adolescents are interested in career counseling and education but may not readily acknowledge their need for help. It is the responsibility of the counselors, then, to make their services available in such a way as to reduce adolescent resistance and avert premature foreclosure. Nearly all young people seem interested in and able to benefit from the help of a concerned adult outside their families during the years when they are commonly faced with both a great deal of pressure and tension and a decreasing willingness to accept parental advice and support. The counselor can be that concerned and helpful adult.

Goals in Counseling Adolescents

Counselors working with young people should be familiar with the typical difficulties and changes of the adolescent years and should be prepared to help students move toward the developmental goals cited earlier in this chapter. The following objectives characterize the goals of most counselors dealing with adolescents:

1. to improve relationships with peers, teachers, and parents
2. to broaden awareness of and information about viable post-high-school options and lifestyles, including both educational and occupational paths
3. to improve planning and decision-making skills
4. to provide opportunity for observation of role models

5. to facilitate development and implementation of realistic and potentially rewarding future plans and goals

6. to encourage development of positive, articulated, and realistic self-concepts

Secondary school counselors tend to emphasize career development much more than do middle and junior high school counselors. According to a survey conducted by Tennyson et al. (1989), secondary school counselors report that their most frequent activities are assisting students to explore career information, helping students with career planning, and helping students select postsecondary educational institutions. A survey of exemplary secondary school counselors (M. J. Miller, 1988a) indicates that they saw counseling and consultation as their primary roles, followed by career assistance. Clearly, then, both adolescents and their counselors emphasize counseling with a career development focus.

Career Counseling With Adolescents

Career Counseling and Special Populations

To provide maximum assistance to high school students, counselors should be aware of the special needs and characteristic difficulties likely to affect the career development of particular groups of young people. African American youth, for example, are likely to focus their career aspirations on helping and teaching occupations and may overlook opportunities in scientific and mechanical occupations that would be more compatible with their interests and abilities (Miller et al., 1988).

Although counselors should be aware of typical differences and gear their approaches to the needs of their students, they should also guard against stereotyping and not assume that people who come from a similar background will have the same difficulties. Studies have indicated that counselors' own stereotypes can limit the options they view as appropriate for some young people. Hopkins-Best (1987), for example, asked counselors to rate their agreement with hypothetical adolescents' career goals. Some of the adolescents were described as male, some as female, and some as having disabilities. Hopkins-Best concluded, "Most occupations were rated differently depending on whether the student was male or female and disabled or nondisabled. This suggests that some stereotyped views still exist among high school guidance counselors about the types of work women and people with disabilities should do" (p. 32).

Female adolescents seem to need special help from counselors because of their tendency to select occupations that do not adequately reflect their interests and abilities. Young women need to explore ways of integrating their personal and career-related needs to find fulfillment in both areas. As McBride (1990) put it, "Learning to make independent choices and to grow toward self-mastery does not mean that women should ignore their affiliative needs. Being autonomous means choosing to take care of oneself as well as give to others" (p. 25). Pedro (1982) found that high-school-age females seem to approach career planning differently than do males their age and tend to seek less career information, perhaps because of their perception that they have limited options. Adolescent females, then, need strong encouragement to seek career-related information to broaden their awareness of their options. Counselors should help young women realize that they will probably spend many years in the labor force regardless of whether they marry or have children. Both male and female adolescents should be encouraged to examine their marriage and family goals as well as their occupational aspirations and should be helped to consider the many possible ways of combining family, leisure, and occupational activities. Farmer (1983) recommended that high school students be given information about dual-career marriages and other paths that people have taken to integrate family and career. Role models of people who have successfully integrated spouse, parent, and worker aspects of their lives can be especially enlightening.

Gender bias seems to have a particularly strong impact on the aspiration levels of adolescents. Social pressures and stereotypes make it difficult for both males and females to translate their interests and abilities into realistic career plans. Males may overaspire to prestigious occupations because they view them as the route to success and may disregard occupations more congruent with their capacities and enjoyments. Females may shun high-prestige occupations as well as occupations involving manual labor because they perceive them as unfeminine or inconsistent with a socially acceptable gender role. Counselors should help both genders to examine their assumptions as well as societal influences to promote positive career development.

Gifted and talented students are another group who seem to have special career counseling needs. According to Frederickson (1986), "Gifted and talented individuals need more information and assistance with career planning than do other persons because of the many options and alternatives they can realistically consider" (p. 556). Often, gifted adolescents have little exposure to the world of work, make frequent shifts in goals in response to fear of failure, tend to be concerned about living up to others' expectations, and may feel overwhelmed by their multipotentiality. In one study (Post-Kammer & Perrone, 1983), one third felt unprepared to make career decisions when they graduated from high school, and one fourth did not understand how interests and abilities related to career options. The emotional development of these young people may not be as advanced as their intellectual development; counselors and parents should not assume that these young people necessarily have greater career maturity because of their academic skills. Peer groups, guest speakers, and field trips seem particularly helpful to gifted adolescents as is information on their relative strengths and weaknesses and the reassurance that there are many choices and lifestyles likely to bring them fulfillment rather than one perfect match to all their needs (Borman, Nash, & Colson, 1978). Gifted girls, who often emphasize relationships over work as a source of satisfaction, may need particular encouragement to keep their options open, particularly in mathematics, science, and music, where early preparation seems critical to later success (S. Wilson, 1982).

Overview of Career Counseling With Adolescents

Holland (1973) stated that the key to satisfactory career planning for high school students was their ability to translate personal characteristics into occupational alternatives and their having the courage and ability to act on their perceptions. Holland believed that high school students needed to develop the following four abilities in order to accomplish effective career planning:

1. translation ability
2. sufficient self-confidence and competency
3. planning ability
4. elementary knowledge of career resources and principles

In other words, young people need self-knowledge, information on occupational and educational options, planning skills, and self-confidence to understand the fit between their personalities and abilities and the career options available to them.

Adolescents' career planning needs have changed little since Holland made his statement. However, the resources available to help young people develop those four key abilities have changed a great deal. Computer-based career information delivery systems, books and films on jobs and colleges, career resource centers, structured career development programs (both inside and outside of the classroom), tests and inventories, and group and individual counseling are available to facilitate the career development of high school students.

Disseminating and Acquiring Career Information

The foundation for career development during the high school years seems to be the acquisition and use of sufficient relevant information about careers and about the self. To help young people acquire such information, counselors first must assess the students' needs to determine what experiences they have had and what they have missed. Counselors then need to determine accessible means for providing missed and needed information and experiences.

Career information has many functions. It can be used for exploration, verification, motivation, discussion, and knowledge. Providing information in response to a perceived or expressed need seems to increase adolescents' motivation to use the information and translate their knowledge into terms relevant to their own career development. Information giving should not involve simply directing someone to a source of information. Rather, information giving is a process that should begin and end with an exploration of the person's perceptions, attitudes, and reactions.

Career Resource Centers

Many high schools have established career resource centers where both counselors and career information are readily available to students. Counselors can tap many sources of information to build up a resource center that is not very costly. Such sources include national and local businesses and industries, state and federal government agencies, unions, colleges and other postsecondary schools, professional associations, and commercial suppliers.

The following might be included in a resource center developed to meet the needs of high school students:

1. material on higher education, including college guides and catalogs for 2- and 4-year colleges

2. information on vocational and other specialized schools
3. information on careers in the military
4. occupational information
    a. *Occupational Outlook Handbook*
    b. *Dictionary of Occupational Titles*
    c. pamphlets and books on specific occupations
5. information for students who will be seeking employment
    a. material on occupations that do not require postsecondary education
    b. information on job application, resume writing, interviewing
    c. information on internships and on-the-job training programs
6. information on financial aid for postsecondary education
7. audiovisual material and equipment
8. file of resource persons who will speak with students about their own careers and provide opportunities for field visits
9. job experience kits, career games
10. computer terminal and computer-based career information delivery systems
11. listing of part-time jobs and volunteer experiences
12. data on graduates, their educations, occupations, and lifestyles

Useful information on career information systems in secondary schools is provided by Chapman and Katz (1983), who surveyed 10% of public secondary schools on their career information resources. They found that 98% had bound references, 95% had school-arranged experiences, 91% had occupational briefs and kits, 86% had educational directories, 86% offered personal contact with staff, 75% had reference books on military occupations, 75% held career days or fairs, 74% had directories for vocational schools, and 70% had college directories arranged by occupation. The *Occupational Outlook Handbook* was the most common single resource, being found in 92% of the schools, and the *Dictionary of Occupational Titles* was second, found in 83% of the schools. The *Occupational Outlook Handbook* and computerized systems of career information were viewed as the most valuable resources. Most schools reported that their greatest problem was not a lack of resources but, rather, that students were not using available resources as well as students' tendency to focus more on immediate concerns, such as course selection, instead of career planning.

Counselors should take steps to understand and reduce student reluctance to use career information. Materials should be arranged in such a way as to maximize use. Counselors might offer workshops on these resources as a way of helping students become aware of their need for career information, familiarizing them with approaches to using occupational information and increasing their familiarity with the services of the counselors.

Computer-Based Career Information Systems

Computer-based career information systems (CBCISs) are probably the newest major addition to career resource centers. Bloch and Kinnison (1989) found that 4.5 million people were using CBCISs at over 13,000 sites. At least 25% of high schools in the United States have CBCISs (Kapes, Borman, & Frazier, 1989). Most cost several thousand dollars per year but can be used for large numbers of students. Surveys indicate that, overall, people report a moderate-to-high level of satisfaction with these systems and that CBCISs seem to have a significant impact on career development when combined with other counseling programs and activities (Bloch & Kinnison, 1989; Kapes et al., 1989). The following are some of the available and widely used systems:

SIGI Plus (Educational Testing Service). This comprehensive system is fairly typical. It includes nine program selections: introduction, self-assessment, what occupations one might like, information on nature and requirements of occupations, self-ratings and skills needed for occupations, preparing to enter an occupation, coping ("Can I do what is required?"), deciding, and next steps (putting the plan into action).

Guidance Information System (Houghton Mifflin). Designed for high schools, colleges, and employment offices, this system provides information on 1,700 4-year colleges, 1,700 2-year colleges, 1,500 graduate and professional schools, 200 careers in the military, and 1,000 occupations as well as information on assessing interests and obtaining financial aid.

Discover (American College Testing Program).

Career Information System (University of Oregon, Eugene).

C-LECT (Chronicle Guidance Publications)

CHOICES (Canada Systems Group)

PLATO (Control Data Corporation). This system is based on Holland's model of career development (see Chapter 1).

Career Exploration and Planning Program (Meridian Education Corporation).

Other Resources

Some resources appropriate for high school students have been presented in the previous chapter. Additional resources, particularly useful for this age group, are listed here.

Occupational Information

1. The *Dictionary of Occupational Titles (DOT)* is available on computer through Wintergreen Software. A fifth edition is anticipated in 1994-95.
2. *Standard Occupational Classification Manual* (U.S. Government Printing Office) provides a classification system that standardizes occupational data, divides occupations into career clusters, and is linked to the *Dictionary of Occupational Titles.*
3. The *Military Career Guide* (U.S. Government Printing Office) describes career paths in the armed forces and relates them to comparable civilian occupations.
4. The *Guide for Occupational Exploration* (American Guidance Service [AGS]) provides help in using the *DOT* as well as information on over 12,000 occupations organized into broad interest areas and work groups; it also lists apprenticeships.
5. The *Occupational Outlook Handbook* (U.S. Government Printing Office), published every 2 years, provides information on employment trends and projections, the nature of many occupations, and sources of additional information.

Postsecondary Educational Information

1. The *Encyclopedia of Careers and Vocational Guidance* is available from Doubleday.
2. The *National College Catalog Library* (Career Guidance Foundation) is a collection of over 3,500 college catalogs available on microfiche; briefer versions can be developed to meet local needs.

Career and Skill Development

1. *Tools for Transition* (AGS) is a kit to prepare students with learning disabilities for postsecondary education.

2. *Designing the Future* (National Occupational Information Coordinating Committee) is an introduction to career development at the high school level, including publications, videos, guidelines for workshops, and suggested activities.

3. *Swimming Upstream: A Complete Guide to the College Application Process for the Learning Disabled Student*, by D. W. Hunt, is available from Hunt House, Austin, Texas.

Financial Aid

1. The *Chronicle Student Aid Annual* is available from Chronicle Guidance Publications.

2. *The Directory of Athletic Scholarships* is published by G. P. Putnam.

3. The *Directory of Financial Aid for Women* is published by Reference Service Press.

4. *How and Where to Get Scholarships and Financial Aid for College* is available from Arco Press.

5. *Lovejoy's Guide to Financial Aid* is published by Monarch Press.

6. *The Scholarship Book* is published by Prentice Hall.

General Resources

1. *Career World* (General Learning Corporation) is a magazine for high school students on careers, jobs, and future planning.

2. Cambridge Career Products publishes a catalog of career, educational, and personal counseling resources on a broad range of topics.

3. VGM Career Horizons publishes a catalog of many books on career opportunities, job seeking, and college selection.

4. Careers, Inc., publishes a catalog of information on career development, job seeking, personal development, financial aid, and college choice. It includes information for special needs students and features the *Desk-Top Careers Kit*, briefs on over 800 careers, updated regularly.

Structured Workshops to Promote Career Development

One of the primary approaches to promoting the career development of adolescents is structured courses, programs, or workshops. Typically, these are time limited and focus on the development of a specific skill, helping a special population, or dealing with a hurdle in career development. Many of these programs are reported in the literature, most achieving a positive outcome. Numerous articles and dissertations present and evaluate such counseling experiences and provide valuable ideas for counselors who want to develop such programs for their own schools. The following is a sampling of some of these workshops.

1. The Indianapolis Public Schools provided over 400 economically disadvantaged young people, aged 16 to 21, with supervised work or internship experiences, career education workshops designed to provide support and increase motivation and awareness of options, and mentors in businesses and the community to serve as role models (Harris, 1983).

2. A weeklong career development workshop was developed for secondary school students with hearing impairments; the workshop was designed to enhance self-image, eliminate occupational stereotyping, and expand career options (Jarchow & Wade, 1983).

3. The Dual Career Guidance Project used materials and models to help 11th- and 12th-grade students become more aware of and skilled in managing dual-worker or dual-career lifestyles. Participants' career maturity was increased by the program (Amatea & Cross, 1982).

4. The Program to Attract Minority Youth to Careers in Engineering and Technology (Project PACE) brought together 50 minority high school students with minority scientists, engineers, and mathematicians for weekly Saturday morning programs. Of the participants, 10 enrolled in 4-year colleges, 9 of them in science or mathematics (*Project PACE*, 1984).

5. A 1-day program used the Self-Directed Search, fantasy of a perfect future day, information giving, and moderate persuasion to encourage gifted boys and girls to establish career aspirations commensurate with their abilities. At a 6-month follow-up, the girls had increased their aspirations although the boys had not (Kerr, 1983).

6. Life Development Visualization is a career exploration program using techniques such as guided imagery, symbolic art, meditation, journal keeping, centering, focusing, awareness activities, and relaxation in a 2- to 3-hour session designed to help high school students answer the questions, Where am I now in my life? Where do I want to go in my life? What is blocking me? How can I get there? (Lampron, 1985).

7. NIEP College Preview Tour Program conducts 3- to 8-day tours of colleges in various regions of the country and has worked with high schools to plan individualized tours.

8. A career decision-making course, taught to 10th graders and consisting of 20 lessons based on Crites' Career Maturity Inventory, significantly improved foresight and reduced decisional difficulties (Savickas, 1990).

These are only a few among the wide range of effective counseling experiences that have been developed by those concerned with the career development of young people.

Career Education Activities to Promote Career Development

Some activities relevant to secondary school students as well as middle and junior high school students were listed in the previous chapter. An additional list of activities, particularly well suited to secondary school students, follows.

Information Giving

1. guided field trips of colleges and job sites
2. discussion of family influences on career development
3. exploration of the relationship between career and lifestyle

Skill Development

1. understanding occupational and personal values using exercises and card sorts
2. completing college applications
3. developing job-seeking skills
4. developing positive work habits
5. making good use of leisure time
6. cognitive-behavioral training in problem solving
7. developing principles of life planning
8. improving decision-making skills
9. conducting informational interviews
10. for parents: understanding their own career development

Support Groups and Services

1. job and internship placement programs

2. job clubs, emphasizing development and rehearsal of job-seeking skills
3. college-bound clubs
4. collaborative job placement programs especially for people with disabilities, reflecting a team effort of vocational teachers, rehabilitation and employment counselors, parents, special education teachers, general counselors, students, and community representatives

Improving Decision-Making Skills

In addition to facilitating the overall career development of young people, there are certain skills and clusters of information that counselors should be familiar with and be able to transmit to their students. One of the most important skills for secondary school students is decision making. Nearly all adolescents will be making tentative occupational choices, making educational decisions, and beginning the process of establishing an adult lifestyle. Sound decision-making skills can maximize the likelihood that young people will make satisfying choices.

Often, young people make decisions on the basis of limited information or knowledge, make decisions by default, or put off that anxiety-provoking task of making decisions so long that options become limited. Young people with many diverse abilities and those with few apparent talents seem to have the greatest difficulty narrowing their choices during these years. Special help in decision making should be extended to these groups.

Many times, young people's decisions are greatly influenced by social and cultural factors and by their reference groups. Personality factors also have a strong effect on the nature of decisions. Decisions may be more a reflection of the response style and background of the decider than they are an appropriate response to available options. People have characteristic styles of decision making, and their choices tend to fall into patterns such as choosing the safest strategy, choosing the most pleasurable alternative, making the most responsible choice, choosing what will please others most, or choosing to avoid consequences. Counselors can help adolescents identify their predominant mode of decision making so that they become more able to make decisions based on thought and awareness rather than on habitual patterns of response.

Positive decision making can be broken down into a sequence of behaviors. These include the following:

1. Define the decision to be made.
2. Generate a list of options or possibilities.
3. Gather information on each possible choice.
4. Clarify relationship of options to one's own values, feelings, self-concept, and long- and short-range goals.
5. Assess the likelihood of success and the potential benefits of each option.
6. Assess the risks and pitfalls of each option.
7. Weigh the options, estimate their probable outcomes, and assess their desirability.
8. Narrow the options and develop compromises if necessary.
9. Formulate a tentative plan of action for implementing the selected option and maximizing the likelihood of a positive outcome.
10. Evaluate both the decision and the process of decision making so that the process can operate even better the next time.

Counselors can facilitate competent decision making by helping students learn and execute this sequence of behaviors. Counselors can also help young people by modeling effective decision making and by encouraging them to assume responsibility for their own choices.

Overcoming Extrinsic Hurdles
to Career Development

Difficulty making sound decisions can be an internal roadblock to positive career development. External as well as internal challenges can hamper career development. More than 50% of all high school students now continue into college. In light of this, the major external hurdles encountered by this age group probably are the cost of higher education and the tests required for admission to many colleges. Counselors can help students negotiate these hurdles by keeping both themselves and the students well-informed on admissions procedures and financial aid programs.

The SAT is the most widely used of the admissions tests as well as the most widely used standardized test in the United States (Avasthi, 1990). It is taken by approximately 1.7 million high school students, including 42% of all high school seniors, each year. The American College Testing Program (ACT), another widely used standardized test of academic abilities, is taken by approximately 1 million people each year (Carvajal et al., 1989). Taking the appropriate tests at the appropriate times is important for admission to a large percentage of colleges.

Knowing how and when to apply for financial aid can also exert a considerable influence on the educational plans of many young people. With costs of many colleges reaching at least $10,000 per year, most families cannot afford the cost of 4 years of college education without assistance. Applying for financial aid, in recent years, has become better coordinated with the use of the Parents' Confidential Financial Statement. Processed by a central clearing house, information from this form is used by most colleges to determine awards of financial aid.

Clearly, the role of the secondary school counselor is multifaceted and challenging. Counselors seem to be meeting this challenge. Engen, Laing, and Sawyer (1988) found, for example, that overall satisfaction of college-bound high school students with the counseling they received increased from 48% in 1973-74 to 59% in 1983-84, whereas dissatisfaction decreased from 28% to 20%. The continuing challenge, however, is to improve the level of satisfaction even further.

Case Study of Bob Questor

Searching for Realism and Separation

The following case illustrates some of the issues and challenges often encountered by high school students and counselors.

Bob Questor was no stranger to his counselor. When she received his note asking for an appointment, she recalled some of the milestones in Bob's last 3 years of high school and the part she had played in them. Her first glimpse of Bob had been of a tall, slender young man, looking confused and overwhelmed on his first day in their large high school. She remembered when Bob's father, who had a degenerative disease, became dangerously ill and she had to call Bob out of class and tell him to hurry to the hospital. She remembered many discussions, talking about course selection, choice of colleges, possible scholarships, and future plans. Finally, she remembered the awards assembly, in which Bob won awards for both athletics and academics. She was quite sure what Bob wanted to talk about from his note: "I got into all three! What do I do now? Help!"

Background

Bob was in the last semester of his senior year of high school. Like many others in his age group, he was having difficulty establishing a clear sense of identity and direction. For several years, he had been anticipating that surely by the time he was ready to graduate from high school he would have made some clear decisions about his future that would integrate aspects of himself, bring coherence to his self-image, and enable him to begin college with some clear choices and plans about his future. Now graduation was imminent, but Bob felt more immobilized than ever by the many options he had open to him. It seemed to him that any choice he made, although opening some doors for him, also closed other doors, and that was the challenge, prioritizing his choices and realizing he probably could not fulfill all his ambitions.

Bob lived with his parents and younger sister, Katie, aged 11, in a suburban community. His father had been a successful attorney, well-known for his skill in the courtroom. However, he had been ill for the past 8 years and had stopped working 3 years ago. Although intellectually unimpaired, Bob's father used a wheelchair and had considerable difficulty with motor activities. His mother was a college professor, teaching sociology at a nearby state university. She often taught evening classes and worked at home on the weekends. Bob and his sister were expected to help out, and each one prepared dinner twice a week and had responsibility for household chores.

Academics had come easily to Bob, and he had been an outstanding student throughout his school years. Although, as he put it, "I can't just get by. I really have to work to get my grades," his grade point average was better than a 4.0, or A average, because his participation in advanced placement classes earned him some extra points. Learning was an exciting challenge for Bob, and he agreed with his family's values that education was important to his future.

Obtaining a clear picture of Bob's relative strengths and weaknesses in academics was difficult because of his uniformly high grades. However, he reported having particular interest in mathematics and history. This year, he took journalism as an elective course and became news editor of the school paper. The many aspects of that role—interviewing, writing stories, managing other writers, editing, and planning the layout for the newspaper—all had been very rewarding to him and had opened up some new career options. Investigative journalism was particularly appealing to him. He reported that, as a young boy, he had been fascinated by his father's stories of criminal cases as well as his mother's stories of her work in social welfare and social policy. He always had wanted to be in an occupation where he could make a contribution to society, and journalism seemed to be one way to accomplish that. Elementary school teaching was another option, a rather unconventional choice for a young man. However, Bob spoke of the importance of the early years in children's development; he recognized the important role a teacher could play in helping children develop values and goals. He said he could easily imagine himself teaching in an inner city school. In addition, Bob had a strong interest in writing and research and considered pursuing a career in either mathematics or history. He had had ample exposure to the university environment over the years and was familiar with his mother's work as a college professor. That role, too, seemed to be one he would enjoy. Like many gifted young people, Bob's multipotentiality offered him many choices. However, because his interests and abilities were so broad and varied, he was having difficulty making choices.

Bob's family situation also seemed to have expanded his options. Both parents had established successful professional careers, and both had contributed to the development of Bob's interests. Because of his father's illness, Bob's mother's career was providing most of the income in the family, and both parents seemed to take pride in his mother's accomplishments, including the publication of her recent textbook.

These events and attitudes seemed to expand Bob's horizons, and he seemed less influenced by gender bias in both his own occupational interests and his family aspirations. Bob stated that he hoped to marry and have several children someday; but he anticipated that both he and his future wife would be involved in graduate study, and so he expected to marry at about age 30 and have children in his mid-30s. He assumed that he and his wife would share household responsibilities as his parents had done and said that his responsibilities for planning and cooking meals at home had prepared him well for that role.

Despite his academic and family responsibilities, Bob found time for many leisure activities. He had been playing golf since his father taught him the game when he was in kindergarten. He enjoyed playing street hockey and talking with his friends and had been dating for the past 2 years, although at this point he preferred to date "girls who are friends" rather than "girlfriends." When he was in elementary school, Bob thought he might like to become a professional golfer. However, by junior high school, he realized that that role was not compatible with his values, his personality, or many of his interests. Golf, then, has remained a rewarding leisure interest for Bob but had been ruled out as a career direction.

When asked how he coordinated his activities, he replied, "Organization. I just make lots of lists and plan where I need to be when, and that seems to work for me. I do have trouble sometimes when other people set deadlines. That makes me worry that I won't be able to do my best in the time I have."

Bob had particular difficulty with the application deadlines imposed by the colleges. He had gathered a great deal of information on possibilities by talking with family, friends, teachers, and his school counselor; he had reviewed catalogs and the extensive amount of literature he had received from colleges; and he and his mother had visited the six universities that most interested him. He finally decided on three options: the nearby state university where his mother taught, a highly regarded liberal arts university that was in his state but about 100 miles from his home, and a very competitive university about 500 miles from his home, primarily for people interested in careers in science and technology. To Bob's surprise, he had been admitted to all three schools, with ample scholarships. Bob knew he would be comfortable at the school closest to home. That would enable him to be available to his family if they needed him, even if he lived on-campus. The other two institutions were less comfortable choices. He worried about being able to handle the academic demands, adjusting to a large institution away from home, and leaving his family without his help. Although both parents encouraged him to make his own choices, family needs were an important consideration for him.

Despite his sense of confusion, Bob had already made several important decisions about his career. He had decided to go to college and said that he hoped he would receive his doctorate some day. He had developed some career possibilities that reflected considerable career maturity in that they reflected Bob's interests, his abilities, his values, and his personality. He also had considered some realistic ways to integrate professional and personal goals and was actively involved in leisure pursuits, despite his academic focus. He felt strongly committed to his family and wanted to continue to help them in some way. Bob might be described as undecided rather than indecisive; he was able to make decisions and had already made many, but he seemed to need some more information and guidance to help him make additional decisions about choice of college, choice of major, and eventual career direction. Bob had shown good ability to make use of information, and when he came to counseling asking, "Aren't there some tests you can give me to help me make a decision? I'll take them all if it will help," the counselor responded by planning, with Bob, a sequence of inventories, coupled with discussion, to help him make some of his decisions.

Assessment of Abilities

As with most college-bound high school students, a great deal of information about Bob's abilities was already available, making the administration of additional test of abilities unnecessary. School grades, particularly those demonstrating high performance in advanced placement courses, gave a clear indication that Bob was a very intelligent, very capable student. This was confirmed by ability tests he had taken previously.

Scholastic Aptitude Test

As part of the college admissions process, Bob took the SAT, consisting of a verbal section, a math section, and a Test of Standard Written English (TSWE), in which respondents are asked to locate grammatical or usage errors in sentences. When combined with consideration of high school grades, the SAT can greatly improve prediction of college performance

(Avasthi, 1990). The verbal and math scores are used primarily as part of admissions decisions, whereas the TSWE score is used more for placement. Scores on the SAT verbal and math sections are reported on a 200 to 800 scale, with an anticipated mean of 500 and a standard deviation of 100. The standard error of measurement (*SEM*) is 30 points above or below a score, and scores are reported in specific numbers, in *SEM* bands, and in percentiles. Bob achieved a score of 550 on the SAT-verbal and 660 on the SAT-math. His verbal score was at the 85th percentile nationwide; his math score, at the 91st percentile. His score on the TSWE, 49, fell at the 66th percentile. Clearly, all scores were well above average, with his math score being particularly outstanding.

Although the SAT has been criticized for being biased against women and minorities, 1,500 or 88% of colleges in the United States use that examination. Presently, it is undergoing revision, and a new version, called the Scholastic Assessment Test, is anticipated for 1994. The revised version of the SAT is expected to place primary emphasis on such skills as critical reading and reasoning, data interpretation, and problem solving.

Tests of Achievement and Proficiency

All students in Bob's high school were assessed with the Tests of Achievement and Proficiency (TAP), part of the Riverside Basic Skills Assessment Program for Grades K through 12 that includes the well-known Iowa Tests of Basic Skills for Grades K through 9 and the TAP for Grades 9 through 12. The TAP is a battery of achievement tests that requires approximately 4 hours for administration. Computerized scoring facilitates presentation of scores in formats requested by each school district, including national and local percentiles, grade equivalents, and stanines. The following lists each section or test, followed by the national percentile (NPCT) and stanine scores (NSTN) Bob received when he completed the TAP in the 11th grade.

Test or Section	NPCT	NSTN
Reading comprehension	91	8
Mathematics	96	9
Written expression	94	8
Sources of information	96	9
Basic composite	96	9
Social studies	99	9
Science	97	9
Complete composite	98	9

Here, too, Bob's scores are very high, even higher than his scores on the aptitude test (SAT). This comparison suggests that Bob is making excellent use of his intellectual abilities and confirms his perception of himself as having many realistic possibilities. His somewhat higher scores on the TAP, as compared to the SAT, have several possible explanations. Bob's TAP scores are being compared with a general group of high school students, whereas most taking the SAT will be college bound, having a higher average academic aptitude than a general group of high school students. In addition, Bob's own high standards, strong motivation to succeed, enjoyment of learning, and organizational abilities probably enable him to use his abilities even better than most.

The combination of achievement and aptitude tests seems particularly useful for high school students thinking about attending college. For most, scores on such inventories will be available through the schools. The SAT and the ACT are the aptitude scores most likely to be available. Many achievement test batteries are available, including the Metropolitan Achievement Test, the Comprehensive Tests of Basic Skills, the Stanford Achievement Tests, and other tests listed in previous chapters. Similar information can be obtained from measures of multiple aptitudes such as the Differential Aptitude Tests and the Armed Services Vocational Aptitude Battery.

Assessment of Career Development

To obtain a clearer understanding of some of the factors that might be hampering Bob's efforts to make decisions, he was asked to complete My Vocational Situation (MVS), developed by Holland, Daiger, and Power and published by Consulting Psychologists Press in 1980. Described by its authors as an experimental diagnostic scheme, the 20 questions on this inventory measure three aspects of a person. *Vocational identity* (VI), the first construct, is defined as "awareness of, and ability to specify one's own interests, personality characteristics, strengths, and goals as these relate to career choices" (Leong & Morris, 1989, p. 117). Having strong VI is believed to facilitate career decision making and confidence in decisions. The second construct, *occupational information* (OI), assesses respondents' perceived need for career information. *Barriers* (B), the third construct, looks at external obstacles or limitations in career planning.

Bob's scores on this inventory were quite varied. Compared with high school males, his VI score was slightly below the mean, his OI score was well below the mean, and his B score was well above the mean. Barriers such as abilities, finances, and family support do not trouble Bob. However, he perceives himself as sorely lacking in career information. Concerns that he indicated on the VI scale included the following: "I need reassurance that I have made the right choice of occupation," "Making up my mind about a career has been a long and difficult process for me" and "I don't know what my major strengths and weaknesses are."

Although the MVS does not have high statistical reliability and seems to measure general adjustment as much as it assesses career development, it provides a useful picture of people's perceptions of their career development, a valuable stimulus for discussion, and insight into understanding the difficulties people want to address in counseling (Leong & Morris, 1989; Lucas et al., 1988). The MVS brief self-scored format is not likely to be threatening and seems useful for high school and college students at all stages of career development.

Assessment of Interests

In an effort to provide Bob some of the direction and information he was lacking and to respond to his interest in taking some inventories to give him that information, two interest inventories were included in his assessment.

Self-Directed Search

The Self-Directed Search (SDS), first published in 1971 by Psychological Assessment Resources, has received wide acceptance among counselors and psychologists (McKee & Levinson, 1990). Based on Holland's (1985) theory of career development, described in Chapter 1 of this book, the SDS consists of 228 items divided into three sets (activities, competencies, occupations), yielding scores on the six scales in Holland's hexagonal framework. A three-digit code, composed of a person's first, second, and third highest scores on the SDS, can be translated into occupations that are congruent with that code. The SDS is available in regular, computerized, advanced, and simplified versions as well as in several languages and can be used by people between the ages of 15 and 70. It is used by over 250,000 people each year (Prediger, 1981). Extensive supplementary materials, including the *College Majors Finder*, the *Occupations Finder*, the *Jobs Finder*, and the *Dictionary of Holland Occupational Codes* as well as an accompanying booklet (*You and Your Career*), facilitate use of this inventory. Most people can score this inventory themselves with some direction, thereby obtaining immediate feedback on their choices. This instrument has been extensively studied, is well-grounded in theory, and has become one of the most useful and flexible tools available to career counselors. Although many balk at Holland's recommendation that most people can use this inventory independent of counseling, when the SDS is combined with some short-term counseling, it seems highly effective at reducing an overwhelming amount of information to a small number of comprehensible factors in a fairly short amount of time (approximately 20 minutes to complete and score the inventory) (Krieshok, 1987).

Bob's scores on this inventory were surprisingly well differentiated. He achieved a very high score in the investigative area, moderate scores in social, conventional, and enterprising areas, and low scores in artistic and realistic areas, yielding a summary code of ISC. None of these three areas are adjacent on Holland's hexagonal framework, perhaps one reason for Bob's occupational indecision. His interests are diverse, and finding an occupation that integrates them well will be challenging. Such occupations as public health microbiologist, scientific linguist, and mathematics teacher have a code of ISC. These are occupations that focus on research and learning, provide some involvement with people, and are fairly well structured and unambiguous. Occupations of several permutations of Bob's code (e.g., SIC, ICS) were also reviewed and discussed with him, but those in the ISC group seemed to capture best Bob's varied skills and interests.

Kuder Occupational Interest Survey—Form DD

The Kuder Occupational Interest Survey—Form DD (KOIS) is part of the Kuder family of interest inventories published by Science Research Associates. The KOIS requires about 30 minutes to complete and must be machine scored. First published in 1966, the present version of the KOIS shows the relationship between the respondent's interest patterns and those characteristic of people in over 100 occupational groups and 48 college majors. The inventory presents 100 triads; for each, respondents indicate their most preferred and least preferred activities. This is a forced-choice ipsative format. Because of this, scores cannot be all high or all low. This format, providing differentiation of interests as well as college major preferences, seemed well suited to Bob's needs. The KOIS can be used by people in high school, college, or adulthood. Supplementary material, such as an interpretive audiocassette and packages of career information, facilitate application of information. Extensive research over its many years of use provides reasonable evidence of the reliability and validity of the KOIS.

Numerical scores on the KOIS are lambda coefficients, representing the degree to which a person's responses are similar to the responses of each criterion group (D. P. Jepsen, 1985). Scores are provided in five areas (see Figure 6.1).

1. *Dependability.* A satisfactory V-score indicated that Bob's profile appeared dependable.

2. *Vocational Interest Estimates.* This section rank orders and reflects strength of interest in 10 broad occupational areas. Respondents are compared separately with both men and women. Bob's highest scores were in literary, scientific, and computational areas; average scores were in social service and persuasive; and low scores were in clerical, musical, outdoor, mechanical, and artistic areas. As with the SDS, Bob's high interest in research and mathematics is indicated, but his interest seems less

Kuder Occupational Interest Survey Report Form

Compared with men
MOST SIMILAR, CONT.

Name

Sex　MALE　　　　Date

Numeric Grid No.　　　SRA No.

1 **Dependability:** How much confidence can you place in your results? In scoring your responses several checks were made on your answer patterns to be sure that you understood the directions and that your results were complete and dependable. According to these:

YOUR RESULTS APPEAR
TO BE DEPENDABLE.

2 **Vocational Interest Estimates:** Vocational interests can be divided into different types and the level of your attraction to each type can be measured. You may feel that you know what interests you have already — what you may not know is how strong they are compared with other people's interests. This section shows the relative rank of your preferences for ten different kinds of vocational activities. Each is explained on the back of this report form. Your preferences in these activities, as compared with other people's interests, are as follows:

Compared with men		Compared with women	
HIGH		HIGH	
LITERARY	97	LITERARY	97
SCIENTIFIC	88	SCIENTIFIC	92
COMPUTATIONAL	82	COMPUTATIONAL	86
AVERAGE		AVERAGE	
SOCIAL SERVICE	55	PERSUASIVE	49
PERSUASIVE	39	MECHANICAL	44
LOW		LOW	
CLERICAL	23	SOCIAL SERVICE	24
MUSICAL	20	MUSICAL	22
OUTDOOR	17	CLERICAL	19
MECHANICAL	13	OUTDOOR	18
ARTISTIC	11	ARTISTIC	05

3 **Occupations:** The KOIS has been given to groups of persons who are experienced and satisfied in many different occupations. Their patterns of interests have been compared with yours and placed in order of their similarity with you. The following occupational groups have interest patterns *most* similar to yours:

Compared with men		Compared with women	
COMPUTER PRGRMR	.50	COMPUTR PRGRMR	.50
OPTOMETRIST	.50	PHARMACIST	.49
PSYCHOLOGIST	.50	PSYCHOLOGIST	.49
STATISTICIAN	.50	ACCT, CERT PUB	.48
MATHEMATICIAN	.49	DENTIST	.47
JOURNALIST	.49	PHYSICIAN	.47
ELEM SCH TEACHER	.48	JOURNALIST	.47
PHYSICIAN	.48	AUDIOL/SP PATHOL	.45
BOOKSTORE MGR	.47	BANKER	.44
CHEMIST	.47	PHYS THERAPIST	.44
ACCT, CERT PUB	.46		
PHYS THERAPIST	.45		

Compared with men	
MOST SIMILAR, CONT.	
LIBRARIAN	.45
DENTIST	.45
LAWYER	.45
AUDIOL/SP PATHOL	.44
THESE ARE NEXT	
MOST SIMILAR:	
PODIATRIST	.43
NURSE	.43
RADIO STATION MGR	.43
FILM/TV PROD/DIR	.43
MATH TCHR, HS	.42
PHARMACIST	.42
METEOROLOGIST	.42
COUNSELOR, HS	.42
CLOTHIER, RETAIL	.41
ENGINEER	.41
SCIENCE TCHR, HS	.41
SOCIAL WORKER	.41
BOOKKEEPER	.41
TRAVEL AGENT	.41
X-RAY TECHNICIAN	.40
PRINTER	.39
FORESTER	.39
ARCHITECT	.39
PHOTOGRAPHER	.39
REAL ESTATE AGT	.38
VETERINARIAN	.35
BUYER	.35
THE REST ARE	
LISTED IN ORDER	
OF SIMILARITY:	
PERSONNEL MGR	.36
TV REPAIRER	.36
SCHOOL SUPT	.35
BANKER	.35
POSTAL CLERK	.35
PLANT NURSRY WKR	.35
INSURANCE AGENT	.33
PHARMACEUT SALES	.33
INTERIOR DECOR	.33
FLORIST	.32
AUTO SALESPERSON	.31
POLICE OFFICER	.31
BRICKLAYER	.31
PLUMBING CONTRAC	.30
SUPERVSR, INDUST	.30
EXTENSION AGENT	.29
WELDER	.29
MINISTER	.29
BLDG CONTRACTOR	.28
ELECTRICIAN	.28
MACHINIST	.27
FARMER	.26

Figure 6.1. Kuder Occupational Interest Survey Report Form

Compared with women		Compared with men		Compared with women
THESE ARE NEXT MOST SIMILAR:		REST, CONT.		
		AUTO MECHANIC	.25	
ENGINEER	.43	PLUMBER	.24	
FILM/TV PROD/DIR	.43	TRUCK DRIVER	.24	
BOOKSTORE MGR	.43	PAINTER, HOUSE	.23	
PERSONNEL MGR	.43	CARPENTER	.21	
LIBRARIAN	.42			
MATH TEACHER, HS	.42			
NUTRITIONIST	.42			
INSURANCE AGENT	.42			
LAWYER	.41			
SCIENCE TCHR, HS	.41			
SECRETARY	.41			
ELEM SCH TEACHER	.40			
NURSE	.40			
SOCIAL WORKER	.40			
POLICE OFFICER	.39			
COUNSELOR, HS	.39			
DIETITIAN	.39			
COL STU PERS WKR	.39			
DENTAL ASSISTANT	.39			
VETERINARIAN	.39			
X-RAY TECHNICIAN	.39			
BANK CLERK	.38			

4 College Majors: Just as for occupations, the KOIS has been given to many persons in different college majors. The following college major groups have interest patterns *most* similar to yours:

	Compared with men		Compared with women	
	MATHEMATICS	.52	PSYCHOLOGY	.49
	PREMED/PHAR/DENT	.50	MATHEMATICS	.48
	PSYCHOLOGY	.50	BIOLOGICAL SCI	.46
	ENGLISH	.49	ENGINEERING	.46
	BIOLOGICAL SCI	.48	ELEMENTARY EDUC	.45
	PHYSICAL SCIENCE	.48	BUSINESS ADMIN	.45
	FOREIGN LANGUAGE	.46	ENGLISH	.44
	HISTORY	.46	HEALTH PROFESS	.44
	ECONOMICS	.46	FOREIGN LANGUAGE	.43
			HISTORY	.43

THE REST ARE LISTED IN ORDER OF SIMILARITY:		THESE ARE NEXT MOST SIMILAR:		THESE ARE NEXT MOST SIMILAR:	
REAL ESTATE AGT	.37	ELEMENTARY EDUC	.45		
ARCHITECT	.37	SOCIOLOGY	.45	POLITICAL SCI	.42
OFFICE CLERK	.37	SERV ACAD CADET	.45	NURSING	.41
OCCUPA THERAPIST	.36	ENGINEERING	.44	PHYSICAL EDUC	.40
BOOKKEEPER	.36	PHYSICAL EDUC	.43	HOME ECON EDUC	.39
INTERIOR DECOR	.34	POLITICAL SCI	.43	SOCIOLOGY	.38
FLORIST	.33	BUSINESS ADMIN	.42		
RELIGIOUS ED DIR	.31	FORESTRY	.40	THE REST ARE LISTED IN ORDER OF SIMILARITY:	
MINISTER	.31				
BEAUTICIAN	.31	THE REST ARE LISTED IN ORDER OF SIMILARITY:		DRAMA	.36
EXTENSION AGENT	.30			MUSIC & MUSIC ED	.34
DEPT STORE-SALES	.28			ART & ART EDUC	.31
		MUSIC & MUSIC ED	.38		
		ANIMAL SCIENCE	.34		
		ARCHITECTURE	.34		
		ART & ART EDUC	.34		
		AGRICULTURE	.33		

Experimental Scales.				V-SCORE	52		
M	.42	MBI	.20	W	.45	WBI	.21
S	.49	F	.40	D	.44	MO	.41

Figure 6.1. Continued

pronounced here than on the SDS in social and conventional areas. A formula is provided in the KOIS manual for conversion of these scores into Holland's RIASEC (Realistic Investigative, Artistic, Social, Enterprising, Conventional) codes.

3. *Occupations.* Here, 119 occupations have been rank ordered according to the respondent's level of interest compared to both men and women in those occupations. Lambda scores are also provided. Both relative and absolute scores are relevant, with a difference of .06 or more in scores likely to be a meaningful difference. Most people receive a score higher than .45 in their own occupations or majors.

Bob received his highest scores (between .50 and .44) in 15 different occupations, including such fields as computer programmer, psychologist, mathematician, journalist, elementary school teacher, physician, chemist, and lawyer. He achieved what the test manual terms a flat profile or a pattern of undifferentiated interests, reflecting either people with broad opportunities or considerable career confusion. Although Bob was pleased that most of his verbalized occupational interests appeared in this list, he was disappointed that a more definitive answer had not been provided.

4. *College Majors.* Bob's scores in the college major scales reflected a similar breadth of interests and included mathematics, premedicine, psychology, English, biological science, foreign language, history, and economics. Interest in mathematics, science, history, and language all seemed strong.

5. *Experimental Scales.* Although little weight should be placed on these scales, they provide some information on level of maturity, sincerity in responses, and similarity of interests to each gender. Bob's scores reflected good maturity and sincerity. His interests did seem as much like those of women as they were like those of men, reflecting his interest in traditionally masculine as well as traditionally feminine fields.

Many interest inventories are available for use with high school students. In addition to those inventories discussed elsewhere in this book, some of these include the following:

- Interest Determination, Exploration, and Assessment System (IDEAS), published by National Computer Systems (NCS) and used with Grade 7 through adult
- Jackson Vocational Interest Survey, for Grade 9 and older and published by Sigma Assessment Systems, designed for people who are college bound

- Ohio Vocational Interest Survey (OVIS—II), for Grade 7 through college, published by Harcourt Brace Jovanovich
- College Major Interest Inventory, published by Consulting Psychologists Press
- ACT Career Planning Program, published by ACT Career Services, widely used as part of the ACT assessment of aptitudes
- Career Assessment Inventory, another NCS publication
- Career Directions Inventory, published by Research Psychologists Press
- U.S. Employment Service Interest Inventory (USES—II), published by the Department of Labor

Assessment of Personality and Values

Few inventories have been developed to assess personality and values of adolescents. The High School Personality Questionnaire (HSPQ), published by the Institute for Personality and Ability Testing, Inc., is one of the few aimed at this age group. It was used with Bob both to help him gain insight into the difficulty he was having with decision making and to help him determine which occupations might be most compatible with his personality.

The HSPQ requires about 45 minutes to complete and consists of 142 items that measure 14 relatively independent dimensions of personality. This widely used inventory can be either hand or machine scored and was designed for students in junior high or high school. Versions of the inventory are also available for children (Early School Personality Questionnaire for ages 6-8 and Children's Personality Questionnaire for ages 8-12) and for adults (16 Personality Factor [16PF]). Despite the extensive use of this family of personality inventories, questions have been raised about their reliability and validity, and caution is suggested in their interpretation (Drummond, 1986).

To facilitate adolescents' understanding of the results of this inventory, a narrative Counseling Feedback Report organizes scores into the following five clusters (see Figure 6.2):

1. *Getting along with others.* Bob's profile indicated that he tended to be very shy and rather reserved around others.
2. *Managing your feelings.* His level of tension was very high, although his scores for troubled/untroubled and self-accepting/self-blaming were close to the mean.
3. *Independence.* Bob had fairly high scores on both group-dependent and submissive dimensions. He was concerned with pleasing others and often had difficulty asserting himself.

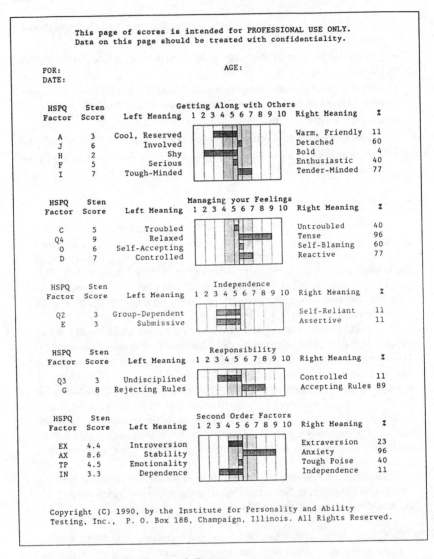

FOR: AGE:
DATE:

HSPQ Factor	Sten Score	Left Meaning	Getting Along with Others 1 2 3 4 5 6 7 8 9 10	Right Meaning	%
A	3	Cool, Reserved		Warm, Friendly	11
J	6	Involved		Detached	60
H	2	Shy		Bold	4
F	5	Serious		Enthusiastic	40
I	7	Tough-Minded		Tender-Minded	77

HSPQ Factor	Sten Score	Left Meaning	Managing your Feelings 1 2 3 4 5 6 7 8 9 10	Right Meaning	%
C	5	Troubled		Untroubled	40
Q4	9	Relaxed		Tense	96
O	6	Self-Accepting		Self-Blaming	60
D	7	Controlled		Reactive	77

HSPQ Factor	Sten Score	Left Meaning	Independence 1 2 3 4 5 6 7 8 9 10	Right Meaning	%
Q2	3	Group-Dependent		Self-Reliant	11
E	3	Submissive		Assertive	11

HSPQ Factor	Sten Score	Left Meaning	Responsibility 1 2 3 4 5 6 7 8 9 10	Right Meaning	%
Q3	3	Undisciplined		Controlled	11
G	8	Rejecting Rules		Accepting Rules	89

HSPQ Factor	Sten Score	Left Meaning	Second Order Factors 1 2 3 4 5 6 7 8 9 10	Right Meaning	%
EX	4.4	Introversion		Extraversion	23
AX	8.6	Stability		Anxiety	96
TP	4.5	Emotionality		Tough Poise	40
IN	3.3	Dependence		Independence	11

Figure 6.2. Counseling Feedback Report

   4. *Responsibility.* An apparent contradiction appeared here: Bob seemed
   very accepting of rules but not very disciplined. Perhaps his strong
   effort to remain organized reflected an underlying tendency to have
   some difficulty maintaining self-control. However, because he valued

approval and success, he had managed to control his tendency to be irresponsible.

5. *Second order factors.* These scores suggested that Bob had high anxiety, was somewhat introverted, and tended to be dependent on others.

Bob found the results of this inventory to be very thought provoking and to reflect some sides of himself that he felt few people knew. He stated that he tried hard to be outgoing and join in group activities, but that was very difficult for him. He was more comfortable by himself or with his family. He reported feeling considerable anxiety in new situations, and unless he was very interested in an activity, he had some trouble maintaining his level of motivation.

Hall Occupational Orientation Inventory

The final inventory that was used with Bob was the Hall Occupational Orientation Inventory (HALL), developed by L. G. Hall and R. B. Tarrier and published by Scholastic Testing Service. The HALL was first developed in 1964. Its theoretical foundation has been derived primarily from three sources: Maslow's (1943) personality-need theory, Roe's (1956) theories of occupational choice (see Chapter 1), and information on worker traits and job content characteristics produced by the U.S. Department of Labor. The purpose of the HALL is to facilitate career planning and decision making by increasing people's awareness of their needs, values, and desires. The HALL is available in three versions (intermediate for Grades 3-7, young adult/college, and adult basic, a simplified version).

The HALL consists of a series of work-related items. The test taker responds by indicating whether each item is *most desirable, desirable, not important, undesirable,* or *very undesirable* to him or her. The HALL is untimed and can usually be completed in 30 to 45 minutes. The answer sheet can be machine scored or self-scored and is designed to involve the test taker in the process of scoring the inventory and plotting the 22 raw scores on a profile sheet that categorizes them as low, average, or high and indicates their relative strengths. Although responses to the HALL can readily be quantified, limited evidence of validity and reliability is available, suggesting that the inventory is best used to promote and focus discussion. It can be particularly useful in a career counseling group.

Bob's highest scores on this inventory (see Figure 6.3) included information, knowledge, and belonging. Other important values were aspiration, esteem, self-actualization, personal satisfaction, creativity and independence, deciding-influencing, and security. Bob was most interested in working with data and was more interested in working with people than with things. Extrinsic work attributes, such as location, monetary concern, or co-workers, held little importance for him. Clearly, intrinsic values were far more important to Bob than were extrinsic ones.

	SCALE NAME	LOW			AVERAGE			HIGH			SCORE DESCRIPTION
	1. CI – Creativity, Independence	0	5	10	15	20	25	30	35	40	See page 5
	2. RI – Risk	0	5	10	15	20	25	30	35	40	See page 5
	3. IK – Information, Knowledge	0	5	10	15	20	25	30	35	40	See page 5
Values and Needs	4. BL – Belongingness	0	5	10	15	20	25	30	35	40	See page 5
	5. SE – Security	0	5	10	15	20	25	30	35	40	See page 5
	6. A – Aspiration	0	5	10	15	20	25	30	35	40	See page 5
	7. ES – Esteem	0	5	10	15	20	25	30	35	40	See page 5
	8. SA – Self-Actualization	0	5	10	15	20	25	30	35	40	See page 6
	9. SAT – Personal Satisfaction	0	5	10	15	20	25	30	35	40	See page 6
	10. RD – Routine-Dependence	0	5	10	15	20	25	30	35	40	See page 6
Job Characteristics	11. DA – Data Orientation	0	5	10	15	20	25	30	35	40	See page 6
	12. TH – Things Orientation	0	5	10	15	20	25	30	35	40	See page 6
	13. PE – People Orientation	0	5	10	15	20	25	30	35	40	See page 6
	14. LO – Location Concern	0		5		10		15		20	See page 7
	15. APT – Aptitude Concern	0		5		10		15		20	See page 7
	16. MON – Monetary Concern	0		5		10		15		20	See page 7
Worker Traits	17. PHA – Physical Abilities Concern	0		5		10		15		20	See page 7
	18. EN – Environment Concern	0		5		10		15		20	See page 8
	19. CW – Co-worker Concern	0		5		10		15		20	See page 8
	20. Q – Qualifications Concern	0		5		10		15		20	See page 8
	21. T – Time Concern	0		5		10		15		20	See page 8
	22. DI – Deciding-Influencing	0	5	10	15	20	25	30	35	40	See page 8

Figure 6.3. Self-Interpreting Profile Sheet for the Hall Occupational
Orientation Inventory

Copyright © 1988 by L. G. Hall. Reprinted by permission of SCHOLASTIC TESTING SERVICE, INC.,
From Hall Occupational Orientation Inventory Self-Interpretative Folder, Young Adult/College form.

Outcomes

Through conversations with his counselor and exploration of his inventory results, Bob came to several conclusions. On a personal level, he
realized that he probably was too closely tied to his family and needed
to branch out and develop his interpersonal skills. He finally came to
believe that his family could manage without him, and he saw some separation as helpful to everyone. At the same time, he recognized that he

tended to be overwhelmed by large, new situations and usually performed best when he was in comfortable and familiar situations. Placing too much pressure on himself would only increase his level of tension and risk impairing his level of organization.

Bob also became more comfortable with the diversity of interests and opportunities open to him. Although he felt that his research interests, supported by inventory after inventory, were particularly strong, he was not yet sure whether to channel those interests into mathematics or one of several other fields in which he had some interest.

Bob decided that he would attend the excellent university in his state, about 100 miles from his home. Although this would allow him some separation from his family, he would be close enough to return home quickly if needed. The local college seemed to offer him too little challenge and separation, whereas the school that was 500 miles from his home, focusing on science and technology, might cause him too much anxiety. In addition, he was not certain that he wanted to limit his career options to the science and technology area but, rather, felt that a strong liberal arts college would enable him to take a variety of courses and participate in some extracurricular activities so that he could develop a clearer picture of his interests. Part-time employment at college might offer another route to clarifying his career-related interests. Because Bob planned on attending graduate school, he could afford to defer his choice of an occupation and a college major for a year or two while developing a strong liberal arts background that would allow him to focus his career in any number of directions. He also developed a systematic plan to gather information on occupations of greatest interest to him that he would pursue during his first year of college. Clearly, Bob had made some definite decisions about his future but, perhaps even more important, he was more comfortable with his many options and interests and had developed some sound plans for exploring them further.

SEVEN

Young Adulthood

Years of Compromise
and Commitment to a Lifestyle

Overview of Young Adult Development

Freud (Brill, 1938) viewed work and love as the two major areas of human endeavor. Freud's words underscore the enormity of the challenge confronting young adults. In a span of about 5 years, generally between the ages of 18 and 23, society expects young adults to demonstrate success in both of these areas. It is not surprising, then, that many people have difficulty negotiating this stage of development with satisfaction and comfort.

Most people in their late teens and early 20s feel some pressure to make a commitment to a mate and an occupation. Ginzberg (1972) and other leaders in career development have emphasized the tenuousness of such early decisions in light of the lifelong nature of career development. The high divorce rate, the large number of single-parent and blended families, and the well-established and widespread pattern of midlife career change bear witness to the often transient and frequently unsatisfying nature of such early decisions over time. However, these theories and trends do not seem to have curtailed the hopes and expectations of young adults that their decisions will withstand the impact of maturation and social change.

Whether choices are made out of wisdom and information, financial and social pressure, or passion, nearly all young adults will have to make choices. Many will postpone career and marriage plans, extending this transitional stage well into adulthood. However, a decision to delay occupational and personal commitments is a choice in itself and is likely to be a strong determinant of lifestyle and emotional development.

Love and work are almost inevitably intertwined in the young adults' life plans. Sound decisions cannot be made about one without consideration of the other. According to Savickas (1991), "Many problems presented by career clients derive from disequilibrium between work and love within their life roles" (p. 315). Consider the case of a young woman entering medical school, engaged to a young man who is entering law school. Both are eager to begin a large family in the near future. For this couple to achieve early success in both their professional and their personal lives seems almost impossible. Priorities will have to be set and compromises made.

Career development is really life planning, the process of finding an integration of occupational, interpersonal, and recreational aspects of life that satisfy one's needs and are consistent with one's values. This is a synergistic process in which success and maturation in one area is likely to enhance and contribute to development in another area. Although this is a lifelong process, young adults probably do more choosing and planning of their lives than does any other age group.

Socioeconomic Influences on Development

Societal patterns, as well as developmental changes, have an impact on young adult decision making. The level of education has been increasing, particularly for women, leading to later entry into the job market. During the third quarter of the 20th century (1950-1975), U.S. Bureau of the Census figures indicate that the average age at first marriage increased to 23.8 for men and 21.3 for women, whereas the birth rate declined from an average of 3.03 children per woman in 1950 to an average of 1.76 children. Generally, people were less interested in early marriage and large families and more interested in their work. However, this trend changed during the last quarter of the century. People placed greater emphasis on leisure and family activities, and the birth rate increased whereas the divorce rate showed some decline. This shift from work to family values has probably been accelerated by the economic difficulties of the early 1990s and the overcrowded and competitive nature of many of the most prestigious professions.

Decision making and planning are difficult in a society in flux that presents many hurdles to occupational and personal success. Overt crisis is most likely to be in evidence toward the end of high school when most students must make a choice. College can provide a moratorium to this time of acute stress, but such a crisis will often reappear toward the end of the college years. A period of anxiety-laden forced choices may lead to impulsive and unrewarding decisions. Although young adulthood is a time of upheaval for many, it is also a time when many developmental trends mesh, leading to improved decision making for many.

Developmental Changes During Young Adulthood

Many terms have been used to describe young adulthood (Thomas & Kuh, 1982). Sheehy (1976) referred to the "trying twenties," Levinson (1986) spoke of "entering the adult world," and Gould referred to "novice adulthood." The following developmental accomplishments seem important for young adults:

1. continued progress in identity development, leading to increased self-awareness and self-esteem
2. development of an independent but accepting and caring relationship with the family of origin
3. establishment of a tentative life plan, including identification of personal and career goals
4. exploration of social and sexual roles and relationships, promoting development of the capacity for communication and intimacy
5. development of relationships with people who are supportive of one's personal and career goals
6. ongoing implementation and reality testing of career choices via education, employment, and other planned experiences
7. establishment of a home base
8. management of the conflict between stability and exploration in career and relationships
9. realistically determining and assessing the compromises that have been and must be made

Erikson (1963) labeled the developmental conflict of the years between 20 and 35, intimacy versus isolation. He pointed out the danger of keeping one's distance from others and observed that some young adults become overly competitive and combative and have difficulty with cooperation and closeness. However, most narrow their circle of close friends and move toward increased intimacy with a few. The peer group, so important during the adolescent years, declines in importance, and special companions and partners are sought. Sexual concerns and a lack of social confidence are common, but these are increasingly resolved through intimate relationships.

Wortley and Amatea (1982) provide a useful overview of the development that typically takes place between the ages of 20 and 30. They view development as occurring in four areas: career, family, intimacy, and inner life, with both exterior and interior changes taking place in all four realms. Developmental milestones include the following:

1. *Career.* Establish and make a commitment to career identity, establish career orientation and initial goals, explore occupational and educational opportunities, make trial entry into the world of work, reevaluate choices.
2. *Family.* Develop identity and social support system separate from the family of origin; develop a couple relationship; establish a new family with its own guidelines for childbearing, child rearing, relationships with extended families, and lifestyle.
3. *Intimacy.* Clarify and stabilize sexual identity, explore and build close and trusting couple and peer relationships.
4. *Inner life.* Develop a sense of personal worth, self-knowledge, and a view of the world, facilitating establishment of oneself as an adult.

Intellectual and Ethical Development

Values continue to develop and become differentiated during the young adult years. Studies suggest that young people of today, particularly young men, are not embracing the traditional values of their parents (Vodanovich & Kramer, 1989). Young women seem to be more androgynous in their values, and the values of both young men and young women are more like those of their fathers than those of their mothers.

Perry (1970) identified four categories of intellectual and ethical development among young adults. *Dualism* involves a dichotomous view of right and wrong as well as unquestioning faith in authority figures. *Multiplicity* involves the recognition that there are many points of view, but emphasis is still placed on finding the right answer. Young people in the stage of *relativism* can place knowledge in context and see that judgments can be made on the basis of evidence. *Commitment*, the fourth stage, involves mature use of reasoning to make decisions and commitments. Many in this age group have developed mature values that include responsibility, independence, and concern for others, whereas some young adults continue to flounder in their value development. Values that seem to be of particular importance to the 18- to 25-year-old include physical activity, advancement, and social interaction, whereas autonomy and working conditions do not have great importance for most in this age group (L. V. Yates, 1990). Values have repeatedly been shown to relate to career development and, for many, continue to need exploration and clarification in young adulthood.

Thinking skills, too, develop during these years and also vary considerably. A study of the distribution of college freshmen (Schwebel, 1975) across Piaget's stages of intellectual development placed 17% at the concrete level, 63% at the lower level of the formal operations stage, and 20% at the upper level of that stage. Although most young adults are able to hypothesize and learn from the experiences of others, many have difficulty with that process and emphasize concrete and egocentric approaches. Use of assessment information may pose particular difficulty for these people. Overall, however, the late teens and early 20s seem to be a period of growth in knowledge, judgment, common sense, empathy, ability for creative and abstract thinking, logic, and ability to deal with generalizations.

Career Development
During the Early Adult Years

Career maturation, too, continues for most as they progress through the young adult years. Preferences expressed and decisions made in these years tend to be more consistent and stable than those made during adolescence. Ginzberg et al. (1951) labeled the phase of career development between the ages of 18 and 24 the realistic stage and divided this stage into three substages: exploration, crystallization, and specification. Super (1963) divided these years into the specification (18-21) and implementation (21-25) stages and described tasks and experiences that generally accompany successful passage through these phases.

According to Super, the specification stage includes the following:

1. a vocational preference an awareness of the need to specify
2. use of resources in specification
3. awareness of factors to consider
4. awareness of contingencies that may affect goals

5. differentiation of interests and values
6. awareness of present-future relationships
7. specification of a vocational preference
8. consistency of preference
9. possession of information concerning the preferred occupation
10. planning for the preferred occupation
11. wisdom of the vocational preference
12. confidence in a specific preference (p. 88)

Similarly, Super describes the implementation stage as including the following:

1. awareness of the need to implement preference
2. planning to implement the preference
3. executing plans to qualify for entry
4. obtaining an entry-level job (pp. 88-89)

Despite the orderly progression described by theorists, rarely does a person negotiate the career development tasks without some faltering. Many obstacles to goals and plans may arise along the way. Super (1985) described four patterns of career exploration and development in early adulthood: systematic exploration, interrupted systematic exploration, fortuitous exploration in which desirable opportunities emerge by chance, and floundering.

Salomone and Mangicaro (1991) described the career transition of early adulthood as "fraught with worry, few work experiences, limited occupational information, unrealistic aspirations, and much self-doubt" (p. 327). They identified three patterns of negotiating this transition:

1. floundering or drifting from job to job, usually accompanied by a poor sense of self and pressure to make decisions
2. moratorium or a delay of commitments, which can reduce anxiety temporarily but that does not resolve deeper psychological needs
3. stabilization or commitment to an appropriate and well-planned career path

Career Decision Making

Career decisions made during early adulthood are not made in a vacuum. They are influenced by 18 or more years of career development, of growing up in a particular family at a certain socioeconomic level, by many years of social experience and personality development, and by a pattern of innate and acquired capacities. For example, Super's (1985) research indicated that a pattern of floundering before and during adolescence typically led to impaired coping later, whereas systematic exploration generally led to a fairly smooth establishment.

Gottfredson (1981) viewed the time of entry into the world of work as a time when many people need to make compromises, focusing first on the least central aspects of the self-concept. She found that, typically, interests are sacrificed first, then job level, then sex type. She concluded, "Compromises continue until eventually most people report being in the type of work they want" (p. 549).

One barrier to career decision making is an uncertain self-image and sense of identity. Some young adults may avoid the risk inherent in seeking a career that implements self-concept if it involves a departure from familial or societal norms. They may seek a safer, though perhaps less rewarding route, and follow the suggestions of parents and teachers on a path to what Brizzi (1986) called *status quo realism*, as distinguished from self-actualized vocational realism. Others may externalize their search and take the first or easiest option, perhaps attending a local college or working in the family business. Some become trapped in undesirable situations, whereas others may become occupational transients, moving from one handy alternative to another. The need to make a choice may produce greater tension than does the need to find a satisfying career, and impulsive and convenient choices may be made during these years.

Anxiety, in the context of career indecision, seems to have a particularly deleterious effect on career development (Lopez, 1989). Young adults who are unusually anxious about their career choices and the possibility of failing or making a mistake tend to set aspirations that are either much lower or much higher than their capacities would indicate so that their abilities will not be put to a meaningful test. Such people also tend to avoid seeking information about themselves and their options in order to delay commitments and perhaps deny the inevitable need to make decisions.

Those young adults who have high anxiety about their choices seem to need extra help from counselors. However, counselors should distinguish between *career indecision* and *career indecisiveness*. The former seems to be a part of career development for almost everyone. Undecided young people may simply need more time or information, whereas indecisive people may require counseling.

In Mauer and Gysbers's (1990) study, 20% of college freshmen expressed anxiety about their career identity, and 50% expressed a need for reassurance about their occupational choices. Mauer and Gysbers also found that limited information was another barrier to decision making; 45% of those surveyed wanted more information about occupations and wanted to increase the number of occupations they were considering.

On the other hand, having high self-esteem and a clear self-concept facilitates the process of choosing an occupation. People with high self-esteem tend to view work positively, enjoy thinking and planning about their careers, and view work as a way of expressing themselves. Such people are more likely to choose occupations that they view as suitable or ideal than are people who view career choices with indifference or anxiety. Self-concept and occupational choice seem to have a reciprocal relationship. Once an occupation is chosen, one's self-concept and image of the chosen occupation tend to be brought into greater alignment.

Family relationships, too, play an important role in career decisions. Career commitment seems easiest for those young people who experience both independence from and attachment to their parents (Blustein, Walbridge, Friedlander, & Palladino, 1991). This combination seems to afford a secure base from which young people can comfortably make their career plans. On the other hand, those young people who are in conflict with their families or who are enmeshed with their families typically have considerable difficulty making career decisions (Kinnier, Brigman, & Noble, 1990; Lopez, 1989). The father-son relationship is another important dimension in young adult career development, with those young men who adopt their fathers' beliefs having the easiest time making a commitment to a career, although their choices may not necessarily be optimal.

Family finances and economic support may also be important determinants of career development. Few young people can attend college without parental assistance. Parents who lack either the financial resources or the willingness to help their children continue their educations may curtail their career options. Some young people will have not only parental wishes to consider but those of a spouse and perhaps children. An early marriage can provide financial and emotional pressure as well as support and can have a strong impact on career development.

Role models, intelligence, personality, goal directedness, realism, achievement orientation, locus of control, gender, and ethnic background are other factors that have an impact on career decisions. These factors will be discussed elsewhere.

In 1960, Super and Overstreet established five criteria for determining the wisdom of career preferences. These criteria still seem useful today:

1. agreement between ability and preference
2. agreement between measured interests and preference
3. agreement between measured interests and fantasies
4. agreement between occupational level of measured interests and level of preference
5. socioeconomic accessibility of preference

Development of a Generation

Young adults are influenced in their choices not only by what has happened inside them but also by the social and cultural milieu in which they have grown up. Changes and characteristics have been noted in the young adults of recent years that distinguish them from their predecessors.

A survey comparing the occupational preferences of students graduating from high school in 1972 and 1980 indicated a shift in interests for both males and females toward professional occupations requiring at least a college degree (e.g., accountant, architect, artist, engineer, nurse, and social worker), whereas interest in those occupations requiring a graduate degree (e.g., attorney, college professor, dentist, physician, scientist) increased for women but decreased for men. For the women, a corresponding decline in interest in clerical, sales, and teaching fields was noted, whereas the young men's interests declined in occupations emphasizing manual labor (Gerstein, Lichtman, & Barokas, 1988). Occupational choices of 1980 were less gender separated than in 1972, but patterns of gender-linked choices were still evident. However, even more young women aspired to professional careers than did the young men (43.1% vs. 38.7%), with both groups manifesting an increase over the 1972 figures.

Distribution of college majors is another sign of change. A comparison of the distribution of majors in 1970-71 with those of 1985-86 indicated growth in business, health sciences, prelaw, engineering, computers and information science, and communication (Gartaganis, 1988;

Kerr & Colangelo, 1988). The percentage of students majoring in history, sociology, foreign languages, English, and education declined, reflecting a shift away from teaching and liberal arts and toward prevocational majors. For most, the primary purpose of college seems to be career training rather than personal and intellectual development.

These trends are reflected in value changes. Pine and Innis (1987) noted a shift during the 1980s toward more traditional, conservative values reminiscent of the 1950s. College students are placing greater importance on the value of material wealth, comfort, power, and status and less importance on altruism and social concerns. These patterns are especially pronounced in young women. Although some tendency has been observed for young men to place increased value on harmony and beauty, in general there has been a decline in such higher-order values as altruism, self-actualization, and beauty. Typically, such a decline reflects a difficult economic climate.

A comparison of college freshmen in 1976 with those of 1986 indicated an increase in distress; the freshmen of 1986 worried more about finances, their health and appearance, their use of leisure time, their adjustment to college, and their future (Koplik & DiVito, 1986). Their major concern was "wondering if I'll be successful in life." The 1986 freshmen were more likely to be employed part-time and to have incurred large loans to pay for their educations.

Growth in special populations has also changed the nature of the cohort of young adults of the late 20th century. Foreign-born students and those of minority ethnic backgrounds are increasing. Dual-career couples, discussed further in the next chapter, are on the increase. Homosexual young adults, constituting about 10% of the population, may not be growing in numbers but have certainly become more open about their needs and concerns, especially in light of the spread of AIDS (Schmitz, 1988).

The young adults of today have many more options than did earlier generations. College is only one of many educational possibilities, including apprenticeship programs, vocational and technical schools, community colleges, on-the-job training, the military, home study courses, and government training and employment programs. Postponing college or combining college and employment, college and child rearing, and employment and child rearing are more prevalent patterns. Increasing societal acceptance of a variety of personal options has increased choices in that area, too. Unmarried men and women living together, single-parent families, blended families, and homosexual life partnerships are only a few of the nontraditional options that have gained increasing visibility and acceptance. The array of options may seem bewildering to young people.

Gender and Career Development

Traditionally, men and women have assumed different roles in adulthood. The man concerned himself with occupational success, and the woman sought success as wife and mother. Although biology has given women more options, they generally have viewed themselves as having fewer options than men. Clear changes in these patterns became evident during the 1970s and 1980s. However, the career development of young adult men and women remains different in many respects. A study of college graduates (Martinez, Sedlacek, & Bachhuber, 1985), for example, indicated that men were more likely to be employed in male-dominated fields, such as engineering and mathematics, whereas women were more likely to be in female-dominated fields, such as education and social sciences, although girls and women outperform boys and men at all educational levels in terms of grades, including college math and science courses (Fitzgerald & Weitzman, 1992). Men were more likely (61% vs. 55%) to report employment in their chosen fields or satisfaction with their positions. They were more likely than women to be hired by large corporations, and their annual salaries were nearly 50% higher. The women were more likely than the men to regret not having had a more practical, job-oriented major and to express a need for help with their career development. The influence of gender needs to be considered to fully understand and facilitate career development.

The Changing Role of Young Adult Women

The days of women choosing between marriage and a career are long gone. Young women are marrying later, planning smaller families, obtaining more education, aspiring to less traditional fields, and endorsing more liberal views of women's roles.

In 1900, only 22.7% of married African American women and 3.2% of married White women were in the labor force (Hansford, 1988). The percentage of women in the labor force increased to 33% in 1948 and to 53% in 1983. In 1988, 65% of women with children under the age of 18 and 52% with children under the age of 6 were employed. By the year 2000, women will compose 47% of the workforce (S. E. Sullivan, 1992). Women in the 20- to 24-year-old age bracket are remaining single longer and having fewer children. The median age for first marriage for women has increased from 20.3 in 1960 to 22.8 in 1983. Economic necessity as well as changing attitudes and opportunities have contributed to the increasing number of women in the workforce. Nearly 50% of marriages since 1970 have ended in divorce, and over 10 million families are supported primarily by women (S. E. Sullivan, 1992).

Today, although nearly 90% of women in the United States marry and most have children, the majority of women spend most of their adult preretirement years in the labor force. This is reflected in the career planning of young adult women. A 1983 survey (Harmon, 1989) indicated that 73% of women intended to work for most of their lives. Generally, young women report that the women's movement has made them more self-confident and assertive and has modified their attitudes toward women's role (Harmon, 1981). Although nearly all wanted to marry, with only 7% viewing being single as ideal, attitudes toward childbearing and employment had changed. Having two children was most likely to be viewed as ideal, and 25% of those surveyed wanted no children. Fifty-five percent viewed family and career as equal in importance, and only 2% anticipated little or no employment. Unlike most men, most young women have split dreams, focusing on both career and family (S. E. Sullivan, 1992).

Women's participation in higher education and nontraditional occupations has also changed over the years. In 1900, 3% of women aged 18 to 24 were attending college. That percentage climbed to 8% in 1940, to 20% in 1972, and to 50% in 1977 (Roark, 1977). Beginning in 1981-82, women earned more bachelor's degrees than did men and dominated fields such as home economics, library science, education, health sciences, public affairs, English, visual and performing arts, recreation, communication, and the social sciences (Gartaganis, 1988). The number of women earning doctoral degrees increased from 4,000 in 1969-70 to 11,800 in 1985-86, constituting over one third of the doctoral degrees awarded at that time (Gartaganis, 1988).

In the 1950s, nearly two thirds of female college students planned careers in education (Super, 1957). Today, women are turning away from careers in the artistic, educational, and social service fields and becoming more involved in business, technical, and professional fields. From 1965 to 1980, the percentage of women increased from 3% to 22% in business administration; from 8% to 28% in architecture; from 14% to 24% in physical science; from less than 1% to 9% in engineering and 13% in dentistry; from 6% to 23% in medicine; from 3% to 30% in law; and from 33% to 42% in mathematics (Hansford, 1988). From 1969 to 1984, the values, expectations, and life plans of college men and women became increasingly similar. Women showed a great increase in status attainment goals while simultaneously maintaining the value they placed on domestic-nurturant goals (Fiorentine, 1988).

Despite these changes, women continue to be concentrated in traditional fields. In 1980, the 10 most popular jobs for women included secretary, cashier, bookkeeper, registered nurse, waitress, elementary school teacher, nursing aide, salesperson or supervisor, and typist. Most of these are low-paying, nonprofessional fields.

In addition, the attitudes of young women toward employment are different from their male peers. A study of college students indicated that women anticipate balancing work and family life, with greater involvement in one area being offset by lesser involvement in the other area (DiBenedetto & Tittle, 1990). Young men, on the other hand, see the two dimensions as independent and do not view themselves as having to prioritize work and family commitments. Harmon (1981) found that 40% of young women planned to interrupt their careers for their families; few young men would advance such career plans. This discrepancy seems supported by the views of both genders; women support men's perceptions of their own roles, and men support women's perceptions of their own roles (Phillips & Johnston, 1985). Young men do not seem to be restraining their female peers, a clear change from the 1970s (K. S. Wilson, 1975). Both men and women are supportive of women's continuous participation in their careers, although both men and women view an interrupted career or a balance of career and family goals as ideal for women. However, women are more likely than men to believe that career and family demands *can* be successfully balanced.

Career Development of Young Adult Women

Osipow (1975) studied the ways in which the career development of females differed from that of males. He identified three major patterns of female career development. The "homemaker" was the woman who had no significant paid work experience. The woman with a "traditional career pattern" may or may not be married but engaged in significant out-of-home employment in a conventionally female field, such as teaching, nursing, secretarial work, or social service. The woman with a "pioneer career pattern" also may or may not be married but engaged in significant out-of-home employment on a regular basis throughout most of her life, often in a male-dominated field and in competition with men. She exhibited a clear commitment to her profession, advanced in it, and often delayed marriage and childbearing to progress in her profession. Although the percentage of women in each of Osipow's three groups has apparently changed over the years, with the first group dwindling in size, whereas the other two grow, Osipow's framework continues to be a useful reflection of women's career patterns and choices.

Research shows that women become less traditional in their thinking as they mature. Harmon (1989) compared female college freshmen in 1983 with women who had been interviewed as college freshmen in 1968. She found that the older women were less traditional than both the 1983 freshmen and the women themselves in 1968, although they more closely resembled the college students of the 1980s. Studies such as this suggest that young women today may still be underestimating the involvement they are likely to have in the labor force as they mature.

Young women seem to go through a different process of career planning and development than do young men, with the young women experiencing more home-career conflict and success avoidance (Karpicke, 1980). Despite patterns of academic achievement, they tend to have low concepts of their self-efficacy in male-dominated fields, such as mathematics and business leadership, leading them to limit their perceived options (Rotberg et al., 1987). In general, women seem to have more difficulty deriving a sense of self-esteem from their accomplishments than do young men.

Although women tend to be satisfied with their college majors and to manifest greater congruence between their inventoried interests and their majors than do men (Slaney, 1980), they are less likely to report employment in their chosen fields or satisfaction with their positions within the first year after their graduation from college. They also express more regrets about their chosen plans and college majors (Martinez et al., 1985). Harmon (1981) found that only 45% of employed women, interviewed 6 years after they entered college, were working in their chosen fields. After high school, the women seemed to have experienced many changes in their career plans, considering an average of nine occupations. Typically, the career development of most young adult women follows a course of considerable change, leading to the establishment of a clear career direction by their mid-20s. Most young women seem ill prepared in their thinking for this pattern of change leading to stability. Granrose (1985) found that the career plans of most college women extended for less than 5 years and about half had not planned beyond college graduation and obtaining an initial job. Only 5% of those interviewed had plans that included more than one job and reflected long-range career planning.

Counselors should be aware that women who negotiate college smoothly and seem to manifest career maturity actually may be experiencing considerable conflict about their future roles and may not achieve the rewards they hope for after graduation. Helping these women to develop their self-confidence and perceived options, then, is important. One way to accomplish this is through role models. Hackett et al. (1989) found that among female college seniors, perceived role model influences, especially parents and teachers, were significantly related to career salience, level of educational aspiration, making nontraditional occupational choices, and college major. Social and family pressures as well as messages from fathers and other important male figures sometimes discourage women from exploring nontraditional options, whereas role models of successful women can exert a positive influence on the possibilities that young women consider.

Self-esteem was another important determinant of young women's career development, with their self-esteem being influenced more by relational events than by work, education, or other experiences (Josselson, 1987). Having adequate career information and being able to make decisions well are also important in women's career development and are related to congruence, sense of vocational identity, self-perceived career maturity, and lower anxiety (Healy & Mourton, 1985).

Gilligan (1982) described three stages in women's identity development that seem related to their career development. In the first or egocentrism stage, young girls have a limited and self-centered view of the world. However, they soon move on to Stage 2, in which they become self-sacrificing and oriented toward pleasing others. Although some women move on to Stage 3, in which they recognize the legitimacy and importance of their own concerns, many become stuck in Stage 2, a pattern often associated with depression in women (Enns, 1991). Josselson (1987) also advanced a three-stage model of women's identity development, based on Marcia's model of young adult development. According to Josselson, young women are first in the foreclosure stage, in which they experience unquestioned adoption of external standards. Next, most move on to the moratorium stage, involving exploration, self-examination, and reflection. In the third and final stage, achievement identity, women establish a positive and flexible self-concept based on exploration and experience.

Traditional and Nontraditional Women and Men

Researchers have distinguished traditional from nontraditional occupations for each gender, with nontraditional occupations, for a given person, defined as those in which 30% fewer of those employed in the occupation are of the person's own gender (Haring-Hidore & Beyard-Tyler, 1984). Those who are happiest in their work are men in male-dominated jobs (traditional) that are congruent with their college majors, whereas women in male-dominated jobs as well as women in female-dominated jobs that are highly congruent with their college major also are generally satisfied with their work. The least happy are women in female-dominated occupations that are not congruent with their majors (T. Adler, 1989). Patterns of both gender dominance and interest, then, seem important in determining career satisfaction. However, women who are more depressed and have lower self-esteem may be more likely to choose traditional occupations because of a fear of failure and of being different (Harlan & Jansen, 1987). The influence of gender distribution in an occupation may be moderated by a selection process in which women who are more optimistic and have better coping skills are more likely to make nontraditional choices and, not surprisingly, are happy with those choices.

Most women have been clustered in a few traditional occupations: social work, nursing, teaching, and office work (Chusmir, 1983). Although, typically, nontraditional occupations offer women better pay, more prestige, and greater opportunity for advancement, many women avoid nontraditional career choices for a variety of reasons, including fear of the unknown, fear of failure, fear of not being accepted, and fear of being viewed as odd or unfeminine. Positive reasons have also been identified for women's preference for traditional occupations, notably women's emphasis on interpersonal relations and concern for others, reflected more in traditional than in nontraditional occupations.

Many women, however, do pursue careers in nontraditional fields. These women tend to emphasize individualism and personal satisfaction, are achievement oriented, and expect to make a life for themselves through their own efforts. They tend to be active, androgynous, autonomous, dominant, expressive, intellectual, responsible, risk taking, self-actualized, self-confident, and sociable. Although these women are concerned with femininity, romance, and marriage, they tend to postpone marriage and seek a spouse who allows them to pursue their own careers. Despite their many personal resources, these women still express concern about the conflict between family and career and about the difficulty of establishing a clear and comfortable sense of their own identity (Chusmir, 1983).

Family backgrounds of women pursuing nontraditional careers tend to differ from those of women following traditional paths. Nontraditional women are more likely to be firstborn and come from relatively small, upwardly aspiring middle-class families where they have few, if any, brothers. Although most of their mothers are homemakers, they tend to be well educated and are more likely to have been employed at some time in their lives. Some of the mothers are themselves in nontraditional occupations, and the prestige of the mother's occupation seems to be positively correlated with the level of the daughter's aspirations (Auster & Auster, 1981). Their fathers tend to be in professional or managerial occupations and seem to have a strong influence on their daughters. Nontraditional women tend to report close relationships with their fathers, with many reporting that they were their father's favorite. These women tend to use their fathers as role models of achievement. Most nontraditional women report having had happy childhoods in which their individuality as well as their educational and occupational aspirations were encouraged. Nontraditional women tend to have a larger number of male friends and are more likely to have peers who support achievement and nontraditional career choices.

One study of women in nontraditional occupations (Stewart, 1989) found that although the women had some problems in relationships with co-workers and lack of opportunity for advancement and supervision, most of the women enjoyed the challenge of their work as well as the opportunity for creativity and collaboration with male workers. Their sources of satisfaction, in order of priority, included the opportunity to do things for others, geographic location, the chance to work alone, the chance to do different things, the chance to use their abilities, the freedom to use their own judgment, the opportunity to be in charge of others, and the opportunity to use their past training. It is interesting that their primary source of satisfaction is one that is consistent with traditional roles for women. For both traditional and nontraditional young women, then, combining nurturance and productivity, mastery and pleasure seems critical for a sense of accomplishment and career satisfaction (Gallos, 1989).

Less research is available on men who follow nontraditional career paths, entering female-dominated occupations. In general, these men are promoted rapidly and seem to be highly valued employees, gaining attention and an economic advantage from being a male minority. However, they tend not to achieve the salaries and prestige levels they might have in traditional jobs (Haring-Hidore & Beyard-Tyler, 1984). Bias seems to occur in attitudes that others hold toward these men, with some viewing them as irrational, inadequate, or ill suited for their occupational choices (Hayes, 1987).

Men who follow nontraditional career paths are more likely to be firstborns, members of racial minority groups, educated beyond college, raised by a homemaker mother in a middle- or working-class family, and have a distant relationship with their fathers (Chusmir, 1990). They have strong social and esthetic values, are more liberal and inner directed, and tend to participate more in rearing their children than do traditional men. Typically, nontraditional men are comfortable with themselves and their masculinity; have good ego strength; and report being involved, satisfied, and committed to their career choices, which, generally, are compatible with their personal needs. Some, however, have difficulty dealing with female supervisors, with having lower occupational status than their spouses, and with role discomfort.

Career Development of Young Adult Men

The overall career development of the young adult man has been explored and described through the major theories of career development (e.g., Super, [1985]; Ginzberg, Ginzberg, Axelrad, & Herma, [1951], discussed elsewhere in this chapter and in Chapter 1). In general, the career development of young men seems more homogeneous than that of young women (Fitzgerald & Crites, 1980). Skovholt and Morgan (1981) identified issues that are likely to play a prominent role in the career development of young men:

1. gender role stereotypes
2. relationship between occupational success and self-esteem
3. balancing work, close relationships, and leisure
4. choice of traditional or nontraditional occupation

In addition, establishing a comfortable separation from one's parents, especially the mother, seems strongly related to young men's ability to establish a clear and positive sense of occupational identity. Paternal role models as well as the educational and occupational accomplishments of both parents also seem to have a strong influence on the career development of young men. Mortimer (1975), for example, found that the combination of a father in a high-income/high-prestige occupation and a close father-son relationship had a great impact on the son's career values and choices.

The Young Adult as Worker

Somewhere between the ages of 16 and 24, most young people enter the labor force. Although the percentage of young people, particularly young women, attending college has increased, the number of young people in the workforce has similarly increased. Most of those receiving bachelor's and master's degrees already have at least 1 year of full-time work experience, and approximately 15% of those receiving bachelor's degrees have at least 5 years of full-time work experience (U.S. Department of Labor, 1990). A pattern of combining education and employment has become very common, especially for those attending community colleges and vocational training programs.

Mobility and Unemployment

Most young adults are confronted with the need to support themselves and perhaps also to finance their education. Frequent job changes characterize the young adults' efforts to find employment that is satisfying and for which they are appropriately qualified. Young people remain in jobs an average of 1.9 years, and five or six job changes between high school and the mid-20s is not unusual (M. Carey, 1990). High rates of unemployment for young adults compound the difficulty of finding rewarding employment. Unemployment is more likely to be due to loss of a position or difficulty in locating an entry or reentry position than to resignation from an unsatisfactory job. Rates of unemployment are negatively related to education and age, with unemployment of young people with a high school education or less often being over 10%. Teenagers constitute 10% of the workforce but as many as 20% of the unemployed (Dayton, 1981). Unemployment rates tend to be higher for people from minority ethnic backgrounds and for young women and have been as high as 34% for young high school dropouts (U.S. Department of Labor, 1976). The unemployment rate for African American males is 250% that of White males, and both minorities and women earn less than do White males during young adulthood (J. V. Miller, 1982).

Although college students and graduates have lower rates of unemployment, a surplus of college graduates in many fields in recent years has led to the underemployment or employment in fields not related to their college majors for many college students. Although college graduates constitute only 20% of the labor force, they accounted for 43% of the growth in the labor force during the 1970s and 1980s, according to the Bureau of Labor Statistics. As a result, many college graduates now hold jobs previously held by workers with less education. One quarter to one half of recent college graduates are overqualified for their jobs (Borgen et al., 1988).

Some college graduates will be disappointed that a college diploma does not offer a guarantee of lucrative and satisfying employment. Shock, disappointment, and job resignations are common responses of new workers as they become aware of the gap between their aspirations and their perceptions of their opportunities (Riverin-Simard, 1990). Adjusting to unanticipated disappointments in salary, supervisors, and co-workers seems even more difficult to handle than surprises about the nature of the work (Hatcher & Crook, 1988). College students need help in obtaining realistic information about occupations from job interviews and other sources of information. Despite the disconcerting experiences of many college graduates, education still does have a strong positive impact on employability, occupational stability, career satisfaction, and opportunities for change. In addition, the oversupply of college graduates seems to be diminishing, and an easing of competition for jobs requiring a college degree is anticipated through the 1990s (Sargent, 1988). Instead, a bipolar economy seems to be developing in which most employment occurs in either high-level managerial jobs or low-paying service jobs.

Frequently, unemployment has a negative impact on the personal and professional development of young people. Borgen and Amundson (1987) studied young people who had been unemployed for at least 3 months and found that, generally, they were confused and frustrated by their situations, turned to parents to help them with their plight, and in many ways dealt with the situation more like adolescents than like young adults, manifesting a slowing down in psychosocial development. These early unsatisfying experiences in the labor force may well affect later career attitudes and adjustment as well as personal relationships, self-esteem, mood, and future plans and decisions (Borgen et al., 1988).

Governmental programs such as the Job Corps, the Career Education Incentives Act, and the Comprehensive Employment and Training Act have been developed to facilitate young people's entry into the workforce. Programs such as these that increase employability by developing job-related skills, career planning, and motivation and also improve labor market transitions by providing information on job openings, job search skills, and ways to succeed on the job seem very useful to young people.

Negotiating and Succeeding in the World of Work

The work-related attitudes and perceptions of young adults tend to change once they enter the labor force, as do their occupational self-concepts. Aspirations are tempered by the reality of the labor market, and goals tend to shift in the direction of increased realism. Maturity seems to be important in determining early adult establishment and satisfaction with one's work. Beginning workers with intrinsic work values and a broad perspective of the meaning of work seem to be more satisfied with their jobs and also more productive than those with extrinsic work values (Kazanas, 1978). The satisfactions of beginning workers tend to focus on intrinsic factors, whereas their expressed dislikes tend to focus on extrinsic factors. For most young workers, job satisfaction starts high, dips to a low, and stabilizes somewhere in the middle, whereas job success starts low and steadily progresses upward (J. V. Miller, 1982).

Women's early participation in the labor force reflects a bimodal pattern (Lassalle & Spokane, 1987). Some have strong attachment to their work, manifest consistent employment, and are more likely to achieve advancement. Others, however, have minimal attachment to their work, giving family goals first priority. Only a small percentage of women vacillate between these two positions, being involved in part-time or sporadic employment.

Most young adults find their early jobs in a rather unsystematic fashion. Their most commonly used job-seeking strategies, in order of frequency of use, include seeking help from friends, searching classified advertisements, selecting a specific job to look for, analyzing their interests and abilities to find the best job, and using summer and after-school work to gain experience and leads. Qualities that enhance young people's success in locating suitable employment include their personalities, their ability to get along well with supervisors and co-workers, persistence and determination in looking for work, and a willingness to work part-time or unusual hours (Dayton, 1981). Confidence or perceived self-efficacy is also correlated with a positive outcome to a job search (Steffy et al., 1989). Other factors contributing significantly to employment of college graduates include the impressiveness of the young adults' references, having employment experience while in school, and their grade point averages in their majors (Marshall, 1985). Overall grade point average and volunteer, leadership, and leisure experiences did not seem to be strong determinants of employability.

In his study of career development during early adulthood, Crites (1976) enumerated the following typical work entry problems of this age group:

   I. On-the-job performance problems
      A. Responsibility, maturity, attitudes, and values
      B. Work habits
      C. Peer and supervisor relations
      D. Communication
      E. New roles
      F. Changing technology
      G. Self-image
      H. Alienation
  II. Job entry, career planning, and management problems
      A. Job seeking
      B. Interviewing and test taking
      C. Geographic mobility
      D. Family and personal situational adjustment
      E. Job layoffs and rejections
      F. Educational preparation and job placement
      G. Career planning and management
      H. Occupational aspirations and job expectations
      I. Youthful image
      J. Military commitments
      K. Prejudice and discrimination
      L. Prior work experience
      M. Labor unions

For young men, the single most critical factor in their failing to succeed in their jobs is the inability to get along well with others (Fitzgerald & Crites, 1980).

Some job-seeking behaviors seem much more effective than others. Cianni-Surridge and Horan (1983) surveyed employer reaction to 16 assertive job-seeking approaches. The best received approaches, in descending order, included the following:

1. writing a thank-you letter after an employment interview, expressing continued interest
2. approaching campus speakers to ask about gaining employment in their fields or organizations
3. volunteering additional information that the applicant believes is important at the close of an employment interview
4. calling to arrange an appointment to discuss employment opportunities with an organization

Strategies that were not well received included requesting a second interview with another person when an interview did not seem to go well, asking for permission to speak with employees about a job opening prior to an interview, rescheduling an interview, and asking interviewers for names of other organizations that might have job openings.

Counselors working with young adults who are entering the labor market should be alert for the presence of any of the areas of concern cited by Crites (1976). They can also help young adults prepare for the all-important employment interview by assisting them to present behaviors cited as desirable by employers. Counselors should help people evaluate themselves in light of the profile of an occupationally successful young adult to maximize their chances of achieving employment that is commensurate with their interests and abilities.

Counselors can be particularly helpful to young women and people from minority backgrounds who have a higher than average rate of unemployment and lower than average earnings. In some cases, discrimination, although prohibited by law, is a factor in reducing the employment opportunities for these groups. Although violations of equal employment opportunity policies are difficult to detect and substantiate, counselors may be helpful to young people by familiarizing them with their rights and helping them to protect those rights.

The Young Adult as College Student

Development is a function of both person and environment. Young adults in a college environment will encounter many experiences and choices that differ from those encountered by young people in the workforce, and those environmental differences will lead to some personal and developmental differences. Chickering's (1969) landmark study identified seven vectors of development in young adulthood: achieving competency, managing emotions, developing autonomy, establishing identity, freeing of interpersonal relationships, developing purpose, and developing integrity. Generally, college counselors, teachers, and administrators are aware of these developmental goals and seek to establish an environment designed to foster positive maturation, unlike the world of work, which typically assumes a maturity that young people may not have. College students, then, may have an advantage over their counterparts who are focusing on employment.

The Changing Nature
of the College Population

By 1970, economic downturns meant that a college education was no longer a guarantee of employment. However, higher education has not been traditionally viewed in the United States as simply a passport to employment. It has been viewed as an important aspect of late adolescent development and has been valued for the personal, social, and educational benefits it offered as well as for its economic benefits. Consequently, the decrease in prestige and economic security associated with a college degree has not led to a significant decline in college enrollment, although most young people entering college do have fairly pragmatic goals. In 1989, the primary reasons that college freshmen expressed for attending college were to be able to get a better job (75%) and to learn more about things that interested them (68%). Their primary goals included being very well-off financially (79.5%), raising a family (68.5%), and becoming an authority in their own field (67%). Clearly, achievement and personal goals are both very important for modern young people. College students of the 1980s were much like those of the 1950s in their emphasis on security, success, and a comfortable lifestyle. Apparently, the economic instability of the 1970s and 1980s has been reflected in a shift in the attitudes of college students from the idealism of the 1970s to increased pragmatism in the 1980s and 1990s (Astin, 1984).

Changing attitudes and opportunities for women and people from minority backgrounds as well as increasing flexibility in the role of the White, middle-class male has led to changes in the nature of the college population. The early and middle 1970s witnessed a downward trend in the college enrollment of the middle-class young adult male. Young men seemed to become less accepting of parental values and societal norms and sought to implement or develop their own value systems during the post-high-school years. This often involved the wish to gain more life experience and self-awareness via travel or early entry into the world of work. College entry was deferred, perhaps indefinitely. The percentage of males in the 18- to 24-year-old age group attending college declined from 42.9% in 1967 to 35.3% in 1976 (Magarrell, 1978). The decline of this group in the colleges made room for groups previously underrepresented, including women, people from minority backgrounds, and older adults. In addition, to keep their classes filled, colleges began to reach out to people from these groups, developing special programs, such as credit for life experience, precollege collaborative programs with high schools, and weekend classes designed to facilitate attendance at college.

From 1972 to 1982, the number of women attending college increased by 61%, with the most rapid growth being among women over the age of 25 (Mathiasen & Neely, 1988). Since 1976, women have generally outnumbered men in colleges. In 1990, women composed 54% of the college population (Chronicle of Higher Education, 1990).

In addition, the enrollment of people from minority backgrounds in colleges has more than doubled over the past 20 years. Particularly rapid growth has been noted among people with Asian or Hispanic backgrounds and among African American females (Evangelauf, 1990). However, most minority groups continue to be underrepresented in college settings. In 1988, a study of people in the 18- to 24-year-old age group indicated that 38.7% of Whites, 30.9% of Hispanics, and 28% of African Americans attended college. Only 19% of college students are from minority backgrounds, although minority as well as international students are predicted to increase throughout the 20th century (Stone & Archer, 1990).

Increasingly prevalent patterns of delaying college entry, returning to college after an extended absence, and attending college part-time have led to an increase in the average age of college students. In 1987, over half of all college students were aged 22 or older, and the average age of college students has continued to increase. Similarly, part-time enrollment has increased much more rapidly than full-time enrollment; in 1990, only 57% of college students attended full-time. The traditional idea of completing college in 4 years is no longer the norm; in recent years, fewer than 20% of students in public colleges and universities graduated in 4 years. After 6 years, however, more than 40% have completed their degrees.

Growth in community colleges has been more rapid than growth in 4-year institutions, and increased availability of community colleges has contributed to the increase in women and people from minority backgrounds attending college. Enrollment in 2-year colleges increased from 600,000 in 1961 to 2.6 million in 1972 (Allen, 1978). Among college students in 1988, 34.1% of Whites, 54.6% of Hispanics, 51.6% of Native Americans, 39.4% of Asians, and 38.3% of African American college students were in 2-year institutions (Evangelauf, 1990). By 2000, 70% of first-time freshmen are expected to be in 2-year colleges.

In 1990, there were 595 public 4-year institutions, 968 public 2-year institutions, 1,532 private 4-year institutions, and 440 private 2-year institutions for a total of 3,535 colleges in the United States. Over the past 20 years, most people who wanted to attend college were able to find an institution they could afford that would accept them as a student. Two thirds attended the college that was their first choice.

Escalating costs of a college education, with costs of $10,000 and more not uncommon for a year of college, have further contributed to the popularity of community colleges. Percentages of people attending college in their home state have also increased because tuition is likely to be lower, living at home can reduce costs, and accessibility facilitates combining employment and college study. In 1989, 81% of freshmen attended college in their home state.

Although college enrollment increased from the early 1970s to the mid-1980s, the number of bachelor's degrees awarded annually is expected to decline from 980,000 to 900,000 by the year 2000, due primarily to a decline of the population in the 18- to 34-year-old age groups (Sargent, 1988). Increasing competition for students may lead colleges to develop even more programs geared to the older or part-time student.

College Expectations and Experiences

College is a time of coping with stressors, of confronting new challenges, and, for most, of significant maturation. Most young adults make at least tentative decisions about their college majors and occupations. Many undergo both personal and intellectual changes. Career development and identity formation continue.

Many find themselves in different and more threatening patterns of competition. Outstanding high school students may feel considerable self-doubt when they discover that almost everyone at highly rated colleges was an outstanding high school student. The same pattern may hold true for the high school athlete who discovers a more challenging level of competition at college. Academic stressors frequently reported by college students include tests and final examinations, performance anxiety, and course scheduling, and important personal stressors include intimate relationships, parental conflict and expectations, and finances (Archer & Lamnin, 1985). Research suggests that the level of psychopathology is increasing among college students (Stone & Archer, 1990). Problems such as eating disorders, substance abuse, sexual abuse and rape, dysfunctional families, and AIDS are becoming more prevalent, or at least more openly expressed by college students.

The experience of attending college, as well as the years of maturation, lead college students to become increasingly tolerant, to improve the quality of their relationships, to develop a stronger sense of identity and more self-confidence, and to manifest a higher level of thinking skills than when they began college (Thrasher & Boland, 1989). Certain experiences at college are particularly likely to contribute to positive development. Students who participated in developmental programs at college scored higher in self-concept, college satisfaction, autonomy, mature lifestyle plans, interdependence, cognitive complexity, sense of purpose, and appropriateness of educational plans than did those who did not attend such programs. Students who live on-campus seem to achieve better social self-concepts and personal adjustment as well as greater independence from their parents than those who remain at home with their families (J. A. Hoffman, 1984). Those who live off-campus, either alone or with peers, achieved even higher levels of development (Wilson, Anderson, & Fleming, 1987). Students in residence halls as well as those living at home manifested slightly better academic performance than did students living in sorority or fraternity houses or in off-campus housing (Blimling, 1989). Involvement in student activities is another factor that contributes to positive development, although young people who are heavily involved in athletic pursuits tend to score lower on measures of development than do those not involved in such activities.

Personal qualities, as well as experiences, contribute to development during the college years. Young people with an internal locus of control seem to adjust better to college and take a more active role in their integration into the college environment than do those with an external locus of control (Martin & Dixon, 1989). Proximity of family, quality of family relationships, and availability of family support combined with emotional independence from family and identification with parents also seems to facilitate adjustment to college (Henton, Lamke, Murphy, & Haynes, 1980; Lapsley, Rice, & Fitzgerald, 1990; Lapsley, Rice, & Shadid, 1989). Positive family relationships also promote development of positive self-esteem, and commitment to goals. A temporary departure from college to enter the work force sometimes is a sign of ambition and a wish to clarify one's career goals and may enable students to return to school with renewed energy and motivation. Certainly, that is reflected in the population of older students, to be discussed in the next chapter.

College leavers seem to be as emotionally healthy and as academically capable as their peers who choose to remain in college. The clearest difference between the two groups seems to be the disappointment, disillusionment, and value conflict that the leavers seem to feel, sentiments that are not outweighed by strong needs to earn a degree and live up to the ideals of their family or socioeconomic group. College leavers seem likely to benefit from counseling. For the most part, they have the ability to complete college and, at one point, planned to do so. However, their chosen college no longer seems to be meeting their needs. Counseling could help these people gain insight into their decision to leave school, review their options, and develop plans so that they have a good chance of going on to another endeavor that will meet their needs, rather than just leaving an experience that has not been all they had hoped it would be.

Making Decisions and Commitments During the College Years

Many students enter college assuming that if they have not already made career plans, they will be made during the college years. The process of career development, especially its decision-making aspect, is very important during these years. College students seem to have become more goal directed and more conscious of the often self-imposed pressure to make career plans during the college years. Most change their choice of major or their career goals during these years. College students average nearly three changes of major during their 4 years of college (Newton, Angle, Schuette, & Ender, 1984). More than half change career goals while in college (Zunker, 1990). However, young people may not realize that uncertainty is the norm during these years and may feel very unhappy about any confusion in their goals and direction. These sentiments may be reinforced by peers and parents as well as by college advisers and teachers who may assume that when young people decided to attend college, they had already chosen a major and formulated career plans.

In general, expressed interests of college students are fairly stable, and changes of major or occupational goals tend to be to similar or related fields. However, a sizable group do change their expressed interests during the college years (Slaney, 1984). According to Betz, Heesacker, and Shuttleworth (1990), "Large numbers of college students continue to choose majors and occupations incongruent with their measured interests" (p. 275). Those who express uncertainty about their interests are more likely to change their majors. Pressures can lead college students to what Tilden (1978) called a sort of "pseudo-crystallization," the premature making of plans or decisions due to external motivations or influences. The comfort level with one's choices rather than whether or not choices have been made, then, is an important clue to identifying those students who are likely to need some help in clarifying goals and choices. Students who are undecided about their career goals are likely to have lower grade point averages than those who are decided, perhaps because the courses they are taking are not a good match for their interests and abilities. On the other hand, for both male and female college students, those with masculine or androgynous personality characteristics are more likely to be using their abilities in their occupational and college major choices than are those with traditionally feminine personalities and those preferring female-dominated occupations.

Level of education seems to be an important determinant of occupational choice. Of those with 4 or more years of college, 70% enter managerial, professional, or technical occupations (Sargent & Pfleeger, 1990). The most common occupational choices for those with 1 to 3 years of college are sales, administrative support, and service. These fields are also popular choices for those without college training, as are craft, operative, labor, and agricultural areas. Popular college majors, in recent years, have been business and technical fields that have ready marketability. The percentage choosing education or liberal arts majors has declined since the 1960s and 1970s. However, patterns do vary from one college to another. Colleges, themselves, seem to have personalities or values that influence the direction and development of student interests and, consequently, their choices of majors and occupations.

Commitment to work seems to be related to career maturity (Nevill & Super, 1988). Interestingly, college women are more committed to both work and family life than are college men, although the women expect to realize more values through the home than do males.

Career Choice and Planning

Many of the factors that seem to have a bearing on the career choices of college students are the same factors that influenced their choices of college major. This is not surprising because, for many, the two choices are actually one, although the major can be chosen first and can determine career choice or the career choice can come first and lead to the choice of a relevant major. Influences on choice include intrinsic dimensions, such as interests, abilities, values, and personality; extrinsic variables, such as salary, occupational requirements, security, location, and available opportunities; and the influence of significant others, such as parents, friends, and academic advisers. All of these factors, and more, have an impact on the career development of most young adults, but which factors exert the greatest influence is related to the strength, clarity, and realism of a person's occupational preference and to the economic climate of the country. The 1990s offer college graduates a more favorable job market than did the 1970s when an influx into the job market of young people born during the so-called baby boom increased competition.

The 1990s have been described as an era of moderate competition; 92% of college graduates between 1988 and 2000 are expected to find college-level jobs (Sargent & Pfleeger, 1990). Historically, the more education people have, the lower their rates of unemployment and the higher their salaries. In 1987, for example, the median income for people aged 25 and older was (a) $20,800 for those who completed high school but did not continue on to college, (b) $24,600 for those with 1 to 3 years of college, (c) $30,100 for those who stopped their formal education at college graduation, and (d) $37,100 for those with more than a bachelor's degree. Unemployment during the 1990s is expected to average about 2% for college graduates and 7% for high school graduates, although the economic difficulties of the early 1990s may alter those projections. Average growth in professional fields is expected to be about 50% from 1988 to 2000. Technical occupations (computer programmer, health technician) are expected to increase by approximately 85%; executive, administrative, and managerial occupations, by about 60%; marketing and sales positions, at the average rate of 50%. Professional specialty occupations, such as teaching, nursing, and engineering, which employ about half of all college graduates, are expected to grow at a slower than average rate of 40%.

During young adulthood, change in career goals is common, as is change in choice of college major. The senior year of college is a time when change is particularly prevalent. In that year, most students apply for employment or graduate school or both. Changes, at that time, can be influenced by many factors, such as need for an income, marital plans, or a rejection by graduate school. Most students in their last year of college are no longer meeting regularly with a counselor or academic adviser (if they ever did). Their college programs have been planned and are nearly completed, and their focus may lie beyond graduation. However, students' need for career counseling is probably as great, if not greater, than at any other time in their college career. Fortunately, many colleges do maintain placement offices that can facilitate employment, but few offer career development and counseling as an integral part of the senior year of college.

Some patterns of change in aspirations have been linked to gender as well as to ethnic and socioeconomic factors. Men's aspirations tend to rise, whereas women's often decline as they decide to marry. Women from minority ethnic backgrounds seem particularly likely to curtail their goals, although this pattern may have changed in recent years. People from upper socioeconomic backgrounds are more likely to decide to continue their education. A sort of regression toward the mean has also been observed, with people who originally aspired to 2-year college degrees raising their sights and those who anticipated receiving their doctorate tending to lower their sights (Winkler, 1976). Another common pattern is a shift toward popular and well-known career choices and away from unusual choices. These patterns suggest that, for the young adult, the process of career choice is often an extension of the process of identity development.

The college years serve as a period of transition for many, having positive effects on both the career development and the occupational opportunities of its students. However, many college students have not made firm career plans by graduation. For some, the years of compromise and commitment extend well beyond the college years, whereas for those who may have made premature commitments based on insufficient thought and knowledge, a shift toward more flexible and tentative career plans may be a sign of positive career development.

The Two-Year College and Its Students

Much of the growth in college enrollment, particularly for women, older adults, and people from ethnic minority backgrounds, has taken place at the 2-year college level. The accessibility of community colleges, in terms of their locations, their course schedules, their relatively low costs, their flexible admissions standards, and their emphasis on career preparation, has attracted a special group of students. Many of these students would not have considered attending college before the growth of the community colleges, and they have different lifestyles, needs, and values than do those students who have enrolled in 4-year colleges. Community college students are more likely than their counterparts in 4-year colleges to come from lower socioeconomic backgrounds, to be older than the average college student, and to be married. Combining school and work or child rearing is common, and a large percentage of 2-year college students attend college on a part-time basis. These students seem particularly interested in college as a way to enhance their opportunities for employment. They may have already sought work or are working in an unsatisfying position. They may be aware that the unemployment rate is particularly high for young adults without college training and are trying to improve their chances of favorable employment. Although 2-year college students may well be interested in the personal and intellectual growth afforded by the college environment, particularly if they are women reentering the academic arena, emphasis is more likely to be on the practical benefits of education. Generally, the 2-year college student is less involved with and influenced by the college environment and more wrapped up in his or her life away from college than is the college student seeking a bachelor's degree (Astin, 1978).

Frequently, these outside commitments lead community college students to leave college before graduation. Good student personnel services should be provided, particularly at the community college level, to prevent outside pressures and commitments from leading a capable and interested student to withdraw prematurely. At the same time, counselors should not assume that attending college is always the best career plan. The high percentage of young people who do attend college along with the availability of the community colleges seems to have established college enrollment as the norm in many parts of the country. Many young adults may enroll in college because their parents view that as desirable or because most of their friends are attending college and they are not sure what else to do. A semester or a course may be enough for them to realize that college is not right for them at the present time. Counselors dealing with college students should acknowledge the broad array of options open to them and recognize that postponement of college studies or even commitment to a less academically oriented path may be the best choice for some. Saltoun (1980) reported that counseling college students, especially those with fear of failure, seemed most effective when it communicated a neutral rather than an achievement-oriented message, treating young people as responsible and capable of establishing their own direction.

Of course, attention also needs to be paid to those community college students who plan to continue their education. Most community college students hope to eventually receive their bachelor's degrees and selection of majors and curriculum should afford flexibility so that pursuing a bachelor's degree is possible while at the same time the associate's degree, itself, confers beneficial knowledge and credentials.

Most community college students begin their education at 2-year colleges. However, a group of students, the so-called reverse transfer students, began their education at 4-year colleges, then transferred to community colleges, and may eventually return to universities. Clearly, these students have gone through some major shifts in goals and could probably benefit from some counseling to clarify abilities, interests, and goals.

The Young Adult as Graduate Student

The number of people receiving graduate degrees has gradually increased. In 1989, a record was set with the awarding of 34,319 doctoral degrees (Mooney, 1990). Women and people from minority backgrounds have been increasing their representation in graduate schools. In 1988, women earned 36.5% of the doctorates awarded, including more than 50% of the doctorates in fields other than science or engineering. On the other hand, increasing numbers of advanced degrees in science and engineering are being awarded to people from minority group backgrounds. In 1989, 55% of the doctorates in engineering awarded in the United States were earned by people who were not U.S. citizens. Although African Americans are the largest minority group in graduate school, they are underrepresented in relation to their numbers in the general population, and the number of doctorates awarded to African Americans has declined nearly 25% during the 1980s. On the other hand, rapid growth in representation of people from Asian backgrounds in graduate programs has been noted (Blum, 1990), reflecting the growth in Asian immigration following the Viet nam war.

College and the Future

During the 1970s, relevance was emphasized in the development of college curricula, and courses of study became increasingly pragmatic. By the end of that decade, however, educators were expressing concern that college students were becoming too job oriented. In response to this concern, many colleges reinstituted or increased their emphasis on providing students a broad exposure to knowledge. This trend seems to have persisted into the 1990s, although student interest in applied fields such as business remains high. A conflict seems present, then, between the colleges' emphasis on a broad, liberal arts education and the students' interest in fields that are useful and marketable. A challenge for the college counselor is helping young people meet their career-related goals while helping them to appreciate the potentially broader objectives of their academic institutions.

Short-term follow-up studies of the college graduates of the 1980s (Braddock & Hecker, 1988; Martinez et al., 1985) indicate that close to 90% are in the labor force, with about 80% of both men and women working full-time. About 25% seem to be underemployed, holding jobs that usually do not require a bachelor's degree. Nearly 25% have gone on to graduate or professional schools, with most of those seeking an advanced degree and more than half attending graduate school full-time. Graduates with majors such as nursing, engineering, computer science, accounting, and education have usually found employment in positions directly related to their course of study, whereas those with majors in economics, history, political science, psychology, and sociology are usually in positions that are, at best, tangentially related to their major areas of study. Although most recent graduates report being satisfied with their education as well as with their present jobs, most also report continuing concerns about their career development. Men, particularly, are concerned with financial planning, applying their education to their job requirements, and dealing with office politics, whereas women are most concerned with adjusting to new schedules and demands and coping with feeling like a novice again (Martinez et al., 1985).

Counseling to Facilitate
Compromise and Commitment

Young adults seem to be impelled by two strong and conflicting motivations—the wish to explore and expand their horizons and the desire for security and protection. Their world is full of options and possibilities that are both alluring and frightening. Establishing a satisfactory balance between taking risks and seeking security seems to be crucial to the positive development of the young adult.

For many in this age group, the identity crisis of adolescence has not yet been resolved. They are still struggling to answer the question, "Who am I?" A sense of panic and anxiety may arise in those young adults who still are searching for a definition of themselves. They may, often erroneously, perceive others as being more self-assured and more able to make appropriate decisions and commitments whereas they continue to flounder. To extricate themselves from these feelings of confusion and isolation, many young adults make premature and unwise commitments. A marriage may be made to escape from parents or an unrewarding job or in the hope that qualities in the spouse will be contagious and will help to define identity and provide security. An occupation may be selected because training or an entry-level position is readily available or because others view it as a wise choice and no other attractive alternatives present themselves.

For some young adults, the fear of commitments that may seem irrevocable and confining may outweigh their need for security. Because many young adults can more easily define what they do not want to do than what they do want to do, those with a fear of commitments may find themselves running away from, rather than running toward, something. Their development may be characterized by a long period of transition in which frequent change is occasioned by evasive, rather than goal-directed, behavior.

Probably the primary role of the counselor of young adults is to help them become aware of their need for self-definition and to assist their efforts to develop a clear, positive, and realistic self-concept, as well as developing relationships, career choices, and plans that complement that self-image. Ideally, their important interpersonal relationships will be based on genuine sharing, intimacy, and appreciation rather than on a need for a vicarious identity or sense of belonging, whereas career plans will be based on an awareness of interests, values, abilities, and opportunities.

A review of the literature led Spokane and Hawks (1990) to identify the following as the most common career-related problems of young adults:

1. making career choices/finding direction
2. conflicts in the workplace
3. conflicts within the family
4. knowledge of the self-occupation relationships
5. indecision

According to Spokane and Hawks, career development and identity development are related and parallel. People having difficulty with career development are likely to have confused self-images. They recommend that counselors promote internal exploration in clients in the early stages of career development and an external exploration or focus on the world of work in people in the later stages of career development. Counselors working with young adults might want to consider incorporating the following elements into their counseling.

1. *Values Clarification.* Although values are relatively well formed by young adulthood, clarification of personal, occupational, and interpersonal/family-related goals can facilitate wise decision making during these years.

2. *Job-Finding Strategies.* This might include developing job leads, informational interviewing, resume writing, interviewing skills, and completing job applications.

3. *Improvement of Coping Skills.* Helping young people develop skills such as decision making, communication, assertiveness, management of anxiety, and self-efficacy can contribute to career development.

4. *Exploration of Family-of-Origin Models and Messages.* Using techniques advanced by Murray Bowen (1978) and other theorists, such as exploration of genograms; birth order; intergenerational patterns; and family rules, norms, and expectations, can help young adults understand the influence their family backgrounds have had on their career development. This can help them make less automatic and more reflective choices about their own careers and relationships and can help them to become more differentiated from their families.

5. *Assessment of Level of Thinking and Decision Making.* Although many young people have not yet established clear career goals, the reasons for their uncertainty vary considerably. Some have the necessary skills to make sound decisions and simply need additional time as well as information on themselves and the world of work before they make firm decisions, whereas others may be immobilized by the belief that there is one ideal decision that they must find, by anxiety, an external locus of control, or by a confused self-image (Fuqua, Blum, & Hartman, 1988; Welfel, 1982). Understanding the nature of the barriers to rewarding career decisions that people are experiencing can guide and improve the counseling process.

6. *Leisure Counseling.* Most young adults make decisions that give shape to their future lives. Although most attend to career and interpersonal decisions, it seems unusual for young people to make a conscious effort to plan the leisure component of their lives. However, attention to leisure and its relationship to and integration with occupational and interpersonal plans can help people establish balanced and rewarding lives. McDaniels (1984) defined leisure as "relatively self-determined activities and experiences that are available due to discretionary income, time, and social behavior; the activity may be physical, intellectual, volunteer, creative, or some combination of all four." He defined career as "the totality of work and leisure one does in a lifetime" (p. 35). Work and interpersonal relationships are unlikely to provide people all the fulfillment or activities they need and, for some, those may not even be their primary source of life satisfaction. Leisure can complement other sources of satisfaction or can compensate for aspects of life that may not be very rewarding. Leisure pursuits can also be tied more closely to interests regardless of talent and so may allow exploration of different areas than are available through career options. For example, a person who loves music may not have

the talent to be a professional performer, teacher, or critic but may have enough knowledge and talent to enjoy playing an instrument for pleasure or listening to others play.

7. *Personal Counseling*. Although beyond the scope of this book, counselors should bear in mind that, often, young adults are coping with such issues as abuse of drugs and alcohol, uncertainty about sexual matters, unplanned pregnancy, family problems, discrimination, and poor interpersonal relations that almost certainly will have an impact on their self-images and goals. Of college students, 22% have been involved in date violence, 20% abuse alcohol, and one third of college women were sexually abused as children (Stone & Archer, 1990). Counselors should be aware of the presence of such difficulties and should either refer a client with these concerns for some personal counseling or expand their goals so that personal as well as career concerns are handled. Making sound career plans and decisions will be difficult if not impossible for a young person coping with upsetting and distracting personal concerns.

Counseling the Young Adult in College

The following developmental tasks of the college years have been proposed (Swain, 1984):

1. learning to use leisure time
2. developing a sense of identity
3. clarifying and implementing values
4. defining and using competencies
5. achieving independence
6. participating in society
7. making an initial job or career choice
8. forming a pattern of healthy and close interpersonal relationships

Nearly all colleges offer some services to help young people accomplish these goals. Surveys of colleges conducted during the 1980s indicated that (a) more than 95% of colleges offer career and personal counseling; (b) 90% offer inventories to assess and clarify interests; (c) over 85% offer career workshops and seminars; (d) approximately 75% offer structured group counseling, crisis intervention, and stress management; (e) 65% offer career courses; (f) approximately 60% offer help with study skills; (g) about half offer career-planning programs, (h) about 40% have academic-advising programs; (i) about the same percentage feature career resource centers; (j) about one third offer placement services; and (k) only about 15% offer help with leisure planning (Goodson, 1982; Weiner & Hunt, 1983; Whiteley, Mahaffey, & Geer, 1987). Despite this broad range of available services, college counseling centers, on the average, had the equivalent of six full-time staff, hardly enough to provide extensive services to all students. In addition, colleges are increasingly providing services to alumni, further limiting services to on-campus students.

Many colleges try to fill in this gap by assigning each student to an academic adviser; however, advisers are usually drawn from the area of the student's declared major. They tend to view their primary function as assisting with program planning, may have little or no training in counseling, and frequently are unable to help the student who is considering a change of major and who needs information about various occupations and areas of concentration. Although faculty may not be able to meet students' needs for career counseling, they can serve an important function by referring students to counseling services. A positive alliance between faculty and campus counselors is, therefore, important in helping students receive needed services.

College students tend to underuse sources of help, typically explaining this by stating that they should have tried harder on their own (Knapp & Karabenick, 1988). One of the challenges, then, in providing counseling and academic advisement to college students is making the services accessible and appealing. To accomplish this, college counseling centers are increasingly being located near other student services, such as veterans affairs, services to students with disabilities, placement, academic advising, offices for foreign students, student health, or academic affairs (Stone & Archer, 1990). In addition, taking a holistic perspective, considering not only career development but also personal growth and adjustment to the campus environment and offering outreach, preventive, individualized, and developmental services, also seems likely to increase student use of counseling programs. Providing child care and evening hours are other approaches. Sensitivity to the special needs of older, minority, foreign-born, and other nontraditional students is integral to developing an effective college counseling program. Minority students, alone, are 18.4% of the college population in the United States. According to Stone and Archer (1990), "The need for psychologically oriented career counseling is great" (p. 550), services that attend not only to young people's career development but also to the relationship of career and personal needs.

Counselors should not assume that those students who have selected majors or who have not sought counseling have no need for assistance. Often, choices are tentative and subject to change during these years and may have been made prematurely to conform to internal or external timetables. In addition, young adults are often still engaged in establishing their independence and so may be reluctant to ask for help. However, studies show that most young adults feel a need for help with their career development and might take advantage of it if it were offered in a way that did not damage self-esteem and made its potential benefits readily apparent.

Research has indicated that long-term interventions such as courses on career development seem more effective than short-term interventions, although both seem to have an impact on career maturation and decision making (Pickering & Vacc, 1984). Career development courses covering topics such as career/life planning, career development theory, decision making, adult development, self-exploration, educational exploration, relationships and society, occupations and their relation to college majors, goal setting, study skills, time management, and job search skills are a popular, appealing, and generally effective approach to making career counseling services widely available.

Research has not found career development services provided in a group context to be inferior to those provided individually (Cooper & Van Matre, 1984). Because few studies have compared the effectiveness of a range of different programs, it is difficult to pinpoint those ingredients that make group approaches to career counseling with college students successful. However, workshops or counseling experiences with young adults do not need to focus directly on career development to have a positive effect on career planning. Career development reflects and is affected by many areas of skill and development, including values clarification, decision making, self-image, and coping with anxiety. Well-planned counseling experiences focusing on any of these or other areas of general concern to the young adult seem likely to enhance career development.

Self-help programs, although cost-effective, seem to be the least helpful mode of intervention and probably are best used in combination with other interventions. At the same time, funds for college counseling services seem to be declining and college counseling services gradually are shifting to a fee-for-service model. Already, 25% charge a fee for the administration of interest inventories and 6.4%

charge for counseling services (Stone & Archer, 1990). Cost, then, must be considered when services are planned.

College students tend to focus primarily on short-range concerns and only approximately one third express a need for help with long-range career planning (Newton et al., 1984). Concerns about self-esteem, independence, relationships, stress, and health seem more important to students than career development needs. Appealing and cost-effective methods are indicated to help college students with career life planning, not just career development. Examples of these include the following:

1. Peer support groups and peer counseling, with supervision by a professional counselor, can be offered.

2. Work-study programs with university or field-based mentors to increase understanding of the self and the world of work can be arranged.

3. College orientation programs, combined with advising and scheduling, provided prior to the beginning of the freshman year have been found to have a positive impact on achievement and retention (Young, Backer, & Rogers, 1989).

4. Skill development workshops can be offered (e.g., study skills, public speaking, decision making, preventing gender bias, assertiveness, time management, job seeking, choosing/changing a major).

5. Semistructured counseling can be provided for several semesters to high-risk students, focusing on improving academic performance and motivation (Hudesman, Avramides, Loveday, Wendell, & Griemsmann, 1986).

6. Focused, time-limited counseling or educational groups can be directed at the needs of special populations (e.g., women, people from minority or lower socioeconomic backgrounds, married students). For example, Asian Americans seem to have lower levels of career maturity and independence as well as a higher expressed need for career counseling than do other large ethnic groups (Leong, 1991). A structured group approach seems likely to be effective in addressing such needs.

7. Computer-assisted career development programs can increase accessibility of services, and they appeal to those students who may be initially uncomfortable speaking to a counselor. These programs can store information on both students and the world of work, they can greatly facilitate the information-gathering process, and they can enable counselors to devote more attention to the emotional needs and difficulties of students. The combined intervention of computer plus counselor seems particularly effective (Marin & Splete, 1991). Generally, college students are highly satisfied with such programs as DISCOVER for

Colleges and Adults (American College Testing Program), PLATO (Control Data), SIGI (Educational Testing Service), Career Navigator (Drake, Beam and Morin, Inc.), and others (Kapes et al., 1989).

8. Volunteer alumni can be matched with undergraduate students and can offer the students opportunities for information gathering, receiving mentoring, and shadowing.

9. Videotapes on such topics as interviewing behavior and communication skills are another low-threat way to provide information and increase familiarity with counseling services.

10. College placement offices, offering full-time and part-time employment listings as well as information on job search strategies, resume writing, the relationship between majors and occupations, interviewing, internships, alumni contacts, and employer interviews, are another important way to involve students in career development services.

11. Interest inventories such as the Strong Interest Inventory, the Self-Directed Search, and the Kuder Occupational Interest Survey are widely used resources to clarify interests and career goals.

Many resources and publications are available to assist the career counselors working with young adults. The following are some of the most useful:

1. *Career Planning and Adult Development Newsletter*—publication listing workshops, jobs for career counselors, conferences, and resources

2. *PATH: A Career Workbook for Liberal Arts Students* (Figler, 1979)

3. *Your Career: Choices, Chances, Changes* (Borchard, Kelly, & Weaver, 1988) —a self-paced workbook for college students and adults

4. *Training for Life: A Practical Guide to Career and Life Planning* (Hecklinger & Curtin, 1987)—a decision-making model designed to facilitate career and life planning

5. Impact Publishers—publications on job seeking and career development (e.g., *High Impact Resumes and Letters, Interview for Success, Careering and Re-Careering for the 1990's*)

6. Peterson's *Guides*—well-known source for guides to colleges, financial aid, programs for learning disabled students, standardized admissions tests, and other areas of interest to young adults

7. *Career Research and Testing*—another good source of materials to facilitate adult personal and professional development

8. *Orchard House, Inc.*—catalog includes handbooks on college admissions, college sports, technical, trade, and business schools, and wall maps of colleges

10. *What Color Is Your Parachute?* (Bolles, 1993)—a classic in the career development/self-help area.

Counseling the Young Adult Worker

The emotional needs and difficulties of the young person entering the labor force may be similar to those of the young college student, but the decisions that must be made and the skills that are required differ somewhat. The young adult worker comes in at least two varieties: the young person who is entering the job market directly from high school and the young person who has some college education but now is seeking employment. Each year, over 1 million college students begin searching for jobs (Arp, Holmberg, & Littrell, 1986). Often, young workers can use counseling to facilitate adjustment to a new lifestyle, a new set of authority figures, and new and often challenging responsibilities. Many young people lack some of the basic skills and information that could help them secure employment and advance rapidly. They may be unfamiliar with exactly what kind of work is performed in various occupations and so may have difficulty deciding what kind of work they are most interested in and most suited for. They may have difficulty asking and answering pertinent questions at employment interviews. They may not know how and where to seek employment, how to write a résumé and a cover letter, or the proper dress and behavior for an interview. A survey of job hunters conducted by C. J. Yates (1987) yielded the following needs, listed in descending order of importance: selling oneself in an interview; what to expect in a typical interview; résumé writing; determining skills, values, and interests; average salaries for specific jobs; budgeting while employed; legal and illegal interview questions; steps involved in a career or occupational decision; using past skills in a new occupation; and knowledge of entry requirements for jobs. Other needed information included how to select and obtain references, using state employment agencies, services for veterans, and job market information.

Hamilton (1984) found that there were five qualities in successful job search training programs: training and rehearsal in interviewing, group emotional support, planned use of the telephone to develop leads and interviews, knowledge of potential employers, and recognition that job seeking is a full-time job of 2 to 6 weeks duration. Several useful models for a support group to improve job seeking, such as Azrin's Job Club, the Job Search Support Group for Adult Students, and the Job Factory, have been widely used. In Azrin's model, for example, participants meet at least once a week. The program seeks to train participants in the life skill of job seeking, emphasizes personal responsibility and development of self-esteem, and focuses on the hidden job market via telephone canvasing (Trimmer, 1984). Job-seeking groups not only accomplish the above goals but support members coping with rejection, provide useful feedback on strengths and weaknesses, improve focus and reality testing, and provide role models and motivation. Such approaches seem both effective and economical.

Some additional resources are available that can be particularly useful to the young adult job seeker. State employment agencies offer a free placement service to job seekers and do find jobs for large numbers of workers. However, the focus of these agencies is primarily on lower-level jobs, and heavy caseloads limit opportunity for individual attention. College placement offices are useful resources for students and alumni. They usually have excellent career libraries, arrange interviews with potential employers, and are particularly good resources for people in high-demand fields requiring a college degree (Bunce, 1984). Typically, private employment agencies specialize in a small group of occupations or an industry. They usually charge a fee, perhaps 10% of 1 year's salary, that sometimes is paid by the employer. These are profit-making organizations and should be evaluated carefully. Executive search firms, charging fees generally paid by employers, also are useful, especially for well-qualified candidates in high-growth fields such as management and computer technology. Exploring a variety of resources seems most likely to help job seekers find the best sources of help in their fields. Many excellent reference books, updated regularly, are also available to help both worker and counselor in these efforts.

Assessment With Young Adults

Assessment procedures have been found to enhance the process of counseling young people. Although expressed occupational preferences of college students are the best predictors of their later occupational choices, abilities, activities, self-estimates, interests, personality, and values all contribute to occupational choices (Gottfredson & Holland, 1974). Assessment can help clarify these factors, thereby facilitating the process of career planning.

However, many young adults have negative views of tests and consequently of the assessment process. They may associate tests with grading and homework and may view the assessment process as another judgment of them. Especially for those young people who do not continue on to college or do not complete high school, assessment may be associated with past failures and may be greeted with resistance. Counselors should be alert to the possibility of such negative feelings, which may adversely affect both the counseling relationship and the validity of the results of the assessment. Formal assessment procedures should be thoroughly discussed with the young adult client before it is used. In addition, counselors should be sure to select instruments for the assessment process that are valid in light of the client's educational and socioeconomic levels.

Case Study of Kerry Kelly

A Young Woman in Search of Herself

"Well, here I am. Fix me," was the way Kerry Kelly began her first counseling session.

"Do you think you need to be fixed?" replied the counselor in private practice she had consulted.

"My mother and father certainly think so. They told me to see you. And I guess I think I need to be fixed, too."

Although most young adults establish at least some independence from their parents in their late teens and early 20s, their sense of identity still may be clouded by missing information about themselves and the world of work and by messages they receive from others. Although Kerry Kelly, at the age of 20, had completed 2 years at a college away from home, her initiation of counseling reflected the strong influence that parental messages continued to have on her.

Background

Kerry was the youngest of three children in her family. Her brother, Edward, 26, had become an accountant like their father and had recently married. Her sister, Maureen, 23, had married soon after high school and now was pregnant with her second child. Kerry's family was Irish Catholic and, with the exception of Kerry, had followed fairly traditional paths. Her father was viewed as the head of the household and made most of the decisions for the family. Although Kerry's mother was now employed as an aide in an elementary school, she had remained home to care for the household and the children until Kerry left for college.

Although education was valued in the Kelly home, both Kerry and her sister had received strong messages that women's primary role was that of wife and mother. Edward, the oldest, was the only child who received strong encouragement to attend college, because he was expected to be supporting his own family.

Maureen and Edward had been comfortable with the roles suggested to them by their parents. Maureen had been an average student who focused her attention on dating and participating in Catholic youth organizations, and Edward had been an above-average student who completed college without difficulty. Kerry, however, resisted family expectations throughout adolescence and was viewed as the rebellious one in the family. Kerry had been an above-average student who excelled in mathematics. She had been active in athletics, playing on soccer and basketball teams. Although interested in dating and socializing in high school, most of Kerry's social life had revolved around group activities and, unlike Maureen, she had done little dating in high school.

In addition to her strengths in mathematics and athletics, Kerry enjoyed crafts, painting, and drawing. She had had a part-time job in a clothing store that emphasized stylish fashions for young women and soon developed a reputation for her flair for combining clothes in striking and flattering ways and for the attractive displays she created in the store.

As a child, Kerry's career goals included actress, model, teacher, and wife and mother. As she matured, she struggled to find a way to integrate her parents' values with her own interests and expressed an interest in becoming an elementary school art teacher, a traditional career choice for women that was acceptable to Kerry's parents. As her mother put it, "I think teaching is a good choice for you. It will help you to understand your own children and, if you do have to work after your children are born, you can be home from school at the same time as your children."

Although her parents suggested she live at home and attend a small local college that focused on teacher preparation, Kerry was eager to separate herself from her parents and increase her independence. She was accepted at a large state university on the West Coast, several thousand miles from her home, and persuaded her parents to pay for her tuition there.

College was quite different from Kerry's small high school, where she was well-known and well-regarded. She felt overwhelmed and confused by all the choices and opportunities. She was lonely and isolated, so far from family and friends. For the first time in her life, Kerry had some difficulty with motivation and study habits. Her grades for her freshman year were Bs and Cs. Although Kerry enjoyed her summer at home after her first year of college, seeing friends and working in the clothing store, she returned to complete her sophomore year of college in California without hesitation.

Toward the end of her freshman year, Kerry had joined a sorority, and she moved into the sorority house for her sophomore year of college.

Although Kerry now felt less lonely and developed some friendships among the women in her sorority, her academic work suffered as she found herself caught up in sorority and fraternity social activities. Alcohol played an important role in parties she attended, and Kerry, who had rarely drunk alcohol before college, found herself drinking before a party to relax herself, drinking during a party to join in with the others, and, often, drinking after a party with a date. She had her first sexual relationship with a young man she met at a party, spending the night in his room when she was too intoxicated to drive home with her friends. Although she was very upset when the young man did not call her after their night together, Kerry soon became sexually involved with another young man. By the end of the first semester of her sophomore year, Kerry's grades had declined to Cs and Ds. She was very disappointed about her academic performance and felt considerable guilt and worry about her drinking and sexual activities, but she did not know how to make a change without losing her friends or, once again, isolating herself. Both Kerry and her parents, who knew about her low grades but were unaware of her sexual activity and abuse of alcohol, thought that Kerry should leave college and return home.

Kerry sought counseling about a month after her return home. She was living with her parents and working at the clothing store. Most of her friends were either married or at college themselves and, although she had made contact with several friends from high school, she felt like she had taken a step backward by returning home. She perceived herself as having failed at her efforts to achieve independence and felt depressed and discouraged.

Planning for Counseling and Assessment

As is often the case, Kerry had sought career counseling because of underlying personal concerns. Goals of counseling with Kerry, then, included both helping her formulate realistic and rewarding career plans and also helping her deal with her affective and behavioral concerns. Initially, counseling focused on Kerry's dangerous behaviors, her alcohol consumption and her sexual activity. Both of these behaviors had stopped when Kerry returned home, and she assured the counselor that she had "learned her lesson" and certainly would avoid those activities in the future. To contribute to Kerry's resolve, her counselor provided her with some literature on alcohol abuse and sexually transmitted diseases and encouraged her to begin attending Alcoholics Anonymous, which Kerry reluctantly agreed to do.

The focus of counseling then shifted to take an integrated look at both Kerry's personal and career concerns. The counselor assumed that if Kerry could establish career goals that were meaningful to her and reflected her interests, abilities, and personality, her self-esteem and optimism would improve, she would be able to establish her independence in a more positive way, and her depression would lift. However, because of her discouragement, counseling needed to emphasize Kerry's accomplishments and strengths and provide information in a way that was empowering, encouraging, and relevant.

Assessment of Abilities

With most adults who have demonstrated their abilities in academic, occupational, and leisure settings, testing of abilities is unnecessary. In addition, such testing may be threatening or uncomfortable to clients and, consequently, may impair the counseling relationship. Particularly for adults who are aiming toward professional careers that require a college education, few measures of abilities are available to assess suitability for specific occupations. Although tests can suggest how well someone is likely to perform at college or graduate school, tests are not available to predict whether someone will be an effective psychologist, a competent art teacher, or a skilled surgeon. No battery of ability tests exists that effectively predicts people's likelihood of success in a broad range of specific professional occupations. For most people, that information is best obtained through history taking and general measures of ability.

For all of the above reasons, no tests of ability were administered to Kerry. Her high school grades, as well as scores received on the Scholastic Aptitude Tests and other standardized tests she had taken in high school, indicated that she had above-average intellectual abilities, with particular strengths in mathematics and spatial relations. Although her college grades had not reflected this level of ability, emotional rather than intellectual factors seemed to have impaired Kerry's performance in college. Available information suggested that, given the right environment, Kerry probably would be able to succeed at college. Building on her strengths— her positive performance in high school and her completion of 39 credits of college course work—gave a positive emphasis to Kerry's counseling.

Genogram

The first instrument used to facilitate counseling with Kerry was a genogram, or family career tree, a nonstandardized tool that can help people delineate family and parental influences, look at personal and occupational roles in their family background, and distinguish their own goals from those of their family (Okiishi, 1987). For Kerry, parental models and influences certainly were important. A genogram, usually a tool presenting little threat, could effectively promote her self-awareness and differentiation from her family.

A review of Kerry's family genogram, emphasizing personal and professional roles (see Figure 7.1), reflects an intergenerational pattern of

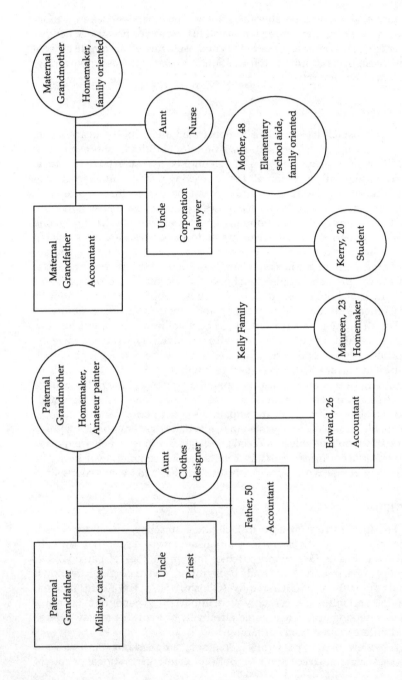

Figure 7.1. Family Career Tree/Genogram

traditional families. Typically, the men entered positions of prestige and authority such as law, the priesthood, accounting, and the military. Most of their roles emphasized involvement with ideas, data, and things rather than with people. The women, on the other hand, focused primarily on their homemaking roles. All the women emphasized nurturing and creativity in their family lives, their leisure activities, and their occupational roles (nursing, teaching, design). Clearly, men and women, in the Kelly family, had a heritage of very different roles. Kerry was the first woman in the family to seek a bachelor's degree, and at least part of the difficulty she encountered in developing and achieving career goals stemmed from the discrepancy between her goals, interests, and abilities and those viewed and modeled as acceptable for women in her family. Through completing and exploring her family genogram, Kerry came to realize that although her parents actually had been very supportive of her career plans by financing her college education, conflict between family messages and her own interests and abilities as well as concern about disappointing her parents and the challenges of following a nontraditional path had interfered with Kerry's clarification and implementation of rewarding career plans.

Assessment of Career Development

The Career Decision Scale (CDS), developed by Samuel H. Osipow (1987) and published by Psychological Assessment Resources, Inc., is a 19-item questionnaire designed to identify barriers preventing people from making career decisions as well as antecedents of educational and occupational indecision. This inventory is particularly useful in helping high school and college students. Allis (1984) wrote of this inventory, "CDS is a useful counseling tool for focusing an individual's attention on which circumstances are causing the indecision and for directing efforts aimed at ameliorating those particular issues" (p. 100). Completion of the inventory yields two scores: certainty and career indecision.

When compared with a norm group of women who were college sophomores, Kerry's score for certainty was low, falling in the 9th percentile, whereas her indecision score was in the middle range at the 59th percentile. Clearly, Kerry was uncertain about her choice of career and major, despite her preliminary selection of art teacher as her occupational choice. According to the manual, the combination of low certainty and moderate indecisiveness characterizes people who have further need for assessment. A review and discussion of items on the CDS that Kerry thought were like her, such as "I feel discouraged because everything about choosing a career seems so 'iffy' and uncertain," "I feel discouraged, so much so that I'd like to put off making a decision for the time being," and "I want to be absolutely certain that my career choice is the 'right' one, but none of the careers I know about seem ideal for me," provided further insight into the barriers to Kerry's career development. Savickas (1984) defined career maturity as "readiness to cope with vocational development tasks" (p. 222). Measures of career development and maturation are particularly useful in counseling young adults who must make important career decisions but who may lack the necessary career maturity to make wise choices. Inventories of career development can shed light on obstacles to development and ways to alleviate them. Other useful inventories of career development include the following:

1. My Vocational Situation, discussed in the previous chapter
2. Career Maturity Inventory, developed by Crites and published by CTB/Macmillan/McGraw-Hill
3. Super's Career Development Inventory, Salience Inventory, and Adult Career Concerns Inventory, published by Consulting Psychologists Press
4. Harren's Assessment of Career Decision Making, published by Western Psychological Services
5. Career Skills Assessment Program, published by the College Entrance Examination Board
6. Gribbons and Lohnes's Readiness for Career Planning Scale (Hood & Johnson, 1991; Savickas, 1984)

Career Decision-Making System

In light of the information obtained from the CDS, further assessments were planned, along with discussion and exploration of occupational information, to promote Kerry's self-awareness as well as her information about career options.

The Career Decision-Making System (CDM), developed by Harrington and O'Shea and published by American Guidance Service, was used primarily to provide information on Kerry's interests. Designed for use with adolescents and adults, the CDM usually requires 30 to 40 minutes for completion of the 120 items. It provides information on occupational preferences, school subject preferences, future educational plans, job values, and abilities and talents. Data are organized according to six major work settings, paralleling Holland's (1985) personality types (discussed in Chapter 1), and 18 career clusters, encompassing 283 occupations that employ the majority of the workforce. The CDM is available in self-scored, machine-scored, and microcomputer editions. According to Hood and Johnson (1991), "It is a simple, yet relatively thorough, instrument that is well integrated with the counseling literature" (p. 133). Data on predictive validity have been viewed as encouraging (Brown, Ware, & Brown, 1985).

Although many inventories are available to assess the interests of young adults (see Chapters 3, 6, and 8 for suggestions), the CDM was selected for use with Kerry because it provides a holistic look at factors to be considered in formulating career choice, integrating data on interests with information on values and abilities. In addition, the self-scored format seemed likely to be less threatening to Kerry than a computer-scored inventory and more likely to engage her actively in the discussion and interpretation of the inventory.

Kerry's completion of the CDM yielded the following summary profile:

I. Stated occupational preferences
   A. First choice: art work
   B. Second choice: data analysis
II. Subject preferences
   A. First choice: mathematics
   B. Second choice: art
III. Future plans: 4-year college
IV. Job values
   A. Independence
   B. Creativity
   C. Working with your mind
   D. Variety-diversion
V. Abilities
   A. Artistic
   B. Computational
   C. Mathematics
   D. Social
VI. Interest scale scores
   A. Crafts—6
   B. Scientific—16
   C. The arts—21
   D. Social—20
   E. Business—24
   F. Clerical—28
VII. Career clusters suggested by your scores for careful exploration
   A. First: data analysis
   B. Second: clerical work
   C. Third: management

Completion of this inventory was very enlightening to Kerry. Although her expressed interest in art was reflected by her scores, both her artistic and her social interests seemed to be secondary to her interest in data analysis, management, and clerical work. Specific occupations in these career clusters that appealed to Kerry included accountant, tax examiner, bank loan officer, business executive, real estate appraiser, and bank manager. Kerry realized that she actually shared many interests with both her father and her brother but, because of messages she had received about appropriate roles for women, she had ignored her interest and ability in mathematics as well as her part-time job in sales and had verbalized occupational preferences that seemed more acceptable. However, her reactions to her high school and college course work confirmed that her strongest interest was in applied mathematics.

Assessment of Personality and Values

Kerry was now poised to make a major shift in her occupational plans. However, in an effort to avert further disappointing choices, her counselor encouraged her to take the time to gather more information about herself and about the occupations she was considering. Inventories of personality and values seemed likely to help Kerry ensure that her occupational choices would be congruent not only with her abilities and interests but also with her personal attributes and values.

The Values Scale, developed by Nevill and Super, and published by Consulting Psychologists Press, was used to assess Kerry's values. Completion of the Values Scale requires approximately 30 to 45 minutes. The inventory consists of 106 items. Hand or computer scoring of the inventory yields scores on 21 intrinsic and extrinsic values. Norms are available for high school and college students as well as adults. According to L. V. Yates (1990), the Values Scale "generally performs as might be expected. The measure might be used by counselors when an assessment of work values would be helpful" (p. 42).

According to the Values Scale, Kerry's strongest values were achievement and economic security, followed closely by personal development. Her least important values included risk, physical prowess, physical activity, and authority. The Values Scales organizes the 21 values into five groups: inner oriented, group oriented, material, physical prowess, and physical activity. Kerry's scores suggested that physical prowess and physical activity had little importance for her. However, the other three groups contained a mix of scores, ranging from very high to below average. Values in the both the inner-oriented group (achievement, personal development) and the material group (economic security) were very high.

When comparing these values to her interests, Kerry concluded that a career in business management, computer programming, or accounting certainly could meet her needs for achievement and economic security. She was less certain about her need for personal development but felt that achieving professional goals that were meaningful to her would contribute to her personal development. Outside interests, such as reading, drawing, and social activities were also seen as contributing to her personal development.

When discussion moved beyond Kerry's career goals, she stated that she hoped to marry and have a family one day, although she did not expect to marry until she had been out of college and had been employed in her chosen profession for a few years. Kerry saw having a family of her own as perhaps the most important way to enhance her personal development.

Finally, a personality inventory, the California Psychological Inventory (CPI), was administered to help Kerry integrate personal and career-related needs and bring the assessment to a close. Developed by Harrison Gough and published by Consulting Psychologists Press, Inc., the CPI is a 462-item true-false inventory that requires 45 to 60 minutes to complete. Designed to provide a comprehensive picture of personality for people in the general population over the age of 12, Van Hutton (1990) described the CPI as easy to complete and score, useful even among people from different cultural groups, extensively researched, and one of the best personality inventories of its kind. Van Hutton found the CPI especially useful in helping students decide "What next?"—the question that was foremost in Kerry's mind. The CPI yields scores on 20 basic scales, 5 special purpose scales and indexes (managerial potential, work orientation, social maturity, leadership, and creativity), and information on which of the following four lifestyles best describes a respondent:

1. Alpha—dependable, enterprising, outgoing
2. Beta—reserved, responsible, moderate
3. Gamma—adventurous, pleasure seeking, restless
4. Delta—private, withdrawn, disaffected

The CPI described Kerry as most like the delta group. According to her profile, "At their best, Deltas are ideationally and imaginatively creative, aesthetically perceptive, and visionary. At their worst, they are fragmented, withdrawn, and at odds with themselves." This last sentence certainly described Kerry when she entered counseling. Most of Kerry's scores on the 20 scales were within 1 standard deviation of the mean, indicating few extreme personality traits. Her highest scores were in communality (fits in easily, sees self as a quite average person), capacity for status (ambitious, wants to be a success, independent), and achievement via independence (has strong drive to do well, likes to work in settings that encourage freedom and individual initiative). Her lowest score was in psychological mindedness, suggesting that she was more interested in the practical and concrete than the abstract and looked more at what people did than what they felt or thought. Special scales indicated that

Kerry's managerial potential was somewhat above average, whereas she was somewhat below average in work orientation (self-discipline, conscientiousness, and reliability as a worker). Of her social maturity, the CPI reported that she accepted the rules and regulations of everyday life, but occasionally found it difficult to do just what she was supposed to do.

Kerry viewed the CPI as an accurate reflection of her personality, highlighting both strengths and weaknesses. In general, she thought it confirmed her present interest in a business/managerial career, although she would need to keep in mind her need for independence and creativity when she was ready to seek employment. The CPI was useful both in enhancing Kerry's self-esteem and in helping her acknowledge and attempt to deal with some of her weaknesses.

Outcomes

Through the process of counseling and assessment, Kerry had obtained a better understanding of herself as well as of some career directions that might be rewarding to her. A computerized guidance information system was used to help her access information about occupations that interested her as well as about colleges that would offer her training in her areas of interest.

Kerry decided to return to college, with a major in business administration. However, rather than going back to California, she decided to live at home for the remainder of her college years. Not only did she think this would improve her study habits and ensure that she would have a more rewarding and positive social life, but she felt it would help her to improve her relationship with her parents. No longer did Kerry have to flee to California to assert her independence. The greater understanding that she had gained through counseling, of family influences and messages as well as her own abilities, personality, and interests, enabled Kerry to separate her own needs from those of her parents and be more comfortable with who she was. By living with her family for the next few years, she and her parents would have the opportunity to get to know each other in a new way, perhaps leading to mutual understanding, acceptance, and appreciation. Kerry decided to continue her art as a hobby and to continue her part-time job in the clothing store. She thought both would give her valuable experience as well as enjoyment. When she spoke of her ideal job, she imagined herself as a business executive for a fashion company or a buyer in an exclusive department store. She also maintained an interest in mathematics and accounting and planned to select courses that would integrate her interest in business and merchandising with her interest in applied mathematics. Developing skills in both areas, she felt, would maximize her opportunities in the labor force.

At a 3-year follow-up, Kerry had graduated from college with a B+ average and had obtained an entry-level management position with a large chain of clothing stores. She reported enjoying her work and thought it reflected and integrated many aspects of herself. Although she had established an active and rewarding social life, she was in control of her behavior and seemed to be making wise choices. Kerry had moved out of her parents' home when she completed college and was saving to purchase the condominium she was renting. The troubled and confused young woman who had sought counseling 3 years earlier had matured into a self-confident woman with a sense of direction and a rewarding personal and professional life.

EIGHT

Middle Adulthood

Years of Consolidating and Redirecting

Middle Adult Years: A Time of Transition

According to Schlossberg (1981), "As people move through life they continually experience change and transition, and . . . these changes often result in new networks of relationships, new behaviors, and new self-perceptions" (p. 2). No longer are the middle adult years regarded as a relatively quiescent period devoted to child rearing and establishment in one's chosen occupation. The high divorce rate of the 1970s and 1980s, the media attention to the so-called midlife crisis, and the prevalence of nontraditional models of work and family life such as dual-career couples, single-parent families, and homosexual couples has brought home the impermanence of choices made during young adulthood. In the middle adult years, many of those youthful choices are no longer rewarding and have failed to fulfill their earlier promise. Feelings of disorientation and disappointment are experienced by nearly all at some point during the middle adult years. For many, these feelings can lead to positive growth and change but rarely without anxiety, pain, and loss.

Labor market statistics give some indication of the prevalence of change during the adult years. Approximately 10% of the population changes jobs each year, with most of those changes being voluntary (M. Carey, 1990). However, approximately 3 million people are forced to leave their jobs each year (Holmes & Werbel, 1992). Average time with a given employer is only 4.2 years, with turnover being particularly high in service and sales occupations, where many opportunities are available. Women have been spending less time as full-time wives and mothers. In 1950, 14% of mothers of preschool children worked outside of their homes; in 1975, 39% of these women were employed; and in the 1990s, approximately 75% of these women are in the labor force (Silverstein, 1991).

Development During
the Middle Adult Years

Many models of adult development have been advanced, with a variety of perspectives. Some view age as the critical variable (Levinson, 1986), some emphasize stage (Erickson, 1963), some focus on transitions or life events (Schlossberg, 1981), and others focus on individual variables in a particular person's life such as background, sequence of events, attitudes, values, and emotions. No one perspective is comprehensive enough to take account of all the important dimensions of adult development.

Patterns of development during the adult years seem to be more linked to external events than they are to a person's chronological age (Schlossberg, Troll, & Leibowitz, 1978). The man whose children are preschoolers when he is in his 40s, for example, may be more like men in their early 30s than like his age peers in terms of his feelings toward himself and his family. Similarly, the woman who deferred childbearing may find she has little in common with her peers while she is in her 20s but is developmentally more like older women who are similarly career oriented. The fullest understanding of adult development, then, seems to emerge from consideration of all these perspectives: age, stage, life events, and individual characteristics and developmental patterns.

Adult development involves interactions of individual, family, and career life cycles (Okun, 1984). Four types of transitions have an impact on these cycles (Schlossberg, 1992). For most, *anticipated transitions*, such as marrying and having a baby in one's mid-20s, are the easiest to negotiate. Literature as well as role models are available to provide information, and support and planning for the event usually facilitates its smooth accomplishment. *Unanticipated events*, such as the early death of a spouse or child or an unplanned pregnancy in a woman in her 40s, can be more difficult to handle. *Nonevents* such as a couple's inability to bear children can also cause stressful transitions, as can long-standing *chronic stressors*, such as a conflicted marriage or dealing with a child with significant disabilities.

Erickson (1963) identified generativity versus self-absorption as the primary crisis of the middle adult years. For most in this age group, generativity will be achieved through development of a family and advancement in one's career. Volunteer work, leisure pursuits, and development of the self, intellectually, physically, and psychologically can also enhance feelings of generativity. Adults in midlife who are fulfilling expected roles successfully seem to be the happiest. Job satisfaction, marriage, high status, and high income all are positively related to satisfaction and a sense of well-being, whereas conflicting work and family responsibilities can reduce satisfaction (Crohan, Antonucci, Adelmann, & Coleman, 1989).

The adult cohort is a large one, with 75 million people born in the baby boom generation (1946-64) now moving into midlife (Tavris, 1989). Several characteristics differentiate this generation from previous ones. They are a generation without rigid timetables; this affords them more flexibility but can also lead to confusion and floundering. People in this generation are more health conscious and report feeling an average of 13 years younger than their chronological age. Couples are marrying later, and more are deciding not to have children. More women are following a traditionally masculine pattern, giving priority to their career development, but have few role models to help them make choices or anticipate the future.

The Early Middle Adult Years

Several substages of middle adulthood have been identified, each with its own needs and characteristics. For most people, the years from the 20s through the early 30s are years of expanding and deepening both family relationships and careers. Levinson (1986) perceived those years as a time of great energy, satisfaction, and stress. People are developing and pursuing their aspirations, establishing their places in society, forming and raising families, and moving ahead in their careers. Important choices are made and considerable responsibility is assumed.

Gould (1978) termed the ages from 28 to 34, "The time of opening up to what's inside," a natural development from the 22- to 28-year-old stage he called, "I'm nobody's baby now." By their 20s, most adults have achieved independence from their families of origin and now are looking inward to clarify the sort of life they really want for themselves. Entering the fourth decade of life triggers a transition for some around age 30, a time for both settling down and reevaluation. As people move through their 30s, major commitments are made to family and career. For many, however, the process of self-examination taking place in the 30s can lead to family and career upheaval, with divorce most likely in the late 20s or early 30s. Changes during these years seem to be part of a continuing quest for the ideal life. Although changes may be accompanied by feelings of anxiety and apprehension, optimism remains fairly high during the late 20s and early 30s, and most early middle adults continue to look forward to the future rather than backward to the past. Goals may be questioned and fears of irrevocable commitment may be heightened but, for the most part, concern is about establishing rather than changing.

R. D. Cox (1970) studied a group of men and women 10 years after college when they were in the 29- to 36-year-old age group. She found six primary activities in which they were engaged: maintaining employment, getting married, sustaining separate households, having and rearing first children, dealing with obligations to parents, and coping with the details of adult living. Despite the high divorce rate during these years, the nuclear family seems to provide security and is not one of the most stressful elements of the period.

Other aspects of adult life, however, do seem to be both stressful and disorganized during these years. Major sources of stress for Cox's sample included disappointing romantic relationships, unsatisfying career development, conflict or divorce in the parents' marriages, and concern about the wisdom of one's career plans. With two of the four primary sources of stress focusing on careers, clearly, career development continues to have importance during these years. Cox found that career success was of considerable importance to both men and women in this age group, with self-actualization and accomplishment through one's career being associated with mental health.

Thomas and Kuh (1982) refer to the early middle adult years as *rethinking adulthood* and view them as characterized by the following processes:

1. revision of personal goals and commitments
2. reexamination of career choice
3. acceptance of similarities and differences between self and significant others, especially parents
4. reflection on the past to guide the future

With most mothers of preschool children in the labor force, a prominent concern for this age group will be the integration of career and family. Maternal employment does not have a clear or consistent impact on either marital relationships or child development (Scarr, Phillips, & McCartney, 1989). The impact is mediated by the psychological wellbeing of the parents, their marital relationships and roles, parent-child relationships, the parents' educations, their social supports, and their distribution of available time (L. W. Hoffman, 1989). Many benefits can result from maternal employment, particularly if the woman is employed by choice: Fathers participate more in child care and household tasks, children develop less stereotyped attitudes about gender roles, both husbands and wives develop more self-esteem because of their ability to successfully manage two challenging roles, children develop more independence, and improved finances relieve family stress and provide a better lifestyle. Maternal employment seems particularly beneficial for daughters, who tend to develop more egalitarian views of roles and relationships. However, commitment overload can also result, impairing self-esteem and family harmony. L. W. Hoffman (1989) suggested that part-time employment is the ideal solution, providing many of the benefits and fewer of the stresses of full-time maternal employment. However, each couple must determine their own preferred style of integrating family and career.

Most people in the early middle adult years accomplish the developmental milestones of finding a person they believe will be their life partner, establishing a home, having a child, and establishing themselves in a career. However, considerable shifting and instability is evident in both careers and marriages, suggesting some restlessness and dissatisfaction.

The Middle Middle Adult Years

Thomas and Kuh (1982) refer to the middle years of adulthood as *differentiated, responsible adulthood* and view most people in this age group as experiencing the following changes:

1. accepting increased responsibility for one's life
2. desire for more authority in career
3. clarification and integration of earlier choices and commitments
4. realization of some earlier goals
5. acceptance of a fuller and deeper range of emotions

6. increased conflict between commitment to one's role in work and a desire for increased freedom
7. continuing to examine earlier decisions and commitments.

Self-awareness and self-interest seem to grow during these years, resulting in a more honest appraisal of the satisfactions, limitations, and disappointments in one's life. Individuation continues and the quality of life improves. Emotional changes include more compassion, greater love of self and others, and more introspection (Levinson, 1986). Value shifts may occur in midlife as people increasingly focus on self-expression (L. V. Yates, 1990). In the middle adult years, people become more specific and concrete about their needs, often leading to a redefinition of goals. Societal changes also have an impact on midlife changes. The ethic of self-fulfillment promulgated during the 1960s and 1970s gave way, in the 1980s, to an emphasis on deeper personal relationships and a shift toward spiritual and expressive values (McIlroy, 1984).

Conflicts of Middle Adulthood

Feelings of dissatisfaction seem to come to a head somewhere between 35 and 45 in what has been referred to as the "deadline decade" (Thomas & Kuh, 1982). O'Toole (1977) reported that more than 80% of those in this age group experience a period of crisis, of questioning and introspection. External events such as the death of a parent, the departure of the youngest child for school, the loss of a promotion to a younger worker, or simply reaching an important age milestone can trigger this crisis. Such events seem to put people in touch with their mortality.

The middle middle adults' time perspective gradually has shifted, and most in this age group think of time left rather than time since birth. Life is half over, and the adult is no longer protected from death by the buffer of the older generation or distracted by the excitement of the early child-rearing years or the first few years of growth and learning in a new occupation. New stressors emerge, including dealing with parental illness and dependency and rearing adolescents. Conflicting needs for action and excitement as well as stability and continuity emerge and must be reconciled (Thomas & Kuh, 1982).

Horizons are no longer limitless, and most realize that talent and determination do not ensure success. The dreams of adolescence are reappraised and often viewed as unrealistic or unimportant. "Is this all there is?" is the question that seems to haunt those in this age group. They are threatened by both the possibility of continuing a lifestyle that is perceived as unrewarding and by the risk involved in making major changes. People may reexperience some of the confusion and floundering of adolescence, particularly if they did not establish a clear sense of identity and direction during those years.

A close and stable relationship with another, generally a spouse, can buffer some of the turmoil of these years (Schlossberg et al., 1978), but for many, the sense of dissatisfaction extends to interpersonal relations as well as to careers. Middle middle adults may leave their marriages in the belief that they must find true love before it is too late or because they have externalized their confusion and blame the spouse for their own dissatisfactions.

Many avenues for handling the crisis or turning point that seems to occur around the late 30s are available. Some look for information or help. They may begin reading more or talking to others in their age group to better understand what is happening to them. Assistance may be sought from a psychotherapist, a support group, or a partner who can provide some needed encouragement. A shift in career or a return to school or the labor force are common ways to achieve new goals and find new sources of satisfaction. In general, dealing with this period of midlife reevaluation in an open and direct way that promotes rewarding change seems preferable to ignoring the problem. Without attention, this period of turmoil can lead to stagnation and disappointment as well as another period of turmoil in later years. Accepting the crisis and striving to change, to establish a lifestyle that is more firmly grounded in one's goals and values, may well be painful and anxiety provoking but is also likely to be a positive experience in the long run.

Dual-Career Couples

Men and women who have given their career a high priority up until this point are likely to be well established in their careers by middle middle adulthood. They probably have considerable responsibility, may have long hours and frequent business trips, and may need to relocate if they are to advance in their careers. Considerable stress may develop in families where both husband and wife have professional careers that are important to them—the so-called dual-career or working family as distinguished from the dual-earner family in which one person is career oriented and the other focuses on household responsibilities, seeking employment only as needed or as time permits (Stolz-Loike, 1992). That stress may be particularly acute for the woman because, as Gilbert and Rachlin (1987) observed, "a career and a family, a 'given' for men, is viewed as 'trying to have it all' for women" (p. 12). Common concerns of these families may occur on four levels: intrapersonal (identity, stress), interpersonal (competition, sharing tasks), organizational (work schedules, career interruptions, advancement), and societal (lack of role models, lack of support) (Wilcox-Mathew & Minor, 1989). However, similarly, benefits of this lifestyle can be identified at four levels: intrapersonal (self-esteem, more areas of accomplishment), interpersonal (job satisfaction, marital solidarity, shared goals, intellectual compatibility, higher standard of living), organizational (help with child care, more resources to allow flexible employment plans), and societal (legislative support, growing social acceptance). Most dual-career couples report having a strong and rewarding marriage. As long as child care is provided that is stable, consistent, and of high quality, the impact of this lifestyle on children seems to be positive, improving their relationships with their fathers, promoting greater self-confidence and self-esteem, and broadening their gender role concepts.

Typically, people in dual-career marriages are between 35 and 50 years of age; are parents of fewer than three children; and tend to be self-reliant, self-confident, and physically fit. Often, one or both partners are in second marriages, and many did not develop dual-career marriages until, with the maturation of the children, the wife began to focus more attention on her career (Maples, 1981). In 1983, there were 3.3 million dual-career marriages in the United States in which both husband and wife simultaneously pursued an active career as well as family life (Wilcox & Minor, 1989).

Three types of dual-career marriages have been identified:

1. *traditional*, in which the woman retains primary responsibility for family and household
2. *participant*, in which the husband shares some responsibility for the household duties but is viewed as helping rather than sharing
3. *role sharing*, in which both husband and wife are actively involved in all areas of child care and household duties

Research suggests that "the degree to which the family accommodates a woman's career is central to the woman's success and satisfaction" (Gilbert & Rachlin, 1987, p. 32). Although role sharing seems the most successful route to eliminating gender-based power structures and affording the woman the time she needs to develop her career, it is not the norm. Most men are less involved than their wives in family and child care roles, even when the husband and wife have similar career responsibilities. Many factors contribute to this pattern, including the wife's guilt at shifting family responsibility to her spouse, the husband's perception that domestic responsibilities will threaten his sense of power and self-esteem, and power struggles between spouses.

Ingredients often leading to successful integration of two professional careers with family life include flexibility, mobility, independence and interdependence, common interests, and self-actualization (Maples, 1981). Creative coping strategies such as cross-country marriages, job sharing, and alternating career-related relocations from one partner to the other are likely to increase with the growth in dual-career couples, rising at the rate of 7% a year since the late 1960s (Parker, Peltier, & Wolleat, 1981).

Patterns of dual-career marriages and deferred childbearing have led to an increase in another pattern, women spending the first 10 or 15 years of adulthood focusing on their career and then cutting back or stepping out of the workforce temporarily sometime around their mid- to late 30s to have a child before it is too late (Sekaran & Hall, 1989). These women, too, have special developmental needs as they cope with their changing roles, the loss of the benefits of their career roles, and perhaps unforeseen challenges of motherhood.

The Later Middle Adult Years

For most of those who have clarified their goals and direction and made wise choices during the sometimes painful years of the late 30s and early 40s, the 40s and early 50s will be years of comfort and restabilization. Work will probably be more rewarding, and careers may seem to be at their height. Marital satisfaction seems to improve after children leave home. If the turbulence of the earlier years led to the end of a first marriage and the beginning of a second one, the new marriage may seem much better than the first, at least in part because it did not have to weather the crisis of the 30s.

For many, the later middle adult years are the best years of their lives. People tend to develop their creativity, their interpersonal relationships, and their self-awareness and self-esteem. They are mature enough to have been enlightened by considerable life experience but still young enough to feel energetic and willing to take risks. People are more concerned with meeting their own needs than with living up to the standards of their families or societies. Interests are better differentiated, and work and family lives are more compatible.

Many people enter the postparental period during these years, when children are no longer living at home. Some may experience loneliness, grief over loss of an important role, and concern about the quality of parenting they had provided (Raup & Myers, 1989). However, relief and enjoyment of a new sense of freedom are also likely to be present. Negative reactions tend to be most pronounced in those who had been overinvested in their parenting roles and had neglected other aspects of their lives as well as those whose children left home under undesirable circumstances. For most, these negative reactions are short-lived and easily managed.

A competitive job market, accompanied by the rising cost of living, has led to an increase in adult children's returning home, many with children of their own following a marital separation. Even the most loving parents may resent this unanticipated intrusion on their newfound freedom, particularly if they are coping with issues of health and independence in their own parents. This so-called sandwich situation (Raup & Myers, 1989) is particularly stressful and can also occur in those who deferred childbearing and are now coping with both young children and aging parents at a time when their contemporaries seem to have considerable freedom.

Physical changes may also begin to trouble adults in the later middle years. The prevalence of both chronic and acute problems increases, potentially adding both financial and emotional pressures. These negative signs of aging may be met with denial or discouragement or may provide a stimulus for future planning. People surviving a life-threatening illness during adulthood are often prompted to reassess their lives and make the most of the time they have left.

Gender Differences in Development During the Middle Adult Years

Although adult men and women both seem to experience the three stages of middle adulthood discussed earlier, the timing and nature of these stages differ somewhat for the two groups as do the changes and choices that are made. For men, the 20s seem to be more positive years than they are for women. Men have been shown to grow in self-confidence during those years, whereas some women decline in self-confidence (Sheehy, 1976). This phenomenon may be because employment tends to enhance self-esteem more than does homemaking and child rearing. This discrepancy seems likely to decline as women increasingly remain in the labor force throughout all or most of the childbearing years.

Once men negotiate the transition at the age of 30, most settle into a relatively peaceful period during the 30s when they are focused on developing their careers and caring for their families (Levinson, Darrow, Klein, Levinson, & McKee, 1978). Men do not seem as prone to the role conflict that many women experience in their 30s when they are striving to balance family and career demands. However, these years may be difficult ones for men and women who do not conform to society's idea of what they should be doing. Approximately 10% of the population is homosexual (Schmitz, 1988), and, for people who are homosexual, efforts to establish a social and occupational role where they can find success and acceptance may extend well into the 30s and even beyond. Similarly, those men and women who do not marry or who do not have children, whether by choice or chance, may have particular difficulty during their 30s.

The period of midlife transition seems to occur at about the age of 40 for most men, somewhat later than it does for women. Perhaps the process of establishing their careers served to defer the onset of the midlife transition in men, whereas in women, who tend to be more family focused, it is often triggered by the departure of the last child for school, an event that occurs when most women are about 35 years of age.

Schlossberg (1992) described the discrepant midlife patterns of men and women as crisscrossing trajectories in which men turn inward and become more introspective, whereas women turn outward and become more involved in the external world. At the time when the woman is beginning to expand her horizons and seek a fuller lifestyle, often through education or employment, the man may still be concerned with establishing himself and may resist the changes introduced by his wife.

Several years later, when the woman is immersed in the early and typically challenging stages of returning to school or embarking on a new occupation, the man may enter a period of crisis. At that time, his wife may not have the time or inclination to provide him needed support; her primary focus may no longer be on her family, and she may resent having to cope with increased conflict at home when she thought she finally had the opportunity to pay attention to her own needs.

These patterns of conflicting needs may be compounded if one or both spouses is in a second marriage and is coping with two levels of responsibility. The man of 55, married to the woman of 35, may be dealing with adolescent and young adult children from his first marriage, young children from his second marriage, and his impending retirement, whereas his wife is focused on the early stages of child rearing and career development.

Men's Development
During the Middle Adult Years

Conflict may become particularly acute when the man experiences a midlife transition. As O'Neil and Fishman (1992) stated, "Many men are socialized to believe that they will earn security and happiness by hard work, success, and achievement" (p. 170). If these rewards are not forthcoming, men may become discouraged and disillusioned, perhaps blaming and rejecting present family and occupational commitments in the hope that new arenas may give them the rewards they are seeking. Men tend to become both more introspective and more self-absorbed as they seek to find a lifestyle that is more meaningful and consistent with present needs and values (Davitz & Davitz, 1976). Although substantive changes in interests and values during the adult years are unusual, the relative importance of these may be altered (Schlossberg et al., 1978). For example, the man who had a lifelong interest in art and painting but could express these only through occasional visits to museums because of his business obligations may realize that the time to actualize these interests is now or never; he may reduce his involvement with his business and begin to paint. Such changes may occasion considerable surprise and dismay in his family as lifestyle and income are modified.

The middle and late 40s and early 50s bring a period of reintegration and stabilization for most men. By those years, most have either established a more rewarding lifestyle for themselves or have gained a new and more positive perspective on their earlier commitments and relationships. Personal growth has also taken place for most; the turbulence of the early 40s seems to lead to an increase in both differentiation and integration for most men. They have developed a clearer sense of their own identities and are more able to balance work, family, and personal needs. Power and competition have declined in importance, whereas intimacy and self-actualization have grown.

Research on career development originally focused almost exclusively on men. During the 1970s, that pattern changed and considerable attention was paid to women's career development. The trend has now shifted again, and the 1990s witnessed a growth in research, writing, and support groups focused on men. Over the next decade, more attention is expected to be paid to the developmental, affiliative, and identity needs of men.

Women's Development
During the Middle Adult Years

Over the past 30 or 40 years, the overall development of the adult woman has increasingly been connected to her career planning. For the man, career plans and lifestyle have always been intertwined. For the woman, however, this represents a significant change that, only in recent years, has gained social acceptance and approval.

Statistics provide considerable information on trends in women's participation in the labor force. According to the U.S. Department of Labor, Women's Bureau (Silverstein, 1991), the number of women in the workforce increased from 44 million in 1979 to 56 million in 1989. In 1988, 81% of women between the ages of 25 and 54 with at least 4 years of college were in the labor force, and 51% of those with less education were employed. Sixty-five percent of mothers with children under the age of 18 and 56% of those with children under the age of 6 were employed outside the home. The number of families headed by never-married mothers has risen sharply, increasing by 365% from 1970 to 1983 (Silverstein, 1991). That the average American family consists of a husband, two children, and a nonworking wife is a myth; that configuration represents fewer than 7% of families (Silverstein, 1991), and 60% of children will spend some time in single-parent families.

Ethnic, socioeconomic, and other demographic factors bear a relationship to the likelihood of a woman's being in the labor force. One in every two marriages now ends in divorce, and divorced or separated women are more likely to be in the labor force than those who are married. African American women are more likely to be heads of households than White women, are less likely to remarry after the end of a marriage, have historically received more family and social support for being employed, and are more likely to be in the labor force (Fitzgerald & Weitzman, 1992). Unfortunately, African American women earn only 92% of the average salary of White women and are more likely to be in clerical, retail, and operative positions rather than professional jobs.

A long-term trend toward fewer children and a longer life span has also contributed to a change in women's careers. In 1890, the average woman was 55 when her last child married; life expectancy tables indicate that, probably, her husband no longer would be living at that point and that she did not have much longer to live. For most of her adult life, then, children had been present to occupy her time and attention and to increase her dependence on her husband.

Today's woman, however, is only in her 40s when her last child marries. In addition, the life expectancy has increased so that she has at least 15 years of potentially productive employment before retirement. The typical young woman of today will have approximately 34 years in the labor force if she marries, and 41 years, if she does not marry, many more years than she will spend in parenting young children.

Career planning for women should take account of these demographic trends, especially those relating to changes in longevity and birth rate. Motherhood now occupies a relatively small proportion of a woman's life. The average woman spends 20 years or 36% of her adulthood with a husband and children but only 7 years or 12% with preschool children. She spends 23 years or 41% of her adulthood with her husband and no children under 18 and spends 13 years or 23% of her adulthood without a husband (Rossi, 1972). Oliver (1975) suggested the importance of both achievement and affiliation needs in women. During the early years of marriage, affiliation needs take precedence. However, 10 to 15 years after marriage, achievement needs seem to come to the fore. Many women choose education or career development as the arena to fulfill their achievement needs.

Women, like men, experience developmental changes that are linked to both age and life situation. Following their passage through the 20s, when most women make important choices about marriage and childbearing, women in their 30s typically become more settled. They place greater emphasis on being themselves and achieving fulfillment (Gallos, 1989). In their 40s, their family responsibilities lessen, and most perceive their 40s as a time of great promise. Regardless of their marital status, women seem to want greater independence as they mature (Hyman & Woog, 1987). Morris (1974) found that women in the 36- to 45-year-old age group were happier and more self-confident than younger women and had stronger needs for introspection, affiliation, and nurturance. Women have what has been called split needs and seem to need to combine nurturance and productivity, mastery and pleasure for a full sense of accomplishment (Gallos, 1989).

Sources of Satisfaction

Women seem able to derive satisfaction from either a homemaker emphasis or a career emphasis. What seems to be important is that women are doing what they prefer. Stafford (1984) found lowest self-esteem in women in a homemaker role who longed for a career. Self-esteem also tends to be low in women who prefer having a job to either a career or homemaking. These women may be working out of necessity rather than choice or may perceive themselves as unable to succeed in demanding endeavors.

Those in homemaker roles find satisfaction via opportunity to make decisions, work independently, try out their own ideas, be of service to others, and exercise authority (Tinsley & Tinsley, 1989). However, they report missing the salary, community recognition, and opportunity for advancement among other aspects of the career role. In general, however, homemaking seemed to meet needs for achievement, autonomy, and security.

Many women combine homemaking with extensive involvement in volunteer activity. Some rise to positions of considerable power and influence. However, because this achievement is not reflected in a title or a salary, women tend to discount the value of these experiences. Such experiences can be of considerable value, however, in helping women become more aware of their interests and abilities. Volunteer experiences should not be neglected by counselors who are helping such women formulate career plans. As much can be learned from an analysis of a woman's performance of and feelings about a volunteer position as can be learned from a discussion of a person's work history.

Like women who focus on homemaking, most women who focus on their career report considerable satisfaction. They seem to have greater power in the marital relationship, better physical and emotional health, more independent children, and a better lifestyle (Fitzgerald & Weitzman, 1992; Silverstein, 1991). Although many women seem troubled by self-doubts in midlife, those women who take on multiple roles, are employed, married, and have children, report particularly high feelings of mastery and pleasure (McIlroy, 1984). However, their roles, too, present conflicts. Employed women with children do report stress and role conflict. The primary source of stress seems to be parenting rather than employment, and the work role actually can ameliorate stress in other roles. Other concerns of women in multiple roles include unequal sharing of responsibility at home, lack of affordable child care, pressure from both themselves and their society to become superwomen and do everything perfectly, gender bias reflected in lower salaries and fewer promotions than their male counterparts, and sexual harassment on the job. According to Fitzgerald and Weitzman (1992), "Of all the barriers to women's career development, none is more dramatic and at the same time more insidious than sexual harassment" (p. 142). As many as 53% of women have experienced harassment on the job (Freiberg, 1991a).

Women's Midlife Transition

Women, like men, seem to experience a transition or crisis sometime in their 30s. The onset of this transition seems to be linked to external events, notably the departure of the last child for school, and may be preceded by some years of pressure and dissatisfaction. During this transition, women's focus seems to shift away from earlier priorities with family-oriented women becoming more interested in career and independence and career-oriented women placing increasing importance on family and friends (Levinson, in press). This transition seems easier for women shifting from career to family than for women making an opposite shift who may lack skills and experience to prepare them to enter the workplace. Women focusing on homemaking may also find themselves simply redefining domestic responsibilities as children leave home but later return, perhaps with their own children, or as women's parents age and need their help. Despite these potential pressures, women who reach midlife toward the end of the 20th century and who probably have already experienced multiple roles are expected to have an easier time dealing with the transition from homemaking to career than did the previous generation (Raup & Myers, 1989).

These are the so-called reentry women, women who probably have experienced a transition or identity crisis in midlife, leading them to have an intense need to bring more meaning into their lives and perhaps shed the role of "vicarious achiever" (McGraw, 1982, p. 469). Although many of these women are well educated, well established, and well respected in the community, some seem to be experiencing feelings of isolation, depression, low self-esteem, and anger toward themselves. They view career satisfaction as a way to ameliorate these negative feelings. Others are returning to school or employment because of a marital change, a need for increased finances, or the appeal of tackling a new area of learning and accomplishment. Reentry women, in both college and employment settings, seem to be a diverse group (Read, Elliott, Escobar, & Slaney, 1988). Most, however, seem decided about their career choices and place considerable importance on their career development.

A study by Mohney and Anderson (1988), focusing on women who entered college for the first time between the ages of 25 and 46, sheds some light on this group. Factors that predisposed the women to enroll in college included needs for competence, security, and independence; a sense of the time being right; role models in their families of origin; the intrinsic rewards of education; and a wish to advance their careers. Barriers to prior enrollment in college included role demands, child-related variables, self-image, messages from family of origin, finances, and unavailability of desired courses. Factors that facilitated their enrollment included a decrease in role demands, support from significant others, financial ability, self-image, and availability of courses. Most of the women were strongly influenced by an interaction of life events and personal goals and were very concerned that others not be adversely affected by their decision to attend college. Despite their concern for others, the primary goal of reentry female students is personal fulfillment and increased knowledge, with the women estimating that about 60% of their future life satisfaction will come from their careers (MacKinnon-Slaney, Barber, & Slaney, 1988).

Women are more likely to make nontraditional career choices in midlife than they are in high school, perhaps because maturity gives them the self-confidence to take more risks and consider more options (Wilson, Weikel, & Rose, 1982). Women making nontraditional choices tend to be only or oldest children, come from better educated families, are employed by choice, and often have husbands who serve as their mentors as they advance in their careers. Women who make nontraditional choices report considerable difficulty with role conflict and experience even more job discrimination than do women in traditional careers. Women hold only 2% of senior management positions, and most women, especially in nontraditional careers, must cope with gender bias (Freiberg, 1991a).

By the late 30s or early 40s, most women have passed through the midlife transition and are hard at work, establishing an altered and more rewarding lifestyle for themselves. For those women who have not resolved the transition of the 30s successfully by establishing some sources of rewards that were not child focused, these years may be difficult ones, accompanied by feelings of loss, isolation, and low self-esteem. However, for most women, the empty nest syndrome is just another myth. Glen (1975) found that, generally, women in midlife whose children had left home reported greater happiness and enjoyment of life than did women of similar age with children still at home. Similarly, the changes associated with menopause seem to cause few significant problems for most women. Although this phase of life has only recently received much attention and there may be some tendency to downplay symptoms of menopause because of feelings of embarrassment, most women report more life satisfaction during the postparental stage than was experienced during the preceding years. Unanticipated events, such as divorce, illness, and bereavement, seem to cause far more difficulty for women in midlife than do anticipated events, such as menopause and children leaving home.

Despite the many conflicts and pressures of this period, midlife is a time of growth and satisfaction for most women, as they reassess their priorities and make changes that better meet their needs. Women seem more likely than at any other time to have the self-confidence and drive that they need to succeed and overcome the obstacles facing them both at home and in the labor force.

Male-Female Developmental Conflicts in Midlife

One unanticipated trend that seems to pose difficulties for many women in this age group is the tendency for men and women to develop in opposite directions during these years. Women move away from their traditional nurturing roles to seek achievement, creative accomplishment, and recognition. At the same time, many men have become disillusioned with the competitive and perhaps unrewarding nature of their occupations and become more concerned with the family. Whereas many men are lowering their career goals and realizing they must alter their dreams, women are raising their career goals and are full of optimism and hopes for success. Just as men are turning to their families for support, women are loosening their ties to the home and are becoming more involved in their occupations or education. Men may react to their wives' endeavors with feelings of anger and jealousy.

Children, too, no longer are readily available to their fathers. Children are probably in their teens or older and are spending most of their time with their peer groups. Although their families still have great importance for them, often, family activities are shunned by teenagers in an effort to emphasize recently gained independence.

All the members of the family, then, seem to be moving in different directions during the middle years of adulthood. These differences often make understanding each other difficult, and the man may feel unloved and neglected, whereas the woman may feel overburdened and confined. Both may feel unappreciated. Some marriages will not be able to sustain the strain of this period. Counselors working with adults in the middle years, then, should be aware not only of the changes their clients are experiencing but also of the effects these changes are having on the clients' family relationships and should address those in counseling.

Career Development
During the Middle Adult Years

Career development continues throughout the adult years, often accompanied by considerable change in goals and plans. Although adults can be found at all stages of career maturation, certain patterns are most likely to characterize career development during these years.

Super (1977) identified five qualities that constitute career maturity in midlife: ability to plan, engage in exploration, gather information, make sound decisions, and be oriented to reality. Adults with career maturity can view career development from a broad perspective and are aware that it is a lifelong and ongoing process. In the past, they explored alternatives, crystallized and specified their goals, and were able to begin implementing them. They have explored themselves and their situations and are aware of resources that are available to them. They are informed on the timing and characteristics of the life stages, have a broad repertoire of coping behaviors, and are aware of opportunities and their likely outcomes. They have a good grasp of the principles and practice of decision making and have a realistic view of themselves. Their career plans are clear and consistent, and the way they see themselves agrees with the way they are perceived by others. In midlife, they are establishing, stabilizing, and advancing their careers. They are aware of the need to keep up with developments in their field, to break new ground, and continue working productively.

Jordaan (1974), basing his model of career development on Super's research, termed the middle adult years of career development the establishment stage. According to Super (1985), establishment is assessed by looking at five factors: attained status, job satisfaction, occupational advancement, career progress, and career satisfaction. Jordaan subdivided the establishment stage into trial (early adulthood to age 30) and advancement (30s to mid-40s). During the trial substage, most adults make a commitment to an occupation and try to establish a place for themselves in that occupation. Super identified four patterns that characterized career development during the early establishment stage (25-35): establishment, establishment with difficulty, establishment with compromise, and impaired establishment.

The advancement substage is characterized by improvement in qualifications, performance, and status. It is a period of consolidation and progress.

Research by Riverin-Simard (1990) delineated a nine-stage model of adult career development:

1. ages 23 to 27—arrival on the job market, experience of shock at discrepancy between goals and perceptions
2. ages 28 to 32—seeking a promising path, questioning goals and beginning to understand the reality of the job market
3. ages 33 to 37—grappling with an occupational role, dealing with renewed objectives and obstacles to moving ahead; focus may be more on the present than the future, creating a plateau in development
4. ages 38 to 42—learning from successes and failures, seeking and testing new guidelines, raising new, more personal questions
5. ages 43 to 47—searching for the guiding thread, trying to make sense of one's life, a period of reflection
6. ages 48 to 52—considering modification of one's trajectories, feeling young but having wisdom, seeking a compromise that respects aspirations but takes account of reality
7. ages 53 to 58—seeking a promising exit, confronting the inevitability of leaving the job market
8. ages 58 to 62—changing gravitational fields, choosing different means of finding rewards
9. ages 63 to 67—coming to terms with the difficulties and advantages of retirement

Although only Stages 2 through 6 are part of middle adulthood, this model provides a useful overview of what Riverin-Simard terms the adult vocational trajectory.

One shortcoming of most models of adult career development is their neglect of the relationship between career development and others aspects of life. Zedeck and Mosier (1990) provide five models for understanding the relationship of career and personal development:

1. *Spillover theory.* Development is similar in both areas with happiness in one leading to happiness in the other.
2. *Compensation theory.* An inverse relationship is found between work and family; people make differential investments in one to compensate for what is missing in the other.

3. *Segmentation theory.* The two areas are distinct and need not influence each other.
4. *Instrumental theory.* One environment is a means by which things are obtained in the other environment (e.g., the primary purpose of employment is to support the family).
5. *Conflict theory.* Satisfaction and success in one area entails sacrifices in the other.

Whatever the relationship between people's careers and other aspects of their lives, a full understanding of the importance of work in people's lives can be obtained only by considering their careers in context. In adulthood as well as in earlier years, career development is affected by family composition and attitudes, ethnic and socioeconomic background, gender, and other aspects of the person.

Career Dissatisfaction in Adulthood

Super (1985) and Jordaan's (1974) models seem to present an ideal view of career development during the adult years. In reality, Super as well as other researchers found that many adults deviate from these models. When Super followed up the men in his Career Patterns Study when they were 36 years of age, he found that 30% had changed fields and 37% were engaged in exploring other career options. About half of those reported initiating exploration after having made what they believed were stable or fixed career plans. Those men who had achieved considerable career success were most likely to have made a commitment to their careers, whereas those with limited success were, not surprisingly, more likely to be engaging in exploration.

A substantial percentage of adults, then, experience career dissatisfaction in adulthood. Crites (1976) found that the cycle of satisfaction with one's career was at its lowest point during the middle years of the establishment stage. At that time, people have been engaged in their careers long enough to have a realistic picture of the rewards of the work and the likelihood of their advancement, and, often, that picture is a disappointing one.

A classic model developed by Marcia (Waterman & Waterman, 1976) sheds light on some of the dynamics of career dissatisfaction. Marcia identified four types of identity formation: moratorium, identity-foreclosed, identity-diffused, and identity-achieved. The moratorium type was characterized by an active search for appropriate commitments. The identity-foreclosed group had made choices with little searching;

they were much influenced by external forces and paid little attention to their own needs and abilities. The identity-diffused group experienced both the external expectations of the foreclosed group and the rootlessness of the moratorium group but were not impelled to seek change; they continued to function adequately but with feelings of discomfort, immobilization, and inferiority. Finally, the identity-achieved group had developed a sense of purpose and satisfactions with their careers as well as a clear and positive sense of identity.

Although many adults do negotiate the stages of career development smoothly and are established in stable and rewarding careers by midlife, many do not follow that pattern. People from disadvantaged or ethnic minority backgrounds seem particularly prone to difficulties in career development because of a combination of factors, including limited resources, limited aspirations, low self-esteem, and discrimination (Manuele, 1984). A 1987 survey focusing on minorities (Hispanics, African Americans, and Asian Pacific Islanders) found that 65% (including 79% of African Americans) would obtain more information if they were starting their careers over, 40% perceived discrimination in their workplace, and one third experienced work-family conflict. Only 41% had gotten started in their careers as a result of a clear plan. For others, chance (18%), family influence (12%), influence of friends and associates (11%), and job availability (12%) were more important determinants than planning. Research has found underemployment to be particularly demoralizing and even to be associated with suicidal ideation (Borgen et al., 1988). Even for people with good incomes, career satisfaction is not likely to be high unless personal qualities and work environment are a good match.

Stress in Adult Career Development

Midlife is a time when career transitions are likely and when dissatisfaction with one's career may come to a head. O'Neil and Fishman (1992, pp. 161-191) list 21 transitions in adult career development, summarized below:

1. initial career choice
2. obtaining training/skill development
3. obtaining a first job
4. career advancement/finding a new job
5. career change

6. loss of interest or meaning in career
7. serious conflicts with supervisors, colleagues, workplace
8. being fired or unemployed
9. rapid career success
10. rapid career failure
11. rapid income loss
12. demotion
13. leveling off/job peaking
14. gender conflicts
15. burnout
16. loss of a mentor
17. becoming a mentor
18. lost career dream or goal
19. aging, loss of stamina or endurance
20. preretirement
21. retirement

Although some of these changes are generally positive, whereas other are generally negative, all are stressful, and most of them (Items 4-18) are most likely to occur during the middle adult years. Other sources of work-related stress include a gap between employee skills and job demands, a perception of danger on the job, electronic monitoring of one's work, lack of participation in decision making, and uncertainty about one's future. The most stressful aspect of work, for most people, is an unsupportive or difficult supervisor, although women also are very concerned about lack of expected promotions (Crabbs, Black, & Morton, 1986). Of adults in a recent survey, 25% reported that job-related stress was so severe, it interfered with their personal relationships, and 20% reported that it had affected their physical health (Brown, Minor, & Jepsen, 1991).

Some occupations seem to be inherently more stressful than others. Jobs that involve danger (e.g., police officer, firefighter), the need for rapid life-or-death decisions (e.g., surgeon, air traffic controller), competition in front of an audience (e.g., football player, jockey), or stressful interpersonal contact (e.g., nurse dealing with people with life-threatening illnesses) are particularly likely to be stressful.

The stress inherent in the work is mediated by the qualities of the person in an occupational role. People are particularly prone to stress, burnout, and dissatisfaction if they perceive their work as a job rather than a career; they have little sense of control over their work; receive little social support; experience frequent psychological demands; and tend to be low in self-esteem, passive, anxious, and socially isolated (Bruhn, 1989).

Burnout is a particular response to job stress, stemming from constant or frequent "emotional pressure associated with intense involvement with other people over long periods of time" (Matthews, 1990, p. 230). Savicki and Cooley (1987) identified three patterns of burnout among mental health professionals: emotional exhaustion (being worn down by the stress of the work), loss of a sense of personal accomplishment, and depersonalization or developing a dehumanizing view of one's clients. Occupations such as physician, teacher, counselor, social worker, and manager have a high positive correlation between dissatisfaction/job stress and burnout.

Typically, burnout is a gradual process, beginning with stagnation and confusion, leading to frustration, and finally despair and apathy (Matthews, 1990). Burnout seems to be exacerbated by lack of progress in one's career, poor communication, lack of recognition, nonparticipation in decisions, role conflict and ambiguity, repetitious and unrewarding tasks, shift work, work overload, limited staff development opportunities, and poor match of person and job. Symptoms of burnout include fatigue, resistance to change, alienation, irritability, decline in social interest, boredom, diminished creativity and work performance, disorganization, procrastination, and a reduced sense of personal accomplishment. Burnout can even lead to physical illness, substance abuse, eating disorders, and suicide (Sauter, Murphy, & Hurrell, 1990). Mental stress as a cause for workers' compensation payments has shown a great increase in recent years.

Other challenges often presented by career development in midlife include overinvesting in one's career, plateauing, and mentoring. Naughton (1987) defined what often is called workaholism as high investment of time and energy in one's job and concomitant reduction of investment in other areas of life. Whereas some people tend to be satisfied with this pattern of working and maintain high interest and performance at work, others feel overloaded and inhibited by work demands, which often leads to impaired performance. This sort of work pattern has been linked with hypertension and physical changes in the heart (Raymond, 1990). Pressures toward overinvestment in work can be particularly troubling to men in midlife who find themselves increasingly drawn toward other, more personal priorities, and to women who have considerable home and family responsibilities.

Plateauing, another pitfall of adult career development, has been defined as that point when further promotions have a low probability, either because the organization does not offer any appropriate opportunities or because the employees' abilities do not match the needs of the next logical step on the career path (Stout, Slocum, & Cron, 1988). People who become plateaued and who do not make career changes tend at least for a time to feel discouraged and resigned; to blame themselves for their failures; and to become less productive, less motivated, and less committed to their work. They may shift their priorities so that other areas of their lives compensate for their career disappointment. This effort may prove difficult, however, because unhappiness in one important area of life tends to color feelings about other areas.

Usually, mentoring is a rewarding aspect of adult career development, but it, too, can be difficult. Mentoring is a professional relationship in which a successful and established worker, the mentor, provides support, guidance, and direction to a less experienced worker, the protégé (Olian, Carroll, Giannantonio, & Feren, 1988). A positive mentoring relationship typically has four stages:

1. The initiation phase lasts 6 to 12 months.
2. The cultivation phase lasts 2 to 5 years and involves coaching, exposure to challenging work, and a developing friendship.
3. Separation, the most difficult phase, is often signaled by the promotion of the protégé up to the level of the mentor.
4. Redefinition usually results in a friendship of peers.

A successful mentoring relationship can be very rewarding to the mentors and can be invaluable to the career development of the protégés, but it can also lead to conflict and disappointment.

Midlife Career Change

Although career development tends to stabilize with age, midlife change, particularly before the age of 45, is fairly common. The average American has eight employers between the ages of 25 and 64 (Wegmann, 1991a) and spends an average of 4.2 years with each employer (M. Carey, 1990). Job tenure tends to be the longest in occupations where opportunities are declining, such as farming, forestry, and fishing, and are the shortest in sales and service occupations, where opportunities are abundant. Of workers in the United States, 8% to 10%, approximately

15 million people, change jobs each year (Kirk, 1989); 40% of these are over the age of 35.

Work seems to have a somewhat different meaning for those who change jobs compared with those who remain in jobs. Although both job changers and nonchangers perceive work as providing them a sense of identity, typically, nonchangers place considerable emphasis on the external rewards of employment (salary, anticipated retirement benefits, status, prestige, power, social interaction, and structure of time) (Kanchier & Unruh, 1989). In contrast, job changers placed greater importance on intrinsic rewards, such as freedom, autonomy, growth, independence, pleasure and achievement. They usually change jobs to find more meaningful work and a better match between their work and their values and interests.

Many men and women seem to experience a sort of renewal stage between the establishment and maintenance stages (to be discussed in the next chapter) in which they reflect on the relationship between their dreams and their reality and either recommit to their present endeavors or pursue other options (Isaacson, 1981). What seems to distinguish the changers from the persisters, then, is not so much the congruence of their work and their personalities but whether their work-related satisfaction is derived primarily from intrinsic or extrinsic sources (Salomone & Sheehan, 1985). Those who emphasize intrinsic rewards and who also experience little job-personality congruence are most likely to make occupational changes in midlife, particularly if they have financial resources to allow a change and confidence in their ability to control their futures and find more meaningful work (Henton, Russell, & Koval, 1983).

Several processes have been identified that can precipitate a career change.

1. A major event, such as the death of a spouse or loved one, a divorce, the departure of the last child from the home, the spouse's relocation, or a change in physical abilities can lead to a reformulation of one's lifestyle and career goals.

2. Gradual disenchantment with earlier career choices can lead to the decision to pursue more rewarding options. This disenchantment could be due either to a change in the person or to a change in the work. Such a person may have made an initial occupational choice because it met family expectations or because it was the first opportunity that presented itself. However, needs have now changed and the work has become less gratifying.

3. Some people experience growth in self-awareness or changes in values along with the realization that potentially more satisfying occupational options are open to them. They are different from the above group in that they are moving toward a goal rather than away from a disappointment. They may still be experiencing considerable success and satisfaction in their jobs but believe that other options will be even more rewarding.
4. A fourth group includes involuntary changers who are fired, laid off, or forced to resign from a position, either because of their own occupational performance or because of economic difficulties in the company.

Involuntary Career Change

Although most occupational changes are made voluntarily, approximately 13% of changes are involuntary (M. Carey, 1990). In 1988, 3,092,000 people lost their jobs (Holmes & Werbel, 1992). These people are likely to have the most difficulty with the process of change as well as the least rewarding outcomes. Wegmann (1991a) found that 70% of voluntary career changes led to higher income, whereas 70% of involuntary changes led to a decline in income. Between 1979 and 1984, 11.5 million workers lost their jobs due to relocations or plant closings; only 60% of them found new jobs in that time period (Liptak, 1991). Most displaced workers are male, older, less educated, union members, with some seniority and above-average wages. A large number have been employed as semiskilled machine operators (U.S. Department of Labor, 1988). Obstacles to future employment include limited basic education and marketable skills.

Although the period of unemployment for people who make involuntary changes averages 2 to 3 months, it varies considerably. Older, college-educated workers often spend 4 to 6 months on a job search. One third of the unemployed leave the labor force at least temporarily before finding a job, the so-called discouraged workers (Wegmann, 1991b). Jones (1989) found that people who lost their jobs fell into five groups, three experiencing low stress and two experiencing high stress. The low-stress groups were described as the unaffected (self-directed mature workers of higher socioeconomic status), those who saw the change as a blessing in disguise, and the cyclers who anticipated periods of unemployment in their careers. Those experiencing high stress included those who were worried about finances and the change in their identity but who were coping actively and the most dysfunctional group, characterized by worry, depression, substance abuse, and either a frantic job search or apathetic inertia. Unemployment has been characterized as a sort of grieving process in which people experience stages similar to those who have experienced a death. Abrego and Brammer (1992) found the following phases to characterize midlife career change: immobilization and shock, minimization and denial, self-doubt, expressions of regret and anger, testing options, searching for meaning, and integration and renewal.

Facilitating Career Change

Many interventions have been developed to assist job or career changers. Identification of people's responses to the change as well as their stage of adaptation to the change can be useful in planning to help them. Anticipated causes of occupational change, both internal (such as increased self-awareness at midlife) and external (such as a promotion or planned retirement) are probably less disruptive than unanticipated causes, such as divorce, illness, and bereavement (internal) or unemployment and work dissatisfaction (external).

Counseling of career changers should probably begin with an exploration of the reasons for the change. Although needs, values, and interests may alter over the life span, motivating a change in middle adulthood to a career that is more congruent with present personality variables, values and interests tend to be fairly stable over the life span. Changes are most likely to be those of focusing, narrowing, and consolidating. Career changers are more likely to remain in areas closely related to their current occupations or to redefine their present work roles rather than shift to an entirely new line of work (Wegmann, 1991a). Values and interests that have been neglected in the past may surface and call for attention. Some of these shifts seem to be age linked. Troll (1975) found, for example, that men in midlife placed more value on independence and control in their work than did younger men. Needs for creativity and helping others are especially likely to surface during the middle years. Adolescent hopes and dreams are likely to return as midlife adults realize this may be the last opportunity for them to pursue that long-buried goal. Family changes may also lead to a shift in needs; parents with several children in college, for example, may have to subordinate other needs to financial ones.

Lifestyle change may be intertwined with career change, and counselors should help people examine the impact of one on the other to determine the most positive way to effect change. Thomas (1977) described three types of career changers. "Changers" are those who make a significant change in both career and lifestyle; "pseudo-changers" change their careers but not their lifestyles; and "crypto-changers" maintain stability in their careers but change their lifestyles and the performance of their work. All three types of change can lead to increased enjoyment and satisfaction; a total change is not always the indicated remedy for midlife dissatisfaction. In fact, Schlossberg et al. (1978) found that even if a change in career or lifestyle is not made, the process of contemplating and anticipating such changes can lead to taking stock and improving adjustment.

Beyond promoting self-awareness, understanding of the reasons behind a wish for change, and an appreciation of available options, the literature suggests the following interventions and resources as useful to the person contemplating a midlife career change:

1. *Leisure counseling.* Particularly during a period of unemployment, leisure can reduce stress and boredom, promote skill development, provide support and networking, develop autonomy, and contribute to self-confidence and a sense of well-being (Liptak, 1991).

2. *Teaching career development skills.* Many people, particularly those who have not previously conducted a thoughtful and systematic job search, may need help in decision making, résumé writing, interviewing, networking, and related competencies. This process should contribute to their sense of self-efficacy as well as to the effectiveness of their job search (Holmes & Werbel, 1992).

3. *Outplacement counseling.* This is most commonly offered to executives leaving large corporations or to groups of employees involved in layoffs or plant closings. Of the 1,500 largest corporations, 75% have outplacement programs for executives (Davenport, 1984). Typically beginning before the layoff occurs, this systematic process can offer peer support, help in dealing with grief and loss, development of job search techniques, identification of options and transferable skills, development of an action plan, and clerical assistance to facilitate the job search.

4. *Inplacement counseling.* This counseling is provided to unsatisfactory employees to facilitate behavioral change so that termination will not be necessary.

5. *Forty Plus Clubs, other job clubs.* These are peer support groups, designed to provide encouragement, job leads, and development of job-seeking skills.

6. *Small business advisory groups.* A substantial percentage of people changing careers, especially those in managerial and professional occupations, start their own businesses. That endeavor seems particularly likely to meet the needs for creativity and independence that tend to strengthen during midlife. Many communities have groups of successful business

owners who are willing to serve as mentors to people establishing new businesses.

7. *Private employment agencies.* Typically, these agencies specialize in a small group of occupations or an industry and charge a fee, usually 10% of 1 year's salary. The fee may be paid by the employer.

8. *Executive search firms.* Similar to employment agencies, these agencies use active recruiting to find the best qualified candidates for positions. Their fees are almost always paid by the employer.

9. *Retraining.* People may be offered retraining by the company that is laying them off, or they may seek retraining on their own initiative to expand their career options.

10. *Computer-based career counseling.* When combined with counseling, such computer-based career development programs as DISCOVER II have been found effective with adults experiencing career transitions as they are with young adults (Marin & Splete, 1991).

In general, the goals of counseling career changers are for clients to

obtain a renewed sense of personal control, experience increased self-esteem and self-confidence, become active rather than passive in finding new career directions and goals, channel their feelings into positive and constructive action, develop a group support network that will help them organize and market their skills, and gain a realistic attitude toward the future that will assist a rapid return to productive employment. (Pedersen, Goldberg, & Papalia, 1991, p. 75)

Counseling programs for midlife career changers are most effective if they maximize participant involvement and initiative, emphasize positive and goal-directed attitudes, encourage family involvement and support, and use multiple strategies. The facility of a person's adaptation to change is mediated by the person's perception of change, so interventions need to focus not only on the pragmatics of career change but also on the experience of change so that before too long the transition is no longer all consuming and becomes a manageable process that leads to a more rewarding career and lifestyle.

In light of the large number of people who change careers in midlife, counselors would do well to prepare young people for this possibility. Anticipated events are generally less difficult to handle than unanticipated ones; adults who experience career dissatisfaction at midlife should be better able to handle those feelings and plan successful career changes if they have regarded career development as a lifelong process rather than as a quest for the one right occupation. As Sheehy (1976) stated, "It will be progress when we come to think of serial careers, not as signifying failure, but as a realistic way to prolong vitality" (p. 282).

The Adult as Student

The past 20 years have witnessed considerable growth in numbers of adult learners. Although many adults enter vocational-technical training programs or enroll in courses designed to enable them to receive high school diplomas, most of this growing group of mature learners are found in the colleges and universities. In 1972, when the increase in adult students was already well underway, 28% of all college students were aged 25 or older. By the year 2000, as many as 50% of college students are expected to be aged 25 or older (Keierleber & Hansen, 1992). More than 60% of these adult students are women (Chartrand, 1990).

Because most older students have family and occupational responsibilities in addition to their academic ones, they attend college in ways that will facilitate its integration with other areas of their lives. They are more likely to attend college part-time and to attend community colleges than are the 18- to 21-year-olds. Proximity, flexible schedules, and a broad selection of occupationally relevant courses are important to older students.

Adult students include not only those who are making a career or lifestyle change but also those who are seeking additional learning to advance in their professions. As increasing numbers of adults have entered higher education, the role of mature student has become socially acceptable and there has been an accompanying shift in how education generally is viewed. No longer is it simply a form of career preparation for the young. The value of education as recreation and as a vehicle for social contact and personal growth has become well accepted. Most adult students are seeking not only career preparation but fulfillment of such values as intimacy, wisdom, self-respect, and independence (Bauer & Mott, 1990).

The older student faces many more areas of concern than does the younger student. These include conflict between the demands of school and other commitments (family, work, leisure, and socialization), feelings of guilt, discomfort in the college environment, worry about academic performance, finances, low self-esteem, and lack of clear goals (Keierleber & Hansen, 1992). Older students tend to be very demanding of themselves and may underestimate their academic abilities because they have been away from school for many years. College can provide an excellent proving ground for such people, a place to test both interests and abilities before entering or reentering the labor force. However, some become discouraged by these pressures. Nontraditional students are less likely to complete a degree than are traditional students. Chartrand (1990) found that mature students who make a strong commitment to the student role manifest better performance but also experience more distress, perhaps resulting from role conflict. Clearly, the challenges of the mature student need special attention.

Many colleges have developed special programs and services to help the adult learner. The College Level Examination Program enables people to receive college credit by demonstrating competency on examinations. Between 700 and 1,000 institutions give college credit for life experience (R. Wilson, 1990). Typically, students must assemble a portfolio of essays, letters of recommendation, awards, licenses, and samples of work to demonstrate the learning they have achieved. This process allows adult students to take advanced courses and complete their degrees more rapidly. Other services such as on-campus child care, support groups for reentry and other adult learners, career development courses, tuition waivers for students of retirement age, external degree programs, interdisciplinary studies, televised courses, and evening and weekend counseling and advising hours are also helpful.

Many employers also have facilitated adults' continuing education by granting paid educational leave. Increasing numbers of workers, especially in industry, education, and government, are being given time during regular working hours that they can use for educational purposes. Some employers also provide tuition reimbursement to employees, particularly if they are taking job-related courses.

Despite these sources of help, often, the adjustment problems of the returning student are significant, particularly for women who may be balancing family, employment, and academic demands. These women may be experiencing guilt, confusion, and self-doubt about their new roles but are often reluctant to seek help from college counseling services. Nevertheless, most adult women attending college experience a growing autonomy, a heightened sense of self-worth, and an improved self-concept. Nearly all older women students seem to view their education as being personally and professionally beneficial (Astin, 1978).

Perhaps because they are more self-motivated and interested, adult students, both men and women, tend to receive better grades than do younger students. Most studies of older students agree that their past experiences, their motivation to learn, and their views of themselves and their goals contribute to making them more successful and more satisfied students than are their younger counterparts. This conclusion, coupled with the finding that high school grades predict the college grades of adult students as well as do the results of any recent tests, suggest that intellectual and academic abilities do not decline through the middle years with either age or absence from school (Lunneborg, Olch, & deWolf, 1974).

Overview of the Middle Adult Years

The middle adult years are a time to reassess one's life, to change and consolidate so that the remaining years will be more rewarding. For most, these years reflect an overall upward trend in adjustment and satisfaction with life. Despite this trend, people typically experience not only positive growth but also difficult and negative change during these years.

Schlossberg (1976) identified five areas of change during adulthood: the inner life, intimacy, family life, community, and career. The inner life of most adults becomes more stable and satisfying. Nevertheless, the middle adult years present most people with a second identity crisis. The self must be reunderstood and reinterpreted. People may experience considerable concern about their physical health and appearance, and an increased awareness of mortality is common. Ideals, values, and beliefs gain in importance, and buried interests and hopes may resurface. These are emotionally rich years, but they may also be troubling ones. Questions are being raised—"Who have I been?" "Who am I?" "Who do I want to be?" "Who will I be?" Answers and the process of finding answers differ from the adolescent identity concerns. Limits are set by the realization that all options are no longer open and by paths already established. However, adults have the benefit of experience and improvements in creativity, flexibility, and the ability to assess situations clearly and realistically to help them resolve their midlife identity questions effectively.

The capacity for intimacy develops during the adult years. Usually, concerns with interpersonal closeness and humanitarian and community endeavors increase, especially among men. At the same time, marital satisfaction may suffer at least a temporary decline; men and women move in opposite directions, and must cope with each other's efforts to find more rewarding lifestyles.

For most, career satisfaction increases as do achievement, recognition, advancement, and responsibility (Heath, 1977). However, gratification with one's career may be tempered by a growing awareness of its limits.

Erikson (1963) termed the crisis of the middle adults years one of generativity versus stagnation. Adults need to be productive and creative during these years, both at home and at work. According to Erikson, adults who cannot achieve productivity may overemphasize intimacy, focusing excessively on themselves or their partners, precipitating feelings of stagnation, emptiness, dependency, and depression. Frequently, such adults have difficulty making a commitment to a career and may feel unsatisfied and fragmented.

The following developmental tasks and coping behaviors for the middle adult years have been adapted from the work of Erikson (1963), Havighurst (1972), and others:

1. achieving adult civic and social interest and responsibility
2. establishing a role in which one can use and develop skills and feel successful, productive, and creative
3. assisting children and young people to become responsible and happy adults
4. developing a gratifying lifestyle that integrates career, family, and leisure pursuits
5. developing intimate, supportive, and mutually satisfying relationships with one's partner, children, parents, and close friends that maintain one's own integrity and individuality
6. accepting, appreciating, and adjusting to the emotional and physiological changes of middle age, maintaining positive health as much as possible
7. reassessing and revising one's values, interests, goals, beliefs, and lifestyle; addressing neglected aspects of the self; and maintaining direction and control over one's own development
8. maintaining a flexible and optimistic outlook that enables one to learn from the past, enjoy the present, and plan for the future.

Counseling the Adult During Midlife

Many adults report a continuing need for counseling on career and related issues. However, counseling with adults is quite different from and perhaps more complex than counseling with children or adolescents. Although some adults may have ready access to counselors in college settings or employee assistance programs, most do not have easy access to counseling services. To obtain counseling, then, they will probably need to familiarize themselves with available resources in their communities and make arrangements for child care or time away from the job to keep appointments. Many adults attach some stigma to the process of counseling; these adults may feel that they should be in the position of helper, not helpee, and are uncomfortable acknowledging their own needs for assistance. In addition, many adults' familiarity with mental health professionals may not go much beyond the school guidance counselor, "who tells you what courses to take," or the psychiatrist, "for sick people." The community counselor and the career counselor are less familiar figures, and many adults are not aware that counselors are available who have been specially prepared to deal with the needs and concerns of adults in midlife. The initial hurdle, then, in providing counseling for adults is acquainting them with the nature and availability of adult counseling and helping them overcome some of their resistance to that process.

Bias in Counseling Adults

Unfortunately, the attitudes of many counselors also interfere with the process of helping adult clients. For example, Fitzgerald and Crites (1980) found that many counselors have negative gender-linked beliefs about career development. They may believe, for example, that women take more sick leave than men, that employing women is harmful to their children, and that most men are uncomfortable having female supervisors, all false beliefs. Inaccurate assumptions about the impact of age and socioeconomic background can also intrude on the counseling process and limit its helpfulness.

Troll and Nowak (1976) identified three types of age bias. *Age restrictiveness* is the setting of arbitrary or inappropriate age limits for any behavior (e.g., a woman should marry in her early 20s and have her children before she is 30). *Age distortion* is the misperception of the characteristics or behavior of any age group (e.g., 50-year-olds are too set in their ways to learn a new field). *Ageism* is the possession of negative attitudes toward any age group (e.g., the view that women become temperamental and depressed during the menopause years). To work effectively with adult clients, counselors must become aware of biases both in themselves and in their clients and should try to examine and eliminate the effect of such potentially destructive views.

Approaches to Adult Career Counseling

Just as adult development is different from the development of the child or adolescent, so are the counseling needs of the adult different from those of the younger person. Counselors working with adults should be cognizant of the predominant concerns and attitudes of this group and of approaches that have been found effective in counseling adult clients. Counselors who treat adults contemplating a midlife career change as they would treat the adolescent who is trying to formulate career plans will probably be unsuccessful and may well alienate the client.

By the time adults contact a counselor, many of them are immersed in a period of crisis or transition. This can be a positive and growth-producing experience. Although people in crisis are likely to be feeling considerable pain and anxiety, these very feelings seem to motivate them to resolve the crisis. People who can draw on their personal resources, assess a situation realistically, formulate sound plans and decisions, and deal positively with their affective reactions to transitions are likely to emerge with renewed self-confidence and coping abilities and more rewarding plans and goals. Counselors who can facilitate this process will probably accomplish a great deal.

Gladstein and Apfel (1987) suggest three essential characteristics of career counseling with adults:

1. Counseling should promote examination of the self and one's life experiences, leading to a dialogue that will clarify and enhance identity.
2. The *process* of career development should be emphasized.
3. A sociological view should be taken that focuses on the interplay between personal identity and a person's society and relationships.

With adults, the possibility for change and growth throughout the life span should be emphasized and the perspective of the counseling process should be a holistic one, recognizing that change in one area of life affects other areas. A constructive-developmentalist perspective, suggested by Carlsen (1988), seems a useful model to guide adult career counseling. In this perspective, counseling is viewed as a dialogue, designed to help people make sense of their lives. Life, itself, is viewed as a self-authored story, whereas career is seen as both a carrier of meaning and a path to give life coherence, focus, and significance. Rather than imposing their theories of career development on people, counselors should help people understand their own ideas about how people develop and relate these to their own lives. This can provide people with a much needed organizing framework for understanding themselves, processing information, and selecting options.

Carlsen suggested four stages to adult career counseling:

1. Establish a relationship and define concerns.
2. Gather historical data relevant to the present situation.
3. Process and reshape a person's patterns of experience.
4. Achieve closure through reintegration.

Anxiety tends to be highest at the beginning and toward the end of the counseling process. Counselors need to address this to prevent premature termination of counseling (Spokane, 1992).

Counseling with midlife adults should not be just a matter of helping them adjust to change or overcome disappointment; rather, it should be a process of helping them to become more like they want to be, to know and feel good about themselves, and to make and implement realistic plans and goals. Some adults feel helpless and no longer have a sense of control over their own lives. They may fear leaving the security of their present situations and competing with younger students and workers. Those who have been at home may feel concerned about their ability to perform effectively at school or work, and those who have been employed may feel self-doubt because they have not been as successful or satisfied as they had hoped when they began their careers.

By drawing on strengths and previous success experiences, counselors can help people improve coping skills and self-esteem. A realistic assessment of the person's current situation and the options it presents can help reduce some the of fear and anxiety. Improved decision-making skills and practice with those skills can help restore people's sense of control over their own lives.Some people can be helped by the realization that at least part of what they are experiencing is a developmental process and is shared by many others of the same age or in similar life situations. However, this approach must be used with care lest people feel that their concerns are being viewed as commonplace or trivial.

The concerns that people have about their lack of skills may be realistic or they may be exaggerated. Counselors can offer some help in this area by clarifying possible misconceptions about the aging process: Intellectual ability does not decline through the middle years, good students in high school are likely to be good students in college at any age, and mature students tend to be more academically successful than those of traditional age (Schlossberg et al., 1978). Often, a genuine lack of skills can be remediated by further education or training. Many adults are concerned about the effect on their families of the changes they are contemplating or experiencing. Counselors can help them to distinguish between actual and expected family resistance, minimize the repercussions of changes, and help families accept, understand, and adjust to the change.

Because of the difficulty usually inherent in midlife career change, people are concerned that the change be a genuinely beneficial one. Counselors can increase the likelihood of positive change by looking closely, with clients, at the degree of congruence between their characteristics, abilities, and values and the attributes of their anticipated roles. Questions might be raised about the proposed changes if they do not seem to be congruent with the person's view of himself or herself or if the proposed changes are less congruent with the person's attributes than are his or her present life roles.

Career Counseling Via
Programs, Groups, or Workshops

Common ingredients of adult career counseling programs include computerized career guidance systems, assessment strategies and techniques, career information, career planning material, seminars, and workshops or group counseling (Gerstein, 1982). Groups may be particularly helpful to people in midlife because a group or workshop offers concrete help in a short period of time and, therefore, is acceptable to most adults. The workshop approach also is helpful in enabling adult clients to realize that others are experiencing difficulties and transitions similar to their own. Manuele (1984) concluded, "Vocational maturity is a characteristic that can be increased or developed in clients if appropriate training is provided" (p. 110).

Brown (1981) described four models for facilitating adult career development through group counseling:

1. The self-help model, in which independent reading and self-discovery is emphasized, assumes considerable initiative and ability on the part of the client.
2. The informational model, often found in libraries, community colleges, and continuing education centers, assumes that people can make good choices for themselves if they are given enough information.

3. The developmental model helps people progress through and understand predictable stages in growth.

4. The structured group model emphasizes group support and commonality rather than individual assessment or concerns.

Job search groups have increased in number in recent years and seem to provide useful help to adults seeking employment or occupational change. Amundson and Borgen (1988) identified 19 factors, in order of importance, that make such groups useful: (a) mutual support and encouragement, (b) job search strategies, (c) information on résumés and correspondence, (d) help in development of self-esteem and a positive outlook, (e) practice in interviewing, (f) development of a telephone script for following up on job leads, (g) a sense of belonging and commonality, (h) job leads, (i) videotaped feedback of role-played interviews, (j) counselors' leadership and direction, (k) giving a sense of structure and accomplishment, (l) secretarial services and supplies, (m) vicarious enjoyment of the enthusiasm and success of others, (n) information and reference material, (o) follow-up and support services, (p) goal setting, (q) reinforcement through peer feedback, (r) feeling a sense of contribution by helping others, and (s) opportunity for ventilating. Clearly, development of specific job-seeking skills such as résumé writing and interviewing are important. However, the emotional support provided by job search groups may be at least as important asthe skill development (Ryland & Rosen, 1987).

The growth of employee assistance programs has led to an accompanying growth in career counseling and development programs at the work site that place particular emphasis on career development in business in industry. Typically, these human resource development programs deal with training and development, needs assessment, employee assistance with personal concerns, career planning and development, consultation on work-related conflicts and dissatisfactions, employee discipline and outplacement, and appraisal (Smith, 1988). Such programs are well positioned to promote adult career development. The following career-related issues can provide an important focus for work site career development programs:

1. helping employees and managers to identify and deal with hazards in the workplace

2. training people to identify and, if appropriate, modify their work styles

3. helping people to understand the effects of repetitive work

4. dealing with job transfer and relocation

5. career development in the dual-career family
6. special stresses on people who experience danger and high interpersonal demands on their jobs
7. preparation for retirement
8. dealing effectively with job and employee evaluation
9. dealing with the special problems of job loss
10. dealing with the special concerns of people in small businesses
11. substance abuse and its impact on the workplace
12. integrating work and leisure
13. promoting self-awareness
14. managing stress
15. developing management skills
16. improving communication and assertiveness skills

In addition to workshops, training, and counseling on these topics, many organizations provide extensive information. One government agency, for example, has a career resource center, focusing on self-managed career-life-planning activities, that provides the following four stations:

1. *Understanding the self*—inventories for values, goals, needs, interests, and skills.
2. *Understanding the environment*—information on educational and occupational options, finances, skill development, and job openings.
3. *Taking action*—job-keeping and job-seeking skills, interviewing, résumé writing, job enrichment, training, and self-development.
4. *Life management*—self-assessment, relationships, parenting, midlife transition, retirement, health, stress, grief, finances, drugs and alcohol, separation and divorce, sexuality, disabilities, and sources of additional help (Blimline, Thorn, Wilson, & Wilcox, 1983).

Counseling for Adults' Special Needs

Leisure Counseling. Only 58% of people report a great deal of satisfaction with their leisure activities (McDowell, 1981). Helping people develop more rewarding use of their leisure time can promote feelings of well-being and fulfillment. Leisure counseling usually takes a holistic approach, exploring the best way to integrate leisure with family and career as well as with existing leisure activities. Consideration of appropriate leisure activities might focus on the following dimensions: involvement, challenge, interpersonal contact and support, structure, feedback on performance, competency building, cost, and integration into life (Blocher & Siegal, 1981).

Reentry Women. Women reentering the labor force after some years at home often need help in integrating perhaps disparate sides of their lives and of themselves. Pirnot and Dustin (1986) found that for both homemaking and career women, the two most important values were aesthetic and economic. Women's need for enjoyment of beauty, self-actualization, individualism, and self-sufficiency may conflict with their practical need for resources for their families and themselves. Workshops, support groups, and career development classes all have been found useful in helping people cope with change in midlife (McGraw, 1982). Common goals of such programs include increased awareness and acceptance of the self, integration of multiple roles, management of transitions, development of confidence and self-esteem, acquisition of occupational and educational information, and clarification of short- and long-term goals.

Dual-Career Couples. For dual-career couples, career development and relationship development are intertwined. Sources of stress that typically need to be addressed in counseling with these families include occupational mobility and job placement, having and rearing children, child care, household responsibilities, time management, and finances. Common issues for husbands include perceived loss of power and prestige and competition with the partner, whereas wives tend to be concerned with unfulfilled expectations for their spouses, redefinition of roles, role conflict, guilt, and self-esteem. Gilbert and Rachlin (1987) found that "having a supportive husband is a key factor in successful dual-career marriages" (p. 28) and "the degree to which the family accommodates a woman's career is central to the woman's success and satisfaction" (p. 32).

Many counselors recommend conjoint counseling for such couples in which both partners are seen together by the counselor. Marital enrichment programs, particularly when used preventively, also help by providing new ideas, role models, and peer support. Interventions such as values clarification, prioritizing strategies, information on stages of family development, teaching communication and problem-solving skills, promoting mutual support and shared goals, contracting for distribution of household responsibilities, helping set realistic standards, planning time alone as well as time together, developing a couples' contract, time management, leisure counseling, clarification of expectations, assertiveness training, using available and innovative career modifications (e.g., parental leave, job sharing, flextime and part-time work, relocation assistance, telecommuting inn order to work at home), and developing a shared vision of success all can be useful.

Today, most dual-career couples follow an egalitarian model in which there are two heads of household; decisions are made democratically; division of labor is based on interests, skills, and availability rather than gender; household and child care responsibilities are shared; and career development is an important and mutual concern that changes little after childbirth (Hazard & Koslow, 1992). Whether a couple is in the early stages of developing a couple relationship, becoming parents, and raising preschoolers; the middle stages of raising school-aged children and maintaining the couple relationship; or in the later stages of weathering adolescents, caring for aging parents, becoming a couple again, and eventually becoming grandparents, counseling focusing on dual-career issues can be useful in promoting individual, relationship, and career development.

Counseling for Burnout. As discussed earlier in this chapter, people sometimes become discouraged and manifest anxiety, impaired performance, and work-related dissatisfaction from job-related stress. This has been called burnout. People in dangerous positions, those where rapid and important decisions must be made, and those who are exposed to constant interpersonal demands are particularly prone to these difficulties. Job-related stress can be addressed either preventively or after it has developed. The following approaches have been effective in improving work motivation and reducing feelings of stress (Bruhn, 1989; Katzell & Thompson, 1990; Sauter et al., 1990):

1. Provide information and training on techniques of stress management.
2. Ensure that personal motives and values are relevant to the job and the organization.
3. Provide appropriate incentives and rewards.
4. Set goals that are specific, clear, appealing, attainable, and challenging.
5. Ensure that workers have adequate personal, social, and material resources.

6. Promote team development and good leadership, using interpersonal and group processes to increase motivation.
7. Maximize the quality of work life.
8. Promote a sense of humor and a sense of control to temper stress.
9. Involve employees in decision making.
10. Maximize person-environment fit via job assignment and change.
11. Provide varied, meaningful, and stimulating work.
12. Make counseling available as needed, especially for people dealing with traumatic incidents.

Development of a stress reduction plan, incorporating at least a few of the above approaches, is likely to result in less stress and greater satisfaction among employees.

Resources for Adult Career Counseling

Adult career development can be enhanced by resources, including computerized career guidance services, printed material, videotapes on occupations and job-finding strategies, and inventories. The following lists some of these resources:

1. *Chronicle Career System (Chronicle Guidance Publications)*. Products include Chronicle Career Quest to assess interests and link them to occupations; C-LECT, a computerized approach to career exploration; Chronicle Occupational Library, printed information on a broad range of occupations; and a video career library.
2. *CHOICES CT.* This a computer-based program for adults in transition that provides assessment of current career-related needs, an inventory of past work experience, a review of self-assessed and transferable skills, a computer printout of compatible occupations, and an action plan (Careerware).
3. *DISCOVER for Colleges and Adults.* This is a comprehensive computer-based career planning system, available through the American College Testing Program Educational Services Division.
4. *The Dictionary of Occupational Titles (DOT).* Published by the U.S. Government Printing Office, the *DOT* is an extensive classification system of occupations. First published in 1939, the *DOT* is perhaps the most important single piece of literature for the career counselor and can be particularly useful in facilitating the transferability of skills of the adult client. The 1991 edition provides information on 12,741 jobs. Related and useful publications, also issued by the U.S. Government Printing Office, include a *Military Career Guide*, a *Guide for Occupational Exploration* that

provides help in using the *DOT*, and the *Occupational Outlook Handbook* (*OOH*). Published every two years, the *OOH* provides information on the occupational outlook, projected trends, the nature of over 300 occupations (nature of work, working conditions, employment statistics, training and other requirements, job outlook, earnings, related occupations), their *DOT* codes, and sources of additional information.

Anita Hirsch and Fred Newman

Two Case Studies of Adults in Midlife

Although any stage of development encompasses considerable diversity, midlife seems to present the most variety. Rather than presenting one extended case study as has been done in previous chapters, two briefer case studies will be presented here to illustrate that variety. The same inventories were administered to both people and both were seeking to make career changes in midlife. Beyond that, their differences outweigh their similarities.

Background of Anita Hirsch

When Anita Hirsch, a 42-year-old Jewish woman, first sought counseling at the Women's Center, she looked tired and depressed. "I finally have everything I want," she said, "but I'm still not happy. Something must be wrong with me. I need some help."

Anita grew up in suburban Massachusetts. Her father was a physician, and her mother was a nurse who had stopped working outside of the home when Anita was born and returned to work in her husband's office when Anita entered high school. As an only child with considerable intelligence, charm, and attractiveness, Anita had received a great deal of attention from family, friends, and teachers. Her parents, who were unable to have other children, focused all their hopes on Anita; her father encouraged her to become a physician and take over his practice, whereas her mother spoke of the joys of marriage and parenthood. Like many young women of her generation and cultural and socioeconomic background, Anita had two goals for herself. Although she wanted to attend college and develop a profession, she also wanted to marry and have children, integrating the goals both parents held for her.

Since childhood, Anita had had a strong interest in foreign cultures. Her interest began through stamp collecting in elementary school, progressed through family trips to Europe and extensive reading in junior high and high school, and led her to major in foreign languages in college. Interests and abilities seemed to coincide in Anita's career development and she enthusiastically studied not only Spanish and French in high school but also Japanese in college and Farsi on her own. A junior year abroad complemented her studies and sparked her interest in foreign cultures even further.

Despite her great interest in other cultures, Anita established fairly conventional career goals, again typical of women of her generation. In addition to her foreign language courses, she also took enough teacher education courses to become certified as a foreign language teacher. She anticipated that she would marry soon after college, perhaps teach for a few years, and then leave teaching to raise her children, following her mother's model.

Initially, Anita's life seemed to go as planned. Shortly after finishing college, she married a man who was completing law school. She obtained a job teaching foreign languages in a high school and looked forward to having children in a few years. Unfortunately, about 3 years after their marriage, Anita's husband was killed in an automobile accident.

Being widowed at age 25 is what might be called a paranormative event, an event that happens at an unexpected time. This was the first of several paranormative events Anita would encounter in her life. Typically, such events are more difficult to handle than events that occur at expected times. Despite considerable support from family and friends, Anita was devastated by her loss and believed that it spelled the end of her personal goals.

Anita had not enjoyed teaching very much but had viewed it as an appropriate temporary job until she and her husband decided to have children. Her primary interest in foreign languages lay in travel and in communication with people from other cultures. With the death of her husband, Anita decided to focus on her career in an effort to find a more rewarding direction. She was soon able to gain employment with an international corporation. Her job involved considerable foreign travel, as well as business dealings with people from a variety of cultures. Success in her job depended on her acceptance of and performance in foreign assignments, and this was just what Anita wanted.

For the first 5 years of working in international business, Anita did very well and was given more responsibility and a promotion. However, when she was in her early 30s, she was given an overseas assignment of several years' duration that involved her working with a supervisor who was not used to dealing with women in professional roles. Instead, he viewed Anita as a potential romantic relationship and began to make overtures toward her. When Anita made clear that this was not acceptable to her, her supervisor escalated his demands and began to assign undesirable tasks to her. At that time, awareness of sexual harassment was limited. Although Anita recognized that her supervisor's behavior was highly unprofessional and inappropriate, she felt that her role in a foreign economy was a precarious one, so she decided "not to make waves" by reporting her supervisor. This experience took its toll on Anita, and she developed some medical problems, eventually diagnosed as ulcers. At about this same time, she received word that her father had died. All of these events were too much for Anita to handle easily; she requested a transfer back to the United States, recognizing that would probably limit her future career advancement.

Although Anita's career was indeed limited by her return to the United States, her personal life was enhanced. Shortly after her return, Anita met the man who would become her second husband. David, divorced and about 10 years older than Anita, had two adult sons. David and Anita were married when Anita was 35, and at 37 she gave birth to their daughter.

Finally, Anita had fulfilled her goals of having a profession, a husband, and a child. However, Anita was now an established professional with a long and generally rewarding career that she was reluctant to abandon. After much thought, she arrived at a compromise in which she obtained her employer's approval to work half-time. Although Anita knew this would be a further setback in her career, she felt it was the best way to meet both her professional and her personal needs.

When she sought counseling, Anita's daughter was nearly 5 years old and Anita had been, as she described it, "Full-time everything with half-time credit. I'm always exhausted, always feel like I'm about to run out of gas. I love my child and I really enjoy my work but lately nothing seems very rewarding any more. I need to get some more control over my life and find more time for me. And for my marriage!" Anita came to counseling for help in reassessing her career and personal goals, in setting priorities, and in developing some plans. She felt strongly committed to her husband and child and did not want to hurt them in any way but, as she said, "Right now, I'm not much good for anybody, including me. I just can't do it all."

Background of Fred Newman

Fred Newman's career and personal development presents a very different picture. Fred was a homosexual man from a Catholic background who had spent most of his 37 years sorting out who he was and what sort of life he wanted. According to Hetherington, Hillerbrand, and Etinger (1989), gay men have higher career uncertainty and dissatisfaction than do either heterosexual men or lesbians.

Fred was the oldest boy and third child in a family of seven children. His father had been a government employee throughout his career. Although he had not found his career very rewarding, it had provided the income and security he needed to support his family. Fred's mother had done bookkeeping at home when the children were young and now worked part-time for a small business.

Fred attended Catholic schools until he completed high school, graduating at the top of his class. He did particularly well in mathematics and science and received a scholarship to attend a nearby engineering college. In retrospect, Fred felt that he had given little thought to his occupational choices; parents and teachers had encouraged him to study engineering, educational opportunities presented themselves, and he graduated from college with a degree in electrical engineering. However, his leisure reading, as a high school student, had focused on art, architecture, psychology, and sociology. He had little interest in tinkering with cars and appliances as had many of his friends who studied engineering. Despite these early signs of limited interest in engineering, Fred followed a career path that had been expected and approved of by others rather than really examining his own interests and abilities.

In his personal life, too, Fred felt as though he had been programmed. He was popular and well liked through high school, where he participated actively in team sports. He had dated little through high school and college, but that was not unusual because he had attended an all-boys high school and a college that was largely male. Although he had several female friends, he felt uncomfortable when dating and never dated the same person more than once or twice.

After college, Fred quickly found employment as an engineer with a electronics firm. Although the work came easily to him and he was rapidly moved ahead in the corporation, he was bored with his work. It seemed routine, and he found himself with little enthusiasm at the end of each day. He did prefer his management and organizational responsibilities to his technical and scientific ones, and when a supervisor at work suggested he get some training in business, that provided the impetus for a career change as well as some personal changes.

While continuing to work in engineering, Fred began study toward a master's degree in business administration. Again, he did very well in his studies but failed to find them very interesting. However, once again he convinced himself that he was on an appropriate path, one that was sanctioned by his family as well as his employers, and he completed his degree.

In graduate school, Fred became friendly with one of his classmates, a man named George. As the two became closer, Fred realized that he had long been drawn more to men than women and, for the first time, acknowledged to himself that he was gay. Although Fred's relationship with George lasted only a few years, it paved the way for his relationship with Jeffrey, the man Fred now refers to as his life partner. The two have been living together for the past 5 years and recently bought a home together.

Although Fred clearly became comfortable and accepting of his own identity as a gay man, he had considerably more difficulty telling family and friends about his preferences. Not until he and Jeffrey felt secure in their relationship did he tell his family about Jeffrey and ask them to meet him. Their initial reactions were disbelief and anger, although in recent years they had begun to include Jeffrey in family events. Most friends and colleagues who were not gay themselves were unaware of Fred's homosexuality. He would not bring Jeffrey to social activities at work and felt as though he were living a lie.

In his work activities, too, Fred felt like he could not really be himself. Although he had completed his MBA and was employed by a large banking firm, he continued to be unhappy with his work. As he stated, "I don't feel well integrated at work. I'm just going through the motions. I want a job that will really be fulfilling to me."

Assessment of Abilities

As with most adults, ample evidence of abilities was available for both Anita and Fred. Both had been strong students throughout their academic careers. Fred demonstrated the multipotentiality typical of gifted students, performing well in areas of high interest as well as in those of moderate interest, whereas Anita was less academically oriented and did much better in courses such as history and foreign languages that interested her. However, both were clearly above average in intelligence. High school and college grades as well as college admissions test scores were available but were at least 10 years old for both and probably would contribute little to the picture of their abilities that could be obtained from a discussion of their academic and employment histories as well as their leisure activities.

Although assessment of abilities is typically far less important with adults than it is with children and adolescents, some adults have little clear evidence of their abilities. Perhaps they had not been in the workforce for many years, had long been out of school, or had little motivation to succeed when they were in school. For such people, assessment of abilities might be useful. However, generally, ample information on adults' abilities will come from sources other than inventories.

Assessment of Interests

The Strong Interest Inventory (SII), published by Consulting Psychologists Press, was selected as the most appropriate inventory to assess Anita and Fred's career-related interests. Although considerable information had already been obtained about their expressed and manifest interests, the SII would provide yet another perspective on those interests, confirming interests already acknowledged or offering new perspectives.

The SII was first published in 1927 as the Strong Vocational Interest Inventory and later was known as the Strong-Campbell Interest Inventory. According to Hood and Johnson (1991), "The Strong has become one of the most frequently used, thoroughly researched, and highly respected psychological measures in existence " (p. 110). Both the concurrent and the predictive validities of the SII have been well established, and SII results have been found to correlate positively with self-reported job and work satisfaction. In addition, the SII has been praised for having high exploration validity, the ability to increase the diversity of people's options (Campbell, 1987). The SII has been used in career counseling, outplacement counseling, college major selection, leadership development, retirement counseling, team development, and leisure counseling. Counseling psychologists use the SII as part of a test battery more than any other instrument (Watkins et al., 1988).

The SII consists of 325 items; respondents indicate their degree of liking for or similarity to each item. The reading level of the inventory is at the junior high school level, although the inventory, providing extensive information on specific occupations, is geared to those aged 17 or older. Younger people or people with extremely vague career goals may be overwhelmed by the amount of material generated from this inventory. Completion of the inventory requires 20 to 60 minutes, with 30 minutes being average for adult respondents. Scoring must be done by machine.

Information on responses to the SII is presented in three categories: general occupational themes, basic interest scales, and occupational scales. In addition, two special scales and administrative indexes are provided. Anita's SII profile has been included in this chapter to clarify the nature of this inventory (see Figure 8.1). Fred's SII profile will be summarized.

The General Occupational Themes (GOTs) are those of Holland's hexagon: realistic, investigative, artistic, social, enterprising, and conventional (see Chapters 1 and 6 for more information). Anita's highest scores were in enterprising and conventional areas; her lowest scores were in investigative and artistic areas. Fred's highest scores were in social, investigative, and artistic areas. This first, broad look at their inventoried interests suggests that Anita's work is congruent with her inventoried interests, but Fred's is not.

Each GOT is divided into two to five basic interest scales, providing more detailed information on patterns of interests; t scores, with a mean of 50 and a standard deviation of 10, based on responses from a general population, are used to report scores on both the GOTs and the basic interest scales. Norms for each gender are indicated by bars printed on each scale. Asterisks plot the respondents' standard scores on the bars representing their gender. Anita's highest scores on the basic interest scales were in office practices, business management, and sales, whereas Fred's were in social service, teaching, religious activities, and art. His score in business management was moderately low.

Finally, scores are presented in terms of 102 occupational scales based on the responses of men employed in their occupations for at least 3 years and reporting satisfaction with their work and 105 occupational scales

STRONG INTEREST INVENTORY OF THE
STRONG VOCATIONAL INTEREST BLANKS

PAGE 1

Anita Hirsch
SEX: F

SPECIAL SCALES: ACADEMIC COMFORT 34
INTROVERSION-EXTROVERSION 54

TOTAL RESPONSES: 325 INFREQUENT RESPONSES: 3

GOT	
R	Mod. Low
I	Low
A	Low
S	Average
E	High
C	High

OCCUPATIONAL SCALES

STANDARD SCORES

REALISTIC

GENERAL OCCUPATIONAL THEME - R
Mod. Low 38

BASIC INTEREST SCALES (STANDARD SCORE)
AGRICULTURE Average 43
NATURE Low 35
ADVENTURE Low 36
MILITARY ACTIVITIES Mod. High 50
MECHANICAL ACTIVITIES Mod. Low 40

		F	M
(CRS)	Marine Corps enlisted personnel	27	
Navy enlisted personnel	41	29
Army officer	34	35
Navy officer	32	21
Air Force officer	33	24
(C)	Air Force enlisted personnel		27
Police officer	27	10
Bus driver	34	35
Horticultural worker	33	25
Farmer		14
Vocational agriculture teacher	24	10
Forester	14	20
(IR)	Veterinarian		16
(SR)	Athletic trainer	4	
Emergency medical technician	34	27
Radiologic technologist	33	33
Carpenter	12	20
Electrician	13	14
(ARI)	Architect	15	
Engineer	21	19

INVESTIGATIVE

GENERAL OCCUPATIONAL THEME - I
Low 37

BASIC INTEREST SCALES (STANDARD SCORE)
SCIENCE Average 43
MATHEMATICS Average 52
MEDICAL SCIENCE Average 45
MEDICAL SERVICE Average 46

		F	M
Computer programmer	33	29
Systems analyst	30	23
Medical technologist	31	17
R & D manager	17	9
Geologist	8	19
Biologist		
Chemist	17	13
Physicist	3	4
(RI)	Veterinarian	17	
Science teacher	23	20
Physical therapist	23	11
Respiratory therapist	29	17
Medical technician	37	27
Pharmacist	39	31
(CSE)	Dietitian	51	
(SI)	Nurse, RN		26
Chiropractor	19	20
Optometrist	38	18
Dentist	20	16
Physician	8	19
(RI)	Biologist		18
Mathematician	19	10
Geographer	33	19
College professor	31	24
Psychologist	12	9
Sociologist	6	5

ARTISTIC

GENERAL OCCUPATIONAL THEME - A
Low 40

BASIC INTEREST SCALES (STANDARD SCORE)
MUSIC/DRAMATICS Low 40
ART Mod. Low 45
WRITING Mod. Low 45

		F	M
Medical illustrator	2	2
Art teacher	4	19
Artist, fine	8	16
Artist, commercial	15	17
Interior decorator	25	41
(RIA)	Architect		13
Photographer	12	18
Musician	23	23
Chef	15	(EA)
Beautician		41
Flight attendant	23	35
Advertising executive	21	21
Broadcaster	20	27
Public relations director	16	18
Lawyer	20	17
Public administrator	28	27
Reporter	7	15
Librarian	34	40
English teacher	21	26
(SA)	Foreign language teacher		37

CONSULTING PSYCHOLOGISTS PRESS, INC.
577 COLLEGE AVENUE
PALO ALTO, CA 94306

Figure 8.1. Anita Hirsch's Strong Interest Inventory Profile

STRONG INTEREST INVENTORY OF THE   PAGE 2
STRONG VOCATIONAL INTEREST BLANKS

PROFILE REPORT FOR: Anita Hirsch   DATE TESTED:
ID: DATE SCORED:
AGE: SEX: F

5 35

OCCUPATIONAL SCALES	STANDARD SCORES F	M	VERY DISSIMILAR	DISSIMILAR	MODERATELY DISSIMILAR	MID-RANGE	MODERATELY SIMILAR	SIMILAR	VERY SIMILAR

SOCIAL

	F	M			15 25 30		40 45 55

GENERAL OCCUPATIONAL THEME - S   Average   49

BASIC INTEREST SCALES (STANDARD SCORE)
TEACHING   Average   47
SOCIAL SERVICE   Mod. High   58
ATHLETICS   Average   41
DOMESTIC ARTS   Average   53
RELIGIOUS ACTIVITIES   Average   43

		F	M
SA (AS)	Foreign language teacher	50	(AS)
SA SA	Minister	14	27
SA SA	Social worker	29	25
S S	Guidance counselor	36	39
S S	Social science teacher	33	23
S S	Elementary teacher	39	24
S S	Special education teacher	36	11
SR SAR	Occupational therapist	25	24
SIA SAI	Speech pathologist	30	25
SI (ISR)	Nurse, RN	31	(ISR)
SCI N/A	Dental hygienist	41	N/A
SC SC	Nurse, LPN	39	46
(RI S) SR	Athletic trainer	(RIS)	15
SR SR	Physical education teacher	16	8
SRE SE	Recreation leader	32	32
SE SE	YWCA/YMCA director	39	28
SEC SCR	School administrator	35	35
SCE N/A	Home economics teacher	36	N/A

ENTERPRISING

	F	M			15 25 30		40 45 55

GENERAL OCCUPATIONAL THEME - E   High   60

BASIC INTEREST SCALES (STANDARD SCORE)
PUBLIC SPEAKING   Mod. Low   41
LAW/POLITICS   Mod. Low   41
MERCHANDISING   Average   54
SALES   High   64
BUSINESS MANAGEMENT   Very High   64

		F	M
E ES	Personnel director	38	19
EA E	Elected public official	28	31
ES ES	Life insurance agent	31	24
EC E	Chamber of Commerce executive	54	30
EC EC	Store manager	49	45
N/A EC	Agribusiness manager	N/A	40
EC EC	Purchasing agent	40	34
EC E	Restaurant manager	47	41
(AR) EA	Chef	(AR)	32
EC E	Travel agent	46	51
ECS E	Funeral director	42	38
(CSE) ESC	Nursing home administrator	(CSE)	49
EC ER	Optician	48	37
E E	Realtor	39	35
E (AE)	Beautician	40	(AE)
EC E	Florist	37	45
EC E	Buyer	38	44
EI EI	Marketing executive	32	35
EIC ECI	Investments manager	19	25

CONVENTIONAL

	F	M			15 25 30		40 45 55

GENERAL OCCUPATIONAL THEME - C   High   65

BASIC INTEREST SCALES (STANDARD SCORE)
OFFICE PRACTICES   Very High   73

		F	M
C C	Accountant	43	27
C C	Banker	48	25
CE C	IRS agent	40	33
CES CES	Credit manager	49	39
CES CES	Business education teacher	39	46
(CS) CES	Food service manager	(CSI)	49
(ISR) CSE	Dietitian	(ISR)	48
CSE (ESC)	Nursing home administrator	42	(ESC)
CSE CSE	Executive housekeeper	43	49
CS (CES)	Food service manager	44	(CES)
CS N/A	Dental assistant	43	N/A
C N/A	Secretary	46	N/A
C (R)	Air Force enlisted personnel	41	(R)
CRS (RC)	Marine Corps enlisted personnel	38	(RC)
CRS CR	Army enlisted personnel	40	35
CIR CIR	Mathematics teacher	42	23

Strong Interest Inventory of the Strong Vocational Interest Blanks®, Form T325.
Copyright © 1933, 1938, 1945, 1946, 1966, 1968, 1981, 1983, 1985 by the Board of Trustees of the Leland Stanford Junior University. All rights reserved. Printed and scored under license from Stanford University Press, Stanford, California 94305. Strong Vocational Interest Blanks is a registered trademark of Stanford University Press.

CONSULTING PSYCHOLOGISTS PRESS, INC.
577 COLLEGE AVENUE
PALO ALTO, CA 94306

ADMINISTRATIVE INDEXES (RESPONSE %)

OCCUPATIONS	36 L %	9 I %	55 D %	
SCHOOL SUBJECTS	47 L %	22 I %	47 D %	
ACTIVITIES	35 L %	10 I %	47 D %	
LEISURE ACTIVITIES	41 L %	1 I %	41 D %	
TYPES OF PEOPLE	38 L %	25 I %	30 D %	
PREFERENCES	37 L %	30 =%	33 R %	
CHARACTERISTICS	29 Y %	27 ?%	43 N %	
ALL PARTS	38 %	17 %	45 %	

Figure 8.1 Continued

based on the responses of similar groups of women. Although information is provided so that a person's scores can be compared with people
of each gender, same-sex norms are emphasized in the presentation of
data and are viewed as having more usefulness. People in those norm
groups had a mean of 50 and a standard deviation of 10 on the scales

reflecting their own occupations. Respondents' scores above 40 indicate similarity to people in an occupation.

Anita had quite a few high scores on these scales, including Navy enlisted personnel, foreign language teacher, travel agent, Chamber of Commerce executive, and banker. In interpreting these scores, efforts should be made to find underlying patterns of interest similarity rather than viewing the high scores as recommended occupations. For example, although Anita had no interest in becoming a travel agent or enlisting in the Navy, those occupations reflected her interest in travel and foreign cultures and in having structure and organization in her work. Fred's highest scores, again, were very different from Anita's and included special education teacher, social worker, and college professor.

The administrative indexes and special scales on the SII profile provide further insight. The academic comfort scale was designed to discriminate people who do well in academic settings from those who do not. People with scores above 50 tend to be interested in studying theory and research, whereas those with scores below 40 typically do not have a strong interest in continuing their education. The scale is weighted toward science and the arts and away from business and applied fields. This scale does not indicate ability; rather, it reflects academic motivation, comfort, and interest. Anita had a fairly low score (34) on this scale, indicating that she probably is not interested in continuing her education, whereas Fred's score was quite high.

On the introversion-extroversion (IE) scale, scores of 55 and above indicate a preference for working with ideas, data, or things, whereas scores of 45 and below suggest a preference for working with people. Both Anita and Fred had scores close to 50, suggesting enjoyment of working both with data and people.

Other scales on the SII indicate the number of questions answered, the number of unusual responses, and the percentages of each type of response. These can be useful, especially in interpreting profiles with little differentiation that may have a high percentage of dislike or indifferent responses.

Assessment of Personality

Myers-Briggs Personality Inventory

The Myers-Briggs Type Indicator (MBTI) was selected to assess personality for Anita and Fred. Published in 1976 for clinical use by Consulting Psychologists Press, the MBTI now is "one of the most widely used tools for working with normal populations" (McCaulley, 1990, p. 181). Based on theories advanced by Carl Jung, the MBTI was developed by Katherine C. Briggs and her daughter, Isabel Briggs Myers. The Center for Applications of Psychological Type and *The Journal of Psychological Type* promote and disseminate information on the MBTI. It has been used in career counseling, leadership development, team building, marital counseling, and self-awareness programs. The MBTI Narrative Report for Organizations and the MBTI Type Differentiation Report elaborate on MBTI preferences in ways that are particularly useful in career counseling or organizational development. The MBTI Relationship Report is designed to help couples look at their similarities and differences.

Although some researchers have expressed reservations about the MBTI, Thompson and Borello (1986) concluded, "Factor adequacy and other results . . . provided positive evidence regarding the validity of the Myers-Briggs Type Indicator" (p. 148). According to Levin (1990), the SII and the MBTI are useful in combination: "The MBTI can serve to complement Strong results. The MBTI can provide clients with *within* occupation information" (p. 1).

The goal of the MBTI is to help people discover and appreciate their own natural styles. Several forms of the MBTI are available, varying in length and nature of scoring. All yield scores on eight dimensions, organized into four bipolar scales. Scores on the four scales as well as their four-letter combination provide insight into preferences. The four scales are as follows:

1. *Extroversion (E)—Introversion (I)*. People with an E preference tend to focus outside themselves and thrive on being in large, active groups, whereas people with an I preference tend to focus inward and feel more comfortable alone or with a small number of close friends.

2. *Sensing (S)—Intuition (N)*. People with an S preference tend to be concrete and practical, focusing on information gathered by their senses, whereas those with an N preference tend to be more imaginative and theoretical, focusing on patterns and possibilities.

3. *Thinking (T)—Feeling (F)*. People with a strong T function tend to be logical, rational, and objective, whereas those with a strong F function typically base their decisions on values, emotions, and subjective assessments.

4. *Judging (J)—Perceiving (P)*. A strong J preference characterizes people who prefer to have their lives organized and planned and who have little difficulty making decisions, whereas a strong P preference characterizes people who prefer to operate spontaneously and want to keep their options open.

On the MBTI, Anita's type was ENTJ, with her J preference being particularly strong (see Figure 8.2). According to Myers (1985), people of this type enjoy administration, like to achieve immediate and tangible results, are practical and realistic, and present oriented. Although they are tolerant of routine, they are stimulated by change and new experiences. This

Report Form for the
Myers-Briggs Type Indicator®

Name: Anita Hirsch

Sex: ☐ Male ☒ Female   Date:

The MBTI® reports your preferences on four scales. There are two opposite preferences on each scale. The four scales deal with where you like to focus your attention (E or I), the way you like to look at things (S or N), the way you like to go about deciding things (T or F), and how you deal with the outer world (J or P). Short descriptions of each scale are shown below.

E You prefer to focus on the outer world of people and things   or   **I** You prefer to focus on the inner world of ideas and impressions

S You tend to focus on the present and on concrete information gained from your senses   or   **N** You tend to focus on the future, with a view toward patterns and possibilities

T You tend to base your decisions on logic and on objective analysis of cause and effect   or   **F** You tend to base your decisions primarily on values and on subjective evaluation of person-centered concerns

J You like a planned and organized approach to life and prefer to have things settled   or   **P** You like a flexible and spontaneous approach to life and prefer to keep your options open

The four letters show your Reported Type, which is the combination of the four preferences you chose. There are sixteen possible types.

REPORTED TYPE: [E] [S] [T] [J]

PREFERENCE SCORES: [ ] [ ] [ ] [ ]

Preference scores show how consistently you chose one preference over the other; high scores usually mean a clear preference. Preference scores do *not* measure abilities or development.

EXTRAVERSION E   I INTROVERSION

SENSING S   N INTUITION

THINKING T   F FEELING

JUDGING J   P PERCEIVING

60 50 40 30 20 10 0 10 20 30 40 50 60

Each type tends to have different interests and different values. On the back of this page are very brief descriptions of each of the sixteen types. Find the one that matches the four letters of your Reported Type and see whether it fits you. If it doesn't, try to find one that does. For a more complete description of the types and the implications for career choice, relationships, and work behavior, see *Introduction to Type* by Isabel Briggs Myers. Remember that everyone uses each of the preferences at different times; your Reported Type shows which you are likely to prefer the most and probably use most often.

Figure 8.2. The Myers-Briggs Type Indicator (MBTI)

411

profile reflects Anita's success in her work as well as her ability to manage her busy life for the past 5 years but also explains her need for change; after 5 years of a demanding routine, she craved some new experiences.

Fred's MBTI preference was ENFJ. People with this combination are curious about new ideas, enjoy theory and academics, and have considerable warmth and insight. According to Myers (1985), "ENFJs do well in many fields, for example, as teachers, clergy, career and personal counselors, and psychiatrists" (pp. 96-97). This profile sheds light on Fred's career development. Although his interest in pleasing others as well as his broad range of abilities led him to achieve success in several fields, neither engineering nor business was fulfilling his strong need to deal with others in a helping way.

For both Anita and Fred, their MBTI preferences are consistent with their SII types. Dillon and Weissman (1987) found that men with NF preferences on the MBTI tend to have high social scores on the SII, whereas women with ET preferences tend to have high enterprising interests.

Maslach Burnout Inventory

To provide further insight into the dynamics of their dissatisfaction with their careers and to provide some direction for change, the Maslach Burnout Inventory (MBI) was administered to both Anita and Fred. This inventory, published by Consulting Psychologists Press, requires about 15 minutes to complete. Respondents indicate how often, on a scale ranging from *never* (0) to *every day* (6), they experience each of 22 states (e.g., I feel like I'm at the end of my rope, I feel very energetic). According to Pelsma, Roland, Tollefson, and Wigington (1989), "In the area of occupational stress, the Maslach Burnout Inventory has been accepted as a psychometrically reliable tool for measuring burnout" (p. 81). Although intended for use primarily with human service professionals, the MBI has been found to have application in a wide range of settings, including parenting.

The MBI yields scores in three areas: emotional exhaustion (EE), depersonalization (DP), and personal accomplishment (PA). The following table indicates the level of Anita's and Fred's scores in the three areas:

	EE	DP	PA
Anita	High	Low	High
Fred	Low	Low	Low

Although neither feels a sense of depersonalization or withdrawal from others, differences in their EE and PA scores reflect differences in their career concerns. Anita feels a strong sense of personal accomplishment from her roles as both parent and employee but feels emotionally exhausted by those roles. Fred, on the other hand, is bored rather than drained by his work and feels little sense of personal accomplishment.

Nonstandardized Tools
to Promote Career Development

Nonstandardized tools, tailored to the needs of a particular person, can play an important role in promoting self-exploration and decision making. They are particularly useful with adults who may be uncomfortable about taking tests or inventories. The following tools were used with Anita:

1. Written list of goals, included the following:
   a. Find more rewards and recognition in my career.
   b. Gain more control over my career.
   c. Come to terms with my decision to have left my overseas assignment.
   d. Have more time for romance in my marriage and enjoyment of my family.
2. Life history questionnaire, designed to provide an overview of career and personal history.
3. Development of a list of strengths and weaknesses, drawn from the spectrum of her work, family, and leisure activities.
4. Prediction of results on the SII, MBTI, and MBI, followed by comparison with inventoried results and discussion.
5. List of options, in which pros and cons for each career alternative were delineated and weighted to facilitate decision making among options such as working full-time in present job, leaving paid employment entirely, becoming a consultant, working fewer hours, seeking a similar position in another setting, or returning to teaching.

Similar tools were used with Fred, with particular emphasis on exploration of career options. Initially, he used brainstorming to develop a list of occupational options that included human resource manager, college professor, manager in a nonprofit organization, administrator in an educational setting, physician, psychologist, architect/designer, public health administrator, and small business owner. He then identified five qualities that seemed essential to his career satisfaction:

1. working with people who respect each other
2. having a job with a mission, a larger social purpose
3. having work that is stimulating and creative, that uses my intelligence and problem-solving ability

4. security and adequate compensation

5. having significant and rewarding contact with people

A list of dislikes also was developed and, after information had been gathered through reading and informational interviews, each career option was evaluated in terms of the two lists.

Outcomes of Career Counseling
With Anita and Fred

Through counseling, Anita realized how important her career was to her. Although she was glad that she had taken time away from work to be with her daughter during her early years, Anita now was ready to return to work full-time. She also realized that her present field combined her interests in foreign cultures and business very well. However, she wanted to maximize her chances of being promoted and of having work that was challenging and interesting where she could use her foreign language skills. Through networking, Anita was able to identify several businesses that would be interested in hiring her. She then went to her present employer and requested the changes that would make her job more rewarding. Rather than lose her to a competitor, her employer allowed her to return to work full-time in a more challenging role that was more likely to be rewarding. A joint session with Anita and her husband helped them to focus on their concerns as a dual-career couple and to make child care arrangements that were acceptable to both of them. This holistic approach helped Anita make both personal and professional changes that were likely to enhance both her career and her family life.

Although Fred thought that he would very much enjoy the roles of psychologist, physician, or college professor, he was reluctant to leave the workforce for 5 or more years to obtain the training needed to make such a radical change in his profession. However, the role of human resource manager, offering him opportunity to engage in training, supervision, staff development, and some counseling, seemed to build on his education and experience in business yet offer him a more rewarding role. After enrolling in some courses in that field, he was able to persuade his employer to modify some of his responsibilities so that he could gradually assume a more people-oriented role in his present company. He also became involved in volunteer work, helping people with AIDS, and took a drawing course as other ways of meeting his needs. In addition, exploration of his sense of identity led him to join a peer support group for gay men. However, in letting go of the traditionally masculine occupational roles that had been prescribed for him and choosing roles that were more reflective of his compassionate and creative nature, Fred already was making strides in becoming the person he wanted to be.

Neither Fred nor Anita made complete changes in their careers, and this is common with adults in midlife who have extensive training and experience as well as commitments that make change difficult. However, research has found that choosing the right niche in an occupational specialty can make a considerable difference in career development and satisfaction (Meir, 1988).

NINE

Later Adulthood

Years of Adapting and Extending

Older Adults—A Growing
Segment of the Population

For many years, two images of older adults have coexisted in the minds of most Americans. In one image, older people look forward eagerly to retirement when they will be free to fulfill the dreams they have neglected throughout their lives—to travel, engage in hobbies, and spend more time with their families. However, in a contrasting image, older people are no longer able to earn a living; they have been abandoned by their children and are forced to live and die in poverty, illness, and unhappiness. People seem able to maintain these conflicting images by assuming that they will eventually move into the role of satisfied retired person, whereas those who have been less provident or less fortunate than they will wind up in the most undesirable of the homes for the aged. However, neither of these extreme images represents the lifestyles of most older people.

Perhaps because the prospects of aging and eventual death are so frightening, many people avoid taking a realistic look at older adults and their needs and lifestyles. In the past 25 years, however, many changes in attitudes, resources, and media treatment of older people have helped both the old and the not yet old take a clearer look at older people and recognize that most are characterized by neither an idyllic retirement nor a long abandonment. For most, the later years are a continuation of the process of development with the degree and direction of change being influenced by a combination of individual and social factors.

One of the reasons for the increased attention being paid to older people is their growing visibility. The declining birth rate and the lengthening life span are increasing both the number and percentage of older Americans in the population. In 1900, only 4% of the U.S. population was 65 or older (Kalish, 1975). In 1990, there were approximately 30 million people, aged 65 and older, in the United States, composing approximately 12% of the population. Over the next 40 years, as the children of the baby boom years (1946-1964) move into their later years, the population of people over 65 is predicted to increase by 105%; it is now the fastest growing segment of the population (Horton & Engels, 1992).

Attention has also been drawn to older people by their own increasing willingness to speak out on their own behalf and make their needs known. The American Association for Retired People (AARP) has approximately 27 million members over the age of 50 and is a powerful source of resources, information, and influence for older people (Horton & Engels, 1992). Films such as *On Golden Pond* and television programs such as *The Golden Girls* as well as documentary programs on older people reduce some of the fear and denial around aging and help us see later life as one more stage in development with both benefits and challenges.

Most people over the age of 65 are reasonably healthy and self-sufficient and have close ties with family and other support systems. Of people over 65, 85% are able to care for themselves without assistance, although most do have one or more chronic medical problems (Smyer, 1984). Of older people, 75% live within 30 minutes' drive of one of their children so that help and support is available if needed, but only 9% live with family members others than spouses. Only 15% of those over 65 suffer serious mental impairment (Tavris, 1989), and only 5% of people in this age group are in institutions (Smyer, 1984).

In 1850, life expectancy was about 40 years; in 1900, approximately 47 years; and in 1950, approximately 68 years. Life expectancy for people born today is approximately 75 years, and people who now are 65 can expect to live another 17 years (Cahill & Salomone, 1987). As life expectancy has increased, so has the difference between the life spans of men and women, with women living, on the average, approximately 8 years longer than men. Among those over 65, there are 148 women to every 100 men; 52% of women aged 65 and older have been widowed, and

70% of those over 75 have been widowed (Glass & Grant, 1983). A large segment of the older population, then, consists of single, widowed, or divorced women. Their special needs should be considered by anyone providing counseling to older people.

Rights of Older People

Many programs and research studies and much legislation to assist older people have been put forth in the past 30 years. Workers over 40 are protected from employment discrimination by the Age Discrimination in Employment Act and other legislation. The mandatory retirement age has been increased from 65 to 70 and has been eliminated entirely for some occupations (Horton & Engels, 1992).

In 1961, the first White House Conference on Aging was held. There, the following Senior Citizen's Charter was adopted (Sinick, 1977):

Each senior citizen, regardless of race, color or creed, is entitled to the right to the following:

1. to be useful
2. to obtain employment based on merit
3. to freedom from want in old age
4. to a fair share of the community's recreational, educational, and medical resources
5. to obtain decent housing suited to the needs of the later years
6. to the moral and financial support of one's family so far as is consistent with the best interest of the family
7. to live independently as one chooses
8. to live and die with dignity
9. to have access to all available knowledge on how to improve the later years of life

Counselors working with older people should help them understand and enhance their own development, so that they can make choices and plans for the future that will ensure their access to these rights and maintain their health and satisfaction with life as much as possible.

Emotional Development in the Later Years

For purposes of this chapter, the later adult years will be defined as the years from 50 onward. Because the focus on this book is career development, emphasis will be placed on the changes taking place during the 50s and 60s, the years when, for most, final career changes are made, retirement planning is done, and full-time paid employment is left behind for the pleasures and challenges of the retirement years.

Nearly all people will have to make some major adjustments during these years. Most will retire, whether or not their place of employment has a mandatory retirement age. Many will have to cope with the death of a spouse and the departure of the last child from the home. Changes in appearance, capacity, and interests will also call for adjustment. Generally, successful adjustment will require extending: reaching out to find new rewards, interests, and activities to replace those that were given up as well as reaching into the self to find the resources, self-confidence, and self-awareness to cope with the transitions of the later years.

Stages of Development

Wortley and Amatea (1982) divided the later years into three stages: stabilization (between 50 and 60), late maturity and retirement (between 60 and 70), and dealing with life review and termination issues (beyond the age of 70). Characteristic changes and transitions occur during each stage with respect to the self, family, and relationships.

During the *stabilization* stage, people typically see a shrinking of the nuclear family as children leave home to pursue their own careers and families. Authority over adult children is relinquished as new, more egalitarian relationships are established with them. New family members enter with the marriages of the children, and relationships need to be formed with in-laws and grandchildren. The couple relationship becomes more important for most, as it was before the children were born. People may delight in the time to rediscover the spouse, or marital problems may surface that were kept out of focus by the busy years of child rearing. Role reversals with parents become increasingly common as the adults in their 50s take on responsibility for parents in their 70s and beyond. Internally, a sense of vulnerability seems to grow as people marshall their energies and support systems, often to make a final push forward in their careers as they near retirement.

Levinson (1986) subdivided the decade of the 50s into the age-50 transition (age 50-55), a time for modifying and improving the structure of one's life, and age 55 to 60, the culminating life structure for middle adulthood. He termed age 60 to 65 the late adult transition, a time for both separation and linking the pre- and post-retirement experiences.

During the decade of the 60s, emphasis is placed on developing and adjusting to retirement. Most people in this age group will have adequate physical capacities to continue energetic, rewarding, and valuable lives (Levinson, 1986). Their last years in the workforce may bring them their greatest sense of responsibility, competence, and seniority. Most will have to cope with the deaths of parents, and many will be widowed during these years. However, freedom from child care, from occupational responsibilities, and, for some, from financial pressure, can provide new opportunities. Often, husband and wife have different goals for this time of life, and compromise must be reached. Friends and family may grow in importance with the loss of socialization opportunities at work. Leisure activities may grow and expand as well. A revised sense of identity may be established, especially for those who derived most of their sense of self from their careers.

These changes continue into the years beyond the age of 70. However, increasingly, people must cope with physical changes and losses. People also may strive to make sense of their lives and clarify its meaning as they move toward the end of their lives.

Integrity Versus Despair

Erikson (1963) labeled the crisis of the later adult years integrity versus despair. According to Erikson, older people whose development has been positive will be able to accept the course of their lives and perceive them as satisfying and meaningful. They will not fear death. They will have feelings of comradeship and love toward other people. They will be able to redirect their energies into new roles and endeavors. According to Gould (1978), they will have achieved true maturity when the earlier issues of childhood and adulthood have been negotiated and they feel competent and successful.

On the other hand, people who are not able to resolve this crisis successfully will feel discouraged and fearful during the later years. They will probably be troubled by regrets and guilt and will not be able to draw much strength from others or from their own endeavors. Depression, the most common mental health problem of these years, increases in prevalence and, often, substance abuse, typically of alcohol or prescription medication, is used as a dysfunctional way of coping with unhappiness (Smyer, 1984).

Gender Differences in Development

Some differences have been found between the emotional development of men and that of women during the later years. Typically, both men and women have coped with the fear of death that surfaced in midlife but also have an increasing realization that life is limited. This can lead to increased stock taking and redefinition of goals. Somehow, women seem to have an easier time of this than do men. This may be because, traditionally, men have been work focused and have therefore had the greater difficulty dealing with the loss of employment during the retirement years, whereas women have been family oriented and have experienced their most significant adjustment in response to changes in their roles as parents during the middle adult years. Retirement may find women appreciating the growth in leisure time that will enable them to put more energy into already established interests, such as grandchildren, homemaking, and volunteer work. However, growing numbers of men and women are abandoning their traditional roles. This will probably be accompanied by increasing numbers of career-oriented women who grieve the loss of employment and family-oriented men who struggle to cope with the children leaving home.

Differences in development begun in midlife continue, with women focusing more on experiences and men focusing more on relationships. With the children grown and the parents aging, men may have more difficulty meeting their shifting needs than do women, who may easily involve themselves in volunteer work, school, or even new occupations.

Adjustment and Satisfaction

For most older people of both genders, adjustment, satisfaction, and self-esteem increase during the later years. This trend is especially likely for those people who already have established a stable and satisfying lifestyle as they enter the later years. Factors such as health, career, marriage, and finances have all been found to be more important in determining adjustment in the later years than is chronological age (Neugarten, 1973). Women's development during these years seems to be more dependent on externals than is men's. The nature of older women's interests and activities are often determined by the circumstances of their children, their marital relationships, and their responsibilities to their parents.

However, aging and its accompanying physical changes can have an impact on self-esteem, at least in part because of society's emphasis on youth. In addition, anxiety and apprehension about the unknown also seem to increase in the later years, and people tend to become less active for both physical and emotional reasons. Common issues of concern for this age group include dealing with age bias at work or school, planning for retirement, dealing with changes in the the spouse's role, relocation, dealing with chronic and life-threatening illness, sexuality, aging parents, late-life career changes, isolation, and bereavement. These concerns are particularly likely to be difficult if they occur "off time" and without time for preparation rather than "on time" and with warning (Latack, 1989). For example, the woman who is widowed at the age of 68 after her husband's long illness is likely to cope more successfully with the event than the woman of 52 whose husband dies in an accident.

For most older people, passage through the later years will parallel their earlier development. Those people who were able to negotiate the earlier stages with success and satisfaction will probably have little difficulty adjusting to the later years. They will have established ways of coping and developed inner strengths and resources that are still with them. However, for those people who have not been able to achieve rewarding lifestyles or satisfactory self-esteem, the later years are likely to be difficult ones. The distractions of work, children, and spouse may no longer be present, making it hard for them to deal with the changes of these years by denial or distraction.

Developmental Tasks of the Later Years

The following developmental tasks of later adulthood are adapted from Havighurst (1972), Erikson (1963), and others:

1. establishing a sense of pride, integrity, and individuality in relation to one's work and family
2. developing new activities and expanding on old ones to replace those that must be put aside
3. having a sense of meaning and coherence about one's life and being able to reflect on it without guilt or regret
4. coping positively with changes in physical strength and health
5. establishing clear ties to one's age group
6. strengthening the quality of the couple relationship but maintaining independence and separateness
7. adopting and adapting social roles in a flexible way

8. establishing satisfactory physical living arrangements and a satisfactory quality of life
9. coping effectively with additions to and losses from the family
10. moving toward a goal, no matter what one's age

Social and Interpersonal Changes During the Later Adult Years

Lowenthal and Haven (1968) found that for older people, the maintenance of a stable intimate relationship was closely associated with good mental health and high morale. However, maintenance of such a relationship is difficult for many in this age group. Some older people suffer from their own ageism, and they shun contact with their peers, viewing them as older than they are and having little to offer. Perhaps contact with their peers reminds them of their own advancing age, so they avoid contact with others their own age. This is unfortunate because it occurs at a time when people are losing many things—employment, youthful appearance, daily contact with children, physical strength—and friendship could serve as an important source of support and compensation. Some older people seek out communities or buildings developed especially for older people to ensure social contact with their peers. However, many cannot afford such living arrangements, whereas others do not want to leave the security of their familiar neighborhoods and may reject the concept of living exclusively with their age-mates.

Most older people do maintain positive relationships with their adult children. Although most older people maintain their own households rather than moving in with their children, a far more common pattern 50 or more years ago, most older people have regular and frequent contact with family members. For many older people, then, their children can provide a significant resource. Typically, children of people in this age group are concerned about and involved with their parents but are also occupied with their own careers and family responsibilities. As a result, they may have less time to spend with their parents than the parents would like.

Widowhood

Many in this age group have been widowed, and increasing numbers of older people are now living alone. The death of the spouse is perhaps the most difficult transition of the later years. Because of the growing disparity between men's and women's life spans and the tendency for women to marry men several years older than they, the average woman now experiences more than 10 years of widowhood. More than half of all women over the age of 65 have been widowed, whereas nearly three quarters of the men in this age group are married (Glass & Grant, 1983). Men and women, then, should be helped to prepare for and deal with different lifestyles in the later years.

Most older people are able to handle the death of a spouse fairly well when it occurs after the surviving spouse is older than 65. Although the bereavement does lead to some loss of life satisfaction, especially for men, it usually does not precipitate social withdrawal or deterioration. A sort of rehearsal for widowhood seems to occur for many older women in which they imagine and prepare themselves emotionally for that event. This seems to help them cope with widowhood, should it occur (Kalish, 1975).

However, women who are widowed at a younger age tend to have more difficulty dealing with that transition. They have not prepared for it emotionally as older women have. They have fewer peers who have gone through similar experiences. In addition, although many of these women perceive themselves as young enough to remarry and establish a new lifestyle, many fewer unmarried men than unmarried women are available in this age group. Efforts to form another marriage, then, may lead only to disappointment for these women.

R. G. Carey (1977) found that about 25% of the widows and widowers he studied were significantly depressed more than a year after the bereavement. Widowers were better adjusted than were widows and were much more likely to have remarried. Adjustment was positively related to age, income, education, and having at least 2 weeks warning of the bereavement. Those who lived alone or with dependent children were better adjusted than were those who lived with independent children, perhaps because they had more sense of purpose. Surprisingly, marital happiness was not found to be related to ability to cope with the bereavement. Adjustment, then, was facilitated by having some time to anticipate widowhood and having resources to fall back on so that the bereaved person did not have to depend excessively on others.

Marital Relationships
During the Later Years

For those who are still married during the later years, the marital relationship often assumes greater importance as work-related interests diminish in importance. Husbands and wives tend to seek common interests and develop an increased focus on each other (Lowenthal, Thurnher, Chiriboga, & associates, 1975). However, the roles of the husband and the wife continue to change. The husband, typically the older and first to retire, may spend more time at home. He may try to become more involved with household duties and seek to spend more time with his wife. The woman, on the other hand, may resent her husband's constant presence in the home and may feel that he interferes with the more independent lifestyle she has been developing since the children left home. In addition, the woman may still be employed, and this reversal of traditional roles may provoke resentment and discomfort in both men and women during the later years. Sexual difficulties are common during these years, and divorce, although less common than at younger ages, is increasing among older couples. Just because a marriage has endured many years does not mean it is sound, and many people have difficulty reestablishing a close couple relationship after the children have left home. Marital conflict and dissatisfaction are common among people coping with the transitions of the later years, and family counseling may be indicated.

Leisure Activities

Improving and increasing leisure activities is one approach to counteract the common decrease in social interaction that occurs among older people. This is particularly important for people who are retiring from a job that provided their primary arena for socialization. Bloland and Edwards (1981) suggest asking the following questions to help older people establish leisure goals: What needs can leisure fulfill? What activities are most likely to meet those needs? Which of those can be provided through leisure and which through employment? Where can those needs conveniently be filled? Providing people with an array of leisure options such as the following may help them to identify activities of interest:

1. sports—health and fitness activities, team sports, adventure, outdoor
2. games—strategy, chance
3. arts—dance, music, painting, theater, as participant or observer
4. crafts—needlework, model building, collecting, food preparation, antiquing
5. social—volunteer work, religious activities, peer support groups, common interest clubs

6. nature—bird-watching, gardening, hiking
7. working leisure—computers, politics
8. knowledge acquisition—reading, research
9. travel

Although a list such as this may prompt some useful discussion of interests, the best source of information on people's interests is their life experiences. Most people do not make radical changes in interests and activities during the later years but, rather, build on and modify existing interests. Someone who has been very invested in work and who has developed few leisure activities, then, may have particular difficulty maintaining a rewarding level of activity and social interaction after retirement.

Theories of Coping With Aging

For many years, *disengagement* was viewed as both the typical and most appropriate way for older people to cope with advancing age. Disengagement theory holds that both society and the aging person withdraw from each other to establish a new equilibrium. The lifestyle of the older person, according to this theory, consists of decreased social interaction and activity and increased freedom from role obligations (Havighurst, Neugarten, & Tobin, 1968). The early stages of this period were believed to be characterized by anxiety, depression, and loss of energy and self-esteem, whereas the later stages reflected a movement toward acceptance, tranquility, and a greater sense of self-worth. Over the last 25 years, this theory has become increasingly controversial. Its many opponents view it as age biased and not reflective of modern patterns of aging (Fry, 1992).

Several other theories have been advanced to explain adaptation to the later years. One that is even more negative than the disengagement theory is *abandonment*, in which people anticipate inevitable social isolation and loss of status. Poor health, decreased income, widowhood, and unemployment all lead to loneliness, depression, and dissatisfaction with life. In this model, older people lead a sort of segregated life, having little contact with the mainstream. Probably, this model does describe the aging process for a small percentage of unfortunate people with limited resources. However, it does not seem widely applicable.

Many theorists today believe that an *activity theory* best characterizes the later years. Activity theory views older people as having the same social and psychological needs as adults in the middle years; the only major changes are thought to be the inevitable physical ones. According to activity theory, then, older people will usually not be contented with withdrawal and reduction of social contacts and activities. Rather, they will seek to maintain their previous levels of involvement and activity by finding suitable substitutes. Research has indicated a strong relationship between activity level and life satisfaction. Ideally, the activities chosen will be stimulating, meaningful, social, instrumental, and expressive. In light of the apparent difficulty people have in developing entirely new interests in the postretirement years, adults moving into the later years are probably wise to begin early to expand and develop their non-work-related interests and activities.

Although the activity model seems most characteristic of modern older people, it may not be realistic for all and may put inappropriate pressure on people who have never had high levels of activity and initiative. These people may prefer a pattern of disengagement, perhaps because it continues an earlier pattern of noninvolvement or because they are relieved to finally be free of pressures and responsibilities.

Several other theories provide further understanding of the later years. *Role theory* postulates that successful aging is characterized by adaptation to role change and assumption of new, more appropriate roles. This is closely related to *developmental theory*, which views life as a predictable sequence of stages and associated roles (Schlossberg, 1992). People who are not able to move smoothly from one role or stage to another are likely to feel some depression and loss of morale. This theory seems particularly important in understanding people in professional positions. Approximately three quarters of white-collar workers express a desire to remain employed well into their later years rather than retire (Fry, 1992). If these people do retire, they may need considerable help in finding roles that are as rewarding to them as their occupations were.

Continuity or life span theory suggests that change is best negotiated by linking the present to the past and building on previous patterns and strengths. Like activity theory, this approach holds that psychological and social needs change little with age and, for most people, continuity of personality, values, wants, and resources into the later years will be evident.

Liberation theories take another positive perspective on the aging process. They remind us that the later years can bring a sense of economic, social, and psychological liberation as people achieve freedom from work, stress, and prior failures.

Finally, the *socioenvironmental* or *cultural theory* emphasizes the importance of viewing people in context. Usually, a dynamic interaction is present between individual and social resources and, whatever theory seems most relevant, a holistic picture should be obtained of each person. People in this mature and experienced population tend to be very heterogeneous, and successful aging seems to be linked to a good person-environment fit.

Transitions or life events must also be taken into account when seeking to understand patterns of the later years. Life events seem to be more important than age in determining lifestyle. For example, couples in their 60s who are dealing with married children and grandchildren are likely to have different needs than couples of the same age who are still coping with young adult children at home. Similarly, the woman who is widowed at 55 may have more in common with the woman who is widowed 10 or 15 years later than she does with her married contemporaries (Schlossberg, 1992).

All of these theories describe the aging of some people more than they do others, and no universal theory of aging exists that captures the later years for everyone. However, for all people, aging seems to involve both continuity and change, both individual and societal variables, both events and ages, and both benefits and losses.

Lifestyles in the Later Years

Older people have also been described by lifestyle as well as by developmental theories. The following lifestyles identify patterns of the later years:

1. family/spouse centered
2. group centered—focus on clubs, religious organizations, politics
3. leisure/hobby focused
4. work centered
5. uncentered—tend to have some important social and family contact spread through many arenas (e.g., children, group member, guest)
6. physically unwell/disengaged

In a 40-year longitudinal study, Maas and Kuypers (1975) found that most older people were functioning quite well. Lifestyle seemed related to gender, with men more likely to be involved with family and hobbies and women more focused on work, groups, spouses, or a wide range of social activities. Continuity of personality was more important for women than it was for men. Women seemed to be coping both with more stress and more opportunity for change than were the men. Interestingly enough, lifestyles of men and women married to each other seemed to have developed independently, and divergent lifestyles often were observed in the same family.

Clearly, many paths are available for living out one's later years. Variables important to satisfactory adjustment during these years include acceptance of the aging process, the ability to accept responsibility for one's life and develop goals that are compatible with previous lifestyle and present needs, and an optimistic attitude. Whether older people feel a sense of completion about their lives and now are ready for a rest or whether they have a continuing need for striving and activity, they can experience happiness and satisfaction as long as the drive and ability to organize a lifestyle that meets those needs is present.

Career Development
During the Later Years

Early research on career development during the later years seemed to draw most heavily on the disengagement theory of aging and viewed the later years of the work life as a process of narrowing and withdrawing. These years were described as consisting of two stages. Jordaan (1974), drawing on Super's research, divided this period into the maintenance stage (mid-40s to retirement) and the decline (retirement on).

Jordaan viewed the maintenance years as a period of trying to preserve status and gains accomplished during the earlier years. For most in the 45 to 65 age group, family and community roles have been established. Workers were assumed to have done their best work by their 40s and to be stabilizing and solidifying earlier gains after the age of 45 rather than breaking new ground. The working years beyond midlife commonly represent the period of highest earnings and the greatest comfort. The upheaval of the earlier years has passed, and this can be a period of increasing inner growth and maximum productivity. However, the maintenance years are not always placid. Super (1957b) described those years as a time of "preserving or being nagged by the self-concept" (p. 147). People may be troubled by their perceptions that they have failed to realize their potential or to accomplish earlier goals and may feel that now it is too late for them to live up to their ideals. Daydreaming, unrest, discouragement, and loneliness may ensue.

According to Super's early writings, the decline stage begins with the preretirement years and continues through the rest of life. Super believed that this stage included three substages: deceleration, retirement planning, and retirement living. Successful adjustment typically involved the establishment of alternate satisfactions and comfortable contemplation of a life that has been productive and rewarding. New strengths emerge, new ties are formed, and an altered but equally rewarding lifestyle is established.

Super's (1982) more recent writing presents a somewhat different picture of the career development process. Super described career development over the life span as a life career rainbow, encompassing nine major life career roles: child, student, leisurite, citizen, worker, pensioner, spouse, homemaker, and parent. The relative importance of these roles changes over the life span, with homemaker, spouse, pensioner, citizen, leisurite, and, possibly, student being the prominent roles of the later years. The salience of each role for a particular person depends on both personal determinants (awareness, attitudes, interests, needs-values, achievement, general and specific aptitudes, and biological heritage) and situational determinants (social structure, historical change, socioeconomic organization and conditions, employment practices, school, community, and family). The life career rainbow better emphasizes both the continuity and the opportunities of the later years than do Super's earlier writings.

Career Satisfaction During the Later Years

During what Super called the maintenance years, career satisfaction and success tend to parallel each other, usually being fairly high at the outset but declining through this stage as people approach retirement (J. V. Miller, 1982). Several reasons have been advanced for this decrease in work-related satisfaction. Most of people's advancement and professional development are behind them by the time they are in their 50s. In part, this is due to the age bias of employers who avoid giving new opportunities to older workers. Attitudinal changes in older workers, themselves, also contribute to this pattern. Flexibility, variety, and advancement become less important, whereas job security and stability become more important values (Krausz, 1982). Frequent job changes are rare among older workers and typical workers, aged 65 and older, report at least 20 years tenure in their present positions, with 20% reporting 40 or more years in the same job (M. Carey, 1990).

As prospects for advancement and recognition decline for older workers, they may feel frustrated, trapped, and limited. They still want to progress and develop but find fewer avenues open to them. Particularly at lower income and employment levels, many people feel that their lives are becoming dull and routinized. For some people, this sense of discouragement will precipitate an early retirement, whereas for others, it will lead to a renewed commitment to their careers. Both of these trends are evident in labor force patterns.

Labor Force Patterns
of Older Workers

The length of the working life has increased significantly for both men and women. In 1900, the average man was employed for 31 years; in 1968, he worked for 42 years (Neugarten & Moore, 1968). For some people, the elimination of mandatory retirement because of age in most positions has extended the work life even further. Increases in the age at which people become eligible for Social Security benefits are another factor in the growing movement to extend the work life (Cahill & Salomone, 1987). The number of workers over 40 is expected to show the largest expansion during the 1990s, with those in the 48- to 53-year-old age group increasing by 67% (Offermann & Gowing, 1990). A growing need for well-trained and qualified workers should make it easier for older people to remain in or to reenter the workforce (Olney, 1988).

However, competing forces are at work. Many government, military, and other positions allow retirement after 20 or 25 years, enabling people to leave the workforce or make a career shift in midlife. Increasing numbers of people are becoming eligible for retirement in their 50s (Fretz & Merikangas, 1992). Age bias, as well as increasing competition for upper-level positions by older workers may also contribute to a wish to leave the workforce. In addition, the lengthened working life, coupled with rapid technological progress, has led to the obsolescence of many areas of knowledge and types of work, forcing many older workers out of jobs. Job stress seems to be another factor leading to early retirement. Despite increases in the life span and improvements in health, the percentage of people between the ages of 55 and 65 in the labor force has fallen from over 90% in the 1960s to 75% in the 1980s (Offermann & Gowing, 1990).

Unemployment in the Later Years

The situation of the unemployed older worker is not an easy one. Workers over 45 are disproportionately represented among the long-term unemployed. Finding a new position seems to be more difficult for the older person than for the adult in midlife. Unemployment, during these years, can cause considerable anxiety, loss of self-esteem, and loss of self-confidence for people who have invested many years in the workforce. These feelings can add to their difficulty in finding new positions. Many unemployed older workers become discouraged and leave the labor force, perhaps retiring at a time when they are neither financially nor emotionally prepared for that step.

Unemployment in the later years may be especially difficult for people at lower socioeconomic levels. They tend to assign older labels to life events than do middle-class workers and perceive middle age as beginning at the age of 35, whereas middle-class workers perceive it as beginning at age 55 (Troll & Nowak, 1976). Workers who are less well educated and more poorly paid, then, may be their own worst enemies in perceiving themselves as too old to begin a new endeavor at a time when their capacities are still undiminished.

Options for Older Workers

Competing forces that both promote and discourage early departure from the workforce seem to have led to the development of new and expanded options for older workers. Changes of position as well as second and third occupations are on the increase among older workers. Self-employment and part-time employment in fields that are less competitive than their former positions are common choices for older people. Flexible employment options, such as job sharing, flextime, alternative work sites (home, satellite office), and part-time and temporary work, are also helpful to older people who want to remain in the workforce but not at their former level. Nearly half of all employers now use part-time workers (Horton & Engels, 1992).

Although many workers do want to scale down their investment in the labor force and most are less willing to retrain or relocate than are younger workers, many people in their later years do seek to prepare for and enter fields that are even more demanding than their earlier occupations (Offermann & Gowing, 1990). This is reflected by the increasing number of older people taking both credit and noncredit courses (Glass & Grant, 1983). Many of these people have not been in an academic environment for 20 years or more, but a great belief in their own self-worth and potential seems to motivate them to return to school (Gilkison & Drummond, 1988). A survey of students between the ages of 50 and 68 indicated that 85% were attending school part-time and 50% were still employed full-time. Attitudes toward returning to school included the following strongly endorsed statements: enjoying of new things, believing that they could master skills necessary for their program, enjoying their classes, feeling comfortable in small-group situations in class, and having family support for their academic goals. Inhibiting factors to continuing their education included high test anxiety and time pressure. Many schools are offering free tuition as well as special programs for older students that provide mutual benefits; schools keep their classrooms full, and older people are helped to embark on new and potentially rewarding ventures.

Growth has also been evident in programs to help older people make appropriate job and occupational changes. Title V of the Older Americans Act, also known as the Senior Community Service Employment Program, is administered by AARP under the auspices of the U.S. Department of Labor. This program provides funding to encourage older people to work in community service agencies, especially those focusing on the needs of older people. AARP also offers a National Older Workers Information System and a structured career development program, AARPWORKS, providing eight 3-hour workshops that include self-assessment, identification of options and preferences, career information, and development of job-finding skills (Horton & Engels, 1992). Participants in that program have an average age of 57.

Some employers are targeting older workers, recognizing that training of older workers is to be cost-effective because they are likely to remain on the job longer than a younger worker (Horton & Engels, 1992). An example of such a program is McDonald's McMasters training program for people over 55. Other employers have job banks of retired workers who want to work part-time or on special projects where their experience can be valuable.

Despite considerable growth in opportunities for older people and awareness of their many strengths, obstacles to their successful continuation in the workforce continue to be present. Many older workers, as well as employers, have negative and inaccurate attitudes toward older workers that can act as a sort of self-fulfilling prophecy in which some older people unconsciously limit themselves because of their self-doubts. Older women who reenter the workforce in midlife often take menial positions with no opportunity for advancement because of their lack of training and experience. Most are earning less than men with comparable positions or skills. However, many of these women have recently been widowed or divorced and have little time for retraining; they must take whatever jobs they can find to support themselves.

Capabilities of Older People

Many older people have beliefs that contribute to the difficulty they encounter in their job searches or career changes. They think, as do many employers, that they cannot perform as well as younger workers and deserve to be rejected. Usually, these beliefs are erroneous. Counselors can help to eliminate some of these misconceptions by making people aware of findings on the performance and abilities of mature workers.

Hiring older workers has not been found to increase employer costs significantly (Sinick, 1977). Any additional pension costs are more than offset by the positive qualities of the older worker. The following have been found to be favorable attributes of the older workers:

1. stability
2. steady work habits
3. less waste of time
4. greater reliability
5. less absenteeism
6. responsibility and loyalty
7. serious attitude toward job
8. less supervision required
9. less distraction by outside interests
10. greater inclination to stay on job

Clearly, the positive work habits and attitudes of the mature worker are very desirable in most positions. Especially in light of the declining growth rate of young workers, the experience, dedication, and stability of older workers can make an invaluable and much needed contribution to the workforce (Horton & Engels, 1992).

Probably, it is easier for most employers to accept the motivational strengths of older workers than it is for them to believe that the skills of those workers show little decline. However, the belief that employees will become forgetful, slow, and less competent in their 50s and 60s is just as erroneous as the belief that older workers will have a high rate of absenteeism.

People experience only a 10% decline in physical strength between the ages of 30 and 60 (Troll, 1975). Although some measurable decrement in speed and ability to do heavy labor is observed in most older workers, few jobs today are so demanding and strenuous that their execution is significantly affected by this change (Offermann & Gowing, 1990). Intellectual ability is even better maintained than physical ability. Longitudinal studies indicate that measured intelligence remains stable or increases slightly up until the period shortly before death when it drops significantly. Although older people commonly experience some mild impairment of short-term memory and spatial reasoning, most people have enough resources to compensate for those changes. Most other abilities, including verbal ability, information, comprehension, judgment, creativity, and learning ability, remain fairly constant throughout the later years (Meier & Kerr, 1976).

Even at age 55, the training of older workers is viable and economically sound. Although these workers may start out more gradually and have more initial difficulty handling new stimuli, older workers soon catch up with younger workers. Although younger workers have more working years ahead, older workers who are retrained are more likely to remain at the place of employment where they were trained, thereby justifying the expense of their retraining.

Most older people seem to be realistic in their assessment of their own health and capabilities. They usually know what they can and cannot do and, generally, will not undertake tasks that they do not have the ability to perform. They are also sufficiently flexible to accommodate to and compensate for most of the gradual changes that do occur during the later years. Findings on physical and intellectual changes during the later years, then, support the conclusion that people can and do perform at a consistently high level throughout life and can be expected to continue to learn and develop until very old age. In light of this, it is indeed unfortunate that many employers continue to discriminate against the older worker and persist in using hiring procedures, such as tests normed on younger respondents, that may contribute to age bias in hiring.

Retirement

For nearly all older people, retirement is a significant transition that will effect marked changes. In recent years, retirement age has increasingly become a matter of choice. Nationwide recognition of the right of older people to work as long as they wished and were able to came with the passage of legislation that eliminated compulsory retirement for federal employees as of September 30, 1978. Subsequent legislation has extended this benefit to those outside of the federal system. It might be inferred from this legislation that most older people want to continue working beyond the age of 65. However, recent trends suggest that only a minority want to continue full-time employment beyond the age of 65. Most prefer to retire before the customary age, and increasing numbers of people are retiring early. A combination of an increased life expectancy and an earlier retirement has lengthened the time that people will spend as retirees. Most people will spend at least 14 years or 20% of their lives in retirement (Fretz & Merikangas, 1992). This is a dramatic change; in 1900, people spent only an average of 2% of their lives in retirement. Retirement no longer is a brief interval between lifelong tenure in a job and death. It is now one of several major changes and adjustments likely to be made by the increasingly mobile modern worker.

Retirement is a process rather than an event. For some, that process is a long and conscious one. For others, who have avoided thinking about retirement, that event may almost come as a surprise. Most people begin thinking about their retirement when they are in their 40s and may spend as many as 25 years anticipating retirement, even though their effective planning may be limited. Initially, most people have positive feelings toward the prospect of retirement, but their feelings tend to become increasingly negative as the event draws closer (Fretz & Merikangas, 1992).

Employers are becoming more aware of the need for preretirement planning, and there is slow growth in work site programs to help people through this stage. Approximately 30% to 45% of all industries offer preretirement programs (Career Planning & Adult Development Network, 1990), although fewer than 10% of older people participate in retirement planning programs (Kragie, Gerstein, & Lichtman, 1989). Aside from some attention to finances, most people do not systematically plan for retirement (Fretz & Merikangas, 1992). This is unfortunate because "recent research has suggested that individuals who plan for retirement are more successful in coping with the transition than those who fail to plan" (Liptak, 1990, p. 360).

Anxiety and apprehension about an impending retirement are most common among people who have a low sense of self-efficacy, a low degree of planfulness, and concerns about finances or health (Fretz, Kluge, Ossana, Jones, & Merikangas, 1989). People with strong commitments to their jobs whose identities are closely linked to their work also have difficulty planning for retirement and developing confidence in their ability to achieve a rewarding retirement. Typically, people who are self-employed, professionals, high-level business persons, or in academic settings are far less eager to retire than are people in blue-collar and clerical positions. Generally, people in occupations that offer continued opportunity for achievement, variety, autonomy, and respons-ibility retire later than do people in positions that do not offer those advantages (Fretz & Merikangas, 1992).

Stages in the Retirement Process

Psychological variables and attitudes seem to be at least as impor-tant as finances and health in determining how people deal with the transition to retirement. Atchley (1976) postulated a seven-stage se-quence in the retirement process. The first stage is the early preretire-ment period. This occurs during early middle age when retirement seems like a remote event. People may ask themselves some general questions such as, What will it be like to retire? Can I afford to retire? What will I do with my time? Feelings toward retirement during this first stage tend to be positive.

The second stage is the near preretirement period when the process of decision making, planning, and disengagement from employment begins. Generally, this stage starts 4 to 7 years before the actual retire-ment. During this stage, most workers become at least somewhat anxious and concerned about the prospect of retirement and begin to think about it more realistically. The first and most critical decision made by most people during this stage is when to retire.

Atchley (1976) also identified five postretirement stages: honey-moon, disenchantment, reorientation, stability, and termination or death. Because most people do little preretirement planning, it is not surprising that the initial enthusiasm for retirement is short-lived and is typically replaced by some disappointment. However, most people seem to cope with this effectively, to formulate or revise goals and plans, and to move on to a stable and fairly rewarding retirement. Of people who retire, 80% report that their preretirement expectations have been fulfilled or exceeded (Fretz & Merikangas, 1992). In fact, men who retire voluntarily seem even happier than those who are still employed.

Generally, those people who derived considerable social benefit from their jobs as well as people who had been heavily invested in their jobs can find the same rewards in other areas of their lives, if they choose to retire. Retirement does not seem to contribute to a decline in health, nor does it seem to precipitate an early death, despite myths to the contrary. Although anxiety about finances is related to adjustment to retirement, as long as income is adequate, money does not seem to be a major factor in satisfaction with retirement.

Involuntary Retirement

However, retirement that is involuntary, due to factors such as the inability of employees to continue in their previous work or to locate jobs that they are able and willing to perform, is likely to be particularly difficult. Such a retirement may permit little time for planning. In addition, in American society, the work ethic and the emphasis on youth are still strong. Inability to live up to the values of this society may lead people who retire involuntarily to view themselves as failures. Depression and loss of self-esteem may result. People who retire involuntarily may be resistant to seeking new avenues of gratification, and many retirees, both voluntary and involuntary, will experience at least some temporary decline in sense of belonging, opportunity for socialization, status, sense of direction, feelings of achievement, and time structure. Some also experience a heightened sense of aging and loss, accompanied by feelings of trepidation and rootlessness. This is a time when many workers are in considerable need of assistance and support.

As with most transitions, adaptation is mediated by the perception of the transition (Schlossberg, 1981). Those people who believe they are retiring at the right time, anticipate gains from the process, have time to prepare for the transition, have a clear and realistic picture of what retirement will be like, have interests and activities to look forward to once they leave full-time employment, have a supportive environment, and a strong sense of their own self-efficacy are more likely to achieve a satisfying retirement than those who lack these attributes.

Planning for Retirement

Satisfaction with retirement depends on a great many factors. Preretirement programs and counselors working with older people should be aware of and attend to the following variables.

External variables

1. Income from present employment, pension plans, social security, savings, and other financial resources

2. Health and ability to perform work and leisure activities
3. Family ties and responsibilities
4. Geographic location, mobility, and preference
5. Financial obligations and standard of living
6. Leisure and social activities

Internal variables

1. Satisfaction with present work
2. Social and personal values
3. Availability of and ability to use support systems (e.g., family, friends, neighbors, social groups)
4. Planning and decision-making ability
5. Awareness of options
6. Self-concept and locus of control
7. Plans, goals, and aspirations
8. Flexibility and willingness to change
9. Interests
10. Perceived societal and cultural norms and expectations

For most preretirees, many possible ways to spend their retirement years are available. Although many retirees can adapt to the loss of full-time paid employment easily, most feel a need for other sources of reward or activity to compensate for what they have left behind. Some older people will continue in their jobs beyond the usual retirement age, maintaining their occupations as their primary focus. However, most will leave the jobs they held in midlife and focus more on interests that are unrelated to or that do not depend on their previous jobs. The task for preretirees is to develop their interests into activities that will be at least as rewarding as full-time employment has been; in that way, their focus can be on what they are moving toward rather than on what they are leaving behind. Vehicles for accomplishing this shift include continuing education, expanded leisure activities, part-time employment or full-time employment in a different area, self-employment, and volunteer work. All of these alternatives can both reflect past interests and abilities and develop new interests and abilities. Retirement is a time when previously suppressed creative drives can surface and finally find expression.

Part-time jobs and volunteer experiences have grown in availability in recent years, with many communities having clearinghouses for volunteer and part-time workers that can match person to opportunity. Part-time employment can be particularly helpful to older adults by serving as a transition from full-time work to full-time leisure activities and can help the retiree to feel productive and valuable.

A substantial percentage of older people return to full-time employment after retiring. For these people, a lifestyle without employment was not sufficiently rewarding. Programs that allow people to reverse their retirement and return to work, have provisions for hiring people over the age of 65, and offer job sharing and flexible schedules can be particularly useful in facilitating the transition to retirement.

Often, leisure planning is a neglected aspect of retirement planning (Liptak, 1990). Although most people make some financial preparations for retirement, careful planning of activities is often not done, and people assume that they will fish or travel or continue previous leisure activities without considering how those interests will change or expand. With only about one third of retirees engaging in paid employment, leisure becomes a major focus for people in the later years (Fretz & Merikangas, 1992). People's reactions to and abilities to use their increased leisure time will reflect lifelong patterns of interests and activities. The person whose life before retirement centered on watching television is unlikely to become an ardent golfer or a gourmet cook after retirement. Although interests and abilities can emerge during the later years, there will probably have been some earlier indication or foreshadowing of their presence.

Preretirement Programs

Preretirement planning programs can be helpful in encouraging people to take account of all aspects of the retirement process. People between the ages of 45 and 55 seem even more receptive to such programs than do older people, perhaps because they do not yet have to come to terms with the imminent reality of retirement (Kragie et al., 1989). Offering such programs to people 15 to 20 years away from retirement, then, is likely to yield a good response and give them an early start on planning for retirement. Such programs should, of course, go beyond financial planning and consider health, work and leisure, and interpersonal relationships. Spouses should be included in such programs to promote collaborative planning. Particular attention should be paid to nontraditional retirees, such as single women, who may have few models to guide them in the retirement process and may not place much emphasis on the importance of preretirement planning. Liptak (1990) suggested focusing initially on wants and fantasies that then can be translated into short-, medium-, and long-term goals. Action plans can be developed to specify what will be done when, to enable people to achieve their retirement goals. Support and encouragement, as well as realistic information and guidelines for planning, can be provided through such programs. In general, retirement seems to be most rewarding when it is a gradual and thoughtful process, when people leave employment with a sense of accomplishment and recognition, and when they consider a broad range of postretirement options and develop plans to move toward one that seems likely to be rewarding (Horton & Engels, 1992). Presently, 30% to 45% of industries have preretirement programs, and the availability of such programs is growing (Career Planning and Adult Development Network, 1990).

Fretz and Merikangas (1992) suggest the following 10 topics for a model preretirement seminar:

1. the retirement experience
2. retiring from your agency
3. social security and retirement
4. you and retirement
5. time and retirement
6. lifestyle
7. financial planning
8. spouse, family, and retirement
9. work and retirement
10. developing a retirement plan

Adjustment to Retirement

Immediately after retirement, most people experience a period when they feel relaxed and elated and have a sense of freedom and opportunity. Atchley (1976) called this the honeymoon period. However, soon the disenchantment stage sets in, signaled by feelings of disappointment and emptiness. Usually, this stage is succeeded by the reorientation stage during which people seek assistance with problems of maintenance and adjustment. Readjustment, accompanied by renewed planning and decision making, characterizes the stability stage. The final stage in Atchley's model is termination, when retirement is ended, due either to a return to full-time employment or to death.

Typically, during the period of adjustment to retirement (the disenchantment and reorientation stages), many changes and emotional difficulties arise. Self-image, social relationships, orientation, motivation, and values are all likely to be disrupted. Retirees may go through a period of depression and mourning when they are dealing with the loss of their former roles and activities and preparing to assume new ones. Feelings of anger, resentment, and fear of death are common. For many people, emotional and economic dependence increases during these years, especially in their relationships with their children. This role reversal, in which parent becomes dependent on child, can cause generational power struggles and hostility at a time when older people are most in need of support and encouragement from their families. Friends and the role of friend become increasingly important as older people seek to compensate for the social contacts lost with retirement and try to find peers with whom to share their experiences.

Reactions to retirement seem to be mediated by people's previous work experiences. Typically, feelings of loss associated with retirement are greatest for those at either end of the spectrum, for those who had been workers of either high or low status. Those who derived a great deal of their self-image and satisfaction from their work often feel a great sense of deprivation with the onset of retirement and tend to be the most dissatisfied group during the retirement years. On the other hand, people from lower socioeconomic backgrounds may lack the resources to provide themselves with a comfortable retirement.

Emotional and economic factors seem intertwined in affecting how people plan for and react to retirement. People with a low sense of self-efficacy tend to be less planful about retirement, have less social support, have less positive attitudes toward retirement, and have more difficulty letting go of the structure provided by their jobs (Fretz et al., 1989).

Despite the emotional and economic challenges presented by the retirement years, most people seem to welcome retirement and use the retirement years for meaningful and rewarding activity. This is most likely to be true of people who have demonstrated career maturity throughout their lives and who have the resources provided by good health, adequate income, and support from family and friends. Personal qualities, such as self-esteem, flexibility, a capacity for intimacy, and a sense of direction and purpose, also facilitate the retirement process. Although not all retirees find satisfaction during the retirement years, relatively few seem to be troubled by the loss of employment. Lidz (1976) found that fewer than 10% of the retired men surveyed reported unhappiness due to the absence of work in their lives. Rather, dissatisfaction during the later years was more likely to be due to economic difficulties, poor health, loss of spouse, or loss of the social contacts and activities provided by work, not loss of the work itself. Most people seem to cope fairly successfully with the changes presented by retirement, and those problems that are encountered can be reduced by preretirement planning programs and counseling.

Counseling the Older Person

Counseling with older people will probably be most effective if it is supportive and oriented toward the development of existing strengths and interests. This does not mean that counselors should never question or explore. On the contrary, many older people are still following paths mapped out by their families or their cultures and may have little awareness of their own needs and values. They may view the age of 65 as the appropriate time for retirement and so will plan to retire then, regardless of their feelings about their work, their capacities, or their interests. Counselors do need to help older people examine their motivations but should do this in such a way as to remain the person's ally and advocate.

Counseling with older people will probably focus on the following:

1. self-image and self-efficacy
2. expectations of and relationships with family and friends
3. life circumstances (e.g., finances, housing, self-care)
4. capabilities
5. leisure and occupational interests and opportunities
6. developmental history and its implications for future development
7. coping with ageism in the self and others
8. expectations and hopes for the future
9. planning
10. programs and resources

Self-Image and Self-Efficacy

Self-efficacy has been found to be an important variable in people coping with retirement. Fretz and his colleagues (1989) suggest four approaches to enhancing self-efficacy related to retirement:

1. exploring past and present performance accomplishments
2. providing role models of people dealing successfully with similar circumstances
3. verbal persuasion, social influence, encouragement
4. active involvement in preretirement planning and tasks

Counseling should enable older people to develop a greater appreciation of themselves. Activities that are rewarding and that seem likely to enhance self-esteem should be encouraged. Lack of self-confidence and feelings of worthlessness and depression may prevent older people from engaging in experiences that are likely to be gratifying and may turn people to drugs or alcohol to help them avoid dealing with the challenges of aging. Counselors can help older people develop self-esteem and, if necessary, obtain counseling for problems of mood disorders or substance abuse that, unfortunately, are quite prevalent during the later years.

Interpersonal Relationships

Most older people have family ties to provide them support, involvement, and, for some, responsibility. Nearly one third of retirees have at least one parent still alive (Fretz & Merikangas, 1992). The older years seem to have little impact on people's patterns of socialization, although they may spend somewhat more time in social activities. However, those people who had little social life before retirement may become socially isolated in the later years when the social contact of the job is no longer available. Although these people might want increased contact with others, they may be fearful of making new friends and may not have well-developed social skills. Counselors can help older people to increase their self-awareness, insight, and communication skills so that they are better able to form friendships. Group counseling, as well as peer support groups, can also help to provide needed interpersonal contact.

Loss of friends and family members to death during these years is likely to be a common focus of counseling. A crisis intervention approach can help people deal with these losses as well as with some of the other crises of the later years. This generally involves the following steps:

1. helping people to clarify and express their feelings about the present crisis
2. developing an accurate assessment of the present situation and its options and limitations

3. assessing people's resources, especially those that were useful in helping them to handle earlier crises
4. formulating plans for resolving the present crisis that draw on those resources

Although people tend to be in a state of considerable stress during a crisis, the very discomfort they are feeling serves to motivate them to make some changes. For this reason, crisis counseling can often accomplish a great deal in a relatively short period of time and can improve people's self-concepts and coping strategies at the same time.

Life Circumstances

Finances seem to receive the most attention in retirement planning. People without adequate resources to provide them a comfortable living situation may find themselves absorbed with fulfilling basic needs during the later years, whereas higher-order needs such as beauty and achievement may be ignored. Although counselors may find it more interesting to help people deal with their higher-order needs, if basic needs for food and shelter are not taken care of, retirement is not likely to be fulfilling. Counseling, then, must have a pragmatic focus at least part of the time to ensure that older people make realistic and adequate financial plans. Counselors should inform themselves about Social Security, Medicaid, Medicare, and other financial programs that are available to older people.

Continuity

Patterns of behavior and adjustment during the later years are a reflection of long-standing strengths and attitudes. Counseling with older people, then, should take a longitudinal and developmental perspective. Continuity rather than change should be emphasized. Earlier experiences of success, indications of capabilities, as well as long held interests and hopes should be emphasized and built on. This process can both increase the self-esteem and self-confidence of older people and facilitate the establishment of rewarding lifestyles during the later years. Many older people are fearful of a sudden loss of capacity through a debilitating physical or psychological illness. Heart disease, Alzheimer's disease, strokes, and cancer are probably the major concerns, especially if a family history of these disorders is present. Although the reality of such conditions cannot be denied, counselors should try to clarify any misconceptions that may be troubling their older clients. Most people do maintain most of their intellectual and physical abilities until they are quite elderly. Even if a person has already encountered difficulty meeting the demands of the job, counselors can and should look beyond the person's work in assessing strengths and interests.

Leisure and Occupational Interests

The transition to the later years and to the period of retirement can be eased if there is a clear relationship between the interests and activities of the older person before retirement and those that are pursued after retirement. For each person, an individual plan for retirement can be developed that meets needs and values, is congruent with interests and abilities, and provides gratification and self-esteem.

Some older people decide to embark on second careers or to seek new types of jobs in their later years. In addition to having many of the same needs and difficulties as other older people, this group also has some special needs and concerns that can often be ameliorated by counseling. Many older people view the world of work in gender-stereotyped terms, look askance at volunteer work because it is unpaid, or feel uncomfortable about accepting a less prestigious position or one that involves competing with younger applicants or trainees. Some older people have little understanding of the transferability of skills and may perceive themselves as suited for only the one sort of job they have held throughout their lives. Older people may need help in expanding the range of options they perceive as open to them, in examining and clearing away stereotypes, and in prompting them to engage in trial experiences.

Developmental History

Nearly everyone has a wealth of experiences and resources that can be drawn on to provide self-esteem and coping skills during the later years. One approach specifically designed to capitalize on these assets is a course for older people developed by researchers at the Andrus Gerontology Center at the University of Southern California (Malde, 1988). The goal of this program is to promote a sense of wholeness and meaning by promoting people's examination of their goals, accomplishments, failures, and regrets. The course consists of four components:

1. lectures on writing and psychological development
2. sensitizing exercises to highlight issues raised by the writing
3. development of a written autobiography, structured according to selected life themes
4. small-group discussion of the autobiographies

Counselors can borrow from and adapt this approach to meet individual needs, such as having people talk into a tape recorder rather than write and using the one-to-one counseling situation rather than the group as the context for the program. This tool seems especially useful for helping people adapt to loss, illness, and retirement.

Coping With Ageism

Younger workers, older workers, employers, and counselors are all prone to having biases against older workers (Cahill & Salmone, 1987). Age prejudice continues to be prevalent among employers despite evidence that it is unwarranted and illegal. Awareness of these negative perceptions, as well as their own misconceptions, can make older people apprehensive about reentering the workforce in later life or making a career shift during the later years. Counselors should be alert for feelings such as these and should seek to dispel misconceptions as well as help older people develop comfortable approaches to job seeking. Computerized job banks, designed to locate suitable employment for older people, have been established in many cities and can reduce some of the anxiety associated with job hunting. Options such as home study and televised courses might offer a less threatening learning environment for older people seeking continuing education or retraining. However, these approaches should be used to build confidence, not to segregate older workers.

Until recent years, older people have probably been the age group most neglected by counseling. Few have had contact with college counselors, and many were reluctant to seek counseling from community agencies or private practitioners. The pride and self-reliance of many older people, along with their unfamiliarity with the counseling process, may lead them to feel uneasy about seeking counseling. Counselors should be aware of the reluctance of many older people to become involved in a counseling relationship. Considerable time and effort may have to be devoted to the building of rapport and trust. Even then, counselors should be cautious not to invade the limits established by older clients and should be sure that the clients understand the relevance of questions that are asked or activities that are proposed.

Counselors also should look closely at their own biases and stereotypes when they are dealing with older clients. Counselors may be having difficulty adjusting to their own parents' aging and the role reversal that may accompany that process; they may unthinkingly relate to older clients as they do to their own parents. Consequently, they may allow more dependence than is necessary and may not concentrate sufficiently on helping older people develop their strengths so that they eventually will no longer need counseling.

In addition, counselors should seek to understand their clients in the context of the clients' generation. People who entered the workforce during the 1940s and 1950s may have much narrower conceptions of career opportunities than people who entered the workforce during the 1960s and 1970s when opportunities were abundant for most and when emphasis was placed on finding rewarding careers. Understanding temporal contexts may be particularly difficult for counselors when their clients are considerably older than they are. Empathy and perhaps even some research may be needed for the younger counselor to develop understanding and acceptance of the older client.

Hopes and Expectations

Minor (1992) wrote of adjustment, "The most powerful of these factors is the magnitude of the discrepancy between what the individual expects to find . . . and what the environment provides" (p. 38). Satisfaction with the later years and the process of retirement, as with the earlier years, depends on a person/environment fit. Exploration of people's hopes and expectations for retirement is an essential ingredient in helping people find satisfaction during the later years.

For most people, retirement does live up to their expectations; approximately 80% report that their preretirement expectations have been fulfilled or exceeded during their actual retirement (Fretz & Merikangas, 1992). With some counseling, that percentage can be increased even further. Although most older people do follow patterns they followed during their younger years, many do develop new areas of endeavor, and people in both groups can make the later years at least as rewarding as the earlier ones.

Planning

Careful and systematic planning is another important ingredient in achieving satisfaction during the later years. Several authors have suggested matrices that can be used to facilitate planning for the later years as well for points of transition during the earlier years (Smyer, 1984; Wadsworth & Ford, 1983). The following is an example of such a matrix:

	Goals		
	Short Term *Specific*	*Medium Term* *Broad*	*Long Term* *Very Broad*
1. Work			
2. Education/ culture			
3. Family life			
4. Social life			
5. Leisure			
6. Personal growth/ psychological			
7. Material/financial			
8. Environmental			
9. Physical/health			
10. Other			

Most people are aware of and can describe personal goals and satisfactions that guide their behavior and can make good use of organizing frameworks such as this to systematize their planning.

Resources

Growth in numbers of older people as well as growth in our awareness of the needs of this group have led to growth in resources available to them. The following is a small sampling of those programs and resources:

1. Senior Community Service Employment Program, administered by AARP under the auspices of the U.S. Department of Labor, provides funds to hire older people to work in community service agencies.
2. Programs such as Retired Senior Volunteers, Foster Grandparents, and Senior Companions, provide travel funds, meals, and small stipends to older people involved in these community service programs.
3. AARP offers programs, services, and information for people over 50, including its publication *Modern Maturity*.

4. Job clubs are available throughout the country to help older people locate part-time or full-time employment.
5. National Older Workers Information System is another useful AARP program.
6. Computer-based systems such as SIGI and DISCOVER can be useful to older people as well as to younger ones (Horton & Engels, 1992).
7. Peer counseling programs for widows and other older people can provide support and understanding.

Successful counseling for older people will develop their sense of self-efficacy, provide information on resources and opportunities, and facilitate effective planning that makes good use of these resources. Counselors can serve as the link between older people and the services designed to meet their needs by helping them to identify and express their needs and develop the confidence and skills they need to take advantage of some of these services.

Case Study of Elizabeth Hepburn

A Woman Engaged in Adapting and Extending

Most career counselors today take a life span approach to career counseling. They assume a broad and longitudinal view of development that considers personal life, leisure, and history among other factors. The importance of context and background becomes particularly clear when dealing with older people. Elizabeth Hepburn is a woman whose life was shaped by her context: messages she received from her parents, husband, and society about women's role; events in both her family of origin and her nuclear family; and her leisure and employment experiences.

Background

Elizabeth sought counseling at the Women's Re-entry Employment Center, providing career counseling primarily to women who had been out of the workforce for some time and now wanted to seek employment. At age 60, Elizabeth decided she was not satisfied with the direction of her life and thought that returning to work might make a positive change.

A short woman with curly white hair and a bright smile, Elizabeth seemed excited yet intimidated by her visit to the counseling center. This was her first experience with counseling, and she was uncertain what to expect. Sensing that Elizabeth would be more comfortable talking about the past rather than the present, her counselor began the counseling process by reviewing with Elizabeth her family background and work history.

The youngest of nine children, Elizabeth was born in a small town in Kansas in 1931. Her father also had been one of nine children. Although he had had little formal education, Elizabeth described him as intelligent and creative, a self-educated electrician. She perceived him as a hard worker, someone who knew right from wrong and who would extend himself to help friends and family. Elizabeth's mother, an only child, was a gifted musician who won a scholarship to college to study the pipe organ. However, during her first year of college, she met her husband-to-be and left college to marry and raise her own family. Although she taught music at home to supplement the family income, she was never employed outside of the home. From her family of origin, Elizabeth received strong messages about the importance of the family, the value of helping others, and women's role.

When Elizabeth was about 6 years old, one of her sisters became ill and died after a long illness. Although their mother had focused considerable attention on her ailing daughter while she was alive, she shifted her focus to Elizabeth after her sister's death. The family's involvement with the medical profession as well as the value her mother placed on the caretaking role led Elizabeth, as a child, to dream of becoming a nurse or a physician. She also shared her mother's love of music and, along with her mother, would sing and play the piano at family gatherings.

Elizabeth had been a capable though unexceptional student through elementary and high school. She reported that she enjoyed both the academic and the social aspects of school and graduated from high school with her class in 1949. Many women had been employed during World War II; by 1949, however, most had resumed traditional roles. Although Elizabeth had maintained her interest in a career in medicine, she stated that she never considered attending college; her parents could not help her financially, and she did not think she could put herself through college. However, their family physician told her about a job opening for a nurse's aide at an Oddfellows home, about 45 miles away. In an early sign of her independent spirit, Elizabeth obtained the job with the endorsement of the family physician and moved into dormitory-like accommodations for nurses employed at the home.

Chance, rather than careful planning, had played the largest role in Elizabeth's entry into the workforce, so it is not surprising that she did not enjoy her duties as a nurse's aide. What appeared glamorous and rewarding from the outside turned out to be demanding and arduous work with long and irregular hours that limited Elizabeth's social life. This was not acceptable to her because it conflicted with her primary goals of getting married, having children, and maintaining a close relationship with her family of origin.

Frequent job changes are common during the early working years, particularly for people without clear professional roles, and that characterized Elizabeth's early career development. She had brief periods of employment as an assistant to a photographer, a dental assistant, and a bookkeeper. Although she had no formal training in any of these areas, she learned quickly and had good technical and interpersonal skills.

While working as a bookkeeper for a large manufacturing company, Elizabeth met her husband, Richard, a tool-and-die maker for the same company. He came from a farming community close to the town of her birth, and the two families had known each other for many years. Elizabeth's family quickly accepted her relationship with Richard; most of their children already had married and they expected Elizabeth, now 21, to marry soon. However, Richard's parents were opposed to the marriage. Richard was an only child who had a very close relationship with his mother. His father reportedly spent most of his time either working or drinking in neighborhood bars with his friends. Their marriage was a conflicted one, and they were not comfortable with Richard's increasing independence. Although Elizabeth and Richard did marry, another sign of Elizabeth's independence, approximately 15 years would pass before Richard's mother, then a widow, would accept the marriage and welcome Elizabeth into her home.

Elizabeth was eager to start a family and became pregnant within a year of her marriage. However, chance factors prevented her from realizing her goal of having a large family. After several miscarriages, Elizabeth and Richard had a daughter, Florence, named after Elizabeth's mother. Further efforts to have more children were unsuccessful. Although Elizabeth once suggested adoption to Richard, he refused, stating that his parents would never be able to accept an adopted child. The topic was not discussed again. According to Elizabeth, "It's no use arguing when Richard has his mind made up. I could have been angry, but what good would that do?" This accepting attitude is not surprising in light of the messages Elizabeth received from family and society while she was growing up.

Elizabeth had left the workforce at the time of her first pregnancy and did not return to paid employment until Florence was in junior high school. However, Elizabeth kept busy with parenting, entertaining friends and family, and extensive volunteer work. She was active in her church and in local politics, where her talents for organizing and fundraising were appreciated. She volunteered in hospitals and at Florence's school, tutoring children with academic problems and leading the children's songs while she played the piano.

Although Elizabeth had established a rewarding lifestyle for herself, Richard was having more difficulty with his life. Always quiet and reserved, Richard gradually withdrew from social activities, increased his consumption of alcohol, and expressed dissatisfaction with himself and his work. He had failed to receive a promotion he thought he deserved and complained about being underpaid and overworked.

Elizabeth took advantage of this situation to persuade Richard to let her return to work. The added income would be useful, but Elizabeth's primary motivation was to give more meaning and focus to her life. As she said, "I really enjoy my volunteer work, but when you're paid for your work, then you know it's really important." Once again, a job presented itself when Elizabeth wanted one; a neighbor heard of her interest in returning to work and offered her a position as a bookkeeper for his company. Elizabeth would remain in that job, a part-time position, for over 15 years, while maintaining active involvement in volunteer work. Florence and Richard were always her first priority and, as she put it, "The work was fine, but it was just a job. The family, the church, my hospital work—that's where my heart was."

In their late 40s and early 50s, Elizabeth and Richard began to talk about their retirement and even established a retirement savings account. Florence was now grown and married, living in Atlanta, and Elizabeth and Richard spoke often of retiring to Florida or Georgia. They anticipated retiring in their early to mid-60s. However, when Richard and Elizabeth both were 55, the company that employed Richard went out of business. Initially, Richard spoke of finding another job, but "evidently being home suited him because he never did go back to work." Finally, Richard told Elizabeth to leave her job, too, so that they would be free to travel or relocate. Although it had been 4 years since she'd resigned from her job, no further discussion of travel or moving ensued. Richard increasingly turned to alcohol and withdrew from Elizabeth. As she put it, "We talked a lot about retirement before it happened but when we did retire, we just stopped talking."

In many respects, Elizabeth's career and personal development had not been unusual up until this time. Like most women of her era, she had a brief period of employment followed by some years at home engaged in child rearing, followed by a return to the labor force. However, her retirement was apparently not going to be the traditional decline or disengagement. Although she had to adapt to changes in her life and in herself, including a heart condition, Elizabeth recognized that her lifelong pattern of finding satisfaction through activity and helping others would not suddenly change just because she was 60 years old.

After 4 years of retirement, Elizabeth was ready to return to work. Her involvement in volunteer activities had grown during those years, and she had discovered a way to combine her interests in music, helping others, crafts, and organizing: She became Sunny the Singing Clown! She had learned to sew her own costumes, did her own makeup, and, as Sunny, visited sick children in local hospitals and medical facilities where she presented programs designed to help them cope with their medical conditions. As with many people beyond midlife, the dreams of Elizabeth's youth had come back to her, though in a somewhat different form, and her interest in medicine and music had resurfaced.

Although Elizabeth described Richard as "supportive up to a point," they had only one car that Elizabeth had not driven in many years, and finances were limited. Elizabeth could not get to the hospitals easily and did not have enough money to buy the fabrics she wanted for her costumes. She responded to this situation by saying, "Having a paying job again will give me the pin money I need and also help me feel better about my life. Retiring was a mistake. I still feel the way I did before I got married, and I'm not ready to spend all day in front of the television. I want to take life as it comes, and I don't believe in crying over spilled milk, but I want to make the most of the years I have left."

Planning the Assessment of Elizabeth Hepburn

Generally, the older and more experienced the person, the more important is his or her history and the less important is testing to the counseling process. However, once Elizabeth overcame her initial apprehensions about counseling, she became an avid client, requesting longer and more frequent sessions and extensive assessment. Counseling provided one of the few opportunities in her life in which she could focus on herself and sort out who she was and what she really wanted. Goals of counseling changed rapidly from helping Elizabeth find part-time employment to helping her understand herself, establish both personal and professional goals that were meaningful to her, and implement those goals. In addition, for Elizabeth, as for many people, personal and career concerns were intertwined and career counseling served as a vehicle for addressing lifestyle concerns as well as occupational ones.

Although establishing optimal testing conditions should always be the goal, the testing environment is particularly important for older people. A quiet, well-lit room; an appropriate room temperature; a comfortable chair and table; clear instructions; and an opportunity to ask questions are important ingredients of testing older clients. In addition, counselors should select inventories carefully, making sure that the print is large enough and that the inventory is appropriate for use with older people.

Generally, ability tests are the least useful form of assessment with older people. Previous education and work history can usually provide sufficient data on the client's overall level of ability. Tests of intelligence and general aptitude are unnecessary unless a decline is suspected or other information on abilities is lacking. Tests of specific aptitude and achievement may be useful if a person is considering entering a new field or is planning to return to school and is uncertain about his or her academic skills. However, information on skills, too, can often be gleaned from the person's history. On the other hand, inventories of interests may be useful in helping counselors to translate interests into vocational and avocational terms, and personality inventories, especially those designed to promote exploration, can be useful in increasing self-awareness and self-esteem and clarifying priorities. Although testing does have a place in career counseling with older people, the role of testing should be de-emphasized, because tests may be threatening to older people and on abilities may be geared more to the needs of younger people. In addition, information can be obtained through discussion.

Although these cautions were kept in mind when Elizabeth's assessment was planned, her interest in developing self-awareness led the counselor to invite her to serve as a case study for this book. She accepted that opportunity with enthusiasm. As a result, quite a few inventories were administered to Elizabeth; usually, such an extensive assessment program would not be established for older people.

Assessment of Abilities

Because Elizabeth did not have specific occupational goals in mind, the counselor decided that a general measure of her intellectual abilities would be most useful and selected the Kaufman Brief Intelligence Test (K-BIT). Developed in 1990 by Alan Kaufman and Nadeen Kaufman and published by American Guidance Service, the K-BIT is an individually administered brief measure of intelligence. The K-BIT has many features that make it appropriate for use with older people. Pictures and print are large, both verbal and nonverbal intelligence are assessed, only one of three sections is timed, sample items are provided, and the K-BIT is recommended for use with people up to age 90. A sample group, although a small one, included people between the ages of 60 and 64. Requiring 15 to 30 minutes for completion, the K-BIT yields three scores: vocabulary, matrices (nonverbal) assessing the ability to solve new problems, and a composite intelligence score. Both standard scores and percentile ranks can be computed.

All three of Elizabeth's scores on the K-BIT were in the above-average range, with her vocabulary score being slightly higher than her matrices score. Elizabeth found this test to be tiring and was often distracted. However, she was pleased to hear how well she had performed. "Well," she said somewhat wistfully, "I guess I could have gone to college after all. I never thought I was smart enough for that." Testing and discussion of the K-BIT, then, not surprisingly revealed Elizabeth to be a woman of good intelligence with some significant self-doubts.

Although test scores do not always boost self-esteem, in this case Elizabeth's self-image was clarified and enhanced by the results of this test. However, considerable thought should be given to the purposes and selection of tests of ability with older people. If used, good choices might be the K-BIT, the individual intelligence tests discussed in Chapter 3 (the Wechsler Adult Intelligence Scale and the Stanford-Binet Intelligence Scale) as well as the Tests of Adult Basic Education, published by CTB/Macmillan/McGraw-Hill, a widely used measure of reading, mathematics, and language skills that was normed on adults.

Assessment of Career Development

The Adult Career Concerns Inventory (ACCI), published by Consulting Psychologists Press, was developed by Super et al. (1988), based on Super's model of career development; it was designed to assess the career concerns of adults of any age or occupation. Although this is a relatively new inventory, first published in 1986, Halpin, Ralph, and Halpin (1990) concluded that the ACCI had good reliability, was psychometrically sound, and appeared to measure what it was designed to measure. Other authors, however, have recommended that the ACCI be used primarily for research and exploration because of limited information on validation (Whiston, 1990). The ACCI consists of 61 statements of career concerns. Respondents indicate their level of concern about each item on a 5-point scale. Completion of the inventory usually requires 15 to 30 minutes, although Elizabeth took 40 minutes. The ACCI yields scores in four stages of career development (exploration, establishment, maintenance, and disengagement) and three substage scales for each of the four stages.

According to her age, Elizabeth would be in the disengagement stage of career development. However, her scores for that scale were the lowest of the four. Her highest score (95th percentile) was in the first stage, exploration, with specification her highest subscale. Scores were also relatively high for establishment (89th percentile) and maintenance (83rd percentile). Elizabeth had little concern with the usual aspects of disengagement: deceleration, retirement planning, and retirement living. Rather, she was much more concerned with finding a job that would be interesting and satisfying to her. Because her career development up to this point had been largely reactive rather than planned, determined by life circumstances and opportunities rather than intention, her career development was, in some ways, more like that of people in their 20s than of people in her age group. Counseling, then, had to help Elizabeth develop a strong foundation for career planning by increasing her information about herself and her options.

Super's (1957a, 1957b, 1985) life span approach to career development is a particularly useful one for older people. Although only one of the inventories from Super's research was used here, other inventories such as the Salience Inventory and the Values Scale that emerged from Super's (1982) International Work Importance Study also might be useful with such clients.

Assessment of Personality and Interests

Assessment of personality and interests was most important in promoting Elizabeth's self-awareness and decision making. One personality inventory, one interest inventory, and a card sort were used. The personality inventory was selected for ease of presentation and interpretation as well as likelihood of yielding useful and positive information.

Adjective Check List

The Adjective Check List (ACL), developed by H. G. Gough and published by Consulting Psychologists Press, consists of a list of 300 adjectives, arranged in alphabetical order from *absentminded* to *zany*. Respondents indicate which terms they consider to be self-descriptive. A second copy of the inventory allows comparison of real and ideal selves, of couples' responses, and of ratings of people both by themselves and by another person. Suitable for use with people in Grade 9 through adulthood, this inventory requires about 15 to 30 minutes to complete and yields scores on 37 dimensions of personality. A narrative report is available, providing additional information. Because of the complexity of scoring, the inventory must be scored by computer.

The ACL was the first inventory given to Elizabeth, chosen to initiate the assessment process because the ACL seemed to pose little threat or pressure to the respondent. However, Elizabeth had difficulty describing her strengths and, at one point during the administration, asked if she could blacken in half-circles rather than whole ones to indicate that an adjective was "a little bit like her." Like many people of her generation, Elizabeth had little experience with self-disclosure and self-exploration, and those processes were difficult for her.

Despite her discomfort with this inventory, Elizabeth's ACL profile seemed to be valid. She achieved high scores in productiveness and nurturing and was described as accepting rather than critical. The narrative report said of Elizabeth, "You probably have a strong sense of duty . . . you steadily pursue your goals and seek stability . . . you probably are strong in interpersonal effectiveness . . . reliable, ambitious, and diligent . . . self-disciplined . . . fun-loving . . . and enterprising . . . adaptable, outgoing, and protective of those close to you and remain cheerful and productive in the face of adversity . . . you are tolerant and usually give in . . . you accept interdependency and probably tolerate the fears and weaknesses of others." Although most of this information could have been inferred from discussion with Elizabeth and a review of her history, this inventory seemed helpful in synthesizing for Elizabeth her most prominent personal characteristics. Even more important, it served as a stimulus for her to talk more openly about some of her disappointments, particularly her concern over her husband's alcohol use and depression and the barriers she faced in talking to him about these issues. Particularly for older people, test results often carry considerable weight and are taken very seriously. Although this can lead to an overreliance on test data, it also can help people to accept and acknowledge aspects of themselves or issues they have been avoiding.

Self-Directed Search

The Self-Directed Search (SDS), developed by John L. Holland and published by Psychological Assessment Resources, was used to assess Elizabeth's interests. This inventory was selected because it is relatively brief, presents items in a clear and well-organized fashion, and yields information that is concise and easily understood. In addition, the SDS integrates information about personality, interests, and abilities and translates that information into occupational terms. (More information on the SDS and its theoretical framework is presented in Chapters 1, 3, and 6.) Other inventories widely used with adults such as the Strong Interest Inventory and the Kuder Occupational Interest Survey present so much information that they might have overwhelmed Elizabeth, whereas simpler inventories such as the Kuder Preference Record are more appropriate for younger people.

Elizabeth's highest scores on the SDS were in the social, enterprising, and artistic areas, yielding a summary code of SEA. Elizabeth's scores were well differentiated and reflected strongest interest in three occupational environments that are adjacent on Holland's hexagon, suggesting compatibility of interests. This pattern of scores suggests that Elizabeth enjoys using verbal and interpersonal skills to help people, can use those interpersonal skills to be persuasive and to gain power, and tends to be creative and imaginative. Occupations that are consistent with the SEA code include family caseworker; director, community organization; manager, employee welfare; director, television; and social worker, among others. Although these specific occupations did not seem appropriate for Elizabeth because of their educational requirements, discussion helped Elizabeth look beyond the job titles to identify characteristics of those occupations that she would find appealing and rewarding. She wanted to work with people in an active way that would be helpful to them and that would allow her opportunity for creativity and interaction.

Retirement Activities Kit

The Retirement Activities Kit (RAK) is an activities package that can be used with individuals or groups. Although not a standardized inventory, exploratory activities, such as vocational card sorts, can be very useful in promoting discussion and exploration in a nonthreatening fashion. A combination of standardized and nonstandardized forms of assessment can be very useful in helping people express themselves. This is especially true of older people who may have some discomfort with tests and inventories.

The RAK, published by Career Research and Testing, consists of a deck of cards, including blank cards as well as cards with activities printed on them, and a manual that suggests many ways to use the RAK. The first step in using this kit is having participants organize the cards into five piles labeled *daily, regularly, occasionally, seldom,* and *never,* reflecting the frequency that the participant engages in each activity. These piles can be processed in a variety of ways, such as comparing pre- and postretirement activities and comparing actual and preferred activities. Goals of the RAK include helping people understand the changes that accompany the retirement years and promoting thinking and planning for avenues of potential growth and satisfaction during these years.

Despite her rejection of retirement, Elizabeth enjoyed the RAK and found it easy to use as well as informative. She used the blank cards to add two activities that were important to her, baking and tutoring. From the RAK, Elizabeth learned that although she does enjoy many of her present activities, there are other activities, such as visiting her family, attending cultural events, and tutoring, that she does seldom but would like to do more often. She also expressed a very strong interest in travel, an activity that was put in the never pile. When asked what kept her from traveling, Elizabeth replied, "Richard never seems to want to travel, and I don't want to tell him that I'd like to travel. If I said it, and he said, 'No,' then I'd know I could never do it. If I keep it inside me, there is still hope." Barriers to her participating more in other preferred activities included lack of transportation, lack of funds, and no one with whom to do the activity. All three of these barriers could potentially be eliminated through part-time paid employment.

Outcome

Through counseling, Elizabeth reaffirmed her wish to return to part-time employment. Now in possession of clear information about herself and her career goals, Elizabeth engaged in a systematic job search, beginning with friends and contacts she had made through her volunteer work. Little time passed before she located a part-time job as a fund-raiser for a church-sponsored program for homeless and abandoned children. Although this was not a high-paying job, Elizabeth was clear about her priorities. As long as the job provided what she called pin money and allowed her to buy a secondhand car, fulfillment of her intrinsic needs for helping others came first. This job seemed likely to be compatible with her SDS code (SEA) as well as her personality. She was hardworking, had considerable initiative and creativity, and good interpersonal skills. With her first paycheck, Elizabeth signed up for driving lessons. Her second paycheck became the beginning of a down payment on a car.

Having brought some resolution to her career plans seemed to give Elizabeth enough self-confidence that she could begin to deal more effectively with her personal life. Her sense of urgency was accelerated when, shortly after Elizabeth began work, Richard had a mild heart attack. As she said to her counselor, "Lots of things don't turn out to be as good as you think they're going to be. Retirement was like that, and I guess my marriage was like that too. I changed my life when I didn't like being retired, and maybe it's not too late to change my marriage too." As a first step, Elizabeth began attending Al-Anon meetings for family members of people with alcohol problems and planned a trip to Atlanta to talk with her daughter about how, together, they might express their concerns to Richard. Although life had handed Elizabeth some disappointments, her spirit, optimism, and resources had enabled her find considerable rewards in her life. As Elizabeth put it, "When life gives you lemons, make lemonade."

TEN

The Future of Career Counseling and Assessment

Trends and Application

State of the Art

Imagine, if you can, that you are a practicing career counselor some time in the future. . . . You have a clear idea about what you want to accomplish, and as your client's story unfolds you draw on the wealth of relevant published research, theory, and case material to form an immediate understanding of the problem the client is facing. The research over the past 20 years or so has been so clear that you can be reasonably sure that the outcome will be positive for the client. Moreover, you have evidence that suggests several specific techniques with enough demonstrated effectiveness to work with this client. . . . The scientific and technical sophistication of the instruments you use is the envy of modern psychology. In short, you are the consummate professional who draws upon a sound scientific base with consistent results. Sound far fetched? Not at all! We are fast approaching this juncture in the career field. (Spokane, 1992, p. 42).

Spokane's encouraging words reflect the considerable progress that has been made in the field of career counseling and assessment. This chapter will provide an overview of current trends and issues in this field. In addition, this chapter provides a model for career counseling and assessment that readers can use to guide their own work as well as a sample interview conducted according to this model.

Overview of Changes in the Field

The field of career counseling and assessment is a dynamic one that has broadened and changed considerably since the pioneering work of Parsons, Super, Roe, and others. Development of the field reflects not only our growing understanding of people's career development and the tools that facilitate that process but also economic and social changes that modify needs and opportunities.

Career counseling, during the 1990s and into the 21st century, almost certainly will continue to take a life span approach, focusing on the interaction of various life roles, their combination and sequence. Growing awareness of the importance of such personal variables as self-efficacy, thinking skills, and empathy in career development will lead to an expanding infusion of developmental psychology and other psychological theory into career development theory.

Concurrently, emphasis on the individual seems likely to increase. So-called meaning making, people's own construction of reality, is being given increasing attention. Helping people to explore theories they have about themselves and their lives (Carlsen, 1988), establishing collaborative rather than subordinate relationships with clients (Healy, 1990), and emphasizing client goals and expectations rather than those of the counselor are all part of the increasing emphasis on the individual.

This growing emphasis on the individual is reflected by the newest counseling theories. Called by names such as constructive-developmentalism (Savickas, 1989) and the developmental-contextual approach (Cook, 1991), these models emphasize the context of a person's life and seek to understand career development in terms of group membership, self-concept, and overall development. Understanding the interactions of development, person, and context; focusing on the whole person; and viewing people as purposive, self-organizing systems are likely frameworks to guide evolution of modern career development theory (Savickas, 1989; Vondracek & Schulenberg, 1986). Hermeneutical inquiry, helping people to look at themes, structures, and patterns in their lives; interpret the stories of their lives; and make sense of them meshes well with the contextual-developmental approaches to career counseling.

Greater awareness of the importance of the individual may lead to a growing interest in matching client to counselor and counseling approach. Preliminary studies have given some support to this. Robbins and Tucker (1986), for example, found that college students with high goal instability preferred and performed better in interactional rather than self-directed counseling, whereas those with low goal instability performed equally well in both conditions, although they, too, preferred interactional counseling. Fretz (1981) found that students with high-average intellectual abilities benefited more from less structured interventions; that group career counseling was particularly effective with inconsistent, nondifferentiated high school students; and that highly anxious students responded better to unstructured study skills counseling, whereas those with low anxiety benefited more from structured counseling.

Although only a small number of studies have focused on matching counseling approach to person, this area of inquiry seems likely to expand along with the growth of the contextual-developmental models. This area of inquiry also seems to reflect an awareness in the field that searching for the one right or best approach to career counseling is likely to be fruitless. Rather, counselors and researchers are probably wiser to develop and refine an array of useful and effective approaches that can be chosen and adapted to meet the individual needs of each counselor and client. As Savickas (1989) stated, "We know that career interventions generally have positive effects. Now we need to determine which interventions work with whom under what circumstances" (p. 107).

Expectations of Career Counseling

One obstacle to providing effective career counseling is an apparent discrepancy between people's anticipations of career counseling and the actual process and outcome. According to Galassi, Crace, Martin, James, and Wallace (1992), college students seeking career counseling think that

> career counseling should take about three sessions. It should result either in a clearer sense of direction about career/major or in confirming one's choice of career/major, with these goals being facilitated, in part, through testing. Moreover, the process should focus on specific career plans and decision making and exploring both careers and oneself, with the counselor as an active, knowledgeable participant who gives advice and uses counseling techniques to facilitate decision making. Between counseling sessions, clients want to be involved in reading and doing research on careers and in interviewing people in various careers. (p. 53)

The students disliked counselors who were perceived as evasive or pressuring or who focused on topics the students saw as unrelated to career counseling. On the other hand, Nevo (1990) found that college students seemed more satisfied with the personal understanding they received from counseling than the help with decision making and that the most satisfied clients were those who reported receiving help with both personal and career aspects of their lives. Discussion with the counselor was reported to be more important than tests or inventories taken. In a similar vein, Savickas (1989) suggested that career counselors should take a more leisurely pace, letting the client's needs and understanding guide the counseling process rather than letting it be driven by the counselor's idea of how career counseling should proceed.

For many people, a conflict may be present between their perceptions of career counseling as a brief, direct, narrowly focused process and the actual process that is most beneficial to them, one that allows time for establishment of rapport and exploration of past development, present concerns, and characteristics and that involves the client in a multifaceted process of exploration, self-discovery, skill development, and decision making. Counselors should be aware that they and their clients may have discrepant ideas of what the counseling process should be like. Discussion, as well as education, may be needed to ensure that counselor and client have a shared view of the process of career counseling and are able to collaborate effectively. Education of the general population also seems needed to help people appreciate the true nature and flexibility of the process of career counseling and assessment and to dispel any misconceptions they may have of it as a mechanistic process that involves telling people what occupations will be best for them.

Changes in the Workplace

The growing emphasis on the contextual-developmental approaches focuses increasing attention on the workplace. The culture of the workplace is affected by a multitude of factors, including human development, motivation, initiative, and satisfaction; sociological changes; and economic changes. To maintain productivity and harmony, the workplace must change to accommodate the shifting needs of its workers. The following are some of the important socioeconomic changes that are having an impact on the workplace:

1. There has been a shift from a goods-producing economy to a service and information economy.
2. There is increasing use of high technology in the workplace.

3. The growth of a global economy affects the workplace.
4. Population shifts have led to growth in the South and West and declines in the Northeast and North Central areas. States such as Florida, Texas, Alaska, Oregon, Washington, Nevada, Utah, and Arizona are showing considerable population growth, whereas states such as Connecticut, Massachusetts, Rhode Island, New York, Illinois, and Pennsylvania are seeing a decline in population.
5. Demographic changes, including the high divorce rate; the growth of single-parent families; the growing number of older workers; a reduction in the number of younger workers entering the labor force; and the population bulge in the baby boom generation, now advancing through their careers, affects the workplace (Gysbers, 1984; Offerman & Gowing, 1990).
6. Increasing numbers of people are self-employed, now approximately 10% of workers (Olney, 1988).
7. Opportunities in manufacturing and retail sales are growing, whereas opportunities in other areas, such as agriculture and fishing, are declining.
8. There has been an increase in complaints of sexual harassment and gender and ethnic bias, in conflicts between work and family demands, and in work-related stress so severe that it can cause disability.
9. An increasingly assertive and articulate workforce is no longer contented just to have a job but demands a job with adequate pay, fair treatment, and appropriate benefits.
10. Increasing numbers of women (particularly women with young children), immigrants, and ethnic minorities are entering the workforce.
11. More jobs are becoming routinized and simplified, offering limited challenge or opportunity for creativity (Hackman & Oldham, 1981).
12. High rates of absenteeism and employee turnover affect the workplace.
13. The increasing impact of personal problems, such as substance abuse and physical abuse, affects people's work performance.
14. A high rate of company failures (57,000 in 1986) has led to employee layoffs (Offerman & Gowing, 1990).
15. Because of increasing automation, there has been a decline in jobs with relatively low skill demands but good salaries.
16. The importance of information, knowledge, and thinking in today's competitive employment market has increased, whereas the importance of physical strength and ability has decreased (Feller, 1991).

Innovative programs have been developed in the workforce in an effort to address and reduce the impact of some of these changes. The following list includes the most popular of these:

1. Flextime allows people to select their own hours, perhaps working four 10-hour days to afford long weekends or working from 7:00 a.m. to 3:00 p.m. to be home early to care for children.

2. Job sharing allows hours and requirements to be divided between two people, sometimes a husband and wife with similar training and experience.

3. A cafeteria approach to benefits allows workers more freedom of choice of benefits, such as health insurance, life insurance, disability insurance, tuition reimbursement, dental insurance, vacation time, stock options, pension plans, and others.

4. On-site child care helps parents with young children maintain employment and return to work quickly after childbirth.

5. Family or parental leave provides paid or unpaid time off for family issues, such as childbearing, adoption, illness of spouse, or illness of parents.

6. Leave banks allow fellow employees to donate vacation days to people with extended illnesses or family problems.

7. A reduction of overtime and relocation demands makes work less stressful.

8. Counseling and other services have been designed to facilitate the transition when a relocation is required.

9. Rapid growth in employee assistance programs, including on-site or contractual counseling services, provides preventive and short-term, problem-focused counseling as well as referral if additional counseling is needed.

10. Outreach, apprenticeship, and on-the-job training programs have been designed to attract workers who are traditionally underemployed (e.g., women, people from minority backgrounds) as well as to facilitate their advancement and skill development. Such training programs are necessitated by myriad economic and demographic changes, including increased technology, growth in numbers of older workers, shifts from manufacturing to service jobs, increased competition from international markets, the growing number of young people with poor skills, and the increasing effort to maximize individual potential (Goldstein & Gilliam, 1990).

11. More convenient workplace locations have been provided, such as branch offices and flexiplace, a pilot program in which government workers are based at home for most of their working hours, using computers or other resources to perform their work away from the office. Such programs are especially beneficial to people caring for family members or people with disabilities.

12. The increasing availability of sabbaticals or leaves of absence offers people some time away from the job for renewal, learning, or new work experi-

ences. Some corporations are offering employees paid leave time for volunteer work, a benefit to the community, the employee, and the image of the company.

13. Early retirement programs give people more time for trying new career directions or for expanding their leisure pursuits.

14. Work-site-based quality-of-work-life programs, including quality circles and other projects, give employees a greater voice and sense of participation in their companies and facilitate efforts to adapt the workplace to employee needs.

Clearly, the career development of the modern worker involves an interaction of personal and socioeconomic ingredients. As Feller (1991) stated, "One's employment and career development are shaped today, much as they were years ago, by job growth, replacement needs, and learning opportunities. Yet, over the next 25 years, what clients need to know, how they access information, and how they plan for multiple routes to economic support will grow increasingly more significant" (pp. 18-19).

The Multicultural Workforce

A particularly strong interaction seems to be present between the growing emphasis on the individual and the increasingly multicultural nature of our population. When there was more homogeneity, at least on the surface of our society, it was easier to believe that one pattern of career development or one theory of career counseling could be right for everyone. However, our present multicultural population makes clear the importance of viewing people in context. One third of new entrants to the labor force will be people from minority backgrounds, with over one half of those having lived in poverty (Offerman & Gowing, 1990).

Career counseling may be particularly important in familiarizing such people with opportunities available to them, common procedures for locating employment and educational opportunities, and their own interests and abilities. A survey of people from minority backgrounds indicated that, overall, 65% would obtain more career information if they were beginning their careers again (Brown et al., 1991). Of the three groups sampled (Hispanics, African Americans, and Asian Pacific Islanders), the African Americans stood out as reporting more need for help, perceiving discrimination, expecting job change, and viewing themselves as taking jobs primarily because of availability. Even more than people from other minority backgrounds, African Americans, who have a long history of underemployment and high unemployment, also have a high level of awareness of their need for career planning.

Ethnic and socioeconomic groups are not the only ones that shape people. The career development of people with strong religious affiliations, people who are homosexual, people who are gifted, people with disabilities, and people with substance abuse or mental illness in their families is also likely to be affected by their experiences and their group affiliations. Some people have strong affiliations to several groups (e.g., the gay Hispanic woman), and the interactions of those groups, their complementary and contradictory messages, need to be explored by both counselor and client.

At the same time, studies typically reveal small differences between groups, and large individual differences within groups (Cook, 1991). What this suggests is that although we should probably pay attention to general information that is available about the development and dynamics of particular groups in our culture, at least as important is the meaning of the group for the individual, the messages and experiences that person has received, and the multipotentiality of the person. Counselors should advocate to expand opportunities, reduce barriers, and help people draw on the special experiences and opportunities they have had because of background and group membership to maximize both the contribution they can make to society and the likelihood of their developing rewarding career and life plans.

Changes in the Process of
Career Counseling and Assessment

As society changes, as the workforce and the economy change, and as theories of career development and counseling change, these changes are reflected in the process of career counseling. The role of the career counselor is likely to become a broader and more comprehensive one, making greater use of technology, seeking greater understanding of individual differences, and cooperating and collaborating more with other specialists and agencies. Specialization is likely to increase because of the wealth of new resources and ideas on the market (Walz & Benjamin, 1984). The counselor is increasingly likely to become an advocate for clients, to be found in community-based facilities such as libraries, community centers, and businesses as well as in schools and counseling agencies. Career counseling is no longer regarded as a service primarily for high school and college students. Rather, as the *NECA Newsletter* stated, "Assistance with job choice and career planning is an immediate and growing need for many employed adults" (National Employment Counseling Association [NECA], 1990, p. 7). Although 81% of Americans report that they are satisfied with their work (McDaniels, 1984), 75% of adults are aware that they would have benefited from some help in career planning and decision making. The importance and effectiveness of career counseling seems well established, with approximately 75% of people reporting satisfaction with their career counseling (Nevo, 1990). Clearly, it is a service that will be growing and changing in the foreseeable future.

The role of the career counselor also seems to be expanding. Career counseling increasingly means career life planning, helping people to examine work, leisure, family, and personal goals and opportunities and determine effective ways to integrate them. Technology is not likely to eliminate the role of the counselor because most people prefer and report a superior outcome for career counseling combining computer-based career guidance systems with a live counselor to use of a computer-based program alone (Hoffman, Spokane, & Magoon, 1981; Marin & Splete, 1991).

At the same time, computers play an increasingly important role in career counseling. Computer-assisted career guidance systems (CACGS) seem to increase career decidedness and commitment to occupational choice, promote decisional skills and general adjustment, and provide a useful service to all age groups in a wide range of settings from schools to businesses to community agencies. CACGS have many uses in the career counseling process (Marin & Splete, 1991; Pyle, 1984). These include word processing, producing mailing labels, facilitating preparation of statistical reports, scheduling interviews with counselors and potential employers, retrieving records, computer-assisted testing, listing job vacancies, matching employer and job seeker, providing a career library indexing system, providing guidelines for résumé preparation, guiding the job search process, promoting interviewing skills, providing information on schools and sources of financial assistance, and promoting development of self-awareness, decision-making skills, and sound and realistic career plans. At least 5 million people each year make use of CACGS, and SIGI (Educational Testing Service), DISCOVER (ACT Educational Services), CHOICES (Canada Systems Group), C-LECT (Chronicle Guidance Publications), and Guidance

Information Systems (Houghton Mifflin) are now well-established aids in the process of career development, counseling, and assessment.

Career Counseling in Groups

Another trend, enhancing the effectiveness and efficiency of career counseling, is the use of groups as a vehicle for counseling. Of course, groups have been used for personal counseling for many years, and groups to facilitate job seeking, usually following the Job Club model initiated by Azrin, have been proliferating for several decades (Trimmer, 1984). Group career counseling was an easy and logical next step and is consistent with the growing emphasis on providing community-based services and using a contextual-developmental approach. Fretz (1981) concluded, as do most studies of the subject, that group career counseling is at least as effective as individual career counseling.

By sharing experiences and ideas with other people seeking career counseling, clients can obtain greater insight into both the developmental patterns they share with others and their own unique and special qualities. According to Butcher (1982), "Groups provide for an economical use of the counselor's time; offer a real-life situation in which members can test reality, share feelings, and receive feedback and support from peers; and maximize a climate of cooperation and interdependence among members" (p. 203). Demonstrated benefits of group career counseling include giving members a sense of universality (we're all in the same boat); instilling hope; developing self-confidence and pride from helping others; and learning from other people's behaviors, insights, and efforts (Kivlighan, 1990). The group setting also facilitates attention to environmental and social issues (Butcher, 1982).

Butcher has suggested the following three-stage model for group career counseling:

1. *Exploration.* This involves self-disclosure and assessment of interests and aptitudes, feedback on assessment, and resolution of discrepancies.
2. *Transition.* When congruence of self-image and feedback has been achieved, the group members are ready to relate self-knowledge to the world of work, to examine work and life values, to receive feedback on their reported and exhibited values and, once again, to resolve discrepancies so that values are clear before moving onto the next stage.
3. *Action.* This third stage encompasses making immediate choices, goal setting, developing action plans, identifying resources to facilitate goal

attainment, information gathering and sharing, and immediate and long-range decision making.

Of course, not all career counseling groups are equally successful and not all people benefit equally from group career counseling. In general, group career counseling seems to be more effective for those in greatest need of help, whereas individual career counseling seems to be more useful to those who already have a fair amount of career maturity (Kivlighan, 1981). Fretz (1981), for example, found that students who had not manifested clear, consistent, and differentiated patterns of career development manifested more growth in career maturation, following group career counseling, than did those who were consistent and differentiated in their career development. In a similar vein, Butcher (1982) found that group career counseling was particularly effective for indecisive clients. Kivlighan (1990) found that the self-disclosure promoted by group career counseling was especially beneficial to people with unstable career goals, with those who had set unrealistically high career goals deriving particular help from the group feedback and process. Kivlighan also found groups to have a greater impact if members were given occupational information before receiving interpretations of tests and inventories that they had completed.

Men and women seem to have different goals when they enter group career counseling. Men are primarily interested in confirmation of choices and decisions they already have made, whereas women are more interested in expanding their options and considering new possibilities. Because of this discrepancy, Kivlighan (1990) has suggested that same-gender career counseling groups might be more effective than combined-gender ones.

The Importance of
the Family in Career Development

Growing emphasis on context and environment, as well as increasing appreciation of the formative role that the family plays in people's development, has led to greater attention to the family in career counseling. Since the early 1980s, there has been a strong interest in incorporating family systems theory into career counseling (Whiston, 1989). Counselors recognize that career development is shaped by many factors in families, such as parental careers and expectations, siblings' career development, birth order, social/cultural/economic background of family, and the level of adjustment and mental health in the family. Bradley and Mims (1992), for example, found that siblings who are adjacent in birth order tend not to follow the same career path, whereas nonadjacent siblings are more likely to follow similar patterns. They also found that roles played in families often establish a prototype for roles that people will assume in their careers; for example, the family caretaker may seek to care for others outside of the family because that is a familiar and rewarding role. Career counseling, therefore, should explore family dynamics, patterns, and influences as part of the process of helping people develop self-awareness and make decisions that are likely to be sound and rewarding.

Increasingly, tools such as genograms, illustrating family roles as well as career and educational patterns over three or more generations, are borrowed from family counseling and integrated into the process of career counseling. Counselors can be creative in developing genograms with their clients that focus on family messages about careers, occupational roles, gender roles, and family rules and norms about the appropriate places of work, leisure, and family in one's life. Exploration of people's families of origin can also help them to clarify and modify dysfunctional attitudes and behaviors, such as chronic indecision or overinvestment in work, that may appear generation after generation in families.

In addition to considering family influences on career development, many career counselors have expanded the boundaries of the career counseling process to include family members as well as the identified client. Whiston (1989), for example, set up a series of group meetings for parents, designed to maximize and guide parental involvement in their children's career development. The goals of the groups included helping the parents facilitate their children's decisions rather than making decisions for them, making the parents aware of sources of career information, helping them to become more conscious of the messages they are transmitting to their children, and promoting the parents' own decision-making skills and awareness of their own interests and abilities. As part of the group process, both children and parents identified their Holland codes (see Chapter 1) and discussed similarities and differences in their career-related interests.

Of people responding to a recent survey, 36% reported frequent conflicts between work and family life, with 17% of women and 19% of men experiencing a great deal of conflict between those two areas (NECA, 1990). In light of that finding, the growing trend to integrate attention to career development and family background seems a sound and important one.

Barriers to Career Development

Socioeconomic changes, the increasingly multicultural population of the United States, and improved understanding of career development have brought increasing attention to some serious and pervasive problems in our society that need to be addressed by career counselors and their clients. Problems such as underemployment; ethnic, age, and gender bias; stressful and even traumatic work experiences; sexual harassment; illiteracy; substance abuse; physical abuse; and poverty are viewed by most as social problems, but they are also career problems. Increasingly, counselors will find themselves called on to address these issues in their counseling sessions as well as to become a public advocate or spokesperson for their clients, seeking to effect social awareness and change as well as awareness and change in the individual. Counselors can play an important part in reducing occupational barriers and expanding opportunities and should look beyond the walls of their office to find ways to promote people's positive career development.

Internal barriers to career development may also present a challenge to counselors. Many people seek career counseling because they perceive it as a nonthreatening way to address personal concerns, whereas others are unaware that they really need personal rather than career counseling. Although optimal mental health is certainly not a prerequisite for clients to engage in productive career counseling, serious problems such as substance abuse, clinical depression, incapacitating anxiety, or obsessive-compulsive disorders must be addressed before people can make sound career plans. Career counselors, then, must make a rapid assessment of the overall level of adjustment of their clients. If concerns surface that would severely limit the benefits people are likely to gain from career counseling, a referral to a personal counselor should be made before career counseling is begun. Even if counselors determine that personal concerns are present but would not impair ability to benefit from career counseling, counselors can be very helpful to their clients if personal concerns that surface are identified and clients are told of ways to obtain help with those concerns.

A Field of Continuing Change

The study of career development is extremely worthwhile and important; having a rewarding career and finding ways to integrate one's career successfully with other aspects of one's life is integral to our general satisfaction with life. Hoyt's (1991) broad definition captures well the modern view of career development as a comprehensive process: "Career development is the total constellation of psychological, sociological, educational, physical, economic and chance factors that combine to shape the career of any given individual over the life span" (p. 23). However, career development is a complex process that is different for each person. Its study will never be an exact science and will always call for creative and intuitive skills as well as technology, research, tools, and resources. It is a field that will probably be ever changing as our society and its people change. Sundal-Hansen (1985) has listed the following changes in goals in today's career counseling:

1. From slotting people into what is to preparing for life choices and options of what might be.
2. From an emphasis primarily on occupational information and choice to an awareness of an individual's own 'career socialization.'
3. From a focus on narrow stereotypic choices to expanding the range of options men and women are able and willing to consider and choose.
4. From a focus strictly on jobs to a systems perspective on new work and family patterns and linkages.
5. From a focus on work alone to emphasis on the relationship of the work role to other life roles. (pp. 208-209)

Career counseling and development is also a field that will always have unanswered questions. The following are some of the questions researchers are presently studying:

1. How can the effectiveness of career counseling and assessment be maximized?
2. How can we build on and appreciate individual differences while still developing theories and tools for general use that will be relevant and effective?
3. How can we humanize the workplace so that work is rewarding and people treat each other with acceptance and sensitivity?
4. How can we provide equal opportunity for career development to all people?

5. How can we best maintain freedom of choice in decision making?
6. What matches of person to counseling approach are most likely to be successful?
7. How should career counseling be integrated with personal counseling; can career counseling be effective if personal difficulties are overlooked or bypassed?
8. How can career counseling receive the recognition and place of importance it deserves rather than being viewed as a secondary service within the counseling discipline (Dorn, 1986)?

The Content and Process of Career Counseling

The importance of individualizing career counseling and gearing it to the developmental needs of the client has been stressed throughout this book. Consequently, the nature of a particular career counseling relationship cannot be proscribed and will be considerably affected by the styles and personalities of both the client and the counselor.

However, there are certain commonalities in career counseling experiences. In addition, in most instances, career counseling follows a relatively predictable pattern. The following outline, with accompanying questions, is provided to better familiarize readers with the nature of career counseling. The questions are not provided as a model to be followed exactly but, rather, as a guide. They were developed to highlight those aspects of clients and their situations that, generally, should be explored and understood by counselors and clients engaged in career counseling. The questions can be borrowed and used, with appropriate modifications, by counselors or they can be used as a checklist to ascertain whether relevant areas have been discussed.

The sample questions can also be used by career counselors to examine their own career development. Counselors can gain a greater appreciation of the scope of career development and the importance of work in people's lives by examining their own career development. It is suggested that counselors write or think through their own responses to the following processes and questions.

Ten Desirable Processes and Goals of Career Counseling

I. Exploration and clarification of presenting problem
   A. When did you first begin to think about seeking career counseling?

    B. What thoughts or experiences led you to decide to seek counseling at this time?

    C. How did you hear about our services?

    D. What sort of help would you like to receive from career counseling?

    E. What do you think career counseling will be like? How do you think it will help you?

    F. Have you received any other counseling or help with career planning? If so, what was that like and what impact did it have on you?

II. Exploration of relevant background and history

    A. What has been your work history?

    B. What volunteer experiences have you had?

    C. How do you spend your leisure time?

    D. What information do the above experiences provide about your likes, dislikes, and abilities?

    E. What has been your educational history?

    F. What kind of student have you been?

    G. What are your academic strengths and weaknesses, likes and dislikes?

    H. What thoughts have you had about furthering your education?

    I. In what type of community or environment did you grow up?

    J. What was the structure of your family?

    K. What were the occupational and educational attainments of your parents and siblings?

    L. What aspirations did your parents seem to have for you?

    M. How did the career choices of your parents and other important family members affect your goals and aspirations?

    O. What other people (teachers, counselors, friends) served as influential role models for you?

    P. What are your present family circumstances and responsibilities?

    Q. What are your family members' present attitudes toward your career plans?

III. Exploration of self-image and self-awareness

    A. What type of person do you perceive yourself to be?

    B. How do you think other people perceive you?

    C. If you could change anything about yourself, what changes would you make?

    D. What discrepancies have emerged between how you see yourself and how others see you and between your self-image and your ideal self? How do you feel about these differences?

    E. What aspects of yourself would you like to know more about or do you find confusing?

    F. What changes have you noted over the years in the type of person you are and in your feelings about yourself?

IV. Establishment of goals
   A. Now that the nature of career counseling and some of the important aspects of your life have been explored, what would you like to accomplish in career counseling?
   B. What questions or decisions do you think are most important to you right now?
V. Assessment of strengths, limitations and interests, leading to greater self-awareness
   A. What occupational possibilities have you been considering?
   B. What occupations appealed to you when you were younger?
   C. What attracts you to each of the occupations you mentioned?
   D. What difficulties or areas of dislike do you anticipate you would encounter in each of those occupations?
   E. What do you enjoy about your present lifestyle and activities?
   F. What things would you like to change?
   G. Tell me about some situations in which you felt you did a good job or felt you demonstrated strong ability.
   H. Tell me about some situations that you found particularly difficult or challenging.
VI. Interpretation of tests and inventories
   A. What do you predict these inventories will show about your interests or abilities?
   B. What understanding do you have of the information provided by the tests and inventories?
   C. What reactions do you have to the results of your tests and inventories?
   D. How do your test protocols relate to other information about you that we have already discussed?
   E. What do you make of any discrepancies between the results of the inventories and your view of yourself?
   F. What interests, abilities, and personality traits are reflected in both the test data and our discussions?
VII. Values clarification
   A. What would be an ideal balance for you of work, leisure, and family activities and responsibilities?
   B. What extrinsic work-related values are particularly important to you (e.g., salary, benefits, hours, working conditions, co-workers)?
   C. What intrinsic work-related values are particularly important to you (e.g., self-actualization, creativity, independence, prestige, power, challenge)?
   D. What ethical, philosophical, or religious ideas are important to you?
   E. What kinds of situations have made you feel proud, guilty, or disappointed?
   F. What accomplishments would lead you to view yourself as successful?

VIII. Development and weighing of alternatives
  A. What career possibilities are generated by the data that have been gathered?
  B. What occupational and educational options seem to hold the most appeal for you?
  C. What changes seem likely to increase your enjoyment of your leisure time?
  D. What would you like your lifestyle to be like next year? In 10 years? At retirement?
  E. What additional information do you need to gain a clear idea of your options?
  F. What are the pros and cons of the alternatives you have identified? (Consider lifestyle changes, entry requirements, congruence with values, interests, and abilities.)
  G. What external obstacles are likely to be inherent in each option? (Consider economic projections as well as qualities of the client, such as age, physical condition, and training, that may make entry and advancement difficult.) How might these be overcome?
  H. What internal obstacles are likely to arise in connection with each option? (Consider motivation, abilities, attitude toward education and training, other obligations, mobility.) How might these be overcome?

IX. Application of decision-making strategies
  A. What knowledge of or experience with decision-making strategies have you had?
  B. What choices or decisions do you want to make at this point in your career development?
  C. What alternative seems best when decision-making skills are used to help you make a choice?

X. Development, implementation, and evaluation of plans
  A. What sequence of plans seems most likely to help you attain your desired objectives?
  B. What are the first steps you should take in implementing these plans?
  C. Would implementation of these plans be facilitated by providing you some help with skills such as locating suitable employment possibilities, preparing résumés and job applications, improving your interview behavior, or completing college and financial aid applications?
  D. What kind of follow-up could be arranged to ascertain whether you have been able to implement your plans with success and satisfaction or whether further counseling is indicated?

Stages of Career Counseling

In general, career counseling will encompass both directive and person-centered interventions on the part of the counselor, with the counseling process following relatively predictable stages. The following would be typical of the pattern of career counseling:

1. *Initial phase.* Establish a positive working alliance with the client, activate hope, develop readiness for the counseling process, clarify the presenting concern, establish a pattern of the client's taking responsibility and continuing the process of career learning outside of the sessions.
2. *Beginning to work together.* Establish tentative goals, develop a plan, and determine inventories and other tools to be used.
3. *Development of self-awareness.* Use discussion and inventories to develop a clear understanding of aptitudes, abilities, interests, lifestyle preferences, goals, resources, and limitations; review and explore the client's history, considering the impact of family and socioeconomic factors; reconcile discrepancies and contradictions.
4. *Making sense of the data.* Translate information into occupational terms and generate alternatives.
5. *Obtaining occupational information.* Gather relevant information on the labor force and career paths of particular interest to the client; with the client, develop an understanding of occupational requirements, prospects and opportunities, work tasks, intrinsic and extrinsic benefits, working conditions, and other aspects. Have the client weigh and test options.
6. *Making choices.* As options are weighed, compromises are made, decisions are made, and decision-making and other skills are improved if necessary. The client come to terms with the choices, projecting his or her lifestyle into the future.
7. *Reality testing.* This involves planning implementation, overcoming roadblocks, evaluating the feasibility of plans, resolving conflicts, and reassessing choices.
8. *Implementation.* This includes following through on occupational and educational plans and choices, improving relevant skills as needed (e.g., interviewing, résumé writing), assessing progress, modifying goals if necessary, coping with and adjusting to new roles, and follow-up.

Characteristics of Career Counseling

Although career counseling is a flexible process, individualized for each client, certain procedures or techniques enhance that process for almost all clients. These include the following.

1. The facilitative conditions (empathy, genuineness, positive regard, and concreteness) are as basic to career counseling as they are to almost all forms of counseling. Consequently, career counselors should make effective use of skills such as minimal encouragers, reflection of feeling, paraphrase, open question, and summarization that have been shown to be effective in communicating the facilitative conditions. Although the nature of career counseling has been illustrated in the previous pages by a series of questions, this does not mean that the role of the career counselor is primarily that of questioner. Rather, the questions should be used as a guide to help counselors identify and explore important aspects and concerns of clients and of the career counseling process and should be well integrated into the counseling process. Although the questions presented here are typical of the process of career counseling, questions should grow out of the words and feelings of clients and should not follow any rigid pattern. Career counselors, like other counselors, must develop rapport, communicate acceptance, and promote exploration and skillful decision making. Counselors who rely too heavily on the technique of questioning may alienate clients and fail to develop a collaborative and cooperative counseling effort.

2. Critical aspects of the counselors' role should be protecting people's freedom of choice, expanding options, and ensuring equity of opportunity for all, regardless of age, gender, culture, or background.

3. Career counselors should take a holistic approach that considers not only work and education but also leisure, social and family life, and other important aspects of a person's life.

4. Considering life span development as well as context and personal meaning of life events is integral to career counseling.

5. Counselors should focus on empowering people, on working with them collaboratively to help them acquire skills, insights, and information that will promote career maturity, a sense of self-efficacy, and a belief that they can establish and achieve rewarding goals.

6. Computers, inventories, videotapes, books, and other resources can enhance and expedite the process of career counseling and development but should never dominate the counseling process.

Duration of Career Counseling

Career counseling tends to be relatively short-term in nature, typically requiring approximately 6 to 12 counseling and assessment sessions. Counselors who find that their career counseling relationships commonly extend over many fewer or many more sessions than this probably should take a closer look at the nature of their counseling.

Counselors who typically use only a few sessions for career counseling may not be taking a sufficiently broad view of the process of career development and may not be encouraging sufficient exploration of the self, the background and development, the context, and the relevant options.

The counselor who spends many months in the process of career counseling may not really be engaged in career counseling. People with serious personality disorders, mood disorders, or family concerns often seek career counseling as a nonthreatening way of obtaining help, a means of making contact with a helping professional without having to acknowledge the seriousness of their difficulties. Counselors should help such people to express their real needs and recognize that career counseling may not be the most immediate of them. Counselors should then determine whether they are qualified to help such people with their redefined concerns. If so, new goals can be established, different and more relevant than those implied by the person's presenting concerns. If the counselor is not qualified to work with such a person, an appropriate referral can be made.

A similar situation can arise when people who seem to have completed career counseling indicate an interest in receiving counseling for other difficulties. Again, counselors must decide whether to renegotiate the counseling contract or to make a referral. In either case, to call counseling that does not have a career development focus "career counseling" is to foster a dishonest and unrewarding relationship, one in which the agreed-upon goals will rarely be met.

Evaluating the Counseling Process

Evaluation is a necessary ingredient of career counseling. For their own benefit as well as for that of their clients, counselors should always make some evaluation of their counseling. The criteria used may vary from one client to another and may include such procedures as follow-up questionnaires, measures of occupational and educational achievement, client reports of satisfaction, reports of teachers or employers, or assessment of the congruence between plans and accomplishments. Evaluation of the counseling process can help counselors improve their skills and become even more effective with future clients. Follow-up done as part of evaluation should also ascertain whether people are in need of additional counseling and, if so, how that might best be provided.

Skills of the Career Counselor

Career counseling is a creative and challenging field that calls for counselors to have competencies in many areas. The following are some of the important skills required by this field. (The material on pp. 482-484 of this volume is reprinted for Volume 34(2) of the *Vocational Guidance Quarterly*, © ACA. Reprinted with permission. No further reproduction authorized without written permission of the American Counseling Association.)

General Counseling Skills. Counseling competencies considered essential to effective vocational-career counseling include the following:

1. Knowledge of general counseling theories and techniques.
2. Skills in building a productive relationship between counselor and client.
3. Ability to use appropriate counseling techniques in effectively assisting individuals with career choice and life-career development concerns.
4. Ability to help the client recognize the relationship between self-understanding and effective life-career decisions.
5. Ability to assist the client in the identification of internal personal factors related to life-career decision making, including personality, values, interests, aptitudes, and motives.
6. Skills in recognizing and modifying stereotypes held by clients related to career choice.
7. Ability to assist the client in the identification of contextual factors in career decision making, including family, friends, educational opportunities, and finances.

Information. Information base and knowledge essential for professionals engaging in vocational-career counseling include the following:

1. Knowledge of education, training, employment trends, labor market, and career resources that provide information about job tasks, functions, salaries, requirements, and future outlooks related to broad occupational fields.
2. Knowledge of basic concepts related to vocational-career counseling, including career development, career paths, and career patterns.
3. Knowledge of career development and decision-making theories.
4. Knowledge of the changing roles of women and men and the linkage of work, family, and leisure.
5. Knowledge of resources and techniques designed for use with special groups.

6. Knowledge of strategies to store, retrieve, and disseminate vocational-career information.

Individual-Group Assessment. Individual-group assessment skills considered essential for professionals engaged in vocational-career counseling include the following:

1. Knowledge of appraisal techniques and measures of aptitude, achievement, interest, values, and personality.
2. Knowledge of strategies used in the evaluation of job performance, individual effectiveness, and program effectiveness.
3. Ability to identify appraisal resources appropriate for specified situations and populations.
4. Ability to evaluate appraisal resources and techniques in terms of their validity, reliability, and relationships to race, sex, age, and ethnicity.
5. Ability to demonstrate the proper administration of appraisal techniques.
6. Ability to interpret appraisal data to clients and other appropriate individuals or groups of people.
7. Ability to assist clients in appraising quality of life and working environments.

Management and Administration. Management-administration skills necessary to develop, plan, implement, and manage comprehensive career development programs include the following:

1. Knowledge of program designs that can be used in the organization of career development services.
2. Knowledge of needs assessment techniques and practices.
3. Knowledge of performance objectives used in organizing career development programs and setting goals and comprehensive career development programs.
4. Knowledge of management concepts and leadership styles used in relation to career development programs.
5. Ability to adjust management and administration methods to reflect identified career development program problems and specified situational needs.
6. Ability to prepare budgets and time lines for career development programs.
7. Ability to design, compile, and report an evaluation of career development activities and programs.

Implementation. Knowledge and skills essential to the adoption of career development programs and strategies in a variety of settings include the following:

1. Knowledge of program adoption and planned change strategies.
2. Knowledge of personal and environmental barriers affecting the implementation of career development programs.
3. Ability to implement individual and group programs in career development for specified populations.
4. Ability to implement a public relations effort in behalf of career development activities and services.
5. Ability to devise and implement a comprehensive career resource center.
6. Ability to implement pilot programs in a variety of career development areas including: appraisal, decision making, information giving, and general career counseling.

Consultation. Knowledge and skills considered essential in relating to individuals and organizations that have an impact on the career development process include the following:

1. Knowledge of consultation strategies and consultation models.
2. Ability to provide effective career consultation to influential individuals such as parents, teachers, employers, community groups, and the general public.
3. Ability to provide career development consultation to business and professional groups.
4. Ability to convey program goals and achievements to key personnel in positions of authority: legislators, executives, and others.
5. Ability to provide data on the cost-effectiveness of career counseling and career development activities.

In addition to developing mastery of the essential skills of career counseling, counselors should also familiarize themselves with ethical standards relevant to the career counselor. These are included in Appendix A of this book.

Case Study of Senesie Robinson: For the Reader's Analysis

The following case study is presented for analysis and discussion. A transcript of parts of the first counseling session with a client is presented, accompanied by the protocols or results of tests and inventories that were administered to that person. All instruments used have been discussed in detail elsewhere in this book so that even if readers have no previous knowledge of the use and interpretation of these instruments, they should be able to discuss these results with little difficulty.

The client, Senesie Robinson, a 26-year-old African American woman, had been referred for career counseling after she was deemed eligible for vocational rehabilitation services. Prior to counseling, Senesie had been employed as a technician at a chemical plant. An accident there had exposed her to toxic chemicals, resulting in burns on her hands and arms. For the past few months, she had been undergoing medical treatment as well as physical therapy. Although her condition had improved considerably, some permanent impairment in her manual dexterity was anticipated, necessitating a change in career direction.

Senesie was a tall, striking woman whose style of dress reflected her African American background. She expressed herself well and seemed both concerned about her situation and eager to formulate some future plans.

The interview with Senesie began after a preliminary meeting in which the nature of the counseling process was explained to her. The interview was designed to be an introductory and information-gathering one. Although some exploration of feelings, attitudes, and experiences was included in the session, the primary purpose of the session was to obtain an overview of Senesie's career and personal development that could be further explored in subsequent sessions.

In analyzing and discussing the interview and assessment results, readers might use the questions provided earlier in this chapter, considering the questions in the sequence in which they are presented. Of course, some of the later questions cannot be answered on the basis of the material presented here because only the first counseling session has been included. However, readers may speculate on the nature and direction of subsequent counseling sessions with Senesie and may use the later questions to guide their consideration of how the counselor could be most helpful to Senesie, what areas require further exploration, and what choices seem most likely to be rewarding to her. Readers are also encouraged to look critically at the counseling and assessment process that is presented here. The following questions may be used to guide that process:

1. How effective was the counselor at establishing a productive and collaborative counseling relationships? Discuss specific counseling interventions to substantiate your conclusion.
2. What aspects or concerns of the client needed further attention in this session? In future sessions?
3. How helpful and appropriate did the inventories seem to be? What changes, if any, would you have made in the selection of tests and inventories used with Senesie?

4. What direction do you think future counseling sessions with Senesie should take?

5. What obstacles or conflicts seem likely to arise during the counseling process?

6. What do you anticipate will be the outcome of these counseling sessions in terms of choices, decisions, plans, and client level of satisfaction?

7. Does a referral or counseling other than career counseling seem indicated for this client? If so, what other types of help would you recommend?

Initial Counseling Session

After preliminary discussion and introductions the following dialogue took place:

Counselor: Senesie, as you know, your rehabilitation counselor suggested that you meet with me for some help with career planning. I have reviewed your medical records and am familiar with the treatment you are receiving. What I would like to focus on today are some other areas related to your career development, such as your family background, your education, and your work history.

Senesie: That's fine with me. I can't wait to get started. You know, I've worked all my life, and it's real hard for me to be out of work now and not know what's going to happen.

Counselor: Yes, I can imagine this has been a difficult time for you. I hope that by working together we can help you develop some rewarding plans.

Senesie: Yes, I'd like that. I guess in a way this is an opportunity for me. I've never been very happy with my work but couldn't afford to make a change. Now maybe I can do that. Where do we start?

Counselor: How about at the beginning? Maybe you can start by telling me something about your family and where you grew up.

Senesie: Well, I grew up in New York City in a pretty bad neighborhood. My mother had been a real good student like I was, and she wanted to get out of Harlem, but things don't always turn out like you want. I was born when my mother was 18, and my sister was born 2 years later. When I was real young, my father was killed, shot, probably by someone who didn't even know him. We were living with my grandmother then and we just stayed there. My mother had been working as a clerk in a food store down the street, and she kept working to support us. My grandmother would take care of us. She was a great woman. She and my mom would always take us places, to try to help us have some goals and stay out of trouble. We would go to plays and concerts in the park, to museums, and in the summer we'd go to the zoo and Coney Island.

Counselor: It sounds like your family was very close and had many good times together.

Senesie: We really did. I barely remember my father, but I certainly got lots of love and attention from my mother and grandmother.

Counselor: Tell me about your education while you were growing up.

Senesie: I was always a good student. I went to a public school in my neighborhood up until high school. I did well in all my subjects, especially math, and I was involved in a lot of singing groups. I would sing at my church and sing at school, and I even was paid to give a couple of performances when I was a kid. I was put in some special program, Upward Bound, I think it was called, and on Saturdays and sometimes after school we would go on field trips and have discussions. They introduced us to computers, and I've really been interested in them ever since. After junior high school, I got into a special high school for people interested in performing arts. That's a public school in New York, but you have to have an audition and go through all sorts of hurdles to get in. I guess my singing was really pretty good and they admitted me. We worked real hard there, on regular subjects as well as music, and we gave performances. I made some friends there I still have. I did alright in my courses, but high school was a lot harder than elementary or junior high school. I was used to being the smartest one in my class, and it was quite a change to just be sort of average, but I wouldn't have missed that experience for anything. My mother and grandmother were so happy when I graduated from high school, I remember them crying when we took pictures.

Counselor: It sounds like your public school years were very rewarding ones for you. What career goals did you have at that time?

Senesie: Well, when I was real young I wanted to be an elementary school teacher or an actress. Then, when I started singing, I thought, this is what I'll do. You know, when I hear Natalie Cole, it sort of makes me sad. I think maybe I could have done that if I had put my mind to it.

Counselor: You feel disappointed that you didn't pursue a career in singing?

Senesie: Yes, I do.

Counselor: What kept you from doing that?

Senesie: Well, that's a long story. My mother really wanted me to go to college, just in case the singing didn't work out. I thought that was a good idea too. So I applied to several colleges and got a scholarship to attend Howard University in Washington, D.C. I was planning to take courses in both math and music and try to develop my skills in both areas. Well, I had never been away from home before and I found it very difficult to be in Washington. I did alright in my courses, not great, but I passed everything. But when I came home after my freshman year, I wasn't sure I wanted to go back. I enjoyed the courses, especially math and computer programming, but I just didn't feel comfortable at Howard.

Counselor: So college had both pluses and minuses for you. How did you go about making the decision whether to return to college?

Senesie: Well, the decision sort of got made for me. I'd had a boyfriend in high school. We wrote to each other when I was in college, and when I came home, things got pretty serious. By the end of the summer, I found out I was pregnant, so going back to college was out of the question.

Counselor: How did you feel about that?

Senesie: I guess I didn't mind being pregnant that much. Partly because it gave me an excuse not to go back to college. But it made things pretty tough. My boyfriend . . . well, now he's my husband . . . he really cared about me, but he sure wasn't interested in getting married. He was still living with his family and was trying to get his career going. He wanted to be a jazz musician then. Things weren't going too well for him, and he said he just wasn't ready to be a husband and father. He was only 19. I talked it over with my mom and grandmother and decided I really wanted to have the baby. They said they would help me, and so I had my son. He's 6 years old now. I was very happy to have the baby, but I figured, good-bye college.

Counselor: How did you handle having a baby?

Senesie: My mom taught me a lot. I wanted to go right to work as soon as I found out I was pregnant to save some money, but my mother said, why didn't I try to get some training so I could get a decent job and not wind up bagging groceries. I talked to some of the high school teachers I had gotten to

know well and one of them found a program to train laboratory technologists. I didn't even know what that was, but
it was a way to get some training fairly quickly.

Counselor: How did that training go for you?

Senesie: I did alright at it. I didn't enjoy it very much, and sometimes I felt pretty bad about giving up college and singing,
but then I reminded myself that I was doing this for my son
and that made me feel better.

Counselor: Did you find work as a laboratory technician right away?

Senesie: Yes, my baby had been born before I finished school, and
as soon as I finished, I found a job. That was at the company
where I had the accident. I worked there about 6 years.

Counselor: What sort of work did you do?

Senesie: Ran tests and things like that. It was pretty routine. I just
did what the scientists told me to do. Sometimes I would get
involved in an experiment and be really interested in the
results, but most of the time I was pretty bored.

Counselor: What led you to stay in that job for 6 years?

Senesie: Well, the pay was good, the hours were good, people
seemed to like me there. It was right on the subway line. And
I guess I had enough to deal with outside of work. About 2
years after my first baby was born, I had another son. My
boyfriend and I were both about 21, and we decided that
this time we would get married before the baby was born
and try to work things out.

Counselor: How has that gone for you?

Senesie: Well, it hasn't been easy. I thought at 21 we were old
enough to get married, but it didn't seem that way. Harold,
my husband, would be out until all hours with musician
friends, and I felt like I was stuck with all the housework.
My grandmother would help out; I'd bring the kids over there
before I went to work and she'd watch them. But things were
pretty tense between Harold and me. Finally, after a really
bad couple of years, we sat down and talked things over and
decided we really wanted to stay together, so since then
we've really been working on our relationship. Things are
much better now, but we really have to make time for each
other and try to enjoy ourselves and the kids.

Counselor: Sounds like you really worked hard to improve your marriage and keep your family together. What sorts of leisure
activities do you enjoy, either with your family or friends or
by yourself?

Senesie: Yes, we do lots of things together. That's what really keeps me going. I still sing, at church and sometimes with my husband's group. We take the kids to shows and concerts, just like my mother did with us. My husband and I like to run together; we're both pretty athletic. I've also been doing some part-time jobs, some runway modeling for a department store. I really enjoyed that, and I'd like to do some more modeling.

Counselor: What did you enjoy about that?

Senesie: It reminded me of high school, when I used to perform in shows, the excitement, the audience. I also like the fashion part. I'm very interested in clothes and fabrics. I even thought I might like to try my hand at designing clothes sometime. People tell me I have a real flair for fashion and that might be something I could do.

Counselor: What other career options have you considered?

Senesie: Well, I still have an interest in math and computers. Maybe something in programming. I don't think I'd mind sitting at a computer as long as I had an interesting project to work on. I hope my hands will heal enough so I can do something like that. Right now I'm not sure.

Counselor: How would you feel about continuing your education?

Senesie: Great! I love my kids, but I wish I'd finished college. I'd have so many more opportunities. I'd really like to go back to school, even if I just get a 2-year degree. And it would make my mom really happy too!

Counselor: So returning to school really appeals to you. How would you describe yourself in terms of your strengths and weaknesses?

Senesie: Well, like I said, I have a good sense of style. I can be artistic and creative and I'm a good singer. I'm pretty practical and down-to-earth, get the bills paid on time and all. I'm a good mother and really value my family. I like to perform but, it's funny, sometimes when I'm around people in other ways, I feel shy. I'd rather be with my husband and kids than at a big party. Sometimes I think I get bored easily, though I did work at my job for a long time and that was pretty boring. I enjoy learning about new things and I'm pretty athletic. I feel self-confident about some things, but when I'm with people who are more educated than I am, sometimes I feel uncomfortable.

Counselor: There seem to be many aspects of yourself you feel proud of.

Senesie: Yes, I've done alright. The one thing that bothers me is not finishing college. You know, my younger brother got a scholarship to college too and he's already gotten his degree. He's working as an engineer. He just got married and seems to be doing great.

Counselor: You sound a little envious.

Senesie: Yes, I guess I am. I haven't had it easy, and now this accident really has me worried. In the beginning, I couldn't even take care of my kids myself, tie their shoes and so on. Things are better now, but it still gets me down.

Counselor: What do you do to handle those feelings?

Senesie: They're not that bad. I just wish I knew what the future held. Every time I seemed to be on track, something would come along and knock me off track and, it's like, here we go again.

Counselor: How do you think that our counseling could help you?

Senesie: This may sound funny, but in some ways, I don't think I really know myself. I've been all wrapped up in my kids since I was 19. Maybe through counseling and that testing you said we would do, I could figure out who I really am and what I could be good at. It would give me a chance to really think about things. I think I need some information about jobs too. I'm interested in computers, for example, but I really don't know what kinds of jobs there are related to computers, how much education I would need for those jobs, or if there are still a lot of jobs for people to work with computers.

Counselor: So counseling that helps to develop your self-awareness as well as your information about occupations and the job market would be useful to you. Are there any personal areas in which you might be able to use some counseling?

Senesie: Well, even though my marriage is much better than it was, maybe it would help to talk about ways my husband and I could talk to each other even better. And if I could stop worrying about my burns and just accept whatever will happen, that would help me.

Counselor: You've given me a great deal of information about your background and present situation, and we'll certainly be talking more about those areas of your life. Before we begin the testing, though, is there anything important that we've left out?

Senesie: I think we've covered most everything. You know, when I think about my future, I remember my mother saying to me, "Senesie, you're so pretty and so talented. Some day you'll be somebody!" I've done a lot in my life so far but I still don't feel like I'm somebody the way Mama wanted me to be. I really want to figure out how to use my abilities and be somebody special.

Assessment of Senesie Robinson

Intelligence

Wechsler Adult Intelligence Scale—Revised
Verbal IQ: 118
Performance IQ: 108
Full-scale IQ: 115 (high average)

Interests

The Self-Directed Search: Summary Code—AES (artistic, enterprising, social)
Strong Interest Inventory: See Figures 10.1a and 10.1b

Personality and Values

Myers-Briggs Type Indicator: See Figure 10.2
Hall Occupational Orientation Inventory: See Figure 10.3

STRONG INTEREST INVENTORY OF THE
STRONG VOCATIONAL INTEREST BLANKS PAGE 1

PROFILE REPORT FOR: Senesie Robinson
ID:
AGE: SEX: F
DATE TESTED: 02/01/
DATE SCORED: 2/ 7/

SPECIAL SCALES: ACADEMIC COMFORT 46
INTROVERSION-EXTROVERSION 52

TOTAL RESPONSES: 325 INFREQUENT RESPONSES: 6

GOT

R	Average
I	Average
A	Mod. High
S	Average
E	Low
C	Mod. High

668

REALISTIC

GENERAL OCCUPATIONAL THEME - R (30 40 50 60 70; F / M)
Average 44

BASIC INTEREST SCALES (STANDARD SCORE)

Scale	Rating	Score
AGRICULTURE	Average	49
NATURE	Average	45
ADVENTURE	Average	51
MILITARY ACTIVITIES	Mod. Low	44
MECHANICAL ACTIVITIES	Average	41

INVESTIGATIVE

GENERAL OCCUPATIONAL THEME - I (30 40 50 60 70; F / M)
Average 47

BASIC INTEREST SCALES (STANDARD SCORE)

Scale	Rating	Score
SCIENCE	Average	53
MATHEMATICS	High	61
MEDICAL SCIENCE	Mod. Low	43
MEDICAL SERVICE	Average	48

ARTISTIC

GENERAL OCCUPATIONAL THEME - A (30 40 50 60 70; F / M)
Mod. High 59

BASIC INTEREST SCALES (STANDARD SCORE)

Scale	Rating	Score
MUSIC/DRAMATICS	High	65
ART	Average	58
WRITING	Mod. Low	46

OCCUPATIONAL SCALES

F	M	Occupation	Standard Score F	Standard Score M	Very Dissimilar (15)	Dissimilar (25)	Moderately Dissimilar (30)	Mid-Range	Moderately Similar (40)	Similar (45)	Very Similar (55)
REALISTIC											
(CRS)	RC	Marine Corps enlisted personnel	(CRS)	26							
RC	RC	Navy enlisted personnel	38	26				*			
RC	RC	Army officer	35	23				*			
RI	RIC	Navy officer	42	23					*		
R	R	Air Force officer	38	16				*			
(C)	R	Air Force enlisted personnel	(C)	22							
R	R	Police officer	36	20				*			
R	R	Bus driver	37	37				*			
R	R	Horticultural worker	39	34				*			
RC	R	Farmer	24	21		*					
R	RCS	Vocational agriculture teacher	29	13			*				
RI	R	Forester	41	22					*		
(IR)	RI	Veterinarian	(IR)	18							
RIS	(SR)	Athletic trainer	20	(SR)		*					
RS	R	Emergency medical technician	28	22			*				
RI	RI	Radiologic technologist	35	27				*			
RI	R	Carpenter	29	13			*				
RI	R	Electrician	29	24			*				
RIA	(ARI)	Architect	31	(ARI)				*			
RI	RI	Engineer	29	19			*				
INVESTIGATIVE											
IRC	IRC	Computer programmer	38	34				*			
IRC	IRC	Systems analyst	45	33						*	
IRC	IR	Medical technologist	36	31				*			
IR	IR	R & D manager	34	22				*			
IR	IR	Geologist	38	37				*			
IR	(I)	Biologist	30	(I)				*			
IR	IR	Chemist	31	31				*			
IR	IR	Physicist	23	21		*					
IR	(RI)	Veterinarian	29	(RI)			*				
IRS	IR	Science teacher	32	36				*			
IRS	IRS	Physical therapist	43	38					*		
IR	IRS	Respiratory therapist	42	29					*		
IC	IR	Medical technician	40	25					*		
IC	IE	Pharmacist	28	14			*				
ISR	(CSE)	Dietitian	21	(CSE)		*					
(SI)	ISR	Nurse, RN	(SI)	15							
IR	I	Chiropractor	27	22			*				
IR	IR	Optometrist	34	31				*			
IR	IR	Dentist	30	26				*			
I	IA	Physician	32	36				*			
(IR)	I	Biologist	(IR)	39							
I	I	Mathematician	37	32				*			
IR	I	Geographer	48	47						*	
I	I	College professor	47	50						*	
IA	IA	Psychologist	35	47				*			
IA	IA	Sociologist	38	43				*			
ARTISTIC											
AI	AI	Medical illustrator	31	32				*			
A	A	Art teacher	15	34		*					
A	A	Artist, fine	40	41					*		
A	A	Artist, commercial	35	40				*			
AE	A	Interior decorator	26	37			*				
(RIA)	ARI	Architect	(RIA)	35							
A	A	Photographer	45	40						*	
A	A	Musician	53	53						*	
AR	(EA)	Chef	38	(EA)				*			
(E)	AE	Beautician	(E)	42							
AE	A	Flight attendant	31	44				*			
A	A	Advertising executive	28	39			*				
A	A	Broadcaster	35	41				*			
A	A	Public relations director	16	12		*					
A	A	Lawyer	36	32				*			
A	AS	Public administrator	33	33				*			
A	A	Reporter	24	37		*					
A	A	Librarian	51	49						*	
AS	AS	English teacher	18	40		*					
(SA)	AS	Foreign language teacher	(SA)	41							

CONSULTING PSYCHOLOGISTS PRESS, INC.
577 COLLEGE AVENUE
PALO ALTO, CA 94306
115 13 2 N

Figure 10.1A. Senesie Robinson's Strong Interest Inventory Profile

494   Developmental Career Counseling and Assessment

Figure 10.1B. Senesie Robinson's Strong Interest Inventory Profile

Report Form for the
Myers-Briggs Type Indicator®

Name: _Senesie Robinson_

Sex: ☐ Male ☒ Female Date: _____

The MBTI® reports your preferences on four scales. There are two opposite preferences on each scale. The four scales deal with where you like to focus your attention (E or I), the way you like to look at things (S or N), the way you like to go about deciding things (T or F), and how you deal with the outer world (J or P). Short descriptions of each scale are shown below.

E You prefer to focus on the outer world of people and things or **I** You prefer to focus on the inner world of ideas and impressions

S You tend to focus on the present and on concrete information gained from your senses or **N** You tend to focus on the future, with a view toward patterns and possibilities

T You tend to base your decisions on logic and on objective analysis of cause and effect or **F** You tend to base your decisions primarily on values and on subjective evaluation of person-centered concerns

J You like a planned and organized approach to life and prefer to have things settled or **P** You like a flexible and spontaneous approach to life and prefer to keep your options open

The four letters show your Reported Type, which is the combination of the four preferences you chose. There are sixteen possible types.

REPORTED TYPE: | E | N | T | J |

PREFERENCE SCORES: | 15 | 39 | 7 | 21 |

Preference scores show how consistently you chose one preference over the other; high scores usually mean a clear preference. Preference scores do *not* measure abilities or development.

EXTRAVERSION **E**   **I** INTROVERSION

SENSING **S**   **N** INTUITION

THINKING **T**   **F** FEELING

JUDGING **J**   **P** PERCEIVING

Each type tends to have different interests and different values. On the back of this page are very brief descriptions of each of the sixteen types. Find the one that matches the four letters of your Reported Type and see whether it fits you. If it doesn't, try to find one that does. For a more complete description of the types and the implications for career choice, relationships, and work behavior, see *Introduction to Type* by Isabel Briggs Myers. Remember that everyone uses each of the preferences at different times; your Reported Type shows which you are likely to prefer the most and probably use most often.

Figure 10.2. Senesie Robinson's Myer-Briggs Type Indicator

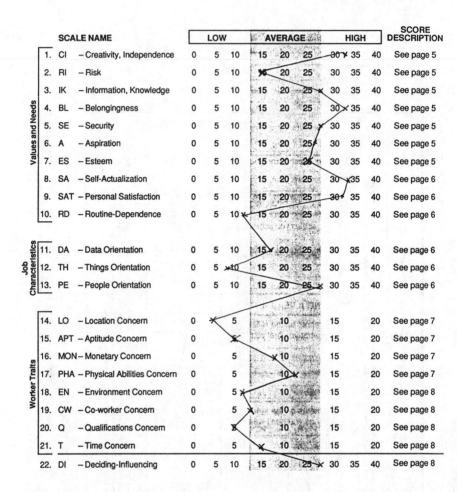

	SCALE NAME	LOW			AVERAGE			HIGH			SCORE DESCRIPTION
1. CI	– Creativity, Independence	0	5	10	15	20	25	30	35	40	See page 5
2. RI	– Risk	0	5	10		20	25	30	35	40	See page 5
3. IK	– Information, Knowledge	0	5	10	15	20	25	30	35	40	See page 5
4. BL	– Belongingness	0	5	10	15	20	25	30	35	40	See page 5
5. SE	– Security	0	5	10	15	20	25	30	35	40	See page 5
6. A	– Aspiration	0	5	10	15	20	25	30	35	40	See page 5
7. ES	– Esteem	0	5	10	15	20	25	30	35	40	See page 5
8. SA	– Self-Actualization	0	5	10	15	20	25	30	35	40	See page 6
9. SAT	– Personal Satisfaction	0	5	10	15	20	25	30	35	40	See page 6
10. RD	– Routine-Dependence	0	5	10	15	20	25	30	35	40	See page 6
11. DA	– Data Orientation	0	5	10	15	20	25	30	35	40	See page 6
12. TH	– Things Orientation	0	5	10	15	20	25	30	35	40	See page 6
13. PE	– People Orientation	0	5	10	15	20	25	30	35	40	See page 6
14. LO	– Location Concern	0		5		10		15		20	See page 7
15. APT	– Aptitude Concern	0		5		10		15		20	See page 7
16. MON	– Monetary Concern	0		5		10		15		20	See page 7
17. PHA	– Physical Abilities Concern	0		5		10		15		20	See page 7
18. EN	– Environment Concern	0		5		10		15		20	See page 8
19. CW	– Co-worker Concern	0		5		10		15		20	See page 8
20. Q	– Qualifications Concern	0		5		10		15		20	See page 8
21. T	– Time Concern	0		5		10		15		20	See page 8
22. DI	– Deciding-Influencing	0	5	10	15	20	25	30	35	40	See page 8

Left side labels: Values and Needs (scales 1–10); Job Characteristics (scales 11–13); Worker Traits (scales 14–21)

Figure 10.3. Self-Interpreting Profile Sheet for the Hall Occupation Orientation Inventory

Copyright © 1988 by L. G. Hall. Reprinted by permission of SCHOLASTIC TESTING SERVICE, INC., From Hall Occupational Orientation Inventory Self-Interpretive Folder, Young Adult/College Form.

Appendix A

National Career Development
Association Ethical Standards *

These Ethical Standards were developed by the National Board for Certified Counselors (NBCC), an independent, voluntary, not-for-profit organization incorporated in 1982. Titled "Code of Ethics" by NBCC and last amended in February 1987, the Ethical Standards were adopted by the National Career Development Association (NCDA) Board of Directors at its April 1987 meeting in New Orleans, LA. Only minor changes in wording (e.g., the addition of specific to NCDA members) were made.

Preamble: NCDA is an educational, scientific, and professional organization dedicated to the enhancement of the worth, dignity, potential, and uniqueness of each individual and, thus, to the service of society. This code of ethics enables the NCDA to clarify the nature of ethical responsibilities for present and future professional career counselors.

Section A: General

1. NCDA members influence the development of the profession by continuous efforts to improve professional practices, services, and research. Professional growth is continuous throughout the career counselor's career and

---

* Reprinted from *Career Developments* I (2), December, 1991, pp. 18-20. © ACA. Reprinted with permission. No further reproduction authorized without written permission of American Counseling Association.

is exemplified by the development of a philosophy that explains why and how a career counselor functions in the helping relationship. Career counselors must gather data on their effectiveness and be guided by the findings.

2. NCDA members have a responsibility to the clients they are serving and to the institutions within which the services are being performed. Career counselors also strive to assist the respective agency, organization, or institution in providing the highest caliber of professional services. The acceptance of employment in an institution implies that the career counselor is in agreement with the general policies and principles of the institution. Therefore, the professional activities of the career counselor are in accord with the objective of the institution. If, despite concerted efforts, the career counselor cannot reach agreement with the employer as to acceptable standards of conduct that allow for changes in institutional policy that are conducive to the positive growth and development of clients, then terminating the affiliation should be seriously considered.

3. Ethical behavior among professional associates (e.g., career counselors) must be expected at all times. When accessible information raises doubt about the ethical behavior of professional colleagues, the NCDA member must take action to attempt to rectify this condition. Such action uses the respective institution's channels first and then uses the procedures established by the American Association for Counseling and Development, of which NCDA is a division.

4. NCDA members neither claim nor imply professional qualifications which exceed those possessed, and are responsible for correcting any misrepresentations of these qualifications by others.

5. NCDA members must refuse a private fee or remuneration for consultation or counseling with persons who are entitled to their services through the career counselor's employing institution or agency. The policies of some agencies may make explicit provisions for staff members to engage in private practice with agency clients. However, should agency clients desire private counseling or consulting services, they must be apprised of other options available to them. Career counselors must not divert to their private practices legitimate clients in their primary agencies or of the institutions with which they are affiliated.

6. In establishing fees for professional counseling services, NCDA members must consider the financial status of clients and the respective locality. In the event that the established fee status is inappropriate for a client, assistance must be provided in finding comparable services of acceptable cost.

7. NCDA members seek only those positions in the delivery of professional services for which they are professionally qualified.

8. NCDA members recognize their limitations and provide services or only use techniques for which they are qualified by training and/or experience. Career counselors recognize the need for, and seek, continuing education to assure competent services.

9. NCDA members are aware of the intimacy in the counseling relationship, maintain respect for the client, and avoid engaging in activities that seek to meet their personal needs at the expense of the client.

10. NCDA members do not condone or engage in sexual harassment, which is defined as deliberate or repeated comments, gestures, or physical contacts of a sexual nature.

11. NCDA members avoid bringing their personal or professional issues into the counseling relationship. Through an awareness of the impact of stereotyping and discrimination (i.e., biases based on age, disability, ethnicity, gender, religion, or sexual preference), career counselors guard the individual rights and personal dignity of the client in the counseling relationship.

12. NCDA members are accountable at all times for their behavior. They must be aware that all actions and behaviors of a counselor reflect on professional integrity and, when inappropriate, can damage the public trust in the counseling profession. To protect public confidence in the counseling profession, career counselors avoid public behavior that is clearly in violation of accepted moral and legal standards.

13. NCDA members have a social responsibility because their recommendations and professional actions may alter the lives of others. Career counselors remain fully cognizant of their impact and are alert to personal, social, organization, financial, or political situations or pressures which might lead to misuse of their influence.

14. Products or services provided by NCDA members by means of classroom instruction, public lectures, demonstrations, written articles, radio or television programs, or other types of media must meet the criteria cited in Sections A through F of these Ethical Standards.

Section B: Counseling Relationship

1. The primary obligation of NCDA members is to respect the integrity and promote the welfare of the client, regardless of whether the client is assisted individually or in a group relationship. In a group setting, the career counselor is also responsible for taking reasonable precautions to protect individuals from physical and/or psychological trauma resulting from interaction within that group.

2. The counseling relationship and information resulting from it remains confidential, consistent with the legal obligations of the NCDA member. In a group counseling setting, the career counselor sets a norm of confidentiality regarding all group participants' disclosures.

3. NCDA members know and take into account the traditions and practices of other professional groups with whom they work, and they cooperate fully with such groups. If a person is receiving similar services from another professional, career counselors do not offer their own services directly to such a person. If a career counselor is contacted by a person who is already receiving similar services from another professional, the career counselor carefully considers that professional relationship and proceeds with caution and sensitivity to the therapeutic issues as well as to the client's welfare. Career counselors discuss these issues with clients so as to minimize the risk of confusion and conflict.

4. When a client's condition indicates that there is a clear and imminent danger to the client or others, the NCDA member must take reasonable personal action or inform responsible authorities. Consultation with other professionals must be used where possible. The assumption of responsibility for the client's behavior must be taken only after careful deliberation, and the client must be involved in the resumption of responsibility as quickly as possible.

5. Records of the counseling relationship, including interview notes, test data, correspondence, audio or visual tape recordings, electronic data storage, and other documents are to be considered professional information for use in counseling. They should not be considered a part of the records of the institution or agency in which the NCDA member is employed unless specified by state statute or regulation. Revelation to others of counseling material must occur only upon the expressed consent of the client; career counselors must make provisions for maintaining confidentiality in the storage and disposal of records. Career counselors providing information to the public or to subordinates, peers, or supervisors have a responsibility to ensure that the content is general; unidentified client information should be accurate and unbiased, and should consist of objective, factual data.

6. NCDA members must ensure that data maintained in electronic storage are secure. The data must be limited to information that is appropriate and necessary for the services being provided and accessible only to appropriate staff members involved in the provision of services by using the best computer security methods available. Career counselors must also ensure that electronically stored data are destroyed when the information is no longer of value in providing services.

7. Data derived from a counseling relationship for use in counselor training or research shall be confined to content that can be disguised to ensure full protection of the identity of the subject/client and shall be obtained with informed consent.

8. NCDA members must inform clients before or at the time the counseling relationship commences, of the purposes, goals, techniques, rules and procedures, and limitations that may affect the relationship.

9. All methods of treatment by NCDA members must be clearly indicated to prospective recipients, and safety precautions must be taken in their use.

10. NCDA members who have an administrative, supervisory and/or evaluative relationship with individuals seeking counseling services must not serve as the counselor and should refer the individuals to other professionals. Exceptions are made only in instances where an individual's situation warrants counseling intervention and another alternative is unavailable. Dual relationship with clients that might impair the career counselor's objectivity and professional judgment must be avoided and/or the counseling relationship terminated through referral to another competent professional.

11. When NCDA members determine an inability to be of professional assistance to a potential or existing client, they must, respectively, not initiate the counseling relationship or immediately terminate the relationship. In either event, the career counselor must suggest appropriate alternatives. Career counselors must be knowledgeable about referral resources so that a satisfactory referral can be initiated. In the event that the client declines a suggested referral, the career counselor is not obligated to continue the relationship.

12. NCDA members may choose to consult with any other professionally competent person about a client and must notify clients of this right. Career counselors must avoid placing a consultant in a conflict-of-interest situation that would preclude the consultant's being a proper party to the career counselor's efforts to help the client.

13. NCDA members who counsel clients from cultures different from their own must gain knowledge, personal awareness, and sensitivity pertinent to the client populations served and must incorporate culturally relevant techniques into their practice.

14. When NCDA members engage in intensive counseling with a client, the client's counseling needs should be assessed. When needs exist outside the counselor's expertise, appropriate referrals should be made.

15. NCDA members must screen prospective group counseling participants, especially when the emphasis is on self-understanding and growth through self-disclosure. Career counselors must maintain an awareness of each group participant's welfare throughout the group process.

16. When electronic data and systems are used as a component of counseling services, NCDA members must ensure that the computer application, and any information it contains, is appropriate for the respective needs of clients and is nondiscriminatory. Career counselors must ensure that they themselves have acquired a facilitation level of knowledge with any system they use, including hands-on application, search experience, and understanding of the uses of all aspects of the computer-based system. In selecting and/or maintaining computer-based systems that contain career information, career counselors,

must ensure that the systems provide current, accurate, and locally relevant information. Career counselors must also ensure that clients are intellectually, emotionally, and physically compatible to using the computer application and understand its purpose and operation. Client use of computer application must be evaluated to correct possible problems and assess subsequent needs.

17. NCDA members who develop self-help, stand-alone computer software for use by the general public must first ensure that it is initially designed to function in a stand-alone manner, as opposed to modifying software that was originally designed to require support from a counselor. Secondly, the software must include program statements that provide the user with intended outcomes, suggestions for using the software, descriptions of inappropriately used applications, and descriptions of when and how counseling services might be beneficial. Finally, the manual must include the qualifications of the developer, the development process, validation data, and operating procedures.

Section C:
Measurement and Evaluation

1. NCDA members must provide specific orientation or information to an examinee prior to and following the administration of assessment instruments or techniques so that the results may be placed in proper perspective with other relevant factors. The purpose of testing and the explicit use of the results must be made known to an examinee prior to testing.

2. In selecting assessment instruments or techniques for use in a given situation or with a particular client, NCDA members must evaluate carefully the instrument's specific theoretical bases and characteristics, validity, reliability, and appropriateness. Career counselors are professionally responsible for using unvalidated information with special care.

3. When making statements to the public about assessment instruments or techniques, NCDA members must provide accurate information and avoid false claims or misconceptions concerning the meaning of psychometric terms. Special efforts are often required to avoid unwarranted connotations of terms such as IQ and grade-equivalent scores.

4. Because many types of assessment techniques exist, NCDA members must recognize the limits of their competence and perform only those functions for which they have received appropriate training.

5. NCDA members must note when tests are not administered under standard conditions or when unusual behavior or irregularities occur during a testing session, and the results must be designated as invalid or of question-

able validity. Unsupervised or inadequately supervised assessments, such as mail-in tests, are considered unethical. However, the use of standardized instruments that are designed to be self-administered and self-scored, such as interest inventories, is appropriate.

6. Because prior coaching or dissemination of test materials can invalidate test results, NCDA members are professionally obligated to maintain test security. In addition, conditions that produce most favorable test results must be made known to an examinee (e.g., penalty for guessing).

7. NCDA members must consider psychometric limitations when selecting and using an instrument, and must be cognizant of the limitations when interpreting the results. When tests are used to classify clients, career counselors must ensure that periodic review and/or re-testing are conducted to prevent client stereotyping.

8. An examinee's welfare, explicit prior understanding, and agreement are the factors used when determining who receives the test results. NCDA members must see that appropriate interpretation accompanies any release of individual or group test data (e.g., limitations of instrument and norms).

9. NCDA members must ensure that computer-generated test administration and scoring programs function properly, thereby providing clients with accurate test results.

10. NCDA members who are responsible for making decisions based on assessment results must have appropriate training and skills in educational and psychological measurement—including validation criteria, test research, and guidelines for test development and use.

11. NCDA members must be cautious when interpreting the results of instruments that possess insufficient technical data, and must explicitly state to examinees the specific purposes for the use of such instruments.

12. NCDA members must proceed with caution when attempting to evaluate and interpret performances of minority group members or other persons who are not represented in the norm group on which the instrument was standardized.

13. NCDA members who develop computer-based test interpretations to support the assessment process must ensure that the validity of the interpretations is established prior to the commercial distribution of the computer application.

14. NCDA members recognize that test results may become obsolete, and avoid the misuse of obsolete data.

15. NCDA members must avoid the appropriation, reproduction, or modification for published tests or parts thereof without acknowledgment and permission from the publisher.

Section D: Research and Publication

1. NCDA members will adhere to relevant guidelines on research with human subjects. These include:
   a. *Code of Federal Regulations*, Title 45, Subtitle A, Part 46, as currently issued.
   b. American Psychological Association. (1982). *Ethical principles in the conduct of research with human participants*. Washington, DC: Author.
   c. American Psychological Association. (1981). Research with human participants. *American Psychologist, 36*, 633-638.
   d. Family Education Rights and Privacy Act. (Buckley Amendment to P.L. 93-380 of the Laws of 1974).
   e. Current federal regulations and various state privacy acts.

2. In planning research activities involving human subjects, NCDA members must be aware of and responsive to all pertinent ethical principles and ensure that the research problem, design, and execution are in full compliance with the principles.

3. The ultimate responsibility for ethical research lies with the principal researcher, though others involved in the research activities are ethically obligated and responsible for their own actions.

4. NCDA members who conduct research with human subjects are responsible for the subjects' welfare throughout the experiment and must take all reasonable precautions to avoid causing injurious psychological, physical, or social effects on their subjects.

5. NCDA members who conduct research must abide by the following basic elements of informed consent:
   a. a fair explanation of the procedures to be followed, including an identification of those which are experimental
   b. a description of the attendant discomforts and risks
   c. a description of the benefits to be expected
   d. a disclosure of appropriate alternative procedures that would be advantageous for subjects
   e. an offer to answer any inquiries concerning procedures
   f. an instruction that subjects are free to withdraw their consent and to discontinue participation in the project or activity at any time

6. When reporting research results, explicit mention must be made of all the variables and conditions known to the NCDA member that may have affected the outcome of the study or the interpretation of the data.

7. NCDA members who conduct and report research investigations must do so in a manner that minimizes the possibility that the results will be misleading.

8. NCDA members are obligated to make available sufficient original research data to qualified others who may wish to replicate the study.

9. NCDA members who supply data, aid in research of another person, report research results, or make original data available must take due care to disguise the identity of respective subjects in the absence of specific authorization from the subject to do otherwise.

10. When conducting and reporting research, NCDA members must be familiar with, and give recognition to, previous work on the topic, must observe all copyright laws, and must follow the principles of giving full credit to those to whom credit is due.

11. NCDA members must give due credit through joint authorship, acknowledgment, footnote statements, or other appropriate means to those who have contributed significantly to the research and/or publication, in accordance with such contributions.

12. NCDA members should communicate to others the results of any research judged to be of professional value. Results that reflect unfavorably on institutions, programs, services, or vested interests must not be withheld.

13. NCDA members who agree to cooperate with another individual on research and/or publication must incur an obligation to cooperate as promised in terms of punctuality of performance and with full regard to the completeness and accuracy of the information required.

14. NCDA members must not submit the same manuscript, or one essentially similar in content, for simultaneous publication consideration by two or more journals. In addition, manuscripts that are published in whole or substantial part in another journal or published work should not be submitted for publication without acknowledgment and permission from the previous publication.

Section E: Consulting

Consultation refers to a voluntary relationship between a professional helper and help-needing individual, group, or social unit in which the consultant is providing help to the client(s) in defining and solving a work-related problem or potential work-related problem with a client or client system.

1. NCDA members acting as consultants must have a high degree of self-awareness of their own values, knowledge, skills, limitations, and needs in entering a helping relationship that involves human and/or organizational change. The focus of the consulting relationship must be on the issues to be resolved and not on the person(s) presenting the problem.

2. In the consulting relationship, the NCDA member and client must understand and agree upon the problem definition, subsequent goals, and predicted consequences of interventions selected.

3. NCDA members must be reasonably certain that they, or the organization represented, have the necessary competencies and resources for giving the kind of help that is needed or that may develop later, and that appropriate referral resources are available to the consultant.

4. NCDA members in a consulting relationship must encourage and cultivate client adaptability and growth toward self-direction. NCDA members must maintain this role consistently and not become a decision maker for clients or create a future dependency on the consultant.

5. NCDA members conscientiously adhere to the NCDA Ethical Standards when announcing consultant availability for services.

Section F: Private Practice

1. NCDA members should assist the profession by facilitating the availability of counseling services in private as well as public settings.

2. In advertising services as private practitioners, NCDA members must advertise in a manner that accurately informs the public of the professional services, expertise, and counseling techniques available.

3. NCDA members who assume an executive leadership role in a private practice organization do not permit their names to be used in professional notices during periods of time when they are not actively engaged in the private practice of counseling.

4. NCDA members may list their highest relevant degree, type, and level of certification and/or license, address, telephone number, office hours, type and/or description of services, and other relevant information. Listed information must not contain false, inaccurate, misleading, partial, out-of-context, or otherwise deceptive material or statements.

5. NCDA members who are involved in a partnership or corporation with other professionals must, in compliance with the regulations of the locality, clearly specify the separate specialties of each member of the partnership or corporation.

6. NCDA members have an obligation to withdraw from a private-practice counseling relationship if it violates the NCDA Ethical Standards, if the mental or physical condition of the NCDA member renders it difficult to carry out an effective professional relationship, or if the counseling relationship is no longer productive for the client.

Section G: Procedures for Processing Ethical Complaints

As a division of the American Association for Counseling and Development (AACD), the National Career Development Association (NCDA) adheres to the guidelines and procedures for processing ethical complaints and the disciplinary sanctions adopted by AACD. A complaint against an NCDA member may be filed by an individual or group of individuals ("complainant"), whether or not the complainant is a member of NCDA. (Action will not be taken on anonymous complaints.)

For specifics on how to file ethical complaints and a description of the guidelines and procedures for processing contact:

Ethics Committee
c/o Executive Director
American Counseling Association
5999 Stevenson Avenue
Alexandria, VA 22304

Appendix B

Sources and Resources for Career Counselors

The following listing includes addresses for publishers of tests, inventories, career information, and career development products that may be useful to the career counselor.

Advocacy Press
P.O. Box 236
Department C1
Santa Barbara, CA 93102
(805) 962-2728

American College Testing Program
Career Planning Services
P.O. Box 168
Iowa City, IA 52243
(319) 337-1349

American College Testing Program
Educational Services Division
P.O. Box 168
Iowa City, IA 52243-9946
(319) 337-1000

American Counseling Association
(formerly American Association
for Counseling and Development)
5999 Stevenson Avenue
Alexandria, VA 22304
(800) 347-6647

American Guidance Service (AGS)
4201 Woodland Road
P.O. Box 99
Circle Pines, MN 55014-1796
(800) 328-2560

American Orthopsychiatric
Association, Inc.
1775 Broadway
New York, NY 10019
(212) 586-5690

Arco Publications
(see Prentice Hall)

Bureau of Labor Statistics
Publication Sales Center
P.O. Box 2145
Chicago, IL 60690
(312) 353-1880

Cambridge Career Products
P.O. Box 2153
Department CC6
Charleston, WV 25328-2153

Career Guidance Foundation
8090 Engineer Road
San Diego, CA 92111-1988

Career Planning and
Adult Development Newsletter
4965 Sierra Road
San Jose, CA 95132
(408) 559-4946

Career Planning and
Placement Service
100 Noyes Hall
University of Missouri
Columbia, MO 65211

Career Publishing, Inc.
910 N. Main Street
P.O. Box 5486
Orange, CA 92613-5486

Career Research and Testing
2005 Hamilton Avenue
San Jose, CA 95125
(408) 559-4945

Careers, Inc.
P.O. Box 135
Largo, FL 34649-0135

Center for Applications
of Psychological Type
2720 N.W. 6th Street
Gainesville, FL 32609
(904) 375-0160

CFKR Career Materials, Inc.
11860 Kemper Road, Unit 7
Auburn, CA 95603
(800) 525-5626

Chronicle Guidance Publications, Inc.
66 Aurora Street
P.O. Box 1190
Moravia, NY 13118-1190
(800) 622-7284

COIN Educational Products
3361 Executive Parkway
Suite 302
Toledo, OH 43606
(800) 274-8515

Conover Company Ltd.
P.O. Box 155
Omro, WI 54963

Consulting Psychologists Press, Inc.
3803 E. Bayshore Road
Palo Alto, CA 94303
(800) 624-1765

Control Data Systems, Inc.
4201 Lexington Ave., No.
St. Paul, MN 55126-6164
(612) 482-2100

CTB
McGraw-Hill Publishing
2500 Garden Road
Monterey, CA 93940
(800) 538-9547

DBM Publishing (Drake, Beam, Morin)
Division of Harcourt Brace & Co.
100 Park Ave.
New York, NY 10017
(800) 345-5627

Doubleday & Co., Inc.
1540 Broadway
New York, NY 10036-4094
(212) 354-6500

Doubleday
Division of Bantam Doubleday Dell
1540 Broadway
New York,NY 10036-4094
(800) 223-6834

EdITS
P.O. Box 7234
San Diego, CA 92167
(619) 222-1666

Educational Resources
Information Center (ERIC)
University of Michigan
Ann Arbor, MI 48109-1259

Educational Testing Service
P.O. Box 6403
Princeton, NJ 08543-5071
(800) 257-7444

Garrett Park Press
Garrett Park, MD 20896
(301) 946-2553

General Learning Corporation
P.O. Box 3060
Northbrook, IL 60065-9931
(800) 323-5471

Harper Collins Publishers
Department 361
10 East 53rd Street
New York, NY 10022-5299

Houghton Mifflin
222 Berkeley Street
Boston, MA 02116
(617) 725-5000

Hunt House Publishing, Inc.
3704 Meadowbank
Austin, TX 78703
(512) 453-1368

Impact Publishers
P.O. Box 1094
San Luis Obispo, CA 93406
(805) 543-5911

Institute for Personality
and Ability Testing
P.O. Box 1188
Champaign, IL 61824-1188
(800) 225-4728

Jastak Associates, Inc.
P.O. Box 3410
Wilmington, DE 19804
(800) 221-WRAT

JIST Works, Inc.
720 N. Park Avenue
Indianapolis, IN 46202

Kendall/Hunt Publishing Company
2460 Kerper Boulevard
P.O. Box 539
Dubuque, IA 52001

Marathon Consulting and Press
575 Anfield Road
Columbus, OH 43209

McBer and Company
137 Newbury Street
Boston, MA 02116

Meridian Education Corporation
236 E. Front Street
Bloomington, IL 61701-9990
(800) 727-5507

Merrill Publishing Co.
P. O. Box 508
Columbus, OH 43216

MetriTech, Inc.
111 North Market Street
Champaign, IL 61820
(800) 747-4868

Monarch Ltd.
P. O. Box. 160
Orangeburg, NY 10962
(914) 359-5300

National Computer Systems
P.O. Box 1416
Minneapolis, MN 55440
(800) NCS-7271

National Occupational Information
Coordinating Committee (NOICC)
1200 M Street, N.W.
Suite 156
Washington, DC 20036
(202) 653-7680

National Wellness Institute
1319 Fremont Street
South Hall
Stevens Point, WI 54481
(715) 346-2172

New Careers Center
1515 23rd Street
P.O. Box 339-UB
Boulder, CO 80306
(800) 634-9024

NIEP College Preview Tour Program
219 Broadway
Suite 321
Laguna Beach, CA 92651

Non-Sexist Vocational Card Set
Route 4, Box 217
Gainesville, FL 32601

Orchard House, Inc.
112 Balls Hill Road
Concord, MA 01742

Paperbacks for Educators
426 W. Front Street
Washington, MO 63090
(800) 227-2591

Peterson's Guides
Department 0318
P.O. Box 2123
Princeton, NJ 08543-2123

Positive Action
P.O. Box 2347
Twin Falls, ID 83303-2347
(800) 345-2974

Prentice Hall
113 Sylvan
Rte. 9W
Englewood Cliffs, NJ 07632
(201) 592-2000

Prentice Hall/Arco Publications
Division of Simon & Schuster, Inc.
15 Columbus Circle
New York, NY 10023
(800) 223-2348

Pro-ed
8700 Shoal Creek Boulevard
Austin, TX 78758-6897
(512) 451-3246

Professional Associates
Box 6254
Harrisburg, PA 17112

Psychological Assessment
Resources (PAR)
P.O. Box 998
Odessa, FL 33556
(800) 331-TEST

Psychological Corporation
Harcourt Brace Jovanovich, Inc.
555 Academic Court
San Antonio, TX 78204-2498
(800) 228-0752

Publishers Test Service
2500 Garden Road
Monterey, CA 93940

Putnam Publishing Group
200 Madison Ave.
New York, NY 10016
(800) 631-8571

Reference Service Press
1100 Industrial Rd.
Suite 9
San Carlos, CA 94070
(415) 594-0743

Research Press
Department B
2612 N. Mattis Avenue
Champaign, IL 61821
(217) 352-3273

Riverside Publishing Company
8420 Bryn Mawr Avenue
Chicago, IL 60631
(800) 323-9540

Scholastic Testing Service, Inc.
480 Meyer Road
P.O. Box 1056
Bensenville, IL 60106-8056
(800) 642-6787

Science Research Associates
155 N. Wacker Drive
Chicago, IL 60606
(800) 621-0476

Scott, Foresman & Co.
1900 E. Lake Ave.
Glenview, IL 60025
(708) 729-3000

Sigma Assessment Systems, Inc.
1110 Military Street
P.O. Box 610984
Port Huron, MI 48061-0984
(800) 265-1285

Slosson Educational Publications, Inc.
P.O. Box 280
East Aurora, NY 14052
(800) 828-4800

Social Studies School Service
10200 Jefferson Boulevard
P.O. Box 802
Culver City, CA 90232-0802

STM Systems Corporation
Careerware
810 Proctor Avenue
Ogdensburg, NY 13669
(800) 267-1544

Sunburst Communications
39 Washington Avenue
Pleasantville, NY 10570-9971

Superintendent of Documents
Government Printing Office
Washington, DC 20402
(202) 783-3238

Teaching Resources Corporation
50 Pond Park Road
Hingham, MA 02043
(617) 749-0461

Ten Speed Press/Celestial Arts
P.O. Box 7123
Berkeley, CA 94707
(800) 841-BOOK

Test Corporation of America
330 W. 47th Street
Suite 205
Kansas City, MO 64112
(800) 822-8485

U.S. Department of Labor
Division of Testing
200 Constitution Ave., NW
Washington, DC 20213
(202) 535-0157

VGM Career Horizons
4255 W. Touhy Avenue
Lincolnwood, IL 60646-1975

Vocational Biographies
P.O. 31
Sauk Centre, MN 56378-0031
(800) 255-0752

Vocational Studies Center
School of Education
University of Wisconsin—Madison
1025 W. Johnson Street
Madison, WI 53706

Wellness Associates
12347 Dupont Road
Sebastopol, CA 95472
(707) 874-1466

Western Psychological Services
12031 Wilshire Boulevard
Los Angeles, CA 90025
(800) 648-8857

Wintergreen Software, Inc.
P.O. Box 1229
Madison, WI 53701
(800) 999-WGSW

Appendix C

Acronyms for Tools of Assessment

ACCI = Adult Career Concerns Inventory
ACDM = Assessment of Career Decision Making
ACL = Adjective Checklist
APP = Advanced Placement Program
ASVAB = Armed Services Vocational Aptitude Battery

BASIS = Basic Achievement Skills Individual Screener

CAI = Career Assessment Inventory
CAPS = Career Ability Placement Survey
CDI = Career Development Inventory
CDI = Career Directions Inventory
CDM = Harrington O'Shea Career Decision-Making System
CDS = Career Decision Scale
CLEP = College-Level Examination Program
CMI = Career Maturity Inventory
COPES = Career Orientation Placement and Evaluation Survey
COPS = Career Occupational Preference System
COPS-P = California Occupational Preference System—Professional
CPI = California Psychological Inventory
CPP = Career Planning Program
CPQ = Career Planning Questionnaire
CTBS = Comprehensive Test of Basic Skills

DAT = Differential Aptitude Tests
DATCPP = Differential Aptitude Tests Career Planning Program
DUSO = Developing Understanding of Themselves and Others

EPPS = Edwards Personal Preference Schedule

GATB = General Aptitude Test Battery

HALL = Hall Occupational Orientation Inventory
HSPQ = High School Personality Questionnaire

ICE = Individual Career Exploration
IDEAS = Interest Determination, Exploration and Assessment System

JVIS = Jackson Vocational Interest Inventory

K-BIT = Kaufman Brief Intelligence Test
KGIS = Kuder General Interest Survey
KOIS = Kuder Occupational Interest Survey

LAQ = Lifestyle Assessment Questionnaire

MAT = Miller Analogies Test
MBTI = Myers-Briggs Type Indicator
MCAB = Minnesota Clerical Assessment Battery
MCMI-II = Millon Clinical Multiaxial Inventory—II
MIQ = Minnesota Importance Questionnaire
MMPI = Minnesota Multiphasic Personality Inventory
MMPI-II = Minnesota Multiphasic Personality Inventory—II
MMY = Mental Measurements Yearbook
MVS = My Vocational Situation

OLSAT = Otis-Lennon School Ability Test
OVIS-II = Ohio Vocational Interest Survey—II

P-ACT = Preliminary American College Test
PCOP = Personal Career Development Profile
PEP = Proficiency Examination Program
PIAT-R = Peabody Individual Achievement Test—Revised
PPVT-R = Peabody Picture Vocabulary Test—Revised
PSAT = Preliminary Scholastic Aptitude Test

RAK = Retirement Activities Kit

SAT = Scholastic Aptitude Test
SDS = Self-Directed Search
SEI = Self-Esteem Inventory
SI = Salience Inventory
SIGI = System of Interactive Guidance and Information
SII = Strong Interest Inventory
16PF = Sixteen Personality Factor

TABE = Tests of Adult Basic Education
TAP = Tests of Achievement and Proficiency
TONI = Test of Nonverbal Intelligence
TSWE = Test of Standard Written English

USES-II = U.S. Employment Service—Interest Inventory

VIESA = Vocational Interest Experience Skill Assessment
VPI = Vocational Preference Inventory

WAIS = Wechsler Adult Intelligence Scale
WISC = Wechsler Intelligence Scale for Children
WJII = Woodcock-Johnson Psycho-Educational Battery II
WPPSI = Wechsler Preschool and Primary Scale of Intelligence
WRAT = Wide Range Achievement Test
WRIOT = Wide Range Interest-Opinion Test

References

Abramowitz, M. W., & Macari, C. (1972). Values clarification in junior high school. *Educational Leadership, 7*, 621-626.

Abrego, P., & Brammer, L. (1992). Counseling adults in midlife career transitions. In H. D. Lea & Z. B. Leibowitz (Eds.), *Adult career development* (pp. 234-254). Alexandria, VA: American Association of Counseling and Development.

Adams, R. L., & Phillips, N. N. (1972). Motivational and achievement differences among children of various ordinal birth positions. *Child Development, 43*, 155-164.

Adler, A. (1931). *What life should mean to you.* Boston: Little, Brown.

Adler, T. (1989, August). Happiest workers are in fields dominated by their own gender. *APA Monitor,* pp. 12-13.

Ahmann, J. S. (1985). Otis-Lennon School Ability Test. *Career Development Quarterly, 17*(4), 226-229.

Allen, R. E. (1978). Factors influencing the compensation of two-year-college alumni. *Vocational Guidance Quarterly, 27*(1), 25-36.

Allis, M. R. (1984). Career Decision Scale. *Measurement and Evaluation in Counseling and Development, 17*(2), 98-100.

Allport, G. S., Vernon, P., & Lindzey, G. (1960). *Study of values.* Iowa City, IA: Riverside.

Amatea, E. S., Clark, J. E., & Cross, E. G. (1984). Life-styles: Evaluating a life role planning program for high school students. *Vocational Guidance Quarterly, 32*(4), 249-259.

Amatea, E. S., & Cross, G. E. (1982). *Evaluating dual career guidance programs for high school and college students* (Final report, Project 2-2F11). Gainesville: University of Florida. (ERIC Document Reproduction Service No. ED 236 450)

American Personnel and Guidance Association. (1972). *AMEG's position paper on the responsible use of tests.* Washington, DC: Author.

American School Counselors Association. (1976). *Standardized group I.Q. testing: A statement of the American School Counselors Association.* Alexandria, VA: Author.

Amundson, N. E., & Borgen, W. A. (1988). Factors that help and hinder in group employment counseling. *Journal of Employment Counseling, 25*(3), 104-114.

Anastasi, A. (1992). What counselors should know about the use and interpretation of psychological tests. *Journal of Counseling and Development, 70*(5), 610-615.

Anderson, R. C., & Apostal, R. A. (1971). Occupational introversion-extroversion and size of hometown. *Vocational Guidance Quarterly, 20*(2), 138-140.

Angoff, W. H. (1988). The nature-nurture debate, aptitudes, and group differences. *American Psychologist, 43*(9), 713-720.

Arbona, C. (1990). Career counseling research and Hispanics. *The Counseling Psychologist, 18*(2), 300-323.

Arbona, C., & Novy, D. M. (1991). Career aspirations and expectations of Black, Mexican American, and White students. *Career Development Quarterly, 39*(3), 231-239.

Archer, J., Jr., & Lamnin, A. (1985). An investigation of personnel and academic stressors on college campuses. *Journal of College Student Personnel, 26*(3), 210-214.

Arp, R. S., Holmberg, K. S., & Littrell, J. M. (1986). Launching adult students into the job market: A support group approach. *Journal of Counseling and Development, 65*(3), 166-167.

Arthur, M. B., Hall, D. T., & Lawrence, B. S. (1989). Generating new directions in career theory: The case for a trans-disciplinary approach. In M. B. Arthur, D. T. Hall, & B. S. Lawrence (Eds.), *Handbook of career theory* (pp. 7-25). New York: Cambridge University Press.

Astin, A. W. (1978). *Four critical years.* San Francisco: Jossey-Bass.

Astin, A. W. (1984). Student values: Knowing more about where we are today. *Bulletin of the American Association of Higher Education, 36*(9), 10-13.

Atchley, R. C. (1976). *The sociology of retirement.* New York: John Wiley.

Aubrey, R. G. (1977). *Career development needs of thirteen-year-olds: How to improve career development programs.* Washington, DC: National Advisory Council for Career Education.

Auster, C. J., & Auster, D. (1981). Factors influencing women's choice of nontraditional careers: The role of family, peers, and counselors. *Vocational Guidance Quarterly, 29*(3), 253-263.

Avasthi, S. (1990, December 6). SAT revisions signal change, prompt criticism. *Guidepost,* pp. 1, 6.

Backover, A. (1991, March 14). Wage gap poses dilemma for women and counselors. *Guidepost,* pp. 1, 8, 10.

Bailey, L. J., & Stadt, R. W. (1973). *Career education.* Bloomington, IL: McKnight.

Baker, S. B., & Popowicz, C. L. (1983). Meta-analysis as a strategy for evaluating effects of career education interventions. *Vocational Guidance Quarterly, 31*(3), 178-186.

Barak, A., Librowsky, I., & Shiloh, S. (1989). Cognitive determinants of interests: An extension of a theoretical model and initial empirical examinations. *Journal of Vocational Behavior, 34,* 318-334.

Barrett, G. V., & Depinet, R. L. (1991). A reconsideration of testing for competence rather than for intelligence. *American Psychologist, 46*(10), 1012-1024.

Bartling, H. C., & Hood, A. B. (1981). An 11-year follow-up of measured interest and vocational choice. *Journal of Counseling Psychology, 28*(1), 27-35.

Baruch, G. K. (1970). Feminine self-esteem, self-ratings of competence and maternal career commitment. *Journal of Counseling Psychology, 20,* 487-488.

Baruch, G. K. (1974). Maternal career-orientation as related to parental identification in college women. *Journal of Vocational Behavior, 4,* 173-180.

Bauer, D., & Mott, D. (1990). Life themes and motivations of re-entry students. *Journal of Counseling and Development, 68*(5), 555-560.

Bauernfeind, R. H. (1991a). Interest Determination, Exploration, and Assessment System (IDEAS). *AMECD Newsnotes, 26*(2), 6-9.

Bauernfeind, R. H. (1991b). Jackson Vocational Interest Survey (JVIS). *AMECD Newsnotes, 26*(3), 6-11.

Bauernfeind, R. H., & Kandor, J. R. (1988). *AMECD committee to screen career guidance instruments.* Alexandria, VA: Association for Measurement and Evaluation in Counseling and Development.

Bayer, D. L. (1986). The effects of two methods of affective education on self-concept in seventh-grade students. *The School Counselor, 34*(2), 123-134.

Beane, J. A. (1986). The self-enhancing middle-grade school. *The School Counselor, 33*(3), 189-195.

Benson, J., Urman, H., & Hocevar, D. (1986). Effects of test-wiseness training and ethnicity on achievement of third- and fifth-grade students. *Measurement and Evaluation in Counseling and Development, 18*(4), 154-162.

Bernardelli, A. (1983). Occupational information-seeking as a function of perception of locus of control and other personality variables. *Canadian Counsellor, 17,* 75-81.

Betz, N. E., Fitzgerald, L. F., & Hill, R. E. (1989). Trait-factor theories: Traditional cornerstone of career theory. In M. B. Arthur, D. T. Hall, & B. S. Lawrence (Eds.), *Handbook of career theory* (pp. 25-40). New York: Cambridge University Press.

Betz, N. E., & Hackett, G. (1981). The relationship of career-related self-efficacy expectations to perceived career options in college women and men. *Journal of Counseling Psychology, 28*(5), 339-410.

Betz, N. E., Heesacker, R. S., & Shuttleworth, C. (1990). Moderators of the congruence and realism of major and occupational plans in college students: A replication and extension. *Journal of Counseling Psychology, 37*(3), 269-276.

Biggs, D. A., & Keller, K. E. (1982). A cognitive approach to using tests in counseling. *Personnel and Guidance Journal, 60,* 528-532.

Blackburn, A. C., & Erickson, D. B. (1986). Predictable crises of the gifted student. *Journal of Counseling and Development, 64*(9), 552-555.

Blimline, C. A., Thorn, M., Wilson, J. C., & Wilcox, J. (1983). Counseling in a government agency: Interventions for employees and supervisors. *Personnel and Guidance Journal, 61*(9), 570-574.

Blimling, G. S. (1989). A meta-analysis of the influence of college residence halls on academic performance. *Journal of College Student Personnel, 30*(4), 298-308.

Bloch, D. P. (1989). Using career information with dropouts and at-risk youth. *Career Development Quarterly, 38*(2), 159-171.

Bloch, D. P., & Kinnison, J. F. (1989). A method for rating computer-based career information delivery systems. *Measurement and Evaluation in Counseling and Development, 21*(4), 177-187.

Blocher, D. H., & Siegal, R. (1981). Toward a cognitive developmental theory of leisure and work. *The Counseling Psychologist, 9*(3), 33-44.

Bloland, P. A., & Edwards, P. B. (1981). Work and leisure: A counseling synthesis. *Vocational Guidance Quarterly, 30*(2), 101-108.

Bloland, P. A., & Walker, B. A. (1981). A humanistic existential perspective on career counseling. *Vocational Guidance Quarterly, 29*(3), 197-204.

Blum, D. E. (1990, May 2). Representation of minorities in graduate programs rose steadily from 1986 to 1988, survey finds. *Chronicle of Higher Education,* p. A13.

Blustein, D. L. (1989). The role of goal instability and career self-efficacy in the career exploration process. *Journal of Vocational Behavior, 35,* 194-203.

Blustein, D. L., Walbridge, M. M., Friedlander, M. L., & Palladino, D. E. (1991). Contributions of psychological separation and parental attachment to the career development process. *Journal of Counseling Psychology, 38*(1), 39-50.

Bolles, R. N. (1993). *What color is your parachute?* Berkeley, CA: Ten Speed Press.

Bolton, B. (1988). Retest reliability of the USES Interest Inventory: A research note. *Measurement and Evaluation in Counseling and Development, 21*(3), 113-116.

Borchard, D. C., Kelly, J. J., & Weaver, N. P. K. (1988). *Your career: Choices, chances, changes.* Dubuque, IA: Kendall/Hunt.

Borgen, W. A., & Amundson, N. E. (1987). The dynamics of unemployment. *Journal of Counseling and Development, 66*(4), 180-184.

Borgen, W. A., Amundson, N. E., & Harder, H. G. (1988). The experience of underemployment. *Journal of Employment Counseling, 25*(4), 149-159.

Borman, C., Nash, W., & Colson, S. (1978). Career guidance for gifted and talented students. *Vocational Guidance Quarterly, 27*(1), 72-76.

Bowen, H. R. (1977, November 28). The differences among colleges. *Chronicle of Higher Education,* p. 9.

Bowen, M. (1978). *Family therapy in clinical practice.* New York: Aronson.

Braddock, D. J., & Hecker, D. E. (1988). The class of '84 one year after graduation. *Occupational Outlook Quarterly, 32*(2), 17-44.

Bradley, R. W. (1982). Using birth order and sibling dynamics in career counseling. *Personnel and Guidance Journal, 61*(1), 25-31.

Bradley, R. W., & Mims, G. A. (1992). Using family systems and birth order dynamics as the basis for a college career decision-making course. *Journal of Counseling Psychology, 70*(3), 445-448.

Brand, L. (1990). Occupational staffing patterns within industries through the year 2000. *Occupational Outlook Quarterly, 34*(2), 40-52.

Breland, H. M. (1974). Birth order, family configuration and verbal achievement. *Child Development, 45,* 1011-1019.

Brill, A. A. (1938). *The basic writings of Sigmund Freud.* New York: Modern Library.

Brizzi, J. S. (1986). The socialization of women's vocational realism. *Vocational Guidance Quarterly, 34*(4), 225-232.

Brolin, D. E., & Gysbers, N. C. (1989). Career education for students with disabilities. *Journal of Counseling and Development, 68*(2), 155-159.

Brook, J. S., Whiteman, M., Persach, E., & Deutsch, M. (1974). Aspiration levels of and for children: Age, race and socioeconomic correlates. *Journal of Genetic Psychology, 124,* 3-16.

Brookings, J. B., & Bolton, B. (1986). Vocational interest dimensions of adult handicapped persons. *Measurement and Evaluation in Counseling and Development, 18*(4), 168-175.

Brown, D. (1981). Emerging models of career development groups for persons at midlife. *Vocational Guidance Quarterly, 29*(4), 332-340.

Brown, D. (1987). The status of Holland's theory of vocational choice. *Career Development Quarterly, 36*(1), 13-23.

Brown, D., Minor, C. W., & Jepsen, D. A. (1991). The opinions of minorities about preparing for work: Report of the second NCDA national survey. *Career Development Quarterly, 40*(1), 5-19.

Brown, D., Ware, W. B., & Brown, S. T. (1985). A predictive validation of the Career Decision-Making System. *Measurement and Evaluation in Counseling and Development, 18*(2), 81-85.

Bruhn, J. G. (1989). Job stress: An opportunity for professional growth. *Career Development Quarterly, 37*(4), 306-315.

Buehler, C. (1933). *Der menschliche Lebenslauf als psychologisches Problem.* Leipzig: Hirzel.

Bunce, M. E. (1984). An examination of placement services available to job seekers: A review of laypersons' literature. *Journal of Employment Counseling, 21*(4), 175-181.

Butcher, E. (1982). Changing by choice: A process model for group career counseling. *Vocational Guidance Quarterly, 30*(3), 200-209.

Cahill, M., & Salomone, P. R. (1987). Career counseling for work life extension: Integrating the older worker into the labor force. *Career Development Quarterly, 35*(3), 188-196.

Calsyn, R. J., Pennell, C., & Harter, M. (1984). Are affective education programs more effective with girls than with boys? *Elementary School Guidance and Counseling, 19*(2), 132-140.

Campbell, V. L. (1987). Strong-Campbell Interest Inventory, fourth edition. *Journal of Counseling and Development, 66*(1), 53-56.

Career Planning and Adult Development Network. (1990). *Career Planning and Adult Development Network Newsletter, 12*(3).

Carey, M. (1990). Occupational tenure, employer tenure, and occupational mobility. *Occupational Outlook Quarterly, 34*(2), 55-60.

Carey, R. G. (1977). The widowed: A year later. *Journal of Counseling Psychology, 24*(2), 125-131.

Carlsen, M. B. (1988). *Meaning-making.* New York: Norton.

Carr, J. V., & Hayslip, J. B. (1989). Getting unstuck from the 1970's: New Hampshire style. *The School Counselor, 37*(1), 41-46.

Carson, A., & Mowsesian, R. (1990). Some remarks on Gati's theory of career decision-making models. *Journal of Counseling Psychology, 37*(4), 502-507.

Carvajal, H., McKnab, P., Gerber, J., Hewes, P., & Smith, P. (1989). Counseling college-bound students: Can ACT scores be predicted? *The School Counselor, 36*(3), 186-191.

Chapman, W., & Katz, M. R. (1983). Career information systems in secondary schools: A survey and assessment. *Vocational Guidance Quarterly, 31*(3), 165-177.

Chartrand, J. M. (1990). A causal analysis to predict the personal and academic adjustment of nontraditional students. *Journal of Counseling Psychology, 37*(1), 65-73.

Chartrand, J. M. (1991). The evolution of trait-and-factor career counseling: A Person × Environment fit approach. *Journal of Counseling and Development, 69*(6), 518-524.

Cheatham, H. E. (1990). Africentricity and career development of African Americans. *Career Development Quarterly, 38*(4), 334-346.

Chickering, A. W. (1969). *Education and identity.* San Francisco: Jossey-Bass.

Chiu, L. (1987). Development of the Self-esteem Rating Scale for Children (revised). *Measurement and Evaluation in Counseling and Development, 20*(1), 36-41.

Chiu, L. (1988). Measures of self-esteem for school-age children. *Journal of Counseling and Development, 66*(6), 298-301.

Chronicle of Higher Education. (1990). *Chronicle of Higher Education Almanac.* Washington, DC: Author.

Chusmir, L. H. (1983). Characteristics and predictive dimensions of women who make nontradtiional vocational choices. *Personnel and Guidance Journal, 62*(1), 43-47.

Chusmir, L. H. (1990). Men who make nontraditional career choices. *Journal of Counseling and Development, 69*(1), 11-16.

Cianni-Surridge, M., & Horan, J. J. (1983). On the wisdom of assertive job-seeking behavior. *Journal of Counseling Psychology, 30*(2), 209-214.

Claiborn, C. D. (1991). The Buros tradition and the counseling profession. *Journal of Counseling and Development, 69*(5), 456-457.

Colangelo, N., Kelly, K. R., & Schrepfer, R. M. (1987). A comparison of gifted, general, and special learning needs students on academic and social self-concept. *Journal of Counseling and Development, 66*(2), 73-77.

Cole, C. (1982). Career guidance for middle-junior high school students. *Vocational Guidance Quarterly, 30*(4), 308-314.

Conoley, J. C., & Kramer, J. J. (Eds.). (1989). *The tenth mental measurements yearbook.* Lincoln: University of Nebraska—Lincoln, Buros Institute of Mental Measurements.

Cook, E. P. (1991). Annual review: Practice and research in career counseling and development, 1990. *Career Development Quarterly, 40*(2), 99-131.

Cooper, S. E., & Robinson, D. A. G. (1989). Childhood play activities of women and men entering engineering and science careers. *The School Counselor, 36*(5), 338-342.

Cooper, S. E., & Van Matre, G. (1984, April). *An investigation of the differential effects of group versus individual treatment on vocational indecision and indecisiveness.* Paper presented at the meetings of the American Educational Research Association, New Orleans, LA. (ERIC Document Reproduction Service No. ED 244 105)

Cosby, A. G. (1974). Occupational expectations and the hypothesis of increasing realism of choice. *Journal of Vocational Behavior, 5*, 53-65.

Cox, R. D. (1970). *Youth into maturity.* New York: Mental Health Materials Center.

Cox, S. G. (1971). Do educational measures predict vocational success? *Vocational Guidance Quarterly, 19*, 271-274.

Crabbs, M. A., Black, K. U., & Morton, S. B. (1986). Stress at work: A comparison of men and women. *Journal of Employment Counseling, 23*(1), 2-8.

Crites, J. O. (1976). A comprehensive model of career development in early adulthood. *Journal of Vocational Behavior, 9*, 105-118.

Crohan, S. E., Antonucci, T. C., Adelmann, P. K., & Coleman, L. M. (1989). Job characteristics and well-being at midlife: Ethnic and gender comparisons. *Psychology of Women Quarterly, 13*, 223-235.

Cytrynbaum, S., & Crites, J. O. (1989). The utility of adult development theory in understanding the career adjustment process. In M. B. Arthur, D. T. Hall, & B. S. Lawrence (Eds.), *Handbook of career theory* (pp. 66-88). New York: Cambridge University Press.

Dahl, P. R. (1982). Maximizing vocational opportunities for handicapped clients. *Vocational Guidance Quarterly, 31*(1), 43-52.

Davenport, D. W. (1984). Outplacement counseling: Whither the counselor? *Vocational Guidance Quarterly, 32*(3), 185-191.

Davitz, J., & Davitz, L. (1976). *Making it from 40 to 50.* New York: Random House.

Dawis, R. B., & Lofquist, L. (1984). *A psychological theory of work adjustment: An individual differences model and its application.* Minneapolis: University of Minnesota Press.

Dayton, C. W. (1981). The young person's job search: Insights from a study. *Journal of Counseling Psychology, 28*(4), 321-333.

Dewey, C. R. (1974). Exploring interests: A non-sexist method. *Personnel and Guidance Journal, 52*, 311-315.

DeWinne, R. F., Overton, T. D., & Schneider, L. J. (1978). Types produce types—especially fathers. *Journal of Vocational Behavior, 12*, 140-144.

Diamond, E. E., Harmon, L. H., & Zytowski, D. G. (1976, September 9). Other-sex norms fulfill "right to know" provision. *Guidepost*, p. 2.

DiBenedetto, B., & Tittle, C. K. (1990). Gender and adult roles: Role commitment of women and men in a job-family trade-off context. *Journal of Counseling Psychology, 37*(1), 41-48.

Dillard, J. M., & Campbell, N. J. (1981). Influences of Puerto Rican, Black, and Anglo parents' career behavior on their adolescent children's career development. *Vocational Guidance Quarterly, 30*(2), 139-148.

Dillard, J. M., & Perrin, D. W. (1980). Puerto Rican, Black, and Anglo adolescents' career aspirations, expectations, and maturity. *Vocational Guidance Quarterly, 28*(4), 313-321.

Dillon, M., & Weissman, S. (1987). Relationship between personality types on the Strong-Campbell and Myers-Briggs instruments. *Measurement and Evaluation in Counseling and Development, 20*(2), 68-79.

Dimock, P. H., & Cormier, P. (1991). The effects of format differences and computer experience on performance and anxiety on a computer-administered test. *Measurement and Evaluation in Counseling and Development, 24*(3), 119-126.

Dorn, F. J. (1986). Needed: Competent, confident, and committed career counselors. *Journal of Counseling and Development, 65*(4), 216-217.

Dorn, F. J. (1988). Utilizing social influence in career counseling: A case study. *Career Development Quarterly, 36*(3), 269-280.

Droege, R. C., & Boese, R. (1982). Development of a new occupational aptitude pattern structure with comprehensive occupational coverage. *Vocational Guidance Quarterly, 30*(3), 219-229.

Drummond, R. J. (1986). A review of the High School Personality Questionnaire. *Journal of Counseling and Development, 65*(4), 218-219.

Drummond, R. J. (1988). Test review: The Values Scale by D. D. Nevill and D. E. Super. *Journal of Employment Counseling, 25*(3), 136-138.

Duckworth, J. (1990). The counseling approach to the use of testing. *The Counseling Psychologist, 18*(2), 198-204.

Duckworth, J. C. (1991). The Minnesota Multiphasic Personality Inventory—2: A review. *Journal of Counseling and Development, 69*(6), 564-567.

Dweck, C. S. (1986). Motivational processes affecting learning. *American Psychologist, 41*(10), 1040-1048.

Eberly, C. G., & Cech, E. J. (1986). Integrating computer-assisted testing and assessment into the counseling process. *Measurement and Evaluation in Counseling and Development, 19*(1), 18-26.

EdITS. (1990, Winter/Spring). *EdITS research and developments*. San Diego, CA: Author.

Elsenrath, D., Hettler, B., & Leafgreen, F. (1988). *Lifestyle assessment questionnaire*. Stevens Point, WI: National Wellness Institute, Inc.

Engen, H. B., Laing, J., & Sawyer, R. (1988). College-bound students' satisfaction with guidance services. *The School Counselor, 36*(2), 112-117.

Engen, H. B., Lamb, R. R., & Prediger, D. J. (1982). Are secondary schools still using standardized tests? *Personnel and Guidance Journal, 60*(5), 287-293.

Enns, C. Z. (1991). The "new" relationship model of women's identity: A review and critique for counselors. *Journal of Counseling and Development, 69*(3), 209-217.

Erikson, E. H. (1963). *Childhood and society*. New York: Norton.

Erwin, T. D. (1987). The construct validity of Holland's differentiation concept. *Measurement and Evaluation in Counseling and Development, 20*(3), 106-112.

Erwin, T. D. (1988). Some evidence for the construct validity of the Map of College Majors. *Measurement and Evaluation in Counseling and Development, 20*(4), 158-161.

Evangelauf, J. (1990, April 11). 1988 enrollments of all racial groups hit record level. *Chronicle of Higher Education*, pp. 1, 37.

Exhibit C: IQ trial. (1978, April). *APA Monitor*, p. 9.

Eyde, L. D., Moreland, K. L., & Robertson, G. J. (1988). *Test user qualifications: A data-based approach to promoting good test use*. Washington, DC: American Psychological Association.

Farinholt, F. W. (1977). The middle school: What? Why? How? *Journal of the National Association of Women Deans, Administrators and Counselors, 40*, 83-86.

Farmer, H. S. (1983). Career and homemaking plans for high school youth. *Journal of Counseling Psychology, 30*(1), 40-45.

Farmer, H. S. (1985). Model of career and achievement motivation for women and men. *Journal of Counseling Psychology, 32*(3), 363-390.

Feller, R. (1991). Employment and career development in a world of change: What is ahead for the next twenty-five years? *Journal of Employment Counseling, 28*(1), 13-20.

Fields, C. M. (1977, September 12). Heredity and environment, but not race, found to influence intelligence. *Chronicle of Higher Education*, p. 9.

Figler, H. E. (1979). *PATH: A career workbook for liberal arts students*. Cranston, RI: Carroll Press.

Fiorentine, R. (1988). Increasing similarity in the values and life plans of male and female college students? Evidence and implications. *Sex Roles, 18*, 143-158.

Fitzgerald, L. F., & Crites, J. O. (1980). Toward a career psychology of women: What do we know? What do we need to know? *Journal of Counseling Psychology, 27*(1), 44-62.

Fitzgerald, L. F., & Weitzman, L. M. (1992). Women's career development theory: Theory and practice from a feminist perspective. In H. D. Lea & Z. B. Leibowitz (Eds.), *Adult career development* (pp. 124-160). Alexandria, VA: American Association for Counseling and Development.

Fleenor, J. (1986). The Personal Career Development Profile: Using the 16 PF for vocational exploration. *Measurement and Evaluation in Counseling and Development, 18*(4), 185-189.

Franco, J. N. (1983). Aptitude tests: Can we predict their future? *Personnel and Guidance Journal, 61*(5), 263-264.

Fredrickson, R. H. (1986). Preparing gifted and talented students for the world of work. *Journal of Counseling and Development, 64*(9), 556-557.

Freeman, S. C. (1990). C. H. Patterson on client-centered career counseling: An interview: *Career Development Quarterly, 38*(4), 291-301.

Freiberg, P. (1991a, January). At work, nobody knows the troubles women see. *APA Monitor*, pp. 24-25.

Freiberg, P. (1991b, April), Self-esteem gender gap widens in adolescence. *APA Monitor*, p. 29.

Fretz, B. R. (1981). Evaluating the effectiveness of career interventions. *Journal of Counseling Psychology, 28*(1), 77-90.

Fretz, B. R., Kluge, N. A., Ossana, S. M., Jones, S. M., & Merikangas, M. W. (1989). Intervention targets for reducing preretirement anxiety and depression. *Journal of Counseling Psychology, 36*(3), 301-307.

Fretz, B. R., & Merikangas, M. W. (1992). Preretirement programming: Needs and responses. In H. D. Lea & Z. B. Leibowitz (Eds.), *Adult career development* (pp. 269-294). Alexandria, VA: American Association for Counseling and Development.

Freud, S. (1962). *Civilization and its discontents* (J. Strachey, Trans.) New York: Norton.

Fry, P. S. (1992). Major social theories of aging and their importance for counseling concepts and practices: A critical review. *The Counseling Psychologist, 20*(2), 246-329.

Fullerton, H. N., Jr. (1989, November). New labor force projections spanning 1988 to 2000. *Monthly Labor Review*, pp. 3-12.

Fuqua, D. R., Blum, C. R., & Hartman, B. W. (1988). Empirical support for the differential diagnosis of career indecision. *Career Development Quarterly, 36*(4), 364-373.

Gade, E., & Peterson, L. (1980). A comparison of working and nonworking high school students on school performance, socioeconomic status, and self-esteem. *Vocational Guidance Quarterly, 29*(1), 65-69.

Galassi, J. P., Crace, R. K., Martin, G. A., James, R. A., Jr., & Wallace, R. L. (1992). Client preferences and anticipations in career counseling: A preliminary investigation. *Journal of Counseling Psychology, 39*(1), 46-55.

Galassi, M. D., Jones, L. K., & Britt, M. N. (1985). Nontraditional career options for women: An evaluation of career guidance instruments. *Vocational Guidance Quarterly, 34*(2), 124-130.

Gallos, J. V. (1989). Exploring women's development: Implications for career, theory, practice, and research. In M. B. Arthur, D. T. Hall, & B. S. Lawrence (Eds.), *Handbook of career theory* (pp. 110-132). New York: Cambridge University Press.

Galton, F. (1883). *Inquiries into human faculty and its development.* London: Macmillan.

Garfield, C. (1986). *Peak performers.* New York: Avon.

Gartaganis, A. (1988). Trends in bachelor's and higher degrees. *Occupational Outlook Quarterly, 32*(2), 9-15.

Gati, I., & Tikotzki, Y. (1989). Strategies for collection and processing of occupational information in making career decisions. *Journal of Counseling Psychology, 36*(3), 430-439.

Gelatt, H. B. (1967). Information and decision theories applied to college choice and planning. In *Preparing school counselors in educational guidance* (Pamphlet). New York: College Entrance Examination Board.

Gellen, M. I., & Hoffman, R. A. (1984). Analysis of the subscales of the Tennessee Self-concept Scale. *Measurement and Evaluation in Counseling and Development, 17*(2), 51-55.

Gerstein, M. (1982). Vocational counseling for adults in varied settings: A comprehensive view. *Vocational Guidance Quarterly, 30*(4), 315-322.

Gerstein, M., Lichtman, M., & Barokas, J. U. (1988). Occupational plans of adolescent women compared to men: A cross-sectional examination. *Career Development Quarterly, 36*(3), 222-230.

Gilbert, L. A., & Rachlin, V. (1987). Mental health and psychological functioning of dual-career families. *The Counseling Psychologist, 15*(1), 7-49.

Gilkison, B., & Drummond, R. J. (1988). Academic self-concept of older adults in career transition. *Journal of Employment Counseling, 25*(1), 24-29.

Gilligan, C. (1982). *In a different voice.* Cambridge, MA: Harvard University Press.

Ginzberg, E. (1972). Toward a theory of occupational choice: A restatement. *Vocational Guidance Quarterly, 20*(2), 169-176.

Ginzberg, E. (1984). Career development. In D. Brown & L. Brooks (Eds.), *Career choice and development* (pp. 169-191). San Francisco: Jossey-Bass.

Ginzberg, E., Ginsburg, S. W., Axelrad, S., & Herma, J. L. (1951). *Occupational choice: An approach to a general theory.* New York: Columbia University Press.

Gladstein, G. A., & Apfel, F. S. (1987). A theoretically based adult career counseling center. *Career Development Quarterly, 36*(2), 178-185.

Glass, J. C., & Grant, K. A. (1983). Counseling in the later years: A growing need. *Personnel and Guidance Journal, 62*(4), 210-213.

Glen, N. D. (1975). Psychological well-being in the post-parental stage: Some evidence from national surveys. *Journal of Marriage and the Family, 37*, 105-110.

Goldman, L. (1971). *Using tests in counseling.* New York: Appleton-Century-Crofts.

Goldman, L. (1972). Tests and counseling: The marriage that failed. *Measurement and Evaluation in Guidance, 4,* 213-220.

Goldman, L. (1990). Qualitative assessment. *The Counseling Psychologist, 18*(2), 205-213.

Goldstein, I. L., & Gilliam, P. (1990). Training system issues in the year 2000. *American Psychologist, 45*(2), 134-143.

Goodson, W. D. (1982). Status of career programs on college and university campuses. *Vocational Guidance Quarterly, 30*(3), 230-235.

Goodyear, R. K. (1990). Research on the effects of test interpretation: A review. *The Counseling Psychologist,18*(2), 240-257.

Gordon, L. V. (1960a). *Survey of interpersonal values.* Chicago: Science Research Associates.

Gordon, L. V. (1960b). *Survey of personal values.* Chicago: Science Research Associates.

Gottfredson, G. D., & Holland, J. L. (1974). *Vocational choices of men and women: A comparison of predictors from the SDS* (Pamphlet No. 175). Baltimore, MD: John S. Hopkins University, Center for the Study of the Social Organization of Schools.

Gottfredson, G. D., & Holland, J. L. (1990). A longitudinal test of the influence of congruence: Job satisfaction, competency utilization, and counterproductive behavior. *Journal of Counseling Psychology, 37*(4), 389-398.

Gottfredson, L. S. (1981). Circumscription and compromise: A developmental theory of occupational aspirations. *Journal of Counseling Psychology, 28*(6), 545-579.

Gottfredson, L. S., & Sharf, J. C. (1988). Fairness in employment testing. *Journal of Vocational Behavior, 33,* 225-230.

Gould, R. (1978). *Transformations: Growth and change in adult life.* New York: Simon & Schuster.

Granrose, C. S. (1985). Plans for work careers among college women who expect to have families. *Vocational Guidance Quarterly, 33*(4), 284-295.

Greenhaus, J. H. (1973). A factorial investigation of career salience. *Journal of Vocational Behavior, 3,* 95-98.

Gribbons, W. D., & Lohnes, P. R. (1968). *Emerging careers.* New York: Teachers College Press.

Gysbers, N. C. (1984). Major trends in career development theory and practice. *Vocational Guidance Quarterly, 33*(1), 15-25.

Hackett, G., Esposito, D., & O'Halloran, M. S. (1989). The relationship of role model influences to the career salience and educational and career plans of college women. *Journal of Vocational Behavior, 35,* 164-180.

Hackman, J. R., & Oldham, G. R. (1981). Work redesigned: People and their work. In J. O'Toole, J. L. Scheiber, & L. C. Wood (Eds.), *Working changes and choices* (pp. 172-184). New York: Human Sciences Press

Hagner, D., & Salomone, P. R. (1989). Issues in career decision making for workers with developmental disabilities. *Career Development Quarterly, 38*(2), 148-159.

Halpin, G., Ralph, J., & Halpin, G. (1990). The Adult Career Concerns Inventory: Validity and reliability. *Measurement and Evaluation in Counseling and Development, 22*(4), 196-202.

Hamachek, D. E. (1988). Evaluating self-concept and ego development within Erikson's psychosocial framework: A formulation. *Journal of Counseling and Development, 66*(8), 354-360.

Hamilton, L. J. (1984). Developing game plans for entry into the post-secondary world: An intensive teaching approach. *Vocational Guidance Quarterly, 33*(1), 82-88.

Hanna, G. S. (1988). Using percentile bands for meaningful descriptive test score interpretations. *Journal of Counseling and Development, 66*(10), 477-483.

Hanselman, P. R. (1989). Countering rejection anxiety. *The School Counselor, 36*(5), 376-379.

Hansen, J. C. (1986). Computers and beyond in the career decision-making process. *Measurement and Evaluation in Counseling and Development, 19*(1), 48-52.

Hansen, J. C. (1987). Cross-cultural research on vocational interests. *Measurement and Evaluation in Counseling and Development, 19*(4), 163-176.

Hansford, S. (1988). Selected trends in the economic status of American women (1900-1986): Implications for employment counselors. *Journal of Employment Counseling, 25*(1), 30-36.

Hanson, G. R., Noeth, R. J., & Prediger, R. J. (1977). Validity of diverse procedures for reporting interest scores: An analysis of longitudinal data. *Journal of Counseling Psychology, 24*(6), 487-493.

Haring-Hidore, M., & Beyard-Tyler, K. (1984). Counseling and research on nontraditional careers: A caveat. *Vocational Guidance Quarterly, 33*(2), 113-119.

Harlan, C. L., & Jansen, M. A. (1987). The psychological and physical well-being of women in sex-stereotyped occupations. *Journal of Employment Counseling, 24*(1), 31-39.

Harmon, L. (1985). Ohio Vocational Interest Survey. *Measurement and Evaluation in Counseling and Development, 17*(4), 224-226.

Harmon, L. W. (1981). The life and career plans of young adult college women: A follow-up study. *Journal of Counseling Psychology, 28*(5), 416-427.

Harmon, L. W. (1989). Longitudinal changes in women's career aspirations: Developmental or historical? *Journal of Vocational Behavior, 35*, 46-63.

Harrington, T. F., & O'Shea, A. J. (1980). Applicability of the Holland (1973) model of vocational development with Spanish-speaking clients. *Journal of Counseling Psychology, 27*(3), 246-251.

Harrington, T. F., & O'Shea, A. J. (1982). *Harrington/O'Shea Career Decision-Making System*. Circle Pines, MN: American Guidance Service.

Harris, J. J., III. (1983). *STARI (Summer Training Achieves Results)*. Bloomington: Indiana University. (ERIC Document Reproduction Service No. ED 247 361)

Harris, T. L., & Wallin, J. S. (1978). Influencing career choices of seventh-grade students. *Vocational Guidance Quarterly, 27*(1), 50-54.

Hatcher, L., & Crook, J. C. (1988). First-job surprises for college graduates: An exploratory investigation. *Journal of College Student Personnel, 29*(5), 441-448.

Havighurst, R. J. (1972). *Developmental tasks and education*. New York: David McKay.

Havighurst, R. J., Neugarten, B. L., & Tobin, S. S. (1968). Disengagement and patterns of aging. In B. L. Neugarten (Ed.), *Middle age and aging* (pp. 161-172). Chicago: University of Chicago Press.

Hawks, B. K., & Muha, D. (1991). Facilitating the career development of minorities: Doing it differently this time. *Career Development Quarterly, 39*(3), 251-260.

Hayes, R. (1987). Men's decisions to enter or avoid nontraditional occupations. *Career Development Quarterly, 35*(2), 89-101.

Hazard, L. B., & Koslow, D. (1992). Conjoint career counseling: Counseling dual-career couples. In H. D. Lea & Z. B. Leibowitz (Eds.), *Adult career development* (pp. 218-233). Alexandria, VA: American Association for Counseling and Development.

Healy, C. C. (1989). Negative: The MBTI: Not ready for routine use in counseling. *Journal of Counseling and Development, 67*(8), 487-488.

Healy, C. C. (1990). Reforming career appraisals to meet the needs of clients in the 1990's. *The Counseling Psychologist, 18*(2), 214-226.

Healy, C. C., & Mourton, D. L. (1985). Congruence and vocational identity: Outcomes of career counseling with persuasive power. *Journal of Counseling Psychology, 32*(3), 441-444.

Hecklinger, F. J., & Curtin, B. M. (1987). *Training for life.* Dubuque, IA: Kendall/Hunt.

Helwig, A. A. (1989, Fall). National Academy of Sciences Report on the GATB and validity generalization. *NECA Newsletter,* pp. 4-5.

Henton, J., Lamke, L., Murphy, C., & Haynes, L. (1980). Crisis reactions of college freshmen as a function of family support systems. *Personnel and Guidance Journal, 58*(8), 508-511.

Henton, J., Russell, R., & Koval, J. (1983). Spousal perceptions of midlife career change. *Personnel and Guidance Journal, 61*(5), 287-291.

Herr, E. L., & Cramer, S. H. (1972). *Vocational guidance and career development in the schools: Toward a systems approach.* Boston: Houghton Mifflin.

Hesketh, B. (1985). In search of a conceptual framework for vocational psychology. *Journal of Counseling and Development, 64*(1), 26-30.

Hesketh, B., Elmslie, S., & Kaldor, W. (1990). Career compromise: An alternative account to Gottfredson's theory. *Journal of Counseling Psychology, 37*(1), 49-56.

Hetherington, C., Hillerbrand, E., & Etinger, B. D. (1989). Career counseling with gay men: Issues and recommendations for research. *Journal of Counseling and Development, 67*(8), 452-454.

Hoffman, J. A. (1984). Psychological separation of late adolescents from their parents. *Journal of Counseling Psychology, 31*(2), 170-178.

Hoffman, L. R., & McDaniels, C. (1991). Career development in the elementary schools: A perspective for the 1990's. *Elementary School Guidance and Counseling, 25,* 163-171.

Hoffman, L. W. (1989). Effects of maternal employment in the two-parent family. *American Psychologist, 44*(2), 283-292.

Hoffman, M. A., Spokane, A. R., & Magoon, T. M. (1981). Effects of feedback mode on counseling outcomes using the Strong-Campbell Interest Inventory: Does the counselor really matter? *Journal of Counseling Psychology, 28*(2), 119-125.

Holland, J. L. (1966). *The psychology of vocational choice.* Waltham, MA: Blaisdell.

Holland, J. L. (1973). *Some practical remedies for providing vocational guidance for everyone* (Pamphlet No. 163). Baltimore, MD: Johns Hopkins University, Center for the Study of Social Organization of Schools.

Holland, J. L. (1980). The influence of vocational interest inventories: Some implications for psychological testing. *The Counseling Psychologist, 9*(1), 83-86.

Holland, J. L. (1985). *Making vocational choices* (2nd ed.). Englewood Cliffs, NJ: Prentice Hall.

Holland, J. L. (1987a). Current status of Holland's theory of careers: Another perspective. *Career Development Quarterly, 36*(1), 24-30.

Holland, J. L. (1987b). *The self-directed search.* Odessa, FL: Psychological Assessment Resources.

Holland, J. L. (1991). *You and your career.* Lutz, FL: Psychological Assessment Resources.

Holland, J. L., Daiger, D. C., & Power, P. G. (1980). *My vocational situation.* Palo Alto, CA: Consulting Psychologists Press.

Holland, J. L., Gottfredson, G. D., & Baker, H. G. (1990). Validity of vocational aspirations and interest inventories: Extended, replicated, and reinterpreted. *Journal of Counseling Psychology, 37*(3), 337-342.

Holmes, B. H., & Werbel, J. D. (1992). Finding work following job loss: The role of coping resources. *Journal of Employment Counseling, 29*(1), 22-29.

Homan, K. B. (1986). Vocation as the quest for authentic existence. *Career Development Quarterly, 35*(1), 14-23.

Hood, A. B., & Johnson, R. W. (1991). *Assessment in counseling: A guide to the use of psychological assessment procedures.* Alexandria, VA: American Association for Counseling and Development.

Hopke, W. E. (Ed.). (1990). *Encyclopedia of careers and vocational guidance.* Chicago: J. G. Ferguson.

Hopkins, K. D., & Bracht, G. H. (1975). Ten-year stability of verbal and nonverbal I.Q. scores. *American Educational Research Journal, 12,* 469-477.

Hopkins-Best, M. (1987). The effect of students' sex and disability on counselors' agreement with postsecondary career goals. *The School Counselor, 35*(1), 28-33.

Horton, G. M., & Engels, D. W. (1992). Career counseling for the mature worker. In H. D. Lea & Z. B. Leibowitz (Eds.), *Adult career development* (pp. 255-268). Alexandria, VA: American Association for Counseling and Development.

Hosie, T. W. (1975). The effects of reinforcing intermediate elementary students to constructively use free time for vocational exploration. *Journal of Educational Research, 69,* 77-81.

Hoyt, K. B. (1987). The impact of technology on occupational change: Implications for career guidance. *Career Development Quarterly, 35*(4), 269-278.

Hoyt, K. B. (1989). The career status of women and minority persons: A 20-year retrospective. *Career Development Quarterly, 37*(3), 202-212.

Hoyt, K. B. (1991). The concept of work: Bedrock for career development. *Future Choices, 2*(3), 23-30.

Hudesman, J., Avramides, B., Loveday, C., Wendell, A., & Griemsmann, R. (1986). Counseling style: Its impact on the academic performance of college students in special programs. *Journal of College Student Personnel, 27*(3), 250-254.

Hughes, C. M., Martinek, S. A., & Fitzgerald, L. F. (1985). Sex role attitudes and career choices: The role of children's self-esteem. *Elementary School Guidance and Counseling, 20*(1), 57-66.

Hughes, K. R., Redfield, D. L., & Martray, C. R. (1989). The Children's Academic Motivation Inventory: A research note on psychometric properties. *Measurement and Evaluation in Counseling and Development, 22*(3), 137-142.

Hyman, R. B., & Woog, P. (1987). The relationship of age and marital status to women's need for interdependence-independence. *Measurement and Evaluation in Counseling and Development, 20*(1), 27-35.

Isaacson, L. E. (1981). Counseling male midlife career changers. *Vocational Guidance Quarterly, 29*(4), 324-331.

Jackson, A. W., & Hornbeck, D. W. (1989). Educating young adolescents. *American Psychologist, 44*(5), 831-836.

Jackson, R. M., & Meara, N. M. (1977). Father identification, achievement and occupational behavior of rural youth: Five-year follow-up. *Journal of Vocational Behavior, 10,* 82-91.

Jarchow, E. M., & Wade, K. (1983). Hearing impairment not equal to career impairment. *Science Teacher, 50*(9), 23-25.

Jepsen, D. A. (1975). Occupational decision development over the high school years. *Journal of Vocational Behavior, 7,* 225-237.

Jepsen, D. P. (1985). Kuder Occupational Interest Survey, Form DD. *Measurement and Evaluation in Counseling and Development, 17*(4), 217-220.

Johnson, G. L., & Hummel, T. J. (1971). The effects of three modes of test administration on the reading achievement scores of fifth graders. *Elementary School Guidance and Counseling, 6*(1), 21-26.

Johnson, R. W. (1987). Review of *Assessment of Career Decision Making. Journal of Counseling and Development, 65*(10), 567-569.

Johnson, W. B. (1987). *Workforce 2000*. Indianapolis, IN: Hudson Institute.

Jones, L. P. (1989). A typology of adaptations to unemployment. *Journal of Employment Counseling, 26*(2), 50-59.

Jordaan, J. P. (1974). Life stages as organizing modes of career development. In E. L. Herr (Ed.), *Vocational guidance and human development* (pp. 263-295). Boston: Houghton Mifflin.

Josselson, R. (1987). Identity diffusion: A long-term follow-up. *Adolescent Psychiatry, 14*, 230-258.

Kalish, R. A. (1975). *Late adulthood: Perspectives on human development*. Monterey, CA: Brooks/Cole.

Kammer, P. P., Fouad, N., & Williams, R. (1988). Follow-up of a pre-college program for minority and disadvantaged students. *Career Development Quarterly, 37*(1), 40-45.

Kanchier, C., & Unruh, W. R. (1989). Work values: How do managers who change jobs differ from those who do not? *Journal of Employment Counseling, 26*(3), 107-116.

Kane, S. T. (1989). A review of the COPS interest inventory. *Journal of Counseling and Development, 67*(6), 361-363.

Kapes, J. T., Borman, C. A., & Frazier, N. (1989). An evaluation of the SIGI and Discover microcomputer-based guidance systems. *Measurement and Evaluation in Counseling and Development, 22*(3), 126-136.

Kaplan, D. M., & Brown, D. (1987). The role of anxiety in career indecisiveness. *Career Development Quarterly, 36*(3), 148-162.

Karmos, A. H., & Karmos, J. S. (1984). Attitudes toward standardized achievement tests and their relation to achievement test performance. *Measurement and Evaluation in Counseling and Development, 17*(2), 56-66.

Karpicke, S. (1980). Perceived and real sex differences in college students' career planning. *Journal of Counseling Psychology, 27*(3), 240-245.

Katzell, R. A., & Thompson, D. E. (1990). Work motivation. *American Psychologist, 45*(2), 144-153.

Kavanagh, H. B. (1980). Some appraised instruments of values for counselors. *Personnel and Guidance Journal, 58*(9), 613-616.

Kazanas, H. C. (1978). Relationship of job satisfaction and productivity to work values of vocational education graduates. *Journal of Vocational Behavior, 12*, 155-164.

Keierleber, D. L., & Hansen, L. S. (1992). A coming of age: Addressing the career development needs of adult students in university settings. In H. D. Lea & Z. B. Leibowitz (Eds.), *Adult career development* (pp. 312-339). Alexandria, VA: American Association for Counseling and Development.

Keller, K. E., Biggs, D. A., & Gysbers, N. C. (1982). Career counseling from a cognitive perspective. *Personnel and Guidance Journal, 60*(6), 367-371.

Kelly, K. R., & Jordan, L. K. (1990). Effects of academic achievement and gender on academic and social self-concept: A replication study. *Journal of Counseling and Development, 69*(2), 173-177.

Kerr, B. A. (1983). Raising the career aspirations of gifted girls. *Vocational Guidance Quarterly, 32*(1), 37-43.

Kerr, B. A., & Colangelo, N. (1988). The college plans of academically talented students. *Journal of Counseling and Development, 67*(1), 42-48.

King, S. (1989). Sex differences in a causal model of career maturity. *Journal of Counseling and Development, 68*(2), 208-215.

Kinnie, E. J., & Sternlof, R. E. (1971). The influence of nonintellective factors on the IQ scores of middle- and lower-class children. *Child Development, 42,* 1989-1995.

Kinnier, R. T., Brigman, S. L., & Noble, F. C. (1990). Career indecision and family enmeshment. *Journal of Counseling and Development, 68*(3), 309-312.

Kirk, J. J. (1989). Job satisfaction among type C career changers. *Journal of Employment Counseling, 26*(4), 161-168.

Kirkland, M. C. (1971). The effects of tests on students and schools. *Review of Educational Research, 41,* 303-350.

Kivlighan, D. M. (1981). Effects of matching treatment approaches and personality types in group vocational counseling. *Journal of Counseling Psychology, 28*(4), 315-320.

Kivlighan, D. M., Jr. (1990). Career group theory. *The Counseling Psychologist, 18*(1), 64-79.

Kline, P. (1975). *Psychology of vocational guidance.* New York: John Wiley.

Knapp, J. R., & Karabenick, S. A. (1988). Incidence of formal and informal academic help-seeking in higher education. *Journal of College Student Personnel, 29*(3), 223-227.

Knapp, R. R., & Knapp, L. (1984). *Manual: COPS Interest Inventory.* San Diego, CA: Educational and Instructional Testing Service.

Knapp, R. R., Knapp, L., & Knapp-Lee, L. (1985). Occupational interest measurement and subsequent career decisions: A predictive follow-up study of the COPSystem Interest Inventory. *Journal of Counseling Psychology, 32*(3), 348-354.

Koch, W. R., Dodd, B. G., & Fitzpatrick, S. J. (1990). Computerized adaptive measurements of attitudes. *Measurement and Evaluation in Counseling and Development, 23*(1), 20-30.

Kolb, D. (1976). *The Learning Styles Inventory technical manual.* Boston: McBer.

Kolb, D. (1984). *Experiential learning.* Englewood Cliffs, NJ: Prentice Hall.

Koplik, E. K., & DeVito, A. J. (1986). Problems of freshmen: Comparison of classes of 1976 and 1986. *Journal of College Student Personnel, 27*(2), 124-131.

Koski, L. K., & Subich, L. M. (1985). Career and homemaking choices of college preparatory and vocational education students. *Vocational Guidance Quarterly, 34*(2), 116-123.

Kragie, E. R., Gerstein, M., & Lichtman, M. (1989). Do Americans plan for retirement? Some recent trends. *Career Development Quarterly, 37*(3), 232-239.

Krantz, L. (1988). *The jobs rated almanac.* Philadelphia: Pharos.

Krausz, M. (1982). Policies of organizational choice at different vocational life stages. *Vocational Guidance Quarterly, 31*(1), 60-68.

Kreps, J. M. (1973). Modern man and his instinct of workmanship. *American Journal of Psychiatry, 30,* 179-183.

Krieshok, T. S. (1987). Review of the Self-Directed Search. *Journal of Counseling and Development, 65*(9), 512-514.

Krumboltz, J. D., Mitchell, A., & Gelatt, H. G. (1976). Applications of social learning theory. *Focus on Guidance, 8,* 1-16.

Kuldau, J. E., & Hollis, J. W. (1971). The development of attitudes toward work among upper elementary school age children. *Journal of Vocational Behavior, 1,* 387-398.

Lampe, R. E. (1985). Self-scoring accuracy of the Kuder General Interest Survey. *The School Counselor, 32*(4), 319-324.

Lampron, D. (1985). *Using life development visualization for high school students and recent graduates for career exploration.* Ann Arbor, MI: Ann Arbor Public Schools. (ERIC Document Reproduction Service No. ED 268 409)

Lapan, R. T., & Jingeleski, J. (1992). Circumscribing vocational aspirations in junior high school. *Journal of Counseling Psychology, 39*(1), 81-90.

Lapsley, D. K., Rice, K. G., & Fitzgerald, D. P. (1990). Adolescent attachment, identity, and adjustment to college: Implications for the continuity of adaptation hypothesis. *Journal of Counseling and Development, 68*(5), 561-565.

Lapsley, D. K., Rice, K. G., & Shadid, G. E. (1989). Psychological separation and adjustment to college. *Journal of Counseling Psychology, 36*(3), 286-294.

Larsen, P., & Shertzer, B. (1987). The high school dropout: Everybody's problem? *The School Counselor, 34*(2), 163-169.

Lassalle, A. D., & Spokane, A. R. (1987). Patterns of early labor force participation of American women. *Career Development Quarterly, 36*(1), 55-65.

Latack, J. C. (1989). Work, stress, and careers: A preventive approach to maintaining organizational health. In M. B. Arthur, D. T. Hall, & B. S. Lawrence (Eds.), *Handbook of career theory* (pp. 252-274). New York: Cambridge University Press.

Lauver, P. J., & Jones, R. M. (1991). Factors associated with perceived career options in American Indian, White, and Hispanic rural high school students. *Journal of Counseling Psychology, 38*(2), 159-166.

Lee, C. C. (1984a). Predicting the career choice attitudes of rural Black, White, and Native American high school students. *Vocational Guidance Quarterly, 32*(3), 177-184.

Lee, C. C. (1984b). Work values of rural Black, White, and Native American adolescents: Implications for contemporary rural school counselors. *Counseling and Values, 28*(1), 63-71.

Leifer, A. D., & Lesser, G. S. (1976). *The development of career awareness in young children.* Cambridge, MA: Department of Health, Education and Welfare.

Leong, F. T. L. (1985). Career development of Asian Americans. *Journal of College Student Personnel, 26*(1), 539-546.

Leong, F. T. L. (1991). Career development attributes and occupational values of Asian American and White American college students. *Career Development Quarterly, 39*(3), 221-230.

Leong, F. T. L., & Morris, J. (1989). Assessing the construct validity of Holland, Daiger, and Power's measure of vocational identity. *Measurement and Evaluation in Counseling and Development, 22*(3), 117-125.

Leung, A. S., & Plake, B. S. (1990). A choice dilemma approach for examining the relative importance of sex type and prestige preferences in the process of career choice compromise. *Journal of Counseling Psychology, 37*(4), 399-406.

Levin, A. (1990). *Using the Strong and MBTI together in career development.* Stanford, CA: Stanford University Press.

Levine, A. (1976). Educational and occupational choice: A synthesis of literature from sociology and psychology. *Journal of Consumer Research, 2,* 276-289.

Levinson, D. J. (1986). A conception of adult development. *American Psychologist, 41*(1), 3-13.

Levinson, D. J. (in press). *The seasons of a woman's life.* New York: Knopf.

Levinson, D. J., Darrow, C. M., Klein, E. B., Levinson, M. A., & McKee, B. (1978). *The seasons of a man's life.* New York: Knopf.

Lewis, R. A., & Gilhousen, M. R. (1981). Myths of career development: A cognitive approach to vocational counseling. *Personnel and Guidance Journal, 59*(5), 296-299.

Lidz, T. (1976). *The person.* New York: Basic Books.

Linn, R. L. (1986). Educational testing and assessment. *American Psychologist, 41*(10), 1153-1160.

Liptak, J. J. (1990). Preretirement counseling: Integrating the leisure planning component. *Career Development Quarterly, 38*(4), 360-367.

Liptak, J. J. (1991). The fourth alternative: Leisure search and planning. *Journal of Employment Counseling, 28,* 57-62.

Livson, N., & Peskin, H. (1980). Perspectives on adolescence from longitudinal research. In J. Adelson (Ed.), *Handbook of adolescent psychology* (pp. 47-98). New York: John Wiley.

Loesch, L. C. (1975). A child's guide to educational and psychological assessment. *Elementary School Guidance and Counseling, 9,* 289-297.

Lopez, F. G. (1989). Current family dynamics, trait anxiety, and academic adjustment: Test of a family-based model of vocational identity. *Journal of Vocational Behavior, 35,* 76-87.

Loughead, T. (1988). The Harrington-O'Shea Career Decision-Making System, microcomputer edition, 1985: A review. *Measurement and Evaluation in Counseling and Development, 21*(1), 36-39.

Lowenthal, M. F., & Haven, C. (1968). Interaction and adaptation: Intimacy as a critical variable. In B. L. Neugarten (Ed.), *Middle age and aging* (pp. 390-400). Chicago: University of Chicago Press.

Lowenthal, M. F., Thurnher, M., Chiriboga, D., & associates. (1975). *Four stages of life.* San Francisco: Jossey-Bass.

Lubin, B., Larsen, R. M., & Matarazzo, J. D. (1984). Patterns of psychological test usage in the United States: 1935-1982. *American Psychologist, 39*(4), 451-454.

Lucas, E. B., Gysbers, N. C., Buescher, K. L., & Heppner, P. P. (1988). My Vocational Situation: Normative, psychometric, and comparative data. *Measurement and Evaluation in Counseling and Development, 20*(4), 162-170.

Lunneborg, P. W., Olch, D. R., & deWolf, V. (1974). Prediction of college performance in older students. *Journal of Counseling Psychology, 21*(3), 215-221.

Lyman, H. B. (1971). *Test scores and what they mean.* Englewood Cliffs, NJ: Prentice Hall.

Maas, H. S., & Kuypers, J. A. (1975). *From thirty to seventy.* San Francisco: Jossey-Bass.

MacKinnon-Slaney, F., Barber, S. L., & Slaney, R. B. (1988). Marital status as a mediating factor on career aspirations of re-entry female students. *Journal of College Student Personnel, 29*(4), 327-334.

Madsen, D. H. (1986). Computer applications for test administration and scoring. *Measurement and Evaluation in Counseling and Development, 19*(1), 6-14.

Magarrell, J. (1978, January 9). Women account for 93 percent of enrollment gain. *Chronicle of Higher Education,* pp. 1, 11.

Malde, S. (1988). Guided autobiography: A counseling tool for older adults. *Journal of Counseling and Development, 66*(6), 290-293.

Manuele, C. A. (1984). Modifying vocational maturity in adults with delayed career development: A life skills approach. *Vocational Guidance Quarterly, 33*(2), 101-112.

Maples, M. F. (1981). Dual career marriages: Elements for potential success. *Personnel and Guidance Journal, 60*(1), 19-23.

Marantz, S. A., & Mansfield, A. F. (1977). Maternal employment and the development of sex-role stereotyping in five- to eleven-year-old girls. *Child Development, 48,* 668-673.

Marin, P. A., & Splete, H. (1991). A comparison of the effect of two computer-based counseling interventions on the career decidedness of adults. *Career Development Quarterly, 39*(4), 360-371.

Marland, S. P., Jr. (1974). *Career education.* New York: McGraw-Hill.

Marshall, A. (1985). Employment qualifications of college graduates: How important are they? *Journal of Employment Counseling, 22*(4), 136-143.

Martin, M. K., & Dixon, P. N. (1989). The effects of freshman orientation and locus of control on adjustment to college. *Journal of College Student Personnel, 30*(4), 362-367.

Martinez, A. C., Sedlacek, W. E., & Bachhuber, T. D. (1985). Male and female college graduates—Seven months later. *Vocational Guidance Quarterly, 34*(2), 77-84.

Maslow, A. A. (1943). A theory of human motivation. *Psychological Review, 50*(4), 379-393.

Mathiasen, R. E., & Neely, R. E. (1988). Developing a support network for reentry adult students. *Journal of College Student Personnel, 29*(6), 557-559.

Matthay, E. R. (1989). A critical study of the college selection process. *The School Counselor, 36*(5), 359-370.

Matthews, D. B. (1990). A comparison of burnout in selected occupational fields. *Career Development Quarterly, 38*(3), 230-239.

Mauer, E. B., & Gysbers, N. C. (1990). Identifying career concerns of entering university freshmen using My Vocational Situation. *Career Development Quarterly, 39*(2), 155-165.

McBride, M. C. (1990). Autonomy and the struggle for female identity: Implications for counseling women. *Journal of Counseling and Development, 69*(1), 22-26.

McCaulley, M. (1990). The Myers-Briggs Type Indicator: A measure for individuals and groups. *Measurement and Evaluation in Counseling and Development, 22*(4), 181-195.

McDaniels, C. (1984). The work/leisure connection. *Vocational Guidance Quarterly, 33*(1), 35-44.

McDowell, C. F. (1981). Leisure: Consciousness, well-being, and counseling. *The Counseling Psychologist, 9*(3), 3-21.

McGraw, L. (1982). A selective review of programs and counseling interventions for the reentry woman. *Personnel and Guidance Journal, 60*(8), 469-472.

McIlroy, J. H. (1984). Midlife in the 1980's: Philosophy, economy, and psychology. *Personnel and Guidance Journal, 62*(10), 623-628.

McKee, L. M., & Levinson, E. M. (1990). A review of the computerized version of the Self-Directed Search. *Career Development Quarterly, 38*(4), 325-333.

McKenna, A. E., & Ferrero, G. W. (1991). Ninth-grade students' attitudes toward nontraditional occupations. *Career Development Quarterly, 40*(2), 168-181.

McMorris, R. F., & Weideman, A. H. (1986). Answer changing after instruction on answer changing. *Measurement and Evaluation in Counseling and Development, 19*(2), 93-101.

McNair, D., & Brown, D. (1983). Predicting the occupational aspirations, occupational expectations, and career maturity of Black and White male and female tenth graders. *Vocational Guidance Quarterly, 32*(1), 29-36.

Medvene, A. M., & Shueman, S. A. (1978). Perceived parental attitudes and choice of vocational specialty area among male engineering students. *Journal of Vocational Behavior, 12*, 208-216.

Meir, E. I. (1988). The need for congruence between within-occupation interests and specialty in mid-career. *Career Development Quarterly, 37*(1), 63-69.

Meier, E. L., & Kerr, E. A. (1976). Capabilities of middle-aged and older workers. *Industrial Gerontology, 3*, 147-156.

Miller, G. M. (1988). Counselor functions in excellent schools: Elementary through secondary. *The School Counselor, 36*, 88-93.

Miller, J. (1977). *Career development needs of nine-year-olds: How to improve career development programs*. Washington, DC: Advisory Council for Career Education.

Miller, J. V. (1982). Lifelong career development for disadvantaged youth and adults. *Vocational Guidance Quarterly, 30*(4), 359-366.

Miller, M. J. (1983). The role of happenstance in career choice. *Vocational Guidance Quarterly, 32*(1), 16-20.

Miller, M. J. (1987). Career counseling for high school students, grades 10-12. *Journal of Employment Counseling, 24*(4), 173-183.

Miller, M. J. (1988a). Career counseling for the middle school youngster: Grades 6-9. *Journal of Employment Counseling, 25*(4), 172-179.

Miller, M. J. (1988b). Restating a client-centered approach to career counseling. *Journal of Employment Counseling, 25*(2), 64-69.

Miller, M. J. (1989). Career counseling for the elementary school child: Grades K-5. *Journal of Employment Counseling, 26*(4), 169-177.

Miller, M. J., Springer, T. P., & Wells, D. (1988). Which occupational environments do Black youths prefer? Extending Holland's typology. *The School Counselor, 36*(2), 103-106.

Miller, R. R. (1986). Reducing occupational circumscription. *Elementary School Guidance and Counseling, 20*(4), 250-254.

Miller-Tiedeman, A. (1988). *Life career: The quantum leap into a process theory of career*. Vista, CA: Life Career Foundation.

Millon, T. (1992). Millon Clinical Multiaxial Inventory: I & II. *Journal of Counseling Psychology, 70*(3), 421-426.

Minor, C. W. (1992). Career development: Theories and models. In H. D. Lea & Z. B. Leibowitz (Eds.), *Adult career development* (pp. 17-41). Alexandria, VA: American Association for Counseling and Development.

Minuchin, P. P. (1977). *The middle years of childhood*. Monterey, CA: Brooks/Cole.

Mitchell, A. M. (1977). *Career development needs of seventeen year olds: How to improve career development programs*. Washington, DC: National Advisory Committee for Career Education.

Mitchell, L. K., & Krumboltz, J. D. (1987). The effects of cognitive restructuring and decision-making training on career indecision. *Journal of Counseling and Development, 66*(4), 171-174.

Mohney, C., & Anderson, W. (1988). The effect of life events and relationships on adult women's decisions to enroll in college. *Journal of Counseling and Development, 66*(6), 271-274.

Mooney, C. J. (1990, April 25). Universities awarded record number of doctorates last year: Foreign students thought to account for much of the increase. *Chronicle of Higher Education*, pp. 1, 11, 18.

Moore, C. L., & Retish, P. M. (1974). Effect of the examiner's race on Black children's Wechsler Preschool and Primary Scale of Intelligence I.Q. *Developmental Psychology, 10*, 115-123.

Moos, R. H. (1987). *The social climate scales: A user's guide*. Palo Alto, CA: Consulting Psychologists Press.

Morris, E. F. (1974). The personality traits and psychological needs of educated homemakers and career women. *Dissertation Abstracts International, 34*, 6934A. (University Microfilm No. 74-9893)

Morse, C. L., Bockoven, J., & Bettesworth, A. (1988). Effects of DUSO-2 and DUSO-2 Revised on children's social skills and self-esteem. *Elementary School Guidance and Counseling, 22*(3), 199-205.

Mortimer, J. T. (1975). Occupational value socialization in business and professional families. *Sociology of Work and Occupations, 2,* 29-55.

Moses, S. (1991, April). Questions surround idea of national exam. *APA Monitor,* pp. 34-35.

Mueller, D. (1985). Career Orientation Placement and Evaluation Survey. *Measurement and Evaluation in Counseling and Development, 18*(3), 132-134.

Murray, H. A., & Kluckhohn, C. (1953). Outline of a conception of personality. In C. Kluckhohn, H. A. Murray, & D. Schneider (Eds.), *Personality in nature, society, and culture* (2nd ed., pp. 3-52). New York: Knopf.

Myers, I. B. (1985). *Gifts differing.* Palo Alto, CA: Consulting Psychologists Press.

National Employment Counseling Association. (1990, Fall). Survey of working America. *NECA Newsletter,* pp. 6-7.

Naughton, T. J. (1987). A conceptual view of workaholism and implications for career counseling and research. *Career Development Quarterly, 35*(3), 180-187.

Neugarten, B. L. (1973). Personality change in late life: A developmental perspective. In C. Eisdorfer & M. P. Lawton (Eds.), *The psychology of adult development and aging* (pp. 311-335). Washington, DC: American Psychological Association.

Neugarten, B. L., & Moore, J. W. (1968). The changing age-status system. In B. L. Neugarten (Ed.), *Middle age and aging* (pp. 5-21). Chicago: University of Chicago Press.

Nevill, D. D., & Super, D. E. (1988). Career maturity and commitment to work in university students. *Journal of Vocational Behavior, 32,* 139-151.

Nevo, O. (1990). Career counseling from the counselee perspective: Analysis of feedback questionnaire. *Career Development Quarterly, 38*(4), 314-324.

Newman, J. L., Fuqua, D. R., & Minger, C. (1990). Further evidence for the use of career subtypes in defining career status. *Career Development Quarterly, 39*(2), 178-188.

Newton, F. B., Angle, S. S., Schuette, C. G., & Ender, S. C. (1984). The assessment of college student need: First step in a prevention response. *Personnel and Guidance Journal, 62*(9), 537-543.

Niles, S., & Herr, E. R. (1989). Using secondary school behaviors to predict career behaviors in young adulthood: Does "success" breed "success"? *Career Development Quarterly, 37*(4), 345-354.

Noeth, R. J., & Jepsen, D. A. (1981). Predicting field of job entry from expressed vocational choice and certainty level. *Journal of Counseling Psychology, 28*(1), 22-26.

Noeth, R. J., & Prediger, D. J. (1978). Career development over the high school years. *Vocational Guidance Quarterly, 26*(3), 244-254.

O'Bryant, S. L., & Corder-Bolz, C. R. (1978). The effects of television on children's sterotyping of women's work roles. *Journal of Vocational Behavior, 12*(2), 233-244.

Offerman, L. R., & Gowing, M. K. (1990). Organizations of the future. *American Psychologist, 45*(2), 95-108.

Okiishi, R. W. (1987). The genogram as a tool in career counseling. *Journal of Counseling and Development, 66*(3), 139-143.

Okun, B. F. (1984). *Working with adults: Individual, family, and career development.* Pacific Grove, CA: Brooks/Cole.

Olian, J. D., Carroll, S. J., Giannantonio, C. M., & Feren, D. B. (1988). What do proteges look for in a mentor? Results of three experimental studies. *Journal of Vocational Behavior, 33,* 15-37.

Oliver, L. (1975). Counseling implications of recent research on women. *Personnel and Guidance Journal, 53*(6), 430-438.

Olney, C. W. (1988). The new job outlook: Preparing for the years ahead. *Journal of Employment Counseling, 25*(1), 7-13.

O'Neil, J. M., & Fishman, D. M. (1992). Adult men's career transitions and gender-role themes. In H. D. Lea & Z. B. Leibowitz (Eds.), *Adult career development* (pp. 161-191). Alexandria, VA: American Association for Counseling and Development.

O'Neil, J. M., Ohlde, C., Tollefson, N., Barke, C., Piggott, T., & Watts, D. (1980). Factors, correlates, and problem areas affecting career decision making of a cross-sectional sample of students. *Journal of Counseling Psychology, 27*(6), 571-580.

Orleans, E. L. (1970). Family interaction, personality development and vocational choice in adolescent males. *Dissertation Abstracts International, 31,* 919B-920B. (University Microfilms No. 70-14, 162)

Orum, L. S. (1982). *Career information and Hispanic high school students.* Washington, DC: National Institute of Education. (ERIC Document Reproduction Service No. ED 238 650)

Osipow, S. H. (1968). *Theories of career development.* New York: Appleton-Century-Crofts.

Osipow, S. H. (1975). *Emerging woman: Career analysis and outlooks.* Columbus, OH: Charles E. Merrill.

Osipow, S. H. (1987). *Career Decision Scale manual.* Odessa, FL: Psychological Assessment Resources.

O'Toole, J. (1977). *Work, learning and the American future.* San Francisco: Jossey-Bass.

Owen, G., & Erchul, W. P. (1987). The Wide Range Achievement Test—Revised: How much has it been improved? *Measurement and Evaluation in Counseling and Development, 20*(1), 44-48.

Parker, H. J., Chan, F., & Saper, B. (1989). Occupational representativeness and prestige rating: Some observations. *Journal of Employment Counseling, 26*(3), 117-131.

Parker, M., Peltier, S., & Wolleat, P. (1981). Understanding dual career couples. *Personnel and Guidance Journal, 60*(1), 14-18.

Parsons, F. (1909). *Choosing a vocation.* Boston: Houghton Mifflin.

Pedersen, P., Goldberg, A., & Papalia, T. (1991). A model for planning career continuation and change through increased awareness, knowledge, and skill. *Journal of Employment Counseling, 28*(2), 74-79.

Pedro, J. D. (1982). Career maturity in high school age females. *Vocational Guidance Quarterly, 30*(3), 243-251.

Pelsma, D. M., Roland, B., Tollefson, N., & Wigington, H. (1989). Parent burnout: Validation of the Maslach Burnout Inventory with a sample of mothers. *Measurement and Evaluation in Counseling and Development, 22*(2), 81-87.

Penick, N. I., & Jepsen, D. A. (1992). Family functioning and adolescent career development. *Career Development Quarterly, 40*(3), 208-222.

Perry, W. G. (1970). *Forms of intellectual and ethical development in the college years.* New York: Holt, Rinehart & Winston.

Peterson, G. W., Sampson, J. P., & Reardon, R. C. (1991). *Career development and services: A cognitive approach.* Pacific Grove, CA: Brooks/Cole.

Phifer, P. (1987, October). *College majors and careers: How to select a college major.* Paper presented at the annual meeting of the Michigan Association for Counseling and Development, Grand Rapids. (ERIC Document Reproduction Service No. ED 292 021)

Phillips, S. D., & Johnston, S. L. (1985). Attitudes toward work roles for women. *Journal of College Student Personnel, 26*(4), 334-338.

Piaget, J. (1963). *The child's conception of the world*. Patterson, NJ: Littlefield, Adams.

Pickering, J. W., & Vacc, N. A. (1984). Effectiveness of career development interventions for college students: A review of published research. *Vocational Guidance Quarterly, 32*(3), 147-159.

Pickney, J. W., & Ramirez, M. (1985). Career-planning myths of Chicano students. *Journal of College Student Personnel, 26*(4), 300-305.

Piers, E., & Harris, D. B. (1983). *Piers-Harris Children's Self-Concept Scales*. Los Angeles: Western Psychological Services.

Pine, G. J., & Innis, G. (1987). Cultural and individual work values. *Career Development Quarterly, 35*(4), 279-287.

Pinkney, J. W. (1985). A card sort interpretive strategy for flat profiles on the Strong-Campbell Interest Inventory. *Vocational Guidance Quarterly, 33*(4), 331-339.

Piotrowski, C., & Keller, J. W. (1984). Psychological testing: Trends in master's level counseling psychology programs. *Teaching of Psychology, 11*(4), 244-245.

Pirnot, K., & Dustin, R. (1986). A new look at value priorities for homemakers and career women. *Journal of Counseling and Development, 64*(7), 432-436.

Post-Kammer, P. (1987). Intrinsic and extrinsic work values and career maturity of 9th- and 11th-grade boys and girls. *Journal of Counseling and Development, 65*(8), 420-423.

Post-Kammer, P., & Perrone, P. (1983). Career perceptions of talented individuals: A follow-up study. *Vocational Guidance Quarterly, 31*(3), 203-211.

Powell, R. (1990). *Career planning today: Hire me* (2nd ed.). Dubuque, IA: Kendall/Hunt.

Powers, S. I., Hauser, S. T., & Kilner, L. A. (1989). Adolescent mental health. *American Psychologist, 44*(2), 200-208.

Prediger, D. J. (1981). A note on Self-Directed Search validity for females. *Vocational Guidance Quarterly, 30*(2), 117-129.

Prediger, D. J. (1987). Validity of the new Armed Services Vocational Aptitude Battery job cluster scores in career planning. *Career Development Quarterly, 36*(2), 113-124.

Prediger, D. J., & Sawyer, R. L. (1986). Ten years of career development: A nationwide study of high school students. *Journal of Counseling and Development, 65*(1), 45-49.

Project PACE final report 1983-84. (1984). Portland, ME: Portland Public Schools. (ERIC Document Reproduction Service No. ED 248 360)

Pyle, K. R. (1984). Career counseling and computers: Where is the creativity? *Journal of Counseling and Development, 63*(3), 141-144.

Quinn, R. P., & Baldi de Mandilovitch, M. S. (1980). Education and job satisfaction, 1962-1977. *Vocational Guidance Quarterly, 29*(2), 100-111.

Raths, L. E., Harmin, M., & Simon, S. B. (1966). *Values and teaching*. Columbus, OH: Charles E. Merrill.

Raup, J. L., & Myers, J. E. (1989). The empty nest syndrome: Myth or reality? *Journal of Counseling and Development, 68*(2), 180-183.

Raymond, C. (1990, April 11). Research notes. *Chronical of Higher Education*, p. A7.

Read, N. O., Elliott, M. R., Escobar, M. D., & Slaney, R. B. (1988). The effects of marital status and motherhood on the career concerns of reentry women. *Career Development Quarterly, 37*(1), 46-55.

Rees, A. H., & Palmer, F. H. (1970). Factors related to change in mental test performance. *Developmental Psychology Monographs, 3*, 1-57.

Reeves, J. W. (1970). What is occupational success? *Occupational Psychology, 44*, 213-217.

Reid, N. (1986). Wide Range Achievement Test: 1984 revised edition. *Measurement and Evaluation in Counseling and Development, 64*(8), 538-539.

Reynolds, C. R., Kamphaus, R. W., & Rosenthal, B. L. (1988). Factor analysis of the Stanford-Binet fourth edition for ages 2 years through 23 years. *Measurement and Evaluation in Counseling and Development, 21*(2), 52-63.

Richman, D. R. (1988). Cognitive psychotherapy through the career cycle. In W. Dryden & P. Trower (Eds.), *Developments in cognitive psychotherapy* (pp. 190-217). London: Sage.

Riverin-Simard, D. (1990). Adult vocational trajectory. *Career Development Quarterly, 39*(2), 129-142.

Roark, A. C. (1977, February 2). First-time college enrollment of women leaps dramatically. *Chronicle of Higher Education*, pp. 1, 10.

Robbins, S. B., & Tucker, K. R., Jr. (1986). Relation of goal instability to self-directed and interactional career counseling workshops. *Journal of Counseling Psychology, 33*(4), 418-424.

Robinson, S. E. (1983). Nader versus ETS: Who should we believe? *Personnel and Guidance Journal, 61*(5), 260-262.

Roe, A. (1956). *The psychology of occupations.* New York: John Wiley.

Roe, A. (1957). Early determinants of vocational choice. *Journal of Vocational Choice, 4*(3), 212-217.

Roe, A. (1964). Personality structure and occupational behavior. In H. Borow (Ed.), *Man in a world at work* (pp. 196-214). Boston: Houghton Mifflin.

Rogers, C. R. (1942). *Counseling and psychotherapy.* Boston: Houghton Mifflin.

Rossi, A. S. (1972). Family development in a changing world. *American Journal of Psychiatry, 128*, 1057-1066.

Rotberg, H. L., Brown, D., & Ware, W. B. (1987). Career self-efficacy expectations and perceived range of career options in community college students. *Journal of Counseling Psychology, 34*(2), 164-170.

Roth, M. J. (1973). Career awareness in the elementary school. *Dissertation Abstracts International, 33*, 5056A. (University Microfilms No. 73-5611)

Rubinton, N. (1985). Career exploration for middle school youth: A university-school cooperative. *Vocational Guidance Quarterly, 33*(3), 249-255.

Ryland, E. K., & Rosen, B. (1987). Personnel professionals' reactions to chronological and functional resume formats. *Career Development Quarterly, 35*(3), 228-238.

Salomone, P. R., & Mangicaro, L. L. (1991). Difficult cases in career counseling: IV. Floundering and occupational moratorium. *Career Development Quarterly, 39*(4), 325-336.

Salomone, P. R., & Sheehan, M. C. (1985). Vocational stability and congruence: An examination of Holland's proposition. *Vocational Guidance Quarterly, 34*(2), 91-98.

Saltoun, J. (1980). Fear of failure in career development. *Vocational Guidance Quarterly, 29*(1), 35-41.

Sampson, J. P., Jr., & Loesch, L. C. (1981). Relationships among work values and job knowledge. *Vocational Guidance Quarterly, 29*(3), 229-235.

Samuda, R. J. (1975). *Psychological testing of American minorities.* New York: Dodd, Mead.

Sargent, J. (1988). A greatly improved outlook for college graduates: A 1988 update to the year 2000. *Occupational Outlook Quarterly, 32*(2), 3-8.

Sargent, J., & Pfleeger, J. (1990). The job outlook for college graduates to the year 2000: A 1990 update. *Occupational Outlook Quarterly, 34*(2), 3-8.

Sauter, S. L., Murphy, L. R., & Hurrell, J. J., Jr. (1990). Prevention of work-related psychological disorders. *American Psychologist, 45*(10), 1146-1158.

Savickas, M. (1984). Career maturity: The construct and its measurement. *Vocational Guidance Quarterly, 32*(4), 222-231.

Savickas, M. L. (1989). Annual review: Practice and research in career counseling and development, 1988. *Career Development Quarterly, 38*(2), 100-134.

Savickas, M. L. (1990). The career decision-making course: Description and field test. *Career Development Quarterly, 38*(3), 275-284.

Savickas, M. L. (1991). The meaning of work and love: Career issues and interventions. *Career Development Quarterly, 39*(4), 315-324.

Savicki, V., & Cooley, E. (1987). The relationship of work environment and client contact to burnout in mental health professionals. *Journal of Counseling and Development, 65*(5), 249-252.

Scarr, S., Phillips, D., & McCartney, K. (1989). Working mothers and their families. *American Psychologist, 44*(11), 1402-1409.

Scarr, S., & Weinberg, R. A. (1986). Care and education of the young. *American Psychologist, 41*(10), 1040-1046.

Schlossberg, N. K. (1976). The case for counseling adults. *Counseling Psychologist, 6*, 33-36.

Schlossberg, N. K. (1981). A model for analyzing human adaptation to transition. *The Counseling Psychologist, 9*(2), 2-18.

Schlossberg, N. K. (1992). Adult development theories: Ways to illuminate the adult experience. In H. D. Lea & Z. B. Leibowitz (Eds.), *Adult career development* (pp. 2-16). Alexandria, VA: American Association for Counseling and Development.

Schlossberg, N. K., Troll, L. E., & Leibowitz, Z. (1978). *Perspectives on counseling adults: Issues and skills.* Monterey, CA: Brooks/Cole.

Schmitz, T. J. (1988). Career counseling implications with the gay and lesbian population. *Journal of Employment Counseling, 25*(2), 51-56.

Schwartz, F. N. (1989, January/February). Management women and the new facts of life. *Harvard Business Review*, pp. 65-76.

Schwebel, M. (1975). Formal operations in first-year college students. *Journal of Psychology, 91*, 133-141.

Sedlacek, W. E. (1977). Test bias and the elimination of racism. *Journal of College Student Personnel, 18*(1), 16-20.

Sekaran, U., & Hall, D. T. (1989). Asynchronism in dual-career and family linkages. In M. B. Arthur, D. T. Hall, & B. S. Lawrence (Eds.), *Handbook of career theory* (pp. 159-180). New York: Cambridge University Press.

Seligman, L., Weinstock, L., & Heflin, E. N. (1991). The career development of 10-year-olds. *Elementary School Guidance and Counseling, 25*(3), 172-181.

Seligman, L., Weinstock, L., & Owings, N. (1988). The role of family dynamics in career development of 5-year-olds. *Elementary School Guidance and Counseling, 22*(3), 222-230.

Sewell, W. H., & Orenstein, A. M. (1965). Community of residence and occupational choice. *American Journal of Sociology, 70*, 551-563.

Sheehy, G. (1976). *Passages.* New York: E. P. Dutton.

Shelver, J. W. (1976). The centering of career in self through an elementary career education program. *Dissertation Abstracts International, 36*, 6488A. (University Microfilms No. 76-8927)

Shostrom, E. L. (1963). *Personal orientation inventory.* San Diego, CA: Educational and Industrial Testing Service.

Silverstein, L. B. (1991). Transforming the debate about child care and maternal employment. *American Psychologist, 46*(10), 1025-1032.

Sinick, D. (1977). *Counseling older persons: Careers, retirement, dying.* New York: Human Sciences Press.

Skovholt, T. M., & Morgan, J. I. (1981). Career development: An outline of issues for men. *Personnel and Guidance Journal, 60*(4), 231-237.

Skovholt, T. M., Morgan, J. I., & Negron-Cunningham, H. (1989). Mental imagery in career counseling and life planning: A review of research and intervention methods. *Journal of Counseling and Development, 67*(5), 287-292.

Slaney, R. B. (1980). Expressed vocational choice and vocational indecision. *Journal of Counseling Psychology, 27*(2), 122-129.

Slaney, R. B. (1984). Relation of career indecision to changes in expressed vocational interests. *Journal of Counseling Psychology, 31*(3), 349-355.

Smith, R. L. (1988). Counseling and human resource development: Response to "Career Development in Business and Industry." *Journal of Counseling and Development, 66*(8), 382-384.

Smith, R. L., Engels, D. W., & Bonk, E. C. (1985). The past and future: The National Vocational Guidance Association. *Journal of Counseling and Development, 63*(7), 420-423.

Smith, R. L., & Karpati, F. S. (1985). Credentialing career counselors. *Journal of Counseling and Development, 63*(10), 611.

Smyer, M. A. (1984). Life transitions and aging: Implications for counseling older adults. *The Counseling Psychologist, 12*(2), 17-28.

Snyderman, M., & Rothman, S. (1987). Survey of expert opinion on intelligence and aptitude testing. *American Psychologist, 42*(2), 137-144.

Sodetz, A. R., & Vinitsky, M. N. (1977). Expanding vocational alternatives: Innovative techniques for interpreting the SCII. *Vocational Guidance Quarterly, 26*(12), 141-146.

Solomon, D., Scheinfeld, D. R., Hirsch, J. G., & Jackson, J. C. (1971). Early grade school performance of inner city Negro high school high achievers, low achievers and dropouts. *Developmental Psychology, 4,* 482.

Spearman, C. E. (1904). General intelligence objectively determined and measured. *American Journal of Psychology, 15,* 201-293.

Spokane, A. R. (1992). Career intervention and counseling theory for adults: Toward a consensus model. In H. D. Lea & Z. B. Leibowitz (Eds.), *Adult career development* (pp. 42-54). Alexandria, VA: American Association for Counseling and Development.

Spokane, A. R., & Hawks, B. K. (1990). Annual review: Practice and research in career counseling and development. *Career Development Quarterly, 39,* 98-128.

Stafford, I. P. (1984). Relation of attitudes toward women's roles and occupational behavior to women's self-esteem. *Journal of Counseling Psychology, 31*(3), 332-338.

Steffy, B. D., Shaw, K. N., & Noe, A. W. (1989). Antecedents and consequences of job search behaviors. *Journal of Vocational Behavior, 35,* 254-269.

Stevens, F. I. (1986). Vineland Adaptive Behavior Scales: Classroom edition. *Journal of Counseling and Development, 65*(2), 112-113.

Stewart, H. R. (1989). Job satisfaction of women in nontraditional occupations. *Journal of Employment Counseling, 26*(1), 26-34.

Stolz-Loike, M. (1992). The working family: Helping women balance the roles of wife, mother, and career woman. *Career Development Quarterly, 40*(3), 244-256.

Stone, G. L., & Archer, J., Jr. (1990). College and university counseling centers in the 1990's: Challenges and limits. *The Counseling Psychologist, 18*(4), 539-607.

Stout, S. K., Slocum, J. W., Jr., & Cron, W. L. (1988). Dynamics of the career plateauing process. *Journal of Vocational Behavior, 32,* 74-91.

Strauss, G. (1976). Worker dissatisfaction: A look at the causes. *Journal of Employment Counseling, 13,* 105-106.

Sullivan, H. S. (1954). *The psychiatric interview.* New York: Norton.

Sullivan, S. E. (1992). Is there a time for everything? Attitudes related to women's sequencing of career and family. *Career Development Quarterly, 40*(3), 234-243.

Sundal-Hansen, L. S. (1985). Work-family linkages: Neglected factors in career guidance across cultures. *Vocational Guidance Quarterly, 33*(3), 202-212.

Super, D. E. (1952). A theory of vocational development. *The American Psychologist, 8,* 189-190.

Super, D. E. (1957a). *The psychology of careers.* New York: Harper & Row.

Super, D. E. (1957b). *Vocational development: A framework for research.* New York: Teachers College Press.

Super, D. E. (1963). Vocational development in adolescence and early adulthood: Tasks and behaviors. In D. E. Super, R. Starishevsky, N. Matlin, & J. P. Jordaan (Eds.), *Career development: Self-concept theory* (pp. 79-95). New York: College Entrance Examination Board.

Super, D. E. (1968). *Floundering and trial after high school.* New York: Teachers College Press.

Super, D. E. (1977). Vocational maturity in mid-career. *Vocational Guidance Quarterly, 25,* 294-302.

Super, D. E. (1982). The relative importance of work: Models and measures for meaningful data. *The Counseling Psychologist, 10*(4), 95-103.

Super, D. E. (1983). Assessment in career guidance: Toward truly developmental counseling. *Personnel and Guidance Journal, 61*(9), 555-562.

Super, D. E. (1984). Career and life development. In D. Brown & L. Brooks (Eds.), *Career choice and development* (pp. 192-234). San Francisco: Jossey-Bass.

Super, D. E. (1985). Coming of age in Middletown. *American Psychologist, 40*(4), 405-414.

Super, D. E., & Bohn, M. J., Jr. (1970). *Occupational psychology.* Belmont, CA: Wadsworth.

Super, D. E., & Crites, J. O. (1962). *Appraising vocational fitness.* New York: Harper & Row.

Super, D. E., Crites, J. O., Hummel, R. C., Moser, H. P., Overstreet, P. L., & Warnath, C. (1957). *Vocational development: A framework for research.* New York: Teachers College Press.

Super, D. E., & Overstreat, P. I. (1960). *The vocational maturity of ninth-grade boys.* New York: Teachers College Press.

Super, D. E., Starishevsky, R., Matlin, N., & Jordaan, J. P. (Eds.). (1963). *Career development: Self-concept theory.* New York: College Entrance Examination Board.

Super, D. E., Thompson, A. S., & Lindeman, R. H. (1988). *Adult Career Concerns Inventory.* Palo Alto, CA: Consulting Psychologists Press.

Swain, R. (1984). Easing the transition: A career planning course for college students. *Personnel and Guidance Journal, 62*(9), 529-532.

Swanson, J. L., & Hansen, J. C. (1988). Stability of vocational interests over 4-year, 8-year, and 12-year intervals. *Journal of Vocational Behavior, 33,* 185-202.

Sweetland, R. C., & Keyser, D. J. (Eds.). (1986). *Tests: A comprehensive reference for assessments in psychology, education, and business* (2nd ed.). Kansas City, MO: Test Corporation of America.

Tavris, C. (1989, July/August). Don't act your age. *American Health,* pp. 49-58.

Taylor, C. (1972). Developmental conceptions and the retirement process. In F. M. Carp (Ed.), *Retirement* (pp. 75-114). New York: Human Sciences Press.

Tennyson, W. W. (1981). *Career education: Some essential learner outcomes.* St. Paul, MN: Minnesota State Department of Education. (ERIC Document Reproduction Service No. ED 220 574)

Tennyson, W. W., Miller, G. D., Skovholt, T. M., & Williams, R. C. (1989). How they view their role: A survey of counselors in different secondary schools. *Journal of Counseling and Development, 67*(7), 399-403.

Tennyson, W. W., & Monnens, L. P. (1973). The world of work through elementary readers. In N. C. Gysbers, W. Miller, & E. J. Moore (Eds.), *Developing careers in the elementary school* (pp. 63-69). Columbus, OH: Charles E. Merrill.

Thomas, D. A., & Alderfer, C. P. (1989). The influence of race on career dynamics: Theory and research on minority career experiences. In M. B. Authur, D. T. Hall, & B. S. Lawrence (Eds.), *Handbook of career theory* (pp. 133-158). New York: Cambridge University Press.

Thomas, K. R., & O'Brien, R. A. (1984). Occupational status and prestige: Perceptions of business, education, and law students. *Vocational Guidance Quarterly, 33*(1), 70-75.

Thomas, L. E. (1977). Mid-career changes: Self-selected or externally mandated? *Vocational Guidance Quarterly, 25*(4), 320-328.

Thomas, L. E., Morrill, W. H., & Miller, C. D. (1970). Educational interests and achievement. *Vocational Guidance Quarterly, 18,* 199-202.

Thomas, M. L., & Kuh, G. D. (1982). Understanding development during the early adult years: A composite framework. *Personnel and Guidance Journal, 61*(1), 14-21.

Thompson, B., & Borrello, G. M. (1986). Second-order factor structure of the MBTI: A construct validity assessment. *Measurement and Evaluation in Counseling and Development, 18*(4), 148-153.

Thornburg, H. D. (1986). The counselor's impact on middle-grade students. *The School Counselor, 33*(3), 170-177.

Thrasher, F., & Boland, P. (1989). Student development studies: A review of published empirical research, 1973-1987. *Journal of Counseling and Development, 67*(10), 547-554.

Tiedeman, D. V., & O'Hara, R. P. (1963). *Career development: Choice and adjustment.* New York: College Entrance Examination Board.

Tilden, A. J., Jr. (1978). Is there a monotonic criterion for measures of vocational maturity in college students? *Journal of Vocational Behavior, 12,* 43-52.

Tinsley, H. E. A., Benton, B. L., & Rollins, J. A. (1984). The effects of values clarification exercises on the value structure of junior high school students. *Vocational Guidance Quarterly, 32*(3), 160-167.

Tinsley, H. E. A., & Tinsley, D. J. (1989). Reinforcers of the occupation of homemaker: An analysis of the need-gratifying properties of the homemaker occupation across the stages of the homemaker life cycle. *Journal of Counseling Psychology, 36*(2), 189-195.

Trimmer, H. W., Jr. (1984). Group job search workshops: A concept whose time is here. *Journal of Employment Counseling, 21*(3), 103-116.

Troll, L. (1975). *Early and middle adulthood.* Monterey, CA: Brooks/Cole.

Troll, L. E., & Nowak, C. (1976). "How old are you?" The question of age bias in the counseling of adults. *The Counseling Psychologist, 6,* 41-44.

Tyler, L. (1984). What tests don't measure. *Journal of Counseling and Development, 63*(1), 48-50.

U.S. Department of Labor, Bureau of Labor Statistics. (1976). *Employment of school age youth.* Washington, DC: Author.

U.S. Department of Labor, Bureau of Labor Statistics. (1988). *Bureau of Labor Statistics reports on displaced workers* (No. 88-611). Washington, DC: U.S. Government Printing Office.

U.S. Department of Labor, Bureau of Labor Statistics. (1990). *Occupational projections and training data* (No. 2351). Washington, DC: U.S. Government Printing Office.

Vale, D. C. (1990). The Minnesota Clerical Assessment Battery: An application of computerized testing to business. *Measurement and Evaluation in Counseling and Development, 23*(1), 11-19.

Van Hutton, V. (1990). Test review: The California Psychological Inventory. *Journal of Counseling and Development, 69*(1), 75-77.

Van Matre, G., & Cooper, S. (1984). Concurrent evaluation of career indecision and indecisiveness. *Personnel and Guidance Journal, 62*(10), 637-639.

Vansickle, T. R., Kimmel, C., & Kapes, J. T. (1989). Test-retest equivalency of the computer-based and paper-pencil versions of the Strong-Campbell Interest Inventory. *Measurement and Evaluation in Counseling and Development, 22*(2), 88-93.

Villemez, W. J. (1974). Ability vs. effort: Ideological correlates of occupational grading. *Social Forces, 53*, 1974.

Vincenzi, H. (1977). Minimizing occupational stereotypes. *Vocational Guidance Quarterly, 25*, 265-268.

Vocational and career counseling competencies. (1985). *Vocational Guidance Quarterly, 34*(2), 131-134.

Vodanovich, S. J., & Kramer, T. J. (1989). An examination of the work values of parents and their children. *Career Development Quarterly, 37*(4), 365-374.

Vondracek, F. W., Hostetler, M., Schulenberg, J. E., & Shimizu, K. (1990). Dimensions of career indecision. *Journal of Counseling Psychology, 37*(1), 98-106.

Vondracek, F. W., & Schulenberg, J. E. (1986). Career development in adolescence: Some conceptual and intervention issues. *Vocational Guidance Quarterly, 34*(4), 247-254.

Wadsworth, M., & Ford, D. H. (1983). Assessment of personal goal hierarchies. *Journal of Counseling Psychology, 30*(4), 514-526.

Wakelee-Lynch, J. (1990, December 27). Testing in the workplace focuses on skills, aptitudes and integrity. *Guidepost*, pp. 1, 6.

Wainer, H. (1988). How accurately can we assess changes in minority performance on the SAT? *American Psychologist, 43*(10), 774-778.

Walsh, W. B., & Hanle, N. A. (1975). Consistent occupational preferences, vocational maturity and academic achievement. *Journal of Vocational Behavior, 7*, 89-97.

Walz, G. R., & Benjamin, L. (1984). A systems approach to career guidance. *Vocational Guidance Quarterly, 33*(1), 26-34.

Waterman, A. S., & Waterman, C. K. (1976). Factors related to vocational identity after extensive work experience. *Journal of Applied Psychology, 61*, 336-340.

Watkins, C. E., Jr., & Campbell, V. L. (1990). Testing and assessment in counseling psychology: Contemporary developments and issues. *The Counseling Psychologist, 18*(2), 189-197.

Watkins, C. E., Jr., Campbell, V. L., & McGregor, P. (1988). Counseling psychologists' uses of and opinions about psychological tests: A contemporary perspective. *The Counseling Psychologist, 16*(3), 476-486.

Weaver, C. N. (1975). Job preferences of white collar and blue collar workers. *Academy of Management Journal, 18*, 167-175.

Wechsler, D. (1958). *The measurement and appraisal of adult intelligence* (4th ed.). Baltimore, MD: Williams & Wilkins.

Wegmann, R. G. (1991a). From job to job. *Journal of Employment Counseling, 28*(1), 8-12.

Wegmann, R. (1991b). How long does unemployment last? *Career Development Quarterly, 40*(1), 71-81.

Weinberg, R. A. (1989). Intelligence and IQ. *American Psychologist, 44*(2), 98-104.

Weiner, A. I., & Hunt, S. L. (1983). Work and leisure orientations among university students: Implications for college and university counselors. *Personnel and Guidance Journal, 61*(5), 537-542.

Welfel, E. R. (1982). The development of reflective judgment: Implications for career counseling of college students. *Personnel and Guidance Journal, 61*(1), 17-21.

Westbrook, B. W., Sanford, E. E., Merwin, G., Fleenor, J., & Gilliland, K. (1988). Career maturity in grade 9: Can students who make appropriate career choices for others also make appropriate career choices for themselves? *Measurement and Evaluation in Counseling and Development, 21*(2), 64-71.

Westbrook, B. W., Sanford, E. E., Merwin, G. A., Jr., Fleenor, J., & Renzi, D. (1987). Reliability and construct validity of new measures of career maturity for 11th grade students. *Measurement and Evaluation in Counseling and Development, 20*(1), 18-26.

Whiston, S. C. (1989). Using family systems theory in career counseling: A group for parents. *The School Counselor, 36*(5), 343-347.

Whiston, S. C. (1990). Evaluation of the Adult Career Concerns Inventory. *Journal of Counseling and Development, 69*(1), 78-80.

White, K. M., & Speisman, J. C. (1977). *Adolescence.* Monterey, CA: Brooks/Cole.

Whiteley, S. M., Mahaffey, P. J., & Geer, C. A. (1987). The campus counseling center: A profile of staffing patterns and services. *Journal of College Student Personnel, 28*(1), 71-81.

Wilcox-Matthew, L., & Minor, C. W. (1989). The dual career couple: Concerns, benefits, and counseling implications. *Journal of Counseling and Development, 68*(2), 194-198.

Wilgus, E., & Shelley, V. (1988). The role of the elementary-school counselor: Teacher perceptions, expectations, and actual functions. *The School Counselor, 35*(4), 259-266.

Wilson, J., Weikel, W. J., & Rose, H. (1982). A comparison of nontraditional and traditional career women. *Vocational Guidance Quarterly, 31*(2), 109-117.

Wilson, K. M. (1975). Today's women students: New outlooks and new challenges. *Journal of College Student Personnel, 16*, 376-381.

Wilson, N. S. (1986). Counselor interventions with low-achieving and underachieving elementary, middle, and high school students: A review of the literature. *Journal of Counseling and Development, 64*(10), 628-634.

Wilson, R. (1990, April 11). More colleges are offering credit to older students for their experiences on the job or at home. *Chronicle of Higher Education,* pp. 35-36.

Wilson, R. J., Anderson, S. A., & Fleming, W. M. (1987). Commuter and resident students' personal and family adjustment. *Journal of College Student Personnel, 28*(3), 229-233.

Wilson, S. (1982). A new decade: The gifted and career choice. *Vocational Guidance Quarterly, 31*(1), 53-59.

Winkler, K. J. (1976, October 18). Black women's career goals found lower than men's. *Chronicle of Higher Education,* p. 12.

Wise, S. L., & Plake, B. S. (1990). Computer-based testing in higher education. *Measurement and Evaluation in Counseling and Development, 23*(1), 3-10.

Worthington, C. F. (1987). Kaufman Test of Educational Achievement, comprehensive form and brief form. *Journal of Counseling and Development, 65*(6), 325-327.

Wortley, D. B., & Amatea, E. S. (1982). Mapping adult life changes: A conceptual framework for organizing adult development theory. *Personnel and Guidance Journal, 60*(8), 476-482.

Yankelovich, D. (1978, May). The new psychological contracts at work. *Psychology Today,* pp. 46-50.

Yates, C. J. (1987). Job hunters' perspectives on their needs during the job search process. *Journal of Employment Counseling, 24*(4), 155-165.

Yates, L. V. (1990). A note about values assessment of occupational and career stage age groups. *Measurement and Evaluation in Counseling and Development, 23*(1), 39-42.

Yost, E. B., & Corbishly, M. A. (1987). *Career counseling: A psychological approach.* San Francisco: Jossey-Bass.

Young, R. B., Backer, R., & Rogers, G. (1989). The impact of early advising and scheduling on freshman success. *Journal of College Student Personnel, 30*(4), 309-312.

Ysseldyke, J. E. (1985). Basic Achievement Skills Individual Screener. *Journal of Counseling and Development, 64*(1), 90-91.

Zaccaria, J. S. (1970). *Theories of occupational choice and vocational development.* Boston: Houghton Mifflin.

Zajonc, R. B. (1986). The decline and rise of Scholastic Aptitude scores. *American Psychologist, 41*(8), 862-867.

Zedeck, S., & Mosier, K. L. (1990). Work in the family and employing organization. *American Psychologist, 45*(2), 240-251.

Zunker, V. G. (1990). *Career counseling: Applied concepts of life planning.* Pacific Grove, CA: Brooks/Cole.

Zytowski, D. G. (1970a). The concept of work values. *Vocational Guidance Quarterly, 18,* 176-185.

Zytowski, D. G. (1970b). *The influence of psychological factors upon vocational development.* Boston: Houghton Mifflin.

Zytowski, D. G. (1986). Comparison of Roe's and Holland's occupational classifications: Diverse ways of knowing. *Journal of Counseling Psychology, 33*(4), 479-481.

Author Index

Abramowitz, M. W., 224
Abrego, P., 385
Adams, R. L., 41
Adelmann, P. K., 360
Adler, A., 40
Adler, T., 30, 317
Ahmann, J. S., 130
Alderfer, C. P., 44
Allen, R. E., 327
Allis, M. R., 164, 351
Allport, G. S., 161
Amatea, E. S., 266, 282, 305, 419
American Personnel and Guidance Association, 64
American School Counselors Association, 132, 187
Amundson, N. E., 30, 321, 322, 379, 396
Anastasi, A., 68
Anderson, R. C., 42
Anderson, S. A., 328
Anderson, W., 373
Angle, S. S., 330, 342
Angoff, W. H., 119, 128, 133
Antonucci, T. C., 360
Apfel, F. S., 393
Apostal, R. A., 42
Arbona, C., 44, 48
Archer, J., Jr., 326, 328, 339, 340, 342
Arp, R. S., 344
Arthur, M. B., 25
Astin, A. W., 325, 333, 389
Atchley, R. C., 437, 441
Aubrey, R. G., 210, 216, 226, 227
Auster, C. J., 318

Auster, D., 318
Avasthi, S., 118, 124, 125, 285, 290
Avramides, B., 342
Axelrad, S., 7, 179, 215, 256, 306, 319

Bachhuber, T. D., 312, 315, 335, 336
Backer, R., 342
Backover, A., 48
Bailey, L. J., 38
Baker, H. G., 136
Baker, S. B., 191
Baldi de Mandilovitch, M. S., 30
Barak, A., 31
Barber, S. L., 374
Barke, C., 38, 260
Barokas, J. U., 310
Barrett, G. V., 129
Bartling, H. C., 35, 138
Baruch, G. K., 39
Bauer, D., 388
Bauernfeind, R. H., 145, 147
Bayer, D. L., 210
Beane, J. A., 207, 210, 213
Benjamin, L., 191, 468
Benson, J., 93
Benton, B. L., 212, 251
Bernardelli, A., 228
Bettesworth, A., 171
Betz, N. E., 2, 30, 52, 113, 115, 137, 159, 330
Beyard-Tyler, K., 317, 319
Biggs, D. A., 22, 70
Black, K. U., 380

Blackburn, A. C., 176, 266
Blimline, C. A., 397
Blimling, G. S., 328
Bloch, D. P., 267, 268, 279
Blocher, D. H., 398
Bloland, P. A., 18, 425
Blum, C. R., 338
Blum, D. E., 335
Blustein, D. L., 36, 309
Bockoven, J., 171
Boese, R., 127
Bohn, M. J., Jr., 31, 119, 221
Boland, P., 328
Bolles, R. N., 344
Bolton, B., 142, 149, 150, 243
Bonk, E. C., 3
Borchard, D. C., 343
Borgen, W. A., 30, 321, 322, 379, 396
Borman, C., 276
Borman, C. A., 279, 343
Borrello, G. M., 410
Bowen, H. R., 271
Bowen, M., 23, 41, 338
Bracht, G. H., 131
Braddock, D. J., 335
Bradley, R. W., 41, 472
Brammer, L., 385
Brand, L., 60
Breland, H. M., 40
Brigman, S. L., 309
Brill, A. A., 302
Britt, M. N., 151
Brizzi, J. S., 308
Brolin, D. E., 54, 55, 195
Brook, J. S., 184
Brookings, J. B., 142, 150, 243
Brown, D., 17, 34, 36, 51, 258, 259, 260,
    262, 263, 315, 352, 380, 395, 467
Brown, S. T., 352
Bruhn, J. G., 36, 381, 399
Buehler, C., 7
Buescher, K. L., 165, 292
Bunce, M. E., 345
Butcher, E., 470, 471

Cahill, M., 417, 431, 447
Calsyn, R. J., 210, 224
Campbell, N. J., 261, 263

Campbell, V. L., 65, 91, 110, 148, 154, 157,
    406
Career Planning and Adult Development
    Network, 436, 441
Carey, M., 320, 358, 382, 384, 431
Carey, R. G., 424
Carlsen, M. B., 393, 462
Carr, J. V., 226
Carroll, S. J., 382
Carson, A., 20
Carvajal, H., 126, 285
Cech, E. J., 96
Chan, F., 57
Chapman, W., 278
Chartrand, J. M., 2, 388, 389
Cheatham, H. E., 45
Chickering, A. W., 325
Chiriboga, D., 425
Chiu, L., 161, 170, 171, 194, 205
Chronicle of Higher Education, 326
Chusmir, L. H., 53, 317, 318, 319
Cianni-Surridge, M., 324
Claiborn, C. D., 63
Clark, J. E., 266
Colangelo, N., 210, 265, 311
Cole, C., 215, 221
Coleman, L. M., 360
Colson, S., 276
Conoley, J. C., 72
Cook, E. P., 462, 468
Cooley, E., 381
Cooper, S., 34, 35
Cooper, S. E., 190, 341
Corbishly, M. A., 1, 2, 28
Corder-Bolz, C. R., 191
Cormier, P., 96
Cosby, A. G., 47
Cox, R. D., 361
Cox, S. G., 115
Crabbs, M. A., 380
Crace, R. K., 463
Cramer, S. H., 85
Crites, J. O., 9, 15, 30, 49, 51, 53, 64, 137,
    164, 218, 219, 264, 283, 319, 323,
    324, 352, 378, 392
Crohan, S. E., 360
Cron, W. L., 382
Crook, J. C., 321
Cross, E. G., 266

Cross, G. E., 282
Curtin, B. M., 343
Cytrynbaum, S., 30

Dahl, P. R., 54, 55
Daiger, D. C., 17, 291
Darrow, C. M., 368
Davenport, D. W., 386
Davitz, J., 369
Davitz, L., 369
Dawis, R. B., 29, 56, 158, 160
Dayton, C. W., 320, 323
Depinet, R. L., 129
Deutsch, M., 184
DeVito, A. J., 311
Dewey, C. R., 166
DeWinne, R. F., 40
deWolf, V., 390
Diamond, E. E., 89
DiBenedetto, B., 314
Dillard, J. M., 43, 45, 261, 262, 263
Dillon, M., 412
Dimock, P. H., 96
Dixon, P. N., 329
Dodd, B. G., 97
Dorn, F. J., 21, 475
Droege, R. C., 127
Drummond, R. J., 157, 160, 297, 433
Duckworth, J., 99
Duckworth, J. C., 158
Dustin, R., 398
Dweck, C. S., 174

Eberly, C. G., 96
EdiTS, 123, 150, 162, 240, 245, 247
Edwards, P. B., 425
Elliott, M. R., 373
Elmslie, S., 13
Elsenrath, D., 162
Ender, S. C., 330, 342
Engels, D. W., 3, 417, 418, 432, 433, 434,
    441, 450
Engen, H. B., 65, 110, 151, 236, 286
Enns, C. Z., 50, 316
Erchul, W. P., 117
Erickson, D. B., 176, 266

Erikson, E. H., 6, 169, 172, 201, 209, 249,
    254, 255, 304, 359, 360, 391, 420, 422
Erwin, T. D., 17
Escobar, M. D., 373
Esposito, D., 51, 316
Etinger, B. D., 403
Evangelauf, J., 326, 327
Exhibit C: IQ trial, 90
Eyde, L. D., 67

Farinholt, F. W., 213
Farmer, H. S., 37, 184, 216, 220, 260, 261,
    266, 275
Feller, R., 138, 465, 467
Feren, D. B., 382
Ferrero, G. W., 219
Fields, C. M., 131
Figler, H. E., 343
Fiorentine, R., 314
Fishman, D. M., 369, 379
Fitzgerald, D. P., 329
Fitzgerald, L. F., 2, 30, 49, 51, 53, 115,
    137, 159, 177, 178, 218, 219, 264,
    312, 319, 324, 370, 372, 392
Fitzpatrick, S. J., 97
Fleenor, J., 28, 156, 220
Fleming, W. M., 328
Ford, D. H., 449
Fouad, N., 46, 48
Franco, J. N., 91, 122
Frazier, N., 279, 343
Fredrickson, R. H., 275
Freeman, S. C., 19
Freiberg, P., 171, 178, 264, 373, 374
Fretz, B. R., 431, 436, 437, 440, 441, 442,
    443, 444, 448, 463, 470, 471
Freud, S., 1, 168, 302
Friedlander, M. L., 309
Fry, P. S., 426, 427
Fullerton, H. N., Jr., 43, 59
Fuqua, D. R., 35, 338

Gade, E., 261
Galassi, J. P., 463
Galassi, M. D., 151
Gallos, J. V., 53, 319, 371

Galton, F., 2, 128
Garfield, C., 32
Gartaganis, A., 310, 313
Gati, I., 20, 21
Geer, C. A., 340
Gelatt, H. B., 19
Gelatt, H. G., 22
Gellen, M. I., 162
Gerber, J., 126, 285
Gerstein, M., 310, 395, 436, 440
Giannantonio, C. M., 382
Gilbert, L. A., 364, 365, 398
Gilhousen, M. R., 22
Gilkison, B., 433
Gilliam, P., 466
Gilligan, C., 50, 218, 259, 316
Gilliland, K., 220
Ginsburg, S. W., 7, 179, 215, 256, 306, 319
Ginzberg, E., 7, 11, 179, 215, 256, 302,
   306, 319
Gladstein, G. A., 393
Glass, J. C., 418, 424, 432
Glen, N. D., 374
Goldberg, A., 387
Goldman, L., 64, 101, 104, 105, 166, 167
Goldstein, I. L., 466
Goodson, W. D., 340
Goodyear, R. K., 92, 97, 101, 106
Gordon, L. V., 161
Gottfredson, G. D., 17, 30, 136, 345
Gottfredson, L. S., 12, 13, 90, 111, 179,
   180, 182, 183, 208, 209, 215, 218,
   219, 257, 308
Gould, R., 304, 360, 420
Gowing, M. K., 59, 431, 432, 435, 465, 467
Granrose, C. S., 316
Grant, K. A., 418, 424, 432
Greenhaus, J. H., 53
Gribbons, W. D., 27, 28, 352
Griemsmann, R., 342
Gysbers, N. C., 6, 22, 26, 54, 55, 165, 195,
   292, 309, 465

Hackett, G., 51, 52, 113, 137, 316
Hackman, J. R., 29, 465
Hagner, D., 55
Hall, D. T., 25, 366
Halpin, G., 456

Hamachek, D. E., 169, 249, 272
Hamilton, L. J., 344
Hanle, N. A., 135
Hanna, G. S., 86
Hanselman, P. R., 270
Hansen, J. C., 95, 136, 142
Hansen, L. S., 388
Hansford, S., 312, 314
Hanson, G. R., 143
Harder, H. G., 30, 321, 322, 379
Haring-Hidore, M., 317, 319
Harlan, C. L., 317
Harmin, M., 224
Harmon, L., 146
Harmon, L. H., 89
Harmon, L. W., 50, 313, 314, 315
Harrington, T. F., 47, 142
Harris, D. B., 205
Harris, J. J., III, 282
Harris, T. L., 228
Harter, M., 210, 224
Hartman, B. W., 338
Hatcher, L., 321
Hauser, S. T., 250, 251, 253
Haven, C., 423
Havighurst, R. J., 185, 272, 391, 422, 426
Hawks, B. K., 43, 48, 49, 151, 174, 337
Hayes, R., 52, 319
Haynes, L., 329
Hayslip, J. B., 226
Hazard, L. B., 399
Healy, C. C., 156, 316, 462
Hecker, D. E., 335
Hecklinger, F. J., 343
Heesacker, R. S., 330
Heflin, E. N., 171, 173, 181, 183, 184
Helwig, A. A., 127
Henton, J., 329, 383
Heppner, P. P., 165, 292
Herma, J. L., 7, 179, 215, 256, 306, 319
Herr, E. L., 85
Herr, E. R., 258
Hesketh, B., 13, 24
Hetherington, C., 403
Hettler, B., 162
Hewes, P., 126, 285
Hill, R. E., 2, 30, 115, 137, 159
Hillerbrand, E., 403
Hirsch, J. G., 174

Hocevar, D., 93
Hoffman, J. A., 328
Hoffman, L. R., 187, 189, 190
Hoffman, L. W., 362
Hoffman, M. A., 469
Hoffman, R. A., 162
Holland, J. L., 2, 15, 16, 17, 30, 40, 56, 64,
   90, 136, 142, 143, 144, 146, 147, 148,
   149, 153, 157, 165, 204, 217, 263,
   276, 291, 292, 296, 345, 352, 458
Hollis, J. W., 182
Holmberg, K. S., 344
Holmes, B. H., 359, 384, 386
Homan, K. B., 18
Hood, A. B., 35, 47, 70, 83, 85, 87, 111,
   119, 125, 138, 141, 142, 149, 153,
   157, 352, 405
Hopkins, K. D., 131
Hopkins-Best, M., 274
Horan, J. J., 324
Hornbeck, D. W., 171, 209, 211, 233
Horton, G. M., 417, 418, 432, 433, 434,
   441, 450
Hosie, T. W., 191
Hostetler, M., 264
Hoyt, K. B., 25, 26, 37, 44, 48, 58, 59, 60,
   474
Hudesman, J., 342
Hughes, C. M., 177, 178
Hughes, K. R., 162
Hummel, R. C., 9
Hummel, T. J., 93
Hunt, S. L., 32, 340
Hurrell, J. J., Jr., 381, 399
Hyman, R. B., 371

Innis, G., 51, 158, 311
Isaacson, L. E., 383

Jackson, A. W., 171, 209, 211, 233
Jackson, J. C., 174
Jackson, R. M., 260
James, R. A., Jr., 463
Jansen, M. A., 317
Jarchow, E. M., 282
Jepsen, D. A., 38, 136, 256, 260, 380, 467
Jepsen, D. P., 146, 293

Jingeleski, J., 219
Johnson, G. L., 93
Johnson, R. W., 47, 70, 83, 85, 87, 111,
   119, 125, 141, 142, 149, 153, 157,
   164, 352, 405
Johnson, W. B., 59
Johnston, S. L., 314
Jones, L. K., 151
Jones, L. P., 384
Jones, R. M., 46, 262, 264
Jones, S. M., 436, 442, 443
Jordaan, J. P., 8, 53, 376, 378, 429
Jordan, L. K., 210, 218
Josselson, R., 316

Kaldor, W., 13
Kalish, R. A., 417, 424
Kammer, P. P., 46, 48
Kamphaus, R. W., 129
Kanchier, C., 383
Kandor, J. R., 147
Kane, S. T., 150, 243
Kapes, J. T., 95, 148, 279, 343
Kaplan, D. M., 34, 36
Karabenick, S. A., 340
Karmos, A. H., 93, 114, 116
Karmos, J. S., 93, 114, 116
Karpati, F. S., 3
Karpicke, S., 315
Katz, M. R., 278
Katzell, R. A., 37, 399
Kavanaugh, H. B., 161
Kazanas, H. C., 322
Keierleber, D. L., 388
Keller, J. W., 65, 154
Keller, K. E., 22, 70
Kelly, J. J., 343
Kelly, K. R., 210, 218
Kerr, B. A., 265, 282, 311
Kerr, E. A., 435
Keyser, D. J., 202
Kilner, L. A., 250, 251, 253
Kimmel, C., 95, 148
King, S., 259, 261
Kinnie, E. J., 93
Kinnier, R. T., 309
Kinnison, J. F., 279
Kirk, J. J., 383

Kirkland, M. C., 91, 92
Kivlighan, D. M., 471
Kivlighan, D. M., Jr., 470, 471
Klein, E. B., 368
Kline, P., 82, 115
Kluckhohn, C., 155
Kluge, N. A., 436, 442, 443
Knapp, J. R., 340
Knapp, L., 138, 150
Knapp, R. R., 138, 150
Knapp-Lee, L., 138
Koch, W. R., 97
Kolb, D., 21, 162
Koplik, E. K., 311
Koski, L. K., 265
Koslow, D., 399
Koval, J., 383
Kragie, E. R., 436, 440
Kramer, J. J., 72
Kramer, T. J., 305
Krantz, L., 36
Krausz, M., 430
Kreps, J. M., 61
Krieshok, T. S., 147, 292
Krumboltz, J. D., 22
Kuh, G. D., 304, 361, 362, 363
Kuldau, J. E., 182
Kuypers, J. A., 428

Laing, J., 286
Lamb, R. R., 65, 110, 151, 236
Lamke, L., 329
Lamnin, A., 328
Lampe, R. E., 145
Lampron, D., 282
Lapan, R. T., 219
Lapsley, D. K., 329
Larsen, P., 267, 268
Larsen, R. M., 110
Lassalle, A. D., 322
Latack, J. C., 422
Lauver, P. J., 46, 262, 264
Lawrence, B. S., 25
Leafgreen, F., 162
Lee, C. C., 262
Leibowitz, Z., 359, 364, 369, 386, 395
Leifer, A. D., 182
Leong, F. T. L., 17, 46, 163, 291, 292, 342

Lesser, G. S., 182
Leung, A. S., 13, 266
Levin, A., 156, 410
Levine, A., 41, 133
Levinson, D. J., 304, 359, 360, 363, 368, 373, 419, 420
Levinson, E. M., 96, 147, 292
Levinson, M. A., 368
Lewis, R. A., 22
Librowsky, I., 31
Lichtman, M., 310, 436, 440
Lidz, T., 442
Lindeman, R. H., 164, 456
Lindzey, G., 161
Linn, R. L., 64, 65, 91, 132
Liptak, J. J., 384, 386, 436, 440
Littrell, J. M., 344
Livson, N., 209
Loesch, L. C., 108, 159, 212
Lofquist, L., 29, 56, 158, 160
Lohnes, P. R., 27, 28, 352
Lopez, F. G., 40, 308, 309
Loughead, T., 144
Loveday, C., 342
Lowenthal, M. F., 423, 425
Lubin, B., 110
Lucas, E. B., 165, 292
Lunneborg, P. W., 15, 390
Lyman, H. B., 84

Maas, H. S., 428
Macari, C., 224
MacKinnon-Slaney, F., 374
Madsen, D. H., 95, 96
Magarrell, J., 326
Magoon, T. M., 469
Mahaffey, P. J., 340
Malde, S., 446
Mangicaro, L. L., 307
Mansfield, A. F., 177
Manuele, C. A., 379, 395
Maples, M. F., 365, 366
Marantz, S. A., 177
Marin, P. A., 342, 387, 469
Marland, S. P., Jr., 187
Marshall, A., 323
Martin, G. A., 463
Martin, M. K., 329

Martinek, S. A., 177, 178
Martinez, A. C., 312, 315, 335, 336
Martray, C. R., 162
Maslow, A. A., 37, 224, 299
Matarazzo, J. D., 110
Mathiasen, R. E., 326
Matlin, N., 8, 53
Matthay, E. R., 270, 271, 272
Matthews, D. B., 381
Mauer, E. B., 309
McBride, M. C., 50, 275
McCartney, K., 362
McCaulley, M., 152, 156, 409
McDaniels, C., 33, 187, 189, 190, 338, 469
McDowell, C. F., 33, 397
McGraw, L., 373, 398
McGregor, P., 65, 110, 130, 154, 157, 158, 406
McIlroy, J. H., 363, 372
McKee, B., 368
McKee, L. M., 96, 147, 292
McKenna, A. E., 219
McKnab, P., 126, 285
McMorris, R. F., 94
McNair, D., 258, 259, 260, 262, 263
Meara, N. M., 260
Medvene, A. M., 40
Meier, E. L., 435
Meir, E. I., 415
Merikangas, M. W., 431, 436, 437, 440, 441, 442, 443, 444, 448
Merwin, G., 220
Merwin, G. A., Jr., 28
Miller, C. D., 137
Miller, G. D., 226, 274
Miller, G. M., 196
Miller, J., 181, 182
Miller, J. V., 321, 322, 430
Miller, M. J., 18, 19, 23, 142, 179, 181, 188, 189, 223, 226, 255, 261, 263, 264, 274
Miller, R. R., 183, 184, 190, 216, 228
Miller-Tiedeman, A., 11
Millon, T., 158
Mims, G. A., 472
Minger, C., 35
Minor, C. W., 365, 380, 448, 467
Minuchin, P. P., 173
Mitchell, A., 22

Mitchell, A. M., 255
Mitchell, L. K., 22
Mohney, C., 373
Monnens, L. P., 182
Mooney, C. J., 334
Moore, C. L., 132
Moore, J. W., 431
Moos, R. H., 161
Moreland, K. L., 67
Morgan, J. I., 52, 167, 319
Morrill, W. H., 137
Morris, E. F., 371
Morris, J., 17, 163, 291, 292
Morse, C. L., 171
Mortimer, J. T., 320
Morton, S. B., 380
Moser, H. P., 9
Moses, S., 114
Mosier, K. L., 377
Mott, D., 388
Mourton, D. L., 316
Mowsesian, R., 20
Mueller, D., 160, 245
Muha, D., 43, 48
Murphy, C., 329
Murphy, L. R., 381, 399
Murray, H. A., 155
Myers, I. B., 155, 409, 410, 412
Myers, J. E., 367, 373

Nash, W., 276
National Employment Counseling Association, 469, 472
Naughton, T. J., 381
Neely, R. E., 326
Negron-Cunningham, H., 167
Neugarten, B. L., 421, 426, 431
Nevill, D. D., 160, 331, 354
Nevo, O., 464, 469
Newman, J. L., 35
Newton, F. B., 330, 342
Niles, S., 258
Noble, F. C., 309
Noe, A. W., 36, 323
Noeth, R. J., 136, 143, 258, 260
Novy, D. M., 48
Nowak, C., 392, 432

O'Brien, R. A., 57
O'Bryant, S. L., 191
Offerman, L. R., 59, 431, 432, 435, 465, 467
O'Halloran, M. S., 51, 316
O'Hara, R. P., 11
Ohlde, C., 38, 260
Okiishi, R. W., 167, 349
Okun, B. F., 359
Olch, D. R., 390
Oldham, G. R., 29, 465
Olian, J. D., 382
Oliver, L., 371
Olney, C. W., 60, 61, 431, 465
O'Neil, J. M., 38, 260, 369, 379
Orenstein, A. M., 42
Orleans, E. L., 40
Orum, L. S., 45
O'Shea, A. J., 47, 142
Osipow, S. H., 164, 218, 314, 315
Ossana, S. M., 436, 442, 443
O'Toole, J., 363
Overstreat, P. I., 310
Overstreet, P. L., 9
Overton, T. D., 40
Owen, G., 117
Owings, N., 180

Palladino, D. E., 309
Palmer, F. H., 131
Papalia, T., 387
Parker, H. J., 57
Parker, M., 366
Parsons, F., 1, 2, 3, 5, 24, 63, 462
Pedersen, P., 387
Pedro, J. D., 259, 264, 275
Pelsma, D. M., 412
Peltier, S., 366
Penick, N. I., 38
Pennell, C., 210, 224
Perrin, D. W., 43, 45, 262
Perrone, P., 265, 276
Perry, W. G., 305
Persach, E., 184
Peskin, H., 209
Peterson, G. W., 19
Peterson, L., 261
Pfleeger, J., 330, 331

Phifer, P., 270
Phillips, D., 362
Phillips, N. N., 41
Phillips, S. D., 314
Piaget, J., 173, 253, 254
Pickering, J. W., 341
Pickney, J. W., 45
Piers, E., 205
Piggott, T., 38, 260
Pine, G. J., 51, 158, 311
Pinkney, J. W., 140
Piotrowski, C., 65, 154
Pirnot, K., 398
Plake, B. S., 13, 95, 266
Popowicz, C. L., 191
Post-Kammer, P., 255, 258, 265, 276
Power, P. G., 17, 291
Powers, S. I., 250, 251, 253
Prediger, D. J., 65, 110, 123, 147, 151, 217, 236, 258, 266, 273, 292
Prediger, R. J., 143
Pyle, K. R., 469

Quinn, R. P., 30

Rachlin, V., 364, 365, 398
Ralph, J., 456
Ramirez, M., 45
Raths, L. E., 224
Raup, J. L., 367, 373
Raymond, C., 381
Read, N. O., 373
Reardon, R. C., 19
Redfield, D. L., 162
Rees, A. H., 131
Reeves, J. W., 31, 32
Reid, N., 117
Renzi, D., 28
Retish, R. M., 132
Reynolds, C. R., 129
Rice, K. G., 329
Richman, D. R., 19
Riverin-Simard, D., 321, 377
Roark, A. C., 313
Robbins, S. B., 462
Robertson, G. J., 67
Robinson, D. A. G., 190

Robinson, S. E., 122
Roe, A., 14, 15, 39, 40, 56, 144, 145, 149,
    150, 160, 183, 193, 241, 299, 462
Rogers, C. R., 224
Rogers, G., 342
Roland, B., 412
Rollins, J. A., 212, 251
Rose, H., 374
Rosen, B., 396
Rosenthal, B. L., 129
Rossi, A. S., 371
Rotberg, H. L., 51, 315
Roth, M. J., 191
Rothman, S., 64, 67, 93, 111, 128, 129,
    133, 134
Rubinton, N., 225
Russell, R., 383
Ryland, E. K., 396

Salomone, P. R., 55, 307, 383, 417, 431, 447
Saltoun, J., 334
Sampson, J. P., 19
Sampson, J. P., Jr., 159, 212
Samuda, R. J., 128
Sanford, E. E., 28, 220
Saper, B., 57
Sargent, J., 321, 327, 330, 331
Sauter, S. L., 381, 399
Savickas, M., 163, 352
Savickas, M. L., 11, 25, 34, 283, 303, 462,
    463, 464
Savicki, V., 381
Sawyer, R., 286
Sawyer, R. L., 217, 258, 266, 273
Scarr, S., 176, 362
Scheinfeld, D. R., 174
Schlossberg, N. K., 358, 359, 364, 368,
    369, 386, 390, 395, 427, 428, 438
Schmitz, T. J., 311, 368
Schneider, L. J., 40
Schrepfer, R. M., 210
Schuette, C. G., 330, 342
Schulenberg, J. E., 254, 264, 462
Schwartz, F. N., 49, 50
Schwebel, M., 306
Sedlacek, W. E., 88, 312, 315, 335, 336
Sekaran, U., 366
Seligman, L., 171, 173, 180, 181, 183, 184

Sewell, W. H., 42
Shadid, G. E., 329
Sharf, J. C., 90, 111
Shaw, K. N., 36, 323
Sheehan, M. C., 383
Sheehy, G., 304, 367, 387
Shelley, V., 196
Shelver, J. W., 191
Shertzer, B., 267, 268
Shiloh, S., 31
Shimizu, K., 264
Shostrom, E. L., 161
Shueman, S. A., 40
Shuttleworth, C., 330
Siegal, R., 398
Silverstein, L. B., 359, 370, 372
Simon, S. B., 224
Sinick, D., 418, 434
Skovholt, T. M., 52, 167, 226, 274, 319
Slaney, R. B., 315, 330, 373, 374
Slocum, J. W., Jr., 382
Smith, P., 126, 285
Smith, R. L., 3, 396
Smyer, M. A., 417, 420, 449
Snyderman, M., 64, 67, 93, 111, 128, 129,
    133, 134
Sodetz, A. R., 104
Solomon, D., 174
Spearman, C. E., 129
Speisman, J. C., 209, 253
Splete, H., 342, 387, 469
Spokane, A. R., 43, 49, 151, 174, 322, 337,
    394, 461, 469
Springer, T P., 142, 263, 274
Stadt, R. W., 39
Stafford, I. P., 372
Starishevsky, R., 8, 53
Steffy, B. D., 36, 323
Sternlof, R. E., 93
Stevens, F. I., 194
Stewart, H. R., 318
Stolz-Loike, M., 364
Stone, G. L., 326, 328, 339, 340, 342
Stout, S. K., 382
Strauss, G., 29
Subich, L. M., 265
Sullivan, H. S., 172
Sullivan, S. E., 313
Sundal-Hansen, L. S., 474

Super, D. E., 5, 6, 7, 8, 9, 10, 11, 12, 25, 28, 31, 53, 64, 119, 137, 160, 161, 164, 179, 187, 215, 216, 221, 256, 257, 258, 306, 307, 308, 310, 313, 319, 331, 352, 354, 376, 378, 429, 430, 456, 462
Swain, R., 339
Swanson, J. L., 136
Sweetland, R. C., 202

Tavris, C., 360, 417
Taylor, C., 27
Tennyson, W. W., 182, 226, 272, 274
Thomas, D. A., 44
Thomas, K. R., 57
Thomas, L. E., 137, 385
Thomas, M. L., 304, 361, 362, 363
Thompson, A. S., 164, 456
Thompson, B., 410
Thompson, D. E., 37, 399
Thorn, M., 397
Thornburg, H. D., 211, 212
Thrasher, F., 328
Thurnher, M., 425
Tiedeman, D. V., 11
Tikotzki, Y., 20, 21
Tilden, A. J., Jr., 330
Tinsley, D. J., 49, 372
Tinsley, H. E. A., 49, 212, 251, 372
Tittle, C. K., 314
Tobin, S. S., 426
Tollefson, N., 38, 260, 412
Trimmer, H. W., Jr., 345, 470
Troll, L., 385, 435
Troll, L. E., 359, 364, 369, 386, 392, 395, 432
Tucker, K. R., Jr., 462
Tyler, L., 67, 107, 112, 128, 139

Unruh, W. R., 383
Urman, H., 93
U.S. Department of Labor, 269, 320, 321, 384

Vacc, N. A., 341
Vale, D. C., 123
Van Hutton, V., 155, 355

Van Matre, G., 34, 35, 341
Vansickle, T. R., 95, 148
Vernon, P., 161
Villemez, W. J., 57
Vincenzi, H., 191
Vinitsky, M. N., 104
Vocational and career counseling competencies, 482
Vodanovich, S. J., 305
Vondracek, F. W., 254, 264, 462

Wade, K., 282
Wadsworth, M., 449
Wainer, H., 125
Wakelee-Lynch, J., 63, 163
Walbridge, M. M., 309
Walker, B. A., 18
Wallace, R. L., 463
Wallin, J. S., 228
Walsh, W. B., 135
Walz, G. R., 191, 468
Ware, W. B., 51, 315, 352
Warnath, C., 9
Waterman, A. S., 378
Waterman, C. K., 378
Watkins, C. E., Jr., 65, 91, 110, 130, 154, 157, 158, 406
Watts, D., 38, 260
Weaver, C. N., 30
Weaver, N. P. K., 343
Wechsler, D., 128
Wegmann, R., 384
Wegmann, R. G., 382, 384, 385
Weideman, A. H., 94
Weikel, W. J., 374
Weinberg, R. A., 128, 131, 176
Weiner, A. I., 32, 340
Weinstock, L., 171, 173, 180, 181, 183
Weissman, S., 412
Weitzman, L. M., 312, 370, 372
Welfel, E. R., 338
Wells, D., 142, 263, 274
Wendell, A., 342
Werbel, J. D., 359, 384, 386
Westbrook, B. W., 28, 220
Whiston, S. C., 10, 164, 261, 456, 471, 472
White, K. M., 209, 253
Whiteley, S. M., 340

Whiteman, M., 184
Wigington, H., 412
Wilcox, J., 397
Wilcox-Matthew, L., 365
Wilgus, E., 196
Williams, R., 46, 48
Williams, R. C., 226, 274
Wilson, J., 374
Wilson, J. C., 397
Wilson, K. M., 314
Wilson, N. S., 176
Wilson, R., 389
Wilson, R. J., 328
Wilson, S., 252, 265, 276
Winkler, K. J., 332
Wise, S. L., 95
Wolleat, P., 366

Woog, P., 371
Worthington, C. F., 194
Wortley, D. B., 305, 419

Yankelovich, D., 29
Yates, C. J., 344
Yates, L. V., 159, 306, 354, 363
Yost, E. B., 1, 2, 28
Young, R. B., 342
Ysseldyke, J. E., 116, 195

Zaccaria, J. S., 6
Zajonc, R. B., 125, 131
Zedeck, S., 377
Zunker, V. G., 36, 37, 149, 226, 330
Zytowski, D. G., 15, 89, 120, 159

Subject Index

AARPWORKS, 433
Ability testing, purposes of, 111. *See also* Ability tests
Ability tests, 110-134
  achievement tests, 110, 113-118
  aptitude tests, 110-111, 119-127
  bias in, 111-113
  intelligence tests, 110, 128-134
Achievement tests, 110, 113-118
  assessment of academic achievement, 117-118
  assessment of basic skills, 116-117
  criterion-referenced, 113
  examples of, 116-118
  norm referenced, 113
  purpose of, 115
  uses of, 113
  See also names of individual achievement tests
ACT Career Planning Program (CPP), 149-150, 297
ACT Career Planning Services program, 149
Adjective Checklist (ACL), 155, 457-458
Adolescence:
  academic difficulties during, 253
  as years of realism and separation, 249-253
  attaining maturity in, 254
  career maturity in, 258-259
  career motivation in, 260
  developmental goals during, 272
  developmental personality changes during, 250-253

developments in thinking ability during, 253-254
emotional development during, 249-253
formulating educational plans and decisions during, 267-271
gender-related patterns of development during, 252-253
making occupational choices during, 259-260
peer relations during, 252
relationships with parents during, 251
sexual identity and behavior issues during, 253
Adolescence, early:
  as years of growth and searching, 207-248
  career development objectives for, 233-234
  career development of, 214-221
  career maturation during, 216-218
  developmental milestones of, 232-233
  development of thinking and values in, 212-213
  identity versus role confusion in, 209
  physical development in, 208-209
Adolescent development, early:
  importance of peer group in, 211-212
  middle school/junior high school environment and, 213-214
  overview of, 207-214
  self-image and self-concept in, 209-211
Adolescents:
  career education activities for, 283-284

improving decision-making skills of,
    284-285
Adolescents, career counseling with,
    272-286
  acquiring and disseminating career in-
    formation, 277
  and adolescents' attitudes toward,
    272-273
  career resource centers and, 277-279
  goals of, 273-274
  overview of, 276-277
  special populations, 274-276
Adolescents, career counseling with
    early, 221-232
  approaches to, 222-226
  developmental group, 223-224
  individual, 222-223
  parent conferences and special parent
    programs, 224-225
  role of assessment in, 234-236
Adolescents, career development in,
    254-267
  computer-based information systems
    and, 279-280
  influence of experiences on, 261-262
  influence of gender on, 263-266
  influence of other people on, 260-261
  influence of socioeconomic and eth-
    nic background on, 262-263
  influences on, 260-267
  overcoming extrinsic hurdles to, 285-
    286
  overview of, 255-256
  stages of, 256-257
  structured career development work-
    shops and, 281-283
Adolescents, career development in
    early, 214-221
  characteristics of, 216-217
  environmental influences on, 218,
    220-221
  ethnic and socioeconomic back-
    ground influences on, 218, 219-221
  family influences on, 218, 220
  gender influences on, 218-219
  influences on, 218-221
  resources to promote, 228-229
  stages of, 215-216

Adolescents, career education for early,
    229-232
Adolescents, career maturation of early,
    227-228
Adult Career Concerns Inventory
    (ACCI), 164, 352, 456
Adult career counseling:
  approaches to, 393-395
  essential characteristics of, 393
  resources for, 400-401
  stages of, 394
  via programs, groups, or workshops,
    395-397
Adult career development:
  burnout and, 381
  mentoring and, 382
  models for facilitating, 395-396
  plateauing and, 382
  stress in, 379-382
  transitions in, 379-380
  workaholism and, 381
Adult college students, young, 325-336
  career choice and planning among,
    331-333
  career counseling resources/
    publications for, 343-344
  career life planning for, 342-343
  counseling, 339-344
  decision making of, 329-331
  expectations and experiences of,
    327-329
  making commitments, 329-331
Adult development, young:
  and development of a generation,
    310-312
  changes during, 304-305
  intellectual and ethical, 305-306
  milestones during, 305
  overview of, 302-310
  socioeconomic influences on, 303-304
Adult graduate students, young, 334-335
Adulthood, later:
  adjustment and satisfaction in,
    421-422
  as years of adapting and extending,
    416-460
  career development during, 429-434
  career satisfaction during, 430-431

developmental tasks of, 422-423
emotional development in, 418-423
gender differences in development in, 421
integrity versus despair conflict in, 420-421
leisure activities during, 425-426
lifestyles in, 428-429
marital relationships during, 424-425
planning for, 449
social/interpersonal changes during, 423-426
stages of development in, 419-420
unemployment in, 432
Adulthood, middle:
as time of transition, 358-359
as years of consolidating and redirecting, 358-415
career development during, 376-388
career dissatisfaction in, 378-379
career maturity in, 376
conflicts of middle, 363-364
developmental tasks and coping behaviors for, 391
development during, 359-376
dual-career couples in, 364-366
early, 360-362
gender differences in development during, 367-369
generativity versus stagnation conflict in, 391
later, 366-367
men's development during, 369-370
middle, 362-364
overview of, 390-391
women's development during, 370-375
Adulthood, young:
as years of compromise and commitment to a lifestyle, 302-357
career decision making during, 307-310
career development during, 306-307
gender and career development during, 312-320
intimacy versus isolation conflict in, 304
Adults, midlife:
as students, 388-390

bias in counseling, 392
counseling, 391-401
counseling for special needs of, 397-400
leisure counseling for, 397-398
Adults, older:
as growing segment of population, 416-418
capabilities of, 434-435
continuity in lives of, 445-446
counseling, 443-450
development history of, 446-447
hopes and expectations of, 448
interpersonal relationships of, 444-445
leisure and occupational interests of, 446
life circumstances of, 445
resources for, 449-450
rights of, 418
self-image and self-efficacy in, 443-444
Adults, young:
as college students, 325-336
assessment of level of thinking and decision making for, 338
assessment with, 345-346
counseling young adults, 336-346
exploration of family-of-origin models and messages for, 338
improvement of coping skills for, 337
job-finding strategies for, 337
leisure counseling for, 338-339
most common career-related problems of, 337
personal counseling for, 339
succeeding in world of work, 322-324
values clarification counseling for, 337
work entry problems of, 323
Advanced Placement Program (APP), 118
Affective education programs, 224
Age bias, 392, 431
Age Discrimination in Employment Act, 418
Age distortion, 392
Ageism, 392
coping with, 447-448
Age restrictiveness, 392
Aging theories, 426-429
abandonment, 426

activity, 426-427
continuity/life span, 427
developmental, 427
disengagement, 426
liberation, 427
role, 427
socioenvironmental/cultural, 428
Al-anon meetings, 460
Alcoholics Anonymous, 348
American Association for Counseling
and Development (AACD), 506, 507
American Association for Retired People
(AARP), 417, 433, 449
National Older Workers Information
System of, 433, 450
American College Testing (ACT) program, 118, 126, 285
American Counseling Association
(ACA), 3, 64, 73
annual convention of, 228
American Orthopsychiatric Association,
158
American Personnel and Guidance Association, 64
American Psychological Association, 504
Aptitudes, types of, 120-121
complex, 120, 121
simple/specific, 120, 121
Aptitude tests, 110-111, 119-127
for college admission, 124-126
for measuring academic aptitude,
123-124
for measuring occupational aptitude,
126-127
multi-aptitude batteries, 121
use and selection of, 121-123
validity of, 122
Armed Services Vocational Aptitude Battery (ASVAB), 110, 123, 291
Army General Classification Test, 64
Assessment:
attitudes toward, 69-70
benefits of, 66-67
client rights in, 108
computer-based, 95-97
factors integral to sound use of, 67
limitations of, 67-68
use of by counseling psychologists,
65, 110

use of by school counselors, 65-66, 110
See also Assessment in career counseling and Testing
Assessment in career counseling:
concerns about, 64
history of, 63-66
purposes of, 63
use of, 63-108
Assessment methods, nonstandardized,
166-167
daydreams and mental imagery, 167
genograms, 167, 349, 350, 472
lifeline exercise, 167
Vocational Card Sort (VCS), 166
Assessment of Career Decision Making
(ACDM), 164, 352
Assessment process:
pitfalls of, 91-97
planning, 70-72
Assessment tools, 109-167
acronyms for, 513-515
categories of, 109

Baby-trackers, 50
Barnum Effect, 106
Basic Achievement Skills Individual
Screener (BASIS), 116, 195
Beck Depression Inventory, 158
Behavioral Academic Self-Esteem Scale,
194
Bender Visual Motor Gestalt Test, 158
Binet, A., 2
B'nai B'rith Vocational Service Bureau, 4
Briggs, K. C., 155, 409
Burnout, 381
counseling for, 399-400
Buros, O. K., 72

California Occupational Preference System Interest Inventory, 78
California Psychological Inventory
(CPI), 154, 155, 355, 356
CAPS Career Profile, 242, 246
Career:
changing scope of, 33
definition of, 25-26
personal need satisfaction and, 25

Career Ability Placement Survey
(CAPS), 150, 240, 241
Career adaptability, 28
process of, 28
Career Assessment Inventory (CAI), 143,
145, 151, 297
Career Awareness Inventory (CAI), 294
Career choice, happenstance in, 23
Career Choices, 232
Career choice theory, Roe's, 14-15
Career counseling:
characteristics of, 479-480
content and process of, 475-481
Depression Era, 3-4
desirable processes and goals of, 475-
478
duration of, 480-481
expectations of, 463-464
impact of family counseling on, 23
in groups, 470-471
stages of, 479
World War II Era, 4-5
Career counseling and assessment:
changes in process of, 468-470
Career counseling and assessment field:
continuing change in, 474-475
future of, 461-496
overview of changes in, 462-463
Career counseling and development:
history of, 1-5
overview of, 1-62
Career counseling lexicon, 25-38
Career counseling process, evaluating,
481
Career counselors:
role of with young adolescents, 226-
228
skills of, 482-484
sources and resources for, 508-512
Career Decision-Making System (CDM),
352, 353
Career Decision Scale (CDS), 164, 351,
352
Career development, 29
abilities and interests and, 54-56
barriers to, 473
characteristics of, 27
definition of, 26-28
emotional factors and, 38

environment and, 42
factors affecting, 38-62
familial factors and, 38-42
gender and, 48-53
importance of family in, 471-473
individual factors and, 38, 53-57
of African Americans, 43, 45-46
of Asian Americans, 46
of disabled people, 54-56
of gifted people, 56
of Hispanics, 43, 44-45
of Native Americans, 46-47
personality and, 56
prestige and, 56-57
psychosocial factors and, 38
race/cultural background and, 43-47
role of leisure in, 32-34
self-esteem and, 53-54
societal factors and, 38
socioeconomic factors and, 38, 42-47
socioeconomic status and, 42-43
styles of, 27
Career development inventories, 352
Career Development Inventory (CDI),
164, 352
Career development organizations, 3.
See also names of individual career
development organizations
Career development theories, 5-25
commonalities in, 23-25
developmental theories, 6-13, 23
learning and social influence theories,
21-22, 24
personality and need theories, 13-18, 23
research on, 13
shortcomings of Ginsberg's, 8
shortcomings of Holland's, 18
shortcomings of Roe's, 15
shortcomings of Super's, 11
social/environmental theories, 22-23,
24
theories derived from personal counseling, 18-22, 23-24
Career development workshops:
for adolescents, 281-283
for hearing-impaired students, 282
in Indianapolis Public Schools, 282
Career Directions Inventory (CDI), 143-
144, 297

Career education, 225
  framework for, 187
  in elementary school, 188-190
  major goals of, 187-188
Career education, elementary school,
  188-190
  children's responses to, 190-191
  for children with disabilities, 195-196
  important goals of, 188-189
  primary goal of, 188
  to reduce stereotyping, 190
Career Education Incentives Act, 322
Career education programs, elementary
  school:
  assessment tools for, 193-195
  characteristics of systematic and
    effective, 191
  common core experiences of, 191
  content of, 191-195
  resources and methods for, 192-193
Career Exploration and Planning Program (CEPP), 166, 232, 280
Career Exploration for Youth, components of, 225
Career indecision:
  categories of people with, 34
  definition of, 34-35
  versus career indecisiveness, 308
Career Information System, 166, 279
Career maturation, patterns of, 28-29
Career maturity, definition of, 28-29, 163,
  352
Career maturity and development measures, 163-165
Career Maturity Inventory (CMI), 164-
  165, 283, 352
Career motivation:
  definition of, 37-38
  factors contributing to, 37
  strategies for improving, 37-38
Career Navigator, 343
Career Occupational Preference System
  (COPS), 123, 244, 245, 246
  Interest Inventory, 15, 151, 240, 243
Career Orientation Placement and Evalu-
  ation Survey (COPES), 150, 159-
  160, 240, 245, 246
Career Pattern Study, Super's, 8-11, 164,
  221, 257, 158, 378

types of female career patterns, 10
types of male career patterns, 9
Career planning programs, 149-150
Career Planning Questionnaire (CPQ),
  150, 242
Career preferences, criteria for determin-
  ing wisdom of, 310
Career-related stress, definition of, 35-36
Career resource centers, 225-226, 397
  for adolescents, 277-279
Career satisfaction, definition of, 29-31
Career self-efficacy, definition of, 36-37
Career Skills Assessment Program, 352
Career success, definition of, 31-32
Careerville, 194
Carl D. Perkins Vocational Education
  Act of 1984, 55, 195
Cattell, J., 2
Childhood:
  as years of identification and differen-
    tiation, 168-206
  career education during, 186-196
  counseling in, 186
  developmental accomplishments of,
    185-186
  development in early, 168-170
  development in middle, 170-178
Childhood, early:
  roots of career development in, 178
Childhood, middle:
  achievement motivation development
    in, 174-176
  gender and sex role identity develop-
    ment in, 177-178
  industry versus inferiority crisis in,
    172
  self-concept and self-esteem in, 170-
    172
  social development in, 172-173
  thought and judgment development
    in, 173-174
Children, career development in, 178-185
  career maturation, 182
  fantasy stage, 179-180
  gender and, 184
  influence of values on, 182-183
  interest stage, 180-181
  occupational self-concepts, 181
  overview of, 185

personal goals and family interactions and, 183-184
Children's Apperception Test, 203
Children's Dictionary of Occupations, 231
Children's Personality Questionnaire, 157, 194
CHOICES, 166, 280, 469
CHOICES CT, 400
Chronicle Career Quest, 400
Chronicle Career System, 400
Chronicle Occupational Library, 400
Circumscription and compromise developmental career theory, Gottfredson's, 12-13
Civil Conservation Corps (CCC), 4
C-Lect, 166, 279, 400, 469
Cognitive-behavioral career counseling approaches, 19-21
techniques used in, 22
College Entrance Examination Board, 118
College-Level Examination Program (CLEP), 118, 389
College Major Interest Inventory, 144, 297
College Majors Finder, 147, 292
College placement offices, 345
College population:
changing nature of, 325-327
in two-year colleges, 333-334
Colleges:
future of, 335-336
two-year, 333-334
Comprehensive Assessment Program, 117
Comprehensive Employment and Training Act, 322
Comprehensive Test of Basic Skills, 117, 194, 242, 291
Computer-assisted assessment, 165-166
Computer-assisted career guidance systems (CACGS), 469
Computer-based assessment, 95-97
advantages of, 95-96
concerns about, 96
levels of, 95
Computer-based career information systems (CBCISs), 165-166, 279-280, 450
Computerized career guidance and assessment, 65-66

Congruence model of career choice, Holland's, 15-18
Coopersmith Self-Esteem Inventories (SEI), 161, 194
COPS—P, 150, 241
COPS II, 241
COPS II Intermediate Inventory, 150
COPSystem Career Guidance Program, 150, 159, 240, 241, 242
COPSystem Comprehensive Career Guide, 241, 244
Culture-Fair Intelligence Test, 130
Culture-Free Self-Esteem inventories, 194
Curriculum Referenced Tests of Mastery, 118

DAT, 242
Decision Making Inventory, 162
Decision theory, 19-21
conjunctive model of, 20
expected utility model of, 20
within-attributes model of, 20
Dental Aptitude Test, 126
Depression, Great, 3-4, 7, 29
Designing the Future, 281
Developing Skills Checklist, 195
Developing Understanding of Self and Others (DUSO), 193
Developing Understanding of Self and Others (DUSO-2-R), 171
Dictionary of Holland Occupational Codes, 147, 292
Dictionary of Occupational Titles, 4, 127, 146, 147, 231, 278, 280, 400, 401
Differential Aptitude Test Career Planning Program (DAT CPP), 150
Differential Aptitude Tests (DAT), 86, 110, 123-124, 241, 291
Directive counseling, 4
DISCOVER program, 123, 165, 279, 450, 469
for Colleges and Adults, 342-343, 400
for junior high and middle schools, 232
DISCOVER II, 387
Dual-career couples, 364-366
counseling, 398-399
Dual Career Guidance Project, 282

Dual-career marriages, 365
  types of, 365

Early School Assessment, 195
Early School Personality Questionnaire, 157, 203
Eating Inventory, 158
Edwards Personal Preference Schedule (EPPS), 88, 154, 155
Elementary school counseling, foci of, 196-197
Elementary school counselor, 186
  role of, 196-197
Employee assistance programs, 396-397
Employment agencies, private, 345
Employment patterns, factors underlying changes in, 60-61
Empty nest syndrome, 374
Encyclopedia of Careers, 231, 280
Equal Employment Opportunity Commission guidelines, 123
Erikson, E.:
  identity concept of, 17
  psychosocial crises of, 11
ETS Test Collection, 73
E-WOW, 194

Family counseling:
  Adlerian approaches to, 23
  impact of on career counseling, 23
Family Education Rights and Privacy Act, 504
Family Relations Inventory, 15
First National Conference on Vocational Guidance, 3
Foster Grandparents, 449

GED, 124
Geist Picture Interest Inventory, 144
General Aptitude Test Battery (GATB), 110, 126-127, 241
Gough, H. C., 155, 355, 457
Graduate Management Aptitude Test, 126
Graduate Record Examination (GRE), 87, 118, 122, 125, 126

Guidance Information System, 166, 279, 469-470
Guide for Occupational Exploration, 280

Hall, G. S., 2
Hall, L. G., 299, 300
Hall Occupational Orientation Inventory (HALL), 15, 160, 299-300
Handbook for Exploring Careers, 146
Harren, V., 164, 352
Harrington/O'Shea Career Decision-Making System (CDM), 18, 144
Head Start, 175
High School Personality Questionnaire (HSPQ), 156-157, 297
Holland's hexagon, 15, 123, 145, 147, 293, 406, 458
House-Tree-Person exercise, 158

Individual Career Exploration (ICE), 144-145, 193
Inferred Self-Concept Scale, 194
Integrative counseling, 101
Intellectual abilities:
  development of, 131-132
  environment and, 131
  family attitudes and, 131
  family composition and, 131
Intelligence, nature of, 128-129
Intelligence tests, 110, 128-134
  and achievement tests, 133
  and aptitude tests, 133
  appropriate use of, 132-134
  criticisms of, 132
  group, 129
  individual, 129
  interpretation of, 134
  nonintellectual factors and, 134
  nonverbal, 130-131
  types of, 129-131
  usefulness of, 132-133
  validity of, 129
Interest Determination, Exploration and Assessment System (IDEAS), 145, 296
Interest inventories, 135-151
  bias/distortion in, 141-143
  development of, 137-138

faking and, 141-143
important/representative, 143-149
selection of, 151
use of, 138-141
Interests:
development of, 136-137
expressed, 135
inventoried, 135
manifest, 135
types of, 135
International Work Importance Study,
Super's, 160, 456
Inventories, 77
evaluating, 72
scoring of, 82
selecting appropriate, 68-74
See also Interest inventories, Personality inventories, *and* Tests
Iowa Test of Basic Skills, 117, 242, 290

Jackson, D. N., 143, 145
Jackson Vocational Interest Survey
(JVIS), 145, 296
Job, definition of, 26
Job Club, Azrin's, 344-345, 470
Job clubs, 386, 450
Job Corps, 322
Job Factory, 344
JOB JUNGLE, 194
Job market changes, 59-61
JOB-O, 204, 205
JOB-O A, 204
JOB-O E, 194, 204
Job search groups, 396
Job Search Support Group for Adult Stu-
dents, 344
Job search training programs, successful:
qualities in, 344
Job-seeking behaviors, best received ap-
proaches to, 324
Jobs Finder, 147, 292
Jobs 1990, 231
Job Training Partnership Act, 195
Johansson, C. B., 143, 145
Jung, C., 78, 155, 409

Kaufman, A., 455

Kaufman, N., 455
Kaufman Brief Intelligence Test (K-BIT),
195, 455, 456
Kaufman Test of Educational
Achievement, 117, 194
Kuder, F., 145
Kuder General Interest Survey (KGIS),
138, 145, 146, 151
Kuder Occupational Interest Survey
(KOIS), 88, 138, 146, 151, 343, 458
Form DD of, 293-297
Report form of, 294-295
Kuder Preference Record, 145, 458
Kuder tests, 110
as ipsative tests, 87
Kuhlmann Anderson Tests, 242

Labor force trends, 58-59
Larry P. v. Riles, 64, 132
Law School Aptitude Test (LSAT), 122,
126
Learning styles, 21
Learning Styles Inventory, 21, 162-163
Learning theorists, techniques used by,
22
Leisure:
role of in career development, 32-34
Leisure counseling, 33
Life-career rainbow, 10
Life career theory, Miller-Tiedeman,
11-12, 13
Life-Centered Career Education
Curriculum (LCCE), 195-196
Life Development Visualization, 282
Life span career counselors, 33
Lifestyle Assessment Questionnaire
(LAQ), 162
Lifestyle Coping Inventory, 162
Looking at MYSELF, 194

Maslach Burnout Inventory (MBI), 163,
412-413
Maslow, A., theories of, 14, 160
Medical College Admission Test, 126
Men, development of during middle
adulthood, 369-370
Men, young adult:

career development of, 319-320
  nontraditional, 319
Men's career development, 51-53
  issues that impact, 52
Mental Measurements Yearbook (MMY),
  4, 72, 121
Mentoring, 382
Metropolitan Achievement Test, 117,
  242, 291
Middle school education, goal of, 233
Midlife career change, 382-384
  computer-based career counseling
    and, 387
  executive search firms and, 387
  facilitating, 385-388
  Forty Plus Clubs and, 386
  inplacement counseling and, 386
  interventions and resources for, 386-387
  involuntary, 384-385
  job clubs and, 386
  leisure counseling and, 386
  outplacement counseling and, 386
  private employment agencies and, 387
  processes that can precipitate, 383-384
  retraining and, 387
  small business advisory groups and,
    386
  teaching career development skills
    and, 386
Midlife developmental conflicts, male-fe-
  male, 375-376
Military Career Guide, 280, 400
Miller Analogies Test (MAT), 122, 126
Millon Clinical Multiaxial Inventory—
  (MCMI-II), 158
Minnesota Clerical Assessment Battery
  (MCAB), 127
Minnesota importance Questionnaire
  (MIQ), 160
Minnesota Multiphasic Personality In-
  ventory (MMPI), 76, 110
Minnesota Multiphasic Personality In-
  ventory—II (MMPI-II), 157-158
Minnesota Report Personnel Selection
  System, 157
Minority career development:
  of African Americans, 43, 45-46
  of Asian Americans, 46
  of Hispanics, 43, 44-45

of Native Americans, 46-47
  recommendations for facilitating, 48
  understanding and improving, 47-48
Missouri Occupational Card Sort, 166
Myers-Briggs Type Indicator (MBTI), 77-
  78, 79, 152, 154, 155-156, 409-412, 413
My Vocational Situation (MVS), 165, 291-
  292, 352

Nader, R., 122
National Board for Certified Counselors
  (NBCC), 497
National Career Counseling Credential-
  ing Examination, 3
National Career Development Associa-
  tion (NCDA), 3, 506, 507
  Ethical Standards of, 497-507
National College Catalog Library, 280
National Computer System (NCS), 76
National Employment Counseling Asso-
  ciation, 3
National Merit Examination, 40
National Merit Scholarship program, 126
National Vocational Guidance Associa-
  tion, 3
Nevill, D. D., 160, 354
New Hampshire, Comprehensive Coun-
  seling and Guidance Program of,
  226
  components of, 226-227
NIEP College Preview Tour Program, 282
Non-Sexist Vocational Card Set, 166

Occupational Outlook Handbook, 145, 149,
  150, 231, 241, 278, 280, 401
Occupational segregation, 46
Occupational Stress Inventory, 163
Occupations:
  declining, 60
  fastest-growing, 60
Occupations Finder, 147, 292
Occupation/vocation, definition of, 26
Occ-U-Sort, 166
Ohio State Center for Vocational and
  Technical Education, 187
  career education framework of, 187

Ohio Vocational Interest Survey—II
(Ovis-II), 146, 297
Older Americans Act, Title V, 433
101 Careers, 231
Otis, A., 63
Otis-Lennon School Ability Test (OL-
SAT), 63, 130, 202, 242

P-ACT, 126
Peabody Early Experiences Kit (PEEK),
193
Peabody Individual Achievement Test,
195
Peabody Individual Achievement Test—
Revised (PIAT-R), 116
Peabody Picture Vocabulary Test—
Revised (PPVT), 124, 195
Peak performers, 32
Peer counseling programs, 450
Personal Career Development Profile
(PCDP), 156
Personality:
influence of on career development,
151-153
Personality inventories, 151-165
career maturity and development
measures, 154, 163-165
clinical, 154, 157-158
general, 154, 154-157
projective tests, 158
selection and use of, 153-154
self-esteem, 161-162
specialized, 154, 158-163
specialized clinical, 158
types of, 154-165
values, 158-161
wellness and leisure, 162
Personal Orientation Inventory, 161
Person-centered career counseling, 18-19
key assumptions of, 19
Piers-Harris Children's Self-Concept
Scale, 161, 194, 205
Plateauing, 382
PLATO, 280, 343
Position, definition of, 26
Positive Action, 232
Preliminary Scholastic Aptitude Test
(PSAT), 125-126

Preretirement programs, 440-441
Primary Test of Cognitive Skills, 195
Proficiency Examination Program (PEP),
118
Progressive Matrices, 130
Project PACE, 282

Readiness for Career Planning Scale, 352
Reliability, test, 84-85
definition of, 84
importance of, 85
internal consistency, 84
of performance tests, 84
of power tests, 84
of speed tests, 84
stability over time, 84
types of, 84
Retired Senior Volunteers, 449
Retirement, 435-443
adjustment to, 441-443
creativity and, 439
involuntary, 438
planning for, 438-440
stages in process of, 437-438
Retirement Activities Kit (RAK), 458-459
Retirement planning, 438-440
external variables, 438-439
internal variables, 439
leisure planning and, 440
Riverside Basic Skills Assessment Program, 290
Roe-Siegelman Parent-Child Relations
Questionnaire, 15
Rogers, C., 5, 18
Rorschach Technique, 158
Rorschach Test, 75, 203
Rosenberg Self-Esteem Scale, 194
Rosie the Riveter, 5
Rotter Incomplete Sentences Blank, 158

Salience Inventory, The (SI), 160, 352, 456
SAT II, 118, 125
Scholastic Aptitude Tests (SAT), 87, 91,
118, 122, 124-125, 126, 263, 285, 289-
290, 291, 349
Scholastic Assessment Test, 290
School dropout rates, 267-268

Self-Directed Search (SDS), 16, 17, 81, 85, 90, 106, 146-147, 151, 157, 282, 292-293, 296, 343, 458
Self-esteem inventories, 161-162, 194
Self-Esteem Rating Scale for Children, 194
Senior Citizens Charter, 418
Senior Community Service Employment Act, 433
Senior Community Service Employment Program, 449
Senior Companions, 449
Sexual harassment, 402
SIGI, 343, 450, 469
SIGI Plus, 165, 279
Sixteen Personality Factor (16PF), 154, 156
Social learning theory, 106
Standard Occupational Classification Manual, 280
Stanford Achievement Test, 242, 291
Stanford-Binet Intelligence Scale, 63, 129-130, 202, 456
State employment agencies, 345
State-Trait Anxiety Inventory, 158
Stressful occupations:
    least, 35-36
    most, 35
Strong, Jr., E. K., 64, 148
Strong-Campbell Interest Inventory, 136, 148
Strong Interest Inventory (SII), 18, 64, 76, 78, 82, 87, 89, 91, 110, 138, 143, 148, 151, 343, 405-406, 413
    validity of, 148
Strong Vocational Interest Blank, 148
Study Attitudes and Methods Survey, 162
Study of Values, 161
Survey of Interpersonal Values, 161
Survey of Personal Values, 161
Survey of Study Habits and Attitudes, 162
Swimming Upstream, 281

TAP, 290, 291
Tarrier, R. B., 299
Tennessee Self-Concept Scale, 161-162, 194, 245
Terman, L., 63
Test administration, 93-95

group versus individual, 80
    timing, 79-80
Test bias, 88-91
    atmosphere, 89
    content, 89
    counselors and reduction of, 91
    gender, 89-90
    racial, 90
    use, 89
Test Critiques, 73
Test forms, 78-79
Testing:
    benefits of, 66-67
    factors integral to sound use of, 67
    limitations of, 67-68
    See also Assessment and Tests
Test interpretation, 97-108
    approaches to, 101-103
    concluding process of, 107-108
    descriptive, 101
    evaluative, 101, 102
    face-to-face, 98-99
    genetic, 101, 102
    Gestalt approaches to, 104, 106
    guidelines for, 99-101
    in group settings, 104-105
    predictive, 101, 102
    reactions to, 105-107
    summary of process of, 108
    types of, 101
    using prediction in, 103-104
    written, 97-98
Test manuals:
    information found in, 74-75
    understanding, 74-91
Test of Nonverbal Intelligence (TONI), 130, 195
Test performance:
    factors affecting, 93
    maximizing, 93-94
Test responses, 88
Tests:
    affective, 77
    cognitive, 77
    criticisms of, 91-97
    diagnostic, 77
    evaluating, 72
    interpretation of, 76
    ipsative, 87

norms and, 82-83
objective, 76
power, 79
prognostic, 77
projective, 75
purposes of, 77-78
reading levels of, 82
reliability, 84-85
selecting appropriate, 68-74
sources of information on, 72-74
speed, 79
standardized, 75
understanding, 74-91
user qualifications, 75-77
validity of, 83-84
See also Inventories *and* names of individual tests
Tests: A Comprehensive Reference, 73, 121
Test scores:
age- or grade-equivalent, 86
percentiles, 86
ranks, 86
standard, 86, 87
stanine, 87
types of, 85-87
z, 87
Test scoring, 81-82
computer, 75-76
hand, 81
machine, 81
of projective, 76
Tests in Print, 72, 121
Tests of Adult Basic Education (TABE), 124, 456
Thematic Apperception Test, 75, 158
Tools for Transition, 281
Trait-and-factor theory, Parsons's, 1-3, 4, 15, 23, 101
Transescence, 207

Unemployment:
among minorities, 44, 58
frictional, 58
in later adulthood, 432
of young adults, 320-322
University of Southern California, Andrus Gerontology Center, 446
Upward Bound, 487

U.S. Bureau of Labor Statistics, 321
U.S. Bureau of the Census, 303
U.S. Department of Defense, 123
U.S. Department of Education, 226, 267
U.S. Department of Labor, 60, 127, 145, 148, 160, 241, 299, 433, 449
Women's Bureau, 370
U.S. Employment Service, 3, 4, 126
U.S. Employment Service Interest Inventory (USES-II), 148-149, 297

Validity, construct, 83
Validity, criterion-related, 83
Validity, test, 83-84
construct, 83
content, 83
definition of, 83
face, 83
importance of, 85
types of, 83
Values, definition of, 224
Values inventories, 158-161
Values Scale, The (VS), 160, 354, 456
Veterans Administration (VA), 4
Vineland Adaptive Behavior Scales, 117
classroom edition, 193-194
Vocational Card Sort (VCS), 166
Vocational Interest Blank, 64
Vocational Interest Experience and Skill Assessment (VIESA), 149
Vocational Interest Inventory, 15
Vocational Preference Inventory (VPI), 157

Wagner-Peyser Act, 3
Wechsler Adult Intelligence Scale (WAIS), 110, 129, 130, 456
Wechsler Intelligence Scale for Children (WISC), 129, 130, 202
Wechsler Preschool and Primary Scale of Intelligence (WPPSI), 129, 130
Wellness and leisure inventories, 162
Wellness inventory, 162
White House Conference on Aging, 418
Whole Work Catalog, The, 231
Wide Range Achievement Test (WRAT), 86, 114, 117, 194, 195

Wide Range Interest-Opinion Test
(WRIOT), 149
Widowhood, 423-424
Williamson, E. G., 4, 5
Women:
    development of during middle adult-
        hood, 370-375
    midlife transition of, 373-375
    reentry, 373, 398
    sources of satisfaction for midlife
        adult, 371-373
    stages in development of identity of, 50
Women, young adult:
    career development of, 314-317
    changing role of, 312-314
    nontraditional, 317-318
    traditional, 317
Women's career development, 5, 48-51
    in young adults, 314-317
    role models in, 51
    social constraints and, 49
Women's movement, 5, 49, 313
Woodcock-Johnson PsychoEducational
    Battery II (WJII), 202
Work:
    definition of, 26
    negotiating and succeeding in, 322-324

world of, 57-62
Workaholism, 381
Workers, older:
    labor force patterns of, 431
    options for, 432-434
    unemployment of, 432
Workers, young adult, 320-324
    counseling, 344-345
    unemployment of, 320-322
Work Importance Project, Super's, 11
Work life:
    changes in, 61-62
    programs to improve quality of, 61-62
Workplace:
    changes in, 464-467
    multicultural, 467-468
    popular innovative programs in,
        466-467
Work Windows, 194
World War I, use of assessment during,
    63-64
World War II, 29
    use of assessment during, 63-64

You and Your Career, 147

About the Author

Linda Seligman is Professor and Coordinator of the Counseling and Development Program at George Mason University, Fairfax, Virginia. Her teaching specializations include diagnosis and treatment planning, career counseling, family counseling, and theories and techniques of counseling.

She is the author of two other books, *Diagnosis and Treatment Planning in Counseling* and *Selecting Effective Treatments*, as well as more than 30 professional chapters and articles. She has lectured widely throughout the United States and Canada. She has been the editor of the *Journal of Mental Health Counseling* and presently is on the editorial board of the *Journal of Counseling and Development*. She has served as president of the Virginia Mental Health Counselors Association. In 1990, she was selected as Researcher of the Year by the American Mental Health Counselors Association.

Dr. Seligman is a licensed psychologist and counselor as well as a certified clinical mental health counselor. She is Director of the Center for Counseling and Consultation in Fairfax, Virginia, and Bethesda, Maryland, where she provides counseling to adults and adolescents. She has served as a psychologist or consultant to many organizations, including the Salvation Army, the Montgomery County Department of Corrections, the Veterans Administration, the federal government, and the American Counseling Association. She received her Ph.D. degree in counseling psychology from Columbia University.